UP AGAINST
THE CORPORATE WALL

Fifth Edition

UP AGAINST
THE CORPORATE WALL

Modern Corporations and Social Issues
of the Nineties

S. Prakash Sethi
Baruch College, The City University of New York
Rensselaer Institute of Technology

Paul Steidlmeier
State University of New York, Binghamton

With contributions from
KAREN PAUL and PAUL SHRIVASTAVA

PRENTICE HALL
Englewood Cliffs, NJ 07632

Library of Congress Cataloging-in-Publication Data

Sethi, S. Prakash.
    Up against the corporate wall : modern corporations and social
  issues of the nineties / S. Prakash Sethi, Paul Steidlmeier ; with
  contributions from Karen Paul, Paul Shrivastava. -- 5th ed.
        p.   cm.
    Includes bibliographical references.
    ISBN 0-13-946237-6
    1. Industry--Social aspects--United States--Case studies.
  I. Steidlmeier, Paul   II. Title.
  HD605.U5S47 1990
  658.4'08--dc20
                                                        90-7351
                                                          CIP

 © 1991 by Prentice-Hall, Inc.
A Division of Simon & Schuster
Englewood Cliffs, New Jersey 07632

Previously published as
Up Against the Corporate Wall: Modern Corporations and Social Issues of the Eighties

Editorial/ production supervision and interior design: Maureen Wilson
Cover design: Marianne Frasco
Manufacturing buyer: Peter Havens

Printed in the United States of America
10 9 8 7 6 5 4 3 2 1

ISBN 0-13-946237-6

Prentice-Hall International (UK) Limited, *London*
Prentice-Hall of Australia Pty. Limited, *Sydney*
Prentice-Hall Canada Inc., *Toronto*
Prentice-Hall Hispanoamericana, S.A., *Mexico*
Prentice-Hall of India Private Limited, *New Delhi*
Prentice-Hall of Japan, Inc., *Tokyo*
Simon & Schuster Asia Pte. Ltd., *Singapore*
Editora Prentice-Hall do Brasil, Ltda., *Rio de Janeiro*

To
those haves and have-nots among us
who still have hopes
that when people of reason get together
they will plan the survival
and not the extinction
of the human race and of humanity,
this book is affectionately dedicated.

It is to this itch of being spoken of,
to this fury of distinguishing ourselves, which
seldom or never gives us a moment of respite,
that we owe both the best and the worst things
among us.

Ralph Waldo Emerson

CONTENTS

GRUMMAN CORPORATION 47
*Relations between Corporate Board and Top Management:
Obligation of Top Management to Implement Board Policies and Directives*

II

Business Strategies and Public Policy

GENERAL MOTORS AND THE CITY OF NORWOOD, OHIO 67
Plant Closings and Their Impact on Affected Communities

GOODYEAR TIRE & RUBBER COMPANY 82
Hostile Corporate Takeovers and Public Interest

INSIDER TRADING: THE LEVINE, BOESKY, AND THE DREXEL BURNHAM LAMBERT CAPER 102
How and Why Do Innovative Entrepreneurs Become White-Collar Criminals?

III

Corporate Advocacy and Grass-Roots Lobbying

CHEMICAL MANUFACTURERS ASSOCIATION, WASHINGTON, D.C. 125
Educational Advertising Campaign to Change Public Perception and Awareness of the Chemical Industry's Activities and Contributions to American Society

AMERICAN FEDERATION OF STATE, COUNTY, AND MUNICIPAL EMPLOYEES (AFSCME), WASHINGTON, D.C. 144
An Advocacy Campaign against Reaganomics

THE NATIONAL RIFLE ASSOCIATION AND GUN CONTROL 160
Lobbying Activities and Their Influence on Government Decision Making

IV

Corporate Actions and Workplace Safety

WARNER-LAMBERT COMPANY   187

Personal Criminal Liability of Senior Executives for Accidents Causing Workers' Death and Injury

WHIRLPOOL CORPORATION   204

*Employee Rights Protection from Employer's Retaliation
for Refusal to Work under Hazardous and Imminently Dangerous Conditions*

IOWA BEEF PROCESSORS, INC. (IBP, INC.)   212

Unsafe Working Conditions and Labor Practices in the Meat Industry

FILM RECOVERY SYSTEMS, INC.   230

*The Extent of Officers' Culpability for Serious Harm, and Even Death, of Workers
Caused by Unsafe Working Conditions*

V

Corporate Actions and Employee Rights

C. ITOH & CO. (AMERICA), INC.,
AND SUMITOMO CORPORATION OF AMERICA   245

*Conflicts between the Personnel Policies of Foreign Multinational Corporations (MNCs)
in the United States and Application of U.S. Civil Rights Laws*

COMPARABLE WORTH   267

A New Approach to Eliminating Sex-based Wage Inequities in Employment

UNITED AIRLINES, INC.   280

A Case of Age Discrimination or a Concern for the Safety of the Flying Public

PREFACE

The last two decades were quite turbulent in the evolving relationship between business, especially the large corporations, and society. It would be presumptuous for someone who has lived through this period and is so close to it to declare that its lessons have been learned and that all that remains is to add up the gains and losses from the experience. For this, we must await the mature perspective which only distance from the present can afford.

Instant history, however, has its uses. For neither now nor in the future can we ignore the recent past. It provides us with a point of departure from which we can measure progress or deflection from it. On the one hand, we are encumbered by the recent past in our perceptual biases about the behavior and motives of the people and institutions we must deal with. On the other hand, however, it provides the context in which we articulate the goals we wish to achieve and the means we would like to employ.

History repeats itself, precisely because we have short memories.

We are all captives of our imaginations, which are constrained to a large extent by our living environment. Societies survive and civilizations flourish because people of wisdom can judiciously combine the lessons of the distant past with the human and material resource constraints. To build a future based solely on historical antecedents that ignore the real concerns of living persons is like casting a grand illusion. There is always a sense of motion, but no progress. To build a future as if it were an incremental step determined solely by the step just taken is ineffective. There is a continued sense of progress but, in an endless chain of actions and reactions, nothing substantive or lasting is ever accomplished.

The conflicts between business firms and various elements of society during the early 1960s arose from long-standing grievances of various disenfranchised groups.

They felt their rightful share of the opportunities, aspirations, and fruits of American society were being denied by powerful vested economic interests supported and protected by a captive political system. Their rebellion was born out of the desperation of those who had nothing to lose. Issues were seen as black or white, groups as villainous or virtuous, causes as holy or satanic, and leaders as saints or charlatans.

The social and political upheavals of the 1960s forced us to face the injustices inflicted on certain social groups in our political and economic order. This was nothing new. We have experienced similar cycles throughout our history, starting with the Industrial Revolution and ending with the Great Depression. During the 1960s, the inequities in opportunity, the lack of caring, and the high proportion of society's rewards going to a few combined to make people doubt the legitimacy of the large corporations that were identified with the socioeconomic order. We saw well-being not only in the aggregate growth, but in terms of those poor who were lost in the counting. We examined political democracy not only in terms of its grand design but in terms of the disenfranchised who did not count at all.

The 1970s brought a partial resolution of these problems: large-scale, overt inequalities were outlawed. In an effort to prevent future inequities and provide fair compensation for past inequities, inequality of opportunity was measured, in a large number of cases, by inequality of outcome. These resolutions of past inequalities have become institutionalized in a plethora of new rights and entitlements. We all claim rights to education, a decent standard of living, support for the family, privacy, a cleaner environment, old age support, and protection from failure. When divorced from any individual obligation or reciprocity, these rights become absolutes with politically strong constituencies to protect and expand them.

An inevitable outcome of this approach surfaced in the 1980s with the emergence of single-issue causes and narrowly based political groups as a dominant feature, and not necessarily a beneficial one, of the American sociopolitical arena. These single-issue advocacy groups brought about a shift in power alliances and yielded highly visible benefits to groups who were previously not so fortunate. The shift in power from producer to consumer groups also brought about a shift in outlook concerning the future of society, from a perspective of eternal optimism and growth to a mood of pessimism and finite resources. Instead of everyone sharing in a common endeavor, we viewed society as a zero-sum game where one's gains must come at someone else's costs.

The 1980s began under the banner of the "me-generation." This self-centeredness was elevated to the status of a noble calling. We became cloistered in our self-ordained virtues. We disdained compromises because to see reason in an adversary is to sully one's own reputation.

Business has not been immune to these changes over the past three decades. Both as a measure of self-preservation and as a consequence of a narrow perspective, business has answered its critics largely with strident intransigence and an uncompromising attitude. Instead of defining corporate interests within the larger framework of the public good, it has often resorted to defining the public interest as if it were a secondary and incidental outcome of corporate interests.

During the early 1960s, when social pressures on business had barely gathered momentum, the business response to opposition groups was generally one of lofty disdain. Business felt that paying these groups any attention would be legitimizing their social credibility. The response was a simplistic one: Pretend they are not there, and they and their complaints will go away.

In the 1970s, business displayed a more conciliatory response to societal concerns.

Although corporations were aggressive in formulating the national agenda, they nevertheless attempted to narrow the gap between societal expectations and corporate performance. Substantive gains were made, some of them only after changes were institutionalized and mandated by law. During the 1980s, corporations became far more sophisticated in managing their relations to society. Confronted with well-organized and articulate adversaries, corporations began to use some of the same tactics. Rhetoric was substituted for substance. Compromises and consensus were discarded in favor of holding firm. Corporations began to speak out on social issues not only by advocating specific public policies, but also by questioning their opponents' motives and even branding them misinformed and ignorant. The polarization of viewpoints had become almost complete.

The tragedy has been the failure of both the corporate community and the social activists to work as partners in finding and developing commonly acceptable solutions to societal problems. The relationship has been an adversarial one, each side attempting to persuade the American public that the opposition is the villain. Each seems more interested in directing attention to deficiencies and labeling the opposition than in acting in the public interest.

The problems of the 1960s and 1970s concerned the correction of flagrant imbalances in the allocation of costs and the distribution of benefits among various societal groups. Business bore the major burden of enacting social changes because it was the repository of the nation's economic resources; it had the management expertise to bring about those changes; and it was most susceptible to public and political pressures for change because it comprised large, private collectives with weak constituencies.

In the 1990s, our problems are infinitely more complex and their solutions immeasurably more difficult. We seem to have reached a watershed in terms of conflict between business and social groups. We have come to realize that big government can be just as insensitive to individual needs as big business. Although big government has solved some problems, it has created others equally ominous: social and economic inefficiencies, erosion of purchasing power through inflation, allocation of increased proportions of Gross National Product to public sector spending, and even invasion of individual privacy. There is a growing aversion toward increased reliance on the government to solve all our problems.

There is also some questioning concerning the viability of solutions offered by social activists. We no longer accept on faith every activist group that purports to speak for the public interest. It is becoming apparent that often in their strident intransigence and uncompromising attitudes the activists may be advancing only their own self-interests. They frequently speak for those who directly and immediately stand to gain from their positions.

The ethical problems of the 1980s and 1990s stemming from the conflict between business and society do not concern obvious right and wrong, guilt and innocence, but one type of inequity over another, giving one group more while taking from another group, the virtue of frugality and the sin of accumulation, and the morality of principles versus the morality of situations. In an unjust world, the distinctions between the guilty and innocent have become ambiguous. We are confronted with the realization that we live in an increasingly interdependent society where individual good is not possible outside the context of common good. It makes no sense to separate moral principles from institutional behavior, political power from economic influence, and environmental values from material rewards. To do so is to divorce the social system from its basic element, the human being, who does not behave in a fragmented manner.

The corporation must become an active agent for social change. The corporation cannot confine its role to responding to societal goals advocated by other groups. As a dominant institution in society, it must assume its rightful place and contribute to the articulation of the public agenda itself. In today's pluralistic society, corporate participation in social policy formulation is not a luxury but a necessity; it must receive top management attention and the corporate resources to do it right and to do it well. The cost of being wrong can be very high. Participation simply to defend the corporate position on a given social issue, to support a political candidate considered friendly to the firm, or to sell the free enterprise system is not sufficient. Effective participation demands the advancement of a coherent political position, something most businesspeople do not have today. Businesspeople cannot participate effectively in the political process until they can articulate who and what they are socially and what role their products and services play culturally. This demands positive political strategies, not ad hoc responses to immediate crises.

This fifth edition of *Up Against the Corporate Wall* presents case studies that will likely become critical issues of conflict between business and society in the 1990s. The challenge is for the business student and business executive to develop innovative and constructive approaches to resolving these issues. The cases represent, in our view, the major areas of concern that will involve the business community and larger segments of the American society in the 1990s. We would have liked to have covered a great many more issues and more cases, but this would have been impossible given the constraints of space and time. We recognize that there may be differences of opinion as to our choices of issues and cases; however, we would hope that such differences are minimal.

Public policy has come to exert an increasingly powerful influence on business strategies. While all of the cases we present reflect this dynamic, seven are particularly centered around public policy regulations and processes. The sociopolitical dimension is reflected in issues affecting personal security. The National Rifle Association and Gun Control case captures the conviction and emotion surrounding the desire for safety in the streets, with protagonists taking radically different approaches to law and order.

Socioeconomic dimensions of corporate policy have riveted the public's attention with the drama of plant closings as corporations struggle for survival in an increasingly competitive world. At the same time, the public has been stunned with disbelief as layer after layer is peeled away from the scandal of insider trading. The saga of Dennis Levine, Ivan Boesky, and the firm of Drexel Burnham Lambert took four years to come to light, and even as this book goes to press the end is not in sight. On the other hand, the multibillion-dollar stakes of the turbulent world of corporate takeovers leave the common person to piece together what happened long after the action has been played out. The drama is epitomized in the struggle that took place between Goodyear and Sir James Goldsmith (see the Goodyear Tire & Rubber Company case).

Corporations do not simply adopt a reactive approach to public policy, however. Increasingly, they take the offensive with advocacy advertising. Both the AFSCME and Chemical Manufacturers cases illustrate the tactics economic agents increasingly employ to shape public opinion and their operating environments.

In the past decades, responsibility for corporate social performance has increasingly been placed on top management. Often, when a scandal is uncovered top management does a disappearing act, leaving subordinates or the nameless system to shoulder the blame. This is examined in the E. F. Hutton check kiting case, the General Dynamics defense industry profiteering case, and the Bank of Boston money laundering case. At the same time, the question of whether boards of directors have any real clout is dramatized in the case of Grumman Corporation, where top management was at odds with its board.

Since the origins of capitalism, the worker has occupied a central place of concern. Our case selection reflects this long-standing orientation, as we devote four cases to workplace safety and four to employee rights. Both the Warner-Lambert and Whirlpool cases examine specific industrial accidents and raise the question of management responsibility. In the IBP case, the focus shifts from a specific accident to a regular pattern of accidents. This case raises classic questions of management practice in a cost-cutting industry when there is a ready supply of unskilled labor. The Film Recovery case focuses on the responsibility of top management when industrial hazards result in the death of an employee.

Our cases on employee rights concern sex discrimination (Comparable Worth), race discrimination (Sears, Roebuck), age discrimination (United Airlines), and alleged race and sex discrimination against American employees by a Japanese company. These cases all raise fundamental questions concerning the dignity of the individual, which lies at the root of democracy.

Two cases focus on the rights of consumers. The case concerning GM's X-car examines the issue of auto safety. At the same time, it draws attention (along with the Sears case) to the problem of regulatory excesses and their impact on affected businesses. The case concerning the role of the tobacco industry in the United States examines consumer welfare and choice in the face of the legal production and marketing of a harmful product.

Finally, we examine the role of multinational corporations in developing societies. The South Africa case examines the role of American corporations in societies which explicitly avow principles of discrimination. The Bhopal case focuses on industrial accidents in settings where the likelihood of implementing safety precautions is marginal at best. The case concerning the tobacco industry in the Third World examines what the tobacco multinationals seek to do in the Third World that they are forbidden to do at home.

We are especially grateful to Professor Karen Paul of the Rochester Institute of Technology for contributing the case on South Africa, and to Professor Paul Shrivastava of New York University for the case of Bhopal. In addition, we would like to thank the staff at the Center for Management at Baruch College of the City University of New York. We particularly note the research assistance of Leo Giglio and Ramesh Gehani, who are doctoral candidates in management at Baruch College. Finally, we are grateful for the typing and word processing chores indefatigably carried out by Ruben Cardona, with additional support from Beulah Babulal and Julie Levine.

S. PRAKASH SETHI
New York City and Troy, NY

PAUL STEIDLMEIER
Binghamton, NY

·I·

Top Management Actions and Corporate Social Performance

E. F. HUTTON & CO., NEW YORK

Check kiting and wire fraud

On May 3, 1985, E. F. Hutton pleaded guilty to 2,000 mail and wire fraud violations arising from allegations that the company engaged in cash management practices that led to unauthorized overdrafts from banks where its various branches held accounts. The guilty plea was a culmination of an extensive investigation lasting over three years and conducted by the office of the U.S. Attorney for the middle district of Pennsylvania. Hutton acknowledged that more than 100 of the company's branches were involved in the cash drawdown scheme.[1] According to Robert Ogren, the head of the Justice Department's white-collar fraud office, there were indications that other firms were using the same type of illegal practices.[2] However, to date, the Justice Department has not charged any other firm for similar crimes.

As a result of the guilty plea and settlement, Hutton agreed to pay $2 million in fines, pay the cost of the government's investigation, and make restitution (variously estimated from $8 to $30 million) to the banks which suffered losses because of Hutton's activities. In addition, Hutton agreed to accept a broad civil injunction, a remedy provided under the Comprehensive Crime Control Act of 1984, which spelled out the ground rules for future cash management practices.[3]

THE CHARGES AND THE BELL INVESTIGATION

The specific accusations against E. F. Hutton under the indictment pertained to the period between July 1980 and February 1982. The company was charged with:

1. *excessive overdrafting*, in which a bank account is drawn in excess of deposits or funds available;

2. *improper chaining* and crisscrossing, which involves a cycle of overdrafted checks that are transferred through an extensive network of different bank branches and Hutton offices;

3. *tampering with the microencoding* on checks, resulting in intentional clearing delays; and

4. *a failure to produce material documents* as requested by a Federal Grand Jury subpoena.

Following the guilty plea, and with a view to undertaking a thorough housecleaning, Hutton's CEO, Robert Fomon, and the company's board of directors decided to appoint a special counsel to investigate the practices that gave rise to the criminal charges and to determine who within Hutton was responsible for those practices.[4] On May 17, 1985, Hutton chose Griffin B. Bell to conduct the investigation. Bell was a former attorney general of the United States under President Carter, and at the time of his appointment he was a member of the law firm of King and Spalding in Atlanta, Georgia. Bell was promised full cooperation from all Hutton employees. The Bell Report was issued on September 4, 1985. The full Report was not made publicly available. However, copies were obtained by various members of the press, and its finding were widely reported.

THE IMPORTANCE OF THE CASE AND ISSUES FOR ANALYSIS

The resulting shock of adverse publicity, loss of customer confidence, and revelations of sloppy management and indifferent and poor internal controls were so severe that the firm was never able to extricate itself fully from the morass. Following the stock market crash of October 19, 1987, the firm faced extreme difficulty and felt that it could not compete effectively in the market. Consequently, in December 1987, E. F. Hutton was acquired by Shearson Lehman Brothers for a total price of about $1 billion ($600 million less than Shearson had bid the previous year).[5]

The Hutton case is one of a handful regarding highly prominent and prestigious firms that were shown to have a dark underside during the turbulent period following deregulation of U.S. financial markets in May 1975.[6] These cases show how a loss of public confidence impacts negatively on a firm's performance and profitability. They also show the risks and adverse public consequences when firms drive themselves to the edge of ethical and prudent business practices in their pursuit of short-term profits.

The issue, therefore, is not simply one of managers acting irresponsibly in their zeal to become more profitable. It is also the relative lack of sufficient internal controls on a firm's top managers by its own board of directors, and external controls through regulatory institutions in the United States.

The Hutton case demonstrates that there is a thin line between aggressive business practices and imprudent, unethical, and illegal business conduct. Moreover, this line is likely to be obliterated by the absence of a strong culture of corporate ethics and by a system of employee compensation and rewards that emphasizes performance but overlooks the process by which such performance is generated. The Hutton case relates to the self-perception of top managers, their egos, management styles, and comparisons with their peers in terms of the size and profitability of their empires. It is tied to the immense financial rewards garnered by them based on the year-to-year performance of their firms, and their relative insulation from the adverse long-term consequences of their actions through such measures as golden parachutes, handsome severance packages, and lucrative consulting contracts lasting far into the future. It shows the consequences that follow when managers fail to develop a system of checks and balances by which top management ensures that employees follow procedures that protect the company, its shareholders, and eventually the employees themselves from the consequences of illegal and unlawful behavior.

Hutton's guilty plea on such a massive scale raised tremendous controversy both within and outside the corporation. A number of people faulted the company for not defending itself vigorously. They believed that the charges against the company were highly technical, and further, that the company stood a reasonable chance of being acquitted. At worst, it could end up settling for fewer and milder charges resulting in nominal penalties or even a consent degree.[7] Hutton's CEO, Robert Fomon, indicated that he pleaded guilty to all the charges because he wanted to get the issue behind him and spare the company from further adverse publicity and deteriorating employee morale. The result, however, was quite the contrary.[8] The company was in the news, all of it negative, for quite some time after the guilty plea, and there was significant erosion of employee morale and many employee defections. At the same time, the U.S. government did not escape criticism. The Securities and Exchange Commission (SEC) and Justice Department were faulted for not prosecuting the case more vigorously and instead settling for fines and letting the corporate executives escape all penalties.[9] They argued that since Hutton settled so quickly, senior executives were probably worried about what might be disclosed in the event of a public trial. In the absence of a trial, the true extent of Hutton's guilt, the culpability of its executives, and the structural and operational aspects of Hutton's management that may have contributed to its illegal and unethical behavior remain unclear and unexplained.

The issues for analysis can be grouped into three areas: those relating to the corporation, the banking and financial system, and the regulatory agencies. In terms of the corporation, we might ask:

1. What were the structural aspects of Hutton's cash flow, reporting, auditing, and corporate reporting systems that contributed to both the high interest earnings and the failure of control mechanisms?

2. To what extent were these failures due primarily to a lack of management actions (i.e., incompetence, indifference, or disregard of sound operating procedures)? What is the extent of responsibility for these failures that can be attributed to various executives, and why?

3. To what extent did the system of compensation, e.g., salaries and bonuses for branch managers, contribute to Hutton's managers abusing overdraft facilities in order to inflate their incomes?

4. How might one describe Hutton's corporate culture, the organization structure, and the decision-making style of its CEO and other top managers? To what extent, if any, might these factors have contributed to Hutton's downfall?

5. What should companies like Hutton do to prevent the occurrence of similar behavior in their own operations?

6. How did the company behave during the investigation? Should its conduct inspire confidence in terms of the veracity of its claims regarding its acts?

7. How effective is the notion of using outside, and presumably highly credible, experts such as former attorney general Griffin Bell as fact finders? How might similar approaches be used by companies in public confidence crises? What are some of the advantages and limitations of such approaches for the company and for the public? Given that Bell was a lawyer, is it possible that his investigation was too confined and narrowly based on a legal framework, which led to neglecting the broader issues of organizational structure, decision-making procedures, corporate culture, and the character and decision-making style of the CEO and other senior executives?

Next, there are questions about the conduct of various banks and indeed the entire banking system, which failed to detect the overdrafts for such a long time, even though they were undertaken on a consistent and regular basis.

8. Should we consider what happened to Hutton as an aberration in a single company, or is it something that could have happened easily in other companies or might still be happening but has not been discovered?

9. What are the vulnerabilities in the U.S. banking system, especially those pertaining to the check-clearing system, that were exploited by Hutton? How might one go about eliminating them without overburdening the system and adding further delays and costs?

10. How did various banks behave in the system? Should one expect these banks to blow the whistle under such circumstances? Why wasn't the system able to discover the broad pattern?

Finally, with regard to the regulatory agencies, we must ask:

11. How might one evaluate the behavior of various regulatory agencies, especially the SEC, and prosecuting authorities during various phases of the investigation, prosecution, and punishment?

12. How adequate was the magnitude and nature of punishment in restoring the losses of various parties, in punishing the wrongdoers, and in setting an example that would act as a deterrent to other companies and individuals? What, if any, additional measures should be taken to make the system of regulatory oversight more efficient, fair, and demonstrably effective?

THE FINANCIAL
SERVICES INDUSTRY

The financial services industry is a highly competitive one. Financial services firms have historically relied on brokerage commissions for a substantial portion of their revenue. In May 1975, the fixed commission rate structure which pervaded the entire industry gave way as deregulation set in. Also, the number of companies in the industry as well as the range of services offered multiplied. Profits were squeezed.

As a result of deregulation, about one-third of New York Stock Exchange member firms lost money in 1977, and the number of New York Stock Exchange member firms fell from 570 in 1970 to 370 in 1977.[10] The remaining firms found that they needed to diversify and utilize all available assets to the fullest extent possible in order to maintain a competitive position. At Hutton, one response to this extremely competitive environment was to stress the importance of improving cash management, particularly of interest income.

HUTTON'S BACKGROUND
AND THE INCIDENT THAT
BROUGHT IT DOWN

E. F. Hutton and Company, Inc., was the second largest independent securities firm in the United States until its acquisition in 1987 by Shearson Lehman Brothers, a unit of American Express. It had been a major broker dealing in securities, options, and commodities; a leading investment bank; a major dealer in corporate, municipal, and government securities; and a large distributor of mutual funds, tax shelters, life insurance, and annuity products. Hutton was a member of the New York Stock Exchange, the National Association of Securities Dealers, and other domestic and foreign securities and commodity exchanges. Hutton had 18,000 employees and 6,500 brokers at 350 outlets. In 1987, it had $28 billion in assets under management. However, it posted a $90.3 million loss in 1986 (a banner year for the rest of the industry). Throughout the 1980s, it consistently trailed its rivals in technology, management innovations, and profitability, which from 1984 averaged well less than 30% of the industry level. After the October 19 crash, its stock fell to $11 contrasted with a book value of $26. Hutton had nowhere to turn.[11]

The first disclosure of the brewing crisis was innocuous enough and showed all signs of being a minor oversight that would easily blow over. That was not to be the case.

On Friday, December 11, 1984, a small rural upstate New York bank, the Genessee County Bank in Batavia, was presented with an $8 million depository check that had been deposited in one of Hutton's New York banks. Genessee also had Hutton checks drawn on the United Penn bank in Wilkes-Barre, Pennsylvania. Concerned about the amount of money involved, the auditor of the Genessee bank telephoned the United Penn bank to verify that the money had in fact been collected in Hutton's account there. The United Penn bank had nothing more than uncollected funds in the form of reimbursement checks deposited a day earlier. The Genessee Bank, on discovering this, did not honor the check, and at the same time it and the United Penn bank refused several others. Although Hutton immediately wired the necessary money to the banks, the two banks, nevertheless, informed the New York State banking authorities and the Federal Deposit Insurance Corporation of the spurious transactions, thereby instigating an extensive investigation.

CASH MANAGEMENT SYSTEM AT HUTTON

Businesses have increasingly come to realize the value of effective cash management. When millions of dollars flow through a company's system every day, it is important that these funds not remain idle. Thus, large corporations have developed very sophisticated systems through which they constantly earn interest income on idle funds while they go through various stages of processing and clearing.

The cash management system at E. F. Hutton was designed by the company's money manager, William T. Sullivan. It was devised as a drawdown system to ensure that only a minimum of cash was left in the banks each day. The initial system worked as follows: Every day, each Hutton branch office would advise its respective regional office of the amount by which its bank deposits exceeded its withdrawals. The regional office had that branch's checkbook and would write a withdrawal check for that amount. It would do the same for each branch office in the area. Later, Hutton's headquarters in New York would take all excess funds out of the bank account of each regional office and its branches. However, two complicating factors made this system inefficient. First, approximately 70% of the deposits of a typical branch were checks written on the same bank, thereby providing immediately available funds. Second, on occasion, checks would not be presented to the bank the following day because of unforeseen delays in the bank's clearing process. As a result, at a West Coast bank, over $400,000 was left in daily balances. All banks, however, did not have such large balances.[12] (See Exhibit 1.)

As William Sullivan, Hutton's executive responsible for developing the cash management system, became aware of these problems, he instituted a revised system that was designed to extract the full value of funds left with the bank less the proper amount of funds to compensate the bank for its services. The revised drawdown system worked as follows: When cash or its equivalent was deposited, that amount was drawn down twice. The rationale was that cash deposits were immediately available to Hutton as funds. One way to retrieve the use of these funds was a withdrawal. However, this was costly and cumbersome. The second way was to issue drawdown checks which had cash value only for the next day. Thus, banks had the use of Hutton funds for two days. By doubling the amount drawn down, Hutton ensured that a bank was not overcompensated. Branch cashiers were instructed to de-

EXHIBIT 1.   How E. F. Hutton Created Interest-Free "Loans"

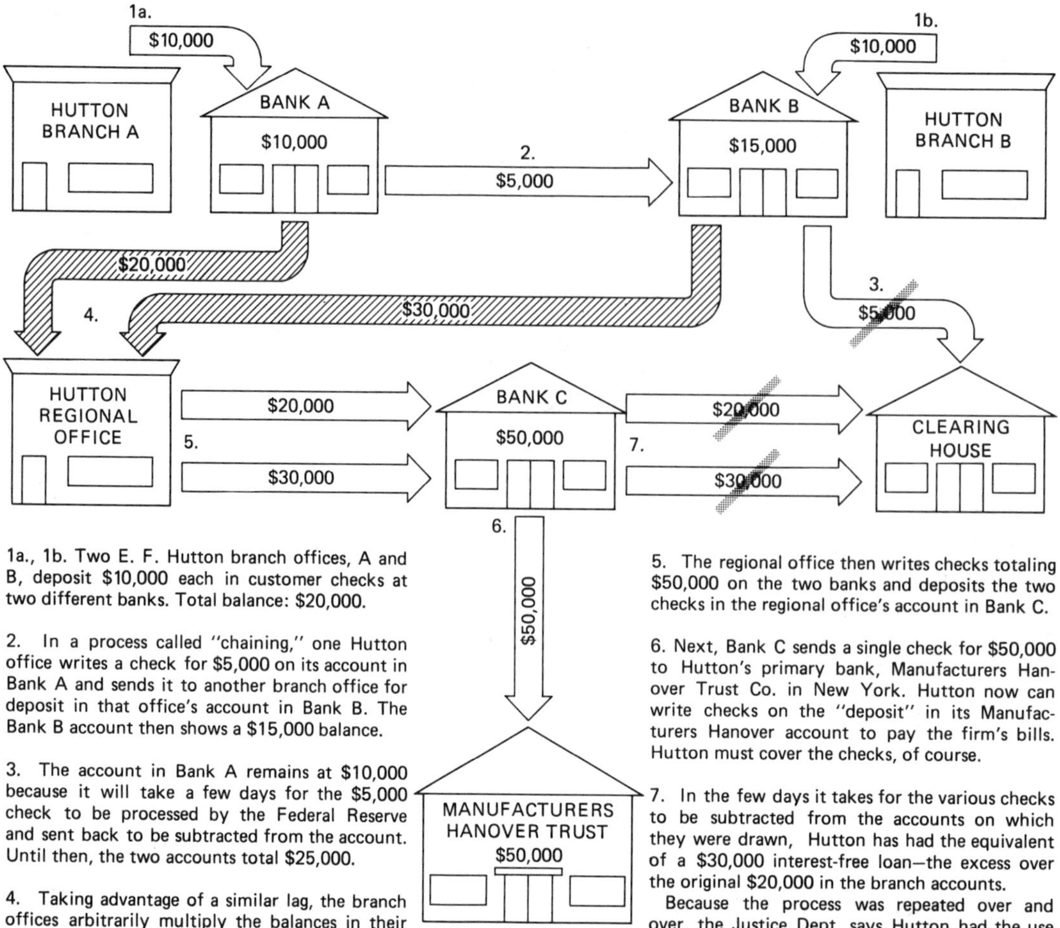

1a. $10,000

1b. $10,000

HUTTON BRANCH A

BANK A $10,000

2. $5,000

BANK B $15,000

HUTTON BRANCH B

$20,000

4. $30,000

3. $5,000

HUTTON REGIONAL OFFICE

5. $20,000

BANK C $50,000

$20,000

7. $30,000

CLEARING HOUSE

5. $30,000

6. $50,000

MANUFACTURERS HANOVER TRUST $50,000

1a., 1b. Two E. F. Hutton branch offices, A and B, deposit $10,000 each in customer checks at two different banks. Total balance: $20,000.

2. In a process called "chaining," one Hutton office writes a check for $5,000 on its account in Bank A and sends it to another branch office for deposit in that office's account in Bank B. The Bank B account then shows a $15,000 balance.

3. The account in Bank A remains at $10,000 because it will take a few days for the $5,000 check to be processed by the Federal Reserve and sent back to be subtracted from the account. Until then, the two accounts total $25,000.

4. Taking advantage of a similar lag, the branch offices arbitrarily multiply the balances in their accounts by two and report that amount to E. F. Hutton's regional office.

5. The regional office then writes checks totaling $50,000 on the two banks and deposits the two checks in the regional office's account in Bank C.

6. Next, Bank C sends a single check for $50,000 to Hutton's primary bank, Manufacturers Hanover Trust Co. in New York. Hutton now can write checks on the "deposit" in its Manufacturers Hanover account to pay the firm's bills. Hutton must cover the checks, of course.

7. In the few days it takes for the various checks to be subtracted from the accounts on which they were drawn, Hutton has had the equivalent of a $30,000 interest-free loan—the excess over the original $20,000 in the branch accounts.

Because the process was repeated over and over, the Justice Dept. says Hutton had the use of "well in excess of $1 billion" during the year and a half the scheme was in operation.

SOURCE: "What Did Hutton's Managers Know—And When Did They Know It?" *Business Week,* May 20, 1985, p. 111.

posit on the next day the excess amount required by the addition of the drawdown with customer payments or a reimbursement check, if necessary. The system recognized where float had occurred and recaptured the corresponding value. Exhibit 2 shows an actual drawdown sheet presented as part of Sullivan's testimony before the House Subcommittee Hearings investigating Hutton.[13]

EXCESSIVE OVERDRAFTING

The objective of excessive overdrafting was to earn interest on funds that did not belong to Hutton and which the company did not actually have on deposit in its bank accounts. The excessive overdrafting resulted in increased interest income for Hutton's

EXHIBIT 2.   Illustration of Sullivan's Addition to Drawdown Sheet

Part One:

Opening bank book balance, as reported to branch by bank	$_____
less local checks issued by branch to customers which they deposited in other banks	$_____
less previous day's drawdown check written off of branch bank account	$_____
Subtotal of Part One	$_____

Part Two:

Wired amounts received in branch account	$_____
Checks deposited by customers of same bank where branch account is located	$_____
less checks paid by branch to person who deposits them in bank where branch account is located	$_____
Subtotal of Part Two	$_____

Part Three:

Subtotal from Part One	$_____
Subtotal from Part Two	$_____
less cash value, if any, owed to bank	$_____
less cash balances left with branch's bank to compensate it for services it provides to branch	$_____
Total to be Added to Day's Drawdown	$_____

SOURCE: Subcommittee on Crime of the House Commitee on the Judiciary, *Hearing on E. F. Hutton Mail and Wire Fraud*, June 19, July 19, August 1, October 3, October 31, December 6, December 11, 1986. Washington, D.C.: U.S. Government Printing Office, p. 480. Hereafter cited as *Hearings.*

participating branches. This, in turn, generated performance bonuses for branch managers since they were tied to the performance of their respective branches. The banks involved, however, felt that Hutton obtained these sizable interest-free loans at their expense.

Two criteria were used in determining which branches had engaged in excessive overdrafting: abnormally high interest income, and excessive use of branch reimbursement checks. Twenty branches were found to have engaged in excessive overdrafting.[14]

The Atlantic, Midwest, Pacific South, Mountain, South Central, and Northwest regions all engaged in excessive overdrafting at the regional level. For example, the branch cashier at the Williamsport office received instructions from the regional operations of the Atlantic division to have the branch bank account drawn down by $925,000 for a significant period of time in 1981. The amount was arbitrary and not related to deposits of the day. Similarly, the Bakersfield branch claimed that Mark Willets, the Regional Interest Specialist, instructed the branch to overdraw in amounts of $500,000 daily. These types of instructions were conveyed to some branches in the aforementioned regions.[15]

Not all excessive overdrafting was initiated at the regional level, however. The Wilkes-Barre branch, on instruction from John Holland, then branch manager, during October alone deposited $21 million in bank reimbursement checks. On occasion, Holland would arbitrarily determine the amount of the overdraft. John Pearce at the Bethesda branch (and later at St. Louis) instructed the cashier to overdraw on a daily basis; the daily drawdown amount was not to exceed $10 million. Both Holland and Pearce defended their actions to be legal and conforming with Hutton's policy of "aggressive cash management."[16]

Variations of this approach were also used by a number of other branch managers in other regions. At the Congressional hearings, all managers who testified stated that they believed their actions were legal, were known by the banks, and were condoned, even encouraged by Hutton officials. Branch managers felt that their system was an extension of Hutton's cash management program.[17]

Hutton maintains that its cash management practices reflected common practices in the financial industry. Critics maintain that what Hutton called aggressive management was in fact excessive and abusive.[18] The excessive overdrafting resulted in increased income for Hutton's participating branches. This, in turn, generated performance bonuses for branch managers. As noted earlier, however, the banks involved felt that Hutton obtained these sizable interest-free loans at their expense. Evidence discovered by the Justice Department in its investigation of Hutton showed that George Ball, Hutton's president from 1980 to 1982, wrote congratulatory and encouraging notes to the branch managers who were most successful in generating interest income.[19]

CHAINING, CRISSCROSSING, AND ENCODING

Evidence presented both at the hearings and discovered through the Bell investigation showed that various Hutton branch managers used these dubious and often illegal methods to increase cash flow and interest earnings.

Chaining occurs when, instead of passing daily branch receipts from a local bank to a regional bank to money center banks, a company sends checks through local banks all over the country before the checks reach the money center.[20] As with excessive overdrafting, improper chaining benefited Hutton and the participating managers because of the delays in the clearing process.

Crisscrossing is designed to increase a company's cash balance by simultaneously issuing checks in the same amounts drawn on two different banks and cross-depositing each check in the other bank. For Hutton, this practice resulted in increased opening balances for Hutton branches, although the level of funds fell later in the day as the checks cleared. Crisscrossing is not illegal, although it is an improper action and one that is not expected by a bank's corporate customer. It is not clear when the practice began, but William Sullivan, Hutton's money mobilizer from 1974 to 1980, stated that the practice had been in existence before 1975. Sullivan was aware of this practice during his time as money mobilizer and did not take any steps to terminate the practice. Under Thomas Morley, money mobilizer after Sullivan, crisscrossing continued, al-

though Morley did not expressly state that it should do so.[21]

It was alleged that Hutton intentionally engaged in the alteration of codes or processing numbers on Hutton checks, or that it failed to correct encoding problems in order to take advantage of the delays created by check encoding or printing errors. Check encoding problems involved three banks: Chemical bank, the Bank of America, and the First National Bank of Pennsylvania.

Hutton's New York Management

At the time of the investigation, Hutton was divided into one international and nine domestic regions, with each region supervised by a vice-president. However, individual regions operated almost exclusively under the control of a sales executive who managed branch office staffing and business production. Each regional operations manager reported to Norman Epstein, head of operations, through Richard Genin, senior vice-president for trading operations. Although selected with the approval of regional vice-presidents, the operations managers reported to these vice-presidents in name only. They were for the most part controlled by Epstein and Genin (see Exhibit 3 on page 11).

The Hutton group could generally be characterized as having a loose management structure. Functions among various groups were to a large degree overlapping, with an unclear division of responsibilities. Dual reporting was not uncommon. The principal operating officers of Hutton during this period were Thomas P. Lynch, executive vice-president and managing director, who served as de facto chief financial officer; Paul G. Hines, head of corporate planning and control; Norman M. Epstein, head of operations; and Thomas W. Rae, head of legal affairs and compliance.

Ball and Morley were the leading advocates of increased interest income profits at

EXHIBIT 3. E. F. Hutton & Co. Organizational Chart[a]

E. F. HUTTON ORGANIZATION, AS OF DECEMBER 31, 1981

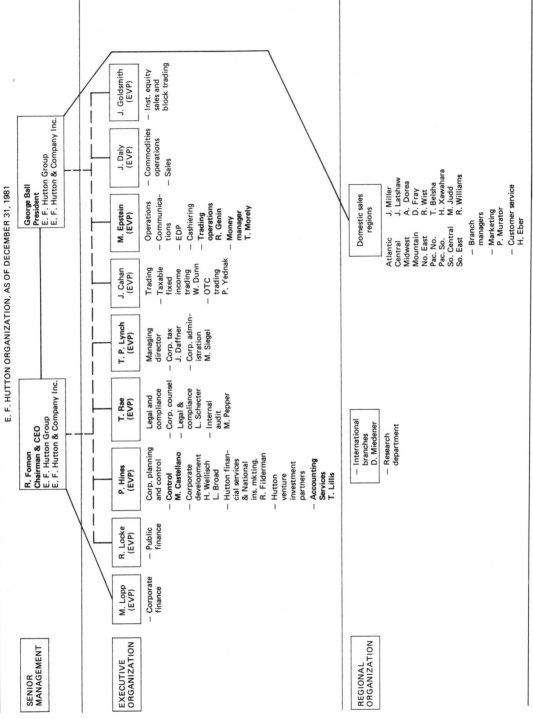

SENIOR MANAGEMENT

R. Fomon
Chairman & CEO
E. F. Hutton Group
E. F. Hutton & Company Inc.

George Ball
President
E. F. Hutton Group
E. F. Hutton & Company Inc.

EXECUTIVE ORGANIZATION

M. Lopp
(EVP)
– Corporate finance

R. Locke
(EVP)
– Public finance

P. Hines
(EVP)
– Corp. planning and control
– **Control**
  M. Castellano
– Corporate development
  H. Wellisch
  L. Broad
– Hutton finan- cial services & National ins. mkting.
  R. Filderman
– Hutton venture investment partners
– **Accounting**
  Services
  T. Lillis

T. Rae
(EVP)
– Legal and compliance
– Corp. counsel
– Legal & compliance
  L. Schecter
– Internal audit
  M. Pepper

T. P. Lynch
(EVP)
– Managing director
– Corp. tax
  J. Daffner
– Corp. admin- istration
  M. Siegel

J. Cahan
(EVP)
– Trading
– Taxable fixed income trading
  W. Dunn
– OTC trading
  P. Yednak

M. Epstein
(EVP)
– Operations
– Communica- tions
– EDP
– Cashiering
– **Trading**
  operations
  R. Genin
– **Money**
  manager
  T. Morely

J. Daly
(EVP)
– Commodities operations
– Sales

J. Goldsmith
(EVP)
– Inst. equity sales and block trading

REGIONAL ORGANIZATION

– International branches
  D. Miedener
– Research department

Domestic sales regions

Atlantic	J. Miller
Central	J. Latshaw
Midwest	A. Dorea
Mountain	D. Fray
No. East	R. Wist
Pac. No.	T. Belsha
Pac. So.	H. Xawahara
So. Central	M. Judd
So. East	R. Williams

– Branch managers
– Marketing
  P. Murator
– Customer service
  H. Eber

Source: *Hearings*, pp. 94.

11

the national level. Regional vice-presidents and regional operations managers also actively encouraged this type of income. Interest profits had become frequent topics at meetings between branch managers and regional personnel. This added to the Hutton overdraft culture.

Hutton's problems developed because its culture allowed improper overdrafts. With rare exceptions, regional and branch personnel contended that improper overdrafting procedures were authorized by or attributable to Morley and New York's money management operations. Such procedures developed to the point that Hutton's accounting department was concentrating on interest earnings rather than interest problems.

Ball, along with the operational executive vice-presidents, reported directly to Robert Fomon, chairman of the board and CEO. Ball was, however, a dominant figure in the company, and other senior officers reported to him primarily in the capacity of support officers. The controller for the accounting department was Michael Castellano. This department published studies and reports on interest earnings, many of which indicated great variances caused by improper overdrafting practices. None of the receivers of these reports, including directors and vice-presidents, took note of these variances. The vice-president of accounting services, Thomas Lillis, wrote memoranda advocating increases in interest earnings. Almost all of Hutton's senior management were focused on increasing interest earnings. Those with low-interest earnings were told to follow the examples of the high earners.

Robert Fomon's leadership style was in part responsible for the company becoming embroiled in the check overdraft scandal. Fomon himself conceded that a tighter rein should have been kept on the company's cash management activities. He was known for keeping subordinates at a distance and letting them work out their own problems as long as they did not diverge from the course he had set.[22] He led Hutton for 15 years in a style not dissimilar from that of a grand monarch. According to various internal sources, he ruled with an iron hand and had little patience for dissent. He was an isolated figure, enveloped in mystery, who never liked to manage people and was extremely reluctant to grab management's reins. His physical health was not good; he suffered two mild strokes in the 1980s. His personal character was also questioned as he became involved in "embarrassing episodes" linked to heavy drinking and the chasing of young women on Manhattan's Upper East Side party circuit. Confidence in his leadership eroded.[23]

THE EXTENT OF TOP MANAGEMENT INVOLVEMENT AND RESPONSIBILITY

Hutton claimed that senior management first learned of the illegal activities when Genessee County Bank of Batavia, New York, first bounced their checks in December 1981. This claim was supported by attorney general Edwin Meese, who explained the government's decision not to prosecute individual employees both in order to avoid lengthy litigation and because it was a corporate scheme and no one personally benefitted from defrauding the banks.[24] On the face of it, this claim sounds preposterous because of the widespread nature of the scheme and the extent to which it permeated various levels of Hutton's organization. Consequently, the Justice Department came under severe criticism for its decision. However, even if one were to suspend credulity and accept Hutton's version, it would seem that the organization lacked appropriate financial and supervisory controls and was instead running amok. If this were the case, then the top management of Hutton must share the blame for being incompetent and must be discharged from their positions. Instead, most of them received golden parachutes when the company was acquired by Shearson Lehman.[25]

Some evidence of the culpability of Hutton's management, or lack thereof, can be evaluated in terms of the company's cooperation in various investigations. Throughout the whole process both the Justice Department and the Subcommittee complained that Hutton frequently only postured at being cooperative. Indeed, at the end of the first day of hearings, the Subcommittee chairman complained to Hutton's chairman Fomon that Hutton had provided 62 cartons of largely irrelevant material in a seeming effort to bury the Subcommittee in paperwork. Only four days after Hutton's guilty plea, the Judiciary Subcommittee voted unanimously to issue subpoenas requiring Fomon and three other senior Hutton executives to testify about the 1980–1982 scheme and the government's handling of the case. They also subpoenaed documents from Hutton and 13 banks. The Energy and Commerce Subcommittee asked Hutton, the Justice Department, and the SEC to turn over a wide variety of documents including reports prepared by examiners for the New York Stock Exchange and National Association of Securities Dealers, who inspected Hutton's books and operations under the SEC's auspices. The documents and witnesses had to be subpoenaed because Hutton refused to provide them for the June 19 congressional hearing.[26]

Findings by the House Judiciary Subcommitee showed that several Hutton senior executives were informed in late 1981 by memo of a pattern of "aggressive overdrafting" of their bank accounts but failed to rectify the matter.[27] These executives included George L. Ball, former president of Hutton and its parent firm, E. F. Hutton Group, Inc. A memo from Thomas Lillis addressed to Ball and three of his top aides commended some of Hutton's branch and regional officers for profitably using overdrafting sub-

stantially, and detailed the extra income gained from the cash management system. Asked how he understood the phrase "overdraft substantially," Ball insisted that he took it to mean that large sums of money were involved, but not large or excessive overdrafts. Even though memos were uncovered in which Ball praised aggressive overdrafters and urged on the less profitable, Ball, now CEO of Prudential-Bache Securities, Inc., said he knew nothing of the memos nor the illegal practices. He insisted that he had no knowledge of details, and instead maintained that it was Thomas Morley, first vice-president and money manager, who really understood the system. Ball left Hutton before the grand jury investigation ended.

Under intense questioning, chairman Robert Fomon and other current Hutton officials insisted that top management was not aware of the fraudulent scheme and ordered it stopped as soon as they learned about it in early 1982. Fomon and Morley both told the Subcommittee that the aforementioned memos referred to overdrafting of Hutton's *own* books and did not necessarily indicate illegal use of bank funds without paying interest. Morley added that in retrospect, some of the material in the memos "should have been a signal" to top Hutton management of banking law violations.[28]

However, later documents suggest that Morley directed the overdrafting operations and that Ball was personally aware of them. These include a memo written by a branch manager, Perry H. Bacon, to another branch manager, Steve Bralove, on April 23, 1982, in which Bacon complained about the overdrafting of Hutton bank accounts. Bacon wrote, "Specifically, we will from time to time draw down not only deposits plus anticipated deposits, but also bogus deposits. I know of at least a dozen managers at E. F. Hutton—managers who along with . . . Tom Morley taught me the system—who do precisely the same thing."[29] But just one day after these memos were presented as evidence, Hutton claimed that the whole thing was a mix-up. The stapling together of two memos led to the erroneous conclusion that Hutton officials were aware of the overdrafting scheme and did nothing to stop it. Hutton claimed that the second memo, praising the overdrafting, had been prepared in March 1982 and was accidentally stapled to a memo dated November 1981. Throughout, Hutton's top management denied that it knew the details of the abuses. Congressman Mazzoli was prompted to characterize top management's strategy as one of "plausible deniability."[30]

THE ROLE OF THE JUSTICE DEPARTMENT

The Justice Department was the subject of lawmakers' and the public's criticism for not identifying the individuals responsible for setting up the system. The House Energy and Commerce Subcommittee on Oversight and Investigations and the House Judiciary Subcommittee on Crime were dissatisfied with the Justice Department's failure to charge any Hutton officials, having negotiated a settlement instead. Stephen Trott, assistant attorney general and head of the Justice Department's criminal division, told the Judiciary Subcommittee that the case was not a "sure winner against individuals" and that prosecutors gathered "sufficient evidence to indict" only two Hutton cash managers, and the odds of convicting them were low because they hadn't "personally profited from the offenses."[31] The Justice Department argued that legal precedents made it difficult to prosecute check kiting. Therefore, the Justice Department thought its best attack was to focus on the legality of Hutton's relations with its banks. In so doing, it anticipated good-faith claims to be made by the defense as well as the argument of caveat emptor. The government believed it had only a 50-50 chance of winning convictions. In addition, in reaching the plea agreement, Justice Department officials forced

Hutton to halt illegal check-writing activity immediately and accept a civil injunction barring the company from further check-writing violations.

There was, however, one event that rankled the Subcommittee: the lunch that Robert Fomon had arranged with then attorney general William French Smith. Fomon forthrightly said that when he had a problem with anyone, his method was to go to the top. And that is what he did in this case. Some of the Subcommittee members tried to portray this event as an example of the Reagan administration's slap-on-the-wrist approach to big business rather than taking more severe measures. In his testimony, however, Stephen Trott explicitly denied that the luncheon meeting had any influence on the Justice Department's decision not to prosecute.[32]

THE BELL REPORT

The mandate for the Bell investigation was to determine in detail what happened, how and why it happened, and what remedial and disciplinary actions Hutton should take in response. Bell and his 14 lawyers interviewed 300 past and present employees, 63 banks, accounting firms, and state and federal regulatory agencies, and shuffled through 40,000 pages of memoranda to write a 138-page report. Additionally interviewed were George Ball, president of E. F. Hutton and Company, Inc.; John S. R. Shad, former vice-chairman of Hutton Group and later chairman of the Securities and Exchange Commission; and Robert Fomon, chairman and CEO of Hutton and Hutton Group. The Report's main conclusion: While Hutton's top managers were obviously guilty of managerial shortcomings, they had not committed any criminal acts. According to Bell, overdrafting is a big business, but at Hutton it became tantamount to a loose cannon fired at will by a minority of Hutton employees. Management was faulted for inadequate internal controls and a "loose management structure'' that allowed massive overdrafting to become a central part of the company's culture in 1981 and 1982 (pp. 168–70).

Bell, in particular, faulted three senior Hutton executives: Thomas Lynch, de facto chief financial officer; Thomas Morley, first vice-president in charge of cash management; and Thomas Rae, general counsel. According to the Bell Report, Lynch should have been aware of the potential abuses. Morley was faulted with ''a failure in duty'' for not acting on repeated warnings about improper or illegal overdrafts. Rae ''bears responsibility'' for the ''incompetence'' and ''failure to systematically search executive files'' that resulted in the company's failure to turn over a number of documents subpoenaed by federal prosecutors over the years. All three men agreed to step down. Robert Fomon and George L. Ball were not found responsible for any improper activity in connection with the overdrafts. The report did, however, describe Ball as one of the ''leading advocates'' of maximizing the interest profits and a ''dominant figure'' in the company who ''constantly exhorted'' branch and regional officials to boost such earnings (pp. 173–75).

Lynch said his treatment by Bell was ''grossly unfair in view of the limited sanctions imposed on the lower-level people'' and the fact that he ''didn't have line responsibility for money management.'' The report did not accuse Lynch or other senior officials of actively promoting or participating in specific illegal activities. However, it recommended a number of administrative and management changes that were intended to prevent the recurrence of improper drawdown. The most far-reaching recommendation was to reshape the parent company's board to give outside directors majority control. The report, in general, was more sympathetic to Hutton and called for fewer sanctions and personnel shake-ups than some company officials and federal prosecutors anticipated. It asserted that the overdrafting was much less widespread and

that banks suffered substantially less damage from the millions of dollars of interest-free loans Hutton was able to secure than Justice Department officials had previously indicated.

Bell suggested in his report that six branch managers be punished for participating in overdrafts that were ''so excessive and egregious'' that ''no reasonable person could have believed that their conduct was proper.'' He recommended fines of $25,000 to $50,000 against Perry Bacon, who was head of the Alexandria, Virginia office; Anthony Read, manager of the Baltimore branch; John Pearce, manager of St. Louis and Bethesda, Maryland; William Shaw, manager of Fresno, California; Robert Clear, manager of Hartford, Connecticut; and John Holland, manager of Wilkes-Barre, Pennsylvania. The exact amount of each fine was left up to Hutton's audit committee, which would also select the charity to which the money would be paid. Bell also called for additional fines to cover restitution to banks that were cheated by Hutton branches.

Bell recognized that his credibility could be in doubt because Hutton paid for the report, but he maintained that his investigation was independent and thorough. Needless to say, lawmakers disputed Bell's conclusion that senior management did not participate in or directly encourage banking activities that were later determined to be illegal. Representative Shaw, a member of the Judiciary Subcommittee, said that that portion of Bell's report ''did leave a lot more questions in my mind than were answered. I can't believe management was as unaware as they say they were.'' Representative William J. Hughes (D-N.J.), the panel's chairman, asserted that the facts don't support many of the report's conclusions that Mr. Ball wasn't responsible (pp. 177–81).

SETTLEMENT OF THE CASE

In pleading guilty to 2,000 counts of mail and wire fraud, Hutton agreed to pay more than

$10 million in criminal fines and restitution. Hutton put aside $2.75 million to cover fines and prosecution costs and an additional $8 million to cover restitution to banks. Following the guilty plea, there were immediate cries of public outrage and some adverse actions on the part of various state and municipal regulatory agencies. However, when it was all over, it appeared that Hutton received only minor punishment. The Bell Report looked for the proverbial smoking gun but failed to find one. With the exception of a few executives who contended that they were made scapegoats, the Bell Report exonerated most others from any specific culpability while pointing a finger at a collective lack of diligence and corporate control of management practices. The Hutton corporation was fined $400,000 after the SEC sued, charging it with violating reporting and internal control requirements. The company consented to a court order enjoining it from future securities law violations, without admitting or denying the charges. E. F. Hutton & Co. was censured for violations related to the overdrafting scheme. They accepted the censure without admitting or denying wrongdoing and agreed to conduct special auditing for the next two-and-a-half years. They also agreed to hire an independent consultant to study and report on Hutton's money-handling practice since 1980.[33]

The same day the guilty plea was announced, Hutton began sending letters of apology to hundreds of bankers with whom it had accounts from July 1980 to early 1982, offering them full restitution. Although Hutton maintained accounts with approximately 400 banks during the period, only 75 to 110 were expected to have been affected by the fraudulent scheme. Former U.S. Appeals Court Judge William Hughes Mulligan was named a special master to oversee the restitution and arbitrated the disbursement of these payments to the banks. By July 25, 1985, about 50 banks where Hutton maintained accounts during those years had formally notified Hutton that they believed

they were bilked by the practices and intended to participate in the court-ordered claims procedure. The filing period expired the same day, but larger banks were given extensions. This was considerably less than many company officials, federal prosecutors, and congressional investigators originally anticipated. Hutton attorneys and federal investigators said many banks decided against seeking claims because they would be required to perform expensive computations of overdrafts and because filing could endanger business relations with Hutton branches, which are major customers for some banks. United Virginia Bank filed one of the largest claims, more than $350,000 as compensation for illegal overdrafts resulting in interest-free loans for Hutton's Alexandria, Virginia branch.[34]

The North American Securities Administrators Association disclosed that it formed a group to investigate and report on Hutton's cash management practices. The Association consists of securities regulators from all 50 states. Hutton's conviction on federal felony charges is grounds in most states for revoking a company's or individual's securities registration. If a state revokes Hutton's registration, the company is effectively put out of business there. Actions taken by states could include fines and censures, as well as suspension or revocation of licenses.

Several states took action. As an example, in Connecticut, banking commissioner Brian J. Woolf planned a hearing to decide whether or not to suspend or revoke Hutton's broker-dealer registration. Connecticut's attorney general argued that Hutton's state license should be suspended for 30 days and the firm should pay a $500,000 fine. On December 19, 1985, six Hutton brokers from the New London, Connecticut office defected to rival Paine Webber Incorporated in response to intense regulatory scrutiny by Connecticut officials. Robert Witt, Hutton's retail sales manager, testified at hearings in Connecticut that the six brokers left Hutton because they had lost some clients, and feared losing more, as a result of the state investigation.[35]

At the same time, most senior officers received golden handshakes.[36] Fomon eventually walked off with more than $3 million severance in the acquisition by Shearson Lehman Brothers. Lynch lost his position but remained a director at full salary. He sued Griffin Bell but in 1988 lost a court challenge. Rae took early retirement, and Morley resigned. Ball was formally censured by the

SEC in 1988. Scott Pierce remained president of E. F. Hutton & Co. Paul Hines, executive vice-president in charge of the control and planning division, assumed authority for treasury functions. He remained chairman of Hutton's insurance group. In the end, the corporate world protected its own. No individual was held accountable in a significant way, even though they engaged in fraud and tore Hutton to pieces in the process.

NOTES

1. Andy S. Pasztor, " 'Lucky Hunch' Led Federal Prosecutor to Begin Three-Year Probe of Hutton." *Wall Street Journal* (May 3, 1985), p. 3.

2. Dan Herzog, "Hutton Pleads Guilty in Fraud Case." *Wall Street Journal* (May 3, 1985), p. 3.

3. 18 U.S.C. 1345, Injunction against Bank Fraud; Griffin B. Bell, *The Hutton Report: A Special Investigation into the Conduct of E. F. Hutton & Company Inc. that Gave Rise to the Plea of Guilty Entered on May 2, 1985.* Atlanta, Ga.: King and Spaulding Law Firm, p. 2. Hereafter cited as *Bell Report.*

4. Subcommitee on Crime of the House Committee on the Judiciary, *Hearing on E. F. Hutton Mail and Wire Fraud,* June 19, July 19, August 1, October 3, October 31, December 6, December 11, 1986. Washington, D.C.: U.S. Government Printing Office, p. 480. Hereafter cited as *Hearings.*

5. *New York Times,* "E. F. Hutton, Losing Two Year Struggle, Is Looking for Buyer," (November 24, 1987), pp. A1, D4.

6. Steve Swartz, "How Eccentric Chief Built Up Hutton, Hastened its Demise," *Wall Street Journal* (February 17, 1988), pp. 1, 16.

7. "They Shouldn't Have Listened" *Fortune* (May 27, 1985), p. 8; and "How They Tore Hutton to Pieces." *New York Times* (January 17, 1988), pp. f1, f6.

8. *Hearings,* pp. 480ff.

9. Andrew S. Pazstor and Bruce Ingersoll, "Justice Department Is Being Investigated for Its Handling of Case Against Hutton." *Wall Street Journal.* (June 7, 1985), p. 5.

10. John S. Pearce and J. Robinson, 1984. *Strategic Management.* Homewood, Ill.: Irwin Publishing Co., p. 664.

11. Alison Leigh Cowan, "Swallowing Hutton in 1,200 Bites." *New York Times* (January 10, 1988), pp. F1, F8.

12. Griffin B. Bell, *The Hutton Report: A Special Investigation into the Conduct of E. F. Hutton & Company Inc. that Gave Rise to the Plea of Guilty Entered on May 2, 1985.* Atlanta, Ga.: King and Spaulding Law Firm, pp. 45–77.

13. William Sullivan, *Hearings,* pp. 999–1019; worksheet presented on p. 1018.

14. *Bell Report,* pp. 58–72.

15. *Bell Report,* pp. 64–67.

16. *Hearings,* pp. 1072–110; *Bell Report,* pp. 67–69.

17. *Hearings,* pp. 1072ff 1200ff; *Bell Report,* pp. 72–77.

18. *Institutional Investor,* September 1985, "The Crisis in Cash Management—The Fine Line between Smart and Criminal." (See the entire issue.)

19. *Hearings,* pp. 1570, 1598.

20. *Bell Report,* pp. 72–76.

21. *Hearings,* pp. 1001–19; *Bell Report,* pp. 107–15.

22. Swartz, "Eccentric Chief," p. 1.

23. Scott Murray, "Hutton's Fomon is in Unaccustomed Spot as Critics of Checking Scandal Abound," *Wall Street Journal* (July 19, 1985), p. 34.

24. Bartlett Naylor, "Meese Defends Record on White Collar Crime; Announces Legislative Initiatives as Congressional Hearings Are Set to Begin Anew." *American Banker* (September 17, 1985), pp. 3–5.

25. "Big Payments for Top Officials at Hutton." *New York Times* (December 21, 1987), pp. A1, D6.

26. *Hearings,* p. 1895. See also Andy Pasztor, "US Officials Examine Whether Hutton Improperly Withheld Certain Documents." *Wall Street Journal* (July 5, 1985), p. 3; and Andy Pasztor and, Lee Berton, "Arthur Young's Work for Hutton Probed by SEC and Two Congressional Panels." *Wall Street Journal* (July 18, 1985), p. 18.

27. *Hearings,* pp. 1654–1672. See also Andy Pasztor and Paul Duke, "Hutton Documents Show Senior Aides Were Told of 'Aggressive Overdrafting'." *Wall Street Journal* (June 20, 1985), p. 3.

28. Andy Pasztor, "E. F. Hutton Cites Amount Mix-Up in Check Scheme." *Wall Street Journal* (June 21, 1985), p. 2.

29. *Bell Report,* 82ff.

30. *Hearings,* pp. 482, 1201ff; *Bell Report,* pp. 181ff.

31. *Hearings,* pp. 1723, 1726–63; Andy S. Pazstor and Bruce Ingersoll, "Justice Department," p. 5.

32. *Hearings,* pp. 1726–63.

33. Andy Pasztor, "Congress Widens Hutton Probe as Panel Learns Auditors Question Overdraft." *Wall Street Journal* (July 22, 1985), p. 4.

34. August Bequal, "If Anything Needs Reform, It's the SEC." *New York Times* (November 30, 1986), p. 1; Dan Hertzgerg, "Hutton Pleads Guilty in Fraud Case." *Wall Street Journal* (May 3, 1985), p. 3; Scott Murray, "E. F. Hutton Appears Headed for Long Siege in Bank Draft Schemes." *Wall Street Journal* (July 16, 1985), p. 10; Andy Pasztor, "Hutton Overdrafting Case Was Settled Only after Sum Miscues on Both Sides." *Wall Street Journal* (April 9, 1985), p. 26; *Hearings,* pp. 1544–98; Phillip Zweig, "Hutton Sends Bankers Written Apology for Scheme, Offering Them Restitution." *Wall Street Journal* (June 17, 1985), p. 9; and "Former US Judge Named Special Master in E. F. Hutton Case." *Wall Street Journal* (June 17, 1985), p. 5.

35. "Hutton Will Pay $65,000 Civil Fine to Massachusetts." *Wall Street Journal* (February 5, 1986), p. 19; Scott McMurray, "Hutton's Cash Management Procedures Probed By Groups Representing 50 States." *Wall Street Journal* (February 8, 1985), p. 6; "Hutton May Get Evicted from Connecticut." *Business Week* (July 15, 1985), p. 3; Scott McMurray, "Georgia Regulations Give E. F. Hutton A Year's Probation." *Wall Street Journal* (September 7, 1985), p. 13; and "E. F. Hutton Draws One-Year Probation from West Virginia." *Wall Street Journal* (May 21, 1986), p. 54.

36. Scott Murray, "Hutton Group Picks Rittereiser to be President." *Wall Street Journal* (June 4, 1985), p. 2; Scott Murray, "Hutton's Report on Check Overdrafting to Implicate about a Dozen Employees." *Wall Street Journal* (September 4, 1985), p. 4; Nathaniel C. Nash, "Two Top Officials of Hutton Resign in Banking Scheme." *New York Times,* (September 6, 1985), pp. A1, D6; and James Sterngold, "Censures in Hutton Case Reported." *New York Times* (February 29, 1988), pp. A1, D4.

E. F. HUTTON & CO., NEW YORK

"Assessing Liability for MICR Fraud." *Alabama Law Review,* 37 (fall 1985), pp. 145–61.

"Bank Check-hold Policies: A Proposal to Protect Consumers." *Journal of Legislation,* 14 (1987), pp. 53–68.

"Banking Abuses: The E. F. Hutton Mail and Wire Fraud Case: An Analysis." *International Currency Review,* 18 (August 1987), pp. 3–11.

"Check Kiting: The Inadequacy of the Uniform Commercial Code." *Duke Law Journal* (September 1986), pp. 728–46.

"Civil RICO and its Application to 'Garden Variety' Fraud within the Sixth Circuit." *Northern Kentucky Law Review* 13 (1987), pp. 463–93.

"Common Law Malpractice Liability of Accountants to Third Parties." *Washington & Lee Law Review*, 44 (Winter 1987), pp. 187–212.

"Computerized Check Processing and a Bank's Duty to Use Ordinary Care." *Texas Law Review*, 65 (May 1987), pp. 1173–200.

"Criminal Law—Mail Fraud—Mail Fraud Statute Restricted to the Protection of Property Rights and Does Not Extend to the Protection of the Intangible Right to Honest and Impartial State Government: McNally v. United States, 107 S. Ct. 2875." *St. Mary's Law Journal*, 19 (1988), pp. 1115–32.

GETTY, R. A. "The Civil RICO Action—A New Weapon for Use in Securities and Commercial Fraud Cases." *Eastern Mineral Law Institute*, 5 (1984), pp. 2.1–32.

"Intra-corporate Mail and Wire Fraud: Criminal Liability for Fiduciary Breach." *Yale Law Journal*, 94 (May 1985), pp. 1427–46.

LEARY, F., JR., and P. B. FRY. "MICR Fraud: A Systems Approach to Foiling the Felon's Fun." *University of Miami Law Review*, 40 (March 1986), pp. 737–90.

"Mail Fraud: Termination of the 'Intangible Rights' Doctrine—McNally v. United States, 107 S. Ct. 2875." *Harvard Journal of Law and Public Policy*, 11 (Winter 1988), pp. 286–95.

"Mail Fraud and Free Speech." *New York University Law Review*, 61 (November 1986), pp. 942–75.

O'BRIEN, C. N. "The Legal Environment of the Accounting Profession." *Duquesne Law Review*, 25 (winter 1987), pp. 283–97.

O'BRIEN, C. N. "SEC Regulation of the Accounting Profession: Rule 2(e)." *Gonzaga Law Review*, 21 (1985/1986), pp. 675–90.

STURM, W. C. "Accountant's Liability to Third Parties." *Commercial Law Journal*, 92 (Summer 1987), pp. 158–67.

"The Accountant-client Privilege: Does It and Should It Survive the Death of the Client?" *Brigham Young University Law Review* (1987), pp. 1271–92.

"The Allocation of Risk of Loss Due to 'MICR Fraud': Is Northpark [*Northpark National Bank* v. *Bankers Trust Co.* 572 F. Supp. 524] a Steadfast Solution or an Evanescent Effort?" *Delaware Journal of Corporate Law*, 9 (1984), pp. 347–84.

United States House of Representatives. Committee on the Judiciary. Subcommittee on Crime. *E. F. Hutton Mail and Wire Fraud: Report, December 1986; Together with Separate, Additional, and Dissenting Views* (99th Congress, 2nd Session; Serial no. 13).

WECHSLER, S. "Delayed Funds Availability." *Syracuse Law Review*, 35 (1984), pp. 1117–214.

GENERAL DYNAMICS CORPORATION

Defrauding the U.S. government:
overcharging on defense contracts

General Dynamics (GD), the second largest U.S. defense contractor with 1987 awards of $7 billion, has been the subject of various government inquiries for almost 20 years. The current charges of fraud and mismanagement were brought out in the process of congressional hearings, Pentagon reviews, and Justice Department proceedings.[1]

The principal charges and accusations included the following:

1. inadequate financial disclosures to the SEC and the shareholders, particularly with respect to the SSN 688 submarine construction contracts;

2. stock manipulation through the cover-up of potential losses, in particular with reference to the Trident program;

3. providing illegal gratuities to military officers (i.e., Hyman Rickover and others), and falsification of records to conceal these illegal gratuities;

4. incorrect procedures involving millions of dollars of "undocumented" expense vouchers and related requests for the government to reimburse the company for its costs; and

5. misuse of corporate aircraft and abuse of executive perquisites.

PREVALENCE OF FRAUD AND MISMANAGEMENT AMONG DEFENSE CONTRACTORS

This was not the first time that charges had been levied against General Dynamics. The company had been beleaguered with similar charges in the past.[2] Moreover, fraud and mismanagement are not confined to General Dynamics in a manner that can be attributed to the company's organizational structure, decision-making procedures, or the caliber and character of its top management. In fact, problems of inefficient management, sloppy record keeping, and financial mismanagement, including fraud, are endemic to large segments of the defense industry.[3]

Examples of such activity include the notorious $600 toilet seat, the $300 coffee pot, and the $9,000 wrench. The issue has been building for a long time. These and similar activities came to a boiling point in 1985. In that year, the Department of Defense (DOD) temporarily or permanently barred over 650 military contractors from doing business with the Pentagon. This was up from only 57 in 1975 and 78 in 1980.[4] The Department of Defense reports that cases under investigation have averaged over 1,000 per year during the past five years. The FBI has said that 680 cases of fraud were referred to the Bureau from October 1983 through May 1987. Of these, 286 are still pending.[5]

The post-Vietnam War years saw the emergence of more scandalous stories that coincided with the military build-up. When Ronald Reagan became President in 1981 and vowed a dramatic increase in defense spending, the stories of fraud and mismanagement served to rouse public opinion against increased spending. Addressing the defense industry's Best Practices Forum Defense, Secretary Caspar W. Weinberger acknowledged the problem: "We all know waste, poor management, and actual criminality are present in many companies." Weinberger underscored the seriousness of the problem when he added, "unless there is [defense] acquisition reform, the defense program is imperiled."[6]

ISSUES FOR ANALYSIS

The issues raised by the General Dynamics case go beyond the narrow confines of the particulars relating to the company. They encompass an array of macro and micro concerns about managing relations between business and government on the one hand,

and determining national priorities on the other hand.

1. Defense procurement, by its very nature, often involves dealing with single-source suppliers. Competition among different suppliers is either nonexistent or nonfeasible. The United States Department of Defense (DOD) annually purchases almost $170 billion in goods and services. It accounts for about 25% of the federal budget and approximately 6% of the Gross National Product (GNP). Defense acquisition is the largest business enterprise in the world. Weapons procurement accounts for approximately 28% of the Pentagon's own budget. The Department also spends huge amounts of money on research and development (R & D).[7] Moreover, procurement often involves both development and production, with uncertain technologies, unforeseen development and manufacturing problems, constant design and specifications changes, and unanticipated cost overruns. Thus, the more complex the project, the greater the difficulty in the monitoring function under these circumstances.

   a. How can defense industry standards be effectively monitored and controlled? Will the codes of ethics mandated by the Defense Department be adequate? Or will they be no more than window dressing?

   b. How should the procurement process itself be structured. What changes are needed at the Department of Defense, in the Congress, in the management policies of corporations, in the Executive Branch, and in the interaction of the foregoing?

2. A related issue concerns the need for maintaining close DOD-contractor relations for smooth functioning of the procurement function, while at the same time maintaining arms-length transactions between DOD employees and defense contractors to ensure honesty and integrity in the oversight function. Under these circumstances:

   a. How does the present system of contracts, including limitations between the two groups, influence these relationships? Relevant points include lobbying by the contractors, employment of former defense personnel by the defense industry, and enforcement procedures by the DOD to root out corruption, bribery, and other abuses among its own employees.

  b. How should disputes in overhead, pricing discrepancies, and progress payments be resolved, and who should resolve them?

  c. To what extent does DOD encourage reporting of illegal activities among its employees and those of its contractors? How does DOD protect whistle-blowers? What additional measures are needed in this area?

  d. What measures, if any, are needed to minimize undue political influence by the nation's defense contractors? Does the revolving-door policy create a conflict of interest when key decision makers at the Pentagon leave their posts to take jobs in defense industries? Do they use their positions at the Pentagon to grant special treatment in order to gain future employment?

  e. How effective are the DOD procedures in detecting fraud, and how energetic is DOD in enforcing these regulations, prosecuting wrongdoers, and seeking restitution? What addtional measures, if any, might be needed?

4. What are the problems related to defense contractors who undertake both private and government projects? To what extent do these problems contribute to a tendency for false claims or overbilling? How might these problems be resolved or minimized?

5. Regarding General Dynamics, what are the characteristics of the company, its corporate culture, organizational structure, product mix, or the quality of its top management that might have contributed to its problems? Should felons such as Lester Crown, who was an unindicted coconspirator in bribery charges, be allowed to sit on the boards of strategically sensitive companies such as General Dynamics?

6. Apart from legal and regulatory measures, what else can American society do to inculcate higher standards of ethical and professional behavior in corporations that produce goods vital to the nation's defense and security?

GENERAL DYNAMICS CORPORATION

As noted earlier, General Dynamics is one of the largest U.S. defense contractors. In 1987, its sales totaled $9.3 billion with a net income of $437 million. From 1983 to 1987, average sales grew at a rate of 9.4%, while net income grew at the rate of 13.9%. Earnings per share in 1987 stood at $10.26, reflecting a 24.3% grow rate over the five-year period.[8]

The corporation is organized into several divisions. The principal divisions are as follows: (1) the Electric Boat division, which produces the SSN 688 and Trident submarines; (2) the Convair, Pomona, and Valley Systems divisions, which produce missiles and gun systems, including the Tomahawk and Stinger missiles; (3) the Fort Worth division, which produces the F-16 as well as military electronics; (4) the Electronics division, which produces military electronics; (5) the Space Systems division, which contracts primarily with NASA and the Air Force for such things as Centaur Rocket Upper Stages; and (6) the Land Systems division, producer of the M-1 tank. In addition, there are other divisions which produce civilian planes, building products, and information systems.[9]

CHRONOLOGY OF EVENTS

1959 to 1974

In 1959, General Dynamics acquired the Crown family's Material Services Corporation and paid Henry Crown $2.1 million in GD preferred stock. During the early 1960s, General Dynamics went through a period of financial instability. Henry Crown clashed with Roger Lewis, General Dynamics chairman and CEO, over policy. In 1965, the management of General Dynamics attacked Crown and voted to recall the family's convertible preferred shares for $105 million in an effort to remove him from the board. Crown took his money, resigned from the board, and then began to acquire systematically all the General Dynamics shares that he could.

By 1970, the Crown family had accumulated 10.5% of General Dynamics' stock and gained 6 out of 14 seats on its board. Crown was in control again and was determined to keep it that way. This was to have serious repercussions for the company during the 1985 congressional hearings. Crown's son, Lester, was named as an unindicted coconspirator in 1974 for bribery involving the Material Services division and Chicago officials. The issue was settled, but there was no doubt of Crown's culpability. He could not, nonetheless, be removed from the board.[10]

In 1970, GD brought in David Lewis from McDonnell-Douglas as CEO to combat a worsening financial position. The company was facing financially difficult times, and omitted its quarterly dividend. GD was indicted by a grand jury (in 1971) for contract irregularities and had a badly tarnished image. As it turned out, Lewis was highly successful in turning the company around. From a $7 million loss in 1970, sales rose to almost $8.1 billion in 1985, and net income rose to $383 million.[11]

An important element of this success was the company's pursuit of gonverment contracts. In 1971, GD received 7 out of 12 contracts from the SSN668 (Los Angeles class) submarine, with the other 5 going to Newport News, a Tenneco company, which also received the design award. In 1973, Electric Boat gained another 11 contracts. To gain this business, GD agreed to a fixed-price contract. It was speculated that Lewis intentionally underbid to buy in hoping to recover his costs and to profit from increases in DOD's purchase price through specification changes. His own corporate people

thought he yielded too much power to Admiral Rickover in order to gain favor.

When it came to producing the submarine and delivering on the contracts, GD was not doing so well, however. Production at Electric Boat was chaotic. In November 1974, Arthur Barton, the comptroller at Electric Boat, predicted an $800 million overrun on the $1.2 billion bid for the 18 submarines. A bearer of bad news, he became anathema to all company officials. By December 1974, the Navy was aware of production problems and had heard of overrun possibilities. It did not want this in the press, so it offered $100 million to GD. By that time, Electric Boat's own internal estimate was revised downward to $500 million. During all this time, Lewis kept the extent of the overrun secret from everyone: the SEC, the Navy, the Board, shareholders, and Arthur Andersen, the company's independent outside accountants. In January 1975, the Electric Boat claims team estimated a $300 to $350 million loss on the first contract alone (7 submarines).[12]

1975 to 1978

In June 1975, Lewis finally told the board that there could be a $100 million loss. Gordon MacDonald was put in charge of operations at Electric Boat.[13] In April 1976, the Navy came through with $97 million. By December 1976, General Dynamics formally filed a $544 million claim with the Navy, which shocked everyone.

In October 1977, Takis Veliotis took over at Electric Boat. A highly energetic and exuberant Greek American, Veliotis had a checkered past. He came to General Dynamics in 1973 as general manager of the Quincy Yard, where he was very successful during his four-year tenure in turning the division around. Veliotis had hopes of eventually succeeding Lewis. Once at Electric Boat, he discovered the Lewis cover-up but decided he had to play along. The cover-up was cemented in place by the career aspirations of both men. Unknown to anyone, however, during Veliotis's tenure at Quincy, he took over $1 million in kickbacks from Frigitemp, a subcontractor. In the end, this was to prove everyone's undoing. Frigitemp went bankrupt in the early 1980s, and the chain of investigations led to Veliotis's indictment in September 1983. He would flee to Greece to avoid being subpoenaed by federal prosecutors.[14] Were it not for this investigation, the whole General Dynamics scam might well have succeeded.

By 1977, General Dynamics was losing $15 mllion a month. Yet it showed no losses on its books from 1975 to 1977. Its stock price hit a high of $65 in 1976. By October 1977, it was still trading around $50. The Navy auditors found that General Dynamics' claim of $544 million in contract overrruns had only $13 million merit. Rickover was furious over the fraud, and he incited his friendly contacts in the Congress, leading Senator Proxmire to hold hearings. To add to the company's troubles, in November 1979 the Navy said that the Trident program was in trouble. It was $400 million over the $1.19 billion budget. Furthermore, the delivery date was set for April 1980, rather than General Dynamics' October 1979 date (which itself was six months after the contract delivery date). General Dynamics was accused of trying to manipulate its stock price by failing to disclose the truth.[15]

After threatening to discontinue production of the SSN668, General Dynamics decided to settle with SSN688 overrun disputes in June 1978. There was pressure to do so both from the Navy and from local members of Congress. The total amounted to $843 million. General Dynamics was paid $125 million for some of its claims which the Navy did not dispute. The disputed remainder of $718 million was to be split evenly between the Navy and General Dynamics. Future overruns of up to $100 million were also to be split evenly. But amounts in excess of $100 million were to be borne by the company.[16] In the end, the Navy paid the equivalent of nearly $639 million. After tax deductions, General Dynamics charged off $180 million against earnings. It also received $300 million in advance from the government, which afforded the company extra earning capacity. Edward Hidalgo, who negotiated the settlement for the Navy, later went on to work for General Dynamics.

1979 to 1985

With overrun disputes finally settled and General Dynamics on a financial upswing, a new problem was on the horizon. The U.S.S. Bremerton, already one year late to delivery, was found to have been built with poor-quality steel and poor welds as well. The problem affected a number of ships. General Dynamics was faced with massive overhaul costs. James Ashton, assistant manager at Electric Boat, estimated cost overruns of between $170 and $200 million. Both Lewis and Veliotis moved to suppress Ashton's findings.[17]

No submarines were produced in 1980 at Electric Boat. To pay for its overruns, General Dynamics named the Navy as the insurer in a suit to get the U.S. government to pay. The ploy was unprecedented. Rickover was furious once again, and more investigations ensued. But in October 1981, there was a settlement which was generous to General Dynamics. George Sawyer, who negotiated the settlement for the Navy, later went on to become an executive vice-president and a member of the board of General Dynamics.

During 1981, things were beginning to improve. Electric Boat turned out six SSN668 submarines and the first Trident submarine. In addition, F-16 aircraft production was rising, thereby giving General Dynamics' profits a much-needed shot in the arm. Lewis had appointed Oliver Boileau as the new president of the company. Veliotis felt that his career was being undermined by some of the moves made by Lewis and Boileau.

Veliotis was involved in the latest overrun controversy. He threatened .o resign from Electric Boat. Lewis still needed Veliotis at this point, and to mollify him he made him an executive vice-president and a member of the board in May 1980. In the end, however, the settlement with the Navy called for Veliotis's removal from Electric Boat as well as the exclusion of Rickover from Navy contracting. The second major overrun controversy seemed to be settled by 1982, and General Dynamics was prospering.

In the meantime, the Frigitemp investigations heated up. Veliotis was indicted in September 1983 and fled the country. In cooperating with the Justice Department's investigations, General Dynamics froze Veliotis's assets. Veliotis, in turn, decided to bury the company while getting the best deal possible for himself. He had copies of key records as well as tape recordings of key conversations, more than enough to prove that General Dynamics' top management was guilty of fraud. In May 1984, Veliotis was interviewed by the Justice Department in Greece, and by October he had turned over the bulk of his evidence.[18]

In May, 1985 the Navy suspended General Dynamics and set strict conditions for future contracts, including formally instituting a code of ethics as well as new accounting and management practices. In addition, certain fines were to be paid. The company was reinstated on August 13, 1985, but then was suspended again from December 3, 1985 until February 7, 1986. Lewis resigned as CEO in December and was succeeded by Stanley Pace.[19]

General Dynamics' Position

General Dynamics' position with respect to the aforementioned charges was set forth by chairman David S. Lewis in testimony before the Subcommittee on Oversight and Investigations of the House Committee on Energy and Commerce on February 28, 1985.[20]

Lewis and MacDonald (in charge of operations at Electric Boat) appeared together and denied most of the serious charges against General Dynamics. These included the Lester Crown affair, the Trident controversy, and improper billing of expenses to the government. Lewis stated that "the activities of the company are guided by policies set forth in written directives that conform completely with U.S. Government laws and regulations." He went on to say that most of the allegations "have emanated from malicious and untrue allegations made by a former employee, Mr. P. Takis Veliotis, who is now a fugitive from justice in Greece."[21] In his testimony, Lewis offered the following explanations in General Dynamics' defense to various allegations.

Inadequate Financial Disclosures Concerned the SSN688 Submarine Contracts. These contracts caused serious difficulties for General Dynamics. The point of contention was whether the status of incurred costs, predicted overruns, claims submittals, and settlements on the SSN688 program were disclosed in a timely fashion. In Lewis's recounting of events, he focused on the second overrun, which followed on the U.S.S. Bremerton problems. It was this particular overrun, together with the Trident issue, that investigators felt provided the major basis for an indictment. Lewis stated that the accusations of overruns apparently stemmed from a telephone conversation taped by Veliotis between himself, Lewis, Gordon MacDonald (executive vice-president of finance), and Warren G. Sullivan (vice-president of industrial relations). The purpose of the telephone conversation was to dissuade Veliotis from immediately discharging James E. Ashton, who was serving as Electric Boat assistant general manager of engineering. Ashton took that position in 1980, when Veliotis told Lewis that he wanted to leave the general manager's position at Electric Boat and move to a higher-level job. Ashton was then brought in as assistant general manager with the goal of growing into the general manager's job. However, almost immediately after his arrival, Ashton had considerable difficulty getting along with Veliotis and others at Electric Boat.

Ashton's testimony followed the joint appearance by MacDonald and Lewis. His testimony indicated a considerable discrepancy between GD's public announcements and his projection, which would later turn out to be far more accurate. Ashton had called Navy officials and corporate officers to tell them that he thought that management's estimates of company losses were far too optimistic. GD maintained that Ashton was not qualified to make such estimates. Furthermore, GD's outside accounting firm, Arthur Andersen and Co., was informed of all the facts and saw nothing out of line with SEC reporting requirements. In fact, Arthur Andersen gave an independent confirmation of the claims.[22] Hence, according to David Lewis's testimony, financial information was, in fact, adequately disclosed to the proper parties in a timely fashion. Lewis's case was based on what he would call best knowledge available at the time. Lewis also contended that Ashton was not doing his assigned duties. Management wanted to fire him, but was reluctant to do so because the company was involved in critical negotiations with the Navy. Thus, according to Lewis, Ashton's dismissal might be construed as a firing for being a troublemaker. It was at this point that the telephone call concerning Ashton took place.

Cost overruns are very difficult to analyze before they happen. They are based on a series of untested probabilities. One estimate of General Dynamics' first set of overruns attributed 35% to inflation, 18.5% to problems with government-furnished equipment not made by General Dynamics, 20% to changes in contract design, and 26.5% to production costs.[23] Design revisions proved to be a major bone of contention. In a taped conversation with MacDonald, Veliotis mentioned 7,000 to 8,000 revisions but asserted that the added costs

were neglible. In another conversation with Rickover, he spoke of 32,000 revisions and implied that the costs were very great indeed.[24] In congressional testimony, the Navy acknowledged some revisions but pointed out that, nonetheless, Newport News produced the same submarine for $50 million less. What all of this shows is that the overrun problem is a hostage to poor accounting and auditing methods. In fact, the industry culture was set in a pattern of bidding low to gain a contract and then proceeding to lock it in so that DOD would come to the rescue of the company.

The Stock Manipulation Charge was Related to the Delivery Date of the First Trident Submarine. The congressional hearing opened with a Veliotis tape of a conversation with MacDonald on November 29, 1977.[25] On the same day, the Navy held a press conference which indicated that a massive cost overrun of $400 million on the Trident program was primarily the fault of Electric Boat and that the Trident program would be unprofitable. The Navy also indicated that its estimate of the delivery date of the first Trident was six months later than the company's estimate.[26] The issue of whether the Trident program would be profitable or would incur a loss was vital with respect to its impact on the price of General Dynamics' stock.

On the next day, Veliotis again taped a telephone conversation with MacDonald. Veliotis alleged that two statements on that tape proved that General Dynamics knowingly quoted an overoptimistic forecast delivery date for the first Trident in order to keep the stock price from sliding. General Dynamics agreed that the stock price was sliding, but attributed it largely to confused and misleading statements made by the Navy in the press conference. General Dynamics protested to the Navy that the press conference inaccurately assigned the whole $400 million overrun to inefficiencies at Electric Boat. In response, the Navy released a memorandum attributing only $114 million to the company. It further stated that the contract ceiling price had not been reached and that General Dynamics would earn a profit on this project.

Veliotis agreed with the company's press conference statement, but he thought the delivery date was too optimistic. He conducted his own study in November 1977, just after he took over at Electric Boat. The study was not completed until February 1978, however, and he then forecast the delivery date as November 1980 or early 1981. Lewis and MacDonald were aware that Veliotis believed the October 1979 date was too optimistic. However, they said that since others were more familiar with the status of the program, they were more confident that the company's quoted date was viable.[27] The company argued that it was the uncertainty of profits, and not the estimates of delivery dates, that were important to the price of General Dynamics' stock, which was trading around $41.50 by March 15, 1978 from its high of $50 in November 1977. Therefore, getting the correct information regarding profits to the stock market was very important. Since General Dynamics' stock had declined by almost 25%, it was obvious that General Dynamics did not manipulate its stock price through more optimistic announcements of delivery dates.

General Dynamics Also Denied the Charges of Illegal Gratuities in Violation of the Submarine Contracts. Related to gifts for Admiral Hyman Rickover and other military officers, the company admitted that two gifts of jewelry costing $1,125 were given to Admiral Rickover for his wife in 1977. Lewis went on to say, "It is unfortunate that the Admiral asked for things and that it is unfortunate that the company gave [gifts] to him, but there was nothing corrupt in any of it."[28] In addition, two other categories of gifts were given. The first consisted of a large number of minor items that were provided to the Navy for Admiral Rickover's use during sea trials of submarines constructed at Electric Boat. The second consisted of gifts made at ceremonial functions at Electric Boat, principally the keel layings and launchings of submarines.

General Dynamics claimed that it understood the breach of the gratuities clause in their contract to mean "the offer of a gratuity to an officer or an employee of the U.S. Government to obtain a contract or to secure favorable treatment in the awarding, amending, or making determinations concerning the performance of a contract."[29] However, since no gift or any other thing of value was ever given to Admiral Rickover by General Dynamics with the intention of corrupting him, no breach could have taken place. With respect to the giving of gifts at launchings, General Dynamics claimed that it was a centuries-old tradition, and that under Navy regulations relative to the receipt of gratuities by Navy personnel, such gifts were specifically recognized as permissible. With regard to the sea trial gratuities, the company maintained that the provisions were requested by the Navy and that they were, in effect, "contract extras" designed for comfort, convenience, and entertainment. In May 1985, the Navy instructed General Dynamics to pay a fine of $676,283.30 (10 times the amount of the gratuities), and Admiral Rickover himself was censured.[30]

Allegations that General Dynamics Submitted Millions of Dollars In "Undocumented" Expense Vouchers to the Government. Lewis maintained that the vouchers were documented to the extent required by the government acquisition regulations. The testimony details a number of expenses.[31] Some, such as MacDonald's boarding of his dog Fursten at Silver Maple Farms for $87.25, are egregiously out of line.[32] Most of the testimony, however, was a sparring contest over the definition of allowable costs. While admitting to some mistakes, Lewis, for the most part, maintained that the government had been asked to reimburse the cost of only those expenses that were properly allocatable to the government's business.

General Dynamics maintained that all defense contracts provide for negotiation of overhead costs when disagreements between the government and the contractor arise. The Defense Contract Audit Agency (DCAA) has access to the contractor's records and, after studying them, issues audit reports which become advisory documents for use by government negotiators in establishing the government's negotiating position. According to GD, in large and complex contracts, it was not unusual to find many items that would be questioned by DCAA and ultimately disallowed by the Administrative Contracting Office (ACO). However, according to Lewis, it was never the company's intention to misrepresent consciously any request for reimbursement of costs incurred.[33] The company agreed that the questions raised by the DCAA should not be considered to be the final word since the role of the DCAA was only advisory. The ACO had the ultimate responsibility for reviewing, negotiating, and settling with a contractor on the contents of the allowable overhead costs. An exhaustive review of ''97 million'' overhead vouchers (primarily at Electric Boat and Pomona divisions) led to a settlement of $57.3 million in the Navy's favor.[34]

Use of Corporate Aircraft for Nonbusiness Purposes and Submitting the Costs to the Government for Reimbursement. The company asserted that its use of corporate aircraft represented an efficient and effective use of an important productivity and security tool. Corporate personnel were required to visit divisional operations in many places in the U.S. In addition, many visits had to be made to other locations where the company had significant business to be carried out with government officials, contractors, and subcontractors concerned with General Dynamics. The disputed cost items centered around business purposes of a more general and indirect nature, e.g., to provide travel to important business meetings and conferences and to meetings of other companies' boards of directors. According to General

Dynamics, the amount of these activities had been greatly exaggerated, and, furthermore, the validity of the items was not in question, just their cost application.[35]

The Government's Position

There was not one government position but two, advanced by two different agencies whose objectives, strategies, and tactics were not necessarily similar. In fact, in some instances, they were diametrically opposed. The two bodies of the government in question are the Department of Defense (DOD) and Congress.

DOD's overriding concern is stability, continuity, and predictability in procurement.[36] DOD wants stability and a reasonable division of labor in the budgeting process. As the system currently works, each year the President prepares a budget for congressional approval. Therefore, each year the amount that the Pentagon receives changes. A weapons development and production system, has long lead times that are not easily changed without serious impact on costs. DOD, therefore, is hard pressed, to keep systems functioning. The contractors know of this instability in government funding and thus are discouraged from making the long-term investment necessary to improve productivity and lower costs. DOD tries to combat its inability to promise a long-term commitment with other inducements. It uses special concessions like highly profitable ''sole source contracts''—thus eliminating the risk of losing a contract to another contractor.[37] It also employs ''unpriced contracts,'' thereby guaranteeing the contractor the reimbursement of virtually *all* the costs and removing any risk of cost overrun. DOD allows for sloppy auditing procedures that ratify unanticipated and questionable expenses ''after the fact,'' e.g., accepting a 50-50 split. DOD also allows for overhead charges and for progress payments—interim monthly payments which reimburse the contractor for up to 95% of costs *before* the performance of the contract is completed.[38]

The DOD contends that these practices are necessary in order to attract high-quality contractors to take on a project, and to keep them interested once production has begun. Such means are deemed necessary because Congress cannot promise contractors any amount beyond the current fiscal year. The DOD also argues that Congress plays too large a role in the weapons development, production, and procurement process.[39] Too often, Congress's interest in a particular weapons system is correlated with the political careers of its members. It is clear that the settlement of both of General Dynamics' cost overruns had the active support of congressional representatives from the affected districts. The settlement of such disputes, as well as the landing of a contract in the first place, means jobs and votes. The success or failure of a program not only has to do with defense but with corporate, political, and military careers. Too often, the latter forces dominate.

Congress, in return, points the finger at the DOD. The first claim, and perhaps the most important one that Congress makes, concerns the need for centralization of procurement. There is no central, senior official in the DOD to handle procurement and associated activities.[40] Keeping in mind that there are four branches of the military (technically the Marines are part of the Navy), it is not difficult to fathom the consequences of having no centralized means of equipment acquisition.

Congress also accuses the DOD of gold-plating the weapons systems, thereby contributing to excessive cost and time overruns. Gold-plating means that the specifications for any system or product are so detailed and customized, that if a contractor can manufacture it at all, it is usually a most inefficient process. For example, specifications on certain computer chips can be so custom tailored, that they end up costing thousands of dollars more and have fewer capabilities than a standard commercial chip.[41]

Congress also accuses the DOD of rushing weapons systems into production without sufficient development and testing of prototype models to eliminate all possible bugs and potential malfunctions.[42] This was the case with the SSN668 submarine. Before it was rigorously tested as a prototype, it was in production as a class of submarines. The SSN668 was in fact an inferior product. It passed the tests of speed and stealth but performed poorly on the depth it could reach.[43]

Another reason for cost overruns, according to congressional sources, was fraud by defense contractors and lenient treatment thereof by DOD. The $9,000 wrench provides a symbolic example.[44] The DOD's accounting procedures are considered so flawed and lax that in some cases R&D and engineering bills were submitted for tools that were produced and paid for under previously satisfied contracts.

The easy informal alliance between the Department of Defense and the industry is further borne out in the rollover of personnel from one to the other. The House hearing devoted considerable time to the case of George Sawyer.[45] He had negotiated the second set of overruns on behalf of the Navy but very favorably for General Dynamics in 1981. By 1983, he was not only a General Dynamics vice-president but a member of the board as well. Company testimony includes documents from Navy officials affirming the lack of a conflict of interest when General Dynamics was in the process of considering Sawyer for employment.

MOVING TOWARD CHANGE

By 1985, it was clear to everyone that defense contracting was in a crisis. Realizing the threat to his administration's defense policy, President Reagan created a 17-member committee to evaluate the current situation and make necessary recommendations. This committee, the President's Blue Ribbon Commission on Defense Management, was set up in July, 1985 under the chairmanship of former defense secretary David Packard (hereafter referred to as the Packard Commission). The Packard Commission report, entitled "A Quest for Excellence," was released in June 1986 and has since become a major document for the development of future policy.[46]

The Commission focused its attention on four topics, i.e., national security planning and budgeting; military organization and command; acquisition organization and procedures; and government-industry accountability.

1. *National security planning and budgeting.* The president and his National Security Council would set forth national security objectives and priorities, and the DOD would draw up military programs accordingly. This conforming would consist of developing a five-year plan of action and a two-year budget, both of which would fit the option the president has chosen. Congress would be asked to approve the two-year budget, and if so, would authorize and appropriate the funds for major weapons systems only at two key milestones of: (a) full-scale R & D (including a prototype); and (b) high rate production (as a weapons class). The DOD would *not* be required to present its budget on a line-item by line-item basis.

2. *Military organization and command.* Several operational changes were suggested in the organization of military command to better facilitate action, and to remove some of the bureaucratic levels of command (management) that existed. Recommended changes allow for better communication between branches, shorter chains of command for quicker action, and in general a better-organized system.

3. *Acquisition organization and procedures.* First and foremost, in the office of the secretary of defense, it was recommended that a statute be passed to create the position of undersecretary of defense-acquisition. This person would have a solid industrial background,

and serve as a full-time defense acquisition executive. He or she would set policy for procurement and R & D, and supervise the overall acquisition system. Further, this position would have administrative oversight for auditing defense contractors. It was further recommended that each branch of the military should create a comparable acquisition position, whose job description would mirror that of the undersecretary.

In addition, the DOD would upgrade the individual acquisition position(s) so as to enable it to attract and hold onto quality acquisition personnel.

The report recommended other changes, including greater use of off-the-shelf items and the increased use of operational testing and prototypes. It also strongly argued for more competition in the acquisition process. Competition does not so much refer to the design of a military system as to its production. The costs of the former may too often be prohibitive. Such a policy would restrict the number of sole-source contracts.

4. *Government-industry accountability.* The Packard Commission recommended that the federal criminal and civil laws pertaining to defense acquisition be aggressively enforced on any and all violators. Further, more effective laws should be passed to prevent fraudulent and/or unethical actions. In addition, ethical guidelines must be drawn up and implemented. In response to the recommendations set forth by the Packard Commission, many defense companies have begun initiatives on business ethics and conduct. Many companies have signed a document called the Defense Industry Initiatives on Business Ethics and Conduct. This document details the following: (a) employees' ethical responsibilities; (b) corporate responsibility to employees; (c) corporate responsibility to the government; (d) corporate responsibility to the defense industry; and (e) public accountability. It.calls for the contractors to adopt and implement a series of principles of business ethics and conduct that acknowledge and address their corporate responsibilities under federal procurement laws. Furthermore, free, open, and timely reporting of violations become the felt responsibility of every employee in the defense industry.[47]

In connection with this, General Dynamics has initiated an updated and strengthened ethics program to ensure that all employees practice and understand the vital importance of the highest possible standards of business ethics and conduct. Beginning in August 1985, the company's newspaper, *General Dynamics World,* has featured regular articles on its new ethics program at all levels throughout the company.[48]

In this program, and as part of a formalized education and training plan, a new booklet entitled "General Dynamics Standards of Business Ethics and Conduct" was distributed to each salaried employee. The booklet defines and discusses explicit standards of employee conduct on a number of specific subjects, including conflicts of interest, pricing, billing, and quality/testing. A comprehensive program to communicate and implement these defined standards was introduced at all divisions.

Finally, the DOD has also begun to implement some changes. As noted earlier, suspensions or debarments of defense contractors have increased dramatically. Settlement agreements now outline specific actions to be taken by contractors to implement comprehensive corporate ethics programs and internal audit and management controls, and to enforce them.[49]

How did it all end? When it was all over, General Dynamics had had its wrists slapped. Although investigations continued for the next two years, little happened. Finally, on Friday, June 19, 1987, the Justice Department dropped all criminal charges against General Dynamics in an investigation of its Pomona division. A civil suit against the company on similar fraud charges was also subsequently dropped. In its announcement, the Justice Department said that a review of documents, found after the original indictment was handed in, showed that General Dynamics was correct in its interpretation of contract provisions pertaining to cost overruns.[50]

If one looks at the nature and scope of government penalties imposed on contractors, three patterns emerge:

1. DOD is extremely dependent on a handful of large contractors for its purchases. The size and complexities of the purchases are such that often it is difficult to draw the line between design charges, unforeseen circumstances, cost overruns due to inefficiencies, and outright contract fraud. Moreover, DOD cannot afford to weaken the contractors, through penalties, so as to reduce their financial and operational strength, thus jeopardizing national security.

2. The long-term nature of supplying complex systems, and even simple purchases, builds a sense of comradery and cooperation between vendors and DOD personnel. While such cooperation is necessary for the procurement effort, it also creates opportunities for collusion and illicit favors. The situation becomes even more complex because of the revolving-door nature of future employment of DOD personnel with the contractors, and the no-competition or single-source nature of many procurement contracts.

3. The long and sustained relationships between DOD and vendor personnel also make it difficult for the former to impose harsh penalties where evidence of clear-cut irregularities exist and where harsher penalties would act as general deterrence without, at the same time, seriously impacting the vendor's viability. Thus, there is a constant attempt on both sides to settle things amicably and to keep disagreements within the "family," with the result that most penalties do not amount to more than a slap on the wrist and have an equally negligible impact on vendor behavior.

Thus, after a few skirmishes and public squabbles, business goes on as usual and the country and society become the ultimate losers. This is evident in the manner in which the charges against General Dynamics were disposed of by DOD. Moreover, as can be seen by the recent evidence in other cases, General Dynamics was not alone in getting off easily, but instead followed a pattern that was only too predictable from similar events in the past and is quite likely to repeat itself in the future.[51]

On June 14, 1988, the Justice Department announced the largest white-collar crime investigation ever in the United States. It may involve a number of large de-fense contractors, defense department officials, consultants, and even, possibly, members of Congress. The alleged activities include bribes, payoffs, bid-rigging, and selling of confidential information to gain competitive advantages in defense contract bidding.[52]

NOTES

1. United States Congress, House of Representatives, Subcommittee on Oversight and Investigations, Committee on Energy and Commerce, 1985. *Oversight of the Federal Securities Laws and Disclosures Thereunder by the General Dynamics Corporation*, February 28, March 25, April 23, April 24, 1985. Hereafter cited as *Hearings*. *Washington Post*, March 1, 1985, "General Dynamics' Officials Grilled," pp. A1, A8.

2. *Business Week*, "General Dynamics Under Fire" (March 25, 1985), pp 70–76.

3. *Newsweek*, "How to Reform the Pentagon's Wasteful Ways" (May 27, 1985), pp. 144–49.

4. *Packard Commission Report*, June 1986. *A Quest for Excellence*, p. 103. (Hereafter cited as *Packard Commission*.)

5. Philip Shenon, "Dept. of Justice Faulted on Drive to Combat Crime." *New York Times* (July 3, 1988), pp. 1, 11. *Newsweek*, "Payoffs At the Pentagon" (June 27, 1988), pp. 20–22.

6. Caspar W. Weinberger, Oct. 30, 1986, "Remarks to the First Annual Best Practices Forum Conference." Press Release, Department of Defense (Xerox).

7. Ruth L. Sivard, *World Military and Social Expenditures*. The Packard Commission, 1985, pp. 48, 73.

8. General Dynamics Corporation, *10-K Report*, 1988.

9. General Dynamics Corporation, *Annual Report*, 1987.

10. Hearings, pp. 8–14.

11. General Dynamics Corporation, *Annual Report*, 1986.

12. Patrick Tyler, *Running Critical: The Silent War, Rickover and General Dynamics*. New York: Harper & Row, 1986, pp. 135–46.

13. Ibid., pp. 146–48, 159–163; *Hearings*, pp. 8–14.

14. Tyler, *Running Critical*, p. 168ff.

15. Ibid., pp. 187–92, 209–14, 220, 231. *Hearings*, pp. 15–49.

16. Tyler, *Running Critical*, pp. 139–46, 176–78, 293–94; *Hearings*, pp. 470–73.

17. Ibid., pp. 258–60, 287; *Hearings*, pp. 76–97, 426ff.

18. *Hearings*, pp. 93ff; Tyler, *Running Critical*, p. 329–41.

19. Joan Nelson-Horschler, "Stan Pace to the Rescue: Creating A New Image at a Scandal Ridden Firm." *Industry Week* (March 31, 1986), p. 81.

20. *Hearings*, pp. 8–14.

21. *Hearings*, pp. 15–49.

22. *Hearings*, p. 470ff.

23. *Wall Street Journal*, "Cost Overruns In the Defense Industry" (December 1, 1977), p. 35.

24. Tyler, *Running Critical*, pp. 152, 239–40.

25. Ibid., pp. 209–12; *Hearings*, pp. 76–89.

26. Tyler, *Running Critical*, pp. 209–14.

27. *Hearings*, pp. 92–97; 171ff.

28. Tyler, *Running Critical*, pp. 162–63, 223–24, 272–73.

29. *Hearings*, p. 258ff.

30. Office of the Assistant Secretary of Defense, Public Affairs, News Release (May 21, 1985).

31. *Hearings*, pp. 180–419.

32. *Hearings*, pp. 197, 205.

33. *Hearings,* pp. 13–14.

34. Assistant Secretary for Defense, Public Affairs, News Release (August 13, 1985).

35. *Hearings,* pp. 12–14.

36. *Packard Commission,* pp. xvii–xx.

37. *Business Week,* "Caspar Weinberger Flies into Heavier Flak" (April 15, 1985), pp. 132–33.

38. Tim Carrington, "Watered-Down Military Procurement Reforms Will Ensure 'Business As Usual,' Critics Charge." *Wall Street Journal* (August 13, 1985), p. 54.

39. *Packard Commission,* pp. xx–xxi.

40. Ibid., p. xxv.

41. Ibid., pp. 60–61.

42. Ibid., pp. xxv–xxvi.

43. Tyler, *Running Critical,* pp. 52–72.

44. *New York Times,* "Another Failure to Fix the Pentagon" (November 21, 1987), p. A18.

45. *Hearings,* pp. 428–527.

46. *Packard Commission,* pp. xvii–xxx.

47. Best Practices Forum, 1986. *Defense Industry Initiatives on Business Ethics and Conduct.* (Reprinted in the *Packard Commission Report,* 1986, pp. 41–45.)

48. General Dynamics Corporation, *General Dynamics World,* January 1986, p. 2. General Dynamics Corporation, *General Dynamics World,* August, 1985, pp. 1–2.

49. Department of Defense, Office of the Inspector General, *Integrity Alerts,* (March 1986). (Xerox).

50. *Packard Commission,* p. xiii.

51. "U.S. Abandons Fraud Case against General Dynamics." *New York Times* (June 19, 1987), p. 18.

52. "The Defense Scandal: The Fallout May Devastate Arms Merchants." *Business Week* (July 4, 1988), p. 28.

GENERAL DYNAMICS CORPORATION

ACKLEY, R. L., J. AGUIRRE, R. C. MCCANN, E. D. MUNNS, JR., and W. E. PEDERSEN. "Recent Developments in Contract Law—1987 in Review." *Army Lawyer* (February 1988), pp. 3–25.

ADAMS, GORDON. *The Iron Triangle: The Politics of Defense Contracting.* New York: Council on Economic Priorities, 1981.

BAXENDALE, SIDNEY J. "Cost Allocation vs. Performance Evaluation: Observations at Five Major Defense Contractors." *Akron Business and Economic Review,* 18 (Winter 1987), pp. 90–97.

BLUM, B., and G. LOBACO. "Following the Money." *California Lawyer,* 7 (May 1987), pp. 36–41.

D'ALOISIO, P. A. "Accusations of Criminal Conduct by Government Contractors: The Remedies, Problems, and Solutions." *Public Contract Law Journal,* 17 (September 1987), pp. 265–319.

DANIELL, R. F. "Easing the Pain of Procurement." *Yale Law and Policy Review,* 5 (Fall/Winter 1986), pp. 120–33.

DITTON, M. H. "The DIVAD Procurement: A Weapon System Case Study." *Army Lawyer* (August 1988), pp. 3–8.

HAZELTON, D. R. "The Federal Circuit's Emerging Role in Bid Protest Cases." *American University Law Review,* 36 (Summer 1987), pp. 919–41.

"International Symposium on Government Procurement Law." *George Washington Journal of International Law and Economics,* 20 (1987), pp. 415–597; 21 (1987), pp. 1–187.

KAESER, R. R. "Major Defense Acquisitions Programs: A Study of Congressional Control over DOD Acquisitions." *Federal Bar News & Journal,* 34 (December 1987), pp. 430–35.

LEIBY, L. R., and R. E. FERENCIK, JR. "Bid Mistakes—When Does it Matter and What Can Be Done?" *Stetson Law Review,* 16 (Summer 1987), pp. 681–704.

MASON, M. "New 'Revolving Door' Restrictions Imposed by the 1986 Defense Appropriations Act." *Federal Bar News & Journal,* 34 (December 1987), pp. 436–40.

MCCHESNEY, KATHLEEN L. "Operation Defcon: A

Multiagency Approach to Defense Fraud Investigations.'' *FBI Law Enforcement Bulletin,* 57 (March 1988), pp. 16–19.

PRESTON, C. A. "The Truth in Negotiations Act: Is a New Definition of 'Cost or Pricing Data' Necessary?'' *Federal Bar News & Journal,* 34 (December 1987), pp. 448–51.

ROLLINS, T. J. "Processing GAO Bid Protests.'' *Army Lawyer* (May 1988), pp. 7–15.

"Set-asides of Local Government Contracts for Minority Owned Businesses: Constitutional and State Law Issues.'' *New Mexico Law Review,* 17 (Spring 1987), pp. 337–59.

United States Congress. *Securities Law Enforcement and Defense Contractors.* Joint Hearings, July 30 and October 28, 1987, before the Subcommittee on Oversight and Investigations of the Committee on Energy and Commerce and the Subcommittee on Criminal Justice of the Committee on the Judiciary (100th Congress, 1st Session) (Committee on Energy and Commerce serial no. 100-86; Committee on the Judiciary serial no. 100-38).

United States Senate. Committee on Governmental Affairs. Permanent Subcommittee on Investigations. *Product Substitution by Defense Contractors.* Hearings, October 15–16, 1987 (100th Congress, 1st Session).

United States Senate. Committee on Governmental Affairs. Subcommittee on Oversight of Government Management. *Wedtech: A Review of Federal Procurement Decisions.* May 1988 (100th Congress, 2nd Session).

VENEMA, W. H. "Substantial Compliance in Fixed-price Supply Contracts: A Call for Commercial Reasonableness.'' *Public Contract Law Journal,* 17 (September 1987), pp. 187–210.

VICTOR, KIRK. "Shooting Back: Defense Contractors, Stung by Spare Parts Scandals and Procurement Reforms, Say that Congress Overreacted and Is Endangering Their Ability to Meet National Security Needs.'' *National Journal,* 20 (May 21, 1988), pp. 1345–49.

THE FIRST NATIONAL BANK OF BOSTON

*Money laundering and other activities by banks
and other financial institutions*

On February 7, 1985, the First National Bank of Boston pleaded guilty to having violated provisions regarding cash transactions of the Bank Secrecy Act of 1970[1] and "knowingly and willfully" failing to report to the Internal Revenue Service cash transactions with foreign banks which totaled $1.22 million over a four-year period. The transactions involved nine foreign banks and 1,163 deposits between July 1980 and September 1984. The Bank of Boston was fined $500,000. The violations were uncovered in the process of a money laundering probe, Operation Greenback, a Treasury Department initiative begun in 1980. The probe was directed at organized crime and was designed to ensure compliance with the Bank Secrecy Act of 1970.[2]

In addition to its international misdealing, the Bank of Boston was also accused of domestic currency violations. Banks are generally required to report cash transactions of $10,000 or more. In this case, the Bank of Boston had placed two real estate firms, Huntington Realty Co., and Federal Investments, Inc., on the list of those exempt from such reporting. These firms were controlled by the Angiulo family, which was reputedly linked to organized crime. The Bank of Boston was not only guilty of illegal currency transactions, it was implicated in money laundering.[3]

Following its guilty plea, the First National Bank of Boston was called before congressional hearings on April 3 and 4, 1985. Upon opening the hearings, Subcommittee chairman Fernand J. St. Germain described the situations as follows:

No one has come forward with evidence that the top officials of the Bank of Boston were in conspiracy with organized crime figures, and we are not suggesting that here today. However, bank officials need not be corrupt or into conspiracies for organized crime; it is enough that bank officials, such as those at the Bank of Boston, be sloppy, and that they operate without controls and without really caring.

Organized crime can make use of any institution that fits that profile, even the purportedly exalted Bank of Boston, and organized crime, drug traffickers, tax evaders are delighted with a regulatory system that hears no evil, sees no evil, speaks no evil, regulators such as we will find at the OCC during this period of time. That is, the Office of the Comptroller of the Currency [sic].[4]

The Bank of Boston case provides a unique exposé of the magnitude and complexity of illegal currency transactions. It reveals an astounding gap between legislative intent and administrative practices in both private banks and public agencies and, in so doing, raises the question as to who is really responsible, and how they are to be held accountable. Further, it calls into question whether the government has any real chance to eliminate money laundering.

ISSUES FOR ANALYSIS

1. To what extent were the mistakes made by the Bank of Boston bureaucratic and administrative errors, rather than a result of benign neglect or a deliberate decision to look the other way?

2. How easy is it for those in the underground economy to take advantage of paperwork foul-ups and communication failures in the banking system, and what can be done about it?

3. To what extent is the management of the Bank of Boston responsible for both the violations of norms for cash transactions and for money laundering? Is it true, as the chairman of the Subcommittee charged, that the Bank of Boston had made noncompliance with the Bank Secrecy Act an art form?

4. What corporate-level and business-level poli-

cies are called for in order to minimize such occurrences in the future?

5. What was the proper role of various government agencies involved, and how well did they execute their responsibilities? Would you agree with the Subcommittee chairman's view that the office of the comptroller of the currency appeared to rise to a high level of efficiency only when it was protecting its own turf?

6. What measures should be undertaken that would ensure better interagency cooperation and would also improve the efficiency of the regulatory process and make it more effective?

7. What, if anything, is morally wrong with violating the administrative norms for cash transactions? Are the norms realistic in today's trillion-dollar economy?

8. What rights do individuals have to privacy regarding their financial situations? Under what conditions is it right for government to invade that privacy?

THE LEGAL AND ECONOMIC CONDITIONS SURROUNDING MONEY LAUNDERING IN THE UNITED STATES

The criminal activities of the Bank of Boston can best be understood within the legal context of the regulatory reporting requirements and their intent in terms of public policy (and the extent to which regulatory processes are inforced and complied with). A second consideration deals with the nature of the underground economy in the United States and the vast sums of money it produces that must be laundered so that they can be used in legal activities. And finally, the laundering activities of the Bank of Boston should also be viewed in terms of how widespread such activities are in the banking industry. The Bank of Boston is not an exception but merely a worst example. This fact suggests that current regulatory processes are grossly inadequate. Profits to be made from money laundering are so enormous that they tempt even the bluest of blue chip banking organizations and financial institutions. In the final analysis, the leaders of these organizations are not only guilty of legal crimes but also of moral and social crimes, in that they participated in the furtherance of organized crime activities in the United States, which undermine the social and moral fabric of society.

REGULATORY ENVIRONMENT: THE BANK SECRECY ACT OF 1970

The Bank Secrecy Act of 1970 was designed to assist the government in its pursuit of the underground economy, especially organized crime and the money that is used in order to attain its goals.[5] This legislation was based on the concept that if a paper trail is established around all large cash transactions, it will deter the flow of illegal funds into the normal banking channels, thereby making their legitimization more difficult. Congress felt that a strong record-keeping system would assist in criminal, tax, and regulatory investigations by tracking sources and uses of cash throughout the banking industry. All insured banks of the United States are required to abide by the rules of this Act. Banks are responsible for keeping proper records. Financial institutions are required to file a CTR (currency transaction report) for amounts in excess of $10,000 with the Internal Revenue Service (IRS) within 15 days of each occurrence. A bank must also identify and record information about the customer who conducts the transaction. The bank must also file a CMIR (currency of monetary instrument report) with the commissioner of customs for any transportation of currency into or out of the United States of $10,000 or more. Penalties under this Act are quite severe and can amount to $10,000 in civil penalties per violation and criminal fines of up to $250,000. These penalties can be imposed either on a bank or an individual, even if the govern-

ment is unable to bring criminal charges regarding how the money itself was accumulated. In other words, a person or a bank can be in trouble for not reporting, even if the money not reported was not involved in a criminal activity.

In the area of domestic transactions, finanical institutions must file a currency transaction report (CTR) with the Internal Revenue Service on each individual deposit, withdrawal, payment, transfer, or exchange of currency by, through, or to a financial institution which involves currency in the amount of $10,000 or more.[6] This report is to be made on form 4789 within 15 days to the IRS.

The sheer size and number of transactions taking place everyday in the vast international banking system makes it absolutely necessary to create some exemptions in order to reduce the incredible level of paperwork that would otherwise be produced. These exemptions have been provided in those areas that are least likely to be connected with any criminal activity. Such exemptions include transactions with the Federal Reserve, Federal Home Loan Banks, transactions between domestic banks, and those between nonbank financial institutions and commercial banks. Additionally, a bank can place certain established depositors on the exempt list if they are U.S. residents and operate a retail business in the United States that generally deals in a large number of cash transactions. The generally accepted exempted businesses are those that operate a sports arena, racetrack, amusement park, bar, restaurant, hotel, licensed check-cashing services, vending machine companies, or theaters. However, these exemptions do not imply that the depositor will never have to file a CTR again; rather, a ceiling higher than that of this Act is installed (based on the average amount of cash transactions for that particular business). When this ceiling is exceeded, a CTR must be filed. Operations that are excluded from this exempt list include automobile, boat, and airplane dealerships. Such exclusions exist purely because those businesses provide an easy and effective way to enter illegal funds into the banking industry. They also supply equipment for the transportation of illegal goods. Finally, transactions by all levels of government may be exempted.

With regard to foreign transactions, the regulation breaks into two components. First, any transaction between a domestic concern and a foreign concern which involves the physical shipment of more than $10,000 of nontraceable funds must be reported to customs through form 4790 (CMIR) and to the currency commissioner through form 4789 (CTR). Second, any standard physical currency transaction from a domestic bank to a foreign bank that consists of at least $10,000 must be filed with U.S. customs officials through the use of form 4790.

The laudable goal of winning the battle against organized crime has, nonetheless, raised questions about the means employed to do so. Specifically, what are the privacy rights of individuals regarding the gathering of necessary information? What methods may the government use to attain information for legal proceedings? The Right to Financial Privacy Act of 1978 restricts the disclosure of information from a customer's records unless he or she has been served with legal papers. Furthermore, the institution must wait 10 to 14 days before furnishing this information to proper authorities. In addition, the government must deliver a statement of compliance with the Privacy Act prior to receiving the requested information. However, this law does not restrict an institution from notifying the government of information which may be related to criminal activity.

THE UNDERGROUND ECONOMY

The real shock in the Bank of Boston case was the realization of how easily the underground economy can use legitimate banking enterprises to achieve its goals. The underground economy deals with tax evasion as well as the rewards of organized crime and other illegal activities.[7] It is estimated to be a $500-billion-a-year industry. It is also growing at an explosive rate. It is based on the false reporting of taxes, nonmarket activities (unreported income earned at home), and illegal activities (drug selling, prostitution, and racketeering).

False reporting of taxes can be accomplished through the nondisclosure of income as well as falsification of records. A prime example of this can be seen on the streets of New York City. It is estimated that there are some 5,000 street vendors who do not disclose any earnings from the sales of their products.

Nonmarket activities include the selling of services through unofficial routes (such as in-home service and repair work) when income so earned is not reported for tax purposes. These two types of activities are functionally legal, but the nondisclosure of income generated therefrom is illegal. The larger the amount of undeclared income, the greater the burden of taxation placed on the declared income, assuming the need for tax revenue to remain constant. The third component of the underground economy is comprised of activities that are illegal per se, e.g., selling illicit drugs and narcotics, selling stolen property, operating prostitution rings, and loan sharking and racketeering, to name a few. Operated by organized crime syndicates or groups, both the activities and the income earned therefrom are concealed from the tax authorities. The magnitude of these activities and their revenues are indeed staggering.

It is estimated that the total revenues of organized crime groups in the United States are greater than the combined revenues of iron, steel, copper, and aluminum manufacturing industries and approximate about 1.1% of the GNP. While it is obvious that this group can operate effectively underground, it also has a problem: These activities generate enormous cash flows that far exceed the needs of the illicit enterprises.

Some means must be found to channel these funds into legitimate enterprises where they can be invested profitably; hence the need for laundering this money and access to the legal banking system. In order to gain entrance to the banking system, organized crime operates various legal enterprises such as construction, entertainment, trucking, and food and liquor wholesaling. Through these companies, organized crime (the "mob") can bring the illegally generated funds into the banking system by making it seem that the cash flows are from these businesses and not from other sources. Once this money is in the banking system, it can be put to use by the mob. It enables organized crime to expand and pursue various illegal goals. The objective of the government, through regulation of the banking system and reporting procedures, is to make such access difficult if not impossible, and to reduce the flow of illegal funds into the normal banking channels.

Another problem caused by the underground economy is the skewing effect it has on various economic indicators, such as the Consumer Price Index (CPI), unemployment rate, and Producer Price Index (PPI). This induces error in the government's assessment of the economy and causes a misdirection of government programs in order to address what is thought to be a problem.

Because of these activities, the government has initiated a number of programs to reduce the impact and scope of the underground economy, with particular emphasis on the activities related to organized crime. These include the Organized Crime Control Act of 1987, The Racketeer Influenced and Corrupt Organizations Act of 1970 (RICO), and the Bank Secrecy Act of 1970. The First National Bank of Boston was charged under the latter.

MONEY LAUNDERING

Money laundering plays a pivotal role in organized crime activity. According to James D. Harmon, executive director of the President's Commission on Organized Crime, cash is "the life support system without which organized crime could not exist."[8] The objective of the U.S. government is to reduce the funds that will be allowed into the system itself. The main laundering objectives include the improved portability (exchanging $20 bills for $100 bills) and nontraceability of funds. This is accomplished by sending funds into little-known banks offshore after converting these funds into more shippable size. Once they are in another country, the funds are exchanged for that or another country's currency. This generally takes place in countries with strong bank secrecy laws, thereby preventing anyone from looking into the source or ownership of these funds.

The use of shell corporations that exist purely to supply a place to run money through is another common method of arriving at the same result. There are numerous other methods, but one of the most common is the use of "smurfs." These people simply go to various banks and branches and make deposits in amounts that are just below the flagging amount of money ($10,000 per deposit). Smurfs can be very effective in the distribution of funds (30 to 40 transactions a day, with a value of $5,000 to $7,000 per deposit). Another method is to purchase nondirected money orders for large amounts and then deposit them into other bank accounts. This effectively eliminates the paper trail because these money orders are purchased with cash and then deposited into accounts as money orders.

The ultimate in money laundering occurs when a depositor can attain exempt status from the CTR lists at a bank. This is a very sought-after privilege since no transactions will be reported to the authorities. All business then falls within the realm of legal transactions for the company in question. As mentioned earlier, there are only certain types of businesses that are allowed to be on this list, and those that fulfill the requirements must provide proof of the source of their cash flows. Placement on the exempt list with a fairly high ceiling is the best of schemes because the transaction costs are much lower (less transactions) and the funds can be processed without concern of the federal involvement.

THE CASE AGAINST
THE BANK OF BOSTON

This is not the first time that the Bank of Boston has flirted with organized crime. In 1978, a loan office of the bank arranged to finance the acquisition of World Jai Alai in Florida for Roger Wheeler, former chairman of Telex Corporation, and John Callahan, former World Jai Alai president and a suspected mobster. As part of the deal, Callahan was to have been reinstated as president of World Jai Alai, if the deal went through. Two years later, Wheeler was murdered. Callahan became the next victim a year later. The two murder cases remain unsolved.

In the current case, the Bank of Boston was charged with two distinct sets of violations: (1) failure to report correctly international currency transactions; (2) failure to report domestic cash transactions. The latter gained particular notoriety because it involved the Angiulo family of Boston, purported to be the biggest Mafia family in Massachusetts and suspected of money laundering.

International Transactions

The first problem deals with overseas transactions with large banks. Commercial banks have long been in the business of receiving shipments from foreign banks for deposit in their own accounts. Most of the action was traditionally handled by New York banks. However, growing logistical problems at Kennedy Airport caused foreign banks to seek alternatives. The Bank of Boston sought this business, and as the letters from the Fed prove, the bank had a large amount of money flowing through its doors soon thereafter. Two separate unrelated shipments would occur. First, small-denomination bills would be received from the foreign banks for credit in their accounts. Then a request would be sent to the Bank of Boston that currency in large-denomination bills be shipped back to the requesting bank. Profits were gained by taking a small percentage of the total amount shipped.

Neither of these transactions was made or received at the explicit request of the Bank of Boston. There were no deposits made to individual or company accounts. It was all inner-bank transactions. There was the possibility that some of the money being received could have originated from illegal activity, but that was not thought to be the responsibility of the Bank of Boston because the Bank could not be expected to find out the origins of the money. This was because the country of origin (for the most part, Switzerland) maintained its own secrecy laws.

The Bank of Boston came under the suspicion of the Federal Reserve Bank of Boston as early as 1977 for its unusually large amount of such transactions.[9] The information brief filed by U.S. attorney William F. Weld and the chief attorney of the New England Organized Crime Strike Force stated the following:[10]

> That the defendant Bank of Boston was required to file a Currency Transaction Report for each of the currency transactions set forth in Appendix A below; and willfully failed to file said Reports, in violation of Title 31, U.S.C. 1081 on transactions occurring before September 14, 1982, and in violation of Title 31, U.S.C. 5313 for transactions on or after September 14, 1982, and in violation of 31 Code of Federal Regulations, Sections 103.22(a) (1980) and 103.25 (1980), which offenses were committed as a part of a pattern of activity involving currency transactions exceeding $100,000.00 within a twelve-month period, to wit:

1980	$ 194,410,422.00
1981	$ 544,722,484.00
1982	$ 269,307,393.00
1983	$ 161,378,672.00
1984	$ 48,864,310.00
TOTAL	$1,212,682,310.00

All in violation of Title 31, U.S.C. Sections 1081 and 1059, and Title 31 U.S.C. Sections 5313 and 5322(b).

The Angiulo Connection

The Angiulo family owned two real estate concerns: Huntington Realty Co. and Federal Investments, Inc. Both firms have been the bank's customers since 1964 at its North End branch. On various occasions, cash deposits large enough to arouse suspicion were made by the two firms. Nevertheless in 1976 Huntington Realty was placed on the exempt list, and in 1979 Federal Investments, Inc. was added to the list.[11] In 1980, new and stricter regulations were announced for the Bank Secrecy Act. The biggest change occurred with the type of companies that would be allowed to stay on the exempt list. In 1980, the Bank of Boston was asked why Huntington Realty and Federal Investments were still on the exempt list given the new changes that were in effect. The Treasury Department requested a copy of the exempt list for examination in April 1982.[12] The Bank of Boston sent the full list. The Treasury Department sent back the list with annotations next to the customers' names about whom it desired more information in order to establish their eligibility. Huntington and Federal were among those questioned.

Hubert Cox, an officer in banking offices administration, Bank of Boston, called Margaret Cushing, the manager of the North End branch, to ask for information about these two accounts.[13] Cushing asked that these companies be allowed to stay on the list since they collected rent and other payments which were mostly in cash. Cox questioned if they should be on the list because

he did not know if they were considered retail operations. Cushing reported that the accounts of Huntington Realty and Federal Investments should be allowed to stay on the list because of the type of business that they were in and because they were long-time customers. It was Cushing's opinion, from experience, that the North End residents tended to pay for their rental payments through the use of cash, which would explain the very high level of cash brought in by these two companies. Cushing also stated that the Angiulos were the primary owners. Cox did not feel comfortable with the situation and asked one of his assistants to follow up on it. This assistant did not do any follow-up. Cox, on his part, never asked his assistant about the outcome. The companies stayed on the list. It was asserted that this was an error of laziness and not one of illegal intent for personal gain either for the bank or any of its employees.

In May 1983, the federal government, in the course of its investigation of the Angiulo family in Boston for racketeering, loan sharking, and murder, subpoenaed the Bank of Boston to provide information regarding its domestic cash transactions. It was dertimined that during 1982, the Angiulos were allowed to purchase $1.765 million worth of cashier's checks, of which more than $250,000 were purchased in cash. Over $270,000 in cashier's checks were made payable to Cowen & Co., where the family maintained 37 brokerage accounts. In all, during the years 1979 through 1983, Huntington and Federal purchased 452 cashier's checks totalling $7,372,343.20. Of these, 163 cashier's checks totalling $2,163,457.50 were for cash and would have been reportable were those firms not on the exempt list. Huntington also engaged in large cash disbursements of the savings account balance at year-end.[14]

On October 10, 1981, the office of the controller of currency (OCC) requested specialized examinations of the Bank of Boston. However, because the examiners were not properly trained in the new regulations and because the new order for specialized examining did not reach the examiners, no violations were found.

In April 1982, treasury deputy Robert E. Powis requested that all Massachusetts banks forward their complete exempt lists to his office for examination. By June 3, Cox forwarded the list to Powis as requested. On June 8, Robert Stankey of the office of enforcement of the department of the treasury returned the list to Cox with several questions regarding individual customers on the list. Both Huntington Realty and Federal Investments were among those questioned.

By summer 1982, OCC was informed by the Treasury Department that it was targeting nine banks in the state of Massachusetts regarding compliance in the matter of 31 CTRs (completion of form 4789). The Treasury Department also requested the assistance of OCC in order to tabulate the currency receipts of the Federal Reserve Bank at Boston relating to the flow of currency. This task was assigned to two assistant national bank examiners.

In September 1982, a regularly scheduled examination of the Bank of Boston took place. On September 21, deputy Powis sent a letter to the OCC chief national bank examiner with the following information:[15]

[C]ompliance with the reporting requirements of the Bank Secrecy Act by banks in Massachusetts [was] very low. [N]otable lack of understanding of the exemption provisions in the [Bank Secrecy Act] regulation.

[T]he number of and dollar amount of CTR reports filed by banks in Massachusetts were not consistent with the large volume of currency activity between the Federal Reserve Bank and its members.

Our review indicates that the First National Bank of Boston, which appears to purchase the largest amounts of currency from the Federal Reserve Bank of Boston . . . has a very low level of compliance with the Bank Secrecy Act.

The officer in charge of currency operations at the bank, in contacts with my office regarding exempt lists, had informed us that he is not completely familiar with the provisions of the Bank Secrecy Act regulations.

A task force was set up in order to assure that the problem recognized by Powis would be effectively reduced and controlled. In April 1983, a national bank examiner in the OCC examination division discussed the matter with the officials of the Bank of Boston. On April 27, the Treasury Department authorized the IRS to undertake an investigation of possible criminal violations of 31 CTRs, Part 103 at the Bank of Boston.

On February 7, 1985, the Justice Department filed criminal felony charges against the First National Bank of Boston, alleging that the bank knowingly and willfully failed to report to the federal government the movement of $1.2 billion between the banks and several Swiss banks. The Bank waived indictment and pleaded guilty to the felony charge. The fine imposed was $500,000.

Bank of Boston's Response

Notwithstanding the guilty plea, William L. Brown, chairman and chief officer of the Bank of Boston, was emphatic that the Bank's international transactions were ''perfectly legal.'' The Bank of Boston began to pursue this business with foreign banks aggressively in the mid-1970s when logistical difficulties at Kennedy Airport led big foreign banks to look outside New York City banking circles.[16] The Bank of Boston dealt principally with Swiss banks. According to Brown:

The international shipments consist of two separate but unrelated elements: first, shipments to Boston consisting mainly of small-denomination bills; and second, shipments to foreign banks consisting largely of new $100 bills. These shipments were always made or received at the explicit request of the foreign bank, not at the instigation of the Bank of Boston. They traveled in a closed, bank-to-bank loop, and no individual depositor had access to them.

It is of course possible that some part of the cash that was deposited into the vaults of the Swiss banks originated from illegal activity. . . . I can only say it was our understanding that Swiss banks served as clearinghouses for other European banks, and Bank of Boston provided a service . . . which we. . . . believe was a legitimate one.[17]

Brown conceded that the only mistakes made by the Bank were in filing the necessary reports. He asserted that this failure was primarily due to "defects in our management systems."[18]

Daniel Dorner, vice-president for deposit operations, gave his account of management confusion over reporting. According to Dorner, the Bank of Boston did in fact file report 4790 which U.S. customs required; it failed, however, to file form 4789 which the IRS required. Dorner, as well as Brown, provided lengthy accounts of how such a mistake was made. The Subcommittee found them barely credible.

In defending the Bank of Boston's domestic transactions, Brown was equally cavalier: The regulations regarding legitimate exemptions from reporting were unclear.[19] In fact, Brown maintained that the pre-1980 regulations were sufficiently broad that the Angiulo enterprises could be properly exempted because the companies regularly dealt in large sums of cash. He concluded:

Without question, that decision represented an exercise of bad judgment; under no interpretation of the 1980 regulations should the two companies have been kept on the exempt list. Nonetheless, our inquiry has revealed absolutely no basis for believing that either the initial placement of the companies on the list or their retention in 1980 and again in 1982 was motivated by any desire for personal gain or other improper purpose.[20]

The response of the Subcommittee

chairman, congressman St. Germain, was incredulous. He queried Brown and Stoddard Colbert, first vice-president in charge of the metropolitan Boston branch system, if they ever read the local papers' articles on the Angiulos:[21]

MR. BROWN: Does it [the article] mention the companies?

CHAIRMAN ST. GERMAIN: Yes, the companies are mentioned, but the fact of the matter is—didn't you, Mr. Colbert and Mr. Brown, know who the controlling parties were in these firms?

MR. BROWN: No.

CHAIRMAN ST. GERMAIN: You don't bother to look? You just take a corporate name at face value and say "Gee, that's a nice name?"

MR. BROWN: It's impossible for me to look at all of our customers. We have hundreds of thousands.

Brown concluded his testimony by asserting that the Bank of Boston admitted its errors and was mending its ways. As proof, he pointed out that there had been a complete audit of all the transactions for the last four years.[22] This audit revealed several missing transactions, and the following supplemental filings were made: (1) a filing on March 7, 1985, involving some 400 transactions that totaled $93,000,000; and (2) a filing on March 27, 1985, involving another 1,200 transactions with a total value of $110,000,000. With these reports, the examiners attested that the Bank of Boston was now under full compliance. To assure that such things would not happen in the future, Brown went on to list some of the changes that would be implemented throughout the Bank of Boston's management.[23] Among these were the following:

1. Final authority for those on the exempt list would be channeled through the upper levels of the law department. To get to this high point, a branch manager must first do a back-

ground check on the customer in question. If the customer passed this test, then the request for exemption would be sent with the branch manager's recommendation to the senior branch administration officer. Final clearance must be given by the law office.

2. A special task force was constructed in October 1984 to develop a comprehensive compliance program that would follow the letter and spirit of all currency reporting. Currency transactions for both domestic and foreign transactions would be signed by the manager of the branch or office they originated from and be signed by a central office, which would control all transaction form logging.

3. Training has become stronger at every level of the company, and this would be ongoing to ensure that training would be up to date with all regulations of the federal government.

4. Manual logs were designed for all tellers to fill out when handling large cash transactions. This log was examined by management every night in search of transactions that would require a CTR to be filed. This log was to be computerized in the near future, and when this occurred it would be possible to total up all deposits for one account throughout the system for that day (thus eliminating the usefulness of the smurfs).

5. Compliance officers had been given increased authority over the groups they managed in order to control them effectively. They also had been given the power to take compliance problems directly to top management.

These changes, as well as those recommended by the President's Commission on Organized Crime, were designed to ensure that the Bank of Boston was in full compliance with the Bank Secrecy Act.

SYSTEMS FAILURE: BUNGLING AND REGULATORY MISMANAGEMENT IN THE OFFICE OF THE COMPTROLLER OF THE CURRENCY

There is little doubt that the Bank of Boston was guilty of showing little or no concern for the various rules of compliance that were necessary for the successful implementation of the Bank Secrecy Act. At the same time, it is also clear that the government agencies charged with implementation of the Act were falling down on the job. The hearings showed that while these government organizations had a common goal, there was a lack of coordination in their actions. In the absence of such cooperation, duplication of work and jurisdictional conflicts were commonplace.[24] In order to alleviate this problem, a document was drawn up between the Department of Justice, Federal Bureau of Investigation, and the four federal banking regulatory agencies. The document was designed to improve detection, investigation, and prosecution of bank fraud.[25]

This document outlined the various responsibilities of each agency as well as restrictions on sharing information between the agencies in order to protect the account holder from invasion of privacy.[26] When and if implemented, this document would most likely aid the effectiveness of each agency. It should bring about reduced duplication of work and enhanced agency communication, which would alert the correct agency of possible problems before they were allowed to reach crisis proportions.

NOTES

1. Subcommittee on Financial Institutions Supervision, Regulations and Insurance of the Committee on Banking, Finance, and Urban Affairs, House of Representatives, *The First National Bank of Boston Hearings*, April 3 and 4, 1985; pp. 1, 139–42, 142ff. (Hereafter cited as *Hearings*); U.S. Department of Justice, Organized Crime and Racketeering Section, Boston Strike Force,

"News Release" (February 7, 1985), in *Hearings*, pp. 139–41; and United States District Court, District of Massachusetts, *United States of America v. The First National Bank of Boston,* "Plea Agreement," in *Hearings,* pp. 142–45.

2. "Appendix to the Statement of C. T. Conover, Comptroller of the Currency," in *Hearings,* pp. 386–87.

3. Permanent Subcommittee on Investigations, Committee of Governmental Affairs, U.S. Senate, *Domestic Money Laundering: Bank Secrecy Act Compliance and Enforcement Report* (December 1986), p. 10ff. (Hereafter cited as *Report.*)

4. Fernand J. St. Germain, *Hearings,* p. 3.

5. *Report,* p. 1ff; Public Law 91-508, Title 27.

6. *Report,* pp. 1–3.

7. *Business Week,* "Money Laundering" (March 16, 1985), pp. 74–80.

8. Ibid., pp. 78–79.

9. Federal Reserve Bank of Boston, "Memorandum" (March 30, 1977), in *Hearings,* p. 13.

10. United States District Court, District of Massachusetts, *United States,* "Information," in *Hearings,* p. 146–148. Bob Davis, "Bank of Boston Unit Currency Transfer Found in Probe of Alleged Crime Family." *Wall Street Journal* (February 11, 1985), p. 11.

11. "Memorandum Concerning Angiulo Transactions at the Bank of Boston," in *Hearings,* pp. 165–75.

12. "Appendix to the Statement of C. T. Conover," in *Hearings,* pp. 386–87; Monica Langley, "Comptroller Concedes Failure to Detect Bank of Boston Currency-Law Violations." *Wall Street Journal* (March 4, 1985), p. 1.

13. William L. Brown, "Statement," in *Hearings,* p. 263; Bob Davis, "U.S. Says Banks of Boston Unit Was Told It Broke Law 2 Years Before Compliance." *Wall Street Journal* (February 28, 1985), p. 11.

14. "Memorandum Concerning Angiulo," in *Hearings,* pp. 170–71.

15. Cited by Conover, "Apendix to the Statement of C. T. Conover," in *Hearings,* p. 389; for full text see Robert E. Powis, "Memorandum" (September 21, 1982), in *Hearings,* pp. 77–78.

16. Brown, "Statement," in *Hearings,* pp. 258–71; also William L. Brown, "Report to the Annual Meeting" (March 28, 1985), in *Hearings,* pp. 177–81.

17. Brown, "Statement," in *Hearings,* p. 259.

18. Ibid., p. 260; *Hearings,* p. 272; *Report,* pp. 4–6; *American Banker,* "Treasury Tightens Rules on Reporting Large Transactions" (June 15, 1980), p. 1.

19. Brown, "Annual Meeting," p. 181ff; Brown, "Statement," p. 263. Bob Davis, "Bank of Boston Faces Image Problem Likely to Linger for Years." *Wall Street Journal* (March 7, 1985), p. 1; *American Banker,* "Boston Bank Chief Defends Actions in Cash Transfers" (February 12, 1985), p. 1.

20. Brown, "Statement," p. 264ff.

21. *Hearings,* p. 252.

22. Brown, "Statement," p.265ff.

23. Ibid., p. 266.

24. *Hearings,* pp. 398–438; Bob Davis, "Bank of Boston Unit's Fine Criticized as Inadequate by House Banking Panel." *Wall Street Journal* (April 4, 1985), p. 8.

25. *Report,* pp. 23–31; Bob Davis and Monica Langley, "Senators Seen Backing Tougher Rules on Bank Cast-Transaction Disclosures." *Wall Street Journal* (March 13, 1985), p. 12; Lois Therrien, "An All-Out Attack on Banks that Launder Money." *Business Week* (March 11, 1985), p. 30.

26. "Appendix to the Statement by C. T. Conover," in *Hearings,* pp. 370–81.

THE FIRST NATIONAL BANK OF BOSTON

"Attorneys Fees and the Money Laundering Control Act of 1986: Further Erosion of Criminal Defense Advocacy." *Georgia Law Review,* 21 (Spring 1987), pp. 929–65.

BYNUM, TIMOTHY S. *Organized Crime in America: Concepts and Controversies.* Monsey, N.Y.: Criminal Justice Press, 1987.

CLARK, R. F., and W. L. COPELAND. "Beware of Columbians Bearing Gifts: What Attorneys Should Know about Currency Transaction

Reporting Requirements." *Alabama Lawyer*, 49 (November 1988), pp. 350–54.

GARLAND, E. T. M., and D. F. SAMUEL. "The Money Laundering Control Act of 1986: Will Attorneys Be Taken to the Cleaners?" *Georgia State Bar Journal*, 24 (May 1988), pp. 186–92.

LYNCH, GERARD E. "RICO: The Crime of Being a Criminal." *Columbia Law Review*, 87, pp. 661–764.

MOKHIBER, RUSSELL. *Corporate Crime and Violence: Big Business Power and Abuse of the Public Trust*. New York: Sierra Club, 1987.

"The Money Laundering Control Act of 1986: Tainted Money and the Criminal Defense Lawyer." *Pacific Law Journal*, 19 (October 1987), pp. 171–92.

NAYLOR, R. T. *Hot Money and the Politics of Debt*. New York: Simon & Schuster, 1987.

PLOMBECK, C. T. "Confidentiality and Disclosure: The Money Laundering Control Act of 1986 and Banking Secrecy." *International Lawyer*, 22 (Spring 1988), pp. 69–98.

"Preventing Billions from Being Washed Offshore: A Growing Approach to Stopping International Drug Trafficking." *Syracuse Journal of International Law & Commerce*, 14 (Fall 1987), pp. 65–88.

TURLEY, JONATHON. "Laying Hands on Religious Racketeers: Applying Civil RICO to Fraudulent Religious Solicitation." *William and Mary Law Review*, 29 (Spring 1988), pp. 441–500.

United States House of Representatives. *Money Laundering Control Act of 1986*, 99th Congress, 2nd Session, September 24, 1986.

United States Senate. *Caucus on International Narcotics Control. Legislation Aimed at Combatting International Drug Trafficking and Money Laundering: a Staff Report*. Oct. 1987, 100th Congress, 1st Session.

United States Senate. Committee on the Judiciary, *Oversight on Civil RICO Suits*, hearings held on May 20, July 31 and September 24, 1985. 99th Congress, 1st Session.

GRUMMAN CORPORATION

*Relations between corporate board and top management:
obligation of top management to implement board policies
and directives*

On January 17, 1979, Grumman Corporation (GC) submitted to the Securities and Exchange Commission (SEC) a report prepared by the audit committee of the board of directors reviewing the audit committee's investigation, findings, and recommendations with respect to the nonmilitary, commercial sales practices of GC and its subsidiaries (collectively called Grumman) for the period of January 1970 to 1979.

The report is one of very few publicly available documents that illuminate the problems of a corporate board in developing an effective monitoring system where top management is deliberately concealing information and actively cooperating with field personnel to evade the letter and spirit of board policies and mandates, and where a large gap exists between the board, senior management, and field personnel regarding

standards of ethical conduct and legal behavior.

In 1977, the U.S. Congress passed the Foreign Corrupt Practices Act (Public Law 95-213). The Act prohibited U.S. companies from bribing or making otherwise illegal payments to foreign officials in order to secure sales. It also imposed heavy bookkeeping and reporting requirements on U.S. companies. American firms have constantly complained that the Act and other related rules and regulations put them at a serious disadvantage in the foreign markets in competition with multinationals from other countries who are under no such restrictions. Since then, there has been heavy lobbying pressure on the U.S. Congress to modify and weaken these laws. However, at the time of this writing, no such changes have been made.

ISSUES FOR ANALYSIS

The problems concerning the gap between corporate policies and operational practices is not unique to Grumman and has always been an aspect of institutional control mechanisms. Field personnel, confronted with realities of day-to-day operations and the need to meet competition on the one hand and the corporation's sales and profit targets on the other hand, often resort to shortcuts that result in sales, believing that in the long run they are acting in the company's interests and that in the end all their actions will be forgiven if they make money for the corporation.

This situation becomes even more serious when it concerns ethical conduct or compliance with laws that are somehow perceived as a public display of corporate morality. The perception of corporate misconduct is further reinforced when there is inadequate follow-through by top management and no serious reprimands for violations or rewards for compliance.

The issues for analysis are as follows:

1. How can a board of directors improve its monitoring ability when senior management is not participating wholeheartedly in ensuring corporate compliance with the board's policies?

2. Given such a condition, what type of insider representation on the board would be desirable? Would increased representation give outside directors greater access to corporate information and diversity of viewpoints? Or would greater representation allow inside directors to keep the outside directors from receiving information showing violations of company policies and programs?

3. In addition to the areas of conflict that are revealed in the Grumman case, what are some of the other areas of potential conflict between boards and top management, and especially between independent outside directors and top management?

4. How can independent directors improve their effectiveness and also limit their liability when senior management has not acted vigorously to ensure compliance with board policies?

5. With regard to the actions of the board in the Grumman case, how well-constructed was the board policy directive of October 1975? Was it possible that the sweeping nature of the resolution made it extremely difficult for employees to comply with?

6. Could internal controls, reporting requirements, and organizational structures have been instituted in a manner that would have made noncompliance difficult if not impossible to conceal?

7. How adequate as an effective deterrent against future violations were the penalties and reprimands meted out to various personnel for violating corporate policies? What other penalties should have been imposed, and with what potential effect?

8. How adequate are the new recommendations likely to be in ensuring compliance with board policies? What additional measures might be suggested?

9. Finally, is it realistic to expect sales representatives in overseas markets not to yield to pressures for such payments, even in contravention of company policy, when: (a) payments are expressly demanded by the purchaser, (b) without such payments no sales would be possible, and (c) the payments do not injure the profitability of GC because they are included in the price to the purchaser with the purchaser's complete understanding and agreement?

THE SEQUENCE OF EVENTS

Grumman Corporation and its subsidiaries are engaged in the design and manufacture of military aircraft and space systems and a diversified line of commercial products and services, such as buses, trucks, fire-fighting vehicles, solar-powered heating, and so on. But the Grumman's principal business is the design, production, engineering, and testing of military aircraft.

In 1979, Grumman Corporation, with sales of $1.47 billion and a net income of $19,571,000, was ranked as the 216th largest corporation according to the *Fortune* 500 ranking. Grumman has several wholly owned subsidiaries: Grumman Aerospace, Grumman Allied Industries, Inc., Grumman Data Systems Corporation, Grumman Energy Systems, Inc., and Grumair Export Sales Corporation. The company is engaged in contracts with the U.S. government for production F-14, A-6E, EA-6, E-2C, and EF-111A military aircraft. It also has contracts with the governments of other countries for military aircraft.

Prior to October 1975, there was a general perception among many companies in the U.S., as well as government officials doing business abroad, that payments to influence potential buyers were a necessary and accepted way of life in many foreign countries. Grumman personnel responsible for selling abroad were no exception. Before October 1975, Grumman had no published corporate policy prohibiting such payments or any other kinds of special procedures for doing businesss abroad, except that instructions had been issued that agreements of sales representatives should be approved by a member of GC senior management. Such instructions were not always complied with, but the agreements actually entered into from time to time followed generally standardized forms. Among the provisions normally included were a specific statement that the sales representative did not have authority to commit or bind Grumman, and a provision that the sales representative would conduct his or her activities in a lawful manner.

In May 1975, in response to public disclosures concerning foreign sales activities of other American corporations, GC's board of directors resolved that all sales representatives be approved by the board. In August of

that year, the audit committee recommended that Grumman's policies and procedures with respect to foreign sales transactions be formalized and expanded. Accordingly, on October 16, 1975, the GC board of directors formally adopted policies and procedures designed to ensure compliance with foreign and domestic law in connection with sales. The salient features of this policy statement included the following:

1. A specific prohibition against making any payments of sales commissions.
2. All sales representatives must be approved by the board.
3. A standard form for contracts must be utilized with prior approval by the chief executive officer and general council of GC of any deviations from the standard form.
4. Periodic reports must be made by sales representatives.
5. Disclosure of the existence of sales representatives must be made to any applicable foreign government purchaser.
6. Receipts must be issued for payments made to sales representatives.
7. The company would make inquiries to foreign government purchasers regarding their policy concerning the engagement compensation of commission agents.
8. Sales representatives must disclose the identity of all persons engaged by them to work on Grumman's behalf.

In October 1976, senior GC management expanded these policies and procedures to specify that the board be given information as to the sales representative's prior experience and suitability, acceptability to the customer, and the status of the requisite notification to the relevant government.

The Audit Committee Review

In February 1977, while believing it had no indication that any improper payments had been made in connection with Grumman's foreign sales, the audit committee felt it would be appropriate to conduct an independent review of the matter, given the current environment. Accordingly, it requested Hurdman and Cranstoun, Grumman's independent certified public accountants, to conduct such a review. On April 28, 1977, the audit committee was informed of the discovery of certain questionable transactions with respect to foreign sales of the Gulfstream Grumman II (G-11 aircraft). These questionable transactions were entered into by Grumman American Aviation Corporation (GAAC), which was then a subsidiary 81% owned by GC. It did not appear that the questionable transactions were material to Grumman's business. Nevertheless, the audit committee ordered a comprehensive review of the corporation's foreign commercial sales activities since January 1970, with particular emphasis on the sales of Gulfstream II. (Gulfstream II is a $6 million twin-engine corporate plane used by many companies around the world.) The purpose of the review was to determine whether there had been any improper payments or misconduct by employees with respect to the sales of commercial aircraft. The review was also to examine the effectiveness of Grumman's current policies and procedures. The audit committee of Grumman's board was composed exclusively of independent outside directors, and no present or former officer of the company was a member.

The audit committee retained the law firm of Cahill, Gordon & Reindill (Cahill Gordon) as its independent outside legal counsel to do the research with the assistance of Hurdman & Cranstoun, which was already working on the investigation.[1] This retention was publicly announced when GC filed a form 8-K report with the SEC on May 5, 1977. The chief executive officers of GC, GAAC, and Grumman International, Inc. (GI), which includes Grumman International and other GI affiliates, were requested to cooperate fully with the review. GI is the

TABLE 1. Cast of Characters

GRUMMAN CORPORATION

John C. Bierwirth, chairman of the board
E Clinton Towl, director emeritus, former chief executive officer and former chairman of the board
Joseph G. Gavin, president
John F. Carr, vice-president, administration, and vice-chairman of the board
Lawrence M. Pierce, vice-president and general counsel
William T. Schwendler, Jr., assistant to the chairman (formerly president of Grumman Ecosystems Corporation)

GRUMMAN AMERICAN AVIATION CORPORATION

Corwin H. Meyer, former president and chief executive officer
Russell W. Meyer, Jr., former president
Charles G. Vogeley, senior vice-president, commercial jet sales
Frank Wisekal, vice-president, administration and resources
Joseph E. Anckner, director of G-II international marketing
Richard Hodge, Latin American regional G-II sales manager
Adel A. Ouban, Middle East regional G-II sales manager
J. Eugene Myers, administrator of G-II international sales
Kenneth Frederick, European regional G-II sales manager

GRUMMAN INTERNATIONAL

Peter B. Oram, president
Robert L. Townsend, former president
Elliot E. Vose, vice-president and treasurer
Edwin V. Zolkoski, consultant (formerly vice-president for Far East marketing
Herbert P. Mosca, Jr., vice-president and director of Far East operations

GRUMMAN ALLIED INDUSTRIES

Robert W. Somerville, president

entity through which Grumman markets most of its products overseas (see Table 1).

INTERIM REMEDIAL ACTIONS

As the investigation progressed, Cahill Gordon conducted intensive discussions with Grumman's management, general counsel, the corporate audit department, and Hurdman & Cranstoun with a view to revisions, expansion, and effective implementation of the board's October 1975 policies and procedures. On January 18, 1978, the management adopted revised procedures (Corporate Directive 5).[2] These procedures were intended to be additional interim procedures, and not in lieu of, previously existing procedures. Corporate Directive 5 included the following procedures:[3]

— In connection with any request for board approval of a sales representative agreement, the chief operating officer and chief sales officer of the subsidiary or division involved must provide a signed, written justification of the reasonableness of the commission contained in the proposed agreement.

— The vice-chairman of the board and the vice-president and treasurer of GC must render a business judgment as to whether the proposed sales representative will serve Grumman's interest.

— The officer or employee most directly involved with the sale of a Grumman product must certify that to the best of his or her knowledge the sale has not and will not violate Grumman's policies and directives (no questionable payments or other improprieties).

— Prior to the retention of any sales representative involved in possible sales to a foreign government, a specified form of letter of notification must be sent to the appropriate official of the foreign government (specified as the head of the department which might purchase Grumman products), informing that government of Grumman's intention to retain the sales representative and inquiring whether such retention would comply with that government's law and whether that government has any adverse information concerning the proposed sales representative.

— All proposed foreign sales representatives must represent and warrant that no partner or owner thereof is, and that the sales representative shall not directly or indirectly retain to perform services on behalf of Grumman for, any public official, political party official, or candidate for public or political office.

— Proposed sales representatives are barred from providing any services on behalf of Grumman until the Sales representative agreement has been approved by the GC board.

— All proposed sales representative agreements must contain specific dollar or percentage commissions (provisions permitting commis-

sions to be negotiated at the time of sale are prohibited).

— Where a high-dollar Grumman product ultimately to be sold to an overseas purchaser is sold to an intermediate party other than the ultimate purchaser, the contract with the intermediate party must contain provisions similar to those required of sales representatives with respect to insuring compliance with Grumman policy.

— Comparable warranties are to be obtained from entities performing finishing work on Grumman products under a separate contract.

SUMMARY OF FINDINGS

The October 1975 policy directive was intended to change the existing way of doing business in foreign countries. However, a full review of the company showed that the directive had little effect on Grumman's foreign sales, especially on foreign G-II sales activities. Many Grumman sales personnel clearly failed to perceive the 1975 and subsequent directives as mandating a prompt and immediate change in conduct. A number of them acceded or actively participated in arrangements involving questionable commission payments.

The committee believed that the most serious problem uncovered by its investigation was the disregard by Grumman's personnel over a period of several years of policies adopted by the board of directors. The committee had no doubt that all the personnel involved were motivated by what they thought to be Grumman's interests. "Nevertheless, disobedience of the instructions of the board of directors, in some cases clearly willful, was so frequent as to raise serious questions concerning the ability of the board of directors to supervise Grumman's business conduct effectively."[4]

The report also found that GC's senior management participated in "restructuring" certain overseas sales transactions in an effort to hide questionable payments, almost simultaneously with their participation in the development of the October 1975 policy directive.[5]

MANAGEMENT RESPONSIBILITY

The ultimate responsibility for policy implementation rests with the corporation president and the managements of the subsidiaries. The managements, in this case, failed in their most important responsibility, which was to exercise policy control over the operating subsidiaries. Indicative of the attitude of Grumman personnel is that as late as mid-1978, approximately 40% of the persons receiving the audit committee questionnaire failed to respond in a timely fashion. Of the 324 Grumman personnel who finally responded to the committee's questionnaire, 35% indicated that they were unfamiliar with Corporate Policy Directive 5, and 49% were unfamiliar with the Foreign Corrupt Practices Act of 1977.

Grumman's corporate structure is such that the marketing function is largely in the hands of its subsidiaries. This lack of control existed at all levels of the corporation.

Senior Management. John C. Bierwirth, GC's chairman of the board, and John F. Carr, GC's vice-chairman of the board and vice-president of the company, permitted the restructuring of two contracts, for Saudi Arabia and Morocco, respectively, which were not in compliance with corporate policy in 1975. Although their effort was to salvage profitable transactions for Grumman, the questionable aspects of the contracts were not eliminated, and if to do so was not possible, the transactions should not have been restructured and consummated. Because these transactions occurred at approximately the same time as the issuance of the October 1975 directives, their consummation created the appearance of approval of these activities and appear to

have been taken by GAAC and GI personnel as models for the future.

GAAC's Management. Corwin H. Meyer was GAAC's president from 1974 until 1978. The report stated that he abdicated his responsibility for enforcing the October 1975 and subsequent directives. G-II sales responsibilities were delegated to Charles G. Vogeley, senior vice-president, and Meyer assumed, without inquiring that G-II foreign sales efforts were being conducted in compliance with corporate policy. Meyer expressly stated that in his opinion the committee's investigation was a needless intrusion on and an interference with GAAC's sales activities. The committee found that Meyer was not in fact aware of any untoward GAAC sales activity. Only in one case, he informed representatives of the committee that during 1977 a GAAC sales official restructured a transaction because of a questionable payment problem and that the restructuring had been approved by an unspecified GC senior official. Meyer made no further inquiries and took no action to prevent the continuation of the transaction. The committee was satisfied, through its own inquiries, that Meyer's assertion about the transaction's approval by a senior GC official was untrue.

Vogeley had de facto responsibility for the conduct of foreign G-II marketing. The committee concluded that insofar as GAAC was concerned (its involvement in questionable transactions and its failure to appraise the GAAC board or the GC board accurately of such activities), the primary responsibility must lie with Vogeley and various sales personnel selected by him. Vogeley resigned on August 15, 1978.

Grumman International, Inc. During the period ending in December 1976, GI automatically renewed 12 pre-October 1975 sales representative agreements without submitting them to the board for approval or converting them to the required standard form of sales representative agreement. When the corporate audit department discovered this total disregard of corporate policy, the GI vice-president responsible asserted: "We have not had the manpower and the time to tackle all of this group of bona fide sales representative arrangements in preference to other, more pressing cases."[6]

Grumman Allied.   Robert. W. Sommerville, president of Grumman Allied since January 1, 1976, permitted Howe, a subsidiary of Grumman Allied, and Wormuth, a division of Grumman Allied, to ignore compliance with corporate directives on the retention of sales representatives. Not until November 1978 did Howe submit to the GC board for approval more than 40 sales representative agreements designed to replace existing agreements, which neither complied with corporate directives as to content nor had been submitted to the GC board for approval. While the committee was unaware of any specific violation of domestic law in connection with Howe's sales activities, the chaotic situation surrounding Howe's noncompliance with corporate policy offered a fertile field for difficulty.

Other Employees.   The committee found that, notwithstanding the ultimate responsibility of senior management for compliance with board directives, in most cases of violation only less senior employees were directly involved. Some of these employees have since left Grumman, while many others still remain. The committee recommended that GC evaluate and consider the conduct of all employees who had played a substantial role in the violation of corporate policy.

ACTIVITIES IN VIOLATION OF CORPORATE POLICIES: GULFSTREAM II SALES

The committee found that during the period covered by the report, "the overwhelming preponderance in dollar amount of questionable sales transactions involved direct or indirect sales of G-II aircraft to foreign governments."[7]

With only one exception, Page Airways, Inc., was involved as the intermediary in every foreign G-II sale covered in the report. Although Page's dealership agreement with GAAC expressly provided for access to Page records, Page refused to cooperate with the audit committee; neither its records nor its personnel were available to the committee for examination and questioning. At the recommendation of the committee, the dealer agreement with Page was not renewed when it expired on December 31, 1977.

The pattern of questionable payments for overseas sales was established with the first sale of a G-II executive jet to the government of Cameroon, where a payment of $300,000 was made through Page. The transaction was described in the report as follows: Certain personnel of GAC and another subsidiary of the company, Grumman International, Inc., and, perhaps, a then member of the company's senior management and board of directors, understood that a significant portion of those funds would or might be paid to third parties, including a person who negotiated for aircraft on behalf of the Cameroon government. The sales representatives had apparently been designated by the negotiator, and a principal of the sales representive acted as the negotiator's interpreter.[8]

In 1973, G-II sales functions and personnel were transferred to GAAC, then a newly formed subsidiary of the company, and GAC ceased to have any function or responsibility with respect to G-II sales. In 1975, GAAC participated in arranging the lease of a G-II from an unaffiliated American corporation to the Cameroon government. Representatives of this other corporation expresssed to an employee of the subsidiary unwillingness to make direct payments of commissions in connection with this transaction to the sales representative, a

Lichtenstein corporation which had succeeded to the business of the New York sales representative. Arrangements were made thereupon for a lessor corporation to pay in excess of $75,000 in commission to the subsidiary, which in turn paid the money to the sales representative.

In a number of the sales that followed, commissions were paid by Grumman directly to sales representatives. However, in the majority of these sales, Grumman sold the aircraft to an intermediate purchaser. In each such transaction, the intermediate purchasers involved said that commissions were involved in the contemplated resale. The planes were sold to Page which, in turn, resold them either to the ultimate purchaser, to a Lichtenstein corporation (believed by GC management at the time to be an established aircraft distributor, which it was not), or to other U.S. companies which had prime contracts with the foreign governments involved. One effect of these transactions involving intermediate purchasers was that commissions were not paid by Grumman or reflected on its books. The majority of these transactions involved GAAC personnel, or prior to the January 1, 1973, GAAC merger, Grumman Aerospace Corporation personnel. GI and/or GC personnel were involved in some of these transactions, in most instances in conjunction with GAAC or GAC personnel.

The committee found that these transactions took place both before the company's 1975 directives and afterward. A selected number of questionable sales and payments discovered by the committee, and their modus operandi, are as follows:[9]

— Sale in 1975 by GAAC to the government of Cameroon, through the Lichtenstein corporation, with $75,000 commission paid.

— Sales of G-IIs in 1972 and 1973 by GAC, GAAC, and GI to the government of the State of Sabah through Page Airways, Inc.

— The people involved in the negotiations were aware that Page intended to pay some of these commissions to the third parties. A total of $925,000 was paid by Page in the two transactions. Some of the money was actually paid to the government officials.

— Sale in 1972 to the government of the Ivory Coast by GAC through Page. Page paid $150,000 as commissions with the knowledge of GAAC and GI personnel.

— Sale in 1973 of one G-II by GAAC to Page for resale to the Republic of Gabon. Page paid between $200,000 and $250,000 to the president of Gabon. In this transaction, Page's price for the aircraft was increased to cover the commission. The president of Gabon made some promises to Page in return. This was denied by Page in the investigation.

— Sale in 1973 of one G-II by GAAC to Page to a Japanese trading company for resale to the Japanese government. A $300,000 commission was paid which was concealed from the Japanese government.

— Sale of two G-IIs to the government of Togo in 1974 and 1975; GAAC paid $1 million to its sales representative.

— Sale of one G-II in 1974 to a Venezuelan company. GAAC paid a commission of $285,000 to an individual designated by the purchaser as its negotiator. An additional $138,000 was paid to the GAAC sales representative for the territory when a GAAC marketing manager had reported to an agent of the purchaser that no such commission would be paid.

— In 1977, in connection with a proposed sale of a used G-II to the same Venezuelan company, employees of GAAC understood that the Venezuelan sales representative intended to make a payment of some part of his commission to an employee of the purchaser. When advised by internal counsel of the subsidiary that payment of the commission under these circumstances would be in contravention of company policy, the employees instead arranged to sell the plane to a Panamanian company controlled by the Venezuelan sales representative for resale to the ultimate purchaser.

— In October 1975, an employee of GI, during negotiations for a sale of a G-II to the government of Morocco, stated that the company would pay no commissions on the sale despite the employee's prior agreement to pay a

$450,000 commission collectively, according to the employee, to a sales consultant of GI and a former official of another government who had performed services in connection with the transaction. On learning of the employee's statement, John Carr, the company's vice-president, administration, suggested that GAAC should sell the aircraft to Page for resale to a Lichtenstein corporation. The Lichtenstein corporation, which Carr then believed to be an established aircraft distribution company, would be introduced as the party through which the plane would be sold to Morocco so that it could be responsible for the payment of commissions, thereby making the employee's statement literally accurate.

— In the sale of a G-II in 1976 to Nigerian Airways, GAAC paid a 6% commission ($425,000) to its Nigerian sales representative. Some of this money might have been passed to the Nigerian government, with the knowledge of both GAAC and GI personnel. Bierwirth, the chief executive officier of the company, decided that no attempt should be made to reduce the commission.

— In connection with the sale of three G-IIs to the United Arab Emirates (April 1975), Oman (December 1975) and Bahrain (1977), GAAC paid approximately $1.3 million to a Lichtenstein corporation that had been retained as its sales representative. Certain officials of the subsidiary believed at the time at which they agreed to compensate the sales representative that significant portions of the payments would be disbursed to other individuals inside the purchasing countries, including, in the case of the United Arab Emirates sales, a diplomatic official (estimated to be $540,000) who negotiated the purchase on behalf of the purchasing country.

— In August 1975, an employee of GAAC contracted to sell two G-IIs to the national airline of Saudi Arabia. Included in the sale price was approximately $4,200,000 to be paid as sales commissions, $1,725,000 of which was to be paid to the subsidiary's Saudi Arabian sales representative, a Saudi company owned by a Saudi businessman. The remaining $2,500,000 was to be paid to an American citizen who was at the time the G-II sales representative for another country and who was also working as a consultant to GAAC's then sales representative in Saudi Arabia. On learning of this deal, senior management of the company became concerned about the magnitude of the commission payments and the prospect that they would be made by the subsidiary to unidentified third parties. Senior management was informed, however, that GAAC had already entered into a binding contract of sale to the Saudi airline. Thereupon, Page personnel suggested to senior management that the transaction to be restructured as a sale to Page for resale to a Lichtenstein corporation for resale to the Saudi airline. The Lichtenstein corporation was to disburse the $2,500,000 at the direction of the consultant and served no other purpose in the transaction. The restructuring of this transaction was approved by Bierwirth and Carr. It does not appear that the company or GAAC personnel considered the company's October 1975 policy applicable to the transaction. In addition, it appears that employees of GAAC did not disclose to the company's senior management all material information in their possession relating to the transaction.

— In 1977, GAAC again sold two G-IIs to Page, for resale to the same Lichtenstein corporation, for resale to the Saudi airline. While this transaction was structured similarly to the first Saudi transaction, senior management of the company has stated that it was not aware that the Lichtenstein corporation made any payments in connection with the transaction.

The aggregate gross contract price to the company's subsidiaries for the aforementioned sales of the G-IIs is approximately $118 million.

Internal Controls: Lack of Compliance with Corporate Procedures

The committee felt that the October 1975 policy directive and procedures should have been adequate to prevent the future occurrence of questionable sales transactions, and that the procedures added in October 1976 should certainly have been sufficient. Instead, not only was the spirit of the directives frequently disregarded, but the specific procedures ordered by the board were often circumvented or ignored.

Board of Directors Approval of Sales Representative Agreements

While GAAC submitted its sales representative agreements to the board with recommendations for approval, information as to the questionable nature of transactions, later discovered, was consistently withheld. As late as June 1977, a GAAC senior marketing officer—a senior vice-president—specifically represented to the board: "I will state that in the marketing of Gulfstream II overseas, we have not done anything that will be embarrassing to Grumman American Aviation Corporation or to the Grumman Corporation."[10]

As mentioned earlier, during the period ending December 31, 1976, GI automatically renewed 12 pre-October sales representative agreements without submitting them to the board for approval. When questioned by the audit department about this violation of corporate policy, the GI vice-president responsible asserted that he did not have the manpower and the time to tackle the problem.[11]

Notification to Foreign Governments

One of the October 1975 policy statements is the requirement that the retention of sales representatives be disclosed to the prospective foreign government purchasers to permit them to raise any legal or other objections they might have to the proposed representative. GAAC until 1978, and GI until 1977, failed to comply with this requirement. The explanation of the responsible GI vice-president was that "the required disclosures and inquiries to the prospective purchasers in these countries must be handled with tact and appreciation of the sensitivities

both of our sales representatives and of the prospective purchasers."[12]

Quarterly Reports

A requirement of the October 1976 policy directive was that marketing personnel obtain quarterly reports from all sales representatives. A major purpose of such reports was to enable management to ensure that the representatives were performing legitimate, definable, and productive business activities which warranted their retention by Grumman. GAAC failed to obtain such reports in numerous instances. Included among the sales representatives from which reports were not obtained were the representatives connected with sales in Saudi Arabia, Oman, and Bahrain. These facts were withheld from the board. At his June 1977 presentation to the GC board, GAAC's senior vice-president represented to the board that GAAC had been requiring "a strict adherence to quarterly report requirements.[13]

Accounting Control

The passing on of commisions by sales representatives and the payment of commissions by intermediate purchasers had the effect of removing them from Grumman's books and records, and it was intended to do so. Nevertheless, even when opportunities existed for subsidiaries' accounting personnel to identify and raise questions as to at least some of these transactions which involved unusual invoicing or other accounting procedures, they either did not seek any answer, or if they sought explanations at all, they were satisfied with questionable assurances from sales or other personnel.

There has not been enough evidence for the committee to eliminate the possibility that Grumman employees personally benefited from any transaction or that the funds were used for purposes other than the specific transactions. On some occasions, at the request of marketing personnel, financial personnel of subsidiaries issued or paid invoices that did not properly reflect the services or goods rendered.

GAAC also had a contractual right to inspect the books and records of Page as they pertained to G-II sales. Until requested to do so by the committee (at which time Page refused), GAAC had never sought to exercise that right.

Relationship with Page Airways, Inc.

An interesting aspect of Grumman's overseas sales of G-IIs is the role played by Page and the personal relationships and organizational needs that brought Page into contact with Grumman.

In 1968, Page was appointed a GAC Gulfstream distributor. This decision was made by the late L. J. Evans, then GC's president, with the concurrence of E. Clinton Towl. Various Grumman personnel believed this appointment was in return for assistance by James Wilmot, the principal stockholder of Page and a substantial Grumman stockholder, in the marketing of various Grumman products to the U.S. government and/or in return for his assistance in thwarting a takeover attempt by another company. Towl understood that Page was chosen because Grumman needed a distributor in the southwestern region of the United States. The relationship between Page and Grumman became sufficiently close that a merger between the two companies was seriously considered.

Page had a twofold responsibility: the marketing of the G-II within its area, and the outfitting of G-IIs when necessary. With respect to its first responsibility, it appears that Page had a marketing organization and was paid a commission ranging from $60,000 to $115,000 only if a sale attributable to it was made. With respect to its second responsibility, Page initially performed as a general

contractor subcontracting the outfitting work to concerns in San Antonio.

In late 1969, Vogeley was hired as marketing manager for the G-II program and was told that he could organize his marketing organization as he saw fit. Shortly thereafter, Vogeley requested that all G-II distributor contracts, including Page's, be terminated. Page complained and within two weeks was reinstated. Vogeley resisted this reinstatement but was overruled by Towl and Evans. According to Vogeley, Evans said that Page was important for other services performed by Grumman, which Vogeley understood to be political in nature.

Shortly after the reinstatement decision, Page entered into a dealer agreement with GAC and continued to assist in nationwide U.S. marketing of the G-II, with a commission ranging from $30,000 to $60,000 on each plane sold in the U.S., whether or not Page assisted in its marketing. Page became involved in international marketing of the G-II on January 1, 1972, with a new worldwide dealer agreement. From January 1, 1972, until December 31, 1977, Page was paid a commission of $30,000 per plane, whether or not it assisted in the sale. Vogeley stated that he included this provision for worldwide operations because he anticipated that Page would request it. The other provisions were negotiated by Evans. The new agreement provided that Page would be the seller of the G-II "if the circumstances of the sale as negotiated by the dealer will better accommodate the ultimate purchaser or lessee."[14] A number of substitutions of Page for Grumman as the final seller to G-II purchasers (Sabah, Ivory Coast, and Gabon) occurred within a short time. The 1972 dealer agreement also required that Page be given the opportunity to bid for all outfitting in the U.S. or abroad. This provision was interpreted by GAC (and later GAAC) to preclude recommending any other outfitter. Indeed, the practice arose whereby Page personnel invariably accompanied GAAC personnel on foreign sales calls.

Immediately after the formation of GAAC in January 1973, Russell Meyer, Jr., stated that Vogeley had little use for Page's domestic marketing activities and urged that GAAC take over these responsibilities. Vogeley told Meyer that he was in favor of Page's continued retention in the international sphere because Page served as an interface between GAAC and the customer. Meyer understood that Vogeley was saying that Page had insulated GAAC from direct involvement in questionable foreign marketing practices.

GAC and Page entered into a new dealer agreement in January 1975. Bierwirth stated that he believed Page had continued utility. The 1975 agreement was essentially identical to the 1972 agreement, except that the 1975 agreement provided that Page would not be paid a commission in the event of a sale to an airline. This provision appears to have been ignored in the sales of five aircraft to Saudia, the Saudi Arabian national airline, and Nigerian Airways. Because of Page's breach of the dealer agreements and because its close relationship with Grumman appeared to have facilitated repeated circumvention of Grumman's October 1975 policy directives, at the recommendation of the committee, the dealer agreement with Page which had expired on December 31, 1977, was not renewed. Page was, however, permitted to continue to pursue G-IIs for its own account so long as it did not receive preferential treatment vis-à-vis any other GAAC customer.

GOVERNMENTAL INQUIRIES

The SEC's Injunction against GC. While the committee was reviewing the company with respect to the policy and payments, the SEC was also investigating the company. In December 1977, the SEC informally notified Grumman that it intended to seek an injunction against GC, GAAC, and certain officers of GC, GAAC, and GI for alleged violations of the securities laws with respect to F-14 sales to Iran and various of the G-II transactions being investigated by the committee. The SEC described payments by Grumman and its subsidiaries of about $9.4 million in connection with overseas sales of Grumman's Gulfstream II twin-engine executive jet. After a series of negotiations in January 1979, without admitting or denying the allegations of the SEC complaint brought in federal court, Grumman consented to the entry of various injunctions against it pertaining to the reporting of questionable payments, to statutory bookkeeping requirements, and to other matters.

The SEC also brought charges against Page for foreign bribery in 1978, charging that Page and six top executives violated securities laws by channeling more than $7.5 million of "corrupt, illegal, improper or unaccountable" payments to promote business abroad from 1972 to 1977.[15]

The Wall Street Journal, in an article headlined "SEC Seen Dropping Foreign Payoff Case against Page Airways at CIA's Request," reported that the SEC was negotiating a settlement whereby it wanted to drop the foreign bribery charges against Page Airways at the behest of the CIA because the SEC could not prosecute Page without disclosing national security secrets.[16] Page was reported to have assisted the CIA in a supporting role in certain foreign activities. Moreover, Page was going to argue in its defense that U.S. government officials knew about the foreign activities that were the subject of the SEC bribery charges.

The Department of Justice Investigation. Along with the SEC, the Department of Justice conducted an investigation of Grumman in 1977. Negotiations between Grumman and the Department resulted in the settlement in January 1979 of GA, as successor to GAAC, pleading guilty to 12 counts of violations of, or aiding and abetting violations of, the Federal False Statement Act with respect to two export-import bank certificates and 10 shipper's export declarations, and paying a fine of $120,000, for which it was reimbursed by GC.

RECOMMENDATIONS

The Committee felt that had the October 1975 policy directive been followed and vigorously enforced, there would have been no further need for corrective action. The committee felt that it was essential that a new attitude prevail among corporate management. Its recommendations were designed to: (1) fill in the interstices of corporate policy relating to sales representatives and related matters; (2) provide an effective enforcement mechanism to ensure compliance; (3) ensure that all key Grumman personnel have an understanding of corporate policy and relevant United States law; and (4) develop policies in areas related to the committee's investigation. These recommendations would be effective only when accompanied by the "unequivocal dedication of GC and subsidiary management to the implementation of corporate policies by effective intra-Grumman dissemination, education, and enforcement. In this respect, it is expected that both the letter and spirit of those policies will be followed and that no Grumman employee will attempt to do indirectly what is forbidden to do directly."[17]

Corporate Directive 5

The committee stated that this directive should be implemented without exception by requiring the following:[18]

1. The chief executive officer of each subsidiary should certify to the chief executive officer of GC that he or she has made a thorough review of the compliance of the subsidiary with Corporate Directive 5 and should detail any noncompliance. Any subsidiary not in compliance should be promptly brought into compliance. GC's chief executive officer should promptly report the results of this review to the committee.

2. Any deviation from the standard forms required by Corporate Directive 5 should be fully disclosed and justified to, and specifically approved by, the board of directors.

3. Senior GC management should develop and submit to the committee for approval procedures to identify and prevent questionable aspects of such intermediate purchaser transactions. The procedures should designate accounting and marketing personnel in the various subsidiaries who shall have responsibility for compliance; include adequate internal reporting requirements; and provide for the termination of any proposed transaction where there is knowledge or belief as to untoward practices.

4. To the extent that there is knowledge or belief that commissions will be paid in the transaction, the intermediate purchaser contract should be submitted to the GC board for approval under procedures comparable to those required for the approval of sales representative agreements.

Enforcement

The committee stated that Grumman's internal audit personnel should be augmented to allow them to undertake systematic compliance reviews of corporate directives. Appropriate steps should be taken to ensure not only that the department maintains its independence, but also that such independence and the importance of the department's functions are clearly perceived throughout Grumman.[19]

Upgrading the Corporate Audit

1. The budget of corporate audit, including the salary of its director, should be placed under the supervision and control of the committee.

2. Upon the board's approval, the committee intends to authorize an increase in corporate audit's personnel to permit it to undertake additional compliance reviews.

3. While the director of corporate audit should continue to report directly to the vice-chairperson of the board (or, in his or her absence, the chairperson) on routine matters, he or she should report directly to the audit committee on all matters relating to material deviations from full compliance with corporate policy.

4. In recognition of the importance of the department and its compliance functions, the director of corporate audit should be appointed a vice-president of GC.

5. The director should be furnished all such proposed agreements, together with all supporting material, sufficiently in advance of submission to the board to permit appropriate review by the department.

General Counsel.   In addition to normal reporting responsibilities, GC's general counsel should promptly report to the committee any material deviations from corporate policy which come to his or her attention.

Outside Compliance Review.   The committee felt that the postdirective problems resulted more from personnel than from procedural deficiencies. Further, the majority of the questionable transactions entailed off-the-books events, and the accounting profession has historically distinguished between its reviews of internal controls incident to rendering opinions on financial statements and more extensive reviews of such controls. Against this background, annual examinations of Grumman's financial statements by its independent certified public accountants would not necessarily, and in fact did not, bring the major problems to light. However, because the events did occur despite internal compliance procedures designed to prevent them, and in view of the express requirements of the Foreign Corrupt Practices Act for devising and maintaining a system of internal controls providing reasonable assurances that specified objectives are met, the committee stated that Grumman's internal controls should be sub-ject to a searching and comprehensive review. Accordingly, the committee recommended that the board of directors authorize the committee to retain, under the supervision and direction of the committee's counsel, a second firm of independent certified public accountants to conduct a review of Grumman's internal controls and to advise as to any modifications required to ensure compliance with the accounting standards of the Foreign Corrupt Practices Act and Grumman policy.

Sanctions.   Senior GC management should submit to the committee for review and approval a statement of policy for distribution throughout Grumman which will unequivocally state that compliance with the highest standards of integrity is required at all times throughout the entire organization. This statement should make clear that there will be no toleration of an employee who in the course of his or her employment knowingly violates or circumvents any laws of the United States or of any foreign country or disregards or circumvents corporate policy or engages in unscrupulous dealings of whatever nature. This statement should make it clear beyond any doubt that any deviation from, or circumvention of, corporate policies will result in the immediate dismissal of the employee or officer concerned. The policy statement should also make it clear that Grumman personnel may not attempt to accomplish indirectly that they are forbidden to do directly, and that any lack of candor or lack of full compliance in these regards will result in immediate dismissal.

Senior GC management should also submit to the committee for review and approval a plan for the creation of a business ethics committee composed of the GC general counsel, the director of corporate audit, and other appropriate Grumman personnel to consider and make determinations concerning the aforementioned matters.

The committee will evaluate the conduct of currently employed personnel who were significantly involved in or responsible for the violations of corporate policy and will make recommendations to the board as to whether any further action is appropriate.

Legal Compliance. GC senior management should issue a directive setting forth the specific procedures to ensure compliance with various United States regulations including those governing the preparation and filing of shipper's export declarations; income tax laws pertaining to the proper deduction of sales commissions; and the laws applicable to all proposed export-import bank filings.

Education: Orientation

Senior GC management should develop a plan for the approval of the audit committee pursuant to which meetings will be held with all key managerial, sales, accounting, and purchasing personnel to explain the Foreign Corrupt Practices Act, Corporate Directive 5, the other directives issued pursuant to the committee report, and the recommendations contained in the report to ensure that corporate policy and the consequences of noncompliance are thoroughly understood. Management shall be responsible for obtaining a certification from all such personnel that the documents reflecting corporate policy have been read and understood.

Formulation of Policies and Procedures

Senior GC management should develop and submit to the committee for approval directives setting forth the following policies:

1. guidelines governing payments or gifts (including entertainment or services) to customers or potential customers;

2. specific rules concerning employee expense accounts and specific review procedures for their enforcement;

3. directives concerning invoices and checks, including unequivocal statements that all invoices issued must accurately reflect the underlying transaction and that checks may be issued only to the contracting party and for the transaction in which the indebtedness accrued; and

4. because the committee has encountered instances in which non-Grumman personnel have, with the knowledge of Grumman officials, held themselves out as officials or employees of Grumman, senior GC management should issue a directive prohibiting this practice.

NOTES

1. *Grumman Corporation Audit Report*, 1977. (Hereafter cited as Report.)
2. *Gruman Corporation Directive 5*, 1977. (Hereafter cited as Directive.)
3. *Directive*, p. 6ff.
4. *Report*, p. 30.
5. *Report*, p. 32.
6. Ibid., pp. 23–29.
7. Ibid., p. 18.
8. Ibid., p. 19.
9. Ibid., pp. 20 and following.
10. Ibid., p. 23.
11. Ibid., pp. 23–29.
12. Ibid., p. 24.
13. Ibid., p. 26.
14. Ibid., p. 27.
15. *The Wall Street Journal*, April 8, 1980, p. 10.
16. Ibid., p. 10.
17. *Report*, pp. 98–99.
18. Ibid., pp. 100 and following.
19. Ibid., pp. 105 and following.

GRUMMAN CORPORATION

BAYSINGER, BARRY D., and HENRY N. BUTLER. "Antitakeover Amendments, Managerial Entrenchment, and the Contractual Theory of the Corporation." _Virginia Law Review,_ 71 (November 1985), pp. 1257–1303.

BEAN, RUSSELL K. "Corporate Director Liability." _Denver University Law Review,_ 65, no. 1 (1988), pp. 59–75.

BENJAMIN, J. J., et al. "How Corporate Controllers View the Foreign Corrupt Practices Act." _Management Accounting,_ 60 (June 1979), pp. 43–45.

BLOCK, DENNIS J., and ELLEN J. ODONER. "Enforcing the Accounting Standards Provision of the Foreign Corrupt Practices Act." _Financial Executive_ (July 1979), pp. 10–26.

BUXBAUM, RICHARD M. "The Internal Division of Powers in Corporate Governance." _California Law Review,_ 73 (December 1985), pp. 1631–1754.

COFFEE, J. "Beyond the Shut-Eyed Sentry: Toward a Theoretical View of Corporate Misconduct and an Effective Legal Response." _Virginia Law Review,_ 63 (1978), p. 1099.

COSH, A. D., and A. HUGHES. "The Anatomy of Corporate Control: Directors, Shareholders and Executive Remuneration in Giant US and UK Corporations." _Cambridge Journal of Economics,_ 11 (December 1987), pp. 285–313.

DALTON, DAN R., and IDALENE F. KESNER. "Composition and CEO Duality in Boards of Directors: An International Perspective." _Journal of International Business Studies,_ 18 (Fall 1987), pp. 33–42.

EISENBERG, MELVIN A. _The Structure of the Corporation._ Boston: Little, Brown, 1976.

GOLDSCHMIDT, H. J., ed. _Business Disclosure—Government's Need to Know._ New York: McGraw Hill, 1979.

HINSEY, JOSEPH. "The Foreign Corrupt Practices Act—The Legislation As Enacted." _Financial Executive_ (July 1979), pp. 13–18.

JACOBY, NEIL H., PETER NEHEMKIS, and RICHARD EALLS. _Bribery and Extortion in World Business._ New York: MacMillan, 1977.

KRIGER, MARK P., and PATRICK J. J. RICH. "Strategic Governance: Why and How MNCs are Using Boards of Directors in Foreign Subsidiaries." _Columbia Journal of World Business,_ 22 (Winter 1987), pp. 39–46.

KRIPKE, HOMER. _The SEC and Disclosure: Regulation in Search of a Purpose._ New York: Harcourt Brace Jovanovich, 1979.

LOEBBECKE, JAMES K., and GEORGE R. ZUBER. "Evaluating Internal Control." _Journal of Acountancy_ (February 1980), pp. 49–56.

MARGOTTA, DONALD G. "Finance Theory: Its Relevance in Corporate Control." _Akron Business and Economic Review,_ 18 (Winter 1987), pp. 18–33.

MCKEE, T. E. "Auditing under the Foreign Corrupt Practices Act." _CPA Journal,_ 49 (August 1979), pp. 31–35.

MCQUEARY, Glen M. II, and Michael P. Risdon. "How We Comply with the Foreign Corrupt Practices Act." _Management Accounting_ (November 1979), pp. 39–43.

"Note: A Congressional Response to the Problem of Questionable Corporate Payments Abroad: The Foreign Corrupt Practices Act." _Law and Policy in International Business,_ 10, no. 4 (1978), pp. 1253–1304.

"Note: The Regulation of Questionable Foreign Payments." _Law and Policy in International Business,_ 8, no. 4 (1976), pp. 1055–82.

PARKER, MARCIA A. "How Corporate Directors Deal with the Boardroom Squeeze." _Buyouts and Acquisitions,_ 4 (July/August 1986), pp. 11–17.

RAMSEYER, J. MARK. "Takeovers in Japan: Opportunism, Ideology and Corporate Control." _UCLA Law Review,_ 35 (October 1987), pp. 1–64.

RICCHIUTE, D. N. "Foreign Corrupt Practices: A New Responsibility for Internal Auditors." _Internal Auditor,_ 35 (December 1978), pp. 58–64.

SCHIFF, MICHAEL, GEORGE H. SORTER, and JEREMY L. WIENSEN. "The Evolving Role of the Corporate Audit Committee." _Journal of Accounting, Auditing & Finance_ (Fall 1977), pp. 19–44.

SUMUTKA, ALAN R. "Questionable Payments and

Practices: Why? How? Detection? Prevention?" *Journal of Accountancy* (March 1980), pp. 50–56.

WEIDENBAUM, MURRAY L. "Battle of the Boardroom: Controlling the Future Corporation; the Proper Function of the Board of Directors." *Business and Society Review* (Summer 1986), pp. 10–12.

WEIDENBAUM, MURRAY L. *Strengthening the Corporate Board: A Constructive Response to Hostile Takeovers.* Center for the Study of American Business, Washington University. September, 1985.

WOODWORTH, WARNER. "The Blue Collar Boardroom: Worker Directors and Corporate Governance." *New Management*, 3 (Winter 1986), pp. 52–57.

WOOLF, E. "Auditing Committees: Are the High Hopes Well-founded?" *Accountancy*, 90 (October 1979), p. 73.

WORTHY, JAMES C., and ROBERT P. NEUSCHEL. *Emerging Issues in Corporate Governance.* Chicago: Northwestern University Press, 1984.

·II·

Business Strategies and Public Policy

GENERAL MOTORS
AND THE CITY OF NORWOOD, OHIO

Plant closings and their impact on affected communities

General Motors has "turned the corner" and is beginning to realize the expected economic results of the reorganization of its North American Automotive Operations. Its $10-billion plant construction and modernization program, and other management actions have created a trimmer and more competitive company.[1]

These were the opening comments of GM's chairman, Roger B. Smith, at a major press conference on November 6, 1986. This upbeat statement, however, was only the prelude to the grim news that was to follow:

A fundamental part of our "Strategy of the Eighties" plan has been to replace obsolete facilities with new or modernized plants. Just as with our reorganization moves, we recognized that for a transition period there would be an inevitable overlapping of capacity and personnel. Now we have progressed to the point where the new plants and equipment

are coming on stream and the expected efficiencies can begin to pay off.[2]

GM's chairman stated that the resulting modernization reorganization would result in the closing of 11 plants that became redundant with the construction of 6 new assembly plants and the total refurbishing of 12 others. GM officials also confirmed that 11 automobile assembly and metal fabrication operations would be closed in the United States and would affect 29,000 employees.

GM estimated that cessation of these operations would result in a fixed-cost reduction of $500 million annually. However, their actions would benefit all who had a stake in the continued well-being of General Motors. This statement was a follow-up on an earlier statement by GM where the company had indicated that it was in the process of reducing its salaried work force by 25% by 1989 to

TABLE 1. GM Assembly and Stamping Plant Closings

PLANT/ DIVISION[a]	LOCATION	MODEL	EMPLOYEES	CLOSING DATE/ REMARKS
1. Assembly (BOC)	Clark Street, Detroit	Cadillac Brougham	3,500	End 1987
2. Stamping (BOC)	Conner Stamping, Detroit	Body panels for Cadillac Brougham Olds '88 Wagon	700	1990
3. Stamping	Fleetwood	Body panels for Cadillac	3,000	—
4. Assembly (CPC)	Pontiac #2	Supreme, Regal, Monte Carlo	1,270	End 1987
5. Assembly (CPC)	Norwood, Ohio	Firebird, Camaro	4,000	Mid-1988
6. Stamping (CPC)	Hamilton/ Fairfield, Ohio	Body Panels for Camaro, Firebird	2,500	1990
7. Stamping (Chicago, BOC)	Willow Spring, Illinois	Lux. reg., midsize car body panels	2,900	Phase out
8. Stamping (BOC)	Flint (Mich.) body assembly	G car bodies	3,230	End 1987
9. Assembly (T & B)	St. Louis, Missouri	Pickup, crewcab	2,200	Mid-1987 (move to Janesville)
10. Assembly (T & B)	Pontiac central	Heavy trucks	2,200	Aug. 1988— trucks sold to Volvo; Sept. 1987— buses sold to Greyhound
11. Assembly (T & B)	Flint line	Pickup	3,450	Aug. 1987

[a]BOC = Buick-Oldsmobile-Cadillac division

CPC = Chevrolet-Pontiac-Canada division

T & B = truck and bus division

SOURCE: Statement prepared by United Auto Workers (UAW) research department (Xerox) based on publicly available information (January 24, 1987, Norwood, Ohio, p. 79). Hearing of Committee on Labor and Human Resources, U.S. Senate 100th Congress, reviewing the reasons behind GM's decision to close 11 plants in four states and to determine ways to keep these plants operating and the employees working.

reduce costs and increase its competitiveness.[3] Over the years, GM had been losing its market share (see Appendix, p. 79). The statement went on to outline the details of the various plants scheduled for closing (see Table 1).

To the city of Norwood, Ohio, the announcement of the GM plant closing came as a thunderbolt from the sky. Its economic impact on the community was nothing short of catastrophic. At one time, the city officials even contemplated declaring a bankruptcy. However, this idea was not seriously pursued.

Although the direct impact of the plant closure would be the dislocation of the plant's 4,300 workers, who relied on General Motors for their livelihood, the indirect impact would be even greater. The plant clo-sure would result in a direct loss of $2.7 million in earnings and property tax revenues to the city of Norwood. This tax loss represented approximately 25% of Norwood's annual operating budget. In addition, the Norwood city school system would also lose $2.3 million in property tax revenues. The city was already in the throes of an economic downturn. Several other Norwood industries had recently announced layoffs and possible closure or relocation. Shortly after General Motors' announcement, the U.S. Playing Card Company announced the layoff of 105 workers, and the Siemens Corporation announced the layoff of 75 workers. These developments had followed an announcement earlier last year that 114 jobs were being eliminated at the Leblond Makino Company. The city had also suffered a loss of $600,000 in federal revenue-sharing funds due to the elimination of the federal revenue-sharing program at the end of 1986. It was estimated that the loss of income from GM jobs would remove over $100 million annually from the greater Cincinnati economy. The multiplier effect of this income loss would further impact service and supply industries throughout the region.[4]

The feelings of Norwood's residents were best captured by a commentary on a local radio station:

LISTEN TO THE HEARTBEAT, MR. SMITH

You became one of the world's largest and richest corporations on the sweat and labor of the people who live in our town. And in the process, the people who made you became dependent on you. They put down their roots, took on 30-year mortgages on 50-foot lots. And whatever else they might have been, or wherever else they might have settled, they didn't because you were here. And, at least for most of them, they gave you everything they had. . . .

There are ways to keep the plants open. The state can help, and the workers are willing to make concessions. True, you might make a little less money, but you can add a human touch. You say, in your commercials, ''Listen to the heartbeat . . . listen to the heartbeat of America.''

To this commentary, I can only add my hope and prayer that the corporate leadership of General Motors will listen to the heartbeat. Listen to the heartbeat of those who built their company—the heartbeat of the workers, families and communities that they are now leaving behind.[5]

ISSUES FOR ANALYSIS

In a changing competitive environment, businesses must relocate plants and facilities and consolidate and expand in order to adapt to market conditions. No one challenges the right of business to make autonomous investment and marketing decisions. At the same time, it is also clear that any sizable move on the part of a business entity has serious economic and sociopsychological impacts on the affected workers, and also on the communities and all those who are directly and indirectly affected by the plant closing. This is particularly true in cases of small communities such as the city of Norwood, where a particular business may represent a disproportionately large segment of its employment and tax base.

The situation is not always one-sided or dismal. Laid-off employees may find new and often more rewarding jobs, pursue new careers, or move to new areas, which job commitments had prevented them to do before. Similarly, communities may find new vigor by bringing in high-growth industries, as well as a diversified economic base and an increased sense of optimism that comes with the process of change.

The primary responsibility of a company in making investment decisions, including plant closings and relocations, is to protect the interests of the owners, i.e., the stockholders, and to ensure the survival of the organization. The next most important consideration is, of course, the employees. Responsible companies make all possible efforts to minimize, if not eliminate, the adverse impact of plant closings on employees as an extension of good employee relations, which are important to the success of a business. Over the years, a large body of federal and state legislation, as well as employment contracts and union agreements, have succeeded in defining and protecting employee rights.

The situation regarding the affected communities, however, is not entirely clear, and considerable controversy exists concerning the rights of communities and the obligation of corporations in the event of plant closures, downsizing, and consolidations.

Some of the important issues for analysis are as follows:

1. What are the legal, social, and moral obligations of a company toward the community where its plant closing will have an adverse economic impact?

2. To what extent would the responsibility of a departing corporation be affected under one or more of the following conditions?

   a. whether or not a company is profitable or is losing money;

   b. the company has been operating in the community for a long time (e.g., over 20 years) or a short time (e.g., less than 10 years);

   c. the company is among the largest, if not the largest employer in the community;

   d. the production is being moving to a poorer and cheaper labor area within the United States;

   e. the production is being moved to a Third World country with cheap labor, or more efficient and economical operating conditions;

   f. the company has recently assumed a large debt as a result of a takeover, leverage buyout, or in an attempt to thwart a hostile or potentially hostile takeover; and

   g. the company's management made some poor strategic choices, or did not anticipate market changes correctly, and must now take radical action to rectify the situation.

3. The adequacy of company's dealings with the community in the event of a plant closing must be analyzed both in terms of process and outcome. How might one evaluate the negotiating process used by GM in its dealings with the city of Norwood officials?

4. Similarly, how might one evaluate the negotiating stance and process used by the city officials? Could the situation, or the final outcome, have been different if either one or both of the parties had used different negotiating strategies and tactics?

5. How adequate was GM's offer to help the city given the overall economic environment and its need to deal with a large number of similar situations?

6. How reasonable were the city of Norwood's demands on GM?

7. What are some of the mechanisms that might prove useful in protecting the legitimate interests of affected communities and in smoothing out the transition process in the event of plant closings? These mechanisms should not harm the process of "creative destruction" that is an indispensable part and inevitable consequence of technological change, human growth, and economic rejuvenation.

THE CITY OF NORWOOD

The city of Norwood is a small town of 2.3 square miles, with a population of approximately 25,000, and is surrounded on all sides by the city of Cincinnati. Norwood is 100 years old and is very proud of its history and traditions. Compared to Cincinnati, it provides a superior level of municipal services including an excellent public school system. The city's population is 95% white. It is almost completely built, and no large vacant tracts of land are available for new industrial development, plant expansion, or multiple-unit high-density housing.

The city is highly industrialized and has a number of plants, of which GM has been by far the biggest (see Exhibit 1). Most of the workers employed in the city's plants, however, do not live there and instead commute from Cincinnati and other neighboring communities. For example, of the 4,300 GM workers employed in the plant, less than 500 lived within the Norwood city limits. Unlike most other cities in the United States, property taxes are not the primary source of revenues for Norwood. Instead, the city levies an earnings tax that is imposed on all wages earned within the city limits. This allows Norwood to provide an unusually high level of services to its residents without burdening them with heavier property taxes.

Even before the current economic slowdown, suggestions had been made that Norwood was too small to sustain itself as an

EXHIBIT 1. Location of GM Plant in Norwood, Ohio

independent town and that it should merge with its larger neighbor, Cincinnati, which surrounds it from all directions. However, the city officials vehemently rejected such a notion and expressed their determination (and that of the citizens of Norwood) to remain an independent municipal entity.

CHRONOLOGY OF EVENTS

Soon after the GM announcement, Ohio state and Norwood city officials initiated discussions with company executives to explore the possibility of keeping the plant open. On January 15, 1987, the Ohio governor met with GM's chairman, Roger B. Smith. This was immediately followed by a congressional hearing held by Ohio Senator Howard W. Metzenbaum on January 26, 1987, at a Norwood junior high school. The hearings included witnesses and testimony from, among others, GM representatives, city officials, UAW representatives, and some affected employees.[6]

GM's Reasons for the Plant Closing

In testifying before Senator Metzenbaum's Committee, GM's president and chief operating officer, James F. McDonald, outlined his company's position for plant closings and restructuring. He argued that his company had no choice but to close obsolete plants and consolidate production in order to meet the competitive challenges faced by the U.S. auto industry in general and his company in particular.

The American automobile industry, more than any other industry, faced the heaviest burden of restructuring and downsizing as a result of changing economic conditions, manufacturing technologies, and fierce competition from Japan and other countries. GM, being the biggest of the "big three" U.S. automobile manufacturers, faced the worst situation. In less than 10 years, its U.S. market share had gone down

to 45% from over 60%, leaving it with a large proportion of redundant capacity, some of which was quite old and economically and technologically inefficient. To meet the new economic and competitive reality, GM launched a $10 billion-plus plant construction and modernization program, which eventually wound up as a $40 billion program, and took other actions designed to create a trimmer and more competitive company.[7]

An integral part of this strategy had been to replace obsolete facilities with new or modernized plants. The strategic plan called for closing 11 plants that had become redundant, with the construction of 6 new assembly plants and the total refurbishing of 12 others. The operations scheduled for closing would affect 29,000 employees. The assembly plant at Norwood, Ohio, was among those scheduled for closing. The closing would directly affect approximately 4,300 workers.

Although GM has apparently turned the corner in its drive to regain profitability and competitive health, it still has much to do in order to survive. Financial analysts and industry observers insist that GM would need further trimming in order to bring its domestic manufacturing capacity in line with its sales prospects. It is estimated that GM would have to adjust downward from a current market share of 43% to an eventual sustainable market share of 35%. And to achieve this, GM would probably have to close an additional half a dozen plants during the next five years, affecting over 100,000 workers.[8]

GM's management accepted that plant closings cause stress and disruption in communities, but felt that unless these painful decisions were made, the long-term health of the entire domestic manufacturing base was at stake.

GM outlined the following reasons for its plants closing:

1. Each of the 11 plants included in the current plan had a different reason for closing. Some

plants making rear-wheel drive cars were to be displaced by more modern plants making front-wheel drive cars. Plants in the truck and bus division were sold to Volvo and Greyhound. Some critics, on the other hand, asserted that GM was closing many plants in order to relocate substantial production capacity overseas, especially for auto parts, and that GM was obtaining more and more automobiles from Korea and Japan.

GM's president McDonald, however, vigorously denied this point. According to his testimony, none of the Norwood city plant's production was to be replaced by overseas production. He also stated that no other American manufacturer could match GM's "committment to the manufacturing base of this country and to maintain American jobs."[9]

2. The Norwood plant was an old, three-story building which could not utilize the latest developments in efficient production systems. Furthermore, as the plant was landlocked, it could not be reconstructed into a modern, single-story production facility. According to GM's president McDonald, Norwood was one of the oldest and least efficient of GM's plants. Therefore, there was no question that in the long run the Norwood plant had to be closed: "It was a matter of when."[10]

3. The Norwood plant produced midsized and sporty cars: Chevrolet Camaro and Pontiac Firebird models. These were also currently produced at the GM's Van Nuys, California, assembly plant. The Van Nuys plant was built in 1947, about a quarter century after Norwood, and was updated at a cost of $22 million in 1985.

4. GM argued that it had to maintain a presence in the highly competitive Californian market. The company felt that by closing the Norwood plant and moving the work to the Van Nuys plant, the latter could be consolidated and made more competitive. GM stressed that they were not sacrificing local production in favor of foreign operations.[11]

United Auto Workers' (UAW) Viewpoint

Owen Bieber, president of the United Auto Workers of America, felt that GM, while ad-

dressing the erosion of its marketshare, "flirted with one quick fix after another."[12] He agreed that in a dynamic economy, some plants are likely to close—but he was convinced that far too many plants were closing needlessly. In his opinion, when a plant closing was justified, its cost must be shared equitably.

From the UAW's point of view, GM invested heavily for a time to gain its market share from domestic and foreign competitors. GM pursued a risky as well as costly strategy—adding capacity at a time when Ford and Chrysler were retrenching, the industry was going through recession, and imports were increasing. GM ran into numerous problems with the expensive technology-intensive strategy. According to the UAW chief, the idle auto capacity in 1986/87 amounted to about 2 million units. General Motors' announcement of its plant closing was likely to reduce work capacity by about 1 million units. With the addition of imports and transplants (foreign companies increasing new production capacity in the United States), the excess capacity by the end of the 1988 model year could be up to 40 million units. This was equivalent to 15 assembly plants, each corresponding to two shifts of 6,000 people per plant. Furthermore, for each job in a domestic American auto assembly plant, 11 additional supplier jobs were created (whereas the transplants generated only 3 jobs). Even leaving aside the nonauto jobs, the numbers amounted to between 300,000 and 400,000 auto workers' jobs.

Bieber also accused GM of diversifying into unrelated industries and buying off its critics when it should be devoting these resources to gaining competitive strength in the automobile industry. In 1984, GM's Hughes Aircraft acquisition cost $5 billion, and its Electronic Data Systems (EDS) acquisition cost another $2 to $4 billion. In December 1986, an additional $750 million was incurred to buy out Ross Perot, EDS's owner.

The UAW chief also charged GM with exporting U.S. jobs. According to Bieber, offshore by 1988, equivalent to two plants, and produce 100,000 to 200,000 vehicles in a GM-Suzuki plant in Canada, to be shipped to the U.S. under the U.S.-Canada Auto Pact. In 1987, GM imported 1 million engines, compared to only 800,000 in 1981. This was equivalent to building a whole new engine plant.

There were some rumors, although denied by everyone at GM, that GM considered the Norwood plant to be afflicted with labor troubles and, therefore, was not anxious to put more money into it. Mayor Sanker admitted that in the past the plant had had more than its share of labor problems, but that these had since been resolved and that labor relations in the plant were excellent. The union felt that workers were not getting "a chance to gain back what had been lost through foreign imports." The UAW was keen to cooperate with the management, as "for instance, during 1984 the Local Agreement was settled on September 10, four days sooner than the National Settlement on September 14."

The local UAW challenged GM's rationale for the Norwood plant closing. Cleon Montgomery, a representative of UAW local 674, contended that "they could build the 1987 model of Camaro and Firebird for $112 million a year cheaper than their sister plant in Van Nuys, and could build the 1988 model $200 million cheaper." Thus, he could not understand General Motors' logic in moving its work to California where "only one out of five automobiles purchased is a General Motors product." He felt that without their "General Motors jobs," they could not buy "General Motors products." Quoting from an article written by the former plant manager Charlie Miller, Montgomery stressed that whereas the media was given the impression that Norwood was an old and outdated plant, it had in fact undergone extensive upgrading, with new equipment and facilities for quality control, checking, and production, and with one of the most modern paint facilities in the world. He

also mentioned that since 1972, there had been very few labor disputes in Norwood. The union's goal was zero grievances. Regarding the Norwood plant being landlocked, Montgomery felt that with the help of the city of Norwood, more acreage could be acquired at very little cost to General Motors. With the close proximity of suppliers (70% within 300 miles) and the just-in-time (JIT) inventory, GM could expand and save money. With the proper layout of docks, the company could easily expand and make money, and the workers were willing and determined to help GM do it.

City of Norwood's Viewpoint

The City of Norwood argued that GM had given short shrift to its efforts in seeking ways to keep the plant operating. According to Mayor Joseph Sanker:

> We have always worked to meet GM's needs, this included redirecting streets, building a new underpass, making zoning changes that GM wanted.
>
> Furthermore, in recent months, the employees of the Norwood assembly plant have proposed a number of changes intended to reduce costs and improve efficiency at the plant. The City of Norwood, State of Ohio, local utilities and suppliers have joined in that effort.
>
> The attitude here used to be "what GM wants, GM gets." Not any more.[13]

Mayor Sanker also pointed out that while General Motors decided to close the Norwood plant, several foreign manufacturers were building or planning to build auto plants along the local Interstate 75 (I-75) corridor that provided access and proximity to suppliers, customers, and skilled labor. Sanker hoped that GM would stay:

> It is our sincere hope that these proposals will be given full consideration by the man-

agement of General Motors. It is our further hope that these proposals combined with the Norwood plant's central location and experienced workforce will lead General Motors to the conclusion that closing the Norwood plant is not a prudent business decision.[14]

GM's Actions in the Norwood Plant Closing

On November 6, 1986, GM announced that the Norwood plant would be closed by mid-1988, giving the city almost 18 months advance notice. However, by early March, GM announced the first date for its plant closing, which turned out to be August 26, 1987. As part of its closing effort, GM developed a comprehensive scheme of worker retraining, job placement, and transfer of workers to other GM locations. Moreover, under the GM-UAW contract, the company was to provide supplemental unemployment benefits, guaranteed income stream benefits, relocation allowances, and continuation of health care coverage. Depending on seniority, hourly laid-off employees with one year or more seniority could receive up to 95% of their take-home pay for up to two years. The combined value of these benefits was estimated to be over $100 million.

At the behest of Ohio's governor, GM agreed to hire independent economic development consultants, the Battelle Memorial Institute, to evaluate the best future use of the plant's facilities and surrounding land. GM also retained West Shell Realtors to market the Norwood property.

General Motors also refrained from seeking property tax reassessment on its plant site, thereby saving the city of Norwood about $2 million in tax revenues. GM also demonstrated its earlier commitment to Norwood as a good corporate citizen by indicating that its Norwood plant and employees had contributed almost $500,000 to local charities in 1986 alone.

The Battelle Institute Report

In August 1987, Battelle Memorial Institute completed its study and submitted a final report. The Battelle study was designed to accomplish three tasks: (1) objectively assess the strengths and weaknesses associated with the Norwood area; (2) identify suitable industries and services for GM sites; and (3) develop strategies to attract new companies to Norwood.

The report identified Norwood's strengths related to factors like multistate market access, transportation, and infrastructure (utilities, communications, health care, etc.) as from excellent to good. It also recognized, however, Norwood's weaknesses—e.g., a poor system of water transportation, the city's perception as a location with high operating costs, etc. Based on its analysis of all relevant factors, the report identified over 100 industries and services that might be prospects for the plant site, and made specific recommendations for its stepwise redevelopment. The Battelle study concluded that the best use for the sight could be served by attracting light manufacturing industries; business-supporting and administrative services; and wholesaling and distribution.[15]

Negotiations Between GM and the City of Norwood

Between November 1986 and March 1987, city and state officials and UAW leaders made numerous representations to GM for keeping the plant open, but these were unsuccessful.

The city immediately launched an effort to cut costs and contain the city's expenses while raising temporary revenues. According to Mayor Joseph Sanker:

> What really hurt us, I guess, is the General Motors' announcement that they were going to leave in mid-1988. We took that to heart

and immediately made cuts. We took some 1.5 million dollars out by payroll deductions. We laid off a total of 37 people. We privatized our waste collection, which saved several hundred thousands of dollars. We did various other things, like letting people go through attrition and giving our appointed people 10% cuts in salary. We couldn't lay off our police and fire department personnel because they were under contract. We have economized while maintaining the quality of the fire and police departments. The 70-man fire department was reduced to 52, and the 56-man-police department was reduced to 48. These were perhaps top heavy. They made the concessions and agreed to reduce the number of people. The city also tried to enact a 10 mill tax levy, but it was defeated by the local voters.

City officials viewed GM's claims of good corporate citizenship as mere puffery designed for public relations effect. They pointed out that $100 million GM would pay in closing its plant were contractual payments that GM was obligated to pay and were in no way a magnanimous gesture designed to help the city.

In its dealings with GM, city officials at first attempted a conciliatory approach, seeking GM's help in tiding the city over its financial difficulties during this transition period. They felt that the large corporation would be willing to help the small town that had come to depend so much on it. Accordingly, on April 17, 1987, city officials sent a letter to GM's chairman asking that GM provide $2.3 million per year for four years in lieu of taxes, during which period the city would redevelop its tax base. GM was also requested to donate immediately to the city its 14-acre lot and two parking garages, and to demolish the plant and clear the site for redevelopment. In May and June, the city also asked GM to withhold payroll city taxes from the laid-off GM employees' supplemental pay (SUB-pay). The city tax commission also subpoenaed key GM plant officials to appear before the commission and pro-

vide information on SUB payments and withholding of taxes, which the tax commissioner estimated to be $2.8 million.

In its reponse, GM rejected the city's request for aid in lieu of taxes. GM feared it would be confronted with similar requests from all other locations with plant closings, which it simply could not meet. Nor would GM withhold payroll taxes of SUB-pay, as the legality of doing so was in question. GM was unwilling to undertake an immediate disposition of its property pending the report from the Battelle Institute. Moreover, in keeping with its policies, GM wanted to undertake a complete environmental clean-up of the property at an approximate cost of $9 million prior to its disposition. Such an action was also necessary to protect GM from any potential liability lawsuits.

Between March and July 1987, discussions and meetings continued between GM representatives and city officials to resolve various outstanding issues arising out of the plant closing. On July 31, 1987, GM released the Battelle Institute report. City officials, however, were not satisfied with either the pace or the progress of negotiations. They had sought the help of state and national political leaders to pressure GM. However, they were singularly unsuccessful in their efforts. Mayor Sanker attributed the failure of these efforts to the politicians' unwillingness to confront GM because the company had many other plants in various congressional districts in Ohio. Sanker further implied that Norwood was a Democratic city in a largely Republican state and, therefore, did not receive much help from Ohio's state and national political leaders.

Undeterred, the city made another strategic change in its efforts to make GM accede to its demands. While discussions with GM were continuing, on August 7, 1987, Norwood filed a suit against GM for $318 million. The city charged GM with breach of contract and fiduciary duty by closing its plant.[16] The city's complaint alleged, among other things, that:

1. GM, during its 64 years of operations, had been storing, burying, or dumping ultrahazardous or toxic materials on its Norwood property, and intended to abandon these at the time of closing its plant.

2. The city had granted GM many concessions on the express and implicit promise that it would retain active manufacturing facilities in the city of Norwood. As a result of the plant closing, the city claimed the following:

   $56,000,000 for the use of tax revenue and commerce
   $ 9,000,000 for the increased cost of fire and police protection
   $ 750,000 for construction of the Forest Avenue underpass
   $ 2,500,000 for the cost of rededicating previously vacated city streets
   $68,250,000

3. GM had created an equitable fiduciary relationship with the city of Norwood because of its largest relative size and longest (64 years) tenure in the city. Closing the plant meant a breach of this equitable fiduciary relationship and caused damages to the city. The city asserted that GM had committed fraud by announcing a latter date of closure and then advancing the date.

At that time, GM was proceeding with the task of finding a suitable developer for the plant site who could come up with a proposal acceptable to the city, the state, and community leaders. At this point, there was some disagreement within the city administration as to the potential uses for this site. The proposed uses ranged from retail-wholesale distribution activities to a high-rise hotel-office complex. On December 12, 1987, GM announced the selection of Miller-Valentine Group, a major developer of office and industrial buildings, to develop the Norwood property. The city officials were pleased with this selection. Miller-Valentine (M-V) was given five months to come up with a development plan.

The Miller-Valentine Plan

The M-V group presented its plan in May 1988. It was developed in close cooperation with the mayor's task force and General Motors. The project was named Highlands Point, after Norwood's title of "Gem of the Highlands," and developed to meet the need for "revitalized, upscale economic development in a highly attractive urban setting." The plan called for a judicious redevelopment of existing properties and construction of several new structures for use by retail, sales/service, industrial purposes, and offices. It projected construction of approximately 1 million square feet of facilities suitable for industrial activity on the 40-acre main plant site, and 90,000 square feet of office development. A 163,000-square feet retail development was planned for the Globe site—a 15-acre parcel adjoining the site. The success of the plan was contingent on the city's cooperation in zoning and street closings, securing a Federal Urban Development grant of $6.2 million, the transfer of property, and other financial considerations for GM.

GM officials, however, were becoming increasingly reluctant to continue working with the city while the lawsuit loomed. Thus, the company advised the city that GM would not make the additional financial commitment required by the V-M group until the city dropped its lawsuit. In a letter to Mayor Sanker, Edmond J. Dilworth, Jr., an attorney and group director of CPC-Public Affairs, stated that while GM had refrained from making any public statements at the city's request, one city official publicly accused GM of "economic terrorism."

> This hysterical and inaccurate characterization unfortunately demonstrates the difficulties we've had in establishing a cooperative relationship with the city. . . . We plan to pursue alternative users for the site, which may involve the sale or lease of the buildings. To do otherwise is a waste of our resources at a time when the corporation is cutting costs to improve our competitive position.

The city officials were stunned by GM's

response. They had hoped that the lawsuit would bring added pressure on GM and force the company to provide greater financial support to the city. In that, they were disappointed. Mayor Sanker observed:

> We had been working very closely with Miller-Valentine. They had great plans and were a responsible development company from Dayton Ohio. The plan was almost ready to be wrapped up and we had a meeting scheduled. They were coming in to give us the final look at the plans. And we met. They showed us the plans, and then the bomb dropped! They said that GM had told them that if we didn't drop our lawsuit GM would not go along with Miller-Valentine.

The city officials refused to withdraw the suit, the GM refused to move further. An impasse had been reached, causing Miller-Valentine to withdraw from the project.

The city suffered another major setback when on September 2, 1988, the Hamilton County Court, Ohio, dismissed the city's suit against GM as totally without merit or basis in fact.[17] In concluding remarks, the Court stated:

> Regrettably, there is no question that the City (and especially its people and the former employees of General Motors in Norwood) has and will continue to suffer from the withdrawal of the Company. A 64-year association that has generally been beneficial to both parties has drawn to a close, but in the broad sense government, all government, exists for the good of the people, not the reverse. The corporate entity of General Motors is one of those "people" for which government exists.[18]

APPENDIX

TABLE 1. Unit Sales of U.S.-Manufactured Cars (in thousands)

YEAR	GM	FORD	CHRYSLER	AMERICAN MOTORS	VOLKSWAGEN	AMERICAN HONDA	NISSAN	TOYOTA	TOTAL
1979	4,887	1,475	909	148	167	—	—	—	8,213
1980	4,117	2,102	660	117	177	—	—	—	6,546
1981	3,797	1,381	730	94	163	—	—	—	6,163
1982	3,516	1,346	692	77	91	—	—	—	5,722
1983	4,054	1,571	842	193	85	50	—	—	6,795
1984	4,588	1,979	987	190	74	134	—	—	7,952
1985	4,608	2,070	1,140	124	78	146	40	—	8,205
1986	4,533	2,067	1,175	73	74	235	53	7	8,215
1987									
1988									

SOURCE: "Auto Sales Data," *Wall Street Journal*, Jan. 8, 1981, p. 17; Jan. 6, 1983, p. 10; Jan. 7, 1985, p. 30; Jan. 8, 1987, p. 13.

TABLE 2. U.S. Sales of Selected Foreign-Made Cars (in thousands) (1979 - 1986)

YEAR	GM	FORD	CHRYSLER (COLT)	TOYOTA	NISSAN/ DATSUN	HONDA	MAZDA	SUBARU	MITSUBISHI	ISUZU	VOLKSWAGEN	VOLVO	MERCEDES BENZ	BMW	AUDI	PORSCHE	FIAT	RENAULT	JAGUAR	SAAB	HYUNDAI
1979	—	—	—	508	472	353	157	128	—	—	99	57	50	38	43	—	37	19	—	—	—
1980	—	—	—	582	517	375	161	143	—	—	125	57	48	35	43	—	59	25	—	—	—
1981	—	—	111	577	465	371	166	152	—	—	82	64	58	42	—	62	32	39	5	15	—
1982	—	—	102	530	470	366	163	150	—	—	67	72	63	52	—	68	14	38	10	18	—
1983	—	—	104	556	522	351	173	157	33	—	77	88	71	57	48	—	—	33	16	26	—
1984	13	—	92	558	485	375	170	158	39	—	104	98	76	69	71	—	—	12	18	33	—
1985	85	9	105	620	535	406	211	174	50	27	141	102	85	85	74	25	—	7	21	38	—
1986	160	14	136	634	494	458	223	179	50	39	143	111	97	96	60	30	—	4	25	48	169
1987																					
1988																					

SOURCE: "Auto Sales Data," *Wall Street Journal*, Jan. 8, 1981, p. 17; Jan. 6, 1983, p. 10; Jan. 7, 1985, p. 30; Jan. 8, 1987, p. 13.

NOTES

1. General Motors Corporation, "Press Release," Detroit, Mich., November 6, 1986, p. 1.

2. Ibid.

3. Ibid.

4. Joseph E. Sanker, Mayor, City of Norwood, "Press Release," January 26, 1987.

5. Ibid.

6. U.S. Congress-Senate, General Motors Plant Closings, Hearings before the Subcommittee on Labor, Committee on Labor and Human Resources, One Hundredth Congress, First Session, January 26, 1987. (Hereafter cited as *Hearings*.)

7. General Motors Corporation, "Press Release," p. 1.

8. S. Prakash Sethi, "Norwood, Ohio, Battles GM over Plant Closing." *Business and Society Review* (1989), in press.

9. *Hearings,* p. 6.

10. Ibid., p. 7.

11. Ibid., pp. 6–25.

12. Ibid., p. 102.

13. Interview with the author. Unless otherwise specified, all direct quotes or paraphrased statements are based on personal interviews or written communications to the author.

14. *Hearings,* p. 93.

15. Battelle Institute, Final Report on Preparation of a Facility Reuse Assessment and Economic Adjustment Strategy for the Norwood, Ohio Area. Columbus, Ohio: Battelle Institute, August 1987.

16. *City of Norwood, Ohio* v. *General Motors Corporation,* Court of Common Pleas, Hamilton County, Ohio, *Complaint and Jury Demand,* Case No. A-8705920, dated August 7, 1987.

17. *City of Norwood, Ohio* v. *General Motors Corporation,* Court of Common Pleas, Hamilton County, Ohio, *Complaint and Jury Demand,* Case No. A-8705920, dated September 2, 1988.

18. Ibid.

GENERAL MOTORS AND THE CITY OF NORWOOD, OHIO

BROWN, SHARON P. "How Often Do Workers Receive Advance Notice of Layoffs?" *Missouri Labor Review,* 110 (June 1987), pp. 13–17.

DENNIS, BARBARA D., ed. "Industrial Relations Research Association Spring Meeting, Boston, Mass. April 20–May 1, 1987." *Labor Law Journal,* 38 (August 1987), pp. 452–538.

DEVENS, RICHARD M., JR. "Displaced Workers: One Year Later." *Missouri Labor Review,* 109 (July 1986), pp. 40–44.

EHRENBERG, RONALD G. "Workers' Rights: Rethinking Protective Labor Legislation." *Research in Labor Economics* (1986), pp. 85–317.

FELDMAN, DIANE. "Hope for Displaced Workers When a Plant Closes." *Management Review* (April 1988), pp. 16–18.

FULMER, WILLIAM E. "A Resurrection Plan for Dying Factories: Saving Jobs through Cooperation." *Business and Society Review* (Summer 1985), pp. 50–55.

GALVIN, MARTIN JAY, and MICHAEL ROBERT LIED. "Severance Pay: A Liability in Waiting?" *Personnel Journal,* 65, (June 1986), p. 126.

HETTINGER, KYLE. B. "NLRA Preemption of State and Local Plant Relocation Laws." *Columbia Law Review,* 86 (March 1986), pp. 407–26.

HORVATH, FRANCIS W. "The Pulse of Economic Change: Displaced Workers of 1981–85." *Missouri Labor Review,* 110 (June 1987), pp. 3–12.

HUDSON, RAY, and DAVID SADLER. "Communities in Crisis: The social and Political Effects of Steel Closures in France, West Germany, and the United Kingdom." *Urban Affairs Quarterly,* 21 (December 1985), pp. 171–86.

KINICKI, ANGELO, et al. "Socially Responsible

Plant Closings.'' *Personnel Administrator,* 32 (June 1987), pp. 116–18.

KOVACH, KENNETH A., and PETER E. MILLSPAUGH. ''Plant Closings: Is the American Industrial Relations System Failing?'' *Business Horizons,* 30 (March/April 1987), pp. 44–49.

LEARY, THOMAS J. ''Deindustrialization, Plant Closing Laws, and the States.'' *State Government,* 58 (Fall 1985), pp. 113–18.

LEE, RAYMOND M., ed. *Redundancy, Layoffs and Plant Closures: Their Character, Causes and Consequences.* London: Croom Helm Ltd., 1987.

O'BRIEN, FRANCIS T. ''Creative Alternatives to Plant Closings: The Rationale for Notice.'' *Labor Law Journal,* 38 (August 1987), pp. 458–60.

PERRUCCI, CAROLYN C., et al. ''Impact of a Plant Closing on Workers and the Community.'' *Research in the Sociology of Work* (1985), pp. 231–60.

''Plant Closings, a Critical Challenge to American Democracy: A Statement by the Research and Policy Committee of the Committee for Economic Development.'' *American Journal of Economics and Sociology,* 46 (July 1987), pp. 257–60.

POPHAM, MITCHELL J. ''Plant Closure Legislation in the United States: Insights from Great Britain.'' *Loyola of Los Angeles International and Comparative Law Journal,* 8, no. 2 (1986), pp. 277–99.

*Ripple Effects of the GM Plant Closings on the Re-*gional Economy. Ohio, Kentucky, Indiana Regional Council of Governments (426 East 4th Street, Cincinnati, Ohio 45202), June 1987.

SCULINCK, MICHAEL W. ''Plant Closings and Mass Layoffs—Toward a Cooperative Approach.'' *Employment Relations Today,* 14 (Summer 1987), pp. 99–106.

SHEEHAN, MICHAEL F. ''Plant Closings and the Community: The Instrumental Value of Public Enterprise in Countering Corporate Flight.'' *American Journal of Economics and Sociology,* 44 (October 1985), pp. 423–33.

STAUDOHAR, PAUL D., and HOLLY E. BROWN. *Deindustrialization and Plant Closure.* Lexington, MA: Lexington Books, 1987.

STROHMEYER, JOHN. ''The Agonizing Ordeal of a One-Company Town.'' *Business and Society Review* (Summer 1985), pp. 45–49.

WILNER, GABRIEL M., and LEE C. DILWORTH. ''Roundtable on Comparative Labor Relations Law: The Law and Measures Affecting Workers in the Context of Voluntary Plant Closings and Workforce Reductions.'' *Georgia Journal of International and Comparative Law,* 16, no. 2 (1986), pp. 219–84.

''Worker Ownership: Buying Control or Selling Out.'' *Multinational Monitor,* 6 (November 30, 1985), pp. 1–6.

ZEITLIN, MORRIS. ''Taking Private Property for Public Use: A Not So Sacred Cow.'' *Political Affairs,* 66 (June 1987), pp. 24–28.

GOODYEAR TIRE & RUBBER COMPANY

Hostile corporate takeovers and public interest

TAKEOVERS IN THE 1980s

The United States has been in the throes of a merger wave in the last few years. Newspapers are replete with stories of billion-dollar companies changing hands overnight, mostly through friendly mergers and management buyouts, but quite often through unfriendly acquisitions or hostile takeovers. For example, in 1986 the number of tender offers stood at 197, up from 97 in 1982. Their value was $65.1 billion, a 17% decrease from 1985 but well above the 1982 figure of $25.8 billion. On the whole, 76.6% of takeovers initiated were successful. The failure rate for uncontested bids averaged 2.45% from 1978 to 1986. The failure rate for contested bids, however, stood at 48.8%; from 1983 to 1985 the average failure rate for contested bids was 68.9%.[1] The number of hostile offers declined from a high of 42% in 1982 to 26% in 1986. On an average, control of the company (rather than a mere stake) was the objective in 73% of tender offers. Of the offers, 89.2% were cash. In 1987, the top 200 deals ranged from a value of $7.6 billion (Standard Oil of Ohio, acquired by British Petroleum) to $152 million. Of all deals, 15% were for over $1 billion, while 35% exceeded $500 million. The median of the top 200 deals was for $365 million.[2] (See Table 1.)

PUBLIC CONTROVERSY

This is not the first merger wave, and it is certainly not likely to be the last one. One only has to go back 25 years to remember the corporate dealings of the 1960s that gave rise to the term *conglomerate*. Mergers and acquisitions are a rather constant feature of the market economy. What makes today's mergers different is that they arise out of the disparity between financial markets and real

TABLE 1. Tender Offers: 1982-1986

	1982	1983	1984	1985	1986
Number of offers	97	74	147	142	197
Number of targets	76	60	125	116	181
Targets' $ value (billions)	25.8	17.3	58.6	78.3	65.1
% Completed offers	73	78	80	76	76
% Hostile offers	42	35	24	30	26
% of offers where control was at stake	73	70	68	72	82
STATUS (%)					
Completed	73	78	80	76	64
Not completed	27	22	20	24	20
Open	0	0	0	0	16
TARGET RESPONSE (%)					
Friendly	43	57	63	62	69
Hostile	42	35	24	30	26
Neutral	15	8	13	8	5
FORM OF OFFER (%)					
Any-or-all	42	64	74	73	85
Partial	37	16	17	23	12
Two-tier	21	20	9	4	3
CONTROL SOUGHT (%)					
Stakehold	19	10	6	9	2
Control	73	70	68	72	82
Lock-up	4	8	14	13	11
Mop-up	4	12	12	6	5
CASH/ EXCHANGE (%)					
Cash	88	91	91	85	91
Exchange/ mixed	12	9	9	15	9
MARKET					
NYSE	37	32	33	41	38
AMEX	16	8	12	8	21
OTC	43	50	49	40	33
Other	4	10	6	11	8

SOURCE: Securities and Exchange Commission, *Monthly Statistics*, vol. 64, no. 2 (1987), pp. 6–9.

product markets. They are undertaken primarily out of financial motives, not production and marketing.

All this frenzy of takeovers has made celebrities of many raiders. The names of T. Boone Pickens, Sir James Goldsmith, Carl Icahn, and Ronald Perlman have become household words. The new entrepreneurs involved in these activities have become multimillionaires many times over. They have also created a new class of millionaires among those who provide support services for these ventures, namely, the arbitrageurs, investment bankers, lawyers, merger specialists, brokers, and others. Many a fortune

has been made almost overnight—although not all of them have been legal or ethical. This is not surprising. In the frenzy of highly pressured activity involving millions of dollars and stock transactions, it is understandable that some shady dealings and unsavory characters will slip through. What is surprising, however, is the evidence that unethical and illegal practices were engaged in by some of the most venerable and blue-chip organizations in the financial community. Witness the prosecution of Ivan Boesky and others on charges of insider trading. Among the Wall Street brokerage, investment, and law firms involved are Kidder Peabody, Drexel Burnham Lambert, as well as numerous lesser luminaries.

The latest merger movement, however, is significant in another important perspective in that both sides, i.e., the acquirers and the acquirees, claim to have similar objectives: to improve America's competitiveness, make companies more efficient and, managers more responsive, and increase shareholder values. On the face of it, there cannot be such a thing as a hostile takeover from the viewpoint of the shareholders. The acquirer must offer a premium over the prevailing market price in order to induce the current shareholders to sell their stock. And these premiums, especially where there has been a bidding war, can be quite handsome.

The issue, therefore, is not merely that of a change in ownership from one group of individuals to another. Instead, it is intertwined with three other equally important issues: first, the role of the private corporations as the primary vehicles of economic activity in free market-oriented societies; second, the relative roles played by different groups in the survival and growth of the corporation and their rights in having a say in the running of the corporation; and third, the changing nature of stockholders and stockholdings and how these might affect the welfare of the corporation and the interests of other stakeholders.

The increased globalization of competition, movement of capital, and almost instant transfer of ownership have created a wide gap between the legal theory of the corporation and its reality and have challenged the myth of shareholder control. In the process, they have raised a number of questions pertaining to the organization of economic activity, the rights and obligations of various stakeholders, and the maintenance of a competitive economy for the benefit of society at large. Nowhere have these issues come to the fore so sharply as in the case of hostile mergers. They place in sharp relief the various perspectives articulated by highly sophisticated advocates. The debate has only begun and is likely to intensify greatly in the coming months and years until such time that a new social consensus emerges concerning the manner in which large corporations should be organized, managed, and held accountable for their activities.

A BRIEF SUMMARY
OF THE GOODYEAR TAKEOVER

The following case study of Goodyear Tire & Rubber Company is typical of many such cases that have come to light. It also provides good insights into the arguments that are made both for and against such hostile takeover attempts.

In November 1986, Sir James Goldsmith proposed to pay $49 a share for the 88.5% of Goodyear that he did not already own. The deal came to about $4.7 billion. Sir James is the chairman of General Oriental Investments Limited—a company based in England. He is among the handful of well-known corporate raiders whose very name strikes terror in the hearts of CEOs of target companies and delights the imagination of those groupies, called arbitrageurs, who follow suit in the hope of making a killing in the stock market by buying and selling the stock of the target company.

Goodyear countered the Goldsmith threat by unveiling an ambitious restructuring plan. The plan included repurchasing as many as 20 million of the company's common shares outstanding and also selling off three major units. The chairman of Goodyear, Robert Mercer, attacked Sir James as a greedy predator who was indifferent to the welfare of the company and its many stakeholders. In addition to using all the usual legal defense strategies against hostile offers, Goodyear also launched a public relations and political pressure offensive by enlisting the support of political leaders and labor unions, among others. When all the dust was settled, Goodyear was still independent. But it had to pay a very heavy price. Sir James was "persuaded" to sell his stock to Goodyear in the process and made a profit of nearly $100 million in greenmail. It is not known how much profit the Goldsmith group actually made. Their original offer was to acquire the 88.5% of the company that they did not already control for $49 a share, or $4.7 billion. According to Mercer, they did acquire 12.5 million shares (while arbitrageurs acquired some 22 million).[3] That would amount to an actual outlay of some $613 million. For that stock, plus what the group already owned, they received about $56 a share. For every $49 share purchased they made $7, over a period of about four months.

The saga of Goodyear escaping the clutches of Sir James Goldsmith enraged many observers because of the alleged greenmail payments. This, along with certain other hostile takeovers, provided the catalyst that led to serious legislative discussion about the need for changes in federal and state laws governing stock transactions and takeover activity. However, to date, no significant legislation has been enacted at the federal level.

ISSUES FOR ANALYSIS

The Goodyear case raises a variety of issues pertaining to corporate governance, stockholder interests, management accountability, and the interests of other important stakeholders, notably the employees and the communities where these corporations are located. At the macro level, they are concerned with the long-term economic viability of these institutions because, more often than not, they take on a heavy debt burden either to fight such takeovers or to pay for them. An additional concern is for the impact of these mergers on the strength and competitiveness of the U.S. economy. Among some of the specific issues are:

1. What are some of the benefits and costs of maintaining an environment of relatively unrestrained merger and acquisition activity in the United States?

2. How effective are the current rules and regulations in maintaining an open environment for investments leading to mergers and acquisitions on a fair and equitable basis so as to minimize illegal activity, e.g., insider trading? If the current regulations are not effective or are insufficient, what additional regulation might be imposed?

3. Should we make a distinction between friendly and unfriendly mergers? Which groups stand to gain the most from friendly mergers, and should protecting these interests have a higher priority?

4. How do the current tax laws and accounting procedures help or hurt friendly and unfriendly mergers? What changes, if any, are needed in these laws and procedures?

5. What are the differences between the financial market value of a transaction and the real product market value, and how do they influence different types of merger activity?

6. How do various groups benefit or suffer from mergers and takeovers, e.g., stockholders, managers (upper, middle, and lower level), workers, lenders, unities where plants and corporate headquarters are located?

7. What are the rights of local communities and workers who are affected by a takeover?

8. What are the rights of shareholders of the target company? Are there significant differences between classes of shareholders? Are

shareholders really dedicated to the well-being of a company? Alternately, why should shareholders be concerned with the welfare of a company when selling it would yield them better returns and thereby maximize their self-interest?

9. How should one evaluate the role of corporate raiders? What service do they provide to current stockholders, other corporate constituencies, and society at large? Are their rewards justified by their services?

10. What are some of the ethical and moral arguments that should be made both for and against friendly and unfriendly mergers?

11. What are some of the recent measures taken by various state legislatures and U.S. courts affecting mergers and takeovers? What do you feel is their impact on the economic activity and rights of various stakeholders affected by mergers and takeovers?

DETAILS OF THE GOODYEAR TAKEOVER

How Goodyear Became Vulnerable

In October 1986, after a month of speculation that it could be a takeover candidate, the Goodyear Tire and Rubber Company (the world's largest tire maker) said it was considering a restructuring.[4] The company retained the investment banking firms of Goldman Sachs & Co. and Drexel Burnham Lambert to assist it with a study aimed at developing a program for maximizing shareholder values over the short-run. This would protect Goodyear's stockholders in the event that a suitor emerged. By October 27, 1986, Goodyear's stock closed at $44.125 a share, up from $32.75 a month earlier.

In the years preceding 1986, Goodyear's chairman and chief executive officer, Robert E. Mercer, and his management group had been attempting to diversify Goodyear through energy and aerospace. Tires accounted for 80% of operating profit. Analysts had speculated that if Goodyear were restructured, shareholders might receive as much as $45 to $52 a share. Goodyear's approximately $109.3 million shares outstanding had a book value of about $34 a share. Most analysts also thought that a restructuring would involve the sale of the company's oil and gas reserves. Goodyear had adopted a portfolio structure-type strategy. In examining what attracted the attack, Mercer found that because the market value of the company's assets exceeded the stock price for the corporation as a whole, the company was left very vulnerable. This was true of energy and aerospace holdings. Another area of Goodyear's vulnerability was its good cash flow, which could be converted by cutting back in areas of advertising, training, and research and development.[5]

The Raid

It soon became apparent that Sir James Goldsmith, an Anglo-French financier and corporate raider, was interested in taking over Goodyear. He owned more than 15% of Goodyear's shares, a stake valued at $781 million based on a price of $47.75 a share. Sir Goldsmith was understood to have amassed the necessary financial resources required to launch a bid for the company if he chose to. Merrill Lynch & Co., Sir Goldsmith's financial adviser, was also rumored to become a principal in any bid for Goodyear.

Although no tender offer had been made, Goodyear's chairman, Robert Mercer, said in a letter to employees that Goodyear was a takeover target. Mercer also told employees that Goodyear was taking every step to avoid a takeover. In a filing with the Securities and Exchange Commission (SEC), Sir Goldsmith said that he would not immediately make a tender offer because the stock price was too high due to market overreaction. In addition, in a letter to Mercer, Sir Goldsmith wrote that he was not interested in receiving any greenmail. A further twist was that Merrill Lynch could collect fees of

$150 to $200 million if Sir Goldsmith succeeded in his quest for Goodyear. In return, Merrill Lynch agreed to provide a $1.9 billion in financing if Sir Goldsmith decided to launch a tender offer for Goodyear. The potential fees and financing commitment were disclosed in SEC filings by Sir Goldsmith. Finally, in November 1986, Sir Goldsmith proposed to buy Goodyear for $49 a share. The fate of Goodyear thus depended on the company's ability to boost its stock price above the $49 offered by Sir Goldsmith.

Goodyear's Defense

In his 1986 testimony before the Senate, Mercer insisted that "Goodyear resisted a takeover in the best interest of the Company" and its "real or long term shareholders, our employees, and plant town communities, suppliers, creditors and, of course, our customers, without whom there would be no business in which to invest."[6]

Stock Repurchase and Restructuring. To do this, Goodyear's restructuring plan called for repurchasing as much as $20 million of its shares outstanding and selling off units of the company. Sir Goldsmith then said that he would not launch a hostile tender offer until the company had a chance to pursue its restructuring. If the stock price got above the offering price, then no deal would occur. Goodyear still refused to accept any offer because it felt that it could do a better job of enhancing shareholder value with its restructuring.

Rallying Shareholders. At the same time, Goodyear's management and its unionized employees tried to rally public opinion and state and federal government leaders to prevent a takeover by Sir Goldsmith. Mercer advised union officials to make elected officials aware of the consequences of foreign takeovers of U.S. companies. In addition, Goodyear announced that as part of its restructuring program, it would offer early retirement to some of the 4,900 salaried employees at its headquarters. Due to the pressure from Goodyear and its employees, congressional hearings were quickly called to investigate this matter. Mercer indicated that he was pessimistic about fighting any acquisition bid by Sir Goldsmith. The question then became whether Sir Goldsmith would be willing to go ahead with a hostile takeover in the face of widespread opposition within Goodyear and political pressure from the communities in which Goodyear had plants.[7]

Mercer warned employees that a rigorous cost-cutting effort would result in layoffs, early retirements, and other curtailments. Goodyear announced that it would close two plants. These closings would result in terminations of about 3,200 hourly and salaried employees. In addition, capital expenditures for the continuing business of tires and related products had to be slashed by $275 million. All of these steps were necessary to provide cash for the debt service and early retirement costs incurred in the takeover battle.

In addition to commenting on the long-term health of the company, Mercer made a strong distinction between Goodyear's "true," "real," and "classic," shareholders who had an interest in the health of the company, and the "elite band of raiders, speculators and financiers [who are] perverting the free market system and dynamic capitalism into a quick money game with America's competitive position, economy and jobs as the chips."[8] It is not clear why Mercer would place a higher degree of trust in "true," "real," and "classic" shareholders. The so-called "elite bond of raiders" were able to become shareholders precisely because the other loyal shareholders were willing to sell their loyalty and long-term interest in the company for immediate profits, reflected in the higher prices the raiders offered for their stock. Mercer considered the shareholders who sold 12.5 million shares to the takeover groups without knowing who they were or what they were up to, as well as those who

sold another 22 million shares to the arbitrageurs, as duped, for they did not have the skills to read the signs and skills of an impending move on the company. It is not clear that these sellers were indeed simpletons who were duped by the raiders. Studies show that raiders acquire their early positions in targeted company stock generally through the purchase of large blocks of stocks from institutional investors, i.e., insurance companies, pension funds, and mutual funds. These stockholders are quite sophisticated and make decisions with full knowledge and understanding of the consequences of their actions.

Mercer contended that raiders were not true investors.[9] He also saw Goodyear's other constituencies—mainly labor and local communities—as ill-served by the raiders. He felt that the raiders' focus on shareholder rights failed to address the legitimate concerns of these other groups, who had a definite stake in the business and whose destinies were interwoven in the corporation with those of the shareholders.

Aftermath

Sir Goldsmith's track record at Crown Zellerbach led people to believe that restructuring would be harsh. Three issues came together: a socially responsible layoff policy, plant closing and relocation policies, and management prerogatives.

In the end, the local community-labor-management coalition prevailed, but the amount of greenmail paid was staggering and made Sir Goldsmith much richer than he would have been otherwise.[10] It also weakened Goodyear considerably. Ironically, Goodyear ended up doing many of the things Sir Goldsmith threatened to do. Management would add that the long-term productive capacity and competitive ability of the United States economy is held hostage to the "efficient financial trading principle" as opposed to efficient production. Thus, there are two sets of consequences which greenmail is allegedly adopted to avoid: (1) whatever adversity might befall the local corporation, community, and labor; and (2) a weakening of the competitive viability of the economy as a whole. For the most part, stockholders who are not included in the corporation-community-labor group resent the practice of greenmail. They contend that soaring debt, falling investment, and curtailed research do not augur well for profits.

In the case of Goodyear, debt rose from $2.6 billion to $5.3 billion. Planned investment fell from $300 million to $270 million, and research from $1.6 billion to $1 billion. Over $2 billion in assets were to be sold off. Sir James Goldsmith walked away with $93 million profit. Stockholders have a hard time seeing themselves as winners. Their only real choice is to stick with management or sell their stock. Management blames Goldsmith's greed for their plight and claims to have done the best it could for shareholders and communities.

Many shareholders question the quality of Goodyear management in the first place. They also object that, in the event that greenmail seems necessary, they should at least have a say in such an important decision. They are demanding shareholder approval for greenmail, poison pills, and parachutes.[11] Furthermore, they object to takeover groups being offered premium prices not available to ordinary shareholders.[12] Shareholders are prevented from cashing in on the premium price takeover groups receive for their shares. They can either stick with the restructured company or sell their stock at the current market price. This apparent disparity between stockholder interests and those of management, labor, and the community have raised a larger issue—corporate governance.

Due to all the political pressure and opposition, as well as opposition from Goodyear, Sir Goldsmith was forced to stop his bid for the company. However, Goodyear had to buy out Sir Goldsmith's stake for $618 million ($49.50 a share) and also make a tender offer for an additional 40 million of its shares at $50 a share, or $2 billion. The two purchases would total about 48% of the company's shares outstanding. They also planned to sell off their oil and gas units, their aerospace unit, and their wheel manufacturing unit. This plan left the company heavily burdened with debt. Sir Goldsmith felt that he had no alternative but to be bought out once he decided against a hostile takeover. He did not feel that this was equivalent to receiving greenmail. Goodyear had to sell 25% of its assets to settle this. After the restructuring, Goodyear's annual sales dropped to just over $8 billion, from $9.6 billion in 1985.

The takeover attempt accelerated restructuring at Goodyear: a 12% downsizing, 4,000 layoffs, R & D and capital expenditures focused on projects with a short-term payoff, and a $4 billion debt which leveraged the company to 80% of debt to total capitalization. Mercer directly countered the argument that takeovers are good for America:

> In 1977, at a time when the tire business was at a low ebb, we invested $260 million in a new state-of-the-art radial auto tire plant in Lawton, to assure our future competitive position in world markets. With the same objective, in the 1970's and early 1980's, we modernized tire plants in Alabama and Tennessee and built up a highly competitive wire plant in North Carolina to provide top quality steel wire for use in our tire products. Then in 1983 we converted a Texas bias-tire plant to radial tires with costs that will meet Korean competition head-on when the startup phase is completed later this month. Because of those investments, Goodyear's U.S. plants can hold their own today in global competition. In many foreign countries, for instance, it takes 25 to 50 man-minutes to manufacture a 13-inch tire. Our modern U.S. plants do it in less than 10. Our advanced equipment and technology make it possible to support higher American wages and benefits—more than $20 an hour versus as low as $1.60 in Korea. Now had we been the target

of a takeover attempt in the mid 1970's, had we been forced then into the short term planning . . . none of these investments would have been made.[13]

THE BATTLE RAGES

Why Takeovers are Good

Proponents rationalize takeovers in terms of increasing economic efficiency. They focus on management errors in strategic planning.

Financially Efficient Asset Use. The classic exponent of takeover benefits and the one to whom everyone defers has been Michael C. Jensen.[14] Jensen summarizes the scientific evidence of research as follows:

1. Takeovers of companies by outsiders do not harm shareholders of the target company; in fact, they gain substantial wealth.

2. Corporate takeovers do not waste resources; rather, they use assets productively.

3. Takeovers do not siphon commercial credit from its uses in funding new plants and equipment.

4. Takeovers do not create gains for shareholders through creation of monopoly power.

5. Prohibition of plant closings, layoffs, and dismissals following takeovers would reduce market efficiency and lower aggregate living standards.

6. Although managers are self-interested, the environment in which they operate gives them relatively little leeway to feather their nests at shareholders' expense. Corporate control-related actions of managers do not generally harm shareholders, but actions that eliminate actual or potential takeover bids are most suspect as exceptions to this rule.

7. Golden parachutes for top-level executives are, in principle, in the interests of shareholders. Although the practice can be abused, the evidence indicates that shareholders gain when golden parachutes are adopted.

Jensen concludes that, in general, the activities of takeover specialists benefit shareholders.

To understand this rationale, it is important to review the main characteristics of corporate strategic planning in the preceding decades. The 1960s and 1970s marked a time of tremendous corporate structural change. Corporations grew through diversification and became conglomerates. In a sense, it was also a takeover period; but, in general, it was the large, established companies that were acquiring the smaller specialty companies. Many companies expanded into unrelated businesses. The underlying logic for such conglomerate diversification was based on a portfolio model of analysis. The corporation was interested in maintaining steady earnings. Diversification provided it with a hedge against losses when one sector or industry had a downturn. But the reverse was also true. Higher profit levels were sometimes foregone in favor of maintaining a steady and safe level of growth and income. To oversimplify, if a conglomerate had 10 divisions, it was most likely at any given time that some would do well while others lagged behind or even incurred a loss. As long as a majority did well, steady profits could be assured. Some might even prove to be cash cows. Only rarely would all do well or fail at the same time. Contemporary takeover entrepreneurs focus on what they call management's strategic mistakes in acquiring unrelated businesses which ended up as underperforming and/or undervalued. Takeover proponents claim that they can improve overall performance by getting rid of such assets and concentrating the business in a few well-chosen lines that promise high efficiency and return.

Interestingly enough, an SEC study which was published in 1988 contended that present takeovers are simply attempts to undo acquisitions that have failed. The conglomerate movement of the 1960s was essentially flawed.[15]

In appearing before Congress in 1985 (in connection with his takeover of Crown

Zellerbach), Sir James Goldsmith decried both socialism and state corporatism and praised the free market.[16] Modern business, he asserted, has a pyramid structure. At the base is big business and big unions; at the peak is government. Sir Goldsmith sees those parties as both needing and taking care of each other, to the exclusion of small- and medium-sized business. He credits the latter with providing 35 million new jobs in the U.S. between 1965 and 1985 and praises their innovativeness and entrepreneurial spirit.

Sir Goldsmith says the debate about takeovers is really about the "new entrepreneurial revolutions and freedoms that have engineered it."[17] Speaking of his experience of companies in France, he added, "the best thing that could happen . . . would be that they should be taken over and that their constituent parts be liberated from the dead hands of established bureaucrats." Sir Goldsmith adds, "Free market forces either force management to get to work or alternately allow new managers and new owners to take over. Artificial devices which inhibit such changes do no more than protect the unsatisfactory. They lead to ossification and decline."[18]

A second point that almost all takeover proponents focus on is organizational inefficiency. They claim that corporate staffs are becoming bloated and inefficient bureaucracies. The term *corpocracy* has been coined to describe the bureaucratization of private enterprise. In their study of corpocracy, Mark Green and John Berry estimate that corporate organizational inefficiency costs $862 billion a year, six times the amount of government waste estimated by the Grace Commission.[19] However tendentious such estimates may be, the traits of corpocracy are more telling: the prevalence of insensitiveness to employees, the encouragement of office politics over productivity, the fostering of secrecy over communication, the diffusion of responsibility through endless meetings, the production of paperwork paralysis,

the neglect of potential markets, the encouragement of short-term thinking, the isolation of management from workers, the discouragement of innovation, and the avoidance of employees who rock the boat. If any of the foregoing is accurate, it is clear that capitalism has moved a long way from the ideals of Adam Smith. In such a situation, overhead costs soar while innovativeness and the ability to move quickly suffer. It is not surprising, then, that proponents of takeovers propose large-scale reorganization with reductions in management and staff along with the selling of unproductive assets.

A third area on which takeover advocates focus is the large amount of cash which is devoted to senior management compensation and perquisites. This has opened managers to the charge that they are primarily out for themselves at the shareholders' expense. Raiders such as T. Boone Pickens and Carl Icahn have remarked many times that top management no longer thinks like shareholders.[20] Their interests and the shareholders' interests no longer coincide.

In his testimony before the House, Pickens put it this way:[21]

> The growing gap between ownership and control has distorted the traditional economic incentives that drive our free enterprise system, and many of our largest businesses have languished as a result. As our largest corporations matured, managers experienced more and more difficulty finding sound investment opportunities within their core businesses. But, rather than distributing returns to the shareholders who had put their money at risk, they frantically diversified into unfamiliar businesses. Slow growth combined with strong cash flows tempted managers to use discretionary income to buy whatever was for sale. The urge to conglomerate overwhelmed any inclination to return cash to owners because managers' careers and financial futures depended more on size than results. Mediocre results pacified shareholders, while an ever-increasing empire jus-

tified higher salaries, more perks, and bigger bonuses. Consequently, performance took a backseat to size.

Long-Term Efficiency of the U.S. Economy. Another issue on which takeover proponents focus is international competitive advantage. Here, they see American industry heading downhill. The former undersecretary of the Treasury and present budget director, Richard Darman, as well as former commerce secretary Malcolm Baldridge, joined the criticism of much of contemporary management for failing to apply and follow through on technology that they invented.[22] The nature of competitive advantage has changed dramatically in the past years due to deregulation of many domestic industries as well as sharply increased foreign competition. This increased competition is due to a number of factors: new cost-cutting technologies, lower labor costs, and intensity of sales efforts. Foreign competitors are not free of allegations of dumping.[23] In most industries, however, it would be difficult to maintain that their competitive advantage was due solely to dumping. To restore the competitive edge of U.S. industry, takeover proponents propose restructuring of production operations. Most often, this means a leaner workforce. Takeover proponents drive a hard economic logic of cost controls and input-output ratios. In addition, they call for tighter financial management and more efficacious sales efforts.

A related reason for takeovers is to expand capacity for production, distribution, and sales. At present it is frequently cheaper to buy than to build. This seems to be the logic operative in Chrysler's $3.5 billion takeover of American Motors, as well as in Emery Air Freight's bid for Purolator.[24] The takeover in this context is based on synergies between related businesses and has good historical prospects for success. A final reason advanced for takeovers is that comparatively low interest rates make takeovers as well as leveraged buyouts more attractive than ever. When low interest is coupled with undervalued assets, the real costs for acquirers are greatly diminished.

G. Chris Anderson made the case for Drexel Burnham Lambert in Senate hearings:[25]

Further legislation of acquisition activity is unwarranted [because]

- Merger and acquisition activity results in a shifting of assets to more productive uses, more efficient forms of distribution and technology transfers which promote new research and development.

- Acquisitions expedite restructuring of unsuccessful conglomerates into more efficient and more highly valued entities.

- Acquisition activity serves to spur management to strengthen company performance and may result in the replacement of ineffective management. The chief executive officers of Walt Disney Productions, Martin Marietta Corp., and Phillips Petroleum Company have all declared that acquisition attempts on their companies have forced management to become more disciplined.

- Tender offers result in substantial gains to shareholders of target firms and benefit shareholders of bidding companies.

- Many defensive strategies available to target management increase shareholder wealth by evoking higher competing offers or deterring inadequate bids.

- Acquisitions result in transfers of wealth to shareholders who normally reinvest the proceeds in the capital markets or purchase goods and services, thereby in either case stimulating economic growth and making money available for investment.

- Acquisition activity has not reduced corporate expenditures for long-term investment.

- Further regulations of acquisitions is unnecessary because the Williams Act strikes an equitable balance between targets and acquirers that allows the market to operate efficiently. The overall balance between acquirer and target has not been upset in recent acquisition activity. Isolated cases of abuse should not be addressed with broad legislative measures, but rather redressed on a case-by-case basis in the courts.

Anderson concluded:

> In sum, Drexel Burnham believes that mergers and acquisitions are a valid business strategy which spurs economic growth and productivity. Acquisitions are motivated by legitimate business objectives such as achieving a better allocation of resources, substituting new management teams, and maximizing other business and economic opportunities. These advantages result, even if the objective of the challenge of the control is to divest part of the target's assets. These transactions almost invariably result in such assets being transferred to stronger or more aggressive managements which more efficiently and effectively deploy the divested assets.

Moral Justification: Self-Interest and the Common Good.   The economic reasons for takeovers have a corollary in moral reasoning, which is rooted in free market ideology. Defenders of takeovers propose three dominant values: individual liberty, fiduciary duties to shareholders, and social utility.

Viewing takeovers in general proponents argue that they can have good consequences for society. The fundamental rationale of this argument reiterates the basic free market premise that individual liberty in economic decision making both protects the rights of the individual to seek his or her self-interest and is in the long-term interest of society. With respect to contemporary takeover activity, proponents argue that the long-term results are in the best interests of society, for the U.S. economy will be healthier. Shareholders are also said to be better served by such a free market. During a takeover, they may divest at a premium. If they

hold their stocks, they will benefit in the long run by the improved economic performance of the company. Those taking over the company, it is argued, are themselves shareholders; their interests coincide with the other shareholders. In the end, it is asserted that a number of operating, financial, and tax benefits for both individuals and society may follow from a corporate takeover. T. Boone Pickens put it this way:[26]

> In the wake of the recent insider trading scandal, the business establishment has raised a hue and cry that unsolicited corporate takeovers must be stopped. Business Roundtable has seized the opportunity to trot out its tired anti-shareholder, pro-management agenda one more time, and Congress has been inundated with pleas for reform.
>
> When the good old boys of corporate America appear before you, look closely at where their interests lie. When they say they are long-termers, ask how much stock they own in the companies they manage. Ask them what percentage of their total personal assets that ownership represents. In other words, ask them if they have made a long-term commitment to their stockholders and employees.

Those in favor of takeovers argue a hard (and theoretical) market logic, primarily in terms of efficiency, competition, and shareholder profits. Their argument is both macro and long term. It is macro because their focus is on the competitiveness of U.S. industry in an increasingly tough international environment. They argue that companies which are the object of takeovers are sick and mismanaged. In the long run, they are headed down the slope to extinction unless drastic measures are taken. The raiders come in, perform surgery, and help bring U.S. industry back to health. It is important to note that the promise is not to bring this or that company back to health exactly as it was. There is a process of restructuring involved. New management may dismantle parts or all of a company while simultaneously building up others. Assets do not vanish, but they take different forms and are managed in new ways.

Antitakeover Forces

At the same time, there is no doubt that takeovers can be like corporate earthquakes that frequently leave formerly standing companies as a pile of rubble. Only very strong institutions withstand the initial tremor and subsequent readjustments.

Taking Care of Shareholders. Often, takeovers are justified as being in the shareholders' interests. Andrew Sigler, who is the head of the Business Roundtable, a business lobby, countered with the following argument:[27]

> Now, I think we have to take a quick look at these shareholders we are all talking about protecting. The shareholders today are principally firms, professionally. Some two-thirds of the equity in the New York Stock Exchange is owned by these funds, and in a company like Champion, over three-quarters of our stock falls into that category.
>
> These are very sophisticated people. They value a company's stock based on its current earnings or its current prospects. They weigh that investment opportunity against their other alternatives. There are no speculative run-ups anymore. The end result of this kind of ownership has been reducing the P/E ratios of companies substantially in the last 4 or 5 years. Of course, that has been greatly pushed along by the high interest rates that we have had.
>
> I think the other part of the shareholders we have to look at is our ownership. We have an ownership today of the economic system of this country that feels that its principal responsibility is to the people whose money it manages, with very little feeling about what its real ownership is. In fact, if I heard him right, I think I heard Mr. LeBaron say that it might be something to think of in terms of

selling that vote—renting, I think was the expression.

The rhetoric of the raider is that he is doing everything for the shareholder. What we are really saying is we are willing to liquidate important parts of the strength of the economy to give more money to our pension funds. The real irony of that is that the assurance that an individual will indeed receive his pension is dependent upon the long-term viability of that institution that he works for. Annual up and down performance of the pension fund has very little to do with guaranteeing the success of that.

Financial and ''Real'' Market Disparities. Opponents of takeovers also underscore the disparity which exists between financial markets and "real product" markets. They assert that the intentions of the takeover artists are to reap short-term trading gains, while committing nothing to R & D and the long-term productive performance of a company or the economy. That is, the raiders skim off profits in the financial markets while creating no real wealth in the product markets. Andrew Sigler commented:[28]

> Behind the smokescreen of doing good for shareholders and punishing stupid, entrenched management, and using the magic cloak of the word "free market," a small group is systematically extracting the equity from corporations and replacing it with debt, and incidentally accumulating major wealth.
>
> Now, anyone who believes that there is no difference between debt and equity in the guts of the economic system just doesn't understand how the system really works. The basic unit we use in this system, basic business unit, is the corporation. We generally measure the strength of that corporation, its ability to perform its normal function to grow, et cetera, by the amount of this equity.
>
> Now, we think it is fiscal insanity to let the country go on with this type of phenomenon because the country loses. When the equity moves out, it does not go into equity of an-

other company, so the economic system in effect is losing the fuel that makes it run.

Those arguing against takeovers focus on what they call the selfish intentions of takeover groups. Do they really mean to increase the economic performance of the assets, or are they opportunists vying for handsome greenmail payoffs? Major criticism ensues when people suspect that those who take over the company do not intend to preserve and further it. Rather, they plan either to be paid greenmail or to strip the company of its valuable (undervalued) assets, pay off the bonds, pocket the difference, and get out. Those who believe in the likelihood of such a scenario not surprisingly see the takeover people as the first cousins of the robber barons. It is only natural that an antitakeover coalition has emerged. Moral objections are based on both the harmful consequences of takeover actions as well as on the greedy and selfish motivation on those launching a takeover attempt. Opposition is composed of management, labor, and communities. They are the ones in line to bear the adverse consequences of restructuring.

Ends and Means

In his testimony regarding takeovers, Felix Rohatyn, a leading Wall Street figure, mentioned abuses brought about by what was happening and suggested the following:[29]

The issues involved here are three-fold:

a. The integrity of our securities markets; b. The safety of our financial institutions; c. The constructive use of capital as an engine for growth.

These are all jeopardized by what is happening today. . . . At the same time, if takeover excesses are curbed, abusive defensive tactics must also be curbed. Not all takeovers are bad, not all managements are good, not all directors represent the shareholders' best

interests. Takeovers do not have to be friendly; they have to be fair and soundly financed. The following should be considered:

1. Outlaw all forms of "greenmail";
2. Re-establish the principle of "one share—one vote";
3. Eliminate any form of "poison pill";
4. Require shareholder vote on any bonafide offer for 100% of a company, or on major restructuring proposals;
5. Eliminate "crown jewel options," "shark repellents," and all other defensive stratagems designed to discourage a bona-fide bidder;
6. Override state takeover statutes which provide management and directors with almost unlimited license to turn away bona-fide bidders and entrench themselves.

Management has developed a number of tools to discourage takeovers. In doing so, they have spawned a new business vocabulary: poison pills, greenmail, white knights, and golden as well as tin parachutes. These tools have one thing in common: to make a takeover so costly that no one would attempt it. It is important to examine what management is doing and whose interests it serves. The same moral scrutiny regarding the intentions of management as well as the consequences of its actions applies.

Takeover groups are criticized for junk bond financing. Junk bonds are highly risky in comparison with other bond offerings. They are not for novice investors. They remain, however, a legitimate financial tool. More important, junk bonds are not the driving force behind takeovers.[30] In 1985, junk bonds financed $6.23 billion of all mergers and acquisitions. This is less than 5% of the $140 billion that figured in all mergers and acquisitions and less than 10% of the $78 billion represented by takeover tender offers. In all, 38.2% of junk bonds in 1985 went for mergers and acquisitions. Even though this trend seems to be increasing somewhat, the mode of financing is not the key issue.

Poison pills have been increasingly used by management to fend off aggressive takeovers. The definition of a poison pill is by no means uniform. In general, it involves the issuance of a pro rata dividend to common stockholders. This dividend comprises stock or rights to acquire stock of (1) the issuer ("flip-in" provisions) or (2) the acquiring persons ("flip-over" provisions) involved in a business combination with the issuer. In addition, poison pills may involve issuing stock with super voting rights ("back-end provisions"), which involve the right of shareholders to tender stock to the issuer for a specified securities package, and convertible preferred stock provisions.[31]

The most important provision is that acquiring persons may be excluded from the exercise of such rights, even though they are stockholders. Poison pill rights cannot be exercises by stockholders unless triggered by specified events, such as a merger, the commencement of the tender offer, or the acquisition of a specific percentage of the issuer's stock. Unless triggered, they are redeemable by the issuer at a nominal price. The intent of such pills is clear: Management hopes to set up insurmountable barriers to hostile outside bidders who would purchase a company's shares. Stockholders are usually not consulted. In imposing prohibitive costs on outside bidders, poison pills effectively give management exclusive authority to decide if an acquisition can proceed. Defenders of the pill say that it buys time. Without it, the object of a takeover has only 20 business days following the beginning of a hostile tender offer in which to respond. Management argues that the additional time to negotiate is beneficial to shareholders in the long run.

The Supreme Court of the state of Delaware upheld the legality of the pill in a 1985 decision, *Moran* v. *Household International*.[32]

In the past few years, over 300 major American corporations have adopted the pill; not all have escaped takeover. Opponents of the pill include both corporate raiders and large institutional investors, who argue that the pill actually works against shareholders. Rarely are they allowed to purchase more shares at a discount. Furthermore, the lethal effects of the pill prevent the stock from rising as it normally would in the course of a takeover and, thus, deprive shareholders of profits they could make by playing the market.

Frequently, in defending itself from a hostile bidder, management will turn to a "white knight."[33] A white knight is a friendly investor who will put away a large block of stock (at a discount price) but who will not pose a takeover threat. In its efforts to avoid being taken over by The Limited, Carter Hawley Hale Stores Inc. turned to General Cinema, which invested $300 million in its stock in 1984. Eventually, in the face of a persistent bid by The Limited, Carter Hawley Hale had to come to an agreement with General Cinema. A white knight strategy does not necessarily save a company from restructuring, but it keeps it out of hostile hands, at least initially. (White knights do not always prove to be benevolent.)

Another device that management uses are golden parachutes (for managers) and tin parachutes (for labor).[34] A parachute affords the relevant party a hefty package of benefits in case it is dismissed. Both labor and management find these parachutes very attractive, for they protect their own interests. Prospective raiders find them unattractive, for they impose increased costs. In terms of the bottom line, it is the stockholder who pays the costs. By far, the most controversial strategy employed by management is the payment of greenmail. When Walt Disney productions bought back Saul Steinberg's shares in 1984, it effectively paid him a $60 million premium not to take over the company. Similarly, Gencorp was (in mid-1987) offering $130 per share for 54% of its stock against an investor group offering $100; the investor group could net nearly $100 mil-lion.[35] In a 1964 ruling, the Supreme Court of Delaware upheld the practice of buying back shares at a premium as long as the directors could show a "legitimate business reason" for doing so.[36] There is a great deal of contro-versy over what constitutes legitimate busi-ness reasons. Increasingly, shareholders are demanding that they get a chance to vote on the matter.

In addition to the aforementioned mea-sures, a number of companies prefer restric-tions tied to the length of time a stock is held.[37] Furthermore, they want types of common stock classified according to voting power. In a related move, some manage-ment groups are putting together their own takeovers by taking the company private in a leveraged buyout.[38] In either case, manage-ment severely restricts those to whom it is accountable.

Finally, a number of management groups are beginning to take a proactive stance to takeovers. They are scrutinizing their company profiles for items a raider would find attractive—large cash surpluses, undervalued assets to strip, overfunded pension funds, bloated staff—and taking measures to correct them before anyone ini-tiates a takeover offer.

CLAMOR FOR ACTION

Business Action

The shareholder is a property owner who does not have full control over his or her property. Often, shareholders are a fickle group. With little or no long-term loyalty to the company, they monitor their portfolio's bottom line and enter and exit accordingly. Any tie to the company is rendered even more remote by techniques of program trad-ing and portfolio hedging. Most observers appeal to management's duties to share-holders to secure an adequate return. The anonymous character and short-term behav-ior of most shareholders suggests that they may have no real commitment to the com-pany. Such a reality calls into question the validity of the principle that the responsibil-ity of management is to the shareholders and makes it imperative to recast the rights (and duties) of shareholders in the context of the rights and duties of stakeholders in a corporation.

Corporate Boards and Governance. The safeguarding of the rights and duties of all the concerned parties is a central respon-sibility of corporate governance. The weak-est link in corporate governance today is found in the board of directors. In theory, the board of directors is charged with secur-ing the best interests of shareholders and monitoring the performance of managers.

F. M. Scherer, who has developed data on over 6,000 mergers, summarized his con-clusion this way:[39]

> You asked the question, how can we im-prove corporate governance? That is really where the problem lies. Let me make a sim-ple proposal. The Congress ought to enact legislation that requires listed companies to have a certain fraction of their directors nom-inated directly by outside shareholders. This nomination would in fact be done largely by financial intermediaries who control for the larger corporations half of the value of shares. The financial intermediaries who now simply follow the Wall Street rule and bail out on short notice, would then have to devote attention to making sure that good outside directors are appointed, to make sure the performance of the corporation is in fact good.

Sir James Goldsmith views the relation between managers and corporate boards as incestuous. It must be remembered that al-most always, directors are not chosen and elected by shareholders. Normally, share-holders are asked to vote on a list of directors proposed by management. There are no primaries, and only rarely, and at a great cost, is an alternative list of candidates proposed to shareholders, and within the context of proxy fights. So, in effect, directors are co-opted by their future colleagues, and shareholders do no more than ratify the proposals.[40] Shareholders have very little effective say. Annual meetings have not offered a fruitful venue for shareholders to communicate with each other, much less organize among themselves. Shareholders are routinely ignored when important issues, such as poison pills or greenmail, are decided on.

In addition, a number of corporations are interested in issuing nonvoting classes of common stock. Such a move is objectionable, for it would further insulate management from market forces of efficiency and competition. The only real power shareholders have is to sell off their shares.[41]

Over the years, an incestuous relationship has emerged between top management and boards. In 75% of large companies, the CEO is also head of the board.[42] In most cases, top management appoints the majority of board members. For the most part, boards of directors simply rubber-stamp what management decides. For some years, there have been calls to make boards more independent by placing more outsiders on them. The issue raised is the moral rectitude of management's intentions. It can no longer be assumed that management seeks the best interests of shareholders or other stakeholders. Nor can it be assumed that the board of directors protects shareholders or other stakeholders. Some argue that it is time for shareholders to gain control of the board and that other stakeholders, such as local communities, labor, suppliers, and consumers, should also be represented.

Be that as it may, such a change in the board would make management's task more difficult. That is exactly what is needed. The prescription is simple: (1) Restore a shareholder's perspective, and (2) take ex-

plicit account of the claims of the various stakeholders in the business enterprise.

Government Action

Many observers look to public policy and legislation to resolve the main issues concerning takeovers. Both the United States Congress and a number of state legislatures have been very active in this regard.

Information and Disclosure. One important issue is the ethics of information. Observers recommend immediate disclosure of a raider's stock position (rather than the current 10-day lag). Disclosure is presently required at 5%, but a lower threshold (1%, for example) may be better. Most important, all secret collusion between acquiring partners, as well as the parking of shares, must be curtailed. Mandatory immediate disclosure at the 1% level would be helpful.

Margin Requirements. In addition, people have proposed changing the margin requirements for trading, linking voting to a requirement that a stock be held for a minimum amount of time, altering the taxation of junk bonds, and installing debt ceilings. Such proposals are all debatable. For the market to be fair, the central issue is to change the rules regarding information.

Restrictions on "Gutting the Assets." A third proposal is to prevent those who take over a company from disposing of its assets for the certain period of time (for example, one year). This would commit those acquiring the company to managing successfully in the product or real wealth market. This measure would help close the gap between financial and product markets.

Monitoring and Surveillance. The SEC is charged, among other things, with ensuring the quality of market information. To do this, it requires additional staff and increased data processing potential.[43] In particular, the SEC's EDGAR system (electronic data gathering, analysis, and retrieval) is essential for timely market surveillance and information. In addition, the monitoring of audit integrity and improved cooperative agreements with other countries are both essential measures.

Stakeholder Actions

Local Communities.   Finally, the volatility of the world economy makes corporate restructuring an increasing likelihood. Labor and local communities must themselves begin to adopt proactive stances. How to do this in the general economy, let alone in the case of takeovers, is not clear. The point is to bridge the gap between micro and macro perspectives. For their part, local communities would be healthier if they moved to diversify their economic base so as to reduce their risk in the face of market readjustments. One-company towns are highly vulnerable. Part of the responsibility of local government is to build up a positive economic base by establishing a favorable business milieu.

Labor.   Labor, too, must begin to build into its policy the likelihood of job turnover rather than persisting in the quest for lifelong security. Job retraining and relocation seem to be a basic feature of modern business. There is considerable scope for labor to change the way it acts on the business scene in other ways, also. For example, it can become a major shareholder through its pension funds. Most important, it must plan for the new emergent international competitive milieu by explicitly gearing its policy and proposals to economic efficiency rather than redundancy.

One perspective of organized labor concerning the impact of mergers on employees is provided by Thomas R. Donahue, secretary-treasurer of the AFL-CIO. In testimony before the Senate Banking, Housing, and Urban Affairs Committee, he listed three areas of injury and harm to workers and employees emanating out of the current wave of takeovers.[44]

First, the takeovers and takeover attempts have led to the elimination of jobs, often those jobs held by long service employees. Although comprehensive data on lay-offs and job eliminations are not available, it is estimated that at a minimum, roughly 80,000 members of unions that are affiliated with the AFL-CIO have been thrown out of work as a direct result of corporate restructuring. And clearly, hundreds of thousands more have been thrown out as an indirect result of those closures and reorganizations.

Second, corporate reorganizations lead to a reduction of wage and fringe benefits through raids on pension funds. Workers are forced to lower their standard of living and get by on less, while their retirement income is jeopardized, all in order to finance the employer's acquisitions or restructuring.

Third, by substituting a new employer for a preexisting employer, takeovers destroy seniority and other expectations that employees build up in their jobs over a period of years. New employers are not bound to honor the expectations of those employees, and those new employers all too often are ready to take advantage of their power in that regard. And the morale of affected workers goes to an all-time low, all the while they listen to an increasing number of lectures about labor-management cooperation.

Donahue went on to make concrete suggestions for changes in stock trading policies and called for new policies to protect local communities and workers.

1. Abolish two-tiered offers which clearly have a coercive impact and are the largest imperfection in the present tender offer system.

2. In case of hostile takeovers or other threats to their jobs, incumbent managers often resort to leveraged buy-outs involving collusive sales of a firm's assets at bargain basement prices. To minimize such abuses corporate directors who receive an offer from incumbent

management for a leveraged buy-out ought to be required to secure legal and investment advice from independent professionals, ought to be required to entertain competing offers from outsiders, and to select the offer that is in the best interest of the stockholders and the stakeholders in the company.

3. Raiders should also be denied the profits arising from the circumstance that their failed raid has inflated the value of the target stock. The mechanism for achieving that goal is quite simple. Section 16(b) of the Securities Act could be amended to grant targets the right to recover from a raider and those acting with a raider to recover any profit realized from the short-swing sales of stock acquired in connection with a tender offer and sold within a defined period of time after the offer expires or is withdrawn.

4. Those mounting a takeover attempt should be required to disclose along with the offer the principal economic assumptions underlying their asset valuation and projections, the sources of and the conditions on the acquirer's financing, the business plans for the target, and any plans of the would-be acquirer with respect to the closing or the sale of any facilities of the target.

5. Fiduciaries, including most particularly institutional stockholders, called upon to decide how to respond to a takeover, should be permitted to take into account the likely community and social impact of their actions and should not feel legally constrained to maximize their short-term profits and to disregard entirely any longer range or broader interests.

6. Contracts voluntarily entered into by a corporation should be binding on the corporate successors or the new owners for the term of those contracts.

7. Acquirers should not be permitted to fund an acquisition or to retire debts assumed in connection with the acquisition by tapping a pension fund and withdrawing the so-called surplus funding from the pension fund.

8. Top managers of an acquired company should not be permitted to escape from a reorganization on golden parachutes at the expense of rank and file workers who are left without any economic cushion whenever their employment is terminated. Just as employers are currently prohibited from discriminating in favor of high paid employees in paying retirement benefits, so too should they be prohibited from discriminating against those high paid employees in the golden parachute arrangements.

NOTES

1. Donald V. Austin and David W. Mandula, "Tender Offer Update: 1986," *Mergers and Acquisitions* (July/August, 1986), pp. 55–57.

2. *Business Week*, "The Top 200 Deals" (April 15, 1988), pp. 53–81. A similar report was issued for 1986 (April 17, 1987); from 1983 through 1985 a report on the top 300 deals was issued.

3. United States Senate, Committee on Banking, Housing and Urban Affairs, *Hostile Takeovers*. Washington, D.C.: U.S. Government Printing Office, 1986, p. 220. Hereafter cited as *Senate Hearings*. United States House of Representatives, Committee on Energy and Commerce, Subcommittee on Telecommunications, Consumer Protection and Finance, *Corporate Takeovers*. Washington, D.C.: U.S. Government Printing Office, 1986, p. 3. Hereafter cited as *House Hearings*.

4. James B. Stewart and Philip Revzin, "Sir James Goldsmith, As Enigmatic As Ever, Bails Out of Goodyear." *Wall Street Journal* (November 21, 1986), pp. 1, 15. James B. Stewart and Daniel Hertzberg, "Goodyear Said to Be Target of Goldsmith." *Wall Street Journal* (October 29, 1986), p. 3. James B. Stewart, "Merrill Lynch Could Get $200 Million in Fees on a Goldsmith Bid for Goodyear." *Wall Street Journal* (November 5, 1986), p. 4. Gregory Stricmarchuk and Ralph B. Winter, "Goodyear's Mercer Tries to Hold off Sir James in a Contest for Company." *Wall Street Journal* (November 5, 1986), p. 28. Jonathan P. Hicks, "Goodyear's Uneasy Aftermath." *New York Times* (November 25, 1986), p. D1.

5. *Senate Hearings,* p. 220.

6. *Senate Hearings,* p. 216.

7. Ibid., p. 217ff.

8. Ibid., pp. 219–20.

9. Ibid., p. 244.

10. Jonathan P. Hicks, "Goodyear's Uneasy Aftermath." *New York Times* (December 5, 1986), pp. D1, D2.

11. Tamar Lewin, "Business and the Law: Suits Aimed at Greenmail." *New York Times* (March 3, 1987), p. D2.

12. *Mergers and Acquisitions,* "SEC's All-Holders Rule" (November/ December, 1986), p. 15.

13. *House Hearings,* p. 217.

14. Michael C. Jensen, "Takeovers: Folklore and Science." *Harvard Business Review* (November/ December, 1984), pp. 109–21.

15. Kenneth Lehn and Mark L. Mitchell, *Do Bad Bidders Become Good Targets?* Washington, D.C.: Securities and Exchange Commission, 1988. Gregory A. Robb, "SEC Study Links Bad Acuisitions to Later Takeovers." *New York Times* (December 5, 1988), p. D2.

16. *Senate Hearings,* p. 1076ff.

17. Ibid., p. 1078.

18. Ibid., p. 1079.

19. Mark Green and John Berry, "Takeovers—A Symptom of Corpocracy." *New York Times* (December 3, 1986), p. A31.

20. T. Boone Pickens, Jr., *Boone.* New York: Houghton Mifflin Company, 1987. T. Boone Pickens, Jr., "How Business Stacks the Deck." *New York Times* (March 1, 1987), p. F2. Steven Prokesch, "America's Imperial Chief Executive." *New York Times* (October 12, 1986), pp. F1, F25.

21. T. Boone Pickens, *House Hearings,* p. 47.

22. *New York Times,* "Looking Who's Bashing Corpocracy" (November 24, 1986), p. 18.

23. Jerry K. Pearlman, "Save the Lectures—Give Us Some Help." *New York Times* (December 14, 1986), p. F3.

24. Teri Agins, "John Emery Looks for a Better Package." *Wall Street Journal* (April 2, 1987), p. 34.

25. Anderson, *Senate Hearings,* pp. 137–38, 490.

26. Pickens, *House Hearings,* pp. 30–31.

27. Andrew Sigler, *Senate Hearings,* pp. 196–97.

28. Ibid., pp. 195–96.

29. Rohatyn, *Senate Hearings,* pp. 101, 109–10.

30. Richard Wines, "The Stock Watch System: Early Warning on Raiders." *Mergers and Acquisitions* (March/ April, 1987), pp. 56–58.

31. Michael S. Helfer and William D. Brighton, "The Federal Reserve's Stand on Junk Bond Takeovers." *Mergers and Acquisitions* (July/ August, 1986), pp. 48–54.

32. Suzanne S. Dawson, Robert J. Pence, and David S. Stone, "Poison Pill Defensive Measure." *The Business Lawyer,* 42 (February, 1987), pp. 423–39.

33. Isadore, Barmash. "Talking Deals–Carter's Ally Calls the Tune." *New York Times* (December 11, 1986), p. D2. Robert Williams, "Taxes and Takeovers—When You Can't Resist a Bear Hug Look for a White Knight." *Journal of Accountancy,* 162 (July, 1986), pp. 86–93.

34. Alison Leigh Cowan, "New Ploy: 'Tin Parachutes.'" *New York Times* (March 19, 1987), pp. D1, D8. David F. Larcher and Richard A. Lambert, "Golden Parachutes, Executive Decision-Making and Shareholder Wealth." *Journal of Accounting and Economics,* 7 (April, 1985), pp. 179–204.

35. Robert J. Cole, "$1.6 Billion Buyback by Gencorp." *New York Times* (April 7, 1987), pp. D1, D7.

36. Tamar Lewin, "Business and the Law: Suits Aimed at Greenmail." *New York Times* (March 3, 1987), p. D2.

37. *Mergers and Acquisitions,* "Failsafe Protection" (November/ December, 1986), pp. 16–17.

38. Louis Lowenstein, "No More Cozy Management Buyouts." *Harvard Business Review,* 61 (January/ February, 1986), pp. 117–27.

39. Scherer, *House Hearings,* p. 156.

40. *Senate Hearings,* p. 1082.

41. Louis Braiotta and A. A. Sommer, *The Essential Guide to Effective Corporate Board Committees.* Englewood Cliffs, N.J.: Prentice-Hall, 1987.

42. Idalene F. Kesner, Bart Victor, and Bruce T. Lamont, "Board Composition and the Commission of Illegal Acts: An Investigation of *Fortune* 500 Companies." *Academy of Management*

Journal, 29, no. 4 (1986), pp. 789–99. Idalene F. Kesner and Dan K. Dalton, "Boards of Directors and the Checks and (Im)balances of Corporate Governance," *Business Horizons*, 29 (October, 1986), pp. 17–23. John D Pawling, "The Crisis of Corporate Boards—Accountability vs. Misplaced Loyalty." *Business Quarterly*, 51 (June, 1986), pp. 71–73.

43. Richard Wines, "The Stock Watch System: Early Warning on Raiders." *Mergers and Acquisitions* (March/April, 1987), pp. 56–58. Roger Oram, "SEC Projects the Case for Defense," *Financial Times* (December 10, 1986), p. 6.

44. *Senate Hearings*, p. 212ff.

GOODYEAR TIRE & RUBBER COMPANY

AUERBACH, ALAN J., ed. *Mergers and Acquisitions.* National Bureau of Economic Research. 1988. (Proceedings of a N.B.E.R. Conference on Mergers and Acquisitions, October 7, 1986). New York, 1988.

BILLINGHAM, CAROL J. "Hostile Corporate Takeovers: Why and How Their Numbers Grow." *Mid-American Journal of Business*, 2 (March 1987), pp. 4–8.

BRUCKMANN, JOHN C., and SCOTT C. PETERS, "Mergers and Acquisitions: The Human Equation." *Employment Relations Today*, 14 (Spring 1987), pp. 55–63.

BUTLER, H. N., and L. E. RIBSTEIN. "Regulating Corporate Takeovers: A Symposium. *University of Cincinnati Law Review*, 57 (1988), pp. 455–656.

CARNEY, WILLIAM J. "Takeover Tussles: the Courts' Tug-of-War With Corporate Boards." *Business and Society Review* (Summer 1985), pp. 64–68.

DAVIS, K. B., JR. "The Risks and Rewards of Regulating Corporate Takeovers: A Symposium" *Wisconsin Law Review* (1988), pp. 353–525.

GORDON, J. N., and L. A. KORNHAUSER. "Discussion of Takeover Defense Tactics: A Comment on Two Models." *Yale Law Journal*, 96, (December 1986), pp. 295–321.

LAMOREAUX, NAOMI. *The Great Merger Movement In American Business, 1895–1904.* New York: Cambridge University Press, 1988.

LEACOCK, S. J., "Restricting Hostile Take-overs in American Law." *Journal of Business Law* (November 1987), pp. 514–19.

MACEY, J. R. "Takeover Defense Tactics and Legal Scholarship: Market Forces versus the Policymaker's Dilemma. *Yale Law Journal*, 96 (December 1986), pp. 342–52.

MAGENHEIM, ELLEN. "Are Corporate Takeovers in the Nation's Interest?" *Forum of Applied Research and Public Policy*, 3 (Spring 1988), pp. 78–87.

MILICH, M. F. "Exclusive Merger Agreements: the Role of the Board of Directors." *Journal of Corporation Law*, 13 (Spring 1988), pp. 823–37.

SUBAK, JOHN T. "Takeovers: Where Are We? Where Do We Go?" *Business Lawyer* 41 (August 1986), pp. 1255–64.

VOLK, S. R., C. O. CONDON, V. I. LEWKOW, W. A. GROLL, R. J. COOPER, and S. M. ROSSOFF. "Developments in the Law of Mergers and Acquisitions: Developments in Defense." *Institute on Security Regulation*, 19 (1987), pp. 287–382.

WEIDENBAUM. MURRAY L., and STEPHEN VOGT. "Takeovers and Stockholders: Winners and Losers:" *California Management Review*, 29 (Summer 1987), pp. 157–68.

WEIDENBAUM, MURRAY L, and KENNETH W. CHILTON, eds. *Public Policy Toward Corporate Takeovers.* New York: Transaction Books, 1988.

INSIDER TRADING: THE LEVINE, BOESKY, AND THE DREXEL BURNHAM LAMBERT CAPER

*How and why do innovative entrepreneurs
become white-collar criminals?*

Private property and voluntary exchange lie at the very core of a market economy and capitalism itself. Thus, availability of information, and its uses and abuses, become critical to the success of the capitalistic system on the one hand, and individual enterprises on the other hand.

To safeguard public trust in the marketplace, public authorities in the United States, and in varying degrees in other nations, have sought to regulate the process by which material information is disseminated in the public domain so that those who are privy to such information because of their official position or status do not use the information for personal gain. In a similar vein, since material information is private property, those gaining unfair advantage from its use are in a sense stealing someone else's property. Hence, insider trading, i.e., entering into transactions for personal gain based on information not normally available to the public,

is considered illegal, unprofessional, unethical, and immoral.

Enlightened self-interest, as espoused by Adam Smith, is not always enlightened and does not always serve public purpose. The line between untrammeled greed and enlightened self-interest is very thin and is constantly blurring.

The case of Ivan Boesky and his cohorts has become the latest, but certainly not the last, episode in one of the longest-running morality plays in the annals of capitalism. It has all the elements of high public drama and a sense of overriding community interest and public welfare. It is also very human in scale, in that the greed and frailties of individuals are hidden behind the masks of professionalism, entrepreneurship, individual enterprise, and optimism. And finally, the fall occurs not because of the failure of vision or idealism gone astray, but because individual greed and instinct for survival have again won over professional standards, individual ethics, or loyalty to employer, colleagues, and friends.

From 1982 to the Fall of 1987, the United States economy experienced one of the most sustained periods of growth in its history. Many fortunes were made during this period, which was characterized by both steady growth as well as by unprecedented takeover activity. The takeover climate in the 1980s, however, was differed drastically between the period of conservative growth in the 1950s and the wild availability of funds in the 1980s. An example of this occurred in the early 1980s, when oil was actually cheaper to buy on the floor of the stock exchange than to discover in the oil fields. This atmosphere strongly supported the insiders' and arbitrageurs' positions. Their opportunities were further enhanced by the huge amounts of merger activity. The takeover climate in this period involved billions of dollars and resulted in huge fees for the people who worked on the mergers. Of course, access to information was a crucial ingredient to financial success and outperforming the market. Also arising from these new mergers was the increased opportunity for insiders—the lawyers, accountants, analysts, secretaries, and, of course, the bankers—all of whom had access to valuable inside information. Additional people who had access to such inside information were the investors themselves, the brokerage firms, the reporters, and even the printers of financial reports and legal documents, to name a few. Almost every week during this period, a new merger was reported to the public. Although the merger activity slackened somewhat in 1989, it is still quite vigorous, and there is no end in sight.

The fuel which was igniting all this growth was the easy availability of funds for the purpose of takeovers. Since takeovers require huge amounts of financing, many forms of financing have developed. The one form which has attracted the most attention is the use of junk bonds to finance acquisitions. The leading underwriter of these bonds is Drexel Burnham Lambert (DBL). Ivan Boesky's story presents an intriguing case study in this regard: He got caught. And he decided to put his former colleagues into play in order to get a good deal for himself. Boesky got his good deal, and he delivered one of the major investment houses—Drexel Burnham Lambert—and the genius behind the 1980s junk bond market—Michael Milken—in securities fraud.

Boesky was the CEO of Ivan F. Boesky & Company, a holding company which held the controlling interests in many different financial services companies. However, the major company in the Boesky empire was his arbitrage unit. During the early 1980s, Boesky gained reknown as a particularly skillful arbitrageur. Riding the crest of his success, he lectured frequently at leading business schools and nurtured a transformation of his public persona by becoming a patron of the arts, a benefactor of higher education, and a mover and shaker of society.[1] In this effort Boesky succeeded admirably, and he basked in his new social role. He was the toast of Wall Street, an upright citizen, a philanthropist, and the conscience of American business. He was in high demand on the lecture circuit.

Boesky's public persona is artfully portrayed in a piece that he authored for the book *Merger Mania*, which was critical of many of the Wall Street's financial maneuvers in this area. He wrote:

> My life has been profoundly influenced by my father's spirit and commitment to the well-being of humanity, and by his emphasis on learning as the most important means to justice, mercy and righteousness. His life remains an example of returning to the community the benefits he had received through the exercise of God-given talents.

> With this inspiration I write this book for all who wish to learn of my specialty, that they may be inspired to believe that confidence in one's self and determination can allow one to

become whatever one may dream. May those who read my book gain some understanding of the opportunity which exists in this great land.[2]

The fall of Ivan Boesky was as steep as was his meteoric rise on the Wall Street and the gain in his personal wealth and public adulation. Public records and available information suggest that his rise from a small-time operator to the peak of financial wealth and the terror of corporate board rooms lasted less than two years. His first use of inside information came about in February 1985, when he persuaded Dennis Levine, an investment banker and a rising star in the Wall Street firm of Drexel Burnham Lambert, to sell him confidential information concerning DBL's involvement in forthcoming tender offers, mergers, and other similar activities which had not yet become public. Levine supplied Boesky with inside information between February 1985 and February 1986 which yielded Boesky some $50 million in profits. Levine, however, was nabbed by the SEC as a result of a follow-up of an anonymous tip. Levine's cooperation with the SEC led to Boesky's downfall and implicated many others. By early summer, Boesky knew his game was up. He wisely enlisted Harvey Pitt (of the New York firm of Fried Frank) as his lawyer. Pitt, who had represented Boesky in various cases dating from 1978, was a former SEC counsel and was well-placed to cut a favorable deal. He did just that. On November 14, 1986, Boesky agreed to plead guilty to one criminal felony charge and pay a $100 million penalty, while agreeing to cooperate with the SEC. On April 27, 1987, he formally entered his guilty plea to a single criminal charge of conspiring to file false statements with the SEC. On December 18, 1987, he was sentenced to three years in prison, and on March 24, 1988, he surrendered to federal authorities.[3]

In an attempt to persuade the government to go easy on him, Boesky eagerly cooperated with federal authorities in ensnar-

ing other Wall Street operators who had allegedly been profiting from inside information. To date, this has resulted in a number of indictments, guilty pleas, fines, and prison sentences. And the investigations are still continuing. The reverberations of the Boesky affair have also crossed the Atlantic and nabbed other perpetrators in Europe, notably England and France.[4] In the process, Wall Street and the financial community have been tarred with scandal and a tremendous loss of public trust in their integrity.[5]

It took less than a year for the SEC to build its case against Boesky and another two years to bring charges against Milken and Drexel Burnham Lambert. On December 22, 1988, Drexel Burnham Lambert settled its case with federal prosecutors. Under the terms of the settlement, DBL agreed to plead guilty to six counts of criminal fraud, pay a fine of $650 million, and cooperate with the government in its ongoing investigation.[6] DBL also agreed to fire Milken and to deny him his 1988 bonus, estimated at over $200 million. In the aftermath DBL filed for bankruptcy in February 1990. Ivan Boesky was released from prison in April 1990. Milken has vociferously denied any wrongdoing and has launched a court challenge against the government. His case does not show signs of an early settlement.[7]

ISSUES FOR ANALYSIS

There are many principles which underlay the fairness of the market system. Perhaps nothing is more important in financial markets than access to information. The debate over insider trading is concerned that the playing field be level in this regard. Issues to be considered include the following:

1. How effective are the current laws and regulations in preventing abuse of insider information?

2. What is the proper role of the SEC in curbing

the use of inside information for personal gain by insiders? How effective has the SEC been in achieving this goal?

3. What are the principles of materiality and disclosure? What are the grounds on which one piece of information becomes material, and how should the information be evaluated?

4. When is information considered to have been properly disseminated and, therefore, in the public domain? What are the implications of constructing a set of broader or narrower boundaries, in terms of time and channels of communication, for the dissemination of information?

5. Who can be defined as an insider and under what circumstances? What are the implications of a narrower or broader definition of *insider* for the financial markets, corporations, large and small stockholders, and for the maintenance of general confidence in the fairness of trading stocks?

6. What are the rights of the stockholders who lost money as a result of insider trading?

7. What is the employer's position when an employee is guilty of insider trading?

8. Is it possible to devise other than public regulatory measures that would curtail the misuse of inside information?

9. If stiffer legislation with respect to insider trading is passed, what will be the implications on the capital markets?

10. As opposed to what is legally wrong, what, if anything, is morally wrong with insider trading?

11. Is it possible for the securities industry to regulate itself? Legal scholars like Henry Manne have argued that insider information is seldom risk-free, and therefore we can largely negate its value by increasing its risk tremendously.

12. What are the moral and ethical implications of the Boesky and other insider trading scandals? What do such scandals tell us, if anything, about our role models, our heroes, and our villains?

13. How might one evaluate the behavior of Ivan Boesky in his postarrest activities? Were these the activities of a contrite and guilt-ridden individual trying to cleanse himself? Or were

these the actions of a chameleon selling his friends and colleagues to minimize for himself the consequences of his illegal and criminal activities?

14. How did Boesky try to portray himself to the public as an upright citizen? What does such behavior tell us about the American society and its value system?

15. What do the Boesky and other related scandals tell us about the American business creed?

16. Finally, how might one judge the behavior of federal prosecutors in settling the Boesky and other related cases, in terms of their equity, fairness, and vigorousness of law enforcement? To what extent should those who cooperate with the SEC be rewarded for informing on others? Are the SEC's actions likely to deter similar crimes in the future?

THE REGULATORY BACKGROUND

With the crash of the stock market in October 1929, the federal government realized the need for increased regulation of the financial markets. The first law enacted was the Glass-Stegall Act of 1933, which separated commercial banks from investment banks. Then, the Securities Act of 1934 created the Securities and Exchange Commission to police all financial markets. In 1940, the Investment Advisers Act permitted the courts to prosecute any operation that led to deceit or fraud of the consumer. In 1968, the Williams Act set a number of restrictions, including one that required that those accumulating a stock give public notice.

With regard to insider information the relevant section of the Securities and Exchange Commission Act of 1934 [15 U.S.C. Sec. 78j(b)] is Rule 10b-5. Section 10 of the Act reads, in pertinent parts, as follows:

It shall be unlawful for any person, directly or indirectly, by the use of any means or instrumentality of interstate commerce or of the mails or of any facility of any national securities exchange. . . .

b) To use or employ, in connection with the purchase or sale of any security registered on a national securities exchange or any security not so registered, any manipulating or deceptive device or contrivance in contravention of such rules and regulations as the Commission may prescribe as necessary or appropriate in the public interest or for the protection of investors.

Rule 10b (17 C.F.R. 240) provides that

it shall be unlawful for any person, directly or indirectly, by use of any means or instrumentality of interstate commerce, or of the mails, or any facility of any national securities exchange,

(1) to employ any device, scheme or artifice to defraud,

(2) to make any untrue statement of a material fact or to omit to state a material fact necessary in order to make the statements made, in the light of the circumstances under which they were made, not misleading, or

(3) to engage in any act, practice, or course of business which operates or would operate as a fraud or deceit upon any person, in connection with the purchase or sale of any security.

Insider Information

The definition of insider trading is set by precedent. Each situation must be looked at case by case. In order to be guilty of insider trading, there must be some kind of a breach of a duty to keep information confidential. Also, a person must act with the intent to deceive or defraud, or with reckless disregard toward deception or fraud.

This definition is often very ambiguous when one considers concrete activities. For example, suppose that an arbitrageur (as noted earlier, one who speculates on the possibility of a merger by purchasing the takeover target's stock in anticipation of a price

increase) calls executives of two companies that he or she suspects are merging. It would be illegal for either executive to disclose or confirm any information pertaining to the situation. However, if the executives' secretaries accidentally let slip the fact that their bosses had been meeting the night before, causing the arbitrageur to act, this would not constitute illegal insider trading. If the arbitrageur sends the secretary a gift in hopes of receiving information which he or she can profitably use, however, such activity is questionable. Of course, if the arbitrageur has the secretary on his or her payroll, paying the secretary a percentage of the profits, the arrangement is definitely illegal. One result of such legal ambiguity is the difficulty prosecutors face in enforcing insider trading laws, which in turn leads to an incredibly low percentage of violators getting caught.

In the last few years, there has been an avalanche of insider cases brought against printers (Chiarella and *Business Week*), reporters (Winans), brokerage house employees (Siegel, Wang), brokers (Jeffries), major executives (Thayer), and lawyers and arbitrage deal makers (Boesky). Major suspicion has centered on Wall Street stalwarts such as Drexel Burnham Lambert, Kidder Peabody, Merrill Lynch, and Goldman Sachs.[8]

Much of the present activity goes back to a landmark case brought by the SEC against Texas Gulf Sulphur (TGS) in 1964.[9] The SEC brought charges against 13 officers and employees of Texas Gulf Sulphur, a publicly held corporation. The trouble started in 1957 when TGS discovered what appeared to be a major lode of copper and silver. The first unofficial press release stated that the find was of major proportion; however, the officers of TGS later stated that this statement was full of rumors. The officers' denial of the first press release negated the excitement that was generated by the report. Later on, however, TGS confirmed the rumors about the huge magnitude of the strike. Before that report was made public, 13 officers and employees purchased stock and options on

TGS stock. Three days later, the report went public. The stock rose in price $7 per share in one day, and in the course of one week it rose to a new high of $57 per share from approximately $30.

Weeks before the actual announcement, rumors had been flying around Wall Street, which aroused the attention of the SEC. Both the wild rumors and the way the officers of TGS handled the initial report caused public criticism to rise. One month after the announcements, the purchases made by the officers were disclosed. The officers had grossed approximately $250,000 in the previous month from TGS stock increases. Later, the SEC charged these individuals with buying shares and options and disclosing information to other parties for their immediate profit. TGS management defended itself by claiming that it quelled the initial rumors because they were unsubstantiated. Management claimed that options and stock it bought were purchased days before the confirmation of the strike. By this time, the extent of the officers' purchases were fully exposed to the public, which reacted with civil suits for damages running into the millions of dollars. The officers agreed to return the profits to the corporation, but the SEC refused. The SEC lost the initial court case, and all charges were dismissed against the alleged defendants. On appeal, a higher court reversed the lower court's decision and found eight of the defendants guilty.

Texas Gulf Sulphur was a landmark case because from it, explicit rules arose pertaining to how and when management can release to the public major corporate developments, the exercise of corporate stock options, and corporate-sponsored investment programs.

At least since the Texas Gulf Sulphur decision, the antifraud provisions of the federal securities laws have come to state, among other requirements, the "disclose-or-refrain" rule. This rule states that persons, or at least some persons, who possess material, nonpublic information pertaining to the value of a corporation's securities cannot buy or sell the securities unless they first disclose the information. This rule was first employed in the interpretation of Rule 10b-5 of the Securities and Exchange Act of 1934, in the context of insiders or the corporation itself trading on inside information about corporate assets or prospects. But it has since been extended under Rule 10b-5 and other antifraud provisions, such as Section 206 of the Investment Advisers Act and the Williams Act, to restrict the conduct of outsiders trading on information that affects securities prices but is unrelated to corporate prospects—e.g., information that someone is about the make a tender offer or publish a sell recommendation that is expected to have a sharp and immediate, if only short-term, impact on stock prices.

The TGS case provided precedents in four major areas of insider trading: (1) It gave a broad definition of who is an insider. (2) It defined *material information*. (3) It clarified what is false and misleading information. (4) It stated how much time must elapse before information becomes public knowledge. Thus, the road to more concise insider trading laws was paved.

The first of these precedents gave the SEC wide latitude in determining the definition of *insider* under SEC Rule 10-5b. Insiders might include employees of a company as well as directors, officers, major stockholders and "tippees" (i.e., lawyers, accountants, financial advisers, or independent contractors whose access to information about corporate affairs is only given for corporate purposes—in other words, a tippee is a person who purchases shares on the basis of advice received directly or indirectly).

The court's definition of *material information* pertained to securities and their values. It stated that material information was "any important development which might affect security values or influence investment decisions of reasonable and objective investors."

In addition, the court ruled on false and misleading information. For fraud to be proven, it had to be shown that there was failure to correct a misleading impression caused by statements already made or by not coming forth and explaining the current situation when there was a duty by law to clarify the situation.

Finally, of great importance to the SEC was the definition of how much time must elapse for a piece of information to become public knowledge. The court held that material information becomes public as soon as an announcement has been made public by the press. Furthermore, the appeals court ruled that to ensure fairness, the time that an insider places the order for the transaction, rather than the time of execution, is what the court rulings are based on.

The definition of *insider* has remained a major bone of contention. The SEC, therefore, has come to base a number of its proceedings on what is known as the *misappropriation theory*. The misappropriation theory holds that it is the theft, or misappropriation, of confidential information by someone such as an investment banker or lawyer entrusted with it that gives rise to criminal liability.[10] It was this theory which was central to the prosecution of R. Foster Winans, which was upheld by the Supreme Court.

In 1984, the Insider Trading Sanctions Act was made law. It gave the SEC the authority to seek monetary penalties and fines up to three times a defendant's illegal profits.[11] The legal basis remained ambiguous, and everyone was clamoring for a clear definition. To this end, the SEC proposed a definition for the Insider Trading Act of 1987. The proposed definition combines elements of misappropriation theory with a portrait of the insider as an agent.[12] It states:

> It shall be unlawful for any person, directly or indirectly, to purchase, sell, or cause the purchase or sale of, any security while in possession of material nonpublic information concerning the issuer or its securities, if such person knows or recklessly disregards that such information has been obtained wrong-

fully or that such purchase or sale would constitute a wrongful use of such information. . . . For purposes of this section information is obtained or used wrongfully if, directly or indirectly, it has been obtained by, or is a result of, or its use would constitute theft, bribery, misrepresentation, or espionage through electronic or other means, or a breach of duty to maintain such information in confidence, or to refrain from purchasing, selling or causing the purchase or sale of, the security, which duty arises from any fiduciary, contractual, employment, personal or other relationships with:

a. the issuer of the security or its security holders;

b. any person planning or engaged in an acquisition or disposition of the issuer's securities or assets;

c. any government or a political subdivision, agency or instrument of a government;

d. any person or any self-regulatory organization registered or required to be registered with the commission;

e. any person engaged in the market for securities or the financial conditions of issuers;

f. any such person that is a member of a class that the commission designates by rule or by regulation where the commission finds that the activities of the members of such a class have a regular nexus to the operation of the nation's securities markets and that such designation is necessary or appropriate to effectuate the purposes of this section; or

g. any other person who obtains such information as a result of a direct or indirect confidential relationship with any persons or entities referred to in paragraphs a–f above.

A few months later, the SEC requested that the Senate Banking Committee's Subcommittee on Securities to include more clearly the misappropriation theory.[13] The Supreme Court Winans decision, while it did uphold misappropriation, proved inconclusive on stock fraud (with the justices split four to four). Investment bankers complained that legal imprecision left too much discretionary power with the SEC. In essence, the Congress, the SEC, and the financial community were moving toward compromise in establishing a clear definition. At present, consensus is building, but the point remained unresolved even in the 1988 congressional legislation on insider trading.[14]

A CHRONOLOGICAL HISTORY OF THE LEVINE-BOESKY-DBL CASE

The speculation about takeover stocks rose to the center of attention in the 1980s. Factors such as undervalued stock, poor management, underutilized assets, large hordes of liquid assets, and the availability of easy credit made companies easy targets for acquisitions and leveraged buyouts. Millions and even billions of dollars changed hands almost instantly. Stock prices fluctuated wildly, and fortunes were made and lost on rumors of takeovers.

The lure of quick fortunes was irresistible even to the most stoic and historically conservative blue-chip financial institutions on Wall Street. The meteoric career success and phenomenal salaries of many young people, who had not matured enough to appreciate the ups and downs of the market, compounded the temptation. Starting at very high salaries and commanding even larger bonuses, they were impatient to make their first million and could not wait for the second. In addition, arbitrageurs emerged, who stood to gain and lose millions on the basis of advance information about takeovers and were willing to pay handsomely to secure this information. Thus, there was a fertile breeding ground for shady deals and financial chicanery.

For all its seriousness and immensity, the unraveling of the Boesky affair had its origins in one of the more ordinary events in the annals of Wall Street. It started in May 1985, when the New York office of Merrill Lynch & Company received an anonymous letter from its office in Caracas, Venezuela, stating that two brokers (Max Hofer and Carlos Zubillaga) in the firm's office were doing extremely well, almost too well, playing takeover stocks. Merrill Lynch's investigation led to a New York stockbroker. As it turned out, the broker was simply acting on orders he received from the Bahamian branch of the Switzerland-headquartered Bank Leu.

Following its regular procedures and policies, Merrill Lynch alerted the SEC's enforcement director, Gary G. Lynch, shortly thereafter. Lynch started pressuring Bank Leu, and the Leu bankers began to worry. It turned out that Bank Leu's Bernhard Meier handled Levine's trades at the bank. Meier subsequently returned to Zurich, where he faced no criminal or civil charges. Bank Leu had been dealing for years with Dennis Levine, a 33-year-old Wall Street investment banker. Levine used various accounts to throw the SEC off his trail. Through these accounts, held in various names such as IGI (International Gold Incorporated), Mr. Diamond (Levine's mother's maiden name), Diamond Holdings, S.A., and Bernhard Meier, Levine made nearly $13 million in profits starting as early as 1980.

The Bank Leu and Levine initially remained silent. Soon, Bank Leu was talking about getting a lawyer. Levine suggested that they obtain Harvey Pitt, who in 1975 at the age of 30 had been a general counsel for the SEC. However, what happened next was not at all what Levine had in mind when he made the suggestion. Pitt worked out a deal for Bank Leu, and the bank named Levine as the man who was doing the trading. On May 12, 1986, Levine was arrested. Within weeks, he was giving the SEC information about the men from whom he had bought tips for his stock transactions.

On May 12, 1986, the SEC filed a complaint alleging that over a five-year period, Levine, who was employed as a mergers and acquisitions specialist, secretly purchased and sold securities through a Bahamian bank account. The SEC alleged that Levine obtained approximately $12.6 million in illegal profits from his scheme of secretly trading the securities of 54 companies.

The official SEC document charged Levine with two major infractions.[15]

1. The defendant Dennis Levine, and all other accounts, directly and indirectly had engaged, and were about to engage in acts, practices and courses of business which constituted, constitute and would constitute violations of section 10(b) of the Securities and Exchange Act of 1934 (''Exchange Act'') [15 U.S.C. ss 78j(b)], and rule 10b-5 [17 C.F.R. ss 240.10b-5] promulgated thereunder.

2. Mr. Levine directly and indirectly had engaged, was then engaged, and was about to engage in acts, practices and courses of business which constituted, constitute and would constitute violations of section 14(e) of the Exchange Act [15 U.S.C. ss 78n(e) and rule 14e-3 [17 C.F.R. 240.14e-3] promulgated thereunder.

After paying $11.6 million initially to settle civil complaints, Levine still had to go to court to face the felony charges. In court, he pleaded guilty to four felony counts, each of which carried a maximum sentence of five years. In the end, Levine only received two years in prison because he gave information to the SEC leading to the greatest string of arrests Wall Street had ever seen. He also had to pay an additional $362,000 in fines.[16]

Those who leaked information to Levine included Ira Sokolow, an investment banker at Shearson Lehman Brothers; Ivan Reich, attorney for Wachtell, Lipton, Rosen and Katz; and, Robert Wilkis, investment banker at Lazard Freres. In addition, Randall Cecola, a Lazard analyst, leaked information to Wilkis and to David Brown, an investment banker at Goldman, Sachs and Co., who leaked information to Sokolow.

Boesky met Levine for the first time in

February of 1985. Because of his employment at Drexel Burnham, Levine learned of confidential information that concerned tender offers, mergers, and other business activities. In addition, Levine also gave Boesky information he had learned from the aforementioned sources in the mergers and acquisitions business. In the spring of 1985, Boesky and Levine made an agreement that would give Levine 5% of the profits made by Boesky on stock transactions based on Levine's tips. Levine would get 1% if the information helped Boesky decide how to play a stock that he already held. Through this agreement, Boesky managed to profit in excess of $4 million in just a few days based on Levine's information.

In the spring of 1986, the deal began to fall apart, and Levine was charged with securities fraud. He was forced to pay fines and also faced the possibility of a prison sentence. In return for a lighter sentence, Levine gave the SEC information pertaining to his dealings with Boesky. Levine agreed to let the SEC tape private conversations he had after he was arrested.[17] One such conversation, according to Wall Street sources, was with Ivan Boesky. This, in time, brought the SEC down on Boesky.

In its complaint against Boesky, the Commission alleged that Boesky exercised investment control over certain entities which engaged in the purchase and sale of publicly traded securities. The Commission also alleged that Boesky obtained from Levine material, nonpublic information concerning tender offers, mergers, and other business activities. Also stated in the complaint was that Boesky knew that the information was confidential and had been obtained through a breach of fiduciary duty on Levine's part. The complaint also stated that during the period from February 1985 through February 1986, Boesky made transactions in certain securities while in possession of this information.[18]

The official complaint against Ivan Boesky pertained to securities fraud and charged, among other things, that defendant Boesky, directly or indirectly, had engaged in acts, practices, and transactions which constituted violations of Sections 10(b) and 14(e) of the Securities Exchange Act of 1934 ("Exchange Act") [15 U.S.C. ss 78j(b) and 78n(e)] and Rules 10b-5 and 14e-3 promulgated thereunder.

According to the SEC, the three largest trades Boesky made (on the basis of profits earned) were as follows:[19]

STOCK	MERGER	PROFIT	DATE
Houston National Gas	with Internorth Inc.	$4,100,000	4/85
Nabisco Brands, Inc.	with R. J. Reynolds	$4,000,000	5/85
FMC, Inc.	restructuring of FMC	$ 975,000	3/85

Boesky had been bargaining with the SEC since July 1987. In September 1987, he reached a settlement with the SEC, which was announced on November 14, 1987. Boesky was ordered to return $50 million in illegal profits and was fined another $50 million. In addition, he was to plead guilty to a single felony conspiracy count. He was also barred from the securities industry for life. Like Levine, he too gave information relating to other insiders on Wall Street who used their nonpublic, material information for personal profit. On April 23, 1987, Boesky entered his plea of guilty. On December 18, 1987, he was sentenced to three years in prison, with the possibility of parole after one year.

During Boesky's questioning, other persons were implicated. One of these was Boyd Jeffries, a broker who was chairman of Jeffries Group Inc. Another was Martin Siegel, who was one of the top investment bankers in the industry. Siegel, of Kidder, Peabody, was accused of passing information pertaining to mergers which he was working on at the time to Boesky in exchange for $700,000 for information. Further, major suspicion was cast on leading figures at Drexel

Burnham Lambert, notably Michael Milken, head of its junk bond department.

Great controversy followed Boesky's settlement. *The Economist* magazine wrote:[20] "The Wall Street crook, Ivan Boesky, pulled off his most audacious insider deal after he was nabbed by the Securities and Exchange Commission. . . . Through a series of maneuvers, his family has salted away at least $160 million." Most people in the field viewed his sentence as very light because after his apprehension he was allowed to liquidate a $400 million portfolio and his other holdings over a period of time, without other investors being any the wiser. This was probably allowed because of Boesky's general counsel, Harvey Pitt, partner for Fried, Frank, Harris, Shriver and Jacobson and former general counsel of the SEC. This was the same Pitt who got Bank Leu off the hook. Boesky also retained another former SEC official, Theodore Levine of the Washington firm Wilmer, Cutler and Pickering. Pitt and Wilmer were both well connected with the SEC, and critics decried another "insider" deal.[21] Table 1 shows Boesky's sentence in comparison with some other equally renowned cases of insider trading convictions.

Suspicions were rife for some time that Boesky had given information on some big traders for the relatively soft terms of his treatment. When the SEC made known its charges against Michael Milken and his associates, as well as against Drexel Burnham Lambert, the financial community was aghast.[22] The charges were detailed in a document nearly 200 pages long; they are summarized in Table 2. The 18 major charges range from insider trading, fraud against clients, failure to disclose, false and misleading books and records, aiding and abetting net capital violations, and fraud in offering materials. Boesky figured in all but four of the deals. Many observers questioned whether a case built on Boesky would hold up. At the same time, others wondered whether Boesky was just a front all along. Not only did the accused face SEC charges; they were also liable to civil suits brought by clients and interested parties. Furthermore, if convicted under RICO premises, they faced treble damages. Initially, DBL vehemently maintained its innocence and mounted a vigorous public relations campaign and legal effort to defend itself. According to some estimates, it spent more than $140 million in legal, public relations, and advertising campaigns—with $46 million paid by Arthur Andersen & Company to copy and collate the 1.5 million pages of documents requested by the government.[23]

On December 22, 1988, however, DBL agreed to plead guilty to six counts of criminal charges and to pay a fine of $650 million. The charges pertained to criminal activities including insider trading, stock manipulation, parking of securities to conceal their true ownership, and false disclosure and bookkeeping. DBL also agreed to have a government-approved accountant pore over any trading records and documents requested by the government. The government agreed not to prosecute DBL for any past crimes. However, no DBL employees were granted personal immunity. Milken

was not a party to this settlement, and he denounced it claiming that some of its provisions violated his rights.[24]

BOESKY FALLOUT: WALL STREET AS THE EVIL EMPIRE

The aftershocks of the Levine-Boesky-Milken-DBL affair are still reverberating throughout the capitalist world. Never had the fault line running between Wall Street and Main Street seemed so pronounced. The giddy takeover period of the 1980s provided Wall Street movers and shakers with unprecedented opportunity. There were 1,889 companies acquired in 1980 at a total cost of $44.3 billion; in 1986 there were 3,356 mergers with a value of $176.6 billion. The head of one of Wall Street's largest investment banks put it this way:[25] "It was like free sex. You definitely saw the abuses growing but you also saw the absence of people getting caught, so the atmosphere grew relaxed. There really was a deterioration in people's caution, and there were so many deals being

TABLE 1. Comparison of Boesky's Sentence with Other Insider Trading Convictions

INSIDER TRADER	PRISON TERM	REMARKS
Paul Thayer	4 years	Former deputy defense secretary; LTV chairman convicted after trial; obstructed justice.
Dennis B. Levine	2 years	Former investment banker at Drexel; implicated Boesky; cooperated after arrest; illegal gain: $12 million.
Israel Grossman	2 years	Former lawyer; leaked information to family members, who made $1.5 million; convicted after trial; no cooperation.
R. Foster Winans	18 months	Former *Wall Street Journal* reporter; paid about $30,000 by Peter Brant, a stockbroker who pleaded guilty but has not been sentenced; cooperated but did not plead guilty; convicted after trial.
James Newman	1 year, 1 day	Former stockbroker; received tips from investment banker Adrian Antoniu; convicted after trial; no cooperation.
Ira Sokolow	1 year, 1 day	Former investment banker, member of Levine group; paid $120,000 for information by Levine; pleaded guilty and cooperated.
Ilan Reich	1 year, 1day	Former takeover lawyer, member of Levine group; took no money; pleaded guilty and cooperated; implicated Randall Cecola.
Robert Wilkis	1 year, 1 day	Former investment banker, member of Levine group; made $3 million; pleaded guilty and cooperated.
David Brown	30 days	Former investment banker, member of Levine group; paid $30,000 by Sokolow; pleaded guilty and cooperated.
Adrian Antoniu	None	Former investment banker; tipped stockbroker James Newman; cooperated, pleaded guilty, implicated others.

SOURCE: "Boesky's Sentence Ends Chapter in Scandal," *Wall Street Journal* (December 21, 1987), p. 2.

TABLE 2. An Outline of the SEC Charges Filed against Drexel, Milken, and Others

TRANSACTION	DREXEL ROLE	BOESKY ROLE	REMARKS
Insider Trading			
Diamond Shamrock/ Occidental Petroleum	An Occidental's investment banker, knew that the company was proposing to merge with Diamond Shamrock	Under instructions from Michael Milken of Drexel, purchased Diamond Shamrock shares and sold Occidental shares short.	Drexel and Boesky agreed to split the profits from the illegal trading. Diamond Shamrock's board voted not to approve the merger.
Storer Communications/ Kohlberg Kravis Roberts	As KKR's investment banker, Drexel knew of a contemplated increase in a buy-out offer for Storer.	Under Drexel's instructions, purchased Storer stock before the increased offer was made public.	Drexel's profits from the insider trading exceeded $1 million.
Lorimar/ Telepictures	Milken, as adviser to both companies, was informed that a merger between the two was likely. Acting before that information was public, Drexel bought Lorimar stock for its own account.	None	The purchases eliminated a short position, enabling Drexel to avoid a loss of approximately $568,000 and obtain a profit of about $1.23 million.
Viacom	Milken was asked to help finance a management buy-out. Before the buy-out was made public, Drexel bought Viacom stock and convertible subordinated debentures for its own account.	None	The purchases eliminated a short position, enabling Drexel to avoid a loss of about $1.78 million.
Fraud against Drexel Clients			
Maxxam Group/ Pacific Lumber	Acted as investment banker for Maxxam. On the day Maxxam publicly announced a tender offer for Pacific Lumber, a dispute developed between Maxxam and Drexel over Drexel's compensation.	Under instructions from Drexel and Milken, purchased Pacific Lumber stock, sometimes at prices that exceeded Maxxam's tender offer price.	Drexel failed to disclose the secret purchases, and received $22 million in fees from Maxxam, reflecting, in part, the increased cost of the tender offer.
Wickes/ National Gypsum	Consulted by Wickes on the possible acquisition of National Gypsum.	Under instructions from Drexel, purchased National Gypsum stock before Wickes' offer was made public.	Drexel failed to disclose to Wickes the purchases. Boesky's purchases resulted in profits for Drexel of about 6.7 million. In addition, Drexel was paid about $1 million in connection with the attempted acquisition.
Stock Manipulation			
Stone Container	Underwriter and manager of an offering of Stone securities that were to be convertible into common stock at a fixed premium over the closing price of Stone common stock on the day of the offering. (Stone told Drexel that it did not want to proceed with the offering until Stone shares reached $46–48.)	At the instructions of a Milken aide, purchased Stone Container stock. On the day before the securities were eventually offered, Boesky's purchases accounted for over 37% of the volume in Stone shares.	The transactions in Stone common stock were done to create apparent active trading in, raise the price of, and induce the purchase of Stone stock and convertible securities.
Wickes Cos.	Underwrote an offering of Wickes preferred stock that could be converted into common stock if Wickes common shares closed above a set price for at least 20 of any 30 consecutive trading days. (Wickes management wanted to call the preferred for conversion as soon as possible.)	Acting under the instructions of a Milken aide, purchased Wickes common stock after it had closed above the threshold on 19 of the previous 27 trading days.	The purchase allowed Wickes stock to close above the threshold price for conversion, and Wickes management was able to redeem the preferred stock. Drexel earned a fee of $2.3 million for agreeing to be standby underwriter for the redemption.

TRANSACTION	DREXEL ROLE	BOESKY ROLE	REMARKS
Failure to Disclose Beneficial Ownership			
Fischbach	Arranged through Milken for Boesky to purchase 10% of Fischbach shares.	Purchased the shares and filed a schedule 13-D reporting that his organization was the beneficial owner of the shares.	The purchases were part of a scheme that would allow Pennsylvania Engineering Corp., controlled by Victor Posner, to get around an agreement that limited its ownership of Fischbach to 24.9% unless a third party acquired 10% of the company. Pennsylvania Engineering eventually acquired 51% of Fischbach's voting stock and Victor Posner was named the company's chairman.
Harris Graphics	Drexel, Milken and various affiliatedcompanies held substantial positions in Harris, much of which was acquired at $1 a share.	Under instructions from Milken, who guaranteed the Boesky organization against any loss, purchased 5% of Harris stock. Then, also at Milken's request, approached Harris management and offered to acquire the company.	Boesky should have stated in his 13-D filing that Drexel was the beneficial owner of the shares. In addition, Milken reportedly did not care whether the Boesky offer was accepted; he was encouraging other Drexel clients to attempt to acquire the company. Eventually, AM International, a Drexel client, acquired Harris for $22 a share.
MGM/ UA	Represented both MGM/ UA and Turner Broadcasting in a deal for Turner to acquire MGM/ UA for $29 a share and then sell UA.	Under instructions from Milken, purchased MGM/ UA securities when the deal was announced and again when the deal had to be restructured. The profits or losses on the purchases were to be shared equally by Drexel and Boesky.	Boesky's filings failed to properly disclose that Drexel and Milken were the beneficial owners of the MGM/ UA shares. Drexel received about $66 million in fees in connection with the TBS-MGM/ UA transactions.
False and Misleading Books and Records			
MCA/ Golden Nugget	In 1984, Drexel purchased Golden Nugget's stake in MCA after Golden Nugget, following Milken's advice, dropped a planned takeover bid for MCA.	At Milken's request, Boesky's broker-dealer Seemala Corp. agreed to purchase the MCA shares from Drexel. Drexel agreed to compensate Seemala for any losses in open market sales of the stock.	Drexel and Seemala's books didn't reflect Drexel and Milken's beneficial ownership of the securities.
Wickes Short Sales	At the direction of Milken and for the benefit of Drexel, Boesky's organization sold Wickes common stock short and engaged in covering transactions. Milken guaranteed Boesky's group against any losses.	Through Drexel, Boesky made a short sale of 5 million when-issued shares of Wickes common stock to Reliance Insurance.	Books kept by Drexel and Boesky's Seemala Corp. failed to reflect Drexel and Milken's beneficial ownership of the Wickes shares.
Tax-Loss Trades	In a series of rigged and prearranged March 1985 transactions, Drexel, Milken, and Boesky sought to create fictitious tax losses for Boesky's Seemala Corp.	Drexel made purported sales of certain securities to the Boesky organization before the dividend record date, and immediately thereafter bought back the securities.	Drexel bore all market risk on the the securities but neither it nor Seemala's records reflected Drexel's beneficial ownership.
Lorimar Short Sales	In 1986, while Lorimar was on its restricted list, Milken instructed Boesky to sell Lorimar common short for Drexel's benefit.	After the Lorimar-Telepictures merger, and its removal from Drexel's restricted list, Drexel sold short shares of the merged company to Boesky to cover Boesky's short position.	Drexel failed accurately to reflect on its books and records its beneficial ownership of Boesky's short position.

TRANSACTION	DREXEL ROLE	BOESKY ROLE	REMARKS
Aiding and Abetting Net Capital Violations			
Phillips Petroleum	Bought Phillips stock in non-bona fide transactions from Seemala Corp., Boesky's company. Drexel held the stock in its own account or in customer accounts. Milken and Boesky agreed that Drexel would be guaranteed against any loss and that any profits would be divided evenly between them.	Semala had sustained substantial losses in connection with some of its transactions undertaken for Drexel and in its own trading of Phillips common stock. The losses created a net capital deficiency of more than $50 million.	The Phillips transactions enabled Seemala to show a smaller capital deficiency, and Seemala was compensated for profits made on the Phillips transaction.
Fraud in Offering Materials			
Hudson Funding Corp.	Drexel was placement agent and Milken was responsible for reorganization and debt offering in connection with the reorganization of Boesky's arbitrage operations.	Sold certain assets to Drexel at below market prices and arranged to pay Drexel a $5.3 million fee for consulting services.	The below-market sales and the consulting payment were actually a way for the Boesky organization to pay Drexel its share of trading profits from transactions undertaken by Boesky at Drexel's request. The offering materials falsely described the $5.3 million payment.
Additional Charges against Victor and Steven Posner			
In addition to the Posners' violations involving Fischbach, Steven Posner contacted the Boesky organization and asked it to buy and hold shares in Burnup & Sims as a favor to Victor Posner in return for a 20% return on the investment. At the time, Victor Posner and companies he controled held over 5% of Burnup & Sims common stock.		Later, a Posner representative told an official of Burnup & Sims that Burnup would have to buy shares owned by persons other than the Posner group as a part of any settlement. The schedule 13-D filed by the Posner group failed to disclose his ownership of Burnup shares held by the Boesky organization.	

SOURCE: James B. Stewart and Daniel Hertberg, ''Letters Are Sent to Milken, Four Others in Drexel Case Indicating Criminal Charges Will Be Sought Soon.'' *Wall Street Journal* (September 9, 1988), pp. 3, 8, 9.

done that people must have felt there was plenty of cover for what they were doing.''

The fallout has taken many forms, two of which are the moral-psychological aspects and the legitimacy of the rules of the game.

What Makes Boesky Run: Profile of an Insider Trader

The moral-psychological debate, as it emanates from business and government circles, generally assumes that the financial system and existing legislation are adequate. The problem is with bad individuals. Why, for instance, would Martin Siegal, who earned in excess of $2 million a year, risk his career and reputation for $700,000? What need did Ivan Boesky have of $50 million in illegal profits when he had (presumably) le-

gitimately amassed over three times that amount? Theories range from the driving compulsions of raw greed to personal insecurity, the feeling that one has not really ''arrived'' in a grand enough way. Surely, no outsider can judge; most likely even those involved would find their actions inexplicable.

Two ingredients make for a criminal—an opportunity and the willingness to exploit it. In that sense, the only difference between the entrepreneur and the criminal is the legality of the opportunity and the means to exploit it. Clearly, given similar opportunities or temptations, relatively few people seem to exploit them in an illegal or criminal manner. It is easy to understand a person's willingness to resort to criminal means when he or she is driven by extremes of physical deprivation. However, criminal behavior is more complex to explain in cases where apparently well-off and affluent people are driven to seek financial gain illegally when they can do without such gain and not suffer any appreciable loss of physical comfort and financial well-being. The following excerpts from an article in *The Wall Street Journal*[26] are revealing:

> No one on Wall Street ever flew as high or crashed as hard as Ivan F. Boesky.
>
> Ivan Boesky and the risk arbitrage movement he dominated transformed the takeovers game. And more than any other person, Mr. Boesky and what he came to represent moved Wall Street's securities firms to stress their trading operations over brokerage, and to seek global trading. Ivan Boesky's spectacular success also helped turn Wall Street's investment bankers into aggressive deal makers rather than consultants.
>
> Ivan Boesky's story—his rise from modest roots as the son of a Russian immigrant delicatessen owner in Detroit to wealth on Wall Street beyond ordinary measure, and his scandalous collapse—will surely become one of American business history's epical dramas.
>
> He is a latter-day Great Gatsby—the self-made Midwesterner struggling to fit in with the East Coast financial establishment—whose compulsion to accumulate a prodigious fortune brings him down catastrophically.
>
> Mr. Boesky came East in 1966, a 28-year old lawyer who had been turned down for jobs with several of Detroit's top firms. As he built his fortune, he studiously affected the trappings of Wall Street prestige. He habituated New York's Harvard Club, his large donations to Harvard having entitled him to club membership. He published a technical, ponderous volume on the art of arbitrage. He adorned his resume with business school lecturing posts, which he seems to have embroidered considerably.
>
> **"It's a Sickness I Have"**
>
> And he continued to make tens of millions of dollars at an obsessive pace, long after he had become one of America's richest men. "It's a sickness I have in the face of which I am helpless," he once told an interviewer. At the crest of his career, this "sickness" apparently drove him to seek still more profits with Dennis Levine through the baldly illegal insider-trading scheme to which he pleaded guilty. . . .
>
> "I don't know what his devils were," said one arbitrager who knows Mr. Boesky well. "Maybe he's greedy beyond the wildest imaginings of mere mortals like you and me," he said. "And maybe part of what drives the guy is an inherent insecurity that was operative here even after he had arrived. Maybe he never arrived."

Boesky was driven by work, was overzealous, and was subject to fast-changing moods. Intimates of Boesky say he vacillated between "being loud, and harsh and aggressive to mellifluously soft-spoken, charming and courtly, and that changes could come abruptly." He was also fiendish about his pursuit of information. "When somebody got an edge on something, he would go bananas."[27] The consistency of his trading successes were so overwhelming that he developed a large following among traders and brokers who would closely watch for clues about his trades and then imitate them. The snowball effect of these trades would create a market frenzy which would become a self-fulfilling prophesy. They would also serve to draw often unwelcome attention to Boesky.

When it came to money and business dealings, Boesky was quite ruthless, pursued his goal with a single-minded purpose, and extracted a high price, almost confiscatory, for his business acumen from his partners. For example, in a 1985 SEC filing, Boesky disclosed that his investors in the original partnership, which was dissolved in 1980, were assigned 45% of the profits, but 95% of any losses, leaving Boesky with 44% of the profits for a mere 5% of the risk.[28]

Although his first love was money, Boesky hankered for the genteel respectability and status that are generally denied the nouveau riche. And yet, he went about achieving them in the flashiest way, which only the new money would aspire to and the old money would despise. In his efforts to adorn himself as the business statesman, Boesky wrote a book (with the help of a professional writer), *Merger Mania,*[29] and set about promoting it with garnishments about his professional credits. The book jacket and the promotional material describe Boesky as serving as adjunct professor both at the Columbia University and New York University graduate schools of business. In fact, he never taught at Columbia and had not taught at New York University since 1984.

Boesky also gave away millions to charities and political activities in his drive toward social acceptance. He became a trustee of New York University, the Jewish Theological Seminary, Brandeis University, and the American Ballet Theater, to name a few. He also thrust himself into Jewish causes and Jewish philanthropies. For example, in 1986, a few months before he was indicted, he became special advisor for Jewish affairs to the Republican National Committee's chairman, and finance director of a Republican Jewish lobbying group. That same year, he was one of a group of Jewish leaders invited to the White House to discuss the proposed sale of American missiles to Saudia Arabia. It is inconceivable that Boesky did not know about his potential troubles with the SEC and that he was very likely to be indicted. And yet, he was not deterred by the prospect of embarrassing his supporters or the charities and causes that he was espousing.

Morality is not, however, identical with the law. The motivations of the insider players raise ethical issues. One result of the Wall Street scandals was a clamoring for ethics training in business schools. To this end, the former head of the SEC, John Shad, gave $30 million to the Harvard Business School. Somehow, it is hoped that people might realize the human carnage created by untrammeled greed and relentless clawing to get to the top. At the heart of the Shad approach is (1) the belief in the goodness of present institutions, and (2) a realization that ethical character must be inculcated. It remains debatable whether educational institutions— and elitist ones at that—are the proper agents for such a task.

While one aspect of the moral-psychological debate focuses on motivation and intention, the other focuses on consequences. One reason insider traders actually commit crimes is that they cannot see any victims because the effects of their crimes are so widely dispersed.[30] They say to themselves that it is legal in Switzerland, so it is not really bad. They believe that everyone is doing it.

In fact, insider trading is viewed differently across international borders. The European Community, West Germany, Italy, Switzerland, and Hong Kong have no insider trading laws. Being an insider is similar to a job prerequisite! France has an $800,000 fine and a two-year maximum jail sentence for insider trading; Britain unlimited fines and two years maximum jail time; the Netherlands a $50,000 fine and two years maximum jail time; and Japan and Canada are more indeterminate.[31] (See Table 3.)

The victimless crime argument has been hotly disputed by investors who have been caught, while Boesky, Milken, and Drexel Burnham Lambert got off with what to them was a mere slap on the wrist. To support the moral unfairness of insider trading, both the SEC and the legal system have left the door open to civil suits for damages.[32]

Another aspect of the moral-psychological debate is that insiders feel they can get away with it. This perception is reinforced by historical evidence, because the courts have dealt leniently with white criminals. The perception does not appear to have changed, despite the recent spate of criminal convictions and sentences. Gary Lynch, the SEC enforcement director and one of the architects behind an aggressive campaign against Wall Street corruption, was quoted

TABLE 3. Insider Trading Regulations in Selected Industrialized Countries

European Community: European Commission expected to require its 12 member countries to outlaw insider trading as soon as 1990.

Britain: Insider trading illegal. Top penalties of two years jail and unlimited fines. Now using recent mutual-aid agreements with the U.S. to probe securities law violations.

France: Insider trading illegal. Maximum penalties of two years jail and $800,000 in fines. But trading on information derived from insiders not banned. Has mutual-aid agreement with the U.S.

West Germany: No insider trading law. Financial industry under voluntary code of conduct prohibiting use of insider information by corporate officials and their bankers. But only one finding of violation since 1970.

Italy: No insider trading law. Dissemination of false information about securities punishable by three years jail and fine up to $38,500. But no convictions since law was enacted in 1942.

The Netherlands: Bill outlawing insider trading likely to pass in 1988. Proposed top penalties: two years jail and $50,000 fine. Agreement with Washington on mutual assistance in criminal matters may allow investigations of securities violations.

Switzerland: Bill outlawing insider trading expected to pass by 1988. Despite bank secrecy laws, Swiss have recently handed over data on several major U.S. insider cases under a 1982 disclosure agreement with Washington.

Canada: Insider trading banned. Ontario recently stiffened insider law. Toronto and Montreal exchanges agree to provide U.S. with data on questionable trading.

Japan: Brokers barred from profiting from inside information. Maximum penalty: three years imprisonment. Has mutual-aid pact with U.S.

Hong Kong: Insider trading not illegal, although authorities can investigate investors' complaints and publish findings. Only two such probes since 1978. Regulators seeking power to cooperate with foreign authorities on securities violations.

SOURCE: "The Insider-Trading Dragnet Is Stretching across the Globe," *Business Week* (March 23, 1987), p. 51.

as saying that severe insider trading penalties were damaging new cases by discouraging potential defendants from cooperating. Lynch suggested that the prospect of imprisonment, civil fines, and financial ruin was convincing some people that "it's better to hunker down than cooperate."[33] It is not clear whether Lynch was arguing for milder sentences or stating that the government could not make these cases effectively without the cooperation of the defendants. If the former is the case, then Lynch was ignoring the deterrent effect of current stiffer sentences on would-be violators. If the latter is the case, then Lynch was either arguing for stiffer laws or for better enforcement procedures and greater allocation of resources to securities laws enforcement.

The Rules of the Game

The heart of the debate over the rules of the game governing financial markets is whether new legislation is needed or whether better enforcement of present rules is called for.

Those arguing for new legislation focus on rules for disclosure and greater clarity in defining the nature of fraud. The federal securities laws impose a system of disclosure which is, in part, mandated and derived from the antifraud provisions of those laws. The mandated disclosure provisions (the registration and reporting requirements of the Securities Acts of 1933 and 1934) require information to be filed with the Commission or an Exchange, and, in that way, to be made available, or in other ways be directly disseminated, to stockholders. These reports come in many forms and with different levels of specificity, such as the 10-K, 14-E, 13-D, and the standard report sent to stockholders. Some of the mandated information is to be furnished in connection with particular transactions or solicitations; other information is required periodically, apart from solicitations or from particular transactions. Many observers wish to tighten disclosure requirements.

The antifraud provisions, in contrast to the mandating provisions, do not call for the filing or reporting of specified items of information. Rather, they require disclosure only when the failure to disclose in particular circumstances leaves a false impression for persons who buy or sell the affected securities or receive services from an investment adviser. The antifraud provisions do not expressly require disclosure when no relevant communication is made as part of a transaction or advisory service. Nevertheless, it is clear from case law that the antifraud provisions do not merely enforce the mandated system of disclosure. "Rather they command disclosure of their own force, and without regard to whether their application is sought in support of mandated disclosure requirements."[34] This means that they function independently—in part to fill in voids left by the system of mandated disclosure, and in part to deter or prevent certain transactions in which one party has an informational advantage over the other.

At the heart of the antifraud measures is a stringent limitation of communication between investment bankers and risk arbitrageurs. This has been compared to the Great Wall of China.[35] "The potential for abuse is astronomical," says Paul A. Fisher, an attorney in Washington with Stoppleman, Rosen and DeMartino and a former official of the SEC, "and the recent allegations make you think they're more common then we had thought." "Chinese Walls didn't keep the Mongols out of China," says House Commerce Committee chairman John D. Dingell, "and they haven't kept the miscreant on Wall St. out of the honey pot either." Dingell added that he was looking at possible remedies, which he declined to specify. The most radical step would be enactment of a law similar to the Glass-Stegall Act, which divorced investment from commercial banking. In this case, investment banks would be barred from arbitrage activities.

The second aspect of the rules of the game debate is how to better enforce existing regulations. This involves surveillance, subpoenaed information, and punishment. Improving surveillance relies on computer systems which efficiently and speedily police the market. The system works based on detecting patterns of trading by charting price increases or decreases. If price jumps occur which are not easily explained and contain suspicious patterns of stock dealings, there is a database which tracks these trades. In this way, the suspicious trades can be traced back to the broker. Computer surveillance can show when, at what price, and for whom the trade was executed. Before the advent of this technology, it took six weeks

to detect who had bought the stock. It now can be done in less than two hours.

The New York Stock Exchange's Automatic Search and Match System (ASAM) was set up in 1985. It stores information about 500,000 American executives. Unbelievably, it stores information pertaining to the clubs they belong to, where they live, and where they used to work.[36] ASAM is used to point out links between names of traders and their backgrounds. The question of whether or not ASAM is an invasion of privacy will probably have to be settled in the courts. Using ASAM, the Stock Exchange has detected many suspicious trades, which the SEC uses as the base of their investigations. Once suspicious patterns are discovered, the SEC has the power to subpoena witnesses for information. It may also investigate whomever it wishes whenever it wishes.

All this modern equipment, however, did not lead to arrests in the Levine-Boesky-Milken-DBL scandal. It took an anonymous postcard from Venezuela to bring these giants down. Many problems still remain. The SEC has major problems dealing with suspects who trade under different names and accounts. Another problem arises with foreign accounts. To remedy this, the SEC, Britain, and Switzerland have mutually agreed to divulge the names behind secretive accounts if the evidence is strong enough. However, the problem remains formidable.

Many people think that stiffer penalties are called for. Currently, the maximum sentence for a defendant in an insider trading case is five years. Perhaps ten years would be more of a deterrent. In addition, the SEC and Justice Department must enforce these penalties and cut down on plea bargaining.

As international trading of equities expands into the future, cooperation between regulators of all countries will have to improve greatly. The government could make these illegal dealings more difficult by unifying takeover rules and requiring prompter disclosure of large shareholdings. Until insider trading has a uniform definition across all borders, it will not be eliminated.

With the addition of modern surveillance equipment, the balance of risk and reward has been pushed to new levels. These regulations will affect the speed and shear numbers which have characterized the rash of mergers and takeovers in the 1980s.[37]

NOTES

1. Tim Metz and Michael W. Miller, "Boesky's Rise and Fall Illustrate a Compulsion to Profit by Getting Inside Track on Market." *Wall Street Journal* (November 17, 1986), p. 28.

2. Ivan F. Boesky, (Jeffrey Madrick, ed.), *Merger Mania.* New York: Holt, Rinehart and Winston, 1985, p. v.

3. Chris Welles and Gary Weiss, "The Man Who Made a Career of Tempting Fate." *Business Week* (December 1, 1986), pp. 34–35; James B. Stewart and Daniel Hertzberg, "Boesky Sentence Ends Chapter in Scandal." *Wall Street Journal* (December 21, 1987), p. 2; and Robert J. Cole, "Guilty Plea Entered by Boesky," *New York Times* (April 24, 1987), pp. D1, D2.

4. *U.K. News,* "Hearing Reveals More of Guinness Jigsaw" (January 28, 1988), p. 11; *Business Week,* "I Say, Old Boy, Did You Hear . . ." (December 5, 1988), p. 49; Blanca Riener, "Insider Trading Shock Rocks the Elysee." *Business Week* (January 23, 1989), p. 54; Steven Greenhouse, "French Report Finds Inside Trading." *New York Times* (February 1, 1989), p. D6; Steven Greenhouse, "Modest Insider Trading Stir Is a Huge Scandal in France." *New York Times* (January 30, 1989), pp. 1, D9; John Rossant and Frank J. Comes, "The Paris Bourse Calls in the Gendarmes." *Business Week* (March 28, 1988), p. 41.

5. *Business Week,* "Just How Corrupt Is Wall Street" (January 9, 1989), pp. 34–36.

6. Ibid.; See also *Business Week,* "And the Next Test Will Be Giuliani vs. Milken" (January 9, 1989), p. 37.

7. Ann Hagedorn and Stephen J. Ader, "Milken Challenge to Parts of Drexel Pact with U.S.—Unlikely to Prevent Settlement." *Wall Street Journal* (February 13, 1989), p. 1; Judith H. Dobrzynski, "After Drexel." *Business Week* (February 26, 1990), pp. 36–40.

8. V. Brudney, "Insiders, Outsiders and Information." *Harvard Law Review,* 93 (1980), pp. 322–26; J. Templeman, "The Insider-Trading

Dragnet Is Stretching across the Globe." *Business Week* (March 23, 1987), pp. 50–51; Gary Weiss and A. Bianco, "Suddenly the Fish Get Bigger." *Business Week* (March 2, 1987), pp. 28–32; *Wall Street Journal,* "What Happened to 50 People Involved in Insider Trading Cases" (November 18, 1987), p. 22; *Chiarella* v. United States, U.S. 63 L. Ed. 2d 348, 100 Stamford, Conn. (1980); *Fordham Urban Law Journal,* "Rule 1065: Birth of the Concept of Market Insider and Its Application in a Criminal Case—United States v. Chiarella," 8, no. 2 (1979–80), p. 457; Bill Sing, "Drexel Takes a Beating But 'Junk Bond' Field Appears Alive and Well." *Los Angeles Times* (December 22, 1988), p. 1.; Stephen Labaton, "Jefferies Says He Destroyed Notes on Trades." *New York Times* (January 6, 1989), p. D4; James B. Stewart and Matthew Winkler, "Merrill Lynch Aide, Israeli Face Trading Charges." *Wall Street Journal* (March 12, 1987), p. 3; James B. Stewart and Daniel Hertzberg, "SEC Charges Insider Trading in Morgan Deals." *Wall Street Journal* (June 28, 1988), p. 3; Karen Blumenthal, "Maxus Sues Kidder, Siegel, Boesky for Damages in Alleged Insider Trades." *Wall Street Journal* (November 24, 1987), p. 2; Andy Pasztor, "Thayer Enters Plea of Guilty in Trading Case." *Wall Street Journal* (March 5, 1985), p. 4; James B. Stewart and Daniel Hertzberg, "Inside Trading Scandal Implicates High Aides at Goldman, Kilder." *Wall Street Journal* (February 13, 1987), p. 1.

9. United States Court of Appeals, Second Circuit, *Securities and Exchange Commission, Plaintiff-Appellant,* v. *Texas Gulf Sulphur Co., a Texas Corporation, et al., Defendants-Appellants,* 401 F.2d 833 (August 13, 1968), 446 F.2d 1301 (June 10, 1971); S. Prakash Sethi, "Securities and Exchange Commission vs. Texas Gulf Sulphur Company," *Up Against the Corporate Wall,* 4th ed. (Englewood Cliffs, N.J.: Prentice-Hall, 1982), pp. 288–316.

10. James B. Stewart, "Death of a Theory? Supreme Court May Revamp Insider-Trading

Law." *Wall Street Journal* (September 30, 1987), p. 39; Stuart Taylor, Jr., "Justices, 8–0, Back Winans Conviction in Misuse of Data." *New York Times* (November 17, 1987), pp. D1, D11.

11. G. Robert Blakely, "RICO's Triple Damage Threat—The Public's Secret Weapon vs. Boesky." *New York Times* (December 12, 1987), p. A1.

12. Gregory A. Robb, "S.E.C. Offers Legal Definition of Insider Trading in Stocks." *New York Times* (August 8, 1987), pp. 1, 34.

13. Thomas E. Ricks, "SEC Proposes Insider-Trading Measure That Includes Misappropriation Theory." *Wall Street Journal* (November 20, 1987), p. 4; Nathaniel C. Nash, "S.E.C. Submits Plan on Insider Trading." *New York Times* (November 20, 1987), pp. D1, D6.

14. Nathaniel Nash, "Stiffer Penalties on Insider Trades and Rewards for Informers Voted." *New York Times* (November 20, 1987), pp. D1, D6.

15. Securities and Exchange Commission, Litigation Release No. 11905, May 12, 1986.

16. Thomas J. Lueck, "Levine gets 2-Year Jail Term." *New York Times* (February 21, 1987), pp. 33, 36.

17. James Sterngold, "Taping by Levine Called Part of U.S. Insider Investigation." *New York Times* (November 24, 1986), pp. D1, D6.

18. Securities and Exchange Commission, Litigation Release No. 11288, November 14, 1986.

19. *New York Times*, "How 3 Insider Deals Worked, as Detailed by U.S." (November 16, 1986), p. 34.

20. *The Economist*, "Ivan Boesky—Who Says Crime Doesn't Pay?" (July 11, 1987), pp. 79–80.

21. Robert J. Cole, "Wall Street's Defensive Line." *New York Times* (March 30, 1987), pp. D1, D6.

22. Stephen J. Adler and Laurie P. Cohen, "Drexel Faces a Stockholder Suit Claiming Injury from Wrongdoing Alleged by SEC." *Wall Street Journal* (September 9, 1988), p. 8.

23. Kurt Eichenwald, "Drexel Burnham Fights Back." *New York Times* (September 11, 1988), pp. F1, F8.

24. *New York Times*, "As Key Executives Face Charges, It Appears Wall St. Itself Is on Trial" (February 15, 1987), p. 38.

25. Tim Metz and Michael W. Miller, "Boesky's Rise and Fall Illustrate a Compulsion to Profit by Getting Inside Track on Market." *Wall Street Journal* (November 17, 1986), p. 28.

26. Ibid.

27. Ibid.

28. Ibid.

29. Ivan F. Boesky, (Jeffrey Madrick, ed.), *Merger Mania—Arbitrage: Wall Street's Best Kept Secret*. New York: Holt, Rinehart and Winston, 1985, p. 30; William Criddle, "They Can't See There's a Victor." *New York TImes* (February 22, 1987), p. D1.

30. *Business Week*, "Across The Globe" (March 23, 1987), pp. 50–51.

31. Templeman, "Insider-Trading Dragnet," pp. 50–51.

32. Fred A. Bleaksdley, "Losses by 'Arabs' Put Near $2 Billion." *New York Times* (November 15, 1986), pp. D1, D9; Stephen Labaton, "Business and the Law: A Green Light in Boesky Suit." *New York Times* (November 23, 1987), p. D2; and Clive Wolman, "Boesky Partners' Assets May Lead to Legal Claims." *Financial Times* (May 7, 1987), p. 7.

33. *New York Times*, "Insider Cases and Penalties" (February 19, 1988), p. D3.

34. Stephen Labaton, "Drexel Concedes Guilt on Trading." *New York Times* (December 23, 1988), p. 1.

35. Chris Welles, "A Big Crack in the 'Chinese Wall.'" *Business Week* (March 2, 1987), p. 33.

36. *The Economist*, "Rules for the City" (February 7, 1987), pp. 17–18, 75–76.

37. *The Economist*, "The Chairman Says" (February 21, 1987), p. 11.

INSIDER TRADING

ALDAVE, B. B. "The Misappropriation Theory: Carpenter [*Carpenter* v. *U.S.*, 108 S. Ct. 316] and Its Aftermath." *Ohio State Law Journal*, 49 (1988), pp. 373–91.

CEUVAS, C. J. "The Misappropriation Theory and Rule 10b-5: Deadlock in the Supreme Court." *Journal of Corporation Law,* 13 (Spring 1988), pp. 793–822.

"A Comparative Analysis of Recent Accords Which Facilitate Transnational SEC Investigations of Insider Trading. *Maryland Journal of International Law and Trade,* 11 (Summer 1987), pp. 243–81.

COX, C. C., and FOGARTY, K. S. "Bases of Insider Trading Law." *Ohio State Law Journal,* 49 (1988), pp. 353–72.

"Defining 'Insider Trading': A Symposium." *Alabama Law Review,* 39 (Winter 1988), pp. 337–558.

DOUGLAS, NORMAN S. "Insider Trading: The Case against the 'Victimless Crime' Hypothesis." *Financial Review,* 23 (May 1988), pp. 127–42.

FRANTZ, DOUGLAS. *Levine & Company: Wall Street's Insider Trading Scandal.* New York: Holt, Rinehart & Winston, 1987.

GARTEN, HELEN A. "Insider Trading in the Corporate Interest." *Wisconsin Law Review,* 4 (1987), pp. 573–640.

GHOSAL, MONOJIT, and KENNETH L. STANLEY. "Insiders Can Disclose and Trade—or Can They?" *Mid-American Journal of Business,* 3 (Spring 1988), pp. 27–31.

HAGEN, W. W. "Insider Trading under Rule 10b-5: The Theoretical Bases for Liability." *Business Lawyer,* 44 (November 1988), pp. 13–41.

"The Impact of the SEC's Cases against Levine and Boesky on the Activities of Investment Bankers and Arbitrageurs. *Washington University Law Quarterly,* 65 (1987), pp. 282–92.

LAWSON, G. "The Ethics of Insider Trading." *Harvard Journal of Law and Public Policy,* 11 (Summer 1988), pp. 727–83.

MACEY, J. R. "Ethics, Economics, and Insider Trading: Ayn Rand Meets the Theory of the Firm." *Harvard Journal of Law and Public Policy,* 11 (Summer 1988), pp. 785–804.

"The Mail and Wire Fraud Statute's Protection of Property Extends to Intangibles such as Confidential Business Information: Carpenter v. United States, 108 S. Ct. 316." *Texas Tech Law Review,* 19 (1988), pp. 1531–55.

MARINELLI, A. J. "Liability for Insider Trading: Expansion of Liability in Rule 10b-5 Cases." *Akron Law Review,* 22 (Summer 1988), pp. 45–60.

"The Misappropriation Theory: The Wrong Answer to the Chiarella [*Chiarella* v. *U.S.,* 100 S. Ct. 1108] Question. *New York Law School Law Review,* 32 (1987), pp. 701–27.

PHILLIPS, D. M. "An Essay: Six Competing Currents of Rule 10b-5 Jurisprudence." *Indiana Law Review,* 21 (Summer 1988), pp. 625–67.

SAMUELSON, S. S. "The Prevention of Insider Trading: A Proposal for Revising Section 16 of the Securities Exchange Act of 1934. *Harvard Journal of Legislation,* 25 (Summer 1988), pp. 511–31.

"SEC Civil Remedies for Insider Trading Actions under Section 10(b) of the Securities Exchange Act of 1934 and rule 10b-5." *University of Cincinnati Law Review* 57 (1988), pp. 679–98.

STEVENS, MARK. *Insiders: The Truth behind the Scandal Rocking Wall Street.* New York: Putnam, 1987.

"Symposium: Defining 'Insider Trading.'" *Alabama Law Review,* 39 (Winter 1988), pp. 337–58.

"To Catch a Thief: The Misappropriation Theory and Securities Fraud." *Marquette Law Review,* 70 (Summer 1987), pp. 692–724.

"Toward a Definition of Insider Trading." *Stanford Law Review,* 41 (January 1989), pp. 377–99.

·III·

Corporate Advocacy and Grass-Roots Lobbying

CHEMICAL MANUFACTURERS ASSOCIATION, WASHINGTON, D.C.

*Educational advertising campaign to change public perception
and awareness of the chemical industry's activities
and contributions to American society*

It does not come as a surprise to any informed reader that the chemical industry has had a poor public image and has suffered a lack of public credibility concerning its commitment to environmental safety. The past decade has witnessed a successive increase in new laws and regulations subjecting the chemical industry to greater restrictions in product development, manufacturing, sales, and waste disposal.

In 1979, the Chemical Manufacturers Association (CMA) convened a special Communications Task Group comprised of selected industry communication managers. Their objective was to consider, develop,

Adapted from S. Prakash Sethi, *Handbook of Advocacy Advertising: Concepts, Strategies and Applications* (Cambridge, Mass.: Ballinger Publishing Company, 1987), pp. 317–36.

and revise the CMA communications program to address the industry's credibility problems. The committee decided to institute a public education and communication campaign to change public opinion about some of the environmental and health hazards commonly associated with the chemical industry. The campaign lasted from 1980 to 1983 and cost almost $8 million. The campaign and the issues it raised for the chemical industry and the business community are the subjects of this case.

The campaign was not an unusual action. An increasing number of corporations, industry and trade groups, religious organizations, public interest groups and community organizations, foreign governments, and even individuals have resorted to advocacy advertising and public communication campaigns to influence public opinion and government policy makers.

WHAT IS ADVOCACY ADVERTISING?

Advocacy advertising, including idea-issue advertising, is part of the genre of advertising known as corporate image or institutional advertising.[1] It is concerned with the propagation of ideas and the elucidation of controversial social issues deemed important in terms of public policy. The managerial context of advocacy advertising is that of defending or promoting a sponsor's activities, modus operandi, and position on controversial issues of public policy. The behavioral and social context of advocacy advertising is that of changing public perception of a sponsor's actions and performance from skepticism and hostility to trust and acceptance—and/or to a more neutral position. The political context of advocacy advertising is that of the constitutional safeguards for freedom of speech; a sponsor is asserting its right to speak out on issues of public importance without any regulation or censorship. Thus, the political context of advocacy advertising encompasses even allegedly purely educational messages where the issues raised involve important matters of public policy, perhaps of a controversial nature, and the sponsor's objective is to heighten public awareness of those issues or some preferred options for their resolution.

Although advocacy advertising has been practiced for a long time in the United States, the latest and perhaps most intensive spurt began with the Arab oil boycott of the early 1970s. No doubt the boycott was spurred in large measure by a spate of advocacy campaigns launched by oil companies, notably Mobil Oil Corporation. Furthermore, in the late 1960s and early 1970s, corporations faced broad public attacks and more intensive government regulation because of increased national concern for a cleaner environment, health and safety, and a better quality of life. Hence, other early entrants into the advocacy advertising fra-

cas, in addition to oil, were chemical, mineral, heavy (smokestack), and forestry industries.

During the mid-1970s, the public gave big business poor marks for credibility and responsibility. In this same period, there was a national trend toward corporations speaking out in print advertising on issues they felt to be important to the public and to themselves. It is in this environment that the chemical industry initiated its advocacy campaign.

ISSUES FOR ANALYSIS

The CMA campaign raised a number of issues that deserve serious consideration:

1. To what extent can advocacy advertising contribute to a greater public understanding of the problems confronted by American business in general and the chemical industry in particular?

2. What is the public perception of such advertising in terms of its accuracy and objectivity? Should such advertising present only the sponsor's viewpoint, or should it present other significant viewpoints?

3. How important, from the public viewpoint, are the various issues selected for such campaigns? What should be the process of identifying salient issues?

4. Should trade associations such as CMA involve themselves in such campaigns, or should the campaigns be the domain of individual companies?

5. What objectives did CMA pursue through this campaign? To what extent were the objectives in the public interest in addition to serving the interests of the industry?

6. What are the options available to the public for hearing opposing viewpoints when the advocacy advertising of large corporations and industry groups overwhelms and distorts the flow of information available to public? Is this a real concern given the large multiplicity of news media and information

channels available to the public? If so, what alternative mechanisms nee 1 to be considered?

7. How effective was the CMA campaign in terms of changing public opinion in the long term?

8. How might one evaluate the effectiveness of copy and media strategies and advertising budgets given CMA's goals and objectives?

CMA: ORGANIZATION, STRUCTURE, AND MEMBERSHIP

The CMA represents the chemical industry in America. Founded in 1872, CMA is the oldest chemical trade organization in the western hemisphere. The association includes about 200 member companies, most in the United States, with some in Canada. The size of CMA's member companies and the products they make are as varied as chemistry itself. Together, they represent a major portion of the productive capacity of the industry.

The association, with headquarters in Washington, D.C., has a permanent staff of approximately one hundred and sixty-five, headed by a full-time president. Its board of directors is composed of major executives of its member companies.

In recent years, CMA's role as the chemical industry's advocate has accelerated, becoming the focal point of many of the association's activities. CMA advocates industry positions in Congress, in the regulatory agencies, and in the executive and judicial branches. Equally important, CMA communicates information to the media across the nation.

According to a CMA brochure, the association has been in the forefront of transportation safety, occupational safety, and health and environmental protection. Recently, it has led the way in energy conservation and in solving waste disposal problems.[2] The CMA brochure describes the benefits of the association to its members in the following terms:

> Measured monetarily, CMA activities are estimated to be worth billions of dollars each year, More than $1 billion are saved annually by reducing future increases in freight charges; more than $100 million are saved each year through the development of proper engineering standards. In a recent year CMA saved several billion dollars by deflecting inappropriate environmental and workplace laws, rules and excessive taxes without endangering public health or employee safety.[3]

CMA's board and executive committees establish policy and define program areas. Responsibility for issue monitoring and development in those areas is assigned to an authorized standing committee. Each committee is usually composed of 15 industry representatives. Under the direction of the association president, the staff is responsible for implementing and communicating policy and helping the committees with their work. The staff is organized into five departments: (1) government relations, (2) technical, (3) communication, (4) administration, and (5) office of general counsel.

The communications department, which is responsible for public communication, is divided into the communications committee and the communications policy review special committee (now defunct). The communications committee has a major influence on the CMA Communications Program and comprehensive public relations activities. These programs communicate the industry's renewed commitment to doing a responsible job of protecting the public and its employees from the health and safety risks of chemicals. The communications policy review special committee was a board of directors committee which reviewed the overall direction, design, and operations of CMA's communication program. This has become the responsibility of the communications committee.

Decision-Making Process and Program Approval

The first step in developing a communications strategy is to decide on the size and shape of the problem and to come up with a tailor-made plan for remedial action. A special task force of 12 industry communication experts spent several months developing such a plan. Although CMA's vice-president for public relations participated in all discussions, the plan was developed by the industry. The next step was to persuade other members to accept this proposal.

In May 1979, the 13-member executive committee of CMA's 45-member board of directors approved the draft plan and appropriated funds for further development. A copy of the draft plan and a request for comments was sent to executives in member companies who acted as contacts with CMA. After receiving members' comments, the task force revised the plan and again sent it to all members. At this time, a public relations consulting agency, a public opinion research firm, and an advertising agency were retained for basic polling, programming, and advertisement development.

Two months later, four regional conferences were conducted across the country to explain the program to industry personnel and to encourage involvement. Different presentations were given to lay out the basics of the plan and to explain the importance of member company participation. Target audiences and major markets were pinpointed, and each communication medium was described along with its role in the overall campaign.

ANTECEDENTS TO THE CAMPAIGN

Research data on public concerns about chemicals and the chemical industry were provided by various companies. Monsanto contributed its proprietary research in its "Chemical Facts of Life" campaign, and Shell contributed data from its 1978 cancer study. Other bits and pieces were also contributed by industry members. The subcommittee reviewed the data and came to the following conclusions:

1. The American public was already convinced that chemicals contributed to the high American standard of living. Thus, the subcommittee felt that there was no need to embark on a campaign to defend that position.

2. The American public was nevertheless apprehensive about hazards to their well-being posed by chemicals in the environment. The subcommittee, accordingly, felt that this was a subject area that the CMA communications campaign might address.

The task force received these conclusions and ultimately accepted them. Accordingly, the theme chosen for the CMA communications program was to increase public recognition that the chemical industry is committed to doing a responsible job to protect the public from the health and safety risks of chemicals.

LINKAGE BETWEEN CMA'S EFFORTS AND MEMBER COMPANIES

No communication program, no matter how good, will achieve its goals if industry performance is not there to begin with. CMA argued that the industry was already paying heavily because of its poor image. For example, the chemical industry was spending more money than any other industry in cleaning up pollution, and had spent $15.3 billion to date on pollution control. However, because of the industry's communication gap, the public did not know about it.

CMA emphasized to its members that

the association's communication effort was intimately related to the total industry communication effort, including the product advertising of individual firms. The CMA Communications Program would emphasize issues, and more importantly, would undertake the difficult but necessary job of dealing with risks. On their part, individual chemical companies would continue to emphasize products and the benefits of chemicals.

This division of effort was based on the fact that associations, rather than companies, can best discuss industry-wide issues, particularly major public issues. Also, an association can act as a lightning rod on controversial issues, taking some of the heat off members.

CMA emphasized to members repeatedly that advertising, while representing the bulk of the program's cost, was one part of a multifaceted program.[4] The association's early efforts to explain the importance of the program to members paid off. In November 1979, the CMA executive committee and the board of directors approved the Communications Program in principle, but they decided that one more across-the-board effort should be made to inform the industry on the plan's objectives, scope, and content. Finally, in January 1980, a full year after planning had begun, the board gave approval to the initial $6.1 million two-year package.

The objective of the program was specifically spelled out to members: to broaden public recognition of the chemical industry's commitment to protecting the public from the health and safety risks associated with its products and services. Five areas were identified as topics to be discussed in the program: transportation safety, environmental protection, product safety, worker safety, and hazardous waste disposal. CMA repeatedly emphasized that the members were themselves primarily responsible for the program's success or failure because, notwithstanding the effectiveness of the communications program, it was industry performance that alone could lend credibility to the program's message.

PROGRAM IMPLEMENTATION

Board approval was followed by a conference in Washington, D.C., in order that people throughout the industry could discuss different ways of implementing the CMA program. The conference underscored several themes: the need for support from chief executive officers, the importance of delegating one person to be in charge of program implementation within a company, a recognition that work on this program would help an employee in his or her career, and the importance of personalizing messages in speeches and letters signed by the chief executive officer.

The CMA board next established a permanent, 15-member communications committee. James Sites, vice-president for communications, served as the committee's staff executive. Working with the CMA staff, the committee guided program development and implementation. A policy review group, made up of five members of the board (now defunct), was also established.[5] Once the program was developed, its implementation was monitored on a continuing basis, eliminating the need for the policy review group.

Once the theme was selected, the task force looked at what syndicated data were telling them. The 1979 Yankelovich Corporate Priorities data, the latest data available at the time, showed that the following proportions of Americans viewed the chemicals industry as doing a poor job in complying with laws and guidelines in the following areas:

Waste disposal	61%
Air pollution	56%
Water pollution	51%
Worker safety	36%
Transportation safety	Data not available
Product safety	32%

The preceding topics, therefore, were selected as themes for the first year's campaign. The task group discussed extensively the unique position of CMA in addressing these themes. It agreed that acknowledging the potential of environmental pollution caused by the chemical industry was not something any one company would wish to do.

After these decisions had been made, the 1980 benchmark survey by Cambridge Reports was designed and carried out. The purpose of the benchmark was to establish precampaign data on the target audiences against which campaign effectiveness could be measured. It examined attitudes toward the chemical industry compared to other business sectors. Among the major findings were the following:

1. The public is well aware of and appreciates the benefits of chemicals; likes what the chemical industry makes; but is afraid the chemical industry is out to poison them through sloppy and irresponsible operating practices.

2. The public sees chemicals as the greatest threat to the environment and a significant cause of cancer. Fifty percent believe the chemical industry does a poor job of controlling water pollution; 44% believe the industry does a poor job of controlling air pollution; 38% think the industry does a poor job of observing worker safety rules. More than 50% believe there is more cancer now than 10 years ago; 47% see chemical food additives as a cause of cancer; 44% see chemical plant air pollution as a cause of cancer; 42% see pesticides as cancer-causing; 33% percent see chemical plant water pollution as cancer-causing. Thirty-three percent see the industry as doing especially poorly in providing enough information to consumers; only 15% see the chemical industry as socially responsible.

According to one leading advertising professional, "[fifteen percent] of any sample are mavericks who like to take the opposite side of any questions. So there is a fair chance that no one really saw the industry as really irresponsible."[5] Half the public said they wanted strong government regulation of the chemical industry, despite the public's bias against further government involvement in most other things.

Faced with these findings, industry executives realized that such a negative image had adverse effects on the industry's public image as well as on its relations with government, employees, and the financial community. Inherent in their objectives was a desire to reduce the public pressure for restrictive legislation. Therefore, the industry required a new approach to help people understand what it was doing to protect them from the health and safety risks of chemicals. What the industry needed most was a dialogue between it and the public to create an agreement on an acceptable balance between risks and benefits.

With much research data in hand, the CMA launched its Chemical Industry Communications Action Program (ChemCAP), now known as the CMA communications program, which was to complement CMA's comprehensive public relations activities. CMA's advocacy advertising was a major element of this program. The objective of the advertising program, like the overall program, was to increase recognition that the chemical industry is committed to doing a responsible job to protect the public from the health and safety risks of chemicals.

THE ADVERTISING CAMPAIGN

Since the CMA program did not have the resources to cover the entire population, certain key groups of individuals that most intimately affect public attitudes and the public policy formation process became priority target audiences. These included politically active individuals, government representatives, educators, communicators, and "plan neighbors"—those living in areas of major chemical plant concentration. Active individuals were defined as the estimated 14 million people who participated in two or more public actions other than voting (such as writing to elected officials or playing leadership roles in local civic or political organizations) within the past year.

The campaign was developed by the Brouillard Communications Division of the J. Walter Thompson advertising agency. It was designed for the print media and included thought-leader magazines and major newspapers in Washington and New York: *Time, Newsweek, U.S. News & World Report, Harper's, Atlantic, Smithsonian,* the *New Yorker, Psychology Today, Natural History,* the *New York Times,* the *Washington Post,* and the *Washington Star.* There were some adjustments in this media schedule from year to year.

Campaign Budget

The advertising expenditures for 1980–1981 were slightly over $3 million. They were reduced to $2.52 million for 1981–1982 and $2.25 million for 1982–1983.

Copy Themes

The first phase (1980–1981) of advertising—a *Scientific American*-type campaign—presented the five areas of concern in such a way as to display the chemical industry as one of high technology and scientific innovations. The first ad dealt with the issue of managing chemical wastes. The second dealt with improving chemical product safety (see Exhibit 1), and the third discussed the issue of worker safety (see Exhibit 2). Although these ads proved to be persuasive and able to communicate a message, they had a low stopping power. The human interest format was adopted when research by Brouillard Communications showed the personalized advertisements to be more effective.

The second phase (1982) was aimed at showing that chemical industry engineers and scientists are just like other citizens,

with normal family concerns; emphasizing that these scientists are responsible citizens and concerned about the environment; and pointing out that they would not be working for the chemical industry if they did not believe that the industry is concerned with producing safe products and also protecting the environment. It was felt that a scientist-employee as a spokesperson would have better public credibility than a professional model, well-known public figure, or corporate executive. Copies of two such advertisements are shown in Exhibits 3 and 4.

In both phases, ads were run in single-page and double-page formats. And in both, the copy themes and layouts were designed to show audiences that the chemical industry was doing a great deal to protect the public from the risks associated with chemicals.

MEASURING AD CAMPAIGN EFFECTIVENESS

CMA undertook two tracking studies in 1981 and 1982 to measure the effectiveness of the ad campaign. The studies were conducted by Cambridge Research Associates. Most of the questions asked in the 1981 and 1982 questionnaires were the same as those asked in the 1980 benchmark survey. Interviews were conducted with 900 politically active individuals and 200 "plan neighbors." The first tracking study to measure the impact of the CMA advertising campaign took place during January and February of 1981. For principal topics were discussed in this survey.

— What is the present image of the chemical industry?

— Have attitudes toward the chemical industry in the target audience (political actives) changed in the last year?

— How aware of the CMA advertising campaign are the target audiences?

— How well is the CMA advertising campaign working?

EXHIBIT 1

Improving Chemical Product Safety

What we're doing to minimize risks to people's health and the environment

America's chemical industry invests millions of dollars each year to make our products as safe as we can. For example, we're building new test facilities and using new, highly sophisticated research equipment. When necessary, we're also searching for alternatives. Still, we're not satisfied. Here's how we're trying to do a better job:

1.
Funding an independent test facility

To supplement their own toxicology laboratories, 35 chemical companies have joined to create the Chemical Industry Institute of Toxicology (CIIT), a $14 million research facility at Research Triangle Park, near Raleigh, North Carolina. The purpose: to develop and use more reliable methods to assess the possible effects of chemicals on people and the environment. The institute has total operating independence. It also operates non-profit and is the first facility of its kind in the world.

CIIT's efforts focus on three mutually supportive areas: testing, research and professional training. At present, CIIT is conducting research on the most commonly used chemicals, evaluating them by today's more stringent standards. Informa-

tion developed by the institute is provided openly and simultaneously to the entire chemical industry, the government and the public. We believe this underscores our entire industry's commitment to making sure our products meet—or exceed—today's exacting health and safety standards.

2.
Increasing on-site research

Seven major chemical companies already have multi-million dollar toxicological laboratories as large as, or larger than, the CIIT facilities. Other chemical companies are opening new research and testing laboratories and adding to existing research facilities. These facilities help companies develop the fullest body of knowledge about their own products should questions

ever arise about their proper use, handling characteristics and overall safety.

3.
Finding safer new chemicals and products

When scientific information casts suspicion on the safety of a chemical substance, we search for safer alternatives and develop safeguards. For example, we helped in the development of biodegradable detergents to replace ordinary detergents that created environmental problems. Another example: cellulose acetate film was developed to eliminate the extreme fire hazard that was posed by nitrocellulose film.

4.
Improving detection methods

Steady, sometimes dramatic improvements in scientific measurement techniques and

EXHIBIT 1 (cont.)

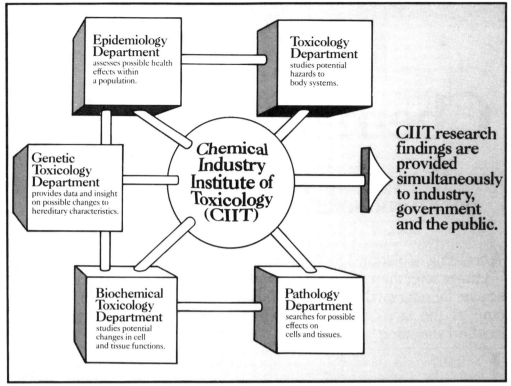

The Chemical Industry Institute of Toxicology, an independent research facility funded by members of the chemical industry, conducts research and testing on commonly used chemicals to help protect people's health and the environment.

equipment have brought about a million-fold increase in our ability to analyze chemicals. One instrument, the gas chromatograph-mass spectrometer, for example, helps us detect materials at levels as low as one part per trillion—equal to one grain in an 18-foot layer of sand covering a football field.

5.
Expanding the flow of safety information

Many member companies of the Chemical Manufacturers Association prepare Material Safety Data Sheets on chemicals and chemical products. These sheets, introduced as a voluntary effort by our industry nearly 50 years ago, are designed to give technical people, plant workers and down-stream processors data to help them safely handle chemical substances. The sheets include information on safe handling techniques, appropriate storage and possible hazards, along with health and emergency instructions in case of chemical accidents.

What you've read here is just an overview. For a booklet that tells more about what we're doing to improve chemical product safety, write to: Chemical Manufacturers Association, Dept. ET-08, Box 363, Beltsville, Md. 20705.

America's Chemical Industry
The member companies of the Chemical Manufacturers Association

EXHIBIT 2

Protecting Chemical Workers

How we're improving one of the best health and safety records in U.S. industry

According to National Safety Council figures, chemical workers are 2.3 times safer than the average employee in American industry. In fact, they are far safer on the job than off. But we're still not satisfied. Here are some of the steps we're taking to make the working environment healthful and safer:

1.
Improving detection techniques

New and more sophisticated devices for monitoring the environment are worn by many workers. Many plants have "area monitoring devices" spotted in strategic locations. Some of these devices change color or sound an alarm to alert workers to even minute traces of contaminants. Others, like the gas chromatograph-mass spectrometer, measure contaminant quantities as low as one part per trillion—equivalent to one second in 32,000 years. Data from these and other measuring devices are analyzed by computer and compared with employee health records to help make sure that exposure is kept at safe levels. (See illustration.)

2.
Upgrading educational programs

Chemical companies are intensifying their safety education programs, especially with videotapes and other visual aid techniques. One company has an 82-page listing of videotape cassettes. It also has an index of safety standards that runs to about 60 pages. And each standard can run as long as 50 pages. The effect of this training goes beyond the plant. Chemical workers learn to "think safety." So they have fewer accidents than the average industrial employee —not only at work, but also on their own time.

3.
Expanding laboratory studies

Throughout the chemical industry, thousands of people are working on new and faster ways to determine the long-term effects of chemicals. It is not an easy job. Doing a study on just one chemical can take over three years and cost more than $1,000,000. To advance this work, 30 chemical com-

EXHIBIT 2 (cont.)

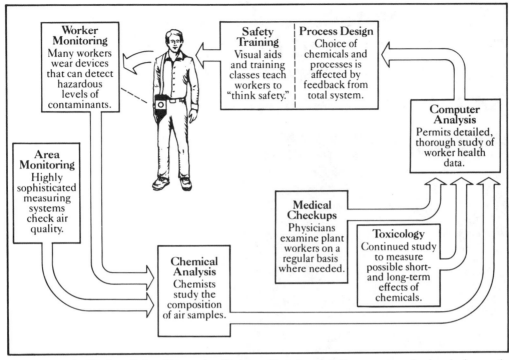

Example of a Worker Safety Protection System: Data from health exams, monitoring devices and laboratory studies are analyzed to identify situations that may require immediate action and to provide information for possible improvements in process design and safety training.

panies have joined to create the Chemical Industry Institute of Toxicology located near Raleigh, North Carolina. The Institute shares its findings with the entire industry, the U.S. Government and the public.

4. "Engineering out"risks

When tests cast suspicion on the safety of a substance, we often find substitutes. There is a constant search for safer chemicals. If necessary, we may redesign the entire manufacturing process to make it safer.

5. Monitoring employee health more closely

The number of industrial hygienists has tripled in the past 10 years. And they are only part of the picture. Many chemical companies now use *interdisciplinary* teams to monitor employee health. A typical team consists of industrial hygienists, physicians, toxicologists and engineers. These teams then multiply their effectiveness by using the latest computer technology to process and study the data they collect. The results help chemical companies anticipate and control threats to worker health and safety better than ever before.

For more information, write: Chemical Manufacturers Association, Department BT-05, P.O. Box 363, Beltsville, Maryland 20705.

America's Chemical Industry
The member companies of the Chemical Manufacturers Association

EXHIBIT 3

"I'm a chemical industry engineer but a concerned father first. I'm working to improve water quality for my kids and yours."

Larry Washington, Manager of Environmental Services for a major chemical company, with daughters Lori and Danielle.

"Clean water is one of our most precious resources," says Larry Washington. "The chemical industry has more than 10,000 specialists working to control pollution and protect the environment.

"One of my responsibilities is to make sure the wastewater discharged from our plant is environmentally acceptable. That means removing suspended solids and using techniques such as carbon adsorption, filtration and biological treatment. It can also mean raising the oxygen content of the water so there's more than enough to support fish in the river.

"I like my job because I know I'm helping the chemical industry improve water quality for my family, yours and for generations to come. We're spending more on pollution control than any other industry. We've already spent $7 billion on protecting the environment, with more than $3.7 billion of that money going just for cleaner water.

"Frequent monitoring is part of our commitment to clean water. We monitor the water as it goes into the river. We monitor the river after our water is mixed with it. At my plant, I know we're doing things right."

For a booklet with more information on how we're protecting people and the environment, write: Chemical Manufacturers Association, Department KY-104, P.O. Box 363, Beltsville, MD 20705.

America's Chemical Industry

The member companies of
the Chemical Manufacturers Association

EXHIBIT 4

"As a chemist who helps decide how industry wastes are managed, my standards are high. As a father, even higher."

Peter Briggs, Senior Advisor, Environmental Analysis, at a major chemical and mining company, with sons Chris and Jonathan.

"I spend most of my time on the job developing progressive company policies to protect the environment. Throughout the chemical industry, there are more than 10,000 specialists like me whose major concern is controlling pollution.

"When I was hired, I was told I was to be the conscience of my company," says Peter Briggs. "I'm concerned about the environment. I want it to be clean for my kids, as well as everybody else's.

"To dispose of chemical wastes, for instance, we use recycling, incineration and other methods, such as building secure landfills with thick, compacted clay linings. Then we check regularly to make sure liquids do not escape.

"In fact, my company has a whole internal Environmental Review Group that works constantly to monitor current operations and improve our standards. They descend on our operations for week-long investigations. Eighteen hours a day, weekends included.

"I know the whole chemical industry is concerned about the environment. We've already spent $7 billion controlling pollution. And our estimates show we'll spend $10 billion more over the next five years on waste disposal alone. So I know I'm not the only one with a conscience."

For a booklet that tells how we're protecting people and the environment, write: Chemical Manufacturers Association, Dept. LM-107, P.O. Box 363, Beltsville, Maryland 20705.

America's Chemical Industry

The member companies of
the Chemical Manufacturers Association

The 1981 Study

The Image of the Chemical Industry.
A majority of people in the study felt that
chemical waste was the major problem related to the chemical industry. Overall, the
public continued to see the chemical industry as paying too little attention to chemical
waste.

The Public's Attitude.   Data were analyzed for two separate groups: opinion
leaders and politically active individuals,
and the chemical industry neighbors. Within
the first group, educators were found to be
most positive toward the industry, but this
group was also less homogeneous. Some
members of this group felt that the industry
was very concerned about the average
person's welfare, whereas others asserted
that this was not so, thereby joining the majority of the public.

In measuring the chemical industry's
favorability and perceived truthfulness, the
industry's position was found to be "not really good" among the six industries tested:
oil, nuclear energy, chemical, retail, banking, and insurance.

*Awareness of CMA Advertising Cam-
paign.*   The study found that people who
saw the ads found them believable; 85% of
the politically active individuals and 87% of
the "plan neighbors" found them very or
somewhat believable. Attitudes of those in
the sample who had been exposed to the ads
improved significantly. Regular readers of
Time and *Newsweek* (where the industry campaign was running) were significantly more
aware than nonreaders of the chemical
industry's effort to inform the public of its
actions to reduce public risk.

There were also some discouraging findings. Sixty percent of those interviewed admitted that they were not aware of any industry efforts; of 40% of those who claimed
awareness of any industry effort to inform
them, about one in four—or 10% of the
total—claimed to have seen any industry

print advertising on what was being done to
reduce risk. When asked about the sponsorship of such advertising, fewer than 10% of
the politically active individuals named any
individual company. And only 1% of the politically active individuals said they were
aware of ad sponsorship by America's
chemical industry.

Effectiveness of the Campaign.   The
communications committee of the CMA concluded that attitudes toward the chemical industry had not changed significantly since
1980. There was no significant level of identification of the CMA advertising campaign.
(According to CMA, this was not a campaign
objective.) There did appear to be somewhat
more awareness of messages in the CMA
advertisements than of CMA's sponsorship
of those messages. Those aware of CMA
messages held more favorable views toward
the chemical industry than those who were
not aware. Clearly very little, if anything,
was accomplished. One can, however, spec-
ulate that the 1981 figures might have been
worse if the industry advertising had not
taken place.

There was only a slight increase in the
awareness of CMA communication efforts,
but there were some positive results:

— The percentages of chemical industry neighbors and politically active individuals who
   wanted information about waste disposal had
   doubled since 1980.

— The percentage of people who felt that the
   chemical industry was concerned rather than
   unconcerned had grown.

— Worker safety and product safety were seen
   by the largest percentages of politically active
   individuals, chemical industry neighbors, and
   educators as areas where efforts at improvement had been displayed.

John Elliott, former chairman of the
board of Ogilvy & Mather, made the following observations concerning CMA's advocacy campaign.[6]

O&M asked Gallup & Robinson to do a computer run of 2,000 corporate advertisements in 1979 and 1980, comparing them on the basis of recall and persuasiveness with the norm for all product advertising. It was found that: Giving all product advertising an index of 100, on the basis of recall and persuasiveness, all corporate advertising got a rating of 81, and institutional/advocacy advertising a rating of 62. The index value of the chemical industry's corporate advertising was 63, compared with the index value of 81 for all corporate advertising.

In Elliott's opinion, by far the most important reason for the slow progress of the chemical industry's campaign was that it was grossly underfunded. Elliott felt that while chemical companies were separately spending millions of dollars in advertising, this effort was largely wasted because it was not well coordinated. Elliott also felt that this modest effort on the part of the chemical industry might be seen by the public as secretiveness and as evidence that the industry did not take the problems seriously and was not doing anything about them. The public might come to the conclusion that others (meaning the government) would have to be given the responsibility to fix things. Elliott commented:

> All the hundreds of millions the industry has already spent to control pollution, to reduce risks, won't count a dime if the public isn't aware of it, or if the public sees it as a reaction to laws made necessary by irresponsible engineering and operations.[7]

Elliott also felt that the chemical industry should bring its messages to the general public, not just to the so-called politically active individuals and the influential:

> I think there is a myth about thought-leaders. The theory goes that if you get your message to them, they'll lead public opinion. It has been repeated so often that a lot of people accept it. But I can't remember an example of the theory working in advertising. It is the general public—all of us—who are besieged daily by front-page stories of spills, leakages,

fires, toxic reactions, etc. Elected officials have an inordinate interest in numbers of votes. It is the general public who are the thought-leaders, the influentials who influence the legislators.[8]

The 1982 Study

The second survey revealed that in general the communications objectives of the CMA campaign were being met, in that those who had seen the industry's communications were more likely than those who had not to concur with messages presented in the communications. However, the communications were reaching a limited audience, and 1982 results showed that this audience had not increased over the past year. As a result, overall public attitudes and perceptions of the chemical industry showed little change over recent years, and much of the impact of the communications was obscured when evaluated in terms of aggregate results.

The tracking study showed that in many aspects, the CMA communications program had mixed results.

1. The ads were reaching a stagnant limited audience; there was no appreciable increase in reach from 1981. However, the 1981–1982 campaign was based on a funding level lower than that of 1980–1981.

2. The awareness of messages communicating the industry's efforts to reduce the risk of potentially hazardous chemicals had dropped 10 points among persons in all groups except politically active individuals, the main target audience. Among the people who could remember the ads, the reactions to the industry's advertising were positive in terms of both the believability and the importance of those ads. At least 7 out of 10 persons from all groups sampled stated that the ads were believable rather than not believable. More than 8 out of 10 politically active individuals who remembered the ads described them as believable.

3. One of the more interesting results was that people who had been exposed to the communication campaign held different opinions of

the chemical industry than those who had not been exposed. However, as one would expect, responses from individuals in each of the three groups were less likely to show difference of opinion on questions that were not related to the advertising messages. Consequently, there were not differences between the views of people in each of these groups when asked about their opinions on the chemical industry, their impressions of the chemical industry's truthfulness, and their personal levels of concern about each of the issues discussed in the advertising.

The most widespread endorsement of the advertising credibility came from the chemical industry's neighbors. More than 9 out of 10 persons in this group said the ads were either very or somewhat believable. In 1981, reactions to the industry's advertising were equally positive among persons in all groups questioned. In determining the impact of CMA's advertisements, the survey used a conservative and narrow definition of opportunity of exposure (see Tables 1 through 3).

Public opinions and perceptions of the chemical industry often differed between the respondents who were probably exposed to and aware of the communications, and those who were probably not exposed to or were unaware of the communications. The most consistent difference between individuals in each of these groups was over perception of the chemical industry's con-

TABLE 2. Changes in Perceptions of the Industry: Industry Effort on Waste Disposal

	1982		1981	
	Exposed	*Unexposed*	*Exposed*	*Unexposed*
Effort (a lot of/ some)	72%	59%	66%	59%
No effort (only a little/ hardly any)	27%	38%	32%	35%

Note: Those exposed have more favorable opinions as to what the industry may actually be doing to manage hazardous waste disposal.

cern and the industry's efforts on each of the five issues discussed in the advertisements. Since the advertising focused specifically on the industry's concern about and efforts on each of these issues, the consistent differences of opinion between the groups confirmed that the advertising was making an impact. However, responses from individuals in each of these groups were less likely to show differences of opinion on questions that related less to the advertising messages.

In general, politically active individuals who were probably exposed to and aware of the communications were 7 to 18 percentage points more likely than their counterparts to believe that the chemical industry was concerned rather than unconcerned about each of the five key issues. In 1982, the widest margin separating individuals in each of these groups was on the issue of chemical waste disposal. In 1981, perceptions of the industry's concern with environmental issues differed on four of the five points, the

TABLE 1. Changes in Perceptions of the Industry: Personal Concern for Waste Disposal

	1982		1981	
	Exposed	*Unexposed*	*Exposed*	*Unexposed*
Concerned (very/ somewhat)	98%	94%	96%	94%
Not concerned at all (not very/ not at all)	2%	6%	3%	6%

Note: This question measures the importance of one of the five designated areas of what the chemical industry is doing to manage chemicals. The response confirms that waste disposal continues to be the most important activity area and that placing the most communications emphasis on this area is warranted. Second, any preexisting difference in the attitudes of exposed and not exposed groups is negligible. This means that such a topic is of major importance to people, whether or not they are likely to be readers of our communications.

TABLE 3. Changes in Perceptions of the Industry: Industry Efforts to Reduce Pollution

	1982		1981	
	Exposed	*Unexposed*	*Exposed*	*Unexposed*
Effort (a lot of/ some)	77%	70%	78%	70%
No effort (only a little/ hardly any)	21%	27%	21%	24%

Note: The activity area of general air and water pollution is second in importance (after waste disposal) to our sample, again confirming previous hypotheses. For this reason, recommendations were made to put approximately 2/3 of the advertising weight behind waste disposal and approximately 1/4 behind the area of air and water pollution. This chart reflects those proportions of communications effort. Once again, we see a favorable difference between those exposed and not exposed. The differences, however, are less dramatic, as one might expect.

exception being the industry's concern with the transportation of chemicals.

The 1982 results showed equally consistent differences between the perceptions of persons in both groups when asked about industry efforts at solving the problems of the five issues. In 1982, those individuals who were probably exposed to and aware of the communications were 6 to 13 percentage points more likely than their counterparts to believe that the chemical industry was making an effort, rather than no effort, concerning the five issues. Once again, the greatest difference between individuals in each group was their perceptions of the industry's effort with waste disposal.

Perceptions of the chemical industry's concern about the average person's welfare also differed between individuals in both groups. The individuals exposed to and aware of the communications were nine points more likely than the group who were neither exposed to nor aware of the communications to view the chemical industry as concerned, rather than not concerned, about the average person's welfare.

There was no sizable difference between both groups on overall opinions of the chemical industry, however. The absence of a difference between both groups on more general questions about the industry, as well as the consistent differences on questions specifically relating to issues discussed in the communications, provides some evidence as to what kind of impact the campaign was having. These findings suggest that those who were exposed to the communications were accepting the specific messages in the campaign. However, this acceptance of the specific messages was not yet being transformed into a general favorability toward the chemical industry.

The Image of the Chemical Industry in Context

Although the communications campaign appears to have had an impact on those ex-

posed to the communications, most of this impact cannot be noticed when we examine the overall attitudes and perceptions of the chemical industry.

Among six major American industries, the chemical industry continued to receive the fifth most favorable rating overall from politically active individuals in 1983. Despite this persistently low ranking, the actual numbers of favorable and unfavorable ratings from politically active individuals show a slight improvement over the 1982 ratings. In 1983 more than two-fifths (43%) of all politically active individuals held favorable, rather than unfavorable, opinions of the chemical industry.

The industry neighbors were also most likely to perceive the industry as least concerned about pollution and waste disposal. Perceptions of the chemical industry's concern about both issues had changed little since 1980. For all three years, the fewest chemical industry neighbors (42%) felt that the industry was concerned about waste disposal, while a moderately larger percentage (52%) felt that the industry was concerned about air and water pollution.

Perceptions of Industry Effort

For the third year in a row, more than one out of every three politically active individuals felt that the industry had made only a little or hardly any effort on waste disposal. Perceptions of the chemical industry's efforts with air and water pollution were more favorable, however. The efforts with air and water pollution ranked third out of the five issue areas examined. The third largest percentage of politically active individuals (72%) stated that the chemical industry was making either a lot of effort or some effort to reduce the risks of air and water pollution.

The percentage of politically active individuals neither exposed to nor aware of the communications who believed that the chemical industry was making only a little effort or no effort at all with waste disposal had grown slightly, from 35% to 38%, from 1981 to 1983. Meanwhile, those individuals exposed to and aware of the communications who believed that the industry was making only a little effort or no effort at all had dropped by five points, from 32% to 27%. What these contrary trends suggest is that those not exposed to the communications viewed the industry's efforts with waste disposal in increasingly negative terms, while those exposed to the communications viewed the industry's efforts in increasingly positive terms.

NOTES

1. John Elliott, Jr., former chairman of the board, Ogilvy & Mather, Inc., "Why Don't You Speak for Yourself, John?" Keynote address, *Issue Advertising: How to Make it Work on Television,* sponsored by AAAA, ANA, PRSA, PUCA, TVB, New York, September 15, 1981.

2. "CMA—What It Is, What It Does." Brochure published by the Chemical Manufacturers Association, Washington, D.C., October 1981, p. 1.

3. Ibid., p. 2.

4. James N. Sites, "Changing Your Image: The Story of How the Chemical Manufacturers Association Mobilized Its Members to Win Public Support." *Association Management* (March 1981), p. 48.

5. Ibid., p. 49.

6. John Elliott, *op. cit.*

7. Ibid.

8. Ibid.

CHEMICAL MANUFACTURERS ASSOCIATION

BIRNBAUM, ALEX, and STEVEN E. STEGNER. "Source Credibility in Social Judgment; Bias, Expertise, and the Judge's Point of View." *Journal of Personality and Social Psychology,* 37 (1979), pp. 48–74.

BOTEIN, MICHAEL, and DAVID M. RICE. *Network Television and the Public Interest.* Lexington, Mass.: D.C. Heath, 1980.

Current Company Practices in the Use of Corporate Advertising, 1981: ANA Survey Report. New York: Association of National Advertisers, 1982.

DARDENNE, PEGGY. "Cost of Corporate Advertising." *Public Relations Journal.* Yearly survey published in November of each year.

HASS, R. GLEN, and DARWYN E. LINDER. "Counterargument: Availability and the Effects of Message Structure on Persuasion." *Journal of Personality and Social Psychology,* 23 (1972), pp. 219–33.

JACCARD, JAMES. "Toward Theories of Persuasion and Belief Change." *Journal of Personality and Social Psychology,* 39 (1980), pp. 752–66.

KAPLAN, STUART J., and HARRY W. SHARP, JR. "The Effect of Responsibility Attributions on Message Source Evaluation." *Speech Monographs,* 41 (November 1974), pp. 364–70.

LUDLUM, CHARLES E. "Abatement of Corporate Image Environmental Advertising." *Ecology Law Quarterly,* 4 (1974), pp. 247–78; "Notes: Freedom of Expression in a Commercial Context." *Harvard Law Review,* 78 (1965), p. 674; "Developments in the Law, Deceptive Advertising." *Harvard Law Review,* 80 (1967), p. 1004.

SETHI, S. PRAKASH. *Advocacy Advertising and Large Corporations.* Lexington, Mass.: D. C. Heath, 1977.

SETHI, S. PRAKASH. Testimony in "IRS Administration of Tax Laws Relating to Lobbying (Part 1)," *Hearings before a Subcommittee of the Committee on Government Operations, House of*

Representatives, 95th Congress, 2nd session, July 18, 1978, U.S. Government Printing Office, pp. 381–455.

SMITH, NELSON, and LEONARD J. THEBERGE, (eds.). *Energy Coverage—Media Panic.* New York: Longman, 1983.

WATSON, FRANCIS W., JR. *The Alternative Media: Dismantling Two Centuries of Progress.* Rockford, Ill: The Rockford College Institute, 1979.

AMERICAN FEDERATION OF STATE, COUNTY, AND MUNICIPAL EMPLOYEES (AFSCME), WASHINGTON, D.C.

An advocacy campaign against Reaganomics

Soon after winning the 1980 presidential election, President Ronald Reagan launched a new economic program, dubbed Reaganomics, aimed at changing the direction of the U.S. economy away from governmental intervention and toward greater reliance on the market system, individual initiative, and private savings and investment. Reaganomics called for a marked reduction in social entitlement programs and a reduction in taxes for both individuals and corporations. The programs scheduled for major cuts included food stamps, aid to families with dependent children (AFDC), school lunches, and student loans. The eligibility criteria for Medicare and Medicaid would be tightened, and there would be a cutback in Social Security benefits.

Reaganomics generated a great deal of controversy in Congress, especially among liberal Democrats, among urban constituencies, and among the poor, all of whom feared that Reaganomics would help the rich and the large corporations at the expense of the poor and minorities. The country's conservative mood, together with the personal popularity of President Reagan and his tremendous media appeal, created such an irresistible force that all opposition to the program was drowned in an avalanche of pro-Reagan publicity.

Against such apparently overwhelming odds, AFSCME decided to launch its ad campaign against Reaganomics and President Reagan's budget proposals. The need for the campaign was best expressed by the late Jerry Wurf, the president of AFSCME, who felt that Reagan's proposals were unfair in all dimensions and would cause the most hardship for working families of moderate income. Moreover, Wurf held that President

Adapted from S. Prakash Sethi, *Handbook of Advocacy Advertising: Concepts, Strategies and Applications* (Cambridge, Mass.: Ballinger Publishing Company, 1987),

Reagan's policies would severely hurt unions like AFSCME since there would be a major cutback in federal programs, which would result in a drastic reduction of public employees at all levels of government, the constituency served by AFSCME. As Wurf said,

> Our union is a union of public sector workers. We don't deal with U.S. Steel at the bargaining table, we deal with the U.S. taxpayer. Our credibility and our standing with the taxpayer translate into better wages and working conditions, and our ability to organize. We see a direct relationship between our public image and our ability to function.

ORGANIZED LABOR AND ADVOCACY ADVERTISING

Unlike business, organized labor has not been a big player in the advocacy advertising arena. It traditionally used grass-roots activity and direct lobbying to influence public opinion and the national agenda. However, during the last 10 years or so, organized labor unions have been taking tentative and somewhat cautious steps in the use of advocacy advertising. The longest running of the current campaigns is for the United Federation of Teachers (UFT). It is also one of the more sophisticated trade union advocacy campaigns in the United States. The ads feature commentaries by the UFT's president, Albert Shanker, bearing the headline "Where We Stand." A variety of education-related issues are discussed. The ad copy follows an editorial format and is crammed with facts and figures. It attempts both to inform and to educate the general public and to present the UFT's viewpoint in a reasoned and low-key manner (see Exhibit 1).

AFSCME has been one of the leading users of advocacy advertising. In 1984, organized labor entered the advocacy arena in a big way. In August, the United Auto Workers (UAW) broadcast TV commercials proclaiming that the UAW's goal in forthcoming contract negotiations with the auto industry was to protect American jobs. The campaign was estimated to have cost $2 million. In September 1984, the AFL-CIO unveiled a nationwide $1 million television campaign focusing on issues affecting American society. Despite the nearness of the presidential election, AFL-CIO's president Lake Kirkland stated that the campaign had "no relationship to the election or to advance the cause of any particular candidate." The three-week campaign consisted of 14 30-second TV spots on six issues: education, jobs, affordable health, trade policy, taxation, and equal rights. It ran on 42 television stations in 24 metropolitan markets around the country, with a potential audience of 38.6 million households, including 8 million union members. In announcing the campaign, Kirkland said that the AFL-CIO hoped to reach its own members with the message that it cared about issues affecting everyone. In addition, a primary campaign goal was to improve the public's attitudes toward organized labor.

Some of the reasons for organized labor's engaging in advocacy advertising are similar to those of the business community—for example, loss of public trust. However, most of the labor campaigns lack a coherent long-term strategy and are not likely to be effective.

1. The overwhelming emphasis is on rhetorical and emotional appeals delivered through 30- and 60-second TV commercials. These commercials may warm the hearts of union members but are likely to do little to improve their understanding of the issues involved or prepare them to discuss these issues with non-union members or the general public.

2. These short TV commercials are inappropriate as educational devices that can inform an increasingly skeptical public about the complexity of the issues, the unions' alleged shortcomings, and the substance of the unions' arguments. Though they may give instant gratification to their sponsors, they

EXHIBIT 1

Where We Stand
by Albert Shanker President United Federation of Teachers

Couple Could Owe $76,000 for College
Plan Saddles Student With High Debt

Last week I gave this space to guest columnist Denis P. Doyle of the American Enterprise Institute, who made two important points. First, he argued that proposed cutbacks in higher education (I would have added elementary and secondary education as well) were very unwise national policy. Our country will need engineers, doctors, physicists, mathematicians. Failure to invest in education today will mean that these skills will not be there when we need them in the years to come. Said Doyle, "It takes 20 years to train the next generation of engineers, scientists, linguists."

But that's not the only point Doyle made. His second dealt with the question of how to pay for college education. Right now students nationally pay about a third of the cost of college. Two-thirds is paid for by previous generations, in the form of tax-supported public colleges and universities, government aid to higher education, student grants and loans and private contributions. We do this because we consider higher education for our people an investment in the future of our country.

Doyle would replace all this with a proposal originally made by John Silber. Under the plan, the federal government would set up a $15 billion fund. All but the wealthiest students would borrow what they needed to get through school and, after graduation, would repay the principal plus interest over a period of years. College graduates who agreed to serve in areas of national need—Doyle gave as examples rural health care or inner-city teaching—would not have to fully repay their loans; they could "work off" all or part of their obligation.

The others, of course, would have to repay the loan—and Doyle fudged the question of interest. He wrote of "an income tax surcharge of several percentage points" when the former student starts working in order for the government to "recover costs." Or, said Doyle, "students could be expected to repay an amount greater than the original advance." But there is clearly going to be interest at a fairly high rate, because Doyle noted that the $15 billion fund would be for the "first five years" and was thereafter expected to become "self-sustaining." In a period of inflation and over a number of years, high interest rates would be necessary in order to sustain the fund and make future loans available.

I received a letter from John P. Mallan, vice president for governmental relations of the American Association of State Colleges and Universities. Mallan points out that AASCU and almost every other higher education group have opposed this college funding idea and a number of variations on it which were promoted by Milton Friedman and Christopher Jencks. It was opposed because it would saddle most college graduates with very high long-term debts from the time of their graduation forward. Buying a college education would be something like buying a house. Mallan wrote:

"Here are some estimates of what the plan might cost at current college prices. A public college student might need $16,000 for four years of undergraduate college. When he pays this back, depending on the interest charged and the period of repaying, his total debt could amount to $38,000—at the age of 22. If he marries [and his wife had also been a student who had borrowed similarly], he and his spouse could begin their married lives with a debt of $76,000!"

(Guaranteed student loans are now at 9% and widely expected to go up; the federal government subsidizes the difference between the 9% and the bank's going rate. Auxiliary loans to assist undergraduates are at an unsubsidized 14%, with repayment to begin at graduation. Checking with a local bank, we learned that if a student takes a $16,000 loan at an interest rate of 14% and expects to repay it over 15 years, he would face payments of $213.09 per month for that time period; if both partners in a marriage were saddled with the same loans from their student days, the monthly tab for 15 years would be $426.18. Each would wind up repaying $38,356.20, or $76,712.40 for the couple.)

Mallan continued: "A private college student might owe $40,000 for four years, plus $30,000 in interest—$70,000 at the age of 22, or twice that if he marries [a classmate].

"Those who went on to graduate or professional school would acquire debts approaching those of smaller Third World nations." (The March 24 *Chronicle of Higher Education* reports a survey by the American Association of Dental Schools showing that 56.1% of last year's graduates had accumulated more than $20,000 in debt by graduation, with the average among those who had debts at $24,700. Dental school officials said they thought that cumulative debts for a new dental school graduate might soon reach $50,000.)

A second important objection to the Silber plan, according to Mallan, is that it would "almost certainly encourage states, institutions, and profit-making schools to raise tuition and other charges, since the lifetime repayment system would be available to pay for it.

"Most important," Mallan wrote, "it would be a radical break with the principle of low tuition and the idea that each generation should pay the costs of college—like elementary and secondary education—for the next generation. At present, students and their families pay about one-third of all college costs and the public much of the rest. Most of us would like to keep it that way. This arrangement has given the United States what is universally recognized as the world's most outstanding and also democratic system of higher education. There is no reason, after two hundred years, to abandon it."

are unlikely to have any lasting impact on the public.

In addition to these campaigns, other unions, notably the United Steel Workers of America, the Postal Workers, the Amalgamated Clothing and Textile Workers, and the International Ladies Garment Workers, have run occasional print ads and television and radio commercials. UAW ads have run the gamut of issues confronting the union and the U.S. steel industry and address topics that are part of the nation's political agenda. Some of these advertisements criticize U.S. Steel Corporation's demand for work rule changes and also oppose the company's plans to import semiunfinished steel from foreign countries. They also support the industry's position for greater protection against foreign imports (see Exhibits 2 through 6). Most of the ads by trade unions, however, have been either of narrow focus or of extremely short duration, with low frequency and reach. Their impact is not likely to be significant.

ISSUES FOR ANALYSIS

1. To what extent can trade union advocacy advertising contribute to increased public understanding of the problems that American workers in general and AFSCME members in particular confront?

2. What is the public's perception of such advertising in terms of its accuracy and objectivity? Should such advertising present only the sponsor's viewpoint, or should it present other significant viewpoints?

3. How important, from the public viewpoint, are the various issues selected for such campaigns? What should be the process of identifying salient issues?

4. Should labor unions engage in advocacy advertising? If so, for whom should they speak? In cases where the issues are of direct or immediate concern to union members, obviously they speak for their membership. However, what happens when unions choose to advocate policy positions of broad public interest, where membership interest is at best indirect?

5. What objectives was AFSCME pursuing through this campaign? To what extent were those objectives in the public interest in addition to serving the interests of the union and/or union members?

6. What are the options available to the public for hearing counterviewpoints when the advocacy advertising of large, organized groups overwhelms and distorts the flow of information available? Is labor advertising a counterpoint to industry advertising, or does it further aggravate the problem of information distortion?

7. How effective is the AFSCME campaign in terms of its long-term goal of changing public opinion?

8. How might one evaluate the effectiveness of AFSCME's campaign, given its goals and objectives?

BACKGROUND OF AFSCME

AFSCME is the fastest-growing union in the AFL-CIO. It has 1.4 million members throughout the United States, including employees of state, county, and municipal governments, school districts, public hospitals, and nonprofit agencies. Members work in blue-collar, clerical, professional, and paraprofessional jobs. White-collar employees account for one-third of the membership.

AFSCME began as a number of separate local unions organized by a group of Wisconsin state employees in the early 1930s. In 1936, AFSCME was chartered by the American Federation of Labor (AFL). Today, AFSCME is organized into more than 2,800 local unions, most of them affiliated with one of 70 district councils. AFSCME's late president, Jerry Wurf, was a vice-president of AFL-CIO. The president, the secretary-treasurer, and 25 vice-presidents comprise AFSCME's international executive board, which meets quarterly to establish policies.

AFSCME is the founder of the Coalition of American Public Employees (CAPE). AFSCME is composed of four public employee organizations with a combined membership of more than 4 million workers. CAPE works to secure equity for all men and women employed in the public sector. AFSCME is a politically active union. Its work is unusual in organized labor, because it is one of the few unions so involved in political education campaigns through the advertising medium.

AFSCME started its educational campaign in the early 1970s. Its first focus was the B-1 bomber. Through advertisements placed in newspapers and leading opinion

EXHIBIT 2

BULLSEYE

Brazil is the latest country to propose sending hundreds of thousands of tons of subsidized steel slabs to the United States for finishing into steel products. The slabs would replace steel made in America, further reduce the steel-making capacity of this country, and throw additional thousands of steelworkers out of work.

The Brazilian deal, being promoted by the Wheeling-Pittsburgh Steel Corporation, mirrors the one new being negotiated between the British Steel Corporation and U.S. Steel.

In each case, a foreign, government-owned steel company would ship huge quantities of subsidized, semi-finished steel to companies in the U.S. American companies would close down steel making facilities and concentrate on turning the foreign steel into finished products.

Wheeling-Pittsburgh proposes to deal with a Brazilian military dictatorship which has "targeted" steel as a loss leader in an effort to tap foreign trade markets. Brazil itself is in the midst of a massive debt crisis—owing $90 billion, more than any other nation.

The government-owned British Steel Corporation is faced with huge financial losses, and the proposed deal with U.S. Steel is widely described in Britain as a "bail-out".

If either or both of these deals should be finalized, we can expect a flood of similar schemes between other American steel companies and foreign governments.

Our country would lose its basic steel-making capacity and become dependent on foreign suppliers. This would seriously jeopardize our national security.

What is happening in the steel industry is a dramatic example of the problem of international targeting of selected industries.

Through targeting, a government gives preferred treatment to a chosen industry—subsidizing its development in many ways until its products can be dumped on foreign markets at prices which do not reflect the true cost of production.

Because of our high consumption and lack of a national industrial policy, the United States is a sitting duck for these practices. Look at what has happened in some other industries which have been targeted:

COMPUTERIZED MACHINE TOOLS: Japan's share of this market in the United States has increased from 5% to 50% since 1976. 24,000 American jobs have been lost.

COLOR TELEVISION: Japan targeted this industry in the 1960's. Since then, 13 American color television producers have dropped out, leaving only five. 27,364 American jobs have been lost. A total of 63,000 have been lost in related consumer electronics industries including radios, tape decks and phonographs.

AIRBUS: Western European countries targeted the world commercial aircraft market in the early 1970's with the creation of a joint venture called Airbus Industries—which now accounts for half of the free world market for widebodied aircraft. This rapid market penetration contributed to Lockheed's decision to stop production of the L1011, with a loss of 4,000 jobs.

This country, its industries, workers and stockholders suffer because of targeting by foreign governments. This situation will continue, and worsen, until we understand targeting and develop a national industrial policy to deal with it.

USA

Brazil Joins Britain In Attack On USA's Steel Independence

UNITED STEELWORKERS OF AMERICA

Lloyd McBride, President
Five Gateway Center
Pittsburgh, Pennsylvania 15222

EXHIBIT 3

ENOUGH IS ENOUGH!

U.S. STEEL HAS RIPPED OFF THE AMERICAN TAXPAYER, THE STATE OF ILLINOIS, THE CITY OF CHICAGO AND THE UNITED STEELWORKERS OF AMERICA!

On December 27, 1983, United States Steel Corporation announced that it had scrapped plans to build a rail mill at Chicago's South Works and would close much of South Works itself, thereby eliminating thousands of jobs. The company blamed the United Steelworkers of America and its members at Local Union 65 for the decision not to build the rail mill.

U.S. Steel has publicly stated that the union did not cooperate to help make construction of the rail mill a reality. *That is completely false.* But no one should be surprised because U.S. Steel is well known for its deceptions.

Here are the facts: In promising to build the rail mill, U.S. Steel made two demands, and much later a third.

U.S. STEEL'S DEMANDS	THE USWA'S RESPONSE
1. A new manning agreement with major labor changes to make the mill economically competitive.	Negotiated a new agreement satisfactory to U.S. Steel, which was ratified by the members of Local Union 65.
2. Repeal of a state sales tax on rails produced in Illinois for sale out of state.	Lobbied the Illinois Legislature and Governor James Thompson. Won repeal of the tax to help U.S. Steel.
3. Overturning of an Environmental Protection Agency consent decree requiring the company to install $33 million worth of pollution control equipment at Gary Works.	Worked closely with Attorney General Neil Hartigan and other public officials in developing a solution to protect the environment and still help U.S. Steel.

In addition, U.S. Steel was the major beneficiary of contract adjustments worth more than $3 billion negotiated between the union and the steel industry last March.

Given the facts, any objective person can only conclude that the USWA and its members at Local Union 65 have done more than their fair share to help U.S. Steel.

UNITED STEELWORKERS OF AMERICA
Five Gateway Center   Pittsburgh. PA 15222

Lynn Williams
Temporary Acting President

Jack Parton
Director. District 31
East Chicago. IN

The union wanted the mill to be constructed.

What did U.S. Steel do? It kept demanding More! It demanded more from the union . . . more from the taxpayers . . . more from the state . . . more from Congress. Well, when a greedy wolf with bared fangs is at your door, threatening your life, you must defend yourself.

U.S. Steel has been deceiving the USWA, the American taxpayer, the City of Chicago, the State of Illinois and the entire nation for too long.

U.S. Steel's deceptions and its slick public relations campaign to discredit the union is a slap in the face to its workers, the union and the nation. Isn't it a shame that at the same time U.S. Steel was demanding sacrifices from its workers, the company found $6.2 billion to purchase Marathon Oil Company. Why didn't U.S. Steel use these $6.2 billion to modernize their entire steel operations? Does U.S. Steel have no allegiance to this country anymore?

U.S. Steel's arrogance and greed, like that of many other corporations, makes it important that this country develop an industrial policy addressing questions such as federal plant shutdown legislation, overseas investment and corporate responsibility to the communities in which they are located.

THESE AREN'T QUESTIONS JUST FOR STEELWORKERS BUT FOR ALL WORKERS . . . ALL AMERICANS.

We are all in this together. We must all help. Here's what you should do to help. Call for a Congressional investigation resulting from the use of the Tax Code in U.S. Steel's shutdown announcement and decision not to build the rail mill at South Works. Fill out the coupon with this ad and send it today to U.S. Representative Daniel Rostenkowski (D-ILL.) as shown. He is Chairman of the House Ways and Means Committee, where all tax legislation begins.

TO: U.S. REP. DANIEL ROSTENKOWSKI
CHAIRMAN. COMMITTEE ON WAYS & MEANS
U.S. HOUSE OF REPRESENTATIVES
ROOM 1102. LONGWORTH BLDG.
WASHINGTON. DC 20515

Dear Congressman Rostenkowski:

I have had enough! U.S. Steel is getting a $1.2 billion tax write-off for putting people out of work, but I know of your concern for working people and appreciate everything you have done on the South Works matter.

Please schedule a full congressional investigation into the impact of tax code advantages from U.S. Steel's shutdown announcement and the decision not to build a rail mill at South Works in Chicago.

Sincerely.

NAME:_____

ADDRESS:_____

CITY/STATE/ZIP_____

EXHIBIT 4

"The British Are Coming, The British Are Coming"

AND AMERICA'S STEEL INDEPENDENCE IS GOING

A Message Especially for Stockholders Of American Steel Companies

As Independence Day approaches this year, Paul Revere's warning takes on a new and dangerous meaning.

If a deal struck by the U.S. Steel Corporation and the government-owned British Steel Corporation goes through as planned, it could be the beginning of the end for America's steel independence. As the union representing America's steelworkers, we find that prospect extremely disturbing, and for reasons that go beyond our self-interest. It is, for example, contrary to the best interests of stockholders of other American steel companies.

Here's what is involved.

U.S. Steel wants to quit making steel at its Fairless Hills plant in Pennsylvania, but continue to operate the Fairless finishing facilities. It wants to accomplish this by importing millions of tons of semi-finished steel "slabs" from the British Steel Corporation's Ravenscraig plant in Scotland.

U.S. Steel says it would be cheaper to do this than to modernize the steel-making facilities at Fairless. To make the deal more palatable for Americans, the British say they will create a so-called "private corporation" just to operate Ravenscraig.

That's supposed to take the sting out of U.S. Steel's importation of subsidized foreign steel. Of course it ignores the fact that the Ravenscraig technology is a direct result of subsidized investment. The same is true for the entire money-losing British steel operation.

The fact is that Ravenscraig would not exist but for this subsidy.

It is indeed ironic that in the past, even U.S. Steel has charged that government subsidies saved British steel from bankruptcy and allowed it to install new technology while encountering huge operating losses.

The logical, fair and reasonable thing for U.S. Steel to do is to forget the British deal and modernize Fairless. Earlier this year, our union negotiated a new contract that will save the steel industry some $3 billion. As the largest steel company, U.S. Steel will realize the largest share of those savings. Our one condition was that these savings be plowed back into existing facilities.

Certainly this is consistent with the industry's long-stated objective of modernizing its facilities to sharpen its competitive edge.

If U.S. Steel is allowed to consummate this unlikely match, it can make other deals with the Europeans, Brazilians, Nigerians, Taiwanese and others who have the capacity to flood the American market with subsidized steel. Then, one by one, other American steel companies will be forced to follow suit to remain competitive. If they don't, they'll be priced out of the marketplace.

The losers in such a scenario would be the thousands of new unemployed American steelworkers, the stockholders of other, smaller American steel companies, and the American people, who would find themselves dependent on foreign producers for our steel needs, including steel for defense purposes.

Smaller steel companies are especially vulnerable. One half or more of their investment in steel properties is tied up in iron and coal mines, and the ovens and furnaces that produce steel. If these facilities are made useless by a national shift to imported raw steel, all of that will have to be written off. The effect on balance sheets and the market value of investments is obvious.

The United Steelworkers of America is determined that this will not happen. We have committed the resources of our union to this total effort. We will employ every legal means at our disposal to block this dangerous precedent.

★ Within recent days, we have engaged counsel to file on our behalf a petition charging that the proposed transaction is illegal under U.S. trade laws.

★ We will press fully our rights under existing collective bargaining agreements with U.S. Steel, as well as our rights under the National Labor Relations Act.

★ We will call for a Congressional investigation of the entire proposed U.S.-British Steel arrangement—including the issuance of subpoenas to examine all documents and notes exchanged by the parties and the relative costs of producing steel at Ravenscraig and the extent of subsidization.

★ We will carry out an extensive information program to provide the public with the facts about this important case.

On April 28, the President of our union, Lloyd McBride, testified before the Steel Caucus of the U.S. House of Representatives about this matter. He closed with these words:

"We may be witnessing here the beginning—for the U.S.—of the internationalization of American steel production. And when steel companies engage in what is essentially unfair trade for the purpose of shifting their production base out of steel for the advantage of their shareholders, then our union and its members are being severely injured and sorely used. Our steel communities are severely impacted. And, I submit to you, our nation is the worse for it. When private decisions have such widespread, devastating consequences on the private and public sectors, those decisions should not be made unilaterally without a thorough investigation of the consequences."

The consequences of U.S. Steel's proposed joint venture with the British Steel Corporation are indeed great. An entire industry as we have come to know it is at stake. U.S. Steel is single-handedly attempting to forge a new national steel policy for America.

The Steelworkers of America are prepared to fight this dangerous proposal at every juncture. And we want your help.

We invite others who share our views on this important matter—especially steel company stockholders—to join us. We'll be glad to provide you with additional information.

United Steelworkers of America
Lloyd McBride, President
Five Gateway Center
Pittsburgh, Pennsylvania 15222

EXHIBIT 5

"...And Then There Were None"

Blast furnaces being demolished last year after U.S. Steel closed its huge Youngstown Works in Ohio.

THE ADMINISTRATION MUST ACT NOW TO SAVE AMERICA'S BASIC STEEL INDUSTRY

Because of the crisis which exists within the American steel industry, we believe it is important to share the following message with the American public.

Our country's basic steel industry is face to face with the greatest crisis in its history. Unless the Reagan administration takes immediate action, the industry will be severely damaged and could disappear.

When Jimmy Carter became President seven years ago, there were 46 large, ore-based steel mills operating in the U.S., capable of producing 145 million tons of raw steel a year. During the Carter years, six of them were closed. Under the current administration, nine have been closed permanently. Two others have been closed for a year. More may close soon, leaving our country dangerously dependent on foreign steel producers.

The national interest is clear. At stake is the loss of hundreds of thousands of jobs connected with the steel industry, the investment of countless steel company shareholders, and the security of our country.

The immediate threat lies in a deal being pressed by the U.S. Steel Corporation and the highly-subsidized, government-owned British Steel Corporation. If this agreement is carried out, U.S. Steel would abandon its steelmaking facilities at its Fairless Hills plant in Pennsylvania but continue to operate the steel-finishing plant at the same location.

U.S. Steel would then buy millions of tons of semi-finished steel "slabs" from two government-owned British plants and finish them at Fairless. U.S. Steel says this would be cheaper than modernizing its own steel-making facilities at Fairless.

This may be true because of the huge subsidies the British government has poured into these plants. Last fall, the Department of Commerce determined that this subsidy amounted to 20.33% of the price of imported British steel.

Since the U.S. Steel deal was announced, Brazil and other countries have rushed to make their own proposals for dumping subsidized steel on the American market. We believe all of these schemes are in clear violation of our domestic trade laws, but laws are meaningless without enforcement.

Executives of other American steel companies have said they will be compelled by competitive pressure to import subsidized raw steel if U.S. Steel gets away with its British Steel plan.

This would destroy the American basic steel industry. During a time of national emergency, dependence on foreign steel would be as disastrous as dependence on foreign oil.

During the presidential campaign, Mr. Reagan often demonstrated an awareness of steel industry problems and made several promises which have not been kept by officials in his administration.

Here are some of them.
• On October 2, 1980, at the Cyclops Mill in Bridgeville, Pa., he promised to do three things which, if carried out, would go far toward resolving the steel industry's problems. He said he would:

1) Enforce anti-dumping steel laws to ensure fair trade in steel;
2) Reinstate the Trigger Price Mechanism for steel;

3) Act vigorously to negotiate reductions in foreign subsidies and trade barriers whenever possible.

These things are not being done. The Trigger Price Mechanism provides a formula for setting fair minimum price for imported steel. It has not been enforced since early 1982. This has encouraged foreign countries to flood our market with subsidized steel.

• In that same speech at Cyclops, he promised to reduce the 13% unemployment rate in the steel industry. Six days later, in Youngstown, Ohio, he said he would do whatever it took to get jobless steelworkers back to work. Since then the steelworker unemployment rate has jumped from 13% to 46%.

Layoffs of a few months have stretched out to continuous years of unemployment for many iron and coal miners, steelworkers and others. Whole communities are being wiped out. Family life is being destroyed for hundreds of thousands of hard-working Americans.

Steel-related unemployment will be much higher if the deal between U.S. Steel and British Steel becomes a reality and sets a precedent for similar schemes with other subsidized foreign producers. They, too, are eager to unload raw steel at prices below the cost of production, thus exporting their unemployment to us.

The President has the power and authority to protect the national interest in this crisis. We ask the President and officials of his administration to understand the urgency of the problem and set in motion the administrative actions which are now so desperately needed.

Specifically, we ask the President to act in these areas:
1) Direct Commerce Secretary Baldrige and Trade Ambassador Brock to launch an immediate investigation to determine if the U.S. Steel-British Steel proposal would violate our domestic trade laws or the United States-European Economic Community Arrangement. This is not a difficult investigation and should be completed within 30 days.
2) Direct Secretary Baldrige to invoke the procedures set forth in the 1982 EEC Arrangement and call for an immediate consultation with the European Coal and Steel Community on the extent and implications of semi-finished steel imports in this country.
3) If consultations do not resolve the problem, the administration should use existing procedures of the federal trade laws to promptly prohibit imports of subsidized steel.
4) Direct the appropriate officials within his administration to carry out the promises he made to steelworkers and the steel industry during the presidential campaign.

Time is short. The powers of the President of the United States are great. The time to act is now. *AMERICAN STEELWORKERS AND THEIR INDUSTRY CANNOT COMPETE WITH FOREIGN GOVERNMENTS.*

United Steelworkers of America
Lloyd McBride, President
Five Gateway Center
Pittsburgh, Pennsylvania 15222

151

EXHIBIT 6

UNCONTROLLED IMPORTS

They have taken nearly a million American jobs in apparel & textiles. They threaten the two million jobs that remain. We have one last chance. And it's in the Congress now.

S680/HR1562:

An urgent, rational bill that will put an end to uncontrolled imports of apparel & textiles, stop the erosion of our industry, save two million American jobs. And still give the nations of the world, poorer ones especially, legitimate access to our market.

THESE AREN'T JUST JOBS. WE'RE TALKING ABOUT TWO MILLION PEOPLE.

And look who they are: 7 out of 10, women. Sitting at sewing machines, standing on their feet in the mills. Supporting their families alone, or making the difference so that the family can live a little better, the kids get a little better chance.

These are people who desperately need work, they want to work and they don't have much choice about where they work.

When their plants close, they can't find jobs in other industries. The lucky ones may find a service job at the minimum wage, if you call it lucky to make $134 a week with a couple of kids to take care of.

More often, it's welfare. And bitterness. For them, dignity, pride, faith in America are wrapped up in paying their own way.

Two million jobs are slipping away.

It's not too late to save them.

WE'RE TALKING ABOUT TOWNS.

There are small towns all over this country where there's only one mill or one garment factory. The people depend on it for a living. And everything else in that town depends on those people: the local department store, the drug store, the movie house, the grocery, the gas station, the garage, the schools and services.

When the plant goes, the town goes. The other businesses fail, taxes disappear, the life of the town crumbles. A little bit of America dies.

It's already happening in many towns. And many more are hanging by a thread.

We think that's urgent. Don't you?

WHY WE NEED THIS BILL RIGHT NOW.

The way things are going, by 1990 we won't have an apparel & textile industry in America at all. It's all here for everybody to see: today 1 out of every 2 garments sold in this country—men's, women's & kids'—is an import. Ten years ago, it was 1 out of 5. In category after category, imports up, up, up. And snowballing.

A FEW HORRENDOUS FACTS.

The Growth of Clothing Imports as a Percentage of the U.S. Market.

	1974	1979	1984
Women's & Children's Coats	22%	38%	52%
Men's & Boys' Shirts (woven, man-made fiber)	19%	42%	55%
Bras	29%	49%	58%
Sweaters (all)	44%	55%	68%

Imports have increased 123% in the past 10 years, 25% in 1983 alone, and a terrifying 32% over that just last year.

YOU CAN SEE WHAT'S HAPPENING WITH YOUR OWN EYES.

In the stores, for example, look for a woman's blouse made here. Instead of there. See how long and hard you have to look. If you find it at all.

Or in those beautiful mail-order catalogs: page after page, see how much is import. How little, USA.

It ought to make us mad.

We are literally being imported out of existence—our mills, our fiber plants, our garment factories, and all the workers who depend on them for a living.

In the last 10 years: nearly a million jobs we had and could have had. Gone.

In state after state, hundreds of garment factories. Gone.

In just one year, February '83-February '84, 50,000 jobs in apparel & knitting. Gone.

In 1984, in North & South Carolina alone: at least 61 textile plants. Gone.

Plant after plant, closing, and among them, just this year: our last remaining manufacturer of corduroy & velveteen, one of the oldest and most prestigious of our mills. Gone.

That's 1 out of 10 manufacturing jobs, more than steel & automobiles combined. And it's frightening.

THIS BILL IS NOT A BAIL-OUT.

Nobody's asking the government to foot the bills for us. Our American apparel & textile industry has become the most modern and productive in the world. It has spent on average a billion dollars a year on new plants and equipment. And it could hold its own against all comers, if those competitors were, like us, competing on their own.

But they're not. Our companies must compete with their governments. And their governments support them with financing, subsidies, tax-relief, and by keeping our goods out. And with workers at wages Americans find hard to believe: 16-cents-an-hour workers, 38-cents-an-hour workers, 63-cents-an-hour workers, $1.18-cents-an-hour workers. Could you live on that? Neither could we.

We can compete in productivity, we can compete in quality. But there is no way American workers can compete with those pitifully, indecently low wages. And there is nobody who thinks we should.

NOT "PROTECTIONISM," FAIRNESS.

Since 1974 we've had a trade agreement, the Multi-Fiber Arrangement (MFA), which was supposed to keep imports in balance. But it's painfully obvious now that the loopholes are big enough to bring down our entire industry.

That's what this bill is all about. Plugging the loopholes which have distorted the MFA,

---

bringing the MFA back to its objectives of an open, orderly market fairly shared by everyone, and giving it the teeth to make it work.

S680/HR1562 doesn't break any new ground. It simply moves to correct the flaws that have damn near destroyed us.

THIS BILL IS EXTRAORDINARILY FAIR.

We're not saying, no more imports. We are saying, give us import levels we can deal with. Make it possible again for American industry and American workers to get a fair share of our own American market.

That's what this bill does. But it's not one-sided.

It recognizes the needs of the struggling economies, the impoverished peoples beyond our borders.

It says to the big exporting countries, you can come in, you can grow as we grow, but you can no longer flood us.

At the same time, it gives the smaller, poorer nations a greater opportunity in our market: more room for their goods, more room to grow.

This is a bill that is not just fair, it is compassionate. A bill every American in good conscience can support.

AND THE SPONSORS SPAN THE POLITICAL SPECTRUM.

They are Republicans and Democrats, conservatives and liberals, moderates on both sides. In the Senate and in the House, they have rallied to this bill.

They have joined forces in common agreement that America cannot afford to lose another great industry, American workers cannot afford to lose one more job.

To date 227 representatives and senators have put their names on the bill.

Even so, we can't take passage for granted. Beyond that, we want the bill to do more than squeak through. We want overwhelming congressional support that will tell the world that we are determined to defend our home markets: they are welcome to come and trade with us, but we are no longer going to sit idly by while our industries are destroyed, our workers deprived of their right to earn a living at a decent American wage.

YOU CAN HELP. BACK S680/HR1562.

Write your representative. Write your senator. Let them know you want this bill. If they're sponsors, they'll know you support them. If they're undecided, they'll know how you want them to decide. If they oppose it, they'll know there is good reason to switch.

America needs this bill. We need this bill.

We're fighting for a fighting chance.

Amalgamated Clothing & Textile Workers' Union

International Ladies' Garment Workers' Union

RALLY: 12 NOON today, Wednesday, April 10, Herald Square.

(34th Street and Broadway)

magazines, the campaign suggested that heavy defense expenditures on such weapon systems as the B-1 bomber are misdirected because they cause a reduction in funding for public education, highway maintenance, and the revitalization of cities and urban areas. One advertisement was headlined, ''One of these could educate every kid in Cincinnati,'' and showed a picture of a B-1 bomber. The copy cited a Brookings Institution study suggesting that no significant military advantages were to be gained by deploying a new penetrating bomber such as the B-1. It said that AFSCME supported a strong national defense but was against spending $100 billion on the B-1 program (see Exhibit 7). The campaign ran for about 12 to 18 months and cost approximately $100,000. Subsequent advocacy advertisements dealt with other public issues, such as deceptive government budget cuts and their consequences, inhuman suffering, and lack of adequate public funding for mental health and human services programs (see Exhibits 7 through 10).

At the time of launching its campaign, AFSCME offered its B-1 ad to other unions who wanted to buy the air time; sponsorship of the B-1 ad would change depending on who bought the air time. As result, the B-1 ad was run in cooperation with AFSCME and other labor unions. The AFL-CIO was one of those who wanted to buy air time to run AFSCME's Social Security advertising.

RATIONALE FOR THE ADVOCACY CAMPAIGN

AFSCME was the first opposition group to start advocacy campaigning against Reaganomics. The union felt that there was a clear need to inform the American public about the problems inherent in Reagan's proposals and to communicate to the public the adverse social consequences that would follow if these proposals were enacted.

DECISION-MAKING PROCESS

There are no formal voting procedures for ascertaining the views of rank-and-file members about undertaking an ad campaign; the decision to launch the ad campaign was made by AFSCME's president in consultation with the executive board. According to a union spokesman, ''The President and the executive board of our union are given wide discretion in terms of expenditures of union treasury money. Those two groups jointly proposed, initiated, approved the original campaigns in the early 70's as well as the present campaigns.''

APPROPRIATION OF FUNDS

The campaign was financed from the union treasury, and the funding came out of membership dues. According to a union spokesman, this was an educational campaign; it was not directed toward any particular candidate, but against specific, and in most cases national, policies and programs. Therefore, it fell outside the jurisdiction of the Federal Election Commission. No political action funds, which are raised in an entirely different manner, were used.

EXECUTION OF CAMPAIGN STRATEGY

The AFSCME campaign strategy had four distinct features:

1. extensive use of public opinion polls prior to campaign launch to determine not only the issues to be advertised, but also the copy themes to be utilized;
2. employment of an outside agency to plan and implement the campaign;
3. use of television as the primary medium; and
4. postcampaign public opinion polls to measure the effectiveness of the campaign.

EXHIBIT 7

"One of these could educate every kid in Cincinnati."

"One brand-new B-1 bomber costs $87 million.

Enough to wipe out the cost of public education in Cincinnati. With enough left over to fund the libraries in the District of Columbia.

A single B-1 could pay for fire protection in Los Angeles for one year. Or finance the entire budget for the city of Atlanta.

Or pay all yearly expenses for streets, parks, and sanitation for Indianapolis, St. Louis, Pittsburgh, Hartford, and Milwaukee. *Combined.*

But what about the military benefits of the B-1?

According to a host of experts, there aren't any.

A Brookings Institution study found: 'No significant military advantages [are] to be gained by deploying a new penetrating bomber such as the B-1.'

Yet, two weeks ago, Congress voted full speed ahead on the most expensive weapon in U.S. history — a 244-plane system that could cost $100 billion.

Our union wants to stop the B-1 funding.

And we urge the Democratic Convention to join us.

We support a military strong enough to deter any aggressor foolish or venal enough to attack us.

But what good is it to be able to destroy Moscow ten times over if our own cities die in the meantime?"

—**Jerry Wurf**, President
American Federation of State,
County and Municipal Employees

AFSCME
the union that cares

American Federation of State, County, and Municipal Employees, 1625 L Street, N.W., Washington, D.C. 20036 Jerry Wurf, President William Lucy, Secretary-Treasurer. In New York City, AFSCME Is The Parent Organization of The 105,000 Municipal Employees Who Belong To District Council 37, AFSCME: And 10,000 Members of District Council 1707, The Community And Social Agency Employee Union.

EXHIBIT 8

"It's easy to cut human services if you don't see human suffering."

"Too many public officials are trying to cure budget problems in state and local government by cutting human services. And by closing their eyes to a lot of human problems we see every day.

Like the 70-year-old widow who has nowhere to live when the state shuts down the nursing home. Or the working mother who's forced onto welfare when the daycare center closes.

Or even the retarded kids who sit in locked rooms because there's no one to care for them.

But human suffering won't go away by ignoring it. Or by blaming the people who work in nursing homes, daycare centers, or mental hospitals.

Our union represents these workers, so we know what the politicians are ignoring. Our goal is to open your eyes."

"The business of government is people."
—Jerry Wurf, President

in the public service

American Federation of State, County and Municipal Employees
1625 L Street, NW, Washington, D.C. 20036

"Some budget slashers are missing the point."

"Budget cutting in state and local governments is politically popular. Unfortunately, it's not always financially smart.

Take New York for example. Without much thought, the state proposed to shut down 135 day care centers, serving 7,500 working families, in hopes of saving $20 million.

In fact, a Columbia School of Public Health study calculated that this 'saving' would have created $18.8 million in spending by other government agencies, both state and federal.

As the union representing state and local government workers, we see these kinds of blind budget decisions being made in every state, every day.

We know legitimate budget cuts are hard enough to live with. But false cuts are intolerable."

"The business of government is people."
—Jerry Wurf, President

in the public service

American Federation of State, County and Municipal Employees
1625 L Street, NW, Washington, D.C. 20036

EXHIBIT 9

According to the new administration, putting our economic house in order is a piece of cake

Now let's give them a tax cut. For a family of four making $100,000 dollars, we'll return $3,300. But, for a family of four earning $15,000, we'll give them back all of $185. Whoops, we forgot the social security tax increase and inflation.

Budget cuts and tax cuts, that's the ticket. If workers run out of unemployment benefits? Tough. If the breadwinner can't find a job? Let him eat cake.

Coming from an administration that says its on the side of the American worker, that doesn't leave much on the plate.

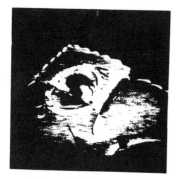

Then lop off medicaid, school lunches, college loans. If middle-income people suffer? Let them eat cake.

If you agree, contact your congressman. The American Federation of State, County and Municipal Employees.

EXHIBIT 10

Don't Do It, Mr. President.

President Reagan still wants to cut Social Security.

We can't afford to let him do it.

Social Security is *not* a handout. It's a contract between the United States Government and the American people — a contract we've earned through lifetimes of hard work.

The Administration and many Republicans want to break that contract. If they do, millions of Americans who paid into Social Security for years — and who have planned their retirement on it — are going to be hurt.

President Reagan wants to cut benefits by more than one-third for over 70 percent of those who retire next year. The worker who retires at age 62 could lose up to $160 a month; by 1986 the loss for an early retiree would more than double. Benefits would also be reduced for families, disabled persons, and workers retiring at 65.

President Reagan's cruelest cut will hurt those of us who must retire early. Over 70 percent of all early retirees don't have a choice. Some are in poor health. Others have lost their jobs. And many more workers, counting on the government's word, have made irreversible decisions to retire.

Right now, the axe is about to fall on the minimum Social Security benefit of $122 a month. This cut will directly hurt more than 1.5 million Americans, many of them women over 70.

President Reagan says he's cutting Social Security to save it. His strategy is to make people believe the system will go bankrupt if benefits aren't cut drastically. That's not true. The cuts President Reagan proposes aren't needed. Even worse, they'd come out of the modest $7,000 the average retired couple on Social Security gets per year. That's not much to live on.

Sure, our Social Security system has problems, caused by high unemployment and inflation. But there are ways to solve them without breaking government's promises to working Americans.

The immediate problem lies within just one of the three Social Security trust funds. The other two trust funds are financially healthy. Simple bookkeeping changes would allow them to make temporary loans to the one fund that needs help.

For a longer-term solution, we should fund Social Security from general tax revenues. Just about every other country does.

Improvements like these would *strengthen* Social Security. They wouldn't undermine it, as President Reagan's plan would do.

Together, we can stop these unfair cuts. Send a letter or mailgram, or call, your U.S. Senators and Representative. Tell them you want the federal government to keep its word. Tell them you've paid into Social Security and want it to be there when you need it.

The Administration and its friends in Congress want to cut Social Security fast, so write or call today. Don't let them take away what we've earned. And don't settle for a compromise that merely pushes back the cuts to a later date. Remember . . .

Social Security is a Contract, Not a Handout!

AFSCME.
American Federation of State,
County, and Municipal Employees

International Union
United Automobile, Aerospace,
and Agricultural Implement Workers of America
UAW

This ad is sponsored jointly by AFSCME and the UAW.

Precampaign Public Opinion Survey

In the spring of 1981, prior to launching the campaign, AFSCME asked the firm, Finger-hut and Granada, to conduct a public opinion survey. This survey was based on 1,500 respondents and was developed to provide a statistically accurate representation of the U.S. population. The primary objectives of the survey were (1) to test the public's knowledge of the budget and tax cuts, and (2) to ascertain public reaction to the specifics of both the tax and budget cuts.

The data showed that there was a clear misunderstanding as to the depth and the magnitude of both the tax and budget cuts, and that specific programs the president was proposing to cut had attracted and continued to attract widespread support. Based on these findings, the union concluded that it was not going to be enough—in terms of the message to be conveyed in those 60 short seconds in the ad—just to make assertions that the president was cutting back on social programs, or that the president was giving money to the rich and was not doing much for working people. The poll indicated that specific details were going to be needed in the advertisements to document the union's assertions.

The campaign strategy benefited from the poll in two ways: (1) It identified specific programs that had high approval ratings. (2) It helped the union develop a message that included information on specific programs and their public impact. AFSCME believes that it probably would not have known either of those things had it not conducted the polls.

1981 CAMPAIGN

Based on the information generated from the survey, AFSCME developed two campaigns with the assistance of the J. Walter Thompson advertising agency. Actual production was done by the agency. The ad concept was developed by the AFSCME public affairs and political affairs departments working with agency writers. The agency was also responsible for buying air time. Philip Sparks, AFSCME director of public affairs, stated:

> In terms of the advocacy campaign, we were interested in states that were urban, and traditionally democratic, with a high concentration of labor union members. Our message in both the spring and the fall campaign was: The administration was proposing things which the Congress opposed. President Reagan had been quite successful in pressuring Congress into passing his program; and people should let Congress know about how they felt about the Reagan program. We were not out to hew a middle of the road line in terms of our ads. We were trying to energize traditional Democratic voters, and labor union members, and get them to counterbalance the pressures that were being put on Congress by the administration.

The first series of commercials and print ads was launched in the spring, the second was launched in the fall of the same year.

The Spring 1981 Campaign

AFSCME's public opinion poll had clearly indicated that President Reagan's overall budget had strong public support which was not going to be diminished by the union's campaign. Therefore, the first round of commercials was not designed to win the battle of the budget, but rather to try to make people aware of the details of the program and to have second thoughts about it. It was hoped that once the program was implemented, those doubts would probably become suspicions and would translate into opposition to further cuts. The spring campaign was the beginning of a long educational program to tell the other side of the story. According to a union spokesman:

"We felt we were absolutely right and on target in what we were doing. Once the cuts go into effect in October 1981, people will realize that it is going to be more than just the welfare cheaters who are going to suffer from the program."

The main copy theme of the spring campaign was, "let them eat cake!" Commercials talked about the budget and tax cuts. One commercial showed an immense cake, the "Republican Economic Policy." It indicated that, according to the new administration, putting our economic house in order was a "piece of cake." Budget cuts plus tax cuts, that was it. It also showed that because of the way in which the cuts were made, it was the workers and breadwinners who suffered. The answer of the administration was to let them eat cake if they did not have enough money to support their families. The commercial asserted that the new administration took care of economic problems by increasing unemployment and cutting the budget for Medicaid, school lunches, college loans, and health and safety agencies.

In terms of the tax cuts, the commercial showed a loaf of bread being given to the rich, while a crumb fell to the working poor. The commercial stated that a family of four earning $15,000 per year would receive only $185 from Uncle Sam if the Reagan proposal was enacted, while a person making $100,000 would get back $3,000 from the government. The commercial asked viewers to write to their congressional representatives expressing their disfavor with the proposed tax cuts. (See Exhibit 9.)

The Fall 1981 Campaign

In the fall campaign, the focus was on Social Security. This ad featured the Social Security tax cuts, and the message was, "Social Security is a contract, not a handout!"

The ad indicated that American workers have contracted with the government to pay each year for their retirement, but the government wants to cut one-third of the amount of Social Security each retiree receives. The ad stated that Social Security is money earned, not a handout. It encouraged the American people to fight for their rights and to write to their congressional representatives expressing their disfavor with the proposed Social Security cuts. (See Exhibit 10.)

EFFECTIVENESS OF THE CAMPAIGN

The purpose of the spring 1981 campaign was to make people aware of the details of the proposed budget cuts so that they would question their value and effect on working people. According to the postcampaign polling, the campaign was successful and had an impact on people, even if that impact was transitory. The polling showed that overall support for the Reagan economic program had dropped by 15 to 20 points among people who had seen the AFSCME ad a number of times.

Although there was no postcampaign polling for the fall 1981 Social Security campaign, the feedback from the House Democratic caucus showed that the campaign generated a substantial amount of mail in opposition to the Reagan Social Security program at a critical time—when the administration was deciding whether it was going to go ahead with the program or back off. As Sparks said, "Our ad was fueling to the fire. . . . I do not have any doubt on social security."

The primary purpose of the spring 1981 ad was to educate people about the problems with the budget proposals. The polling conducted afterward showed significant success in this regard. However, there was a secondary purpose for this ad campaign, and that was to translate the education into opposition for future proposed cuts. This was a longer-term commitment, and its effects were to be seen in later years.

Note that the references following the Chemical Manufacturers case on p. 143 also apply to this case.

THE NATIONAL RIFLE ASSOCIATION AND GUN CONTROL

Lobbying activities and their influence
on government decision making

In 1981, President Ronald Reagan was the object of an assassination attempt at the hands of John Hinckley, who weeks before had easily purchased a handgun in a Dallas pawnshop. The White House press secretary, James S. Brady, was seriously wounded in the head and remains disabled to this day. Once again, the nation faced the paradoxical myth of the frontier, which combines liberty with license, personal safety with danger to others.

Reaction to the assassination attempt was swift on all sides. Two communities—Morton Grove, Illinois, and Kennesaw, Georgia—came to symbolize the polarization gripping the nation. Morton Grove passed the nation's first ordinance banning both the sale and the possession of handguns. This inflamed passions in Kennesaw, some 600 miles to the southeast. The officials there passed an ordinance of their own: Provided that they were neither lame nor mentally impaired, the heads of all households were to be required, under penalty of law, to keep a working gun in their residences.[1]

Since then, the political battle has been raging on local, state, and federal levels. Lobbying groups such as Handgun Control, Inc. (which was founded in 1974 following the assassination attempt on President Ford) call for strict federal legislation which would override any state or local ordinances. The National Rifle Association (NRA), which was founded in 1871, vehemently opposes federal gun control; at the same time it fears that local ordinances may sweep across the nation. It has campaigned in 17 states for laws preempting rights of municipalities to enact gun control measures. Nowhere was it more successful than in Florida, where the state government passed a law which would grant virtually anyone a permit to carry a hidden pistol, while guns in plain view carried no restrictions at all. On the other side, the state of Maryland in May 1988 passed a law banning the sale of pistols which are easily concealed, unsafe, or poorly made. The law set up a special board to determine which pistols should be banned. The law was unsuccessfully challenged in a 1988 statewide referendum.[2]

On the national level, the two sides disputed over the proposed McClure-Vollmer Act of 1985. This act, which passed the Senate easily without public hearings, would have gutted the 1968 Gun Control Act. It was eventually defeated. In 1988, antigun proponents succeeded in winning Senate approval of a bill proposed by Howard Metzenbaum (D-Ohio) which would require a seven-day waiting period (for a background check) when purchasing a handgun. When a similar measure was proposed in the House by Edward Feighan of Ohio in the summer of 1988, it was eventually defeated by a vote of 228 to 182. Neither side can work its will.[3]

It would appear that the nation, Congress, the presidency, and the NRA keep going through cycles of high activity after a national crisis (like the assassination of President Kennedy), followed by a weak gun control bill, if any, and then business as usual, where the NRA largely has its way. President Johnson's success in securing a gun control law, albeit a weak one, could appear from hindsight as no victory at all, because the law has been poorly enforced by the Bureau of Alcohol, Tobacco, and Firearms (ATF), and there have been continuous NRA efforts to further weaken the law.

The unparalleled congressional nonresponse to consistent and overwhelming public support for gun control legislation is the achievement of the gun lobby, spearheaded by the National Rifle Association. The success of the gun lobby is not due to a lack of proposals by the forces favoring gun control legislation. There has been a steady flow of bills at the federal, state, and local levels with, as noted, increased activity following actual or attempted assassinations of public figures. Every year, numerous gun control bill are introduced in Congress.

However, with a few minor exceptions (the NRA calls them "major setbacks"), none of these bills is enacted. Public opinion polls taken since 1934, the height of the Prohibition-sparked gangster era, have shown that an overwhelming majority of the American public supports some kind of restriction on the sale and possession of guns.[4] Table 1 summarizes the response to a 1985 Gallup poll regarding two issues: (1) the registration of handguns, and (2) banning handgun sales.

Seventy percent favor registration and they have consistently done so since at least 1972; at the same time, only 40% favor banning sales altogether. The only contrary information to date has emerged in a 1979 poll of 1,500 respondents conducted by Decision Making Information (DMI), a California-based polling firm sponsored by the National Rifle Association.[5]

Official gun control supporters include the National Riot and National Crime Commission, the American Bar Association, the National Council on Crime and Delinquency, the General Association of Women's Clubs, Women's Clubs of America, the National Association of Sheriffs, the American Civil Liberties Union, the AFL-CIO, the United Auto Workers, Americans for Democratic Action, and the Leadership Conference on Civil Rights (with 40 affiliated organizations).

The opposition to gun control legislation includes some libertarian groups, conservation groups, and some right-wing extremists. It is, however, almost entirely focused on the National Rifle Association, which has proven to be a most effective lobbying agent.

ISSUES FOR ANALYSIS

The success of the NRA and its allies raises a number of questions about the NRA's role in the legislative process.

1. Is the NRA, as it claims, protecting the consti-

TABLE 1. A. Respondents Reporting Whether They Favor or Oppose the Registration of All Handguns, by Demographic Characteristics, United States, 1985 (Percent)

Question: Do you favor or oppose the registration of all handguns?

	FAVOR	OPPOSE	NO OPINION
National	70	25	5
Sex:			
Male	64	33	3
Female	77	16	7
Age:			
Total under 30 years	73	21	6
18 to 24 years	72	22	6
25 to 29 years	75	20	5
30 to 49 years	69	27	4
Total 50 years and older	69	25	6
50 to 64 years	70	25	5
65 years and older	68	26	6
Region:			
East	78	16	6
Midwest	74	21	5
South	65	31	4
West	62	32	6
Race:			
White	69	25	6
Nonwhite	79	19	2
Black	81	16	3
Hispanic	68	29	3
Education:			
College graduate	72	25	3
College incomplete	72	22	6
High school graduate	68	26	6
Less than high school graduate	70	26	4
Politics:			
Republican	66	28	4
Democrat	75	20	5
Independent	68	29	3
Occupation:			
Professional and business	66	28	6
Clerical and sales	70	25	5
Manual worker	72	24	4
Skilled worker	70	26	4
Unskilled worker	74	22	4
Household income:			
$50,000 and over	65	29	6
$35,000 to $49,999	68	29	3
$25,000 to $34,999	70	26	4
$15,000 to $24,999	66	29	5
$10,000 to $14,999	72	23	5
Under $10,000	75	18	7
$25,000 and over	68	28	4
Under $25,000	72	23	5
Religion:			
Protestant	67	27	6
Catholic	75	21	4

SOURCE: Adapted from George Gallup, Jr., *The Gallup Report*, Report No. 237 (Princeton, N.J.: The Gallup Poll, June 1985), pp. 16 and 17. Reprinted by permission.

B. Attitudes Toward Laws Banning the Sale and Possession of Handguns in Own Community, by Demographic Characteristics, United States, 1985 (Percent)

Question: Some communities have passed laws banning the sale and possession of handguns. Would you favor or oppose having such a law in this city/community?

	FAVOR	OPPOSE	NO OPINION
National	40	56	4
Sex:			
Male	30	67	3
Female	48	46	6
Age:			
Total under 30 years	41	55	4
18 to 24 years	44	51	5
25 to 29 years	35	61	4
30 to 49 years	38	59	3
Total 50 years and older	41	54	5
50 to 64 years	39	57	4
65 years and older	42	51	7
Region:			
East	56	39	5
Midwest	36	59	5
South	30	66	4
West	38	58	4
Race:			
White	38	58	4
Nonwhite	50	47	3
Black	51	45	4
Hispanic	48	49	3
Education:			
College graduate	41	57	2
College incomplete	39	56	5
High school graduate	39	57	4
Less than high school graduate	40	55	5
Politics:			
Republican	36	60	4
Democrat	44	51	5
Independent	35	62	3
Occupation:			
Professional and business	37	60	3
Clerical and sales	39	58	3
Manual worker	39	57	4
Skilled worker	33	63	4
Unskilled worker	44	51	5
Household income:			
$50,000 and over	38	61	1
$35,000 to $49,999	35	63	2
$25,000 to $34,999	33	63	4
$15,000 to $24,999	37	58	5
$10,000 to $14,999	44	53	3
Under $10,000	47	46	7
$25,000 and over	34	63	3
Under $25,000	43	52	5
Religion:			
Protestant	33	62	5
Catholic	49	47	4

SOURCE: Adapted from George Gallup, Jr., *The Gallup Report*, Report No. 237 (Princeton, N.J.: The Gallup Poll, June 1985), pp. 16 and 17. Reprinted by permission.

tutionally guaranteed freedom of millions of men, women, and children to keep and bear arms in the interests of sports, liberty, and the American way of life? Or is it working to protect special interests?

2. Does the NRA's ability to prevent the enactment of legislation signal the strength of a system that enables citizens to protect their rights? Or does it point out the vulnerability of a system that can be virtually paralyzed by a small but vocal and organized minority protecting its privilege against the contrary demands of public opinion, the public interest, and the general welfare?

3. In either case, is it acceptable for any special interest group to ensure that Congress does not act contrary to the group's own view of public welfare? Or is it Congress's responsibility to regulate the activities of such groups to ensure that their limited definitions of the public interest do not completely override broader and more generally accepted ones?

4. Where does the proper compromise lie between individual rights and liberties and collective or societal necessity? Is such a compromise either possible or in the public interest?

THE HISTORY OF REGULATION

State and Local Regulation

Although legislation restricting a citizen's right to carry arms in public predates nationhood (Massachusetts, for example, enacted such a law in 1692), the concept of legislation to control the purchase and ownership of guns did not appear in this country until 1911. At that time, the state of New York enacted its still-controversial Sullivan Law, which requires a license to purchase or own a handgun or other concealable weapon. The other 2,000 or so state laws dealing with the manufacture, sale, and use of firearms which existed as of 1988 are less effective in controlling or recording the rapidly proliferating possession of guns by the general public. In the past decades, a number of states have passed more restrictive gun legisla-

tion.[6] A summary of state legislation is presented in Table 2.[7]

As of 1984, only 6 states required registration and 13 a permit to purchase a handgun. Twenty states imposed a waiting period. Only 18 states required a license to carry a handgun openly, while 33 required a license if the handgun was carried concealed.

To counter the lack of effective control at the state level, various municipalities have enacted their own more stringent regulations. Some local communities have historically had requirements covering such areas as dealer registration, purchase permits, waiting periods, permits for possession, regulations on indiscriminate firing of guns, and, in some cities, the registration of all handguns.

Federal Regulation

Congress enacted two minor pieces of legislation during the 1920s; a 1924 excise tax on gun and ammunition sales, and a 1928 prohibition, with some exceptions, of handgun shipments by mail (avoided by express shipment). These attempts at federal regulation did not deal with the issue of controlling the purchase and possession of guns. The attention of an increasingly crime-conscious nation came into abrupt focus with the February 15, 1933, attempted assassination of president-elect Franklin D. Roosevelt. In a pattern to become fearfully familiar in the ensuing 40 years, national shock was soon translated into stringent gun control demands. During 1933, 12 gun control bills were introduced in Congress—seven in the House, five in the Senate. These laws, as originally proposed, required record keeping at the time of sale of small, concealable handguns, such as pistols and revolvers, as well as such "gangster" weapons as machine guns, silencers, sawed-off shotguns, and rifles. The penalty for illegal possession was to be up to five years in prison. The intent of the law was to discourage weapons use and to afford another device for arrest-

TABLE 2. Statutory Restrictions on the Purchase, Carrying, and Ownership of Handguns, by State, as of July 1985

State	Purchase				Carrying				Ownership	
	Application and waiting period	License or permit to purchase	Registration	Record of sales sent to state or local government	Carrying openly prohibited	Carrying concealed prohibited	License to carry openly	License to carry concealed	Owner licensing or identification card	Constitutional provision
Alabama	✓			✓			✓ᵃ	✓		✓
Alaska										✓
Arizona						✓				✓
Arkansas				✓ᵇ		✓ᵇ				✓
California	✓			✓		✓		✓		
Colorado						✓		✓		✓
Connecticut	✓			✓			✓	✓		✓
Delaware						✓		✓		
Florida	✓ᶜ	✓ᶜ	✓ᶜ	✓ᶜ			✓	✓		✓
Georgia							✓	✓		✓
Hawaii	✓	✓	✓				✓	✓		✓
Idaho								✓		✓
Illinois	✓	✓	✓ᵈ,ᶜ	✓ᶜ	✓ᶠ	✓			✓ᵍ	✓
Indiana	✓			✓			✓	✓		✓
Iowa		✓		✓			✓	✓		
Kansas	✓ᶜ	✓ᶜ	✓ᶜ			✓			✓	
Kentucky						✓				✓
Louisiana		✓ʰ				✓		✓		✓
Maine						✓		✓		✓
Maryland	✓			✓			✓	✓		
Massachusetts		✓		✓			✓	✓	✓	✓
Michigan		✓	✓ⁱ	✓			✓ᵃ	✓		✓
Minnesota	✓	✓		✓			✓	✓		
Mississippi			✓			✓				✓
Missouri		✓		✓		✓				✓
Montana						✓		✓		✓
Nebraska						✓				✓
Nevada						✓ʲ		✓		
New Hampshire						✓		✓		✓
New Jersey	✓	✓		✓			✓	✓	✓	✓
New Mexico						✓				
New York		✓	✓	✓			✓	✓	✓	✓
North Carolina		✓		✓		✓				✓
North Dakota				✓	✓ᶠ			✓		✓
Ohio	✓ᶜ	✓ᵏ		✓ᵏ		✓				✓
Oklahoma				✓ᶠ		✓				✓
Oregon	✓			✓		✓		✓		✓
Pennsylvania	✓			✓			✓ᵃ	✓		✓
Rhode Island	✓			✓			✓	✓		✓
South Carolina				✓			✓	✓		✓
South Dakota	✓			✓				✓		✓
Tennessee	✓			✓	✓ᵇ	✓ᵇ				✓
Texas					✓	✓				✓
Utah					✓ᶠ	✓				✓
Vermont					✓ˡ	✓ˡ		✓		✓
Virginia	✓ᶜ	✓ᶜ								✓
Washington	✓			✓			✓ᵃ,ᶠ	✓		
West Virginia				✓			✓	✓		✓ᵐ
Wisconsin	✓					✓				
Wyoming						✓		✓		✓
District of Columbia		✓ᵉ	✓ᵉ		✓ᵉ	✓ᵉ			✓ᵉ	

ᵃLicense to carry in a vehicle either openly or concealed.

ᵇArkansas prohibits carrying "with a purpose to employ it as a weapon against a person." Tennessee prohibits carrying "with the intent to go armed."

(cont.)

ing gangsters. The NRA reacted; pistols, revolvers, handguns, and semiautomatic rifles were eliminated from the list of weapons. The final version of the law, enacted over the opposition of the NRA, was the National Firearms Act of 1934. This law, which excludes handguns, provides for a prohibitive tax on the manufacture, sale, or transfer of machine guns and other fully automatic weapons, sawed-off shotguns and rifles, mufflers, and silencers. Although useless in controlling the flow of handguns to the general public, the act did eliminate the "smoking tommy gun" as the symbol of organized crime and ended much of the more open underworld warfare.

The Federal Firearms Act, a second bill enacted in 1938, makes the interstate shipment of firearms a criminal offense if a dealer knows or has reasonable cause to believe that the recipient is a criminal. Since it is one thing to prove that a gun was shipped to a convicted felon, but quite another thing to prove that the dealer knew the recipient was a felon, the law was almost ineffectual.

Such was, with a few minor exceptions (such as the Federal Aviation Act of 1958, which prohibited carrying weapons in an airplane) the state of federal gun control laws until 1968.

The Gun Control Act of 1968. The assassinations of Martin Luther King, Jr., in April of 1968 and of Senator Robert Kennedy in June of that year finally broke the resistance of Congress, which had not acted following the deaths of President John F. Kennedy, Malcolm X, George Lincoln Rockwell, and Medgar Evers. On June 7, 1968, the day after Senator Robert Kennedy's assassination, the House passed the 1968 Omnibus Crime Bill, Title IV, which contained restrictions on the sale and possession of handguns. The bill originally covered rifles and shotguns as well, but this coverage was deleted in the Senate, which had earlier passed the bill. In the interests of capitalizing on the national shock of Senator Kennedy's death, President Johnson urged immediate passage of the Omnibus bill as a first step but not a final solution. When he signed it on June 20, he called on Congress to take more decisive action: "We must go further and stop mail order murder by rifle and shotgun. . . . What in the name of conscience will it take to pass a truly effective gun control law?"[8]

Congress complied, and in October, President Johnson signed the second major federal gun control legislation of the last three decades. The Gun Control Act of 1968 was a compromise bill whose passage was made possible by concessions to those who were opposed to further federal controls and those who wanted extensive further involve-

---

^cCertain cities or counties.

^dChicago only.

^eApplies only to preregistered firearms. No new handguns can be brought into the city.

^fLoaded.

^gHandguns prohibited in Evanston, Oak Park, and Morton Grove.

^hNew Orleans only.

ⁱHandguns must be presented to the city chief of police or county sheriff to obtain a certificate of inspection.

^jPermission to carry concealed may be granted by county sheriff on written application.

^kSome municipalities control the possession, sale, transfer, or carrying of handguns, e.g., Cleveland and Columbus require a police permit for purchase; Toledo requires a handgun owner's identification; Cincinnati requires application for purchase.

^lProhibits carrying a firearm "with the intent or purpose of injuring another."

^mConstitutional provision to be on November, 1986, ballot.

Note: These data were compiled by the National Rifle Association's Institute for Legislative Action. In addition to state laws, the purchase, sale, and in certain circumstances, the possession and interstate transportation of firearms are regulated by the Federal Gun Control Act of 1968 and Title VII of the Omnibus Crime Control and Safe Streets Act. Also, cities and localities may have their own firearms ordinances in addition to federal and state laws. State firearms laws are subject to frequent change. State and local statutes and ordinances, as well as local law enforcement authorities, should be consulted for full text and meaning of statutory provisions.

Constitutional provision can be defined by citing Article 1, Section 15 of the Connecticut State constitution as an example of the basic features contained in the constitutions of many states. It reads: "Every citizen has a right to bear arms in defense of himself and the State."

SOURCE: Table provided by the National Rifle Association, Institute for Legislative Action.

ment. The main objectives of the act were as follows:

1. eliminating the interstate traffic in firearms and ammunition that had previously frustrated state and local efforts to license, register, or restrict ownership of guns;
2. denying access to firearms to certain congressionally defined groups, including minors, convicted felons, and persons who had been adjudicated as mental defectives or committed to mental institutions; and
3. ending the importation of all surplus military firearms and all other guns unless certified by the Secretary of the Treasury as "particularly suitable for . . . sporting purposes."

The act also extended the coverage and relative prohibitive taxes to "destructive devices" first imposed in the 1934 Act, and it mandated additional penalties for persons convicted of committing federal crimes with firearms.

Interstate Traffic

As a result of the Gun Control Act of 1968, interstate traffic in firearms was prohibited except by federally licensed dealers. It was also declared unlawful for any unlicensed person to engage in the manufacture and sale of firearms, regardless of whether or not such a business involved interstate commerce. Federal licenses were also subjected to minimum standards established by the Treasury. The Act also provided for criminal penalties for law violations.

A dealer selling firearms was required to seek identification from the purchaser establishing that he or she was not an out-of-state purchaser, and to keep such records for inspection by the Bureau of Alcohol, Tobacco, and Firearms. Any violation of the law would require either a falsification of documents on the part of the purchaser or willful violation by the dealer. The system of recordkeeping was deliberately kept highly decentralized by the Treasury, with the concurrence of Congress, in order to avoid any

potential charge of encouraging "gun registration," even though doing so made detection of any law violation and enforcement extremely expensive.

Denial of Access

The 1968 Act expanded the categories of persons named in the Federal Firearms Act of 1938 who were banned from owning firearms or ammunition. Federal licensees were banned from the knowing transfer of guns or ammunition to the following:

1. minors (under 18 for shotguns and rifles; under 21 for handguns);
2. persons convicted of a state or federal felony, as well as the fugitives and defendants under indictment covered by the 1938 Act;
3. adjudicated mental defectives and any person who has been committed to a mental institution; and
4. persons who are unlawful users of or "addicted to marijuana or any depressant or stimulant drug . . . or narcotic drug."

The purpose of these prohibitions was to deny access to guns and ammunition to these defined special risk groups or, failing that, to punish possession of a firearm as a federal offense, whether or not the possession was in violation of local law.

Limitation of Imports

The Act banned importation of any firearm or ammunition into the United States except when specifically certified by the Secretary of the Treasury as particularly suitable for sporting purposes. The primary aim of this provision was to ban the import of cheap guns, called "Saturday Night Specials." Testimony before Congress suggested that the cheap imported guns were considered unsafe and were associated with easy availability to a specific class of people regarded as violence-prone.

Since 1968, many new bills have been

introduced in Congress each year to both ease and tighten various provisions of the 1968 law. The most significant of these are the McClure-Vollmer Act of 1985 and the 1988 Feighan-Metzenbaum legislation. The provisions of both proposals as seen by Handgun Control, Inc. are summarized in Table 3.

THE ARGUMENTS: PRO AND CON

For over four decades, those on both sides of the gun control debate have held firm positions. There are three basic arguments: constitutional, crime, and public health.

The Constitutional Argument

Many critics of handgun control seeking legislation see gun control as an attack on civil rights. An official NRA study stated the following:[9] "Today grave dangers and assaults from many directions threaten all the individual rights of the people. The most fierce assault is the erosion of rights by legal process, a procedure most dangerous because it is so effective."

Article II of the Bill of Rights (the Second Amendment to the Constitution) states: "A well regulated militia, being necessary to the security of a free State, the right of the people to keep and bear Arms, shall not be infringed." The NRA interprets this statement literally. According to the statement of policy of the National Rifle Association:[10]

The NRA is opposed to the registration on any level of government of the ownership of rifles, shotguns, pistols or revolvers for any purpose whatever. Regardless of professed intent, there can be only one outcome of registration, and that is to make possible the seizure of such weapons by political authorities, or by persons seeking to overthrow the government by force. Registration will not keep guns out of the hands of undesirable

persons, and few people seriously claim that it will.

Supreme Court cases have established two conceptual interpretations of the Second Amendment. In *United States* v. *Miller*, 306 U.S. 174, 178 (1939), the Supreme Court upheld the conviction of two men who transported in interstate commerce a shotgun, which came within the definition of a firearm under the National Firearms Act of 1934 and was not registered as required by the Act nor covered by a stamp-affixed order. The Act was challenged on constitutional grounds. The Court found that the Second Amendment did not guarantee the keeping and bearing of any weapon not having a reasonable relationship to the preservation or efficiency of a well-regulated militia. The Court stated that the obvious purpose of the Amendment was to ensure the continuation and render possible the effectiveness of the militia subjected to call and organization by Congress under Article I, section 8, clause 15 and 16 of the Constitution, and the Amendment must be interpreted and applied with that end in view.

In *Presser* v. *Illinois*, 116 U.S 252 (1886), the Supreme Court upheld an Illinois state law that forbade drilling or parading with arms in cities and towns unless authorized by law. The Supreme Court defined the well-regulated militia as a governmentally controlled body rather than a privately organized army, and this is the definition generally accepted today. This definition guarantees a collective right to keep and bear arms in order to preserve a militia. A question arises as to the type of arms included with the protection of the provision.

The majority of state cases follow the doctrine expressed in *Commonwealth* v. *Murphy*, 44 N.E. 138 (Mass. 1896) that "it has been almost universally held that the legislature may regulate and limit the mode of carrying arms." Therefore, a state statute regulating or sometimes prohibiting the carrying of enumerated weapons is not in opposition

TABLE 3. A. Provisions of the McClure-Volkmer Bill, 1985

WHAT THE NRA WANTED: ORIGINAL BILL	$.49 AS PASSED
End federal licensing of individuals who make "occasional sales, exchanges or purchases" of firearms. Pawnbrokers and part-time dealers escape federal record keeping requirements and oversight.	Retains federal controls over pawnbrokers and part time dealers. *New Senate bill, when passed by House, will close loopholes on dealers who provide guns for criminal or terrorist purposes.
Allow mail-order gun sales.	Continues prohibition on mail-order gun sales.
Allow interstate over-the-counter gun sales from individuals, making it easier to buy and sell guns across state lines without keeping any records.	Continues prohibition of interstate handgun sales. Permits individuals to purchase rifles or shotguns interstate from licensed dealers only, with proper records maintained.
Allow dealers to sell guns from "private collections" without keeping any records of sales.	Permits dealers to make unrecorded sales from personal collections if (1) firearm was held in personal collection for one year and (2) the firearm was not transferred to personal collection for purposes of evading recordkeeping.* New Senate bill, when passed by House, will require dealers to keep a record of these sales.
Prohibit all surprise inspections of gun dealers. Required "probable cause" before records could be inspected.	Permits Bureau of Alcohol, Tobacco and Firearms to make annual surprise inspection. Also permits review of records for tracing, in connection with other criminal investigations or upon showing of "reasonable cause" to believe a criminal violation occurred.
Void laws requiring licenses to carry handguns in many states.	Permits limited right to transport firearms from one state where gun is legally owned and carried to another where gun may be legally owned and carried if firearm is unloaded and not readily locked in a case, separate from ammunition. Weapons cannot be in glove compartment.
Bar prosecution for most criminal violations discovered during surprise inspections. For example, if government agents discovered illegal narcotics or evidence of a murder, no charges could be brought.	Provision dropped.
Expand provision allowing for loan of firearm to out-of-state resident for lawful sporting purpose to allow loan for any lawful purpose.	Provision dropped.
Provide "simple carelessness" as a defense for record keeping violations.	Dropped simple carelessness defense. Reduced penalties for record keeping violations.
Weakened mandatory sentence law by requiring prosecutor to prove that gun was actually used to further a crime and providing a "self-defense" exception for criminals using guns in crime.	Provision dropped.
Allow dealers to sell guns from "temporary locations" including any sidewalk stands and yard sales.	Permits dealers to sell firearms only at gunshows sponsored by any national, state, or local firearm organization as is currently allowed by regulation.
Loosen importation criteria to require U.S to permit importation of more Saturday Night Specials.	Retained current criteria for importing Saturday Night Specials, i.e., handgun must be "generally recognized as *particularly* suitable for sporting purposes."

B. Provisions to Strengthen Gun Laws Not Originally Contained in Mcclure-Volkmer

Closed loophole in 1968 Gun Control Act by expanding ban on importation of Saturday Night Specials to include ban on importing parts.	Expands definition of machine gun to include parts used for converting semi-automatics to machine guns, and bans sale, transfer and possession of conversion kits not lawfully owned today.
Bans sales, transfer and possession of machine guns not lawfully owned today.	Expands regulation of silencers to include silencer kits or parts.

C. Proposals of the Feighan-Metzenbaum Bill, 1988

Handgun Control seeks to pass federal legislation to keep handguns out of the wrong hands. Our legislative agenda includes provisions which police and other law enforcement experts have demanded for years:

- **a waiting period and background check** to screen out illegal handgun purchasers, such as convicted felons and drug users;

- **a mandatory jail sentence** for using a handgun in the commission of a crime;

C. Proposals of the Feighan-Metzenbaum Bill, 1988 (cont'd)

- **a license-to-carry law,** requiring a special license to carry a handgun outside one's home or place of business;

- **a ban on the manufacture and sale of snub-nosed handguns,** the Saturday Night Specials used in two-thirds of handgun crime;

- **restriction on the sale of UZI-type assault weapons,** the weapons of war like that used in the 1983 McDonald's massacre in California;

- **a ban on the manufacture and sale of plastic handguns** which made metal detectors and airport screening devices useless. '' . . . The International Association of Chiefs of Police urges the law enforcement community within each state to support and encourage the enactment of legislation pertinent to the screening of handgun purchasers.''

SOURCE: The International Association of Chiefs of Police, 1981 Resolution.

to the Second Amendment or its counterpart in a state constitution. No infringement would bear upon the amendment with acts barring deadly weapons or requiring licenses.

Recently, the NRA has also emphasized the relevance of the first and fourth amendments in interpreting the Second Amendment. Critics of the NRA interpretation of the Second Amendment right to bear arms interpret the term *people* collectively. However, such a restrictive reading of the First Amendment right of assembly or the Fourth Amendment ''right of the people to be secure in their persons, houses, papers and effects, against unreasonable searches and seizures'' would surely be an erosion of individual rights, which those amendments have traditionally been construed to protect. The context suggests that the Second Amendment be interpreted individually, rather than merely collectively.[11]

The Supreme Court, however, has struck down one provision of the 1934 Act on constitutional grounds. In 1968, the Court declared unconstitutional a portion of the law's registration system. The Court's decision was, however, based on the Fifth Amendment, not the Second: The Court held that the registration system in effect required persons to testify against themselves.[12]

Gun control proponents hold that the federal government has full power, under the Constitution, to control firearms in the United States. The power of Congress to regulate firearms under the taxing and commerce clause is clear. Recent Supreme Court decisions have reaffirmed congressional power to enact a broad range of regulatory legislation under the taxing provisions of the National Firearms Act as a legitimate exercise of the United States Congress's power to tax. If Congress were to find that sale and possession of firearms affects interstate commerce or should be taxed, it may take whatever regulatory steps it desires.

The NRA has continued to maintain that the right to possess arms, including shotguns and rifles for sports, in the interest of a prepared citizenry is fundamental to Americans. The NRA further insists that this liberty, far from being a privilege, is a necessity for the protection of the nation from its enemies, both foreign and domestic. The NRA has not wavered from its position stated over 30 years ago in *The American Rifleman:*[13]

> Fighting in the next major war will not be confined to the battlefield alone. It is inevitable that our homeland will be attacked. . . . More than ever, the individual soldier and the individual citizen will be forced to rely on the weapon with which he is armed, and on his ability to use it effectively, if he is to survive.

The Crime Argument

The crime argument is related to the number of guns available in the United States, the lack of adequate controls to prevent acquisition by unauthorized persons, the number of crimes committed with handguns, the number of homicides involving handguns, and the potential deaths and injuries that could possibly be eliminated with better handgun controls. There are numerous controversies over the correct interpretation of statistics. Both sides employ unverifiable rhetoric: "Less crimes are committed because the intended victims had guns to use for self-defense and, thereby, frightened away criminals," or "Crimes would surely be less if guns were not so easily available." The use of such rhetorical devices suggests that the statistical evidence is itself ambiguous.

Advocates make three arguments in favor of gun control. First is the danger-of-proliferation approach—that is, more guns lead to more crimes and killings using guns. The second related argument is the use of guns by citizens in noncriminal situations; the third is the "weapons sickness" approach—that is, that mere possession alters consciousness, predisposing the owner to violence.

During the years from 1976 to 1985, total crime decreased by 1.5% (see Table 4). Although property crime decreased by 3.5%, violent crime increased by 18.9%. The high-growth categories were forcible rape (up by 37.6%) and aggravated assault (up by 29.9%). Robbery was up by 4.6%, but murder actually decreased by 10.2%. That urban area rates were consistently above the city rates is relevant to the regional strength of the pro- and antigun lobbies, especially as manifested in congressional votes.

Firearms figured in 59.1% of murders, 34.3% of robberies, and 21.3% of aggravated assaults; firearms usage in these crimes actually declined slightly from 1982 to 1985 (see Table 5A, B, C, D). The decrease from 1975 to 1985 is even more dramatic: from 65.8% to 58.7% for murder; from 24.9% to 21.3% for aggravated assault, and from 44.8% to 36.3% for robbery.

What sense is to be made of such trends, especially when gun control advocates

imply that the number of handguns in circulation has actually increased? The NRA contends that there is little connection between carry laws and crime rates (see Table 5D). Clearly, analysts must consider all relevant factors when determining the origins of crime. The least restrictive areas (see Table 5D) are more rural, crime rates are socioculturally lower, and therefore there is little social impetus for restrictions. At the very least, the NRA contends that carry laws are not the determining variable in crime rates.[14]

James D. Wright, former Speaker of the House and formerly a strong proponent of gun control, changed his position:[15] "As far as I can tell, the arguments in favor of 'stricter gun control' fail nearly every empirical test, although in many cases, I hasten to add, the 'failure' is simply that the appropriate research is not available."

The analysis of the issue has clearly suffered from the single-variable approach adopted by both sides. In this, Wright may be correct in calling for "appropriate research." Furthermore, the NRA would have to assess whether the rate of gun-related crime might actually be lessened by appropriate legislation. The needed comparison is not between low crime/less restrictive areas and high crime/more restrictive areas but between high crime/nonrestrictive and high crime/restrictive areas.

People question whether accurate data are available on the number of handguns and other firearms in the possession of civilians in the United States. As seen in Table 6, a 1984 survey shows that 45% of all households possess a firearm and 21% possess a pistol.

In another survey of motives for firearm ownership, 65% (of the 42% who said they were gun owners) said that they owned the gun for recreation, 20% for protection, 12% for both recreation and protection, and 2% expressed no opinion.[16] In all, 37% link gun ownership to protection.

Moreover, the data on the sale and manufacture of domestic handguns are also dis-

TABLE 4. Crime Rates, 1976-1985
A. Selected Crime Rates

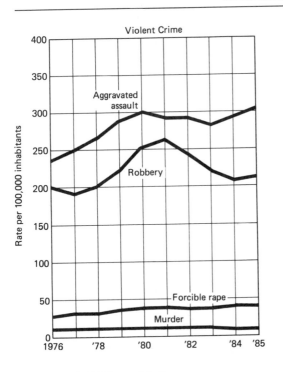

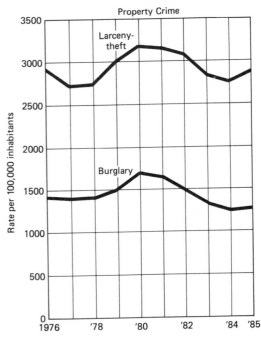

Chart prepared by U.S. Bureau of the Census

puted. Under the law, The Bureau of Alcohol, Tobacco, and Firearms (ATF), a bureau of the U.S. Treasury Department, can require such data and make it public. As seen in Table 6B, handgun production in the U.S. has hovered around 2 million from 1973 to 1982, the low being 1.7 and the high 2.6 million pieces.

The United States is the only industrialized nation that does not have strict firearms regulation on a national basis. In Britain, for example, the purchaser of any gun, even for hunting, must obtain a permit, and all sales are registered with the police. France and Italy have similar regulations, and background investigations of would-be gun purchasers in those countries may take up to six weeks. Spain imposed the additional restriction that only 50 rounds of ammunition may be purchased at one time. In West Germany, citizens may own handguns only upon showing a specific need for personal protection, such as dangerous occupations or living quarters, and permits are required for purchase and carrying. Opponents of controls frequently point to Switzerland as an example of a country where gun ownership is universal. Virtually every male of military age is required to keep his military equipment in his home, including weapons and ammunition. Procontrol advocates counter that each of these guns is registered and every round of ammunition for them must be accounted for. The purchase and ownership of nonmilitary weapons is as strictly regulated in Switzerland as in other European countries. These countries, all with stricter firearms controls than the United States, also

Crime Rates, 1976-1985

B. Crimes and Crime Rates, by Type
(Data refer to offenses known to the police. Rates are based on Bureau of the Census estimated resident
population as of July 1, except 1980, enumerated as of April 1.)

ITEM AND YEAR	Total	VIOLENT CRIME					PROPERTY CRIME			
		Total	Murder[a]	Forcible rape	Robbery	Aggravated assault	Total	Burglary	Larceny—theft	Motor vehicle theft
Number of offenses (1,000):										
1976	11,350	1,004	18.8	57.1	428	501	10,346	3,109	6,271	966
1977	10,985	1,030	19.1	63.5	413	534	9,955	3,072	5,906	978
1978	11,209	1,086	19.6	67.6	427	571	10,123	3,128	5,991	1,004
1979	12,250	1,208	21.5	76.4	481	629	11,042	3,328	6,601	1,113
1980	13,408	1,345	23.0	83.0	566	673	12,064	3,795	7,137	1,132
1981	13,424	1,362	22.5	82.5	593	664	12,062	3,780	7,194	1,088
1982	12,974	1,322	21.0	78.8	553	669	11,652	3,447	7,143	1,062
1983	12,109	1,258	19.3	78.9	507	663	10,851	3,130	6,713	1,008
1984	11,882	1,273	18.7	84.2	485	685	10,609	2,984	6,592	1,032
1985	12,430	1,327	19.0	87.3	498	723	11,103	3,073	6,926	1,103
Percent change, number of offenses:										
1976–1985	9.5	32.2	1.1	53.0	16.4	44.5	7.3	− 1.1	10.5	14.2
1981–1985	− 7.4	−2.5	-15.7	5.9	− 16.0	8.9	− 8.0	−18.7	−3.7	1.4
1984–1985	4.6	4.3	1.6	3.7	2.7	5.5	4.7	3.0	5.1	6.8
Rate per 100,000 inhabitants:										
1976	5,287	468	8.8	26.6	199	233	4,820	1,448	2,921	450
1977	5,078	476	8.8	29.4	191	247	4,602	1,420	2,730	452
1978	5,140	498	9.0	31.0	196	262	4,643	1,435	2,747	461
1979	5,566	549	9.7	34.7	218	286	5,017	1,512	2,999	506
1980	5,950	597	10.2	36.8	251	299	5,353	1,684	3,167	502
1981	5,858	594	9.8	36.0	259	290	5,264	1,650	3,140	475
1982	5,604	571	9.1	34.0	239	289	5,033	1,489	3,085	459
1983	5,175	538	8.3	33.7	217	279	4,637	1,338	2,869	431
1984	5,031	539	7.9	35.7	205	290	4,492	1,264	2,791	437
1985	5,207	556	7.9	36.6	209	303	4,651	1,287	2,901	462
Percent change, rate per 100,000 inhabitants:										
1976–1985	− 1.5	18.9	−10.2	37.6	4.6	29.9	− 3.5	− 11.1	− .7	2.7
1981–1985	− 11.1	− 6.4	−19.4	1.7	− 19.4	4.6	− 11.7	− 22.0	− 7.6	2.7
1984–1985	3.5	3.1	—	2.5	1.5	4.4	3.5	1.9	3.9	5.7

—Represents zero.
[a]Includes nonnegligent manslaughter.
Minus sign (−) indicates decrease.
SOURCE: U.S. Federal Bureau of Investigation, *Crime in the United States,* annual.

have a much lower fatality rate than does this country, as shown in Table 7A.

To the opponents of gun control, however, all these arguments are contrived, based on abuse or misuse of statistics, and are advanced to support a predetermined position. Blackman raised the criticism that such comparisons are too facile and neglect the other determinants of the homicide rate—notably cultural differences and different modes of law enforcement.[17]

The NRA holds that even if gun control laws were relevant to crime statistics (which they deny), they could not be enforced anyway. The result would be that law-abiding citizens would be at a serious disadvantage in facing the criminal element. Given that there are between 50 and 100 million handguns in the U.S., the NRA asks how we are supposed to cope with the problem of enforcement when even a small minority refuses to comply. Even if a majority of owners

C. Crimes and Crime Rates, by Type and Area: 1984 and 1985
(In thousands, except rate. Rate per 100,000 population. Estimated totals based on reports from city and rural law enforcement agencies representing 97 percent of the national population.)

| TYPE OF CRIME | 1984 | | | | | | 1985 | | | | | |
| | MSAs | | OTHER CITIES | | RURAL AREAS | | MSAs | | OTHER CITIES | | RURAL AREAS | |
	Total	Rate	Total	Rate	Total	Rate	Total	Rate	Total	Rate	Total	Rate
Total	10,268	5,717	1,015	4,451	599	1,774	10,767	5,921	1,051	4,580	612	1,803
Violent crime	1,148	639	71	313	55	162	1,197	658	73	319	56	168
Murder and nonnegligent manslaughter	16	9	1	5	2	5	16	9	1	5	2	6
Forcible rape	74	41	5	21	6	17	76	42	5	21	6	18
Robbery	470	262	10	44	5	15	483	266	10	44	5	15
Aggravated assault	588	327	55	243	42	124	622	342	57	249	44	129
Property crime	9,120	5,078	944	4,139	545	1,613	9,569	5,262	978	4,262	555	1,635
Burglary	2,558	1,424	220	967	206	610	2,632	1,447	229	999	212	625
Larceny—theft	5,605	3,121	681	2,988	306	905	5,915	3,253	704	3,067	307	906
Motor vehicle theft	957	533	42	183	33	98	1,023	562	45	195	35	104

SOURCE: U.S Federal Bureau of Investigation, *Crime in the United States,* annual.

were willing to give up their guns, the owners of 1 out of 3,000 handguns involved in murders are unlikely to do so. Thus, enforcement of the laws would have to exceed 99% effectiveness before even one murderer would be disarmed.[18]

The NRA argues, suppose that between 10% and 25% of handgun owners refuse to comply with any law pertaining to handgun registration or confiscation, a not unrealistic presumption: What would be the alternative? Such a situation could mean massive police searches, violation of individual privacy, and tremendous cost of enforcement with dubious benefits.

The Public Health Argument

In recent literature, much mre attention has been focused on guns as a public health hazard (see Table 7B). The data indicate that accidents caused by firearms declined from 1.2% in 1970 to 0.7% in 1983, and the gross number declined from 2,406 to 1,695. Handgun Control, Inc., has focused on the family tragedies involved, especially the cases of violent family situations and suicide. 1983 Gallup polls suggested that 26% of respondents felt that stricter gun laws would reduce deaths due to family arguments "a great deal," while 28% said "quite a lot,"

25% said "not very much," and only 18% "not at all." When asked the same question regarding accidental deaths, the responses were practically identical.[19] The NRA questions whether gun control would actually resolve those problems. The tragedy remains nonetheless, and the question is whether public policy is called for to prevent such accidents or self-inflicted harm.

POWER AND JUSTICE: THE MORALITY OF STRATEGIES AND TACTICS

In a democratic society, laws invariably reflect lawmakers' perceptions of the long-term public interest—perceptions often tempered by lobbyists for special interests. Therefore, the fate of gun control efforts must be analyzed not only by the rationale of various sociopolitical, legal, or economic arguments pertaining to society overall, but also on the strengths, weaknesses, and influence of vested interests, most notably the NRA.

The gun lobby, spearheaded by the NRA, includes manufacturers of guns and related equipment (including clothing manufacturers, sportsmen and women, target shooters, conservation groups, and right-wing extremist groups).

Table 5. A. 1986 Crimes by Weapon

CRIME	FIREARMS	KNIFE	PERSONAL[a]	OTHER
Murder	59.1%	20.5%	6.8%	13.5%[b]
Robbery	34.3	13.5	42.6[c]	9.7
Aggravated assault	21.3	22.0	24.8	31.9

[a]Hands, feet, etc.

[b]Includes murders where weapon was unknown

[c]Strong-arm tactics

Note: Percentages may not add to 100 because of rounding.

SOURCE: FBI, *Crime in the United States, 1986.* Cited in D.S. Greene,
"Gun Control" *Editorial Research Reports* (November 13, 1987),
pp. 592–93.

B. Guns and Murders

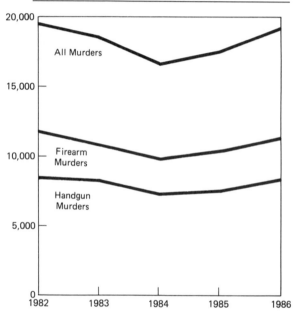

SOURCE: FBI, *Crime in the United States, 1986.* Cited in D.S. Greene,
"Gun Control," *Editorial Research Reports* (November 13, 1987),
pp. 592–93.

The National Rifle Association

The National Rifle Association was founded in 1871 by a few National Guard officers to enhance the peaceful and safe use of firearms. It gained tax exemption at its founding and is not a registered lobby group, since only a small part of its funds go to legislative work. During the 1970s, NRA membership was aroud 1 million, but by 1986 it had risen to 3.1 million. The NRA seems to attract two groups of constituents: the sports-minded (hunting, marksmanship) and the paramilitary. As the organization grew and broadened its membership, its goals also broadened. These restated aims are: to promote social welfare, public safety, law, order, and the national defense; to educate and train citizens of good repute in the sale and efficient handling of small arms and in the techniques of design and production; to increase the knowledge of small arms and promote efficiency in the use of such arms on the part of members of law enforcement agencies, the Armed Forces, and citizens who would be subject to service in the event of war; and to encourage the lawful ownership and use of small arms by citizens of good repute. In pursuit of these goals, the NRA sponsors firearms safety and marksmanship courses, as well as thousands of shooting matches each year. It also selects the rifle and pistol teams that represent the United States in the Olympics and other international competitions.

The main tactic employed by the NRA is to exhort members to write to their congressional representatives and thus register their opposition to any pending gun control legislation. The clearest self-portrait of the NRA is provided in an article by Paul Blackman and Richard Gardiner.[20]

NRA members are reached via two channels: the well-edited and widely circulated *American Rifleman,* the official organ of the NRA sent free to all dues-paying members; and legislative bulletins sent to members in localities considering firearms legislation. Other tactics include editorials in the *American Rifleman* and assistance in the election or defeat of candidates based on their gun control position. The *American Rifleman,* besides carrying articles of interest to gun enthusiasts, fills two important and related functions for the NRA: It provides a major

C. Firearm Usage in Selected Crimes, by Region: 1982 to 1985
(In percent. Murder includes nonnegligent manslaughter.)

REGION	MURDER				AGGRAVATED ASSAULT				ROBBERY			
	1982	*1983*	*1984*	*1985*	*1982*	*1983*	*1984*	*1985*	*1982*	*1983*	*1984*	*1985*
U.S. total	60.2	58.3	58.8	58.7	22.4	21.2	21.1	21.3	39.9	36.7	35.8	35.3
Northeast	52.2	50.5	51.1	50.9	14.9	14.1	13.6	13.5	33.2	30.6	29.7	28.3
Midwest	60.6	59.0	60.5	60.7	23.1	22.2	21.8	22.2	38.9	34.7	36.8	37.2
South	65.8	63.8	63.2	63.1	26.1	24.9	25.3	25.4	47.3	44.3	42.1	41.7
West	55.1	53.6	54.9	54.3	22.0	20.4	20.5	19.9	41.2	37.2	35.7	35.1

SOURCE: U.S. Federal Bureau of Investigation, *Crime in the United States,* annual. Cited in *United States Almanac, 1987,* p. 161.

D. Carry Laws and Crime Rates (Rates per 100,000)

	LEAST RESTRICTIVE[a] (CONCEALED WEAPONS)	MODERATELY RESTRICTIVE (OPEN CARRYING)	MOST RESTRICTIVE (LITTLE OR NO CARRYING, OPEN OR CONCEALED)
Homicide rate	6.0	6.8	9.2
Handgun-related rate	2.5	3.0	4.1
Robbery rate	112.7	126.6	268.8
Street robbery rate	52.6	69.4	153.5
Gun-related robbery rate	42.5	49.2	95.4
Aggravated assault rate	199.1	219.7	309.2
Gun-related assault rate	41.4	49.1	65.1

*Least restrictive: Alabama, Connecticut, Georgia, Indiana, Maine, New Hampshire, North Dakota, Vermont, and Washington.
SOURCE: Paul Blackman, "Firearms and Violence, 1974–1984," NRA, Washington, DC, 1985, p. 31.

revenue source through advertising sales (11% of the NRA's 1987 $71.1 million income); the balance of income is principally derived from $20 membership dues assessed for each of the 3.1 million members.[21] In a monthly column called "What the Lawmakers Are Doing," the *American Rifleman* carries "a concise bill-by-bill summary of firearms proposals and legislative action at both the federal and state levels." Other magazines carrying the NRA message are *Field and Stream, Outdoor Life,* and *Sports Afield.*

The NRA denies that it is simply obstructionist:[22] "Our critics and adversaries often proclaim by word of mouth and on the printed page that the NRA is for minimum firearms controls or no gun regulation at all. This is, of course, completely untrue," said the NRA's late executive vice-president Franklin Orth. But the NRA "looks on the vast majority of bills for firearms legislation as the misdirected efforts of social reformers, do-gooders and/or the completely unin-

formed who would accomplish miracles by the passage of another law." In its opposition to the 1968 gun control law, Frank C. Daniel, the NRA's secretary, explained that the NRA had been unable to support a specific bill because no one had been able to come up with a definition of a Saturday Night Special that was agreeable to the organization.

While the NRA may have been more approchable even a decade ago, critics maintain that an internal power struggle has seen hard-liners come out on top. Some suggest that the theme of the present leadership is to take no conciliatory stances. This was evident in congressional hearings on firearms that can escape detection and armor-piercing ammunition and the ciminal misuse and availability of machine guns and silencers.[23] The NRA criticized former governor Cecil Andrus of Idaho, who favored legislation against armor-piercing bullets, labeling him a "lap dog for the national gun control movement."[24]

TABLE 6. A. Respondents Reporting a Firearm in Their Home, by Demographic Characteristics, United States, Selected Years 1973-1984

Question: "Do you happen to have in your home (or garage) any guns or revolvers?"

	1973	1974	1976	1977	1980	1982	1984
				(Percent reporting having guns)			
National	47	46	47	51	48	45	45
Sex:							
Male	53	51	52	55	56	54	53
Female	43	42	43	47	41	39	40
Race:							
White	49	48	58	53	50	48	48
Black/other	38	32	37	34	29	30	30
Education:							
College	45	42	44	45	41	39	42
High school	50	48	50	54	51	51	48
Grade School	44	49	42	51	51	41	43
Occupation:							
Professional/business	48	45	46	48	45	42	42
Clerical	42	43	40	49	45	39	41
Manual	48	48	48	52	48	49	48
Farmer	83	79	62	66	81	77	84
Income:							
$15,000 and over	55	52	53	57	56	53	53
$10,000 to $14,999	58	51	54	56	46	49	39
$7,000 to $9,999	44	48	42	50	45	43	39
$5,000 to $6,999	43	40	44	38	38	28	27
$3,000 to $4,999	35	38	35	39	26	26	31
Under $3,000	30	34	30	35	24	26	26
Age:							
18 to 20 years	50	34	38	54	48	51	44
21 to 29 years	43	48	45	45	48	41	37
30 to 49 years	51	49	52	55	50	51	48
50 years and older	46	44	44	49	46	44	49
Region:							
Northeast	22	27	29	32	27	32	32
Midwest	51	49	48	53	52	48	44
South	62	59	60	62	59	52	52
West	47	42	44	46	44	47	49
Religion:							
Protestant	56	52	53	57	56	52	52
Catholic	35	37	36	39	36	36	34
Jewish	14	7	26	17	6	11	22
None	32	40	43	50	39	37	36
Politics:							
Republican	53	49	50	56	53	50	56
Democrat	44	45	45	49	46	44	42
Independent	49	47	48	50	47	44	40

SOURCE: Table constructed from data provided by the National Opinion Research Center; data were made available through the Roper Public Opinion Research Center.

The Gun Industry

Critics question the NRA's links to the gun manufacturing industry. According to the *Wall Street Journal:*[25]

> Gun manufacturers play an important part in bankrolling the thus-far largely successful fight to minimize gun legislation. Money from gun makers and sellers, either through outright subsidy or indirectly in the form of advertising in membership journals and the like, helps finance such leaders in the anti-gun fight as the National Rifle Association and the National Shooting Sports Foundation.

In 1986, the small arms (under 30 milli-

B. Respondents Reporting a Firearm in Their Home, by Type of Firearm and Demographic Characteristics, United States, 1984

Question: "Do you happen to have in your home (or garage) any guns or revolvers?"
If yes, "Is it a pistol, shotgun, rifle, or what?"

GUNS IN THE HOME

	All Types	Pistol	Shotgun	Rifle
		Type of firearm		
National	45	21	28	27
Sex:				
Male	53	28	34	34
Female	40	16	23	23
Race:				
White	48	22	30	30
Black/ other	30	15	16	12
Education:				
College	42	21	26	25
High school	48	24	29	31
Grade School	43	11	29	20
Occupation:				
Professional/ business	42	23	26	25
Clerical	41	19	22	26
Manual	48	23	30	30
Farmer	84	23	61	48
Income:				
$15,000 and over	53	28	32	33
$10,000 to $14,999	39	16	28	23
$7,000 to $9,999	39	14	18	21
$5,000 to $6,999	27	10	12	14
$3,000 to $4,999	31	12	13	19
Under $3,000	26	8	16	14
Age:				
18 to 20 years	44	11	27	29
21 to 29 years	37	17	23	22
30 to 49 years	48	24	30	30
50 years and older	49	23	29	28
Region:				
Northeast	32	13	21	19
Midwest	44	18	31	28
South	52	28	32	27
West	49	24	23	35
Religion:				
Protestant	52	24	32	31
Catholic	34	16	20	23
Jewish	22	7	7	7
None	36	22	20	17
Politics:				
Republican	56	23	31	36
Democrat	42	22	26	24
Independent	41	20	27	24

SOURCE: Table constructed from data provided by the National Opinion Research Center; data were made available through the Roper Public Opinion Research Center.

meter) industry shipped $918 million in ammunition and $1,030 million in small arms. The industry employed 20.7 thousand workers and met a payroll of $531.3 million.[26]

While by no means one of the largest industries in the U.S., it does have clout.

The split in NRA ranks that has developed over the past 10 years leaves the firearms industry in a quandary. While it looks favorably on and wishes to maintain vigorously its markets in hunting, sports shooting, and personal security areas, it is not very comfortable with the hard-line paramilitary groups, much less criminals, if for no other reason than trying to maintain a positive public image.

The industry exerts considerable economic clout and generates important advertising revenues for the NRA. Industry group representatives include the National Shooting Sports Foundation (NSSF), founded in 1961, and the Sporting Arms and Ammunition Manufacturers' Institute (SAAMI), founded in 1926. While neither group has favored gun control legislation, they have been historically more conciliatory than the recent hard-line NRA stances.

Conservation Groups

Conservation groups make strange bedfellows with gun control opponents. Hunting is, however, part of the conservation strategy for managing the ratio of wildlife to resources. Also, conservation groups depend heavily on the financial support of the firearms and ammunitions industry. Furthermore, a sizable portion of the federal funds earmarked for wildlife and conservation are directly related to gun and ammunition manufacturing. Under the Pittman-Robertson Act (the Federal Aid in Wildlife Restoration Act) of 1937, which was supported by the gun industry, an 11% excise tax on the manufacture of sporting arms and ammunition is used for aiding state fish and game agencies. In 1987, the excise taxes brought in by firearms broke down as follows: $26,261,000 from a 10% tax on pistols and revolvers; $42,182,000 from an 11% tax on firearms; and $34,978,000 from an 11% tax on shells and cartridges.[27]

C. Firearms Manufactured in the United States, by Type of Firearm, Fiscal Years 1973 to 1982

		HANDGUNS			LONG GUNS		
	TOTAL	TOTAL HANDGUNS	PISTOLS	REVOLVERS	TOTAL LONG GUNS	RIFLES	SHOTGUNS AND COMBINATION GUNS
1973	4,844,565	1,734,154	564,919	1,169,235	3,110,411	1,830,285	1,280,126
1974	5,639,601	1,714,989	398,606	1,316,383	3,924,612	2,099,372	1,825,240
1975	5,767,820	2,023,601	456,182	1,567,419	3,744,219	2,123,166	1,621,053
1976	5,345,179	1,832,785	455,167	1,377,618	3,393,209	2,091,797	1,301,412
Transition quarter	1,234,606	431,120	96,269	334,851	803,486	494,294	309,192
1977	5,015,963	1,868,062	452,667	1,415,395	3,147,901	1,922,858	1,225,043
1978	4,865,537	1,888,660	463,426	1,425,234	2,976,877	1,781,001	1,195,876
1979	5,322,998	2,126,017	612,918	1,513,099	3,196,981	1,877,890	1,319,091
1980	5,646,218	2,370,714	765,522	1,605,192	3,275,504	1,936,094	1,339,410
1981	5,773,791	2,537,231	835,169	1,702,062	3,236,560	1,680,945	1,555,615
1982	5,157,499	2,628,623	853,444	1,775,179	2,528,876	1,622,890	878,568

Note: These data were provided by federally licensed firearms manufacturers. The figures do not include firearms manufactured for use by the military. The data presented for years prior to and including 1976 coincide with former federal fiscal years. The transition quarter refers to the period July 1, 1976 to Sept. 30, 1976. The fiscal year for the federal government is now from Oct. 1 to Sept. 30.
SOURCE: Table adapted from tables provided by the U.S. Department of the Treasury, Bureau of Alcohol, Tobacco, and Firearms.

Further cementing the relationship between conservation activities and anticontrol sentiment is that hunting license revenues are also applied to state and local wildlife programs. According to a 1987 publication of the Fish and Wildlife Service (commemorating the fiftieth anniversary to the Pittman-Robertson Act), revenues from the firearms industry have been instrumental in restoring America's wildlife.[28]

In addition, the Virginia Commission of Game and Inland Fisheries wrote to a congressional subcommittee in 1968 in opposition to controls, stating that if it became more difficult legally to obtain, possess, transport, and use firearms for legitimate purposes, there would be less and less participation in hunting and other shooting sports. Since hunting licenses and taxes on sporting arms and ammunition support virtually all government programs for wildlife protection and management, the wildlife resources of the nation would be endangered to the same degree that interest in shooting sports would wane. Not all conservationists share in the gun industry's financial support or in the concept of managing wildlife for the benefit of hunting activities. But the National Wildlife Federation and the Wildlife

Management Institute, two of the largest beneficiaries of industry support, were created with the help of the industry and have numerous industry representatives as officers and directors. The current president of the World Wildlife Fund's American chapter and the honorary president of World Wildlife, C. R. Gutermuth, is the second-ranking officer of the NRA. John Olin, retired chairman of Olin Corporation (a manufacturer of arms and ammunition), is a director of World Wildlife. Thomas Kimball, executive director of the National Wildlife Federation, testified in 1968:[29]

TABLE 7. The Role of Handguns in Killings and Accidents

A. Killings Due to Handguns, Selected International Comparisons, 1983

COUNTRY	NUMBER OF KILLINGS
Australia	10
Canada	6
Japan	35
Sweden	7
Switzerland	27
United Kingdom	8
United States	9,014

SOURCE: Handgun Control, Inc., "Handgun Facts," Washington, D.C., 1987.

B. Death and Death Rates of Accidents, by Type, 1970-1983

TYPE OF ACCIDENT	DEATHS					RATE				
	1970	1980	1981	1982	1983	1970	1980	1981	1982	1983
Accidents and adverse effects	114,638	105,718	100,704	94,082	92,488	56.4	46.7	43.9	40.6	39.5
Motor-vehicle accidents	54,633	53,172	51,385	45,779	44,452	26.9	23.5	22.4	19.8	19.0
Traffic	53,493	51,930	50,196	44,713	43,428	26.3	22.9	21.9	19.3	18.6
Nontraffic	1,140	1,242	1,189	1,066	1,024	.6	.5	.5	.5	.4
Water-transport accidents	1,651	1,429	1,219	1,297	1,316	.8	.6	.5	.6	.6
Air and space transport accidents	1,612	1,494	1,575	1,664	1,312	.8	.7	.7	.7	.6
Railway accidents	852	632	580	545	544	.4	.3	.3	.2	.2
Accidental falls	16,926	13,294	12,628	12,077	12,024	8.3	5.9	5.5	5.2	5.1
Fall from one level to another	4,798	3,743	3,540	3,471	3,372	2.4	1.7	1.5	1.5	1.4
Fall on the same level	828	415	417	420	432	.4	.2	.2	.2	.2
Fracture, cause unspecified, and other and unspecified falls	11,300	9,136	8,671	8,186	8,220	5.6	4.0	3.8	3.5	3.5
Accidental drowning	6,391	6,043	5,233	5,258	5,254	3.1	2.7	2.3	2.3	2.2
Accidents caused by:										
Fires and flames	6,718	5,822	5,697	5,210	5,028	3.3	2.6	2.5	2.2	2.1
Firearms	2,406	1,955	1,871	1,756	1,695	1.2	.9	.8	.8	.7
Electric current	1,140	1,095	1,008	979	872	.6	.5	.4	.4	.4
Accidental poisoning by—										
Drugs and medicines	2,505	2,492	2,668	2,862	2,866	1.2	1.1	1.2	1.2	1.2
Other solid and liquid substances	1,174	597	575	612	516	.6	.3	.3	.3	.2
Gases and vapors	1,620	1,242	1,280	1,259	1,251	.8	.5	.6	.5	.5
Complications due to medical procedures	3,581	2,437	2,549	2,585	2,660	1.8	1.1	1.1	1.1	1.1
Inhalation and ingestion of objects	2,753	3,249	3,331	3,254	3,387	1.4	1.4	1.5	1.4	1.4
All other accidents	10,676	10,765	9,105	8,945	9,311	5.2	4.7	4.0	3.9	4.0

SOURCE: *United States Alamanac, 1987*, p. 182.

The reason a wildlife conservation organization such as ours is interested in gun legislation revolves around the fact that hunters contribute materially to the wildlife managment programs of this country through their license fees, and that they are quite interested in seeing that legislaion that is considered by the Congress does not materially and adversely affect this interest. . . .

For this reason, the Federation is vitally interested in preventing any unnecessary discouragement of law-abiding citizens desiring to purchase, possess, and transport arms for hunting purposes, while at the same time it is anxious to help reduce the crime rate.

Lax Enforcement:
Friends in High Places

More important are NRA links to the Treasury and State Departments as well as to the Justice Department and law enforcement agencies. These groups oversee enforcement of gun control laws. The loopholes in the gun control laws are more than matched by the lax attitude of the federal bureaucracy charged with enforcing federal laws. For example, although the authority existed under the 1930 and 1934 laws, the Treasury Department did not collect any figures on the production of different types of guns in the United States. In 1968, the only figures available were those collected by the Bureau of the Census for 1963. The State and Treasury departments have not done enough to execute the gun control laws of which they are the chief custodian. Specifically, this is the fault of particular bureaucrats. More generally, it is a reflection of governmental nonchalance toward gun control measures. The pervasive attitude is summed up in acting assistant secretary William Dickey's comment that "there was no requirement" for his office to collect information legitimately requested by a senator and that he did not intend to collect it. For more than 30 years, bureaucratic neglect of gun control duties has increased on two fronts: gun dealer supervision, and the State Department attitude toward gun imports. The attitude toward the importation of guns is reflected in the words of John Sipes, director of the Office of Munitions Control (OMC) of the State Department. Sipes admitted that his agency is authorized to keep out arms that it believes to be detrimental to the security of the United States, but does not have the authority to ban firearms for which there is a legitimate commercial market just because there is the possibility that these guns may end up in the hands of dangerous people.

The issues of armor-piercing bullets and guns that can escape detection saw the NRA pitted against many of its traditional allies. In early 1989, a man brandishing a semiautomatic weapon shot and killed several children in a schoolyard in Stockton, California. Following that tragedy, there was a renewed impetus to ban such weapons "whose only purpose was to kill another human being." Los Angeles police chief Daryl Gates testified in favor of strict legislation on behalf of law enforcement officers across the country, saying, "I don't want that gun on the street." The NRA, of course, opposed such legislation. They were joined in their opposition by President George Bush:

Look, if you're suggesting that every pistol that can do that [referring to a recent shooting in the Wasington, D.C., area] or every rifle [referring to the Stockton massacre] should be banned, I would strongly oppose that. I would strongly go after the criminals who use these guns. But I am not about to suggest that a semi-automated *hunting rifle* should be banned. Absolutely not.[30] (emphasis added)

Extremist Groups

One final component of the lobby, and probably the least savory, must be mentioned. Various extremist and paramilitary groups, such as the Minutemen, Ku Klux Klan, Breakthrough, and Revolutionary Action Movement, have more of an ideological than an economic interest in protecting their freedom of access to firearms. They nonetheless are able to benefit from the economic and political muscle of the rest of the lobby, and are equally vociferous in protecting their right to own guns. These groups frequently form or join organizations which through NRA affiliation are eligible for special discount rates on surplus military weapons and ammunition. The NRA repudiates these groups and does not knowingly allow them to join the association, but it lacks screening procedures to identify such individuals.

NOTES

1. Gun Control Act of 1968, 18 U.S.C. Sec. 925(d)(3)(1970). Gun Control Act of 1968, U.S.C. Sec. 992(d)(3)(1970). William E. Schmidt, "Pressure for Gun Control Rises and Falls, but Ardor for Arms Seems Constant." *New York Times* (October 25, 1987), p. E5.

2. George Volsky, "Guns in Florida: This Week It Suddenly Becomes a Lot Easier to Be Legal." *New York Times* (September 27, 1987), p. 26; *New York Times*, "New Law In Maryland Bans Sale and Manufacture of Some Pistols" (May 24,

1988), p. 27; *New York Times*, "Maryland Gun Ban Is Hotly Debated" (October 9, 1988), p. 35.

3. Address by Sarah Brady to the National Press Club, Washington, D.C., September 29, 1988; *Congressional Quarterly Weekly Report*, "NRA Shows It Still Has What It Takes . . . to Overcome Gun Control Advocates" (September 17, 1988), pp. 2564–65; *Criminals Don't Wait; Why Should You?—The Case against Waiting Periods*. Washington, D.C.: NRA, January 1987.

4. U.S Department of Justice, Bureau of Justice Statistics, *Sourcebook of Criminal Justice Statistics—1985.* Washington, D.C. 1986, pp. 195–201; James D. Wright, "Second Thoughts about Gun Control." *Public Interest,* no. 91 (spring 1988), pp. 34–35; *Newsweek,* "A Goetz Backlash?" (March 11, 1985), pp. 50–53; Howard Schusser and Stanley Presser, "Attitude Measurement and the Gun Control Paradox." *Public Opinion Quarterly,* 41 (winter 1977–1978), p. 427.

5. A. O. Sulzberger, Jr., "Rifle Association Poll Says Majority Oppose More Gun Legislation." *New York Times* (March 10, 1979), p. 25; *Ten Myths about Gun Control.* Washington, D.C.: NRA, March 1985, pp. 1–4; Don B. Kates, "Reflections on the Relevancy of Gun Controls." *Criminal Law Bulletin,* 93 (March/April 1977), pp. 119–24.

6. Wright, "Second Thoughts," pp. 24–25.

7. D. S. Greene, "Gun Control." *Congressional Quarterly Editorial Research Reports* (November 13, 1987), pp. 594–95.

8. *New York Times,* "Transcript of Johnson's Statement on Signing Crime and Safety Bill" (June 20, 1968), p. 23.

9. David I. Caplan, *Constitutional Rights in Jeopardy.* Washington, D.C.: NRA, December 1986.

10. Appendix V, "Statement of Policy of The National Rifle Association," cited in Carl Bakal, *The Right to Bear Arms.* New York: McGraw-Hill, 1966.

11. Caplan, *Constitutional Rights,* pp. 1–9.

12. *Haynes* v. *U.S.,* 390 U.S. 85, 98 (1968).

13. *American Rifleman,* May 1957, p. 12ff.

14. Paul H. Blackman, *Firearms and Violence, 1974–84.* Washington, D.C.: NRA Institute for Legislative Action, July 1985.

15. Wright, "Second Thoughts," p. 35.

16. Cited in U.S. Department of Justice, *Sourcebook—1985,* p. 194, based on a January 11–16, 1985 ABC News *Washington Post* poll.

17. Blackman, *Firearms,* p. 19ff.

18. Ibid., pp. 21–23.

19. Jeffery H. Boyd and Eve K. Moscicki, "Firearms and Youth Suicide." *American Journal of Public Health* (October 2, 1986), pp. 1240–42; Arthur L. Kellermann and Donald T. Reay, "Protection or Peril? An Analysis of Firearm Related Deaths in the Home." *New England Journal of Medicine* (June 12, 1986), pp. 1557–60; Garen J. Wintemute, Stephen P. Teret, and Jess F. Kraus, "The Epidemiology of Firearm Deaths among Residents of California." *Western Journal of Medicine* (March 1987), pp. 374–77; U.S. Department of Justice, *Sourcebook—1985,* pp. 201–2.

20. Paul H. Blackman and Richard E. Gardiner, *The N.R.A. and Criminal Justice Policy: The Effectiveness of the National Rifle Association as a Public Interest Group.* Washington, D.C.: National Rifle Association Institute for Legislative Action, November 1986.

21. Jeffrey H. Birnbaum, "Surprise Setback—Mighty Gun Lobby Loses Its Invincibility by Taking Hard Line." *Wall Street Journal* (May 24, 1988), pp. 1, 25; Blackman and Gardiner, *NRA,* p. 2.

22. Robert Sherill, "Lobby on Target." *New York Times Magazine* (October 15, 1967), p. 112.

23. Committee on the Judiciary, Subcommittee on Crime, *Hearings on Armor Piercing Ammunition and the Criminal Misuse and Availability of Machine Guns and Silencers* (May 17, 24, and June 27, 1984), 98th Congress, 2nd Session; Committee on the Judiciary, Subcommittee on Crime, *Hearings on Firearms that Can Escape Detection* (May 15, 1986), 99th Congress, 2nd Session.

24. Sarah Brady, Address to the National Press Club, September 29, 1988; *New York Times,* "Rifle Association Power Struggle Pits Board against Conservatives" (January 28, 1987), p. D26; Peter Wiley, "Idaho Feud Finds NRA Under Fire." *Wall Street Journal* (December 21, 1987), p. 20; *Business Week,* "The NRA Shoots Itself in the Foot—Extremism Is Souring Lawmakers" (May 16, 1988), pp. 44–45.

25. David Gumpert, "The Gun: To the Arms Industry, Control Controversy Is a Business Problem." *Wall Street Journal* (May 21, 1972), p. 21.

26. U.S. Department of Commerce, Bureau of the Census, *1986 Annual Survey of Manufacturers,* "Statistics for Industry Groups and Industries," pp. I-18, I-19. Washington, D.C.:, 1987.

27. Internal Revenue Service, Public Affairs Division, "Internal Revenue Report of Excise Taxes," News Release IR-88-22 (April 11, 1988).

28. United States Fish and Wildlife Service, *Restoring America's Wildlife, 1937–1987.* Washington, D.C.: 1987.

29. U.S. Congress, Senate Committee on the Judiciary, Subcommittee to Investigate Juvenile Delinquency, *Hearings on Federal Firearms Legislation*, June 26, 27, 28 and July 8, 9, 10, 1968, pp. 499–540.

30. Gerald M. Boyd, "Bush Opposes Ban on Assault Firearms But Backs State Role." *The New York Times* (February 17, 1989), pp. A1, A20; Robert Reinhold, "Effort to Ban Assault Rifles Gains Momentum." *The New York Times* (January 28, 1989), pp. 1, 9.

THE NATIONAL RIFLE ASSOCIATION AND GUN CONTROL

"Ammunition for Victims of Saturday Night Specials: Manufacturer Liability under Kelley v. R. G. Industries, Inc. [497 A.2d 1148 (Md.)]". *Washington & Lee Law Review*, 43 (Fall 1986), pp. 1315–49.

BASKIN, MYRNA G., and LAURA M. THOMAS. "School Metal Detector Searches and the Fourth Amendment: An Empirical Study." *University of Michigan Journal of Law Reform*, 19 (Summer 1986), pp. 1037–1106.

BATEY, ROBERT. "Strict Construction of Firearms Offenses: The Supreme Court and the Gun Control Act of 1968." *Law and Contemporary Problems*, 49 (Winter 1986), pp. 163–98.

"Common Law Strict Liability against the Manufacturers and Sellers of Saturday Night Specials: Circumventing California Civil Code Section 1714.4." *Santa Clara Law Review*, 27 (Summer 1987), pp. 607–35.

Federal Firearms Regulations. U.S. Bureau of Alcohol, Tobacco, and Firearms, 1988.

Firearms and Explosives Operations Brief: State Laws and Published Ordinances: Firearms. Bureau of Alcohol, Tobacco, and Firearms, 1987.

FOSTER, CAROL D. *Gun Control: Restricting Rights or Protecting People.* Plano, Tex.: Instructional Aids Press, 1987.

HALBROOK, S. P. "Firearms, the Fourth Amendment, and Air Carrier Security." *Journal of Air Law and Commerce*, 52 (Spring 1987), pp. 585–680.

"Handguns and Products Liability." *Harvard Law Review*, 97 (June 1984). pp. 1912–28.

HARAN, JAMES F., and JOHN M. MARTIN. "The Armed Urban Bank Robber: A Profile." *Federal Probation*, 48 (December 1984), pp. 47–53.

HARDY, D. T. "The Firearms Owners' Protection Act: A Historical and Legal Perspective." *Cumberland Law Review*, 17 (1986/1987), pp. 585–682.

KATES, D. B., JR. "The Battle Over Gun Control." *Public Interest* (Summer 1986), pp. 42–52.

KATES, D. B., JR., ed. "Gun Control." *Law and Contemporary Problems*, 49 (Winter 1986), pp. 1–267.

KATES, D. B., JR. "Handgun Prohibition and the Original Meaning of the Second Amendment." *Michigan Law Review*, 82 (November 1983), pp. 204–73.

KLECK, GARY. "Crime Control through the Private Use of Armed Force." *Social Problems*, 35 (February 1988), pp. 1–21.

"Large Majority Favors Handgun Registration." *Gallup Report* (June 1985), pp. 15–19.

LEDDY, EDWARD F. *Magnum Force Lobby: The National Rifle Association Fights Gun Control.* University Press of America, 1987.

"Legal Limits of a Handgun Manufacturer's Liability for the Criminal Acts of Third Persons: Richman v. Charter Arms Corp. [571 F. Supp. 192]." *Missouri Law Review*, 49 (Fall 1984), pp. 830–53.

LESTER, DAVID. *Gun Control: Issues and Answers.* Springfield, Ill: Charles C. Thomas, 1984.

LUND, NELSON. "The Second Amendment: Political Liberty, and the Right to Self-Preservation." *Alabama Law Review*, 39 (Fall 1987), pp. 103–30.

MALCOLM, J. L. "The Right of the People to Keep and Bear Arms: The Common Law Tradition." *Hastings Constitutional Law Quarterly*, 10 (Winter 1983), pp. 285–314.

"Maryland Holds Manufacturer of 'Saturday Night Specials' Strictly Liable for Injuries Suffered by Innocent Victims of Criminal Handgun Violence: Kelley v. R. G. Industries, Inc. 497 A.2d 1143 (Md.)." *Suffolk Uni-*

versity Law Review, 20 (Winter 1986), pp. 1147–77.

"Products Liability and Handguns." 1986 *Annual Survey of American Law* (April 1987), pp. 1–29.

"Quilici v. Village of Morton Grove [532 F. Supp. 1169]: Ammunition for a National Handgun Ban." *De Paul Law Review,* 32 (Winter 1983), pp. 371–97.

"The Right to Bear Arms and Handgun Prohibition: A Fundamental Rights Analysis." *North Carolina Central Law Journal,* 14 (1983), pp. 296–311.

"Strict Products Liability: Application of Gun Dealers Who Sell to Incompetent Purchasers." *Arizona Law Review,* 26 (1984), pp. 889–905.

"Symposium on Firearms Legislation and Litigation." *Hamline Law Review,* 6 (July 1983), pp. 277–487.

TONSO, WILLIAM R. "Gun Control: White Man's Law." *Reason,* 17 (December 1985), pp. 22–25.

WAEGEL, WILLIAM B. "How Police Justify the Use of Deadly Force." *Social Problems,* 32 (December 1984), pp. 144–55.

WRIGHT, JAMES D., "Second Thoughts about Gun Control." *Public Interest* (Spring 1988), pp. 23–39.

WRIGHT, JAMES D., and PETER H. ROSSI. *Armed and Considered Dangerous; A Survey of Felons and Their Firearms.* 1986.

WRIGHT, JAMES D., and PETER H. ROSSI. *The Armed Criminal in America: A Survey of Incarcerated Felons.* United States National Institute of Justice, 1985.

ZIMRING, FRANKLIN E. *Citizen's Guide to Gun Control.* New York: Macmillan, 1987.

·IV·

Corporate Actions
and Workplace Safety

WARNER-LAMBERT COMPANY

Personal criminal liability of senior executives for accidents causing workers' death and injury

At 2:40 A.M. on Sunday, November 21, 1976, a large section of a five-story manufacturing plant owned and operated by the American Chicle Division (ACD) of the Warner-Lambert Company (W-L) was destroyed by an explosion and fire that reached 1,000° F. The explosion originated in and involved the Freshen-Up® gum department on the fourth floor. One hundred and eighteen employees were working on the morning shift at the time of the explosion. Forty-eight received burns or other injuries; many required extended hospitalization. Six other employees died as a direct consequence of second- and third- degree burns over most of their bodies and from related complications.[1]

On August 1, 1977, the Grand Jury for Queens county returned a 12-count indictment (six counts of manslaughter in the second degree and six counts of criminally negligent homicide) against the Warner-Lambert Company (American Chicle Division), and against five individuals, all of whom were corporate officers of Warner-Lambert Company.[2] All five respondents entered pleas of not guilty on August 18, 1977, and subsequently argued that there was insufficient evidence to support the grand jury indictment. The trial court, the Supreme Court of the State of New York for the County of Queens, agreed with the respondents and on February 15, 1978, dismissed the indictments. After considering further arguments by the district attorney of Queens county, the trial court reaffirmed its dismissal of the indictments on July 26, 1978. The district attorney appealed to the Appellate Division, Second Judicial Department. On July 9, 1979, the Appellate Division reversed the order of the trial court, reinstated the indictments, and directed that the trial proceed.[3]

ISSUES FOR ANALYSIS

The Warner-Lambert indictments present a number of crucial issues in the area of corpo-

rate liability and the susceptibility of corporations and executives to criminal sanctions
for failure to provide a safe working environment.

1. What are the standards by which one might
   judge hazardous or unsafe conditions in the
   workplace? Should safety standards be based
   on *known* dangers, or on dangers that should
   have been *anticipated*? What are the relevant
   criteria for determining that due diligence
   was exercised by responsible executives to
   protect workers from previously unknown
   dangers?

2. Could the explosion at the American Chicle
   Company have been prevented through effective communication, reporting, and control mechanisms within the corporate hierarchy? The record shows that Warner-Lambert
   plant management took numerous measures
   to keep the plant safe and dust-free and
   urged the Warner-Lambert head office to install a comprehensive exhaust system. Could
   the company have foreseen the circumstances that caused the accident? If so, what
   changes should be made in the American
   Chicle Division's and Warner-Lambert's decision-making process and structure?

3. Is it possible that the company kept postpon-
   ing the installation of exhaust equipment or
   making other changes in the plant in order to
   meet the tremendous demand for their product? Did the company compromise on safety
   to protect large sales and profits generated by
   Freshen-Up® chewing gum?

4. Can a corporation be charged with causing
   the death of an employee because of an alleged failure to provide a safe workplace?

5. Should a corporate officer be held criminally
   liable for the death of an employee because
   his or her job description and organizational
   function include taking appropriate action to
   provide a safe working environment?

6. To what extent are the courts a proper societal
   mechanism for determining whether a safe
   working environment has been provided
   and, if it has not, who within the corporate
   structure should be held responsible?

7. What are the responsibilities of workers,

unions, and government agencies in ensuring a safe workplace?

8. What else might be done through the courts
   or other societal mechanism to increase the
   degree of care and responsibility that management assumes for worker health and
   safety?

   In the Warner-Lambert case, the foregoing issues are complicated by disagreement
among the parties (the district attorney for
Queens county and the respondents) over
the events which took place prior to the explosion, the cause of the explosion, and the
law's role in affixing responsibility for the
deaths that resulted.

THE RESPONDENTS: WARNER-LAMBERT

The Warner-Lambert Company, conducting business under the name of Warner-
Lambert Company and the American Chicle
Division, maintains a manufacturing plant at
3030 Thompson Avenue, Long Island City,
Queens county, New York. Several products are manufactured at this facility, including Freshen-Up® chewing gum.[4]

Arthur Kraft is Warner-Lambert's vice-
president in charge of manufacturing, with
offices at Warner-Lambert's corporate headquarters in Morris Plains, New Jersey. Ed
Harris is director of corporate safety and security for Warner-Lambert, with an office at
the corporate headquarters in Morris Plains.
While both men visit the Long Island plant
on occasion, neither official was responsible
for the day-to-day operations of the plant.[5]

James O'Mahoney is plant manager of
the manufacturing facility in Long Island
City where the explosion occurred. His offices are located on the fifth floor of the
Thompson Avenue plant, and he is involved
in day-to-day operations. John O'Rourke is
the plant engineer at the Long Island City
facility, and his office is in that building. He

worked in the Freshen-Up® department on an almost daily basis.[6]

The Introduction of Freshen-Up Gum into the American Market

In the latter part of 1969, the Research and Development Department at Warner-Lambert's Long Island City factory began a market project to introduce a new chewing gum product. Subsequently sold as Freshen-Up gum, it was unique because of its flavored-liquid or jelly-filled center. The product had been previously introduced and successfully marketed in both Europe and Asia. By 1972, experimentation and development had proved so encouraging that Warner-Lambert decided to go into limited production. A pilot or prototype manufacturing operation was established on the first floor of the Long Island City factory to support limited production for the purpose of testing consumer interest and marketing potential.[7]

Consumer reaction to Freshen-Up gum was extremely favorable, leading Warner-Lambert to set up full-scale production under the aegis of its manufacturing division in September 1974. The company invested $10 million in manufacturing equipment and expanded operations to include six processing lines on the fourth floor of the Long Island City plant operating 24 hours a day, six days a week. The Freshen-Up department became fully operational in December 1975. By the fall of 1976, production had risen to some 2 million packages of gum per day. At a price of 20¢ per package, Freshen-Up generated retail sales of over $400,000 per day. The new product sold better than any other chewing gum on the market, and Warner-Lambert found that it could sell all that it could produce. Freshen-Up was given priority status over such other well-known Warner-Lambert items as Chiclets®, Dentyne®, Trident®, Dynamints®, and Certs®. Efforts were made to reduce all downtime.

Supervisory personnel were promised bonuses for increased productivity.[8]

EVENTS PRECEDING THE EXPLOSION

The basic facts that led Warner-Lambert into the manufacture and marketing of Freshen-Up gum are not in dispute; it is the events that preceded the explosion which might demonstrate Warner-Lambert's failure to take appropriate action to protect its employees from a safety hazard. The Warner-Lambert case really began in February 1975, when the Freshen-Up operation was still located on the first floor of the Long Island City plant and the six processing lines on the fourth floor had not yet become operational.

The Freshen-Up Manufacturing Process

The manufacturing process developed by the corporation provided for slabs of basic gum product to be introduced into the processing line through a hopper located above a batch-forming complex called the extructor-extruder. As the gum passed out of the extruder in the form of a "rope" approximately two inches in diameter, its center was injected with a variably flavored liquid or jelly filling. The product was then moved through a rope sizer, wherein the gum strip was further reduced in diameter to a workable 1/2 inch. On leaving the sizer, the gum rope was drawn through an open transition plate. At this point, among others, a powdered lubricant or metallic and organic compound known as magnesium stearate (MS) was applied to prevent sticking.

The product was then introduced into a tablet-forming machine called the Uniplast. The gum rope passed into a rotating die head, furnished with plungers and guiding cams, for the stamping and formation of 38 separate pieces of liquid-filled gum, each approximately $3/8$ inch in thickness and $5/8$ inch square. To facilitate release of the tablets and prevent adherence of the gum to the dies, the dies were sprayed with a cooling agent known as liquid nitrogen (LN_2), which produced temperatures in and around the machinery sufficiently cold to form ice on the die head and base. (A temperature of $-320°$ F exists at the point of LN_2 emission, compared with the freezing of water at $+32°$ F.) On leaving the Uniplast, the newly formed gum pieces were conveyed into a cooling tunnel. From there, they moved to an adjacent wrapping section for other processing and packaging.

The district attorney contended that the Uniplast machine, the centerpiece of the processing line, was designed by a German concern for the manufacture of hard candy at warm or room temperatures. This contention was based on the manufacturer's brochure and supported by testimony of the manufacturer's representative. It was not designed for gum production in the kind of extreme cold and dust environment created in the manufacture of Freshen-Up gum. The Uniplast machine was made of cast iron and other brittle, low-alloy metals not suitable for use under the extreme cold conditions produced by the application of liquid nitrogen. Nor was the machinery made to operate in a continuously cold environment 24 hours a day, six days a week. The district attorney argued that this extremely cold environment induced embrittlement or structural weakness of the metals and caused them to lose ductility or the capacity to withstand fracture when subjected to impact or temperature changes. The district attorney further contended that the machine's motor was not sealed to prevent electrical spark or arc emission or to prevent the entry of dust—features necessary in any process that generates industrial dust. The machines used in the production of Freshen-Up gum were specifically modified and adapted by Warner-Lambert to produce Freshen-Up gum. In the opinion of

the district attorney, they were not suitable for the manufacturing process established by Warner-Lambert.

The 1975 Pilot Project

As early as February 1975, while the Freshen-Up operation was still located on the first floor of the Long Island City plant, an employee observed a small flash explosion of magnesium stearate produced from an electrical extension cord lying on the floor. When he reported the incident to the assistant production manager, he was told: "... yeah, well, it's one of the problems we have to work out." Based on what he had seen, the employee made an entry in a corporate journal, as required under company rules, recommending that the use of MS be discontinued.[10]

Anticipating similar problems with the move upstairs, another employee made an inquiry and was led to believe that effective dust-collecting equipment would be provided in the new fourth-floor department. This apparently was not outside the realm of possibility, because local dust exhaust systems had been installed over the processing machines in the Dentyne Gum department on the plant's third floor prior to the November 1976 explosion. Warner-Lambert questioned these statements of its employees, contending that the employee mentioned above was only a college intern on the payroll for a total of six months. According to the employee's grand jury testimony, there was no explosion but "sort of a white flash, like similar to a small flashbulb going off." This occurred when another employee kicked a household electrical cord being used to operate a $1/4$- inch drill with a brush on it to clean out the die punches. The corporate journal was, in reality, the employee's own log book. The facts of this particular incident were not officially recorded, and the employee made only a vague reference to eliminating MS.[11]

The grand jury investigation, however, showed that the problem of MS dust was becoming serious. It was aggravated substantially by the use of air hoses to blow dust away from the machinery. In June 1975, Warner-Lambert's manager of safety and fire protection, who worked directly under the supervision of Ed Harris, dispatched Warner-Lambert's own industrial hygienist to the Freshen-Up department for the purpose of determining employee exposure to MS dust and making appropriate recommendations. The manufacture of Freshen-Up utilized large quantities of MS, raising concern regarding the nuisance level of the dust and the health problems that might arise from the workers' exposure to the dust, as opposed to an explosion hazard. The industrial hygienist issued a report in March 1976 recommending (a) use of local exhaust systems; (b) substituting a vacuum unit for compressed air in the cleaning of machinery; (c) vacuuming, not sweeping, the floors; and (d) issuance of face masks until the recommended controls could be instituted by plant engineers. The face masks were issued, but the other recommendations were never implemented.

Notwithstanding, based on the data furnished by the hygienist, Ed Harris concluded in an analysis around December 1975 that the concentration of ambient MS was *not* sufficient to create a dust explosion. However, the hygienist's survey (the basis of Harris's conclusion) was conducted at a time (November 1975) when only three processing lines were in operation on the plant's fourth floor.[12]

The Fourth-Floor Manufacturing Operation

In August 1975, the Freshen-Up project moved to the fourth floor of the plant, and Warner-Lambert put the six production lines in operation. In establishing operations on the fourth floor, the electrical contractors who were installing power lines and control panels were never informed that the operations would involve a combustible dust or that the equipment had to comply with standards and regulations for hazardous locations as set forth in the national and New York City electrical codes. Instead, emphasis was placed on establishing a production line that would satisfy the City Health Department regulations affecting food processing plants. The company's own electrician, who was aware of the amount of MS dust being generated on the first floor during the pilot project, specifically asked the plant engineer, John O'Rourke, whether he wanted a "dust-proof" installation. He was told no, because "there will be no dust."[13]

In October 1975, Warner-Lambert's manager of safety and fire protection, who worked directly for Ed Harris, submitted a report to Warner-Lambert's Rockford, Illinois, plant warning of the explosive nature of MS and the proper venting ratios to be used to protect plant equipment in the event of an explosion. In November 1975, Warner-Lambert's own industrial hygienist again recommended major changes in the fourth-floor venting system to minimize workers' exposure to MS dust. Warner-Lambert contended that this inspection clearly established, apart from the issue of a worker health hazard, that the nuisance level of dust from the standpoint of employee health was, at most, one-one-thousandth of the lowest level at which the dust would explode. Therefore, no fire or explosive hazard was present.[14]

On February 24, 1976, Factory Mutual, a loss prevention consultant employed by Warner-Lambert's insurance carrier (Arkwright-Boston Company) made an inspection of the Freshen-Up department. It determined that "the magnesium stearate dust in the fourth story Freshen-Up gum manufacturing area presents a serious explosion hazard." The consultant recommended the installation of a central vacuum cleaning system, removal of accumulated dust, and modification of all electrical equipment to conform to national electric code standards for "dusty locations." The implementation of these measures was necessary "to prevent a serious dust explosion." The consultant's findings and advice were relayed to the plant engineer, John O'Rourke, on the premises and "in detail." O'Rourke assured the Factory Mutual consultant that Warner-Lambert would comply with the recommendations. The inspector's report also indicated that Harris's prior determination of no explosion hazard was based on dated information and was no longer valid. A written version of the report and advice was sent to Ed Harris. It emphasized the deficiency and requested serious consideration of the recommendations. When no reply was received, a follow-up letter was sent to Harris in June 1976, emphasizing once more "the possibility of a dust explosion due to the use of magnesium stearate powder."[15]

Under established corporate procedures, loss prevention reports were distributed to Harris's department (the division of corporate safety), the corporation's insurance department, and the plant manager (James O'Mahoney). It was the plant manager's duty to review recommendations, propose appropriate action to the division of corporate safety, and then initiate a proper request for action. The safety department under Harris, in turn, was to assist the plant manager in complying with the report recommendations and then give the insurance carrier the company's response.[16]

In April 1976, the New York City Fire Department inspected the Freshen-Up department. According to Warner-Lambert, the New York City Fire Department did not report any explosive conditions whatsoever or indicate the need for any action on the part of the corporation. The following month, a compliance officer from the Occupational and Safety Health Administration (OSHA) of the U.S. Department of Labor visited the plant. According to Warner-Lambert, the OSHA inspection established that

the airborne dust was below the nuisance level of milligrams per meter; OSHA's only recommendation was to have a class A fire extinguisher on hand. The district attorney for Queens county disagreed with this factual summation and contended that the OSHA inspector discussed personally with defendants O'Rourke and O'Mahoney the dust problem and the need to eliminate its source. On May 5, 1976, the plant's chief engineer also gave the same defendants a written report that MS use "continues to be our greatest problem."[17] (New York State, for budgetary reasons, lets OSHA handle inspection chores. But OSHA had no comprehensive standards against explosion hazards, while New York State labor law did.)

On May 25, 1976, a formal proposal for the purchase of a central dust removal system, at a nominal cost of $33,000, was submitted to O'Mahoney for transmittal to corporate headquarters. Also submitted was a separate capital expenditure request covering the proposed exhaust system. The request apparently met with initial rejection from the corporation's engineering division (headed by Joe Zagvali) as a short-term solution. The executives at the plant were very unhappy with this approach. The manager of the Freshen-Up department, in a memo to O'Mahoney (with a copy to O'Rourke) stated bluntly: "[while] Joe Zagvali . . . reinvent[s] the wheel . . . an expenditure of $35,000 [sic] is a small price to pay to get out of the problems we now have and to show our good faith to our employees who are putting up with a very unpleasant environment."[18]

Warner-Lambert continued to conduct dust tests in June of 1976 for the purpose of determining the nuisance level of the dust in the department. According to Warner-Lambert, these tests established that the density of airborne dust was well below the lower explosive limit. On July 7, a meeting was held at corporate headquarters for the purpose of considering the capital expense request of $33,000 to purchase a central dust removal system. Present at this meeting were defendants Kraft and O'Rourke, among others. The purchase request was determined to be "a waste of good money" and was therefore rejected. A decision was made to embark on a long-range solution to eliminate the use of MS altogether from the Freshen-Up production process. Arthur Kraft endorsed the decision and placed a hold on the written request. The topic of dust collection systems for the Freshen-Up gum operation was never again considered by top corporate management prior to the explosion. On July 13, 1976, the corporation's manager of safety and fire protection sent a brief note to O'Mahoney notifying him that the insurance carrier's February 1976 recommendation to eliminate the dust hazard would not be followed.[19]

On August 10, 1976, O'Mahoney sent a memorandum to his staff recommending measures to reduce the use of MS because it was a "major problem—having a deleterious effect on employee health and safety." During the first two weeks of August 1976—the usual time when plant operations shut down every year and everyone takes a vacation— the entire department was cleaned and dust accumulations eliminated. Along with the August 10 memorandum, eleven "strict" procedures were promulgated concerning control procedures upon reopening of the department. These steps included tighter control over the amount of MS used in each shift, improved clean-up, and strict disciplinary measures for failure to conform with the guidelines. Coarser-grade MS was utilized so that ambient dust levels would remain reduced. The cooling tunnel on processing line A was modified so that MS could be eliminated from the process altogether. Warner-Lambert later argued that these cleaning procedures and the decision to modify all the cooling tunnels to run without MS obviated the necessity for the installation of either a dust collection or vacuum system as recommended on May 25, 1976.[20]

On September 16, 1976, a second loss prevention report was filed with the respondents based on an inspection made by a representative of the insurance carrier, Factory Mutual. Warner-Lambert contended that this report established that "the present dust concentration is well below the lower explosive limits." Thus, at the time of the accident, no risk of any kind—possible or probable—could have been perceived by anyone familiar with the circumstances at the plant.

On November 15, 1976, the plant's chief engineer notified O'Mahoney and O'Rourke that the coarser grade of MS was still fouling up the fourth-floor air conditioning system and that the concentration of ambient MS dust in the Freshen-Up department was substantial. Although work had begun to modify one of the processing lines to eliminate MS use (at a cost of some $40,000), no decision had been made to modify the other five lines. In fact, by the fall of 1976, public demand for Freshen-Up gum had forced production up to 2 million packages of gum per day, and six processing lines operated 24 hours a day, six days a week. At 2:40 A.M. on Sunday, November 21, 1976, the Freshen-Up operating came to a halt with an explosion that resulted in the death of six employees and injuries to 48 others. A large section of Warner-Lambert's five-story manufacturing plant was devastated.

THE CAUSES OF THE EXPLOSION

The cause or causes of the explosion are a matter of controversy, and two versions have emerged: one offered by Warner-Lambert and its experts, and the other by the Queens county district attorney and his experts.

The District Attorney's Version[21]

According to the district attorney, the deaths, injuries, and physical damage resulted from the explosion of a heavy concentration of ambient MS dust present in the Freshen-Up department during the early morning hours of November 21, 1976. Testimony was offered to the grand jury by employees as to the existence of a fog-like atmosphere just prior to the explosion. A substantial residue of MS dust in the area involved was also reported after the explosion. The windows on the fourth floor and elsewhere in the plant had been blown out and then in, as the explosive pressure first vented itself out, creating a vacuum into which air from outside the building was then drawn. Broken glass and other damaged items from the plant's fourth floor were strewn all over the street and on the roofs of adjacent buildings, which were themselves damaged by flying debris and the force of the explosion. The Freshen-Up department was found to be in shambles, with the interior walls pushed down; machinery and fixtures displaced, shattered, and twisted; and small pockets of fire in existence among the materials. These are all characteristics of a dust explosion. The ceilings, walls, and overhead areas showed charring or scorching, indicating not general fire damage, but the burning of ambient MS dust. Clothing had been blown off of many of the employees, further evidence of the explosive quality of the ambient MS dust.

The district attorney contended that a dust explosion results when sufficient quantities of a combustible material, pulverized in a finely subdivided state and suspended in a confined atmosphere, are ignited. The ignition is followed by the rapid propagation of flame (as the ambient material is consumed), intense heat, expansion of the air pressure, and finally, a bursting effect. An explosion will occur when there are three essential elements: (1) a combustible fuel, (2) oxygen from the air, and (3) ignition sufficient to initiate combustion and reaction among the dust particles. Although MS dust in a settled state will burn, it is not regarded as explosive unless it is dispersed in the air

in heavy enough concentrations. It is then rated as a severe, strong, or very strong explosive hazard. At the time of the explosion in question, the Freshen-Up gum department was using approximately 500 pounds of MS per day, six days a week, or about a ton-and-a-half per week. A minimum of 25 pounds of MS was allotted to and used by each of the six processing lines per eight-hour shift, with more being used merely on request.

The powdered MS lubricant was applied by hand (by throwing), by can, or by dumping all along the processing line constantly and in large quantities. This sanctioned method of use caused or contributed to the ever-present fog or mist of ambient MS dust in the department. Thick quantities settled in and around the machinery and over all the flat surfaces, including the overhead areas. The dust condition reached a point where employees were forced to wear (and were observed wearing) the face masks and goggles to protect their eyes and breathing passages prior to the explosion. Just prior to the explosion, several processing lines were still in operation, and many engaged in the weekly duty of general clean-up. MS dust was removed from overhead areas and machinery by knocking the dust from overhead areas with brooms and air hoses and sweeping the dust from one end of the department to the other. One employee, standing very close to one of the Uniplast machines, observed a "sparkle" or "spark" in the area of one of the processing lines. According to the employee, "the next thing I knew a big boom, that was the fire." Other employees positioned further away thought they heard two explosions almost simultaneously and that with the second, "just everything caught on fire."[22]

According to the district attorney's experts, there was low-order detonation at the base of the D assembly line Uniplast machine, followed by a major dust explosion. The ignition or primary detonation was attributed to a mechanical sparking or heat-induced break-up of the parts of the Uniplast equipment on line D. The use of LN_2 had completely iced the rotating die head, which then jammed. The equipment, because it was not made to be used with liquid nitrogen, lost its ductility and became extremely brittle. The machine, operating under a tremendous strain just prior to explosion because of the jammed rotating die head, overloaded the motor as it drew more electrical current to meet the resistance of the slowed-up gears. The machinery began to break apart due to the vibration or slippage of the components. The resulting heated metal, mechanical sparking, or friction ignited the settled or ambient MS dust at the base of the Uniplast equipment, causing a violent reaction or detonation in what may have been an oxygen-enriched atmosphere containing ambient MS dust in sufficient quantities for an explosion.[23]

Warner-Lambert's Version[23]

Warner-Lambert contended that liquid nitrogen is basically noncombustible and vaporizes quickly without dangerous effects when exposed to room temperatures. Because of its inherent stability, it is often used in fire extinguishers. MS, in bulk, inert, or settled form, does not create an explosive risk. If ignition is applied, it will only burn or smolder. If it is dispersed into the air at or above the lower explosive level (LEL), it will create a serious risk of explosion if ignited. Warner-Lambert contended that minimum combustible densities of cornstarch, flour dust, peanut hulls, and powdered sugar create a greater danger of explosion than MS dust.

In addition to the lower explosive level, there is also a nuisance level of dust established by OSHA. This level identifies the point at which exposure to dust will cause irritation and difficulty in breathing. Warner-Lambert argued that the nuisance level for MS is one-three-thousandths of the LEL, and that since the nuisance level was one-three-thousandths of the lower explosive level for MS dust, there was an insufficient concentration of ambient MS dust in the air to support an explosion. If there had been a sufficient concentration, it would have been humanly impossible for employees to work in the area without continuous respiratory assistance. Since the Freshen-Up department was in full production and the three shifts operated six days a week, despite whatever subjective testimony there may have been that conditions were foggy or cloudy, the objective fact was that production workers did function with ease and in so doing established clearly that the MS dust in the air was below the lower explosive level.

Warner-Lambert's experts contended that there was a powerful primary detonation caused by a cryogenic phenomenon called liquefaction. This phenomenon results when volatile liquid oxygen is formed due to the exposure of the atmosphere at the base of the Uniplast machine to extremely cold, but otherwise harmless, liquid nitrogen. This detonation then ignited settled MS dust at the bore of the Uniplast machine. The crucial point made by the experts for Warner-Lambert was that the explosion did not involve the two alleged hazardous elements, MS or liquid nitrogen. But for the unforeseen cryogenic phenomenon involving liquid nitrogen, the quantity of MS at the base of the Uniplast equipment actually presented no risk of fire or explosion. Warner-Lambert's experts further testified that the creation of volatile liquid oxygen from the use of stable liquid nitrogen could not reasonably have been foreseen. Liquification is not regarded as a credible hazard in the use of liquid nitrogen. Warner-Lambert's supplier of liquid nitrogen, its insurance carrier, and the various governmental agencies, such as the New York City Fire Department and OSHA, never indicated, suggested, or warned of any risk associated with the use of liquid nitrogen. Consequently, the explosion and the resulting deaths occurred as a result of a hazard that could not have been foreseen by Warner- Lambert, thus clearly indicating Warner-Lambert's lack of responsibility for the incident.

THE LEGAL ISSUES AND LEGAL PROCEEDINGS

The respondents in this matter were charged with: (1) manslaughter in the second degree, and (2) criminally negligent homicide. Under the Penal Law of the State of New York, Section 125.15, Subdivision 1, a person is guilty of manslaughter in the second degree when he or she "recklessly causes the death of another person." Subdivision 3 of the Penal Law, Section 15.05, defines *recklessly* as follows:

> A person acts recklessly with respect to a result or to a circumstance described by a statute defining an offense when he is aware of and consciously disregards the substantial and unjustifiable risk that such results will occur or that such circumstance exists. The risk must be of such a nature and degree that disregard thereof constitutes a gross deviation from the standard of conduct that a reasonable person would observe in the situation.

Therefore, to establish manslaughter in the second degree, the prosecution must prove beyond a reasonable doubt that: (1) the defendants, by their actions, created a substantial risk of death; (2) they were aware of this risk; (3) the defendants consciously disregarded this substantial and unjustifiable risk; and (4) that the risk itself must be of such a nature and degree that disregard therereof would constitute a gross deviation from the standard of conduct that a reasonable person would observe in the situation. (This is the burden of proof required at the trial, not during a grand jury proceeding.)

Under the New York Penal Law, Section 125.10, a person is guilty of criminally negligent homicide when with criminal negligence he or she causes the death of another person. Subdivision 4, Penal Law, Section 15.05, defines *criminal negligence* as follows:

> A person acts with criminal negligence with respect to a result or to a circumstance described by statute defining an offense when he fails to perceive that a substantial and unjustifiable risk that such result will occur or that such circumstances exist. The risk must be of such nature and degree that the failure to perceive it constitutes a gross deviation from the standard of care that a reasonable person would observe in the situation.

The distinction between criminal and negligent homicide in manslaughter in the second degree lies in their differing mental states. The reckless offender (manslaughter, second degree) is aware of the risk and consciously disregards it; the criminally negligent offender is not aware of the risk created and hence cannot be guilty of consciously disregarding it. The criminally negligent offender's liability rises from a culpable failure to perceive the risk. This culpability is appreciably greater than that required for ordinary civil negligence by reason of the substantial and unjustifiable character of the risk involved and the factor of gross deviation required from the ordinary standard here.

In order to establish criminally negligent homicide, the district attorney must prove beyond a reasonable doubt: (1) a culpable failure to perceive, (2) a substantial and justifiable risk, and (3) that the failure to perceive the risk was so flagrant as to be deemed a gross deviation from the standard of care a reasonable person would observe. (Decisions by the courts of New York have defined the conduct prescribed by these provisions as that involving a "flagrant disregard of a known risk of death to others, which risk is both substantial and unjustifiable.")[25] In essence, the district attorney must establish more than a failure to act or negligent action on the part of the defendants. There must be a substantial and un-justifiable risk of death and a gross deviation from the standard of conduct than an ordinary person would observe in the situation to establish criminally negligent homicide.

The trial court dismissed the indictment on the ground that the evidence presented to the grand jury was legally insufficient to establish either manslaughter in the second degree or the lesser offense of criminally negligent homicide.

THE CASE BEFORE THE APPELLATE DIVISION OF THE NEW YORK SUPREME COURT

The district attorney appealed the decision of the trial judge. The prosecution argued that:

1. The defendant's conscious disregard of the risk specified in the prosecution's charge was shown in the constant existence of dust like "heavy fog" in the plant, and communications among the various plant executives cited in the indictment, complaints from workers, and reports from the insurance company inspectors. The prosecutor stated that despite the evidence indicating hazardous working conditions, one Freshen-Up department supervisor unabashedly told the grand jurors "that the entire dust condition was created by 'careless employees.'"[26]

2. The district attorney argued, "Based on the grand jury testimony, there appears to be no escape from the conclusion that the defendants, each and all, were 'aware of . . . a substantial and unjustifiable risk' of death."[27] Thus, the charge of manslaughter in the second degree. However, it can also be argued from the facts that the acts of omission and commission amounted to criminally negligent homicide and not recklessness.

3. The evidence demonstrated that the defendants created and tolerated a substantial and unjustifiable risk of death (through dust explosion) in just about every phase and facet of the Freshen-Up operation imaginable. They

ignored, disregarded, or refused to consider seriously any and all advice rendered to them by those whose only concern was the welfare of the company and the employees.

In summary, the prosecution contended that there was absolutely no question—a matter of considerable proof—that the deaths, injuries, and physical damage resulted directly from the explosion of a heavy concentration of ambient magnesium stearate dust (both preexistent and explosion-generated) present during the early morning hours of November 21, 1976. Among other things, the pattern and extent of damage and the nature of injuries received bore this out. Even though use of MS was cut down after the August 1976 clean-up, allotments over a ton-and-a-half per week were excessive and still fell within the explosive use range. While there was a continuous stream of corporate memoranda regarding the dust problem and clean-up methods, the old procedures remained intact. No type of dust removal equipment was ever installed or purchased, including portable vacuum cleaners. The only clean-up tools available to workers were air hoses and brooms. No changes in electrical equipment or wiring were made to eliminate potential ignition sources. The use of LN_2, with its tendency to embrittle metal, was also unchanged. Even after receipt of advice as to the existence of a definite explosion hazard, no measures were ever implemented to inform the employees of the fact and instruct them on work safety measures.

Based on the grand jury testimony and the exhibits admitted as evidence, there appears to be no escape from the conclusion that the defendants, each and all, were "aware of . . . a substantial and unjustifiable risk" of death—hence, the charges of manslaughter in the second degree. But it is possible to find from the facts that the acts of omission and commission amounted alternatively or also to criminally negligent homicide, and not just recklessness—that is, some or all of the defendants perhaps did not realize the risk involved. Whether that be conceivable or not, the evidence is no different. The same proof actually supports both charges, distinguished by the degree or state of mental culpability.[28]

After an investment of $10 million, the cost of a dust exhaust system at a mere $33,000 became "a waste of money" where lives, property, and the future of a highly profitable operation were at stake. That is what the evidence established, and that constituted a gross deviation from the standard of conduct or care a reasonable person would have observed in the situation.[29]

Warner-Lambert's Brief

The W-L brief argued that although the evidence before the grand jury showed that the explosion in the case involved magnesium stearate dust, MS was not the cause of the explosion. "The evidence is clear and uncontroverted that MS can only explode when it is airborne in a well-defined concentration called the lower explosive limit (LEL)."[30] The brief contended:

> The unanimous testimony of the expert was that the cause of the explosion which killed the employees was a primary detonation at the base of one of the production machines. The experts also agreed that the cause of this primary detonation was not and could not have been an MS dust explosion, but rather most likely was the result of a freak cryogenic phenomenon called "liquefaction". . . . There was absolutely no evidence presented before the Grand Jury which tended to show that any defendant-respondent was aware of the possibility, let alone a substantial risk, of liquefaction.[31]

According to W-L, the central fact that emerges from an objective reading of the evidence before the grand jury is that the explosion at the plant resulted from a cryogenic phenomenon which was unforeseen and unforeseeable. That conclusion, according to W-L, does not depend on weighing conflicting evidence or assessing the credibility of divergent testimony. Rather, it stems from the consistent and undisputed testimony of all the witnesses before the grand jury who analyzed the complex chain of events that caused the explosion.[32]

The W-L brief pointed out that none of the outside institutions involved with W-L in this case, (the governmental agencies which regularly inspected the plant, the LN_2 suppliers, the production machinery suppliers, and W-L's insurer) ever warned W-L of any risks associated with the use of LN_2. For example, although the district attorney called several representatives of the New York City Fire Department to testify before the grand jury, he failed to call Fire Commissioner O'Hagan, who after the accident publicly stated:

> No, I would not say it amounts to negligence in any way. I think that the magnesium stearate powder in an undispersed form, in a powder form, is not combustible, and it is so described in several chemical dictionaries. . . . I think it was a case of a highly unusual set of circumstances that provided the environment that led to the explosion.[33]

Thus, "to hold Warner-Lambert criminally liable under such circumstances is manifestly unsupportable in view of the essential element of the alleged crimes; that is that, Warner-Lambert acted in a manner grossly deviant from a standard of reasonable care."[34] W-L also contended that it had made continuous and successful efforts at reducing the dust levels and controlling MS use. According to W-L, following the explosion, representatives of OSHA, the National Bureau of Standards, the Mining Enforcement and Safety Administration of the United States Department of the Interior, the New York City Fire Department, and others investigated the explosion to determine its cause. "Although the testimony involved complex technical matters, there was substantial agreement among the experts as to the unique chain of circumstances which resulted in the explosion."[35]

The brief argued that evidence provided by the people was circumstantial. While W-L's objective tests showed dust levels to be at most, "one-one thousandths of the LEL," the prosecution relied on workers' "subjective" testimony of fog-like conditions in the processing plant. The testimony also showed that on the day of the accident, the Freshen-Up area "was as clear as this jury room" and that "only forty-five minutes before the accident—after clean-up was in progress—there was no visible dust and everything seemed normal."[36] According to the W-L brief, the prosecution's presentation of the causes of the accident were theories and not incontrovertible facts. For example, the notion that machinery might have failed because it was not designed to work under the extreme cold temperatures was based on the testimony of an expert who stated that he was "dancing a little bit" in stating that "possibly the machinery may have broken apart. . . . There's really no way of actually telling."[37] This expert performed no metallurgical tests on the equipment, and therefore his speculation was incompetent and inadmissible. Furthermore, there was no evidence to show that defendants-respondents were or should have been in any way aware that liquid nitrogen might cause the Uniplast to become brittle. Since the cause of explosion could only be established by circumstantial evidence, it must be shown that the evidence established that cause to a moral certainty—that is, it must exclude any reasonable hypothesis of causation under which defendants would not be criminally responsible. W-L contended that the state's case failed to establish to a moral certainty an essential element of the crime charged. The W-L brief raised similar arguments against all the evidence presented by the prosecution as to the cause of the accident and stated that regardless of the source of detonation, there was no evidence that the defendants-respondents were aware of its existence.

Briefs of James O'Mahoney, John O'Rourke, Arthur Kraft, and Ed Harris

At the time of the accident, O'Mahoney and O'Rourke were the plant manager and plant engineer, respectively, of the American Chicle facility. They both argued that all the evidence before the grand jury demonstrated that they were extremely conscious of the situation about the dust problem at the Freshen-Up plant and took vigorous steps which resulted in bringing the dust level considerably below LEL.[38] In support of these efforts, the brief cited extracts from the opinion of the lower court which completely absolved O'Mahoney and O'Rourke of any wrongful acts and instead commended them for the diligent discharge of their duties.

At the time of the accident, Arthur Kraft and Ed Harris were vice-president in charge of manufacturing and director of corporate safety and security, respectively, of the American Chicle's parent, Warner-Lambert Company. Their brief contended that evidence against them was very sparse and that their names were mentioned only a few times in the course of the lengthy grand jury proceeding. After summarizing the essential facts of the case in a manner similar to that of other defendant-respondents, Kraft and Harris cited the lower court opinion that there was no adequate proof to "establish any criminal liability associated with their explosion."[39]

On March 8, 1979, the Appellate Division of the New York Supreme Court reversed the lower court's decision and ordered the matter to trial so that a jury could determine whether or not the elements of criminally negligent homicide or the more serious offense of manslaughter in the second degree had been established beyond a reasonable doubt by the district attorney.

*The Next Legal Step—Court of Appeals
of the State of New York*

Warner-Lambert and the four defendants appealed the decision of the Appellate Division to the highest court in New York State, i.e., the Court of Appeals of the State of New York. The petitioners asked the court to dismiss the indictments for second degree manslaughter and criminally negligent homicide. The court agreed with the petitioners and on November 20, 1980, dismissed the indictments on grounds that "there was not legally sufficient evidence in this case on the premise of which any jury could permissibly have imposed criminal liability on any of these defendants."[40]

The victims and their families also filed a number of civil law suits for damages against Warner-Lambert, various suppliers of chemicals and machinery, and cleaning companies.

These suits were all combined and were settled by the different parties. The judgment, approved by the court on October 3, 1984, involved more than $16 million to be paid: Warner-Lambert $11 million; $0.5 million each from Hamac-Hansella, a West

German machinery manufacturer; Petrochemicals, Ft. Worth, Texas; and Liquid Carbonics, Belleville, New Jersey. Additional payments ranging from $200,000 to $10,000 were made by 12 other defendants.[41]

The Chicle factory itself was closed in late 1981. Warner-Lambert transferred the production to its more modern and efficient plants in Rockford, Illinois, and Anaheim, California, where there was excess capacity. The company, however, made considerable efforts to help employees cushion the shock of plant closing. At a total cost of over $7 million, W-L provided severance benefits plus employee benefits, such as health insurance. Employees were offered jobs at the company's other locations, with the company picking up relocation costs. W-L also provided job search assistance, resume typing, and the services of an outplacement firm. Most employees appeared to have agreed with the findings of the court that the danger of explosion at the plant could not have been foreseen. During the shutdown after the explosion, many of them had petitioned the New York City administration to allow the plant to be reopened.[42]

NOTES

1. Appellant's Brief, *The People of the State of New York* v. *Warner-Lambert Company, et al.* Indictment No. 915-77, filed September 1978 by the district attorney, Queens county (hereafter cited as DA Brief), p. 4.

2. Record on Appeal, Volume I, *The People of the State of New York* v. *Warner-Lambert Company, et al.* Indictment No. 915-77 (hereafter cited as *Record*), pp. 12, 128, 144; *DA Brief*, pp. 3, 4; Brief of Defendant-Respondent Warner-Lambert Company, *The People of the State of New York* v. *Warner-Lambert Company, et al.* Indictment No. 915-77, filed September 1978 by attorneys for Warner-Lambert Company (hereafter *W-L Brief*), p. 5; Opinion of the Appellate Division, Supreme Court, Second Judicial Department, July 9, 1979,

The People of the State of New York v. *Warner-Lambert Company, et al.* (hereafter *Opinion*), pp. 2, 3.

3. *Record*, pp. 1, 2; *DA Brief*, pp. 1, 2; *W-L Brief*, p. 1–3; *Opinion*, p. 2.

4. *Record*, p. 12; *DA Brief*, p. 1; *Opinion*, p. 2.

5. *Record*, p. 37; Brief of Defendants-Respondents, Arthur Kraft and Ed Harris, *The People of the State of New York* v. *Warner-Lambert Company, et al.*, filed December 11, 1978, by attorneys for Kraft and Harris (hereafter *Kraft Brief*), p. 8; *Opinion*, p. 3.

6. *Record*, p. 37; Brief of Defendants-Respondents, James O'Mahoney and John O'Rourke, *The People of the State of New York* v. *Warner-Lambert Company, et al.*, filed December 1978 by attorneys for O'Mahoney and O'Rourke (hereafter *O'Mahoney Brief*), p. 5; *Opinion*, p. 3.

7. *DA Brief*, p. 5.

8. *Record*, pp. 13, 102; *DA Brief*, p. 7.

9. *Record*, p. 14; *DA Brief*, pp. 5–7, *Opinion*, pp. 3, 4.

10. *DA Brief*, p. 17.

11. *W-L Brief*, pp. 24, 25.

12.. *DA Brief*, pp. 21, 22; Court of Appeals, State of New York, Respondent against Warner-Lambert Company, et al., Defendant, Appellants, filed March 1980, p. 21.

13. *Record*, p. 13; *DA Brief*, pp. 17, 18; *Opinion*, p. 5.

14. *Record*, p. 91; *DA Brief*, p. 19–22; *W-L Brief*, p. 11.

15. *Record*, pp. 100, 140; *DA Brief*, pp. 20, 23; *Opinion*, p. 7.

16.. *DA Brief*, pp. 23, 24.

17. *Record*, p. 91.

18. Cited in *Respondent's Briefs* (State of New York), March 1980, p. 24.

19. *DA Brief*, p. 25.

20. Ibid., pp. 25, 26; *Record*, p. 102.

21. *DA Brief*, pp. 8–14.

22. Ibid., pp. 12, 13.

23. Ibid., pp. 13, 14; *Opinion*, pp. 4–6.

24. *Record*, pp. 15–17, 87–90, 96, 97, 129–33, 145–49.

25. *People* v. *Montanez*, 41 N.Y., 2nd 53, 390 N.Y.S., 2nd 861, 359 N.E., 2nd 371 (1971), cited in *W-L Brief*, p. 8.

26. *DA Brief*, p. 27.

27. *DA Brief*, pp. 27–28, 35, 36.

28. *Respondent's Brief* (State of New York), pp. 26–28.

29. Ibid.

30. *W-L Brief*, p. 3.

31. Ibid.

32. Court of Appeals, State of New York, *The People of New York* v. *Warner-Lambert Company*, November 29, 1979, Brief of Defendant-Appellant Warner-Lambert Company, p. 4.

33. Cited in Brief of Defendant-Appellant Warner-Lambert Company, p. 16.

34. *W-L Brief*, p. 4.

35. Cited in Brief of Defendant-Appellant Warner-Lambert Company, pp. 19, 20.

36. *W-L Brief*, p. 11.

37. *W-L Brief*, p. 19.

38. *O'Mahoney Brief*, pp. 9–10, 12–14.

39. *Kraft Brief*, p. 15.

40. *Record*, pp. 159–65.

41. *Martinez* v. *Warner-Lambert*, 16062/79, cited in *New York Law Journal*, pvd. 192, no. 66 (October 3, 1984), pp. 1, 30.

42. Sandra Salmans, "Chicle Closing: Family Sorrow." *New York Times* (April 25, 1981) p. 19, 21.

WARNER-LAMBERT COMPANY

"A Comprehensive Approach: Director and Officer Indemnification in Wisconsin." *Marquette Law Review*, 71 (Winter 1988), pp. 407–43.

"A Liability Ruling That Has Business Alarmed." *Business Week*, (February 27, 1984), pp. 41–42.

American Bar Association. *American Bar Association Standards Relating to the Administration of Criminal Justice: Sentencing Alternatives and Procedures. Second Tentative Draft. American Bar Association Standards of Criminal Justice*, Washington, D.C. (Summer 1979).

BEAN, R. K. "Corporate Director Liability." *Denver University Law Review*, 65 (1988), pp. 59–75.

BEQUELLE, ASSEFA. "The Cost and Benefits of Protecting and Saving Lives at Work: Some Issues." *International Labour Review*, vol. 123 (January–February 1984), p. 1.

BROWN, M. M., and V. M. DAVIS. "Indemnification of Directors and Officers and Limitations on Director Liability." *Institute on Security Regulation*, 18 V2, (1986), pp. 117–77.

CARROLL, DONAL S. A. "Managing Relations with

Government and Society—The Business Perspective." *Long Range Planning,* vol. 16 (April 1983), pp 6–18.

COFFEE, JOHN, JR. ''Corporate Crime and Punishment: A Non-Chicago View of the Economics of Criminal Sanctions." *American Criminal Law Review,* 17 (1980), pp. 471–85.

COFFEE, JOHN, JR. ''Making the Punishment Fit the Corporation. The Problem of Finding an Optimal Corporation Criminal Sanction." *Northern Illinois University Law Review,* (1980), pp. 78–89.

''Comments: Criminal Sanction for Corporate Illegality." *Journal of Criminal Law and Criminology,* 69, no. 1 (Spring 1978), pp. 15–24.

''Construction Managers' Liability for Job-site Safety." *University of Bridgeport Law Review,* 8 (1987), pp. 105–32.

CONYERS, JOHN, JR. ''Corporate and White-Collar Crime: A View by the Chairman of the House Subcommittee on Crime." *American Criminal Law Review,* 17, no. 3 (Winter 1980), p. 287.

''Corporate Directors—An Endangered Species? A More Reasonable Standard for Director and Officer Liability in Illinois." *University of Illinois Law Review* (1987), pp. 495–521.

CROCKER, E. M. ''Controlling Smoking in the Workplace." *Labor Law Journal,* 38 (December 1987), pp. 739–46.

DEMOTT, D. A. ''Limiting Directors' Liability." *Washington University Law Quarterly,* 66 (1988), pp. 295–323.

''Developments in the Law—Corporate Crime: Regulating Corporate Behavior through Criminal Sanction." *Harvard Law Review,* 92 (April 1979), p. 1227.

''Director Liability Dilemma: Providing Relief for Executive Anxiety." *UMKC Law Review,* 56 (Winter 1988), pp. 367–86.

''Director Liability: Michigan's Response to Smith v. Van Gorkom [488 A.2d 858 (Del.)]." *Wayne Law Review,* 33 (Spring 1987), pp. 1039–66.

FLETCHER, GEORGE P. ''The Theory of Criminal Negligence: A Comparative Analysis." *University of Pennsylvania Law Review,* 119, no. 3 (January 1971), p. 401.

FREDERICK, T. W. ''Indemnification and Liability of Corporate Directors and Officers." *Journal*

of the Missouri Bar, 43 (July/ August 1987), pp. 287–92.

''Getting away with Murder: Federal OSHA Preemption of State Criminal Prosecutions for Industrial Accidents." *Harvard Law Review,* 101 (December 1987), pp. 525–54.

GLABERSON, WILLIAM B. ''A Liability That Has Business Alarmed." *Business Week* (February 27, 1984), p. 41.

HANSELL, E. F., B. L. AUSTIN, and G. B. WILCOX. ''Director Liability under Iowa Law—Duties and Protections." *Journal of Corporation Law,* 13 (Winter 1988), pp. 369–429.

HAZEN, T. L. ''Corporate Directors' Accountability: The Race to the Bottom—Second Lap." *North Carolina Law Review,* 66 (November 1987), pp. 171–82.

HUBBELL, J. W. ''Emerging Issues in Directors' and Officers' Liability Insurance Coverage." *Colorado Lawyer,* 17 (June 1988), pp. 1031–36.

''Hyatt Hotel Engineers Cited for 'Negligence.''' *Engineering News Record* (February 9, 1984), p. 14.

''Indirect Criminal Conduct of Corporate Officers—Law in Search of a Fair and Effective Standard of Liability." *Delaware Journal of Corporate Law,* 13 (1988), pp. 137–64.

''The Limitation of Directors' Liability: A Proposal for Legislative Reform." *Texas Law Review,* 66 (December 1987), pp. 411–52.

MCADAMS, TONY, and C. BURK TOWER. ''Corporate Personal Accountability." *American Business Law Journal* (Spring 1979), pp. 67–82.

MCADAMS, TONY, and ROBERT C. MILJUS. ''Growing Criminal Liability of Executive." *Harvard Business Review* (March–April 1977), pp. 36–40.

MCVISK, WILLIAM. ''Toward a Rational Theory of Criminal Liability for the Corporate Executive." *Journal of Criminal Law and Criminology,* 69, no. 1 (Spring 1978), pp. 75–81.

MUKATIS, W. A., and P. G. BRINKMAN. ''Managerial Liability for Health, Safety, and Environmental Crime: A Review and Suggested Approach to the Problem." *American Business Law Journal,* 25 (Summer 1987), pp. 323–43.

NIELSON, RICHARD P. ''Should Executives Be Jailed for Consumer and Employees Health Violations?" *Journal of Consumer Affairs* (Summer 1979), pp. 128–34.

"Officer and Shareholder Liability under CERCLA: United States v Northeastern Pharmaceutical and Chemical Co., Inc., 810 F. 2d 726." *Washington University Journal of Urban & Contemporary Law*, 34 (Fall 1988), pp. 461–72.

ORLAND, LEONARD. "Reflections on Corporate Crime: Law in Search of Theory and Leadership." *American Criminal Law Review*, 17, no. 4 (Spring 1978), pp. 501–20.

POSNER, RICHARD A. "Optional Sentencing for White Collar Criminals." *American Criminal Law Review*, 17, no. 4 (Spring 1978), pp. 409–18.

"Reflections on White Collar Sentencing." *Yale Law Journal*, 86, no. 4 (March 1977), p. 589.

"The Rising Cost of Corporate Guilt." *Business Week* (November 8, 1970), pp. 36–37.

SCHLEIBA, S. *When the Law Ends: The Social Control of Corporate Behavior*. New York: Harper & Row, 1980.

SEALY, L. S. "Directors' 'Wider' Responsibilities—Problems Conceptual, Practical and Procedural." *Monash University Law Review*, 13 (September 1987), pp. 164–88.

SETHI, S. PRAKASH. "Corporate Law Violations and Illegality." *Journal of Criminal Law and Executive Liability. Testimony on H.R. 4973 before the Subcommittee on Crime of the House Judiciary Committee* (December 13, 1979).

SETHI S. PRAKASH. "Liability without Fault? The Corporate Executive as an Unwitting Crimi-

nal." *Employee Relations Law Journal* (Autumn 1978), p. 185.

SULLIVAN, C. D., and R. P. BARRY. "The Directors and Officers Liability Policy: An Overview." *Defense Counsel Journal*, 55 (July 1988), pp. 248–54.

"Toward a Rational Theory Criminal Liability for the Corporate Executive." *Journal of Criminal Law and Criminology*, 69, no. 1 (Spring 1978), p. 75.

WEINFELD, SHARON R. "Criminal Liability of Corporate Managers for Deaths of Their Employees: People v. Warner-Lambert Co." *Albany Law Review* (Winter 1978), pp. 655–85.

"Why More Corporations May Be Charged With Manslaughter." *Business Week* (February 27, 1984), p. 62.

WILLIAMS, C. R., B. J. KUSHNER, and G. L. WARE. "A Comparison of Statutory Solutions to Directors' Exposure to Liability." *Federation of Insurers and Corporate Counsels Quarterly*, 38 (Spring 1988), pp. 215–45.

YODER, STEPHEN A. "Comments: Criminal Sanctions for Corporate Illegality?" *Journal of Criminal Law and Criminology*, 69, no. 1 (Spring 1978), pp. 40–50.

YOHAY, S. C., and G. E. DODGE. "Criminal Prosecutions for Occupational Injuries: An Issue of Growing Concern." *Employee Relations Law Journal*, 13 (Autumn 1987), pp. 197–223.

WHIRLPOOL CORPORATION, MICHIGAN

Employee rights protection from employer's retaliation for refusal to work under hazardous and imminently dangerous conditions

On February 26, 1980, the U.S. Supreme court upheld[1] the decision of the U.S. Court of Appeals, Sixth Circuit[2] stating that an employee had the right to refuse work when it exposed him or her to imminent danger of bodily harm and even death; that an employer could not reprimand or otherwise discriminate against the employee for such refusal.

The case involved two employees of Whirlpool Corporation who had refused to follow their foreman's orders to undertake maintenance activities under conditions which they considered unsafe. The foreman's orders were contrary to the company's policies and specific procedures. The two employees, Virgil Deemer and Thomas Cornwell, reported the existence of unsafe working conditions to OSHA. The incident occurred on July 10, 1974. Upon their refusal to work, the foreman asked Cornwell and Deemer to leave. Although they were allowed to return to work the following day, the company, nevertheless, docked their pay for the lost time and put reprimand letters in their personnel files.

ISSUES FOR ANALYSIS

An industrial organization must have a reasonable degree of control over its employees in order to plan and manage its operation efficiently. At the same time, an employee should not be expected to take unreasonable risks in order to keep a job. The question is one of balance between the rights of an employer and that of an employee. Often, this right is established through contractual arrangements between employee and employer. In other circumstances, market or competitive conditions, or the state of technology, may prescribe the acceptable level of risks that a worker may be expected to assume in a given type of manufacturing operation.

Underlying all these conditions, two other factors prevail. One, there may be statutory or legal requirements that set a minimum level of safety conditions which must be maintained as a society's expression of concern to protect its citizens from certain types of risks where market or contractual arrangements are not deemed sufficient. Two, society may want corporations to provide a level of safety for their workers, higher than minimally required by statute, because such levels are economically and technically feasible and because corporations are expected to demonstrate socially responsible behavior. Thus, an analysis of this case must deal with the twin issues of competing rights and mutual obligations. More specifically:

1. What are the likely implications of the Supreme Court's decision in terms of impact on employers, employees, and regulatory agencies? Or, what type of precedent is set by this decision and with what potential effect on the manufacturing operations of companies in the United States?

2. Whirlpool based its defense on narrow legal grounds of violation of statutory authority by OSHA. Are there other substantive issues that could have been raised? If so, with what justification?

3. How else might Whirlpool have handled the situation to settle the problem more amicably?

4. The appeals court argued that exposing workers to unreasonable risks is economically unjustifiable because it would have the effect of raising Whirlpool's insurance premiums and, therefore, its costs under the Workmen's Compensation Act. Is it possible that these costs are not high enough to encourage employers to be more safety conscious? What other measures can be used to make both employers and employees more safety conscious?

THE FACTS OF THE CASE

Whirlpool maintains a manufacturing plant at Marion, Ohio, where it produces household appliances. The Marion plant has 13 miles of overhead conveyors that transport components throughout the plant. In order to prevent injury should a component fall from one of the conveyors, the company installed a huge guard screen approximately 20 feet above the plant floor. The guard screen is suspended over one-third of the total floor area. As part of their regular duties, maintenance employees spend several hours each week removing fallen parts from the screens and replacing paper spread on the screen to catch grease drippings. In addition, the overhead conveyors occasionally need maintenance. In order to perform their duties, maintenance workers usually are able to stand on the iron frame, but sometimes they must step onto the steel screen itself.

In 1973, the company began to install heavier wire in the screen because its safety had been questioned. Several employees had fallen partly through the old screen, and on one occasion an employee had fallen completely through to the floor below but had survived. A number of maintenance employees had reacted to these incidents by bringing the unsafe screen conditions to the attention of their foremen. The company's safety instructions admonished employees to step only on the angle-iron frames.

On June 28, 1974, a maintenance employee fell to his death through the guard screen in an area where the newer, stronger mesh had not yet been installed. As a result of this fatality, the U.S. Secretary of Labor conducted an investigation that led to the issuance of a citation charging the company with maintaining an unsafe walking and working surface in violation of 29 U.S.C. 654(a)(1).[3] The citation required immediate abatement of the hazard and proposed a $600 penalty. However, it took nearly five years, following the accident, for the Occupational Safety and Health Review Commission to affirm the citation, but the Commission decided to permit the petitioner six months in which to correct the unsafe conditions.[4]

Following this incident, Whirlpool undertook some repairs and issued an order strictly forbidding maintenance employees from stepping on either the screens or the angle-iron supporting structure. An alternative but somewhat more cumbersome and less satisfactory method was developed for removing objects from the screen. This procedure required employees to stand on power-raised mobile platforms and use hooks to recover the material.

On July 7, 1974, two of Whirlpool's maintenance employees, Virgil Deemer and Thomas Cornwell, met with the plant maintenance superintendent to voice their concern about the safety of the screen. The superintendent disagreed with their view but agreed to inspect the screen with the two men to determine dangerous areas needing repair. Unsatisfied with the superintendent's response to the results of the inspection, Deemer and Cornwell met on July 9 with the plant safety director. At that meeting, they requested the name, address, and telephone number of a representative of the local office of the Occupational Safety and Health Administration (OSHA). Although the safety director told the men that they "had better stop and think about what they were doing," he furnished the information they requested. Later that same day, Deemer contacted an official of the regional OSHA office and discussed the guard screen.

The next day, Deemer and Cornwell reported for the night shift at 10:45 P.M. Their foreman, after himself walking on some of the angle-iron frames, directed the two men to perform their usual maintenance duties on a section of the old screen. (This order appears to have been in direct violation of the outstanding company directive that maintenance work was to be accomplished without stepping on the screen apparatus.)

Claiming that the screen was unsafe, Deemer and Cornwell refused to carry out this directive. The foreman then sent them to the personnel office, where they were ordered to punch out without working or being paid for the remaining six hours of the shift. The two men subsequently received written reprimands, which were placed in their employment files. Both employees apparently returned to work the following day without further incident.

A little over a month later, the secretary of labor filed suit in the United States District Court for the Northern District of Ohio, alleging that the company's actions against Deemer and Cornwell constituted discrimination in violation of 11(c)(1) of the Occupational Health and Safety Act. As relief, the complaint asked that Whirlpool be ordered to expunge from its personnel files all references to the reprimands issued to the two employees, and for a permanent injunction requiring the company to compensate the two employees for the six hours of pay they had lost by reason of their disciplinary suspensions.

Following a bench trial, the district court found that the regulation in question justified Deemer's and Cornwell's refusals to obey their foreman's order on July 10, 1974. The court found that the two employees had "refused to perform the cleaning operation because of a genuine fear of death or serious bodily harm," that the danger presented had been "real and not something which [had] existed only in the minds of the employees," that the employees had acted in good faith, and that "no reasonable alternative had realistically been open to them other than to refuse to work." The district court nevertheless denied relief, holding that the secretary's regulation was inconsistent with the act and therefore invalid.[5] The Court of Appeals for the Sixth Circuit reversed the district court's judgments. Finding ample support in the record for the district court's factual determination that the actions of Deemer and Cornwell had been justified under the secretary's regulation, the appellate court concluded that the regulation is invalid. It accordingly remanded the case to the district court for further proceedings.[6] The Supreme Court agreed to consider the case because the decision of the court of appeals in this case conflicted with those of two other courts of appeals on the important issue.[7]

The court then took up the major question in the case: whether the secretary of labor's regulation authorizing "self-help" in some circumstances is permissible in the Act.

THE DECISIONS
OF THE SUPREME COURT
AND THE COURT OF APPEALS

The Supreme Court declared that the Act itself created a mechanism for protecting workers from employment conditions believed to pose an emergent threat of death or serious injury. Upon receipt of an employee inspection request stating reasonable grounds to believe that an imminent danger is present in a workplace, OSHA must conduct an inspection. In the event that this inspection reveals conditions or practices that "could reasonably be expected to cause death or serious physical harm immediately or before the imminence of such danger can be eliminated through the enforcement procedures otherwise provided by" the Act, the OSHA inspector must inform the affected employees and the employer of the danger and notify them that OSHA is recommending to the secretary of labor that injunctive relief be sought. At this juncture, the secretary can petition a federal court to restrain the conditions or practices giving rise to the imminent danger. By means of a temporary restraining order or preliminary injunction, the court may then require the employer to avoid, correct, or remove the danger or prohibit employees from working in the area.

To ensure that this process functions effectively, the Act expressly accords to every employee several rights, the exercise of which may not subject him or her to discharge or discrimination. An employee is given the right to inform OSHA of an imminently dangerous workplace condition or practice and request that OSHA inspect that condition or practice. He or she is given a limited right to assist the OSHA inspector in inspecting the work place, and the right to aid a court in determining whether or not a risk of imminent danger in fact exists. Finally, an affected employee is given the right to bring an action to compel the secretary of labor to seek an injunctive relief if he or she believes the secretary has wrongfully declined to do so.

In light of this detailed statutory scheme, the secretary of labor is obviously correct when he acknowledges in his regulation that, "as a general matter, there is no right afforded by the Act which would entitle employees to walk off the job because of potential unsafe conditions at the workplace."[8] By providing for prompt notice to the employer of an inspector's intention to seek an injunction against an imminently dangerous condition, the legislation obviously contemplates that the employer will normally respond by voluntarily and speedily eliminating the danger. And in the few instances where this does not occur, the legislative provisions authorizing prompt judicial action are designed to give employees full protection in most situations from the risk of injury or death resulting from an imminently dangerous condition of the worksite.

As this case illustrates, however, circumstances may sometimes exist in which employees justifiably believe that the statutory arrangement does not sufficiently protect them from death or serious injury. Such circumstances will probably not often occur, but such a situation may arise when (1) the employee is ordered by an employer to work under conditions the employee reasonably believes pose an imminent risk of death or serious bodily injury, and (2) the employee

has reason to believe that there is not sufficient time or opportunity to seek effective
redress from the employer or to apprise
OSHA of the danger. Nothing in the Act
suggests that those few employees who
have to face this dilemma must rely exclusively on the remedies expressly set forth in
the Act at the risk of their own safety. But
nothing in the Act explicitly provides otherwise. Against this background of legislative
silence, the secretary of labor has exercised
his rule-making power under 29 U.S.C.
657(g)(2) and has determined that, when an
employee in good faith is in such a predica-
ment, he or she may refuse to expose himself or herself to the dangerous condition
without being subjected to "subsequent discrimination" by the employer.[9]

This Act also prohibits retaliation against
employees for exercising their rights under
the statute by declaring:

> No person shall discharge or in any manner
> discriminate against any employee because
> such employee has filed and compliant is in-
> stituted is caused to be instituted any pro-
> ceedings under or related to this chapter or
> has testified or is about to testify in any such
> proceedings or because of the exercise by
> such proceeding or because of the exercise by
> such employee on behalf of himself or others
> of any right afforded by this chapter.[10]

The Supreme Court concluded that the
regulation in its face appeared to further the
overriding purpose of the Act.

The appeals court's decision further
elaborated on this point and is worth mentioning here. It stated that as a rule, administrative regulations properly promulgated
under statutory authority were presumed
valid. An administrative officer exercising
rule-making powers delegated by Congress
may adopt regulations so long as they are
reasonable and consistent with the intention
of Congress as expressed by the statute.[11] It
has been axiomatic in federal practice that a
statute which is remedial, and intended to
protect worker safety, must be given a liberal

construction: Since the Act in question is a
remedial and safety statute, with its primary
concern being the preservation of human
life, "it is the type of enactment as to which
a 'narrow or limited construction is to be
eschewed.' "[12] Furthermore, under the Act
every employer must "furnish to each of his
employees, employment and a place of employment which are free from recognized
hazards that are causing, or are likely to
cause, death or serious physical harm to his
employees."[13] This clause imposed a duty
on employers to furnish a workplace free
from recognized deadly hazards.

That the Act is remedial and has thus
been broadly construed by the courts is of
great relevance to this inquiry. Its requirement that employers not retaliate against
complaining employees should be read
broadly; otherwise, the Act would be gutted
by employer intimidation. Congress was
aware of the shortage of federal and state
occupational safety inspectors and placed
great reliance on employee assistance in enforcing the Act.[14] Furthermore, it is clear that
without employee cooperation, even an
army of inspectors could not keep America's
workplaces safe. Safety and profit are sometimes mutually exclusive. In the words of the
appeals court: "Safety costs money. The
temptation to minimize compliance with
safety regulations and thus shave costs is
always present."[15] The regulation does not
affect the vast majority of responsible employers who would never consider forcing
workers to labor under imminently hazardous conditions. Only a handful of irresponsible employers are affected, and the regulation may benefit them. If death or injury
occurs on the job, the employer faces potential liability under OSHA or state health and
safety codes. Indeed, a willful violation of
OSHA which results in death to an employee may subject an employer to criminal
prosecution. And since state workmen's
compensation statutes are experience-
based, the employer would end up paying in
the long run as well.[16]

The Appeals Court's decision elaborated

on some of these points and is worth mentioning here. According to the Appeals Court, to invalidate the regulation would lead to absurd results. Consider the following cases:

1. An employee is faced with an imminent hazard on the job. He leaves the job to telephone the local OSHA office and requests an immediate inspection. The employer cannot lawfully discharge the employee.

2. An employee is faced with an imminent hazard on the job. She goes to a telephone, but is unable to reach an OSHA inspector (or there is no telephone available). The worker goes to her car and personally locates an inspector. The worker and the inspector return to the job site. The employer cannot lawfully discharge the employee.

3. An employee is faced with an imminent hazard on the job. He telephones an OSHA inspector, but refuses to subject himself to the perceived hazard until the inspector arrives. Apparently, the employer is free to discharge the employee.

4. An employee is faced with an imminent hazard on the job. She is unable to raech an OSHA inspector by telephone, and has no automobile available to look for one personally (or the nearest OSHA inspector is 100 miles away). Instead of conducting a futile quest on foot, the employee resolves to withdraw from the danger and try to locate an inspector later. Apparently, the employer is free to discharge the employee.

These illustrations demonstrate the reason for the secretary of labor's regulation. The knowledgeable employee who withdraws from the imminent job hazard and immediately takes steps to locate an inspector is protected from retaliation. Yet, without the regulation's protection, the employee who withdraws from the danger but reasonably waits, or must wait, to summon an inspector or for one to arrive can be fired without recourse—no matter what hazard he or she faced. The outcome should not hinge on whether an employee knows enough to keep within OSHA's protections by making an obvious effort to find an OSHA inspector immediately.[17]

The Appeals Court also noted that other remedial acts passed by Congress contain similar provisions protecting employees against retaliation. These include the National Labor Relations Act,[18] the Coal Mine Safety and Health Act,[19] Title VII of the Civil Rights Acts of 1964,[20] and the Fair Labor Standards Act.[21] Commenting about the Whirlpool case, an editorial in *The New York Times* stated:

No matter what ground for compliant business may have had against the Occupational Safety and Health Administration it was reckless to take the agency to the Supreme Court over a rule protecting workers against imminent danger. The temerity of the Whirlpool Corporation deserved the unanimous rebuff it received from the Court....

If Whirlpool had won, workers could have been left to choose between risking their lives and their jobs. Business should be fighting on higher ground. With or without legal protection, it takes a lot of courage for employees to stand up for safety. The employer in this case merely had a lot nerve.[21]

NOTES

1. *Whirlpool Corporation* v. *Ray Marshall*, Secretary of Labor, 76-1870, BNA February 26, 1980, 48, 4189.

2. *Marshall* v. *Whirlpool*, 593 F2d 715 1979.

3. *Occupational Safety and Health Act of 1970*, Public Law 91-596.84, Statute 1590 (1973 as amended by Public Law 95-251.92, Statute 183) 1978 29 U.S.C. 651 et. seq.

4. Whirlpool Corporation, *3 CCH Employee Safety and Health Guide 23.552* (May 11, 1979).

5. *Usery* v. *Whirlpool Corp.*, 416 F. Supp 30. 32-34 N.D. Ohio, 1976.

6. *Marshall* v. *Whirlpool*, 715, 719, 736.

7. *Marshall* v. *Daniel Construction Co.* 563 F.2d 707 (CA. 5 1977); *Marshall* v. *Certified Welding Corp.* F.2d (CA 10 1978).

8. *Whirlpool Corp.* v. *Ray Marshall*, p. 4191.

9. Ibid., p. 4192.

10. 29 U.S.C. 660(c)(1), 1976.

11. *Marshall* v. *Whirlpool*, p. 722.

12. Ibid., p. 722.

13. 29 U.S.C. 654.

14. *Leg. Hist.*, pp. 151–52, 161, 399, 1852–61.

15. *Marshall* v. *Whirlpool*, p. 22.

16. Ibid.

17. Ibid., p. 723.

18. 29 U.C. 158 provides that it shall be an unfair labor practice for an employer ''…. (4) to discharge or otherwise discriminate against an employees because he has filed charges or given testimony under this [Act].''

19. 30 U.S.C. 815(c)(1), 1977.

20. 42 U.S.C. 2000(e)–3.

21. ''Nerve in the Workplace,'' editorial, *New York Times* (March 3, 1980), p. A18.

WHIRLPOOL CORPORATION

BEHR, PETER. ''Controlling Chemical Hazards.'' *Environment*, 20, no. 6 (July/August 1978), pp. 25–29.

BIDDLE, T. M., T. C. MEANS, and P. K. LEVINE. ''Protected Work Refusals under Section 105(c)(1) of the Mine Safety and Health Act.'' *West Virginia Law Review*, 89 (Spring 1987), pp. 629–44.

BINGHAM, EULA. ''The New Look at OSHA.'' *Labor Law Journal* (August 1978), pp. 487–92.

BLAIR, IAN C. ''The Safety Blitz: Whether Mandated by OSHA or Management, Safety Awareness is Playing a Greater Role in the Beverage Workplace.'' *Beverage World*, 107 (January 1988), pp. 49–50.

BRICKEY, KATHLEEN F. ''Death in the Workplace: Corporate Liability for Criminal Homicide.'' *Notre Dame Journal of Law, Ethics and Public Policy*, 2 (Summer 1987), pp. 753–90.

CLEARY, TIMOTHY F. ''Inter-Agency. Relationships under OSHA: A Brief Review of OSHRC Decisions.'' *Labor Law Journal* (January 1978), pp. 3–8.

ENGLISH, JAMES D. ''A Union Viewpoint.'' *Labor Law Journal* (August 1978), pp. 499–502.

ESKRIDGE, NANCY K. ''OSHA/AIHC Clash on Carcinogen Proposal.'' *BioScience*, 28, no. 5 (May 1975), pp. 311–12.

GREER, EDWARD. ''OSHA's Benzene Standard— Lives in the Balance Sheet.'' *Nation* (May 19, 1979), pp. 562–64.

IRWIN, MICHAEL H. K. *Risks to Health and Safety on the Job.* Washington, D.C.: Public Affairs Committee, 1986.

MCADAMS, TONY, and ROBERT C. MILJUS. ''OSHA and Warrantless Inspections.'' *Labor Law Journal* (January 1978), pp. 49–60.

MENDELOFF, JOHN M. *The Dilemma of Toxic Substance Regulation: How Overregulation Causes Underregulation at OSHA.* Cambridge, Mass.: Massachusetts Institute of Technology, 1988.

NICHOLS, ALBERT J., and RICHARD ZECKHAUSER. ''Government Comes to the Workplace: An Assessment of OSHA.'' *Public Interest*, 49 (Fall 1977), pp. 30–69.

OLDHAM, J. C. ''OSHA May Not Work in Imminent Danger Cases.'' *American Bar Association Journal*, 60 (June 1974), p. 690.

PENDERGRASS, John A. ''Safety: An Investment That Pays.'' *Labor Law Journal*, 37 (November 1986), pp. 747–51.

ROBINSON, RUTH O. ''Another Viewpoint.'' *Labor Law Journal* (August 1978), pp. 503–5.

ROSNER, DAVID, and GERALD MARKOWITZ, eds. *Dying for Work: Worker's Safety and Health in Twentieth-Century America.* Indiana University Press, 1987.

SMITH, R. JEFFREY. ''Toxic Substances: EPA and OSHA are Reluctant Regulators.'' *Science*, 203 (January 5, 1979), pp. 38–52.

SOUTAR, DOUGLAS. ''A Management Viewpoint." *Labor Law Journal* (August 1978), pp. 492–98.

Supreme Court Opinions. "Opinions Announced." *United States Law Week*, 48 (February 26, 1980), pp. 4189–95.

SUSSER, PETER A., and DAVID H. JETT. "*OSHA's Recordkeeping Enforcement Campaign.*" *Employment Relations Today*, 14 (Winter 1987/88), pp. 331–38.

SWAIN, J. H. "Protecting Individual Employees: Is it Safe to Complain about Safety?" *University of Bridgeport Law Review*, 9 (1988), pp. 59–139.

United States Bureau of Labor Statistics. *Occupational Injuries and Illnesses in the United States by Industry, 1985.* Washington, D.C.: May 1987.

U.S. Supreme Court. "Marshall v. Whirlpool Corp." 529 Federal Reporter 2nd Series, pp. 715–36.

VISCUSI, W. K. "The Structure and Enforcement of Job Safety Regulation." *Law and Contemporary Problems*, 49 (Autumn 1986), pp. 127–50.

WOHLNER, J. S. "The Evolving Doctrine of Union Liability for Health and Safety in the Workplace. Warning: Collective Bargaining Can Be Hazardous to Your Union's Health." *Pepperdine Law Review*, 14 (March 1987), pp. 601–46.

IOWA BEEF PROCESSORS, INC. (IBP, INC.)

Unsafe working conditions and labor practices
in the meat industry

Janet Henrich was 18 when she went to work at IBP, Inc.'s (formerly known as Iowa Beef Processors, Inc.) hog slaughter plant in Storm Lake, Iowa. She had been working about a week—three days on a pork butt skinner—when the machine with tooth rollers and a fixed blade grabbed her gloved right hand and pulled it through, skinning it like another piece of meat. There was no safety switch on the machine. Janet suffered four severed tendons and damaged nerves in her hand and fingers. As Janet went to the hospital, the machine was hosed off and work continued. The union and workers claim that such incidents are not uncommon.[1] In fact, they maintain that unhealthy and dangerous working conditions are endemic to the entire meat packing industry, of which IBP, the largest company, is the prime example.

The industry has had a sorry record of worker safety from its early days. If the current industry-injury rates are any indication, the situation has not changed substantially when compared with improvements in other industries.

In 1906, Upton Sinclair stunned the public when he published *The Jungle*,[2] which exposed the brutal working conditions of the Chicago slaughterhouses. Now over 80 years later, the meatpacking industry remains one of the most hazardous occupations in the U.S. From the setting of *The Jungle* until now, a meatpacking house is a grim place to work. The atmosphere of the workplace hearkens back to an earlier period of the industrial revolution, as chronicled, for example, in *Hard Times*,[3] by Charles Dickens. In the meatpacking plant, the worker seems to be an "appendage of the machine."

THE MEATPACKING INDUSTRY

The meatpacking industry employs about 100,000 people. The meatpacking industry is one of the most dangerous in the entire economy, as even meat industry analysts attest.[4] At 26.3 injuries per 100 full-time workers, it ranked fourth in 1985 behind manufacturers of structural wood members (28.3), sawmill operations (27.8), and mobile home manufacturers (27.3). These rates, as well as others in the 20-plus range, reflect the nature of the industries in which they occur: industries characterized by hard physical labor involving tools that can do bodily harm if not used properly.

At one end of the meatpacking plant are the yards full of livestock ready to be slaughtered. At the other end, processed meats emerged cut up and boxed ready for market. The technology of the industry has changed considerably since Upton Sinclair wrote his novel. Yet meat processing follows basically an assembly-line process. A job in the meatpacking industry does not demand great skills, but it does call for vigilance and attention.[5] Any momentary lapse can result in serious injury. An overwhelming majority of workers perform monotonous, repetitive-motion jobs at their assigned stations on the assembly line. Depending on where people are stationed, the temperatures may be extremely hot or cold. Workers often stand shoulder to shoulder, plying their trade with power saws, specialty knives, and machines such as slicers. Both grease and blood from the animals tend to make floors and tools slippery. The tools and conditions spell a formula for accidents. Workers are especially accident prone when they experience fatigue. Working conditions combine a constant roar from machinery, a strong stench from open bladders and stomachs, and monotony which sets in when people perform the same tasks—often simply cutting the same part from a carcass moving by on an overhanging conveyor—hour after hour. A person may perform the same cuts a thousand times an hour. There is constant pressure to keep pace with the conveyor belt. The work force comprises largely inexperienced and unskilled workers due to low comparative wages and high turnover rates.

This worker inexperience, combined with unsafe machinery and hazardous working conditions, creates fatigue and lapses of attention and thus contributes to the high accident rates prevailing in the industry.

At the same time, there is intense competition in the industry.[6] Most meatpackers are straining to implement low-cost production strategies. On the one hand, they introduce more automation. On the other hand, the supply of labor is greater than the demand, with the result that the bargaining power of unions is weakened as they themselves fight for survival. Furthermore, worker health and safety regulations are either often weak or poorly enforced.

IBP AND THE OCCUPATIONAL SAFETY AND HEALTH ADMINISTRATION (OSHA)

On July 21, 1987, The Occupational Safety and Health Administration, a branch of the Labor Department, proposed a $2.59 million fine against IBP, Inc., the nation's largest meatpacking company.[7] This investigation followed from a complaint filed against IBP by the IBP workers' union, the United Food and Commercial Workers Union (CFCW).[8]

The charges were that IBP failed to report 1,038 job-related injuries and illnesses at its plant in Dakota City, Nebraska, from January 1985 through December 1986. In announcing the action, assistant labor secretary John A. Pendergrass said, "This case is the worst example of underreporting injuries and illnesses to workers ever encountered by OSHA in its sixteen year history." Under the law, such fines take effect in 15 days unless contested.

Gary Mickleson, a spokesman for IBP, provided the initial company response: "We did not willfully violate OSHA's record-keeping requirements and we will not pay the proposed penalties. We wish to have and will have an opportunity to show our side of the story.''

ISSUES FOR ANALYSIS

The IBP case raises a number of issues for discussion. They pertain to the nature of the industry, including its competitive character; the organizational characteristics and corporate culture and management attitudes at IBP; the composition of the work force and the attitudes of the union; the adequacy of the regulatory and enforcement procedures; and society's perception of the problem and its willingness to take appropriate measures to correct it. In particular:

1. What are some of the dimensions where improvements can be made to make the meatpacking industry safer for workers and more efficient for employers? To what extent have these measures been taken by IBP and the meatpacking industry, and what additional efforts are called for?

2. What has been the attitude of management in the meatpacking industry regarding working conditions? Have they been reactive or proactive, and why?

3. How would one evaluate the management attitude and performance of IBP both prior to the OSHA investigation and subsequent to the filing of the complaint by the United Food and Commercial Workers Union (CFCW)? If the management performance is wanting, what measures can be suggested to induce or compel managers to pay more attention to worker safety?

4. How effective have the unions been in protecting the workers? What are the sources of either their successes or failures? Are changes needed in the way meatpacking workers are organized and represented to help them better protect their lives and limbs, and their other rights?

5. What should be our assessment of the performance of OSHA in this case as well as other situations within the framework of its operational philosophy and enforcement proce-

dures? Is this performance satisfactory? If not, what are some of the factors that might account for OSHA's failure in protecting workers from unsafe working conditions?

6. What sort of regulations are called for both with respect to prevention of injury and compensation?

7. What changes in the external sociopolitical environment have had a strong bearing on the corporate, union, and government policies in the IBP case?

IBP, INC.

IBP, Inc. is a subsidiary of Occidental Petroleum and lists sales of $6.82 billion a year. Occidental acquired IBP in 1981 for $795 million. In 1980, IBP had profits of $53 million on sales of $4.6 billion. On the day before the OSHA announcement, Occidental was reported ready to sell some 40% of IBP for an estimated $600 million.[9]

In 1986, IBP and two small unrelated units which comprise Occidental's Agribusiness Division earned $58.8 million, or 6% of the company's operating profits of $963 million. The sale had been rumored since 1984 and was not directly linked to the OSHA complaint.

IBP employs 18,000 workers (roughly 18% of the industry work force) in 10 beef plants and four pork plants located in eight states. About half of the company's processing capacity is located close to suppliers in the upper Midwest. In 1986, IBP processed 7.9 million cattle and 4.4 million hogs, a record for the company.

IBP is a giant in the meatpacking industry (Table 1). Unions, and even consumer groups and public officials, have charged it with being ruthless and striving to attain and exercise monopoly power, with all the excesses that such power entails. IBP accounted for 45% ($6.5 billion) of Occidental Petroleum's 1985 sales of $14.5 billion. From 1981 to 1985, it experienced healthy growth in both sales and earnings.

TABLE 1. IBP Sales and Operating Earnings

YEAR	SALES (BILLIONS)	EARNINGS (MILLIONS)
1985	$6.5	$144.6
1984	$6.6	$108.2
1983	$6.1	$120.4
1982	$5.0	$127.9
1981	$5.0	$104.8

THE COMPLAINT AGAINST IBP: THE UNITED FOOD AND COMMERCIAL WORKERS UNION'S (CFCW) POSITION

In filing its complaint against IBP, The UFCW alleged that IBP kept a fraudulent set of books regarding job safety with the intent of deceiving OSHA and forestalling plant inspections. This complaint led to the $2.46 million fine assessed against IBP by OSHA.[10] The complaint was filed against a background of bad relations between the union and the corporation. A summary of the union's view of the struggle follows.[11]

The union sees IBP's management as concerned only with the bottom line. This goal is so paramount that management will trade workers' safety to enhance it. Furthermore, they see the company as embarked on a strategy of union busting. The twin issues of worker safety and union busting frame the debate. The struggle at Dakota City began as follows:

On December 14, 1986, IBP gave their Dakota City employees an early Christmas present— IBP locked the workers out. This heartless action came after UFCW Local 222 members rejected IBP's so called "last-best-final proposal" 2,250 to 50. And while the membership soundly rejected the company's proposal, they offered to work without a contract while the parties continued to negotiate, which IBP rejected out of hand.

Struggle is no stranger to the IBP Dakota City

workers—the 1986 Christmas lockout is the fifth time in seventeen years that Local 222 members have had to struggle on the picket line against IBP's ruthless tactics and greed. In fact, IBP's labor policies are as bloody as the cattle slaughtering business of which IBP is the undisputed king: 1969—seven and one-half month strike, 1972—eight month lockout, 1977–78—fifteen month strike, 1982—four month strike. All tallied, IBP Dakota City workers have struggled on the picket line for economic justice, worker dignity and a safe place to work for an aggregated three of the last seventeen years. Their plight is no way the result of their lack of militance or resolve. (*IBP Dakota*, p. 1)

The General Picture

The foregoing setting serves as a symbol of a whole set of grievances:

—How the world's largest and one of the most profitable beef packers uses its size, power, and ruthless tactics to smash competition and destroy industry wages, benefits, and working conditions.

—How for the fifth time in seventeen years the IBP Dakota City workers have been forced to the picket line to struggle against the savage attacks of IBP.

—How workers employed by the world's largest beef packer have not had a general increase in five years and, under the company's current proposal, would not receive a wage increase for another four years making it almost a decade without any kind of wage increase whatsoever.

—How many of the new IBP workers earn just $21.50 a week above the U.S. poverty line and qualify for food stamps and other welfare assistance. All of this while being employed for a company that had an operating income of $144 million in 1985.

—How workers risk life and limb daily to labor away in an industry that the U.S. Department of Labor classifies as one of the most dangerous occupations in the nation.

—How workers at the IBP Dakota City plant work in one of the most unsafe meat packing plants in the country that in 1985 had an injury and illness rate that is 23 percent higher than the outrageously dangerous industry average. (*IBP Dakota*, p. i)

Attack on Workers by Corporate America

Clearly, the union sees IBP as out to bust the union. It is clear that IBP thinks the union is recalcitrant and the cause of trouble at Dakota City. The UFCW sees the union movement as the target of an all-out corporate attack. It notes that since 1973 the average weekly earnings of middle-income families have declined by 14.3% in real terms (*IBP Dakota*, pp. 7–10). Union analysis concludes:

> Without question, the economic plight of U.S. workers is the direct result of a savage attack by Corporate America on worker's wages, benefits and working conditions. Furthermore, such an assault is compounded by the Reagan administration's anti-union policies and its cozy relationship with the wealthy and powerful of this nation. The tools of destruction utilized by the corporate community entail forced wage concessions with threats of plant closings, capital flight to low wage markets, Chapter 11 bankruptcy ploys, corporate spinoffs and subcontracting arrangements. Tactics that cut across all industries and negatively impact tens of millions of American workers. (*IBP Dakota*, p. 2)

In the union view, corporate greed and hardheartedness are the main problem. The UFCW is not attacking IBP alone. In an August 1987 study, it also criticized another giant meatpacker, John Morrell, in a report entitled, "The John Morrell Workers' Struggle."[12]

Wages

As far as the union is concerned, wages are as important as the job safety issue. The general wage picture is as follows:

TABLE 2. IBP Plant Locations in the United States

FEDERAL INSPECTION NUMBER	PLANT LOCATION	NUMBER OF WORKERS
245C	Dakota City, Nebr.	2,800
245	Denison, Iowa	240
292A	Luverne, Minn.	150
245B	West Point, Nebr.	200
245D	Emporia, Kans.	2,000
278	Garden City, Kans.	950
245E	Amarillo, Tex.	1,700
9268	Pasco, Wash.	n/a
245G	Boise, Idaho	250
245J	Joslin, Ill.	1,500
2923	Madison, Nebr.[a]	250
244	Storm Lake, Iowa	750
244L	Columbus Junction, Iowa	200
244C	Council Bluffs, Iowa	350

[a]Subcontractor for Conagra.

Currently, the IBP Dakota City workers who are not on a starting wage rate receive a base labor rate of $8.20 an hour in the slaughter division and $7.90 an hour in the processing division. Based on a 40 hour workweek, which many weeks the workers do not receive, their annual income falls below the "low-family budget" of $17,567 as of October 1, 1986, according to the Bureau of Labor Statistics information (and updated by the AFL-CIO Economic Research Department). (*IBP Dakota*, p. 9)

Some 15% of IBP's total work force is employed at Dakota City, the principal location of the union's complaint, making it the largest plant work force. Table 2 lists IBP's beef and pork plants in the United States.

To complicate the matter, the IBP Dakota City workers had not had a general pay increase in the five years from 1981 to 1986. The IBP proposal to the union, which the membership rejected by a vote of 2,250 to 50, called for a four-year wage freeze extending to 1990. In addition, the IBP 1986 proposal called for a permanent two-tier wage structure for new workers. This would mean that after 30 months at starting rates, this new category of workers would still work for $0.68 an hour less in slaughter and $0.47 an hour less in processing, standing side by side with workers earning more while doing the same. (*IBP Dakota*, p. 9) IBP reportedly also wanted other concessions regarding overtime, reduced wage rates for certain job classifications, and greater worker contributions to their monthly health insurance premiums. The union also claimed that from 1983 to 1986, IBP extracted a $1.07 per hour wage cut that represented an annual loss of $2,225.60 for each worker, or a total three-year wage loss of $6,676.80 per worker. The union maintained that IBP's profit picture did not warrant such action.

To emphasize its point, the UFCW claimed that the IBP wage rates had barely kept a worker with a family above the poverty line. According to CFCW, under the old labor agreement, new workers were required to work for one year at $2.00 under the base labor rate, which placed their hourly rate at $6.20 for slaughter workers and $5.90 for processing workers. Based on a 36-hour work-week, a worker with a family qualified for food stamps. Many IBP workers had been receiving food stamps while working full-time because their wages were so low. Because of a massive work force turnover (100% plus a year), it was estimated that over 40% of the 2,800 workers at the Dakota City plant were new hires working at the starting rate. A new worker employed at the IBP processing division working a 40-hour workweek earned just $21.50 a week above the U.S. poverty line.

The union also specifically countered the IBP position that it had to cut labor costs in order to be competitive in the industry. (*IBP Dakota*, pp. 18–20) It asserted that the company's position was self-serving, for it ignored that it was IBP who drove down wages in the first place, and for all practical purposes IBP was the wage pacesetter. The company was paying what the market would bear. The union contended that the wage rate did not reflect just compensation either with respect to the hazard involved, the cost of living, or the company's profit picture. The union's position was that wage rates in the meatpacking industry were what IBP made them. IBP's competitive strategy is described by the union as follows:

> During the 1960s, into the mid 1970s, Armour, Swift, Wilson, John Morrell and many independents paid the prevailing national wage rate to their beef workers. When IBP first came into the industry in 1961 and expanded into the mid 1970s, IBP maintained they were going to be a low cost producer, which translated into being a low wage operator. IBP forced its employees to work at $2.00 and $3.00 an hour less than what IBP's competitors paid their employees.
>
> As a result of such a labor cost advantage, IBP could pay more for live cattle, which took the raw product away from competitors or forced them to match IBP's bids on top of a higher labor cost, which squeezed profit margins. On the other end of the business, IBP could sell their products cheaper to the retailers which took the marketplace away from competition, or forced them to sell their products at a loss in trying to compete with IBP's low wage operation.
>
> Now this all sounds fine for the livestock producers and the consumers, except for one overlooked fact. IBP drove Wilson, Swift, Armour and several independents out of the beef business. As studies would later show, with such big operators out of the business, with thousands of jobs lost and communities devastated, IBP was dictating prices to be paid for livestock and those prices were much lower than when there was still competition, for example, say in the Southwest part of the United States. And again studies showed consumers did not realize any savings in the price of beef at the retail meat counter. No one—workers, communities, livestock producers and consumers—derives any benefit from IBP's domination of the industry. (*IBP Dakota*, p. 19ff)

IBP's ABUSE OF MARKET POWER

The CFCW maintained that the way IBP handled labor revealed a pattern of using its size and power to beat down all people it dealt with: customers, competitors, suppliers, and the communities which vied with one another to land one of its plants. For example, IBP had been accused in the federal court by the Bohack retail chain of illegal price discrimination, and two New York juries, in 1981 and 1982, agreed with Bohack. IBP has also been the subject of antitrust suits, brought by Cattle Feeders, now awaiting trial in federal court in Texas. In addition, IBP has been the object, through its domination of the market, of investigations by the Department of Agriculture, the U.S. House of Representative's Small Business Committee, and the Justice Department in order to shed light on its marketing practices. One of these investigations revealed that IBP was withholding Grade 2 and 3 carcasses from the market, in order to "hasten the conversion of chain stores from carcass beef to boxed beef," which had higher profit margins for IBP. (*IBP Dakota*, p. 5)

The union also sees IBP as a burden on local communities. It wrings concessions from local communities in terms of water treatment facilities, tax breaks, and other subsidies. At the same time, it squeezes wages so that these communities are denied the anticipated spending of employees. The union contends that at Dakota City "wages are low enough that some employees who work full time are still eligible for welfare and food stamps." (*IBP Dakota*, p. 6)

WORK-RELATED INJURIES IN THE MEATPACKING INDUSTRY

The UFCW complaint underscores that the meatpacking industry is one of the most dangerous in the U.S. Citing statistics for 1985, the union states that there were 30.4 work-related injuries and illnesses for every 100 workers in meatpacking; of these, 15.1 (per hundred) led to time away from work. It is, however, important to evaluate the job-related injury figures in the meatpacking and other industries in a proper context.

According to the American Meat Institute, the industry's trade and lobbying group, because the nature of meatpacking, and other industries where injury incidence rates are high, is different from what workers in the service and information sector are used to, it is best to focus on what is being done to reduce injury rates, rather than the rates themselves, and on the progress that has been made to date.

The injury incidence rate in meatpacking has declined by 23% since 1979. This reduction has been larger than those for all food manufacturing (down 18%) and all manufacturing (down 22%). In human terms, the reduction in meatpacking injuries translates into between 16,000 and 17,000 fewer workers hurt on the job today than in 1979. Still, there is room to improve, and the industry continues to move in that direction.[13] (See Exhibits 1 through 4, and Table 3.)

WORK-RELATED INJURIES AT IBP

The union's assessment of IBP is severe. (*IBP Dakota*, pp. 11–17) According to IBP's own official records filed with OSHA, for the year 1985, "IBP may be the worst of the worst." For 1985, IBP listed 1,049 illnesses and injuries requiring more than just first aid. Of these, 649 involved lost workdays. Since there were approximately 2,800 workers at IBP's Dakota City plant, this worked out to an illness and injury rate of 37 per 100 workers, which was 23% higher than the already outrageous industry average. The horrendous safety problem at the IBP Dakota City plant, according to the union, was the result of a number of factors: excessive chain speeds, work force turnover, improper training, and production receiving priority over worker safety.

First, IBP workers labor with one of the fastest meat packing line speeds in the world.

On a normal two shift workday, 3,200 cattle are slaughtered and 5,600 slaughtered cattle are disassembled and put into boxes. The working conditions are cramped, with lines of people working side by side with approximately 48 inches of workspace wielding razor sharp knives and power tools, frantically trying to keep up with a relentless chain bringing production to their work station. Most workers toil away in numbing cold temperatures of 30 to 35 degrees, standing in blood and animal fat which creates a dangerously slippery floor.

Second, IBP has programmed into its system of operation a workforce turnover that is close to 100 percent a year. The IBP Dakota City plant employs approximately 2,800 workers. Such turnover translates into a con-

stant flow of new workers at the work stations every day. This in and of itself is a dangerously intolerable situation where large numbers of inexperienced workers are placed on a fast moving chain, crowded with workers using razor-sharp knives, trying to meet IBP's production quota demand.

Third, all too often, IBP provides little meaningful training for new workers. The worker turnover is so great and IBP's production demands take priority over all else, that new workers are thrown into the system with little training of even the basics of how to maintain their equipment, not to mention, the damages that lurk on the line to body and limb. New workers have to rely on older workers, who are already overworked with excess chain speeds and unqualified help, for

EXHIBIT 1. Injuries and Rate of Incidence in Meatpacking

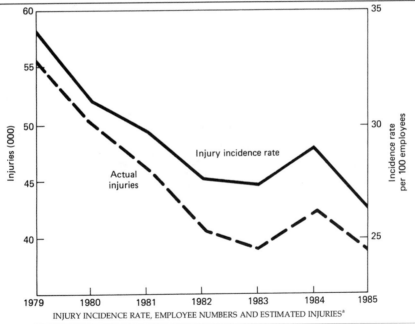

INJURY INCIDENCE RATE, EMPLOYEE NUMBERS AND ESTIMATED INJURIES[a]

	1979	1980	1981	1982	1983	1984	1985
Injury incidence rate (per 100 employees)	34.2	31.0	29.7	27.7	27.4	29.0	26.3
Employees (thousands)	162.6	161.4	155.2	146.9	143.4	146.7	148.5
Injuries[a] (thousands)	55.6	50.0	46.1	40.7	39.3	42.5	38.9

[a]Incidence rate multiplied by employees.
SOURCE: "Update on Injuries." Memo from Jene Knutson to Manly Molpas, the American Meat Institute, Washington, D.C., July 28, 1987.

tips on how to do the job, the proper maintenance of equipment and safety procedures.
This procedure creates dangerous working
conditions for new and older workers alike.

Fourth, production at IBP takes priority over
all else. A battalion of foremen hyped up by
the corporate office to meet staggering production quotas create pressure-cooker working conditions for the workers. Even though
meat packing is one of the most unsafe occupations in the country and IBP is worse than

the industry average, production, not safety,
is the daily drumbeat coming for IBP.

There were numerous injuries. In a three
month period, between May and July of
1985, there were over 1,800 visits to one
nurse's station that didn't even cover the
whole plant. And the workers don't just run
to the nurse for every scratch and fall.

The chain is moving so fast that they can only
break away when they are really in trouble
and only with the foreman's approval.

EXHIBIT 2. Index of Incidence of Occupational Injuries

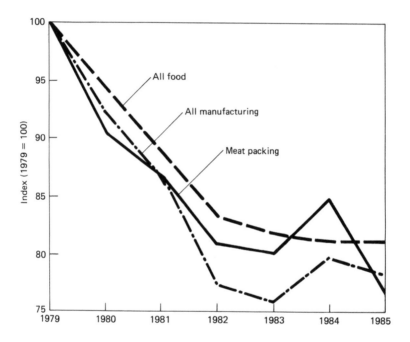

OCCUPATIONAL INJURY INCIDENCE RATES, 1979–1985

	1979	1980	1981	1982	1983	1984	1985	% change 1979–1985
All manufacturing	12.8	11.8	11.1	9.9	9.7	10.2	10.0	− 21.9%
Index (1979 = 100)	100.0	92.1	86.7	77.3	75.8	79.7	78.1	
All foods	19.2	18.1	17.1	16.0	15.7	15.8	15.8	−17.7%
Index (1979 = 100)	100.0	94.3	89.1	83.3	81.8	82.3	82.3	
Meatpacking	34.2	31.0	29.7	27.7	27.4	29.0	26.3	− 23.1%
Index (1979 = 100)	100.0	90.6	86.8	81.0	80.1	84.8	76.9	

SOURCE: "Update on Injuries." Memo from Jene Knutson to Manly Molpas, the American Meat Institute, Washington, D.C., July 28, 1987.

EXHIBIT 3. Injuries and Illnesses and Rate of Incidence in Meatpacking

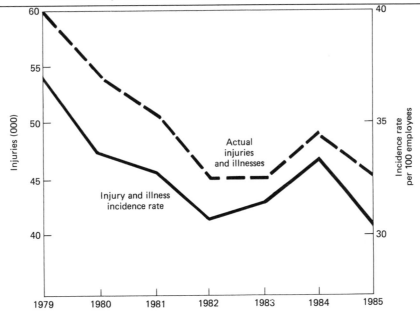

INJURY AND ILLNESS INCIDENCE RATE, EMPLOYEE NUMBERS, AND ESTIMATED INJURIES AND ILLNESSES[a]

	1979	1980	1981	1982	1983	1984	1985
Injury incidence rate (per 100 employees)	36.9	33.5	32.8	30.7	31.4	33.4	30.4
Employees (thousands)	162.6	161.4	155.2	146.9	143.4	146.7	148.5
Injuries and illnesses (thousands)	60.0	54.1	50.9	45.1	45.0	49.0	45.1

[a]Incidence rate multiplied by employees.

SOURCE: "Update on Injuries." Memo from Jene Knutson to Manly Molpas, the American Meat Institute, Washington, D.C., July 28, 1987.

The union report illustrates each of these points with individual examples of people who have had accidents, and it indicates how easily these accidents could have been avoided.

UNION'S LACK OF BARGAINING POWER AND INABILITY TO PROTECT WORKERS

The union felt that industry concentration on the one hand and changing worker demographics on the other hand had seriously impacted its ability to protect workers. Thus, although the Dakota City workers rejected the company offer by the overwhelming vote of 2,250 to 50 (out of 2,800 workers), the union was unable to force IBP to renegotiate. Part of the explanation is found in the ready availability of unorganized workers.[14]

According to CFCW, there is a problem of high turnover among workers. Turnover is considered profitable for meatpacking companies. It affects every aspect of the workers' lives, and it also defeats unions. The new breed of workers are generally young, between the ages of 18 and 25, and are primarily often with very young children, and are of Mexican and Southeast Asian descent. The system which these employers have created is designed to increase employee turnover. The companies do not want employees to stay. Employees with more seniority cost them more money. These companies bank on turnover and, according to CFCW, view it as a profit enhancer. Turnover rates of 500% per year are not uncommon. Thus, most employees are at the low entry level. The companies' health insurance costs are negligible because most of the work force does not have the required six months seniority to be eligible for coverage. In addition, there are certain tax incentives available to employers who hire more of a particular category of employees. The constant turnover apparently does not affect

production nor result in sufficient losses to counter the obvious economic incentives in favor of turnover. For union organizing, the system of turnover prevents employees from becoming knowledgeable and more sophisticated because they simply are not there long enough.

The workers also have no ties with the community. Their relations with the community are hostile. They are ostracized. They put a strain on the community resources. The hospitals are reluctant to treat indigents. The schools dislike teaching English to non-English-speaking children. Police enforce the criminal laws more restric-

EXHIBIT 4. Index of Incidence of Occupational Injuries and Illnesses

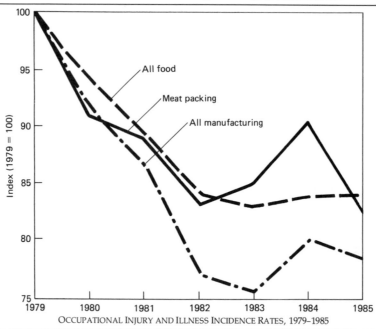

OCCUPATIONAL INJURY AND ILLNESS INCIDENCE RATES, 1979–1985

	1979	1980	1981	1982	1983	1984	1985	*% change 1979–1985*
All manufacturing	13.3	12.2	11.5	10.2	10.0	10.6	10.4	− 21.8%
Index (1979 = 100)	100.0	91.7	86.5	76.7	75.2	79.7	78.2	
All foods	19.9	18.7	17.8	16.7	16.5	16.7	16.7	− 16.1%
Index (1979 = 100)	100.0	94.0	89.4	83.9	82.9	83.9	83.9	
Meatpacking	36.9	33.5	32.8	30.7	31.4	33.4	30.4	− 17.6%
Index (1979 = 100)	100.0	90.8	88.9	83.2	85.1	90.5	82.4	

SOURCE: "Update on Injuries." Memo from Jene Knutson to Manly Molpas, the American Meat Institute, Washington, D.C., July 28, 1987.

TABLE 3.[a] Meatpacking Industry—SIC 2011 Injuries by Selected Source of Injury and Type of Injury U.S. 1976-1981 (inclusive)

	STRUCK BY NEC[b]	LIFTING OBJECT	STATIONARY OBJECT	PULLING OBJECT	OVER-EXERTION	FALLING OBJECT	WORK SURFACE	THROWING OBJECT	CAUGHT IN NEC	BY ABSORPTION	SUB-TOTAL	OTHER AND UN-CLASSIFIED	TOTAL
Knife	16,904	6	1,358	111	993	519	4	927	11	2	20,835	2,819	23,654
Meat products	789	3,241	155	2,557	1,950	962	8	1,428	64	368	11,522	712	12,234
Containers NEC[b] barrel, box	350	3,255	350	488	610	758	9	458	151	2	6,431	497	6,928
Body motion	10	14	3	21	198	0	13	7	1	0	267	6,384	6,651
Floor	2	0	66	3	6	6	4,182	0	16	0	4,281	2,153	6,434
Animals and related Products	1,655	495	516	781	345	267	5	205	64	413	4,746	891	5,637
Metal item(s)	1,008	218	1,118	164	84	863	14	44	137	9	4,659	1,008	4,667
Machine NEC	170	43	339	55	117	75	1	25	513	2	1,340	600	1,940
Nonpower vehicles[b]	332	64	148	451	65	130	6	25	111	1	1,333	361	1,694
Hand tool	889	3	87	16	20	76	0	8	5	0	1,104	368	1,472
Subtotal	22,109	7,339	4,140	4,647	4,388	3,656	4,242	3,127	1,073	797	55,518	15,793	71,311
other and unclassified	3,870	1,751	3,258	1,322	1,513	1,770	1,054	670	1,674	1,474	18,356	15,034	33,390
TOTAL	25,979	9,090	7,398	5,969	5,901	5,426	5,296	3,797	2,747	2,271	73,874	30,827	104,701

[a]Adapted from BLS/ SDS, 1976–1981.
[b]Not elsewhere classified.
[c]Hand trucks, etc.
SOURCE: "Update on Injuries." Memo from Jene Knutson to Manly Molpas, the American Meat Institute, Washington, D.C., July 28, 1987.

tively against the workers. In short, according to CFCW, the workers in the IBP plants were working under subhuman conditions, under a system fostered by tax incentives and a hostile and indifferent local community.[16]

IBP AND THE MEATPACKING INDUSTRY's RESPONSE

In May of 1987, the Subcommittee on Employment and Housing of the U.S. House of Representatives House Government Operations Committee held hearings on safety in the meat industry. Testimony was provided by C. Manly Molpas, president of the American Meat Institute (AMI), and Robert L. Peterson, chairman and chief executive officer of IBP, Inc.[18]

Molpas underscored the commitment of the meat industry to safety. He went on to define safety in two ways. The first aspect of safety he discussed was the provision of safe products for the consumer. He stated:

Toward this end, we work on a daily basis with USDA inspectors who administer the most intensive health-related regulatory program in government. All livestock is subject to veterinary examination by USDA both before and after slaughter. Our plant sanitation is monitored on a daily basis, including a pre-operational check by an inspector before each shift begins. This comprehensive regulatory scheme even extends to areas such as blueprints, equipment and labeling materials, all of which must be approved by USDA prior to their use. We are extremely proud of the track record that comes out of this partnership, with the result being the American consumer enjoys the world's safest supply of meat products. (Peterson, 1987)

Molpas listed in detail the concrete measures the American Meat Institute had taken to achieve the goals of safety in the workplace. First, the AMI had been a cosponsor in conjunction with the National Safety Council and Georgia Tech University of an annual meat industry safety workshop. In addition, the AMI had sponsored a number of seminars and workshops which have dealt with the reduction of accidents, improving loss prevention, and implementing OSHA's work hazard communication standards.

Molpas then went on to stress the interrelation between product safety and safety in the workplace:

> Our employees work with live animals, heavy machinery, knives and a variety of other cutting and trimming implements. In such an environment, it is imperative to maintain a constant on-going focus on human safety. First and foremost, this must be done in order to eliminate unnecessary human suffering. Second, good safety is good business. Accidents and injuries impose impediments to productivity and efficiency and add significant costs to businesses that have traditionally operated with low profit margins. (Peterson, p. 2)

According to Molpas, the Bureau of Labor Statistics (BLS) reports that meatpacking plants (SIC Code 2011) reduced their injury incidence rates by 23% during the period from 1979 to 1985.

These same statistics show that the combined injury and illness figures for the meatpacking industry dropped a total of 9% in a single year from 1984 to 1985. The industry affirmed that it was not content with past successes. In February 1987, the AMI board of directors approved as a priority objective the establishment of a broader, industry-wide safety program. The board subsequently appointed an industry-wide task force and charged it with publishing and distributing an ergonomics handbook for the meat industry, developing a national safety seminar, and sponsoring a meat industry safety ward program in conjunction with the National Safety Council.

Molpas then addressed the issue of OSHA's record keeping requirement. (Peterson, p. 4ff) He noted that, given the nature of the meatpacking business, all meat compa-

nies were forced to operate at rates that kept them in the high-hazard category under OSHA's inspection targeting program. He denied that companies intentionally misreported in order to avoid OSHA inspections. Rather, he suggested that reporting requirements should be more clearly written and be simple and easily understood. Otherwise, the policy would not work properly.

As an example, he pointed out that OSHA felt it necessary to issue an 84-page booklet to explain how to fill out Reporting Form 200. He cited a number of ambiguities in the regulations regarding repetitive motion trauma, which is not as easy to spot ahead of time and document as, for example, a broken arm or a cut. Spotting repetitive motion trauma is like spotting fatigue before the consequences of fatigue—for example, an accident ensuing from a lapse of attention. On this basis, Molpas emphasized what he called a critical distinction between a conscious attempt to circumvent the law and an honest difference in judgment.

Molpas, however, did not adopt an uncooperative posture. He expressed a desire to move beyond simply criticizing the present program and make efforts to improve on it and maximize compliance within the industry. He mentioned the following three areas for further exploration:

1. Initiation of a comprehensive program to identify and clarify the areas of ambiguity in OSHA reporting requirements which may be unique to our industry.

2. Institution of a broad based industry information and training program, utilizing outside experts as appropriate, in order to assure the broadest possible understanding and application of record keeping requirements.

3. A broad review of injury and illness data relating to our industry to determine whether the current information base is adequate. (Peterson, pp. 7–8)

In his testimony, Peterson, the chairman and CEO of IBP, Inc., noted that since he joined IBP as a cattle buyer in 1961, the economies of mass production had revolutioned the industry:

> Today, beef and pork are processed at packing plants through a labor intensive production process. After slaughtering, the livestock are put on a line where they are processed by workers who stand at work stations and make various cuts on the meat with sharp knives as it passes along the disassembly line. These pieces of meat are then vacuum packed and boxed in sturdy corrugated containers and shipped to various wholesale and retail customers throughout the United States.
>
> There are many benefits from this modernization process. Locating plants near major livestock production centers lowers the transportation costs and reduces shipping damage. Mass production allows us to take advantage of scale economies. In addition, boxed meat is easier to ship over long distances, has a longer product life, and is more sanitary for shipping and storage. The bottom line is that these changes keep costs lower and ensure that consumers get more value for their dollar. In fact, meat processing is one of the few labor intensive industries in which the vast majority of jobs has remained here on our shores.
>
> After six years devoted exclusively to meat slaughtering, IBP began meat processing operations in 1967 with the construction of the Dakota City plant. . . . (Peterson, p. 1)

Peterson saw IBP as an industry leader. Of IBP's 14 plants, only the Dakota City plant was represented by the United Food and Commercial Workers Union (UFCW). Peterson went on to say: "We are currently involved in a bitter strike at this plant, our fifth in five negotiations. Two of our other large operations have contracts with another major union and have never experienced a labor dispute." (Peterson, pp. 3–4)

Peterson directly countered the testimony of UFCW witnesses before the Subcommittee. He denied that meat processing

plants were unclean and unsafe, noting that they were subject to frequent and unannounced OSHA inspections. In addition, he said that there were 200 inspectors from the Department of Agriculture constantly in the plants to ensure that the plant and equipment were clean and that the meat was processed under stringent sanitary conditions. He then asserted that many of the UFCW claims were demonstrably untrue: (pp. 4–5)

- Contrary to what the UFCW said, most workers do not work in 20 to 30 degree temperatures on the processing floor. In fact only three percent of our employees—those who work in the meat coolers—face these temperatures, and these people are issued special clothing for their protection.

- Contrary to what the UFCW claimed, "most workers" are not forced to stand in blood. This condition is applicable only to the three to five workers per shift directly involved in the slaughter of the animals and affects less than 0.4 percent of the workforce.

- Contrary to what the UFCW claimed, our floors are not "treacherously slippery." In 1985 and 1986 we spread over two million pounds of salt on our floors to keep them as safe as possible. In Dakota City alone 36 individuals are continuously cleaning the floors to remove all debris and eliminate slippery conditions. We have spent well over $1.0 million in 1985 and 1986 to keep our floors clean and reduce the chance of slipping. (Peterson, pp. 3–4)

Peterson then affirmed IBP's commitment to safety in the workplace. He contended that safety was good human relations and sound economics. Every worker's compensation payment, every work stoppage due to an injury, every lost work day or light-duty day has an impact on the bottom line. (Peterson, p. 6)

Peterson insisted that IBP management was not indifferent to safety considerations. He indicated that IBP had adopted 10 specific measures to maximize workplace safety: (1) safety equipment; (2) executive safety committee; (3) human resources policy; (4) corporate safety department and safety coordinators; (5) employee safety committees; (6) safety training for new workers; (7) safety training observation program (STOP); (8) supervisors' daily safety inspection; (9) facility safety inspection; and (10) accident investigation regarding safety equipment. (Peterson, pp. 6–13)

According to Peterson,

> IBP employees are issued, at company expense, and are required to wear extensive personal protective equipment. . . . To train workers in the use of safety equipment, the appropriate offices have been provided with a training video which both instructs workers in the safe use of knives and demonstrates the use of proper safety equipment. (Peterson, p. 7)

Though there are others, these 10 policies represent the core of IBP's safety policy. Peterson claimed that the results have been good. In support, he cited the declining number of worker's compensation claims:

> I am pleased to report that over the last several years, IBP's worker's compensation claim rate has dropped dramatically. According to figures supplied by our worker's compensation adjusters, total claims filed has declined in each of the last four years—despite the fact that total manhours has increased. The percentage of total worker claims filed per 200,000 manhours (the same standard used by OSHA) has declined by approximately two-thirds since 1983. The totals are as follows:

YEAR	TOTAL CLAIMS	TOTAL MANHOURS	CLAIMS PER 200,000 MANHOURS
1983	7942	25,906,000	61
1984	6588	26,614,000	50
1985	5188	30,235,000	34
1986	3546	33,397,000	21

(Peterson, p. 13)

Peterson also accused the CFCW for being uncooperative.

We have actively sought UFCW cooperation in these efforts, but often the union has been a roadblock to mandatory use of safety equipment. For example, during the term of the recently expired collective bargaining agreement the UFCW filed eight grievances resisting safety gear requirements we established at Dakota City after safety studies led us to conclude that they were necessary. (Peterson, p. 7)

> Our Dakota City plant, which the UFCW criticized so severely in your last hearing on this issue, has four Safety Committees—each with UFCW representatives on it. It is unfortunate that many of the alleged safety problems the union described in its earlier testimony never were bought to our attention at Dakota City Safety Committee meetings. (Peterson, p. 10)

In the final part of his testimony, Peterson discussed IBP's compliance with OSHA's record keeping requirements. (Peterson, pp. 14–20). Labeling the allegations levelled by UFCW as "sensational and blatantly untrue," he denied that IBP ever kept two sets for safety books in order to deliberately deceive OSHA and, thereby, avoid inspections. He stated that IBP kept detailed records of injuries and illnesses as well as medical history. The records were kept in various forms because reporting requirements differed for different regulations.

Peterson insisted that contrary to the union's claims, there was nothing sinister or suspicious in any of this record keeping. And, most importantly, there was no effort to mislead OSHA. In fact, the extraneous entries made it extremely easy when OSHA conducted inspections in 1985 and 1986 to determine whether any dispensary visit constituted a recordable entry for OSHA purposes. Moreover, in 1987, when OSHA inspectors examined the revised log as part of their record keeping examination, IBP also provided them with the comprehensive dispensary log. Thus, at no time was the revised log used to hide any visits by Dakota City workers to medical dispensaries.

Peterson attributed much of the confusion to the ambiguity of OSHA's regulations. He cited testimony by other witnesses at the earlier hearing, and also the Bureau of Labor Statistics guidelines, showing that OSHA rules and guidelines were not precise. They required frequent interpretations and many good-faith judgment calls. Peterson went on:

> That review is underway. While the final results are not yet available, it is clear that some changes to our OSHA No. 200 records for prior years will be needed to bring IBP into complete compliance with OSHA's new guidelines. It is also likely that our recordable injuries for the years 1982–86 will increase, in part because of our instructions to make sure that we call the close ones in favor of recording. (Peterson, p. 11)

Finally, Peterson charged that a complaint with OSHA on January 22, 1987, was part of the union's "corporate campaign" against IBP. As a result, OSHA began an investigation, and Peterson affirmed that IBP was cooperating. He affirmed that IBP was committed to improving its own performance.

IBP CHANGES ITS COURSE

Subsequent to the initial OSHA fine, IBP began a plan to modernize its Dakota City facility and also opted a more conciliatory stance toward the Union. CFCW had launched a major publicity campaign highlighting IBP's unsafe working conditions while at the same time displaying a willingness to work with IBP. The congressional hearing further intensified the negative public image of IBP, which was heightened when OSHA refused to accept IBP's modernization plan and hit IBP with another fine of $3 million, for a total of $5.6 million—the agency's largest fine ever.

In a major change of stance, IBP voluntarily recognized the union (CFCW) at its Joslin, Illinois, plant where it had been resisting the union's efforts toward worker organization. This was a major turnaround and, as a result, put the union on a growth path. The union plans to launch more organizational drives at other nonunion packers. Finally, there is peace at IBP. Whether it will be a lasting peace, only time will tell.

NOTES

1. Gene Erb, "Newspaper Finds 'Injury Epidemic' at Storm Lake." *No Bull Sheet* (September 1987), p. 4.

2. Upton Sinclair, *The Jungle*. Cambridge, Mass.: R. Bentley, 1946.

3. Charles Dickens, *Hard Times*. New York: Hearst's International Library Co., 1968.

4. Alan Pezaro, *Critical Review Analysis for Injury Related Research in the Meatpacking Industry (SIC 2011)*. Washinton, D.C.: American Meat Institute, January 1984.

5. William Glaberson, "Misery on the Meatpacking Line." *New York Times* (June 14, 1987), pp. F1, F8.

6. William Robins, "A Meatpacker Cartel Up Ahead?" *New York Times* (May 29, 1988), p. F4.

7. Philip Shabecoff, "OSHA Seeks $2.59 Million Fine for Meatpacker's Injury Reports." *New York Times* (July 22, 1987), pp. A1, A20.

8. Ibid.

9. Andrea Adelson, "Occidental Hints at IBP Sale." *New York Times* (July 21, 1987), pp. D1, D17.

10. Shabecoff, "OSHA Seeks," pp. A1, A20.

11. United Food and Commercial Workers International Union, *IBP Dakota City Workers' Struggle,* Washington, D.C. and Sioux City, Iowa, January 1987.

12. Ibid., page cited in text.

13. "Update on Injuries." Memo from Jene Knutson to Manly Molpas, the American Meat Institute, Washington, D.C., July 28, 1987.

14. United Food and Commercial Workers International Union, *The John Morrell Workers' Struggle,* Washington, D.C., August 1987.

15. "How OSHA Helped Organize the Meatpackers," *Business Week* (August 29, 1988), p. 82.

16. United Food and Commercial Workers International Union, *General Report: 1986 National Packinghouse Strategy and Policy Conference,* Washington, D.C., April 10, 1987.

17. C. Manley Molpas, "Testimony Regarding Safety in the Workplace before the House Government Operations Committee, Subcommittee on Employment and Housing, U.S. House of Representatives," American Meat Institute, Washington, D.C., May 6, 1987.

18. Robert L. Peterson, "Testimony before the Subcommittee on Housing and Employment, House Government Operations Committee," American Meat Institute, Washington, D.C., May 6, 1987.

IOWA BEEF PROCESSORS, INC.

ADUDDELL, ROBERT M., and LOUIS P. CAIN. "The Consent Decree in the Meat Packing Industry, 1920–1956." *Business History Review,* 55 (August 1981), pp. 359–78.

ADUDDELL, ROBERT M., and LOUIS P. CAIN. "Public Policy Toward the Greatest Trust in the World." *Business History Review,* 55 (Summer 1981), pp. 217–42.

BLAIR, IAN C. "The Safety Blitz: Whether Mandated by OSHA or Management, Safety Awareness is Playing a Greater Role in the Beverage Workplace." *Beverage World,* 107 (January 1988), pp. 49–50.

BUTZ, DALE E., and GEORGE L. BAKER. *The Changing Structure of the Meat Economy.* Cambridge, MA: Harvard Business School, 1960.

CAPPELLI, PETER. "Plant-level Concession Bargaining." *Industrial and Labor Relations Review,* 39 (October 1985), pp. 90–104.

CARNES, RICHARD B. "Meatpacking and Prepared Meats Industry: Above-average Productivity Gains." *Missouri Labor Review,* 107 (April 1984), pp. 37–42.

"Carving Up the Meat Industry: 'New Breed' Packers Grind Workers Down." *Dollars and Sense* (Fall 1983), pp. 8–9.

CLEMEN, RUDOLF A. *The American Livestock & Meat Industry.* New York: Ronald Press Co., 1923.

COREY, LEWIS. *Meat and Man: A Study of Monopoly,*

Unionism and Food Policy. New York: Viking Press, 1950.

DENSFORD, LYNN E. "A New Era on Inspection." *Progressive Grocer* (March, 1980), pp. 26–29.

FAMINOW, M. D., and M. E. SARHAN. "Wholesale Meat Pricing in the United States." *Canadian Journal of Agricultural Economics* (1980), pp. 100–109.

Federal Trade Commission, *Investigation Report on the Meat Industry,* Washington, D.C.: Federal Trade Commission, 1919.

FRUMIN, E. "Conflict and Cooperation in Resolving Workplace Safety and Health Disputes." in *New York University Conference on Labor,* 41 New York: New York University (1988), pp. 1.1–.32.

HARWELL, EDWARD M. *Meat Management & Operations.* Lebhar Friedman, 1985.

IRWIN, MICHAEL H. K. *Risks to Health and Safety on the Job.* Washington, D.C.: Public Affairs Committee, 1986.

LEONARD, RODNEY E. "Meat Inspection is a Lot of Bull: Does the Government Adequately Inspect the Meat We Eat?" *Business and Society Review* (Fall 1983), pp. 56–60.

McCOY, J. H., and M. E. SARHON. *Livestock & Meat Marketing* (3rd ed.). Van Nostrand Reinhold, 1988.

MOLPAS, C. MANLY. "Outlook for the Meat Industry." *Food Processing* (January 1980), pp. 8–10.

"Monfort: A Meatpacker Tries a Comeback by Trimming Labor Costs." *Business Week* (March 15, 1982), p. 52.

PEARSON A. M., and THAYNE R. DUTSON. *Advances in Meat Research.* Greenwich, CN: AVI Press, 1987.

PENDERGRASS, JOHN A. "Safety: An Investment That Pays." *Labor Law Journal,* 37 (November 1986), pp. 747–51.

RICE, JUDY. "Noncontinuous Inspection of Meat and Poultry Plants." *Food Processing* (November, 1982), p. 4–7.

RICE, JUDY. "Voluntary QC Systems for Meat/Poultry Plants." *Food Processing* (December, 1980), p. 18–20.

ROSNER, DAVID, and GERALD MARKOWITZ, eds. *Dying for Work: Workers' Safety and Health in Twentieth-Century America.* Bloomington, IN: Indiana University Press, 1987.

SKAGGS, JiMMY M. *Prime Cut: Livestock Raising & Meatpacking in the United States.* College Station, TX: Texas A&M University Press, 1986.

SMITH, NEAL. "The Monopoly Component of Inflation in Food Prices." *University of Michigan Journal of Law Reform,* 14 (Winter 1981), pp. 149–72.

SUSSER, PETER A., and DAVID H. JETT. "OSHA's Recordkeeping Enforcement Campaign." *Employment Relations Today,* 14 (Winter 1987/88), pp. 331–38.

SWANSON, WAYNE, and GEORGE SCHULTZ. *Prime Rip.* Englewood Cliffs, N.J.: Prentice-Hall, 1982.

"Swift: Cutting Costs and Adding Products to Beat a Profit Deadline." *Business Week* (June 21, 1982), p. 65.

UNIPUB. (United Nations Publications). *Legislation Controlling the International Beef & Veal Trade.* United Nations, 1986.

UNIPUB. *International Markets for Meat.* United Nations, 1988.

UNIPUB. *The International Markets for Meat 1986–87.* United Nations, 1987.

UNIPUB. *The World Meat Economy in Figures.* United Nations, 1985.

United Nations. *Meat Processing Industry.* (UNIDO Guides to Information Sources, No. 1). UN.

United States Bureau of Labor Statistics. *Occupational Injuries and Illnesses in the United States by Industry, 1985.* May 1987.

United States Department of Agriculture. *Quality Control in Small Plants: A Guide for Meat and Poultry Processors.* 1981.

United States House Committee on Small Business. *Small Business Problems in the Marketing of Meat and Other Commodities: Hearings April 29–May 19, 1980.* 1980.

U.S. Congress. *Unfair Trade Practices in the Meat Industry.* Hearing before the Subcommittee on Anti-trust and Monopoly, 85th Congress, 1st Session.

USDA Economic Research Service. *Structured Changes in the Federally Inspected Meat Processing Industry 1961–1964.* Agricultural Economic Report No. 129.

U.S. District Court for the Northern District of Illinois. Opinion of the District Judge, *U.S. v. Swift and Company, et al.,* Docket No. 580613.

WALSH, MARGARET. *The Rise of the Midwestern Meat Packing Industry.* Lexington, KY: University Press of Kentucky, 1982.

WARD, CLEMENT. *Slaughter-cattle Pricing and Procurement Practices of Meatpackers.* United States Department of Agriculture, 1979.

WILSON, JAMES. "Work Related Injuries: A Statistical Highlight of 1984." *Alaska Economic Trends,* 6 (October 1986), pp. 1–6.

YEAGER, MARY. *Competition & Regulation: The Development of Oligopoly in the Meat Packing Industry.* Greenwich, Conn.: JAI Press, 1981.

FILM RECOVERY SYSTEMS INC.

The extent of officers' culpability for serious harm, and even death, of workers caused by unsafe working conditions

On June 14, 1985, Judge Ronald J. P. Banks, sitting on a nonjury trial, convicted three executives of National Film Recovery Systems, a small firm then based in Elk Grove, Illinois, of murder in the death of one employee, Stefan Golab, 61, a Polish immigrant who had been on the job for only two months.

In Illinois, murder is the first degree of homicide, higher than voluntary manslaughter. Defendants are often charged with killing someone by acting with a reckless lack of caution. According to the Illinois Criminal Code, "A person who kills an individual without lawful justification commits murder if, performing such acts, (one) creates a strong probability of death or great bodily harm to the individual or another."[1]

The Film Recovery case is a landmark in that it marks the first time corporate officials have been found guilty in a job-related death. There have been other cases where corporations and their executives have been charged with manslaughter. However, more often than not, it is the corporation that ends up paying the fines, and the executives get off with a slap on the wrist.[2]

The victim, Stefan Golab, left his native Poland in November 1981 to start a new life in the United States. On December 26, 1982, he began work as a laborer for Film Recovery Systems, which operated to recover silver from used photographic film. He was on the job barely two months when on February 10, 1983, he met his death.[3] On that day, Golab arrived for work as usual at 7:00 A.M. and began working with a Polish coworker, Roman Guzoski, around the cyanide-filled vats. After pumping cyanide solution into the tanks at 9:30, Golab went over to disconnect a pump. Upon moving a few steps, he slumped against the wall. His coworkers told him to leave the area. He did so, going to the locker area and (later) to the lunchroom. Shortly thereafter, he slumped over in his chair. His coworkers gathered around to help. Emergency aid was summoned to no avail. Upon arrival at Alexian Brothers Hospital at 10:50 A.M. Stefan Golab was pronounced dead.

A grand jury, convened in October 1983, indicted the companies involved—Metallic Marketing Inc. (MMI), Film Recovery Systems Inc. (FRS), and B. R. McKay and Sons. On November 21, 1983, they reached the consensus that the companies were guilty of involuntary manslaughter. The same grand jury found the corporate management (Steven O'Neil, president of FRS; Gerald Pett, vice-president of FRS; Charles Kirschbaum, plant manager at Elk Grove; Daniel Rodriguez, job supervisor at Elk Grove; and Michael McKay, a director of FRS whose company, B. R. McKay and Sons, owned half of FRS) with 20 violations of the reckless conduct statute. On May 1, 1984, another grand jury (which was convened in April) indicted these same individuals for murder because they knowingly caused the death of Stefan Golab by exposing him to unsafe working conditions in the FRS work environment.[4]

ISSUES FOR ANALYSIS

1. Under what conditions, if any, should the top managers of a company or a plant be held responsible for the death or serious injury to workers? Were these conditions met in the Film Recovery case?

2. What are minimum conditions of adequacy of care that must be met before managers or plant supervisors can be charged with criminal behavior against the person or workers?

3. In the case of a corporate policy or practice causing harm to others, who should ultimately be held responsible: the owners, (shareholders), the board of directors, top, middle, or low management? Alternately, how should responsibility be apportioned among these groups?

4. What is the responsibility of the workers themselves to see to it that their working environment is safe?

5. What is the responsibility of public agencies such as OSHA to see to it that work environments are without serious problems?

6. Are there specific industry, company, or management characteristics that make some firms more prone to reckless disregard of worker saftey? If so, what might these conditions be? In particular, are smaller companies more prone to engaging in such criminal behavior as compared to larger companies?

7. Is the behavior of Film Recovery Systems' managers an aberration, or is it symptomatic of conditions that are more prevalent in plant operations in the United States?

8. What are some of the changes that one might make in orgainzation structure and manager behavior to minimize the occurrence of incidents such as that at Film Recovery Systems?

9. What are the moral and ethical dimensions of the managers' behavior in this case? How are they different from standards of legal culpability? How might one go about inducing higher moral and ethical standards among plant managers in protecting the lives and health of their workers?

FILM RECOVERY SYSTEMS INC.: THE COMPANY PROFILE

Film Recovery Systems (FSM) was formed in late 1979 with the purpose of extracting silver from used film. It was founded by Steven O'Neil together with Michael McKay and Alvin Tolin, whom O'Neil met at a conference of the Radiological Society of North America. O'Neil was 25 years old at the time. He had studied commercial photography at Colorado Mountain College for two years, leaving in 1974. He immediately went to work for RKS Future Industries, a silver recycling firm in Denver. While there, he learned the cyanide wash system. In this process, sodium cyanide was diluted into a caustic solution, which went into holding tanks of approximately 1,000 gallons. The mixture of sodium cyanide in the solution registered as a 2% cyanide solution. Used film was then granulated and placed in the holding tanks. The solution extracted silver from the film product. After that, the cyanide solution and the extracted silver were drained from the holding tanks into electronically charged 125-gallon plating tanks. The extracted silver would adhere to the plates. Later, the plates were removed from the tanks, and the workers scraped the silver from them. The company then shipped the silver to refineries for processing. Workers would also remove the remnants of granulated film product from the holding tanks by climbing into them and shoveling the film residue out. The silver removal process took about three days.[5]

O'Neil worked at RKS full-time until 1977, at various positions both inside and outside the plant. This work experience proved to be important to his case, for he claimed that during these three years he suffered no injury or illnesses.[6] O'Neil then moved to Chicago, where he worked as a trader, purchasing used film and then selling it to processors. In so doing, he traveled extensively. As a result, he met Bob Fields of Drum Silver Company in Norman, Oklahoma. Fields agreed to buy film product from O'Neil. He had modified the cyanide wash system by installing a vacuum system to remove remnant film product from the holding tanks—a safer system.

In late 1977 and early 1978, O'Neil formed Metal Marketing Systems, Inc. (MMI) with two other individuals. MMI continued the film purchase and resale business. But by late 1978, a dispute arose with Drum Silver. In a settlement, MMI received money and one-half of Drum's plant equipment, which it proceeded to install in Wheeling, Illinois. O'Neil was intimately involved in plant operations at Wheeling. He also modified the evacuation system in such a way as to prevent workers from coming into contact with the cyanide solution. Again, he was to claim he never suffered any injury or illness.[7]

When FRS was formed, it acquired MMI's Wheeling plant and entered into a noncompetition pact where MMI would confine its operations to Florida. In return, MMI obtained 51% of FRS stock; O'Neil himself owned 51% of MMI. The Elk Grove plant opened in 1980. All went well. The plant expanded from 80 tanks in 1980 to 120 in 1981 and 140 in 1982. According to the defendants, additional ventilation fans were installed. Only two-thirds of the vats were used at one time, half for holding and half for plating. Both of these points were important in estimating the degree of toxicity in the air.[8] It was in this work environment that Stefan Golab collapsed and died.

FACTS OF THE CASE

During the nonjury trial, the defendants and the prosecution presented the work environment in the FRS plant in totally different terms; the former asserting that it was safe within the context of the essentially hazardous nature of the chemicals being handled at the plant. The defendants also contended that any infractions of safety regulations were at best minor, and that, in many cases, workers' discomfort arose out of their disregard for properly following safety regulations. In addition, the defendants held that the events and the circumstances surrounding them in no way justified the charges for which they were indicted.

Stefan Golab

According to the defendants, Golab had a history of heart problems, including evidence of an earlier heart attack. When he began working at FRS, he smoked cigarettes and suffered from a heart condition, which included an enlarged heart and a 50% blockage in the two major arteries to the heart. He last visited a doctor before coming to the

United States from Poland in November 1981. Thus, FRS was unaware of Golab's physical condition.[9] On the day of his collapse at the plant, all signs indicated a heart attack. When paramedics arrived at the plant to provide emergency medical aid, Golab lay in the company's parking lot. His face was grayish-blue in color. He already had convulsed and foamed at the mouth, all symptoms of a heart attack. As a consequence, the paramedics administered life support procedures, but they were of no avail.

The next day, the Cook county medical examiner performed an autopsy on Golab. He found that Golab suffered from a heart condition, including pulmonary edema (fluid in the lungs), coronary atherosclerosis (artery blockage), and hyperthrophy (thickening) of the heart's left ventricle. He concluded that the condition could cause death. Based on these findings, the medical examiner reported to an Elk Grove village police investigator on February 12, 1983, that he saw no indication during the autopsy that Golab died of anything other than a heart attack. However, he reserved providing a definitive cause of death until he received the results of toxicological laboratory tests on Golab's blood and other bodily specimens. On May 6, 1983, after receiving an toxicological laboratory report dated March 17, 1983, the medical examiner ruled that Golab died from acute cyanide poisoning through the inhalation of cyanide fumes in the air at FRS.[10] In all, two medical examiners and two toxicologists were called in to discern the cause of death. They came up with a split verdict. One medical examiner and one toxicologist found that Golab died of heart failure; the others cited cyanide poisoning. Contrary to the defendant's assertion that Golab died of heart failure, the prosecution claimed that Golab suffered a fatal cyanide blood concentration.

The preceding events led to the indictments against the defendants for murder, involuntary manslaughter, and reckless conduct. The murder indictment alleged that the individual defendants (who as "officers and high managerial agents" operated FRS, a business engaged in the use of cyanide in its industrial process) hired Golab as an employee of FRS without informing him of the company's use of cyanide and of safety procedures pertaining to the use of cyanide and failed to provide necessary safety equipment and adequate storage facilities for cyanide. As a consequence of these acts, the indictment alleged that the individual defendants, knowing that the hazards and dangers of cyanide created a strong probability of death or great bodily harm, caused Golab's death on February 10, 1983.

The involuntary manslaughter indictment charged only the coporate defendants. It alleged that the corporate defendants, while engaged in the silver recovery business, unintentionally killed Golab through acts authorized and commanded by the individual defendants named in the murder indictment. According to the involuntary manslaughter charge, the individuals acted recklessly in their capacities as "officers, board of directors and high managerial agents" and "within the scope of their employment" with the corporate defendants.[11]

Twenty reckless conduct charges accompanied the involuntary manslaughter charge.[12] These charges named both the corporate defendants and the individual defendants. The charges maintained the latter acted within the scope of their employment as officers, board of directors, high managerial agents and employees of the corporate defendants. They also dealt with various employees of the corporate defendants, including Golab, who purportedly sustained injuries as a result of toxic exposure to cyanide in the work environment. Specifically, the reckless conduct charges alleged that the defendants, acting in a reckless manner, hired the named employees without disclosing the use and attendant dangers of cyanide in the workplace and failed to provide necessary safety equipment and adequate storage facilities for cyanide. As a result, the employees purportedly sustained injuries which occurred both before and after Golab's death.

Significantly, the indictments charged as defendants both corporations engaged in business as well as individuals, in their capacity as corporate officials acting within the scope of their employment. The indictments also named employees as victims of injuries purportedly sustained during working hours on the business premises. In addition, the indictments described the employee injuries as arising from the toxic exposure to a chemical used in the normal industrial process of the corporations. In short, the charges related to working conditions provided by employers and employee injuries purportedly arising from those conditions.

The Labor Safety Record in the FRS Plant at Elk Grove

The labor force at Elk Grove was largely composed of illegal immigrants of both Mexican and Polish origin. In all, there were some 89 Hispanic and 15 Polish employees. According to the defendants' own admission, most of the plant workers neither spoke nor read English. The defendants also claimed that the employees were neither underpaid nor mistreated.[13] Indeed, many of the workers sought jobs at Elk Grove for their relatives and friends. Many of the workers never missed work.

The plant, nevertheless, had a high odor threshold and a history of minor health problems: eye irritation, headaches, dizziness, and nausea. However, only one or two employees incurred injuries that required subsequent medical attention. When workers complained about feeling sick, they were generally told (by Rodriguez and Kirschbaum) to go outside for some fresh air. Cloth gloves and cloth face masks were generally available at the plant. Some workers also wore rubber boots, rubber gloves, and rubber aprons. Though this safety equipment

was available, many of the workers refused to wear it. According to the defendants' brief, on many occasions some workers refused to comply with specific requests to wear the safety equipment. FRS also purchased face shields, eye goggles, ear phones, and hard hats. Moreover, the plant contained at least one oxygen tank and several gas masks.

FRS had at least nine ceiling exhaust fans which recycled the air in the plant three times per minute. The plant also had cyanide air test kits, two cyanide antidote kits, eye washes, deluge showers, and fire extinguishers. FRS regularly stocked the medicine cabinet with pain pills and other first aid equipment.[14]

When FRS first opened its Elk Grove facility in 1980, an employee tested for cyanide exposure twice a week for approximately a year. On one occasion, the reading showed a hazardous level of cyanide directly over the plating tanks while they were operating. Thereafter, the company prohibited employees from working over those tanks while they were in operation. Following 1980, the same employee measured cyanide levels in the plant on a regular basis at least until October 1982. The highest reading obtained as result of these tests reflected levels within applicable standards promulgated under the Occupational Safety and Health Act. The employee communicated the readings to defendant O'Neil. After October 1982, defendant Kirschbaum measured air quality in the plant on four or five occasions. Like the earlier readings, these tests reflected permissible levels of cyanide fumes in the plant environment.

The workers painted a far more grim picture of safety conditions, and many of them later filed suit. Golab's friend and coworker, Roman Guzoski, also testified that Golab had felt so ill before his death that he was actually seeking a job transfer.[15]

Workers were not told specifically that they were dealing with cyanide, although the cyanide drums contained the skull and crossbones symbol. The word *poison* was printed in bold red letters on the walls on the plant in English and Spanish.

Inspections by Government Agencies and an Insurance Carrier

From 1980 through 1983, governmental agencies and a private insurance company made numerous inspections of the plant. In November 1982, an inspector from the Occupational Safety and Health Administration came to the plant and, after reviewing company records relating to worker injuries, determined that no follow-up investigation was required. There were eight or more inspections by the Metropolitan Sanitary District between 1981 and 1983. Although odor was detected, the inspectors never reported any violations concerning improper waste discharge or pollution problems. Similarly, inspections by the Elk Grove Village Fire Department during 1980 and 1981 did not indicate any ventilation problems.

In addition to governmental inspections, Film Recovery's insurance company regularly inspected the FRS plant. Thus, when FRS first sought insurance coverage in 1980, the insurance company sent an industrial hygienist to inspect the plant. After the inspection, FRS obtained insurance. Thereafter, the insurance company conducted thorough yearly inspections covering all aspects of the plant's operation. On each occasion, the insurance company made recommendations, and the FRS company always obtained insurance coverage after the inspections. Indeed, the insurance company characterized FRS as a fair insurance risk.

After Golab's death, OSHA carried out an inspection. As a consequence, on March 11, 1983, OSHA issued citations against FRS for using unapproved respirators; having no training program regarding cyanide exposure and the use of respirators; using inappropriate gloves; and providing no emergency eyewash, protective eye gear, or antidote for cyanide poisoning. OSHA proposed fines of $4,850. Judge Josephine O'Brian later settled the issue with FRS for a sum of $2,425. (She defended the sum saying that FRS was in dire financial straits.)[16] In their appeal, the defendants questioned the validity of the OSHA inspection. OSHA apparently tested the plant at full capacity conditions and thus overestimated the toxicity of the environment; the plant normally ran at two-thirds capacity.[17]

The Corporate Involvement of the Individual Defendants

FRS employed the individual defendants in markedly different capacities. Steven O'Neil was the president of FRS. His defense tried to distance him from daily operations.[18] While the plant was getting underway in 1980, he was present continuously. Thereafter, he worked off-site, procuring film for processing and marketing the retrieved silver. In 1981, he visited the plant twice a week for two- to three-hour periods, and in 1982 his visits declined to about 20. In 1983, he stopped visiting the plant, devoting himself entirely to off-site duties. No one in the plant had much contact with him, especially after 1980. In his absence, Gerald Pett, Fred Kopp (who was not indicted), or Charles Kirschbaum ran the plant. The judge acquitted Pett, so the onus fell on Kirschbaum.

Kirschbaum, who had two years experience with another silver extraction firm, joined FRS in July 1981. His defense portrayed him as follows:[19] His responsibility was to monitor film product from the time it was received until it was processed; he also supervised the workers. He himself was on the plant floor six to eight hours a day; he never wore safety equipment and suffered no adverse effects. He did try, however, to get workers to use such equipment, but with little success—even claiming to have fired some who resisted. From July 1981 to summer of 1982, Kirschbaum monitored the production process and supervised the workers to assure that they were performing their jobs correctly. In September 1982, he moved his office to a newly acquired building located adjacent to the plant building. However, during all this period, he was in the plant area six to eight hours a day, six days a week, and never wore anything on his face when he was in the plant.

As part of his duties and pursuant to company policy, Kirschbaum attempted to get workers to wear rubber boots, rubber gloves, rubber aprons, and eye goggles. However, some workers did not like to wear the equipment. As a result, Kirschbaum fired some workers who refused to wear the equipment. Kirschbaum took orders from Fred Kopp, Gerald Pett, Steven O'Neil, and B. R. McKay in Salt Lake City.

Daniel Rodriguez was a shop floor manager. In his defense, he denied being a foreman.[20] He came to the United States in 1979 and went to work at FRS in 1980 on the recommendation of another Mexican worker. Rodriguez worked full-time on the floor doing all jobs. He knew that he was working with poison, as did all the other workers, but he did not know exactly what cyanide was. He observed that workers were getting sick and (together with Kirschbaum and Kopp) advised them to wear safety equipment. He frequently acted as interpreter for the Spanish workers.

Decision of the Lower Court

In rendering his decision, Judge Banks observed that he had reviewed and taken into consideration the oral testimony of the defendants and all the exhibits which were presented; he had also weighed the credibility of all the witnesses who appeared before the Court. More importantly he stated, ''During my deliberations and evaluations of all the evidence, let it be known that I never forgot the most important concept in criminal law, that being the defendants are presumed in-

nocent and that it is the burden of the State that they must prove guilt beyond a reasonable doubt.[21]

Judge Banks had earlier acquitted Pett of all charges and acquitted the other defendants of six reckless conduct charges. This took place on May 14, 1985, at the close of the prosecution's direct case.

Thus, on June 14, 1985, at the close of all the evidence and after argument of counsel, Judge Banks found the remaining individual defendants guilty of murder and 14 counts of reckless conduct. He also found the corporate defendants guilty of involuntary manslaughter and the 14 reckless conduct charges.

On July 1, 1985, Judge Banks sentenced the individual defendants to 25 years in the custody of the Illinois Department of Corrections and fined them $10,000 each on the murder conviction. In addition, he sentenced them to a concurrent period of 364 days in the custody of the Illinois Department of Corrections on the reckless conduct convictions. With respect to the corporate defendants, Judge Banks fined them $10,000 each on the involuntary manslaughter conviction and $14,000 each for the reckless conduct convictions.

McKay's indictment was related to his being a majority owner of FRS. Furthermore, a month before Golab's death, his company, B. R. McKay and Sons, went through the motions of taking over FRS because of unpaid debts. Both O'Neil and McKay claimed that the other was in charge at the time of Golab's death. (It is interesting to note that McKay never faced trial. The governor of Utah refused the State of Illinois's request to extradite him.)

On February 6, 1984, Governor Scott M. Matheson of Utah, describing McKay, a Salt Lake City businessman, as ''an exemplary citizen,'' refused to extradite him to Illinois to face murder and other related criminal charges. Among his reasons, he cited the ''unique and sensational'' nature of the charges and publicity in the news media that made him "very concerned" about McKay's "chances for a fair trial in Illinois." That led Governor James R. Thompson of Illinois to retort: "The pretrial publicity, while novel for Utah, was not novel for the state of Illinois. Maybe Utah's sensibilities are more easily shocked."

Richard Daley, son of the former Chicago mayor, accused Governor Matheson of "abusing his responsibility to justice and law enforcement." That brought a response from one of McKay's attorneys, David K. Watkiss, who said, "What the hell does Mr. Daley know about law and order?"[22]

Governor Matheson refused Illinois's request for extradition a second time later that year, arguing that Illinois could not directly link McKay to Golab's death. On June 16, 1985, the new governor of Utah, Norman H. Bangster, refused a third request from Illinois to extradite McKay, ruling that the facts in the case had not changed since former governor Matheson denied the original request. He also added: "The case represents an unprecedented attempt to expand the liability of a corporate official for consequences which are not demonstrably connected to official's knowledge or actions."[23]

Defendants Appeal the Lower Court's Verdict

In their appeal of Judge Bank's decision, the defendants raised the following issues pertaining to the interpretation of evidence and applicability of pertinent laws.

1. The state of Illinois was wrong to apply its criminal laws to regulate working conditions provided for employees in the industrial workplace by employers engaged in business in interstate commerce. The federal law pertaining to industrial work environments, i.e., the Occupational Safety and Health Act of 1970, 29 U.S.C. S651 et seq., preempts state laws.

2. The due process rights of defendants requires that prosecution must prove violation of applicable occupational safety and health standards before convicting employers and their officers and agents of state law crimes for alleged injuries sustained by employees from unsafe working conditions in the industrial workplace.

3. The evidence does not support the defendants' convictions for state crimes arising from injuries allegedly sustained by employees from unsafe working conditions in the industrial workplace. The evidence failed to establish the existence of a dangerous work environment, the requisite mental states for the defendants, and the cause of death of an employee who died at the workplace.

4. The murder findings against the individual defendants were inconsistent with the voluntary manslaughter findings against the corporate defendants, where both the individual and corporate defendants were charged and convicted because of the acts and statements of the individual defendants, acting in their capacity as officers and high managerial agents of the corporate defendants.

5. The murder findings against the individual defendants were inconsistent with the conduct findings against the same defendants.

In an interview with us (the authors) the attorney who represented Steven O'Neil, FRS, and MMI maintained that the preemption argument was the cornerstone of the defense. In short, the defense maintained that (1) Illinois law is not relevant, and (2) the defendants broke no federal law.

The preemption doctrine provided the foundation of the defense. The defendants' explanation of this doctrine follows:[24]

The preemption doctrine strikes the distribution of federal and state power in our federal system of government. It grants the federal government, in the exercise of a constitutionally granted power, the ability to completely occupy a particular field or activity to the exclusion of all state action. Whether the federal government preempts a given area depends solely upon the congressional intent underlying a particular enactment. As a consequence, federal preemption becomes largely a matter of statutory construction. Once Congress expresses a preemptive intent, however, no state action, either through conflicting with the actual congressional enactment or intruding upon a field that Congress validly reserved to federal control, will stand. Though controversial at its inception in the early nineteenth century, the preemption doctrine now stands as an established principle of law without exception or challenge, which all courts, federal or state, must enforce.

. . . The Occupational Safety and Health Act Congress, pursuant to its constitutionally authorized power to regulate interstate commerce and provide for the general welfare, enacted OSHA in 1970 "to assure so far as possible every working man and woman in the Nation safe and healthful working conditions and to preserve our human resources." 29 U.S.C. S665 (b) (5). Once promulgated, the statute intended the standards to provide guidelines for employer administration of the workplace and to define acceptable working conditions. Indeed, the statute directs that enacted standards, "(whenever practicable . . . shall be expressed in terms of objective criteria and of the performance desired." 29 U.S.C. S655(b)(5)

. . . Central to OSHA is the primacy accorded to the standards established by the Secretary of Labor to regulate the work environment. First, OSHA standards apply without exception to all employers engaged in business in interstate commerce and their employees. Compliance is mandatory.

. . . Moreover, though the states are permitted a role in the field of occupational safety and health, OSHA permits independent state action only in carefully circumscribed situations. Section 667(a) of OSHA provides that where no federal standard is in effect as to a given occupational safety or health issue, federal law does not prevent a state agency or court from asserting jurisdiction over that issue under state law. 29 U.S.C. S667(a). If, however, a federal standard exists as to a given health and safety issue, the only manner in which a state may attempt to exercise jurisdiction over that issue is to submit an enforcement plan to the United States Secre-

tary of Labor for approval. Section 667(b) of OSHA states in material part: Any State which, at any time, desires to assume responsibility for development and enforcement therein of occupational safety and health standards relating to any occupational safety or health issue with respect to which a Federal standard has been promulgated... shall submit a State plan for the development of such standards and their enforcement. 29 U.S.C. S667(b). When a plan is submitted, the submitting state continues to be barred from acting within the occupational safety and health field until the Secretary of Labor approves the plan. The requirements for approval are stringent. Among other things, the plan must:

1. Designate a state agency responsible for the administration of the plan;

2. Provide for the development and adoption of standards that are at least as effective as comparable OSHA standards and;

3. . . . with assurances that the State will devote adequate funds to the administration and enforcement of such standards.

29 U.S.C. S667(c)(1), (2), (4) and (5). Thus, OSHA premises the acceptance of a state plan and the ensuing state regulatory action in the field of occupational safety and health, on the adoption of (1) published standards "at least as effective as" their OSHA counterparts and (2) an effective and adequately funded enforcement program.

. . . In order to obtain approval of such standards, the submitting state must show that there are compelling local circumstances justifying such differences and that the different standards will not impose an undue burden on interstate commerce. 29 U.S.C. S667 (c) (2). In short, the more stringent state standards must be compelled by local conditions and cannot impose an undue burden on interstate commerce. Otherwise, OSHA will preempt their application in the work environment. Finally, OSHA requires a state plan to provide for a procedure of granting variances which correspond to variances granted by the Secretary of Labor under federal standards.

Succinctly, OSHA provides an express preemption provision where Congress preempted state regulation in the field of occupational safety and health with respect to issues for which federal standards exist and then delegated to the Secretary of Labor the discretion to allow state participation in the regulated field after state meets certain statutory prerequisites.

UNRESOLVED LEGAL BATTLES

As of spring 1989, the defendants' appeal was still pending, and it seemed unlikely to be resolved before 1990. The court in the Film Recovery case was awaiting an Illinois Supreme Court decision in a similar case brought against Chicago Magnetic Wire Corporation. The management of that corporation was indicted in 1984 for aggravated battery and reckless assault in the injury of its employees.

The case against Chicago Magnetic Wire reached a milestone when, on February 2, 1989, The Illinois State Supreme Court ruled that OSHA does not bar states from presecuting corporate officials.[25]

This decision is a landmark and has opened the way for similar sanctions against corporate executives by other states, where some eight actions were pending in early 1989. The matter is surely to be appealed to higher courts. The U.S. Chamber of Commerce filed an amicus brief on behalf of the Chicago Magnetic Wire officials. In the meantime, in Chicago the State's attorney Richard Daley vowed to seek the extradition of Michael McKay from Utah and to proceed with prosecution.

The attorney for the defendants vowed in an interview to continue appeals and ruled out any possible out-of-court settlements in the case.

NOTES

1. *The People of the State of Illinois* v. *Film Recovery Systems, et al.,* Circuit Court of Cook County, Fourth Municipal Division, No. 83-11001 and No. 94-5064, June 14, 1985.

2. Steven Greenhouse, "3 Executives Convicted of Murder for Unsafe Workplace Conditions." *New York Times* (June 15, 1985), pp. 1, 29; Mary Breasted, "4 Are Indicted in Fire Fatal to 6 at Chicle Plant." *New York Times* (July 23, 1977), p. 1; Donald Janson, "Great Adventure Owners Cleared of Criminal Charges in Fatal Fire." *New York Times* (July 21, 1985), p. 1; David R. Spiegel, "The Liability of Corporate Officers." *ABA Journal, The Lawyer's Magazine,* 71 (November 1985), pp. 48–52.

3. *People of the State of Illinois* v. *Steven O'Neil, et al.,* Appellate Court of Illinois, First Judicial District, 85-1853, 1854, 1855, 1952, 1953 Consolidated, Brief of Appellants, May 10, 1986, pp. xiii–xv. (Hereinafter cited as *Appellants' Brief*)

4. *Apellants' Brief,* p. xiii; E. R. Shipp, "Workplace Death Prompts a Dispute: 5 Executives Are Accused of Murder—Utah Governor Will Not Extradite One." *New York Times* (February 20, 1984), p. A9; The April 1984 Grand Jury of the Circuit Court of Cook County, May 1, 1984, pp. 1–2.

5. *Appellants' Brief,* p. 6ff.

6. Ibid., p. 7ff.

7. Ibid., pp. 8–9.

8. Ibid., pp. 9–10.

9. Ibid., p. 1.

10. Ibid., pp. 2–3.

11. Ibid., pp. 4–5.

12. Ibid., pp. 10–11.

13. Ray Gibson, "Murder Trial Set for Execs of Factory." *Chicago Tribune* (April 14, 1985), pp. 1–2.

14. *Appellants' Brief,* pp. 10–12.

15. Debbe Nelson, "Foul Haze Veiled Factory Death." *Daily Herald* (April 16, 1985), pp. 1, 3; Debbe Nelson, "Victim Sought Job Transfer—

Cyanide Work Made Him Sick." *Daily Herald* (April 17, 1985), pp. 1, 3.

16. Patrick Owens, "Death of Worker Puts Factory Safety on Trial." *Newsday* (June 6, 1985), pp. 30–31.

17. *Appellants' Brief,* p. 15ff.

18. Ibid., pp. 16–17.

19. Ibid., pp. 17–19.

20. Ibid., pp. 19–20.

21. Decision of Judge Banks, pp. 5–6; *Appellants' Brief,* pp. 21–25; Jackie Koszcuk,

"Judge Frees One Exec in Cyanide Trial." *Daily Herald* (May 15, 1985), p. 1.

22. E. R. Shipp, "Workplace Death," p. A9.

23. *Wall Street Journal,* "Illinois Extradition Bid for Utah Man is Rejected" (June 17, 1985), p. 4.

24. *Appellants' Brief,* pp. 24, 31–32, 35–37.

25. Susan B. Garland, "The Safety Ruling Could Be Hazardous to Employers' Health." *Business Week* (February 20, 1989), p. 34; Bill Richards, "Corporate Officials Ordered to Face Criminal Trial for Worker Injuries." *Wall Street Journal* (February 3, 1989), p. 86.

FILM RECOVERY SYSTEMS, INC.

AMCHAN, A. J. "The Future of OSHA." *Labor Law Journal,* 35 (September 1984), pp. 547–59.

BALLAM, D. A. "The Occupational Safety and Health Act's Preemptive Effect on State Criminal Prosecutions of Employers for Workplace Deaths and Injuries." *American Business Law Journal,* 26 (Spring 1988), pp. 1–27.

BRICKEY, KATHLEEN F. "Death in the Workplace: Corporate Liability for Criminal Homicide." *Notre Dame Journal of Law, Ethics and Public Policy,* 2 (Summer 1987), pp. 753–90.

"Corporate Criminal Liability for Work-site Deaths: Old Law Used a New Way." *Marquette Law Review,* 71 (Summer 1988), pp. 793–814.

"Corporate Criminal Liability for Homicide: The Need to Punish Both the Corporate Entity and Its Officers." *Dickinson Law Review,* 92 (Fall 1987), pp. 193–222.

DIMOND, DIANE. "Know-how or No Way? Some Manufacturers are Stifling Innovation and Abandoning New Technologies Out of Fear of Potential Lawsuits and Mounting Liability Costs." *Insurance Review,* 48 (October 1987), pp. 34–38.

EDWARDS, F. L. "Worker Right-to-Know Laws: Ineffectiveness of Current Policy-making and a Proposed Legislative Solution." *Boston College Environmental Affairs Law Review,* 15 (1987), pp. 1–58.

"The Extent of OSHA Preemption of State Haz-ard Reporting Requirements." *Columbia Law Review,* 88 (April 1988), pp. 630–46.

GEPHART, ROBERT P., JR. "Organization Design for Hazardous Chemical Accidents." *Columbia Journal of World Business.* 22 (Spring 1987), pp. 51–58.

"Getting Away with Murder: Federal OSHA Preemption of State Criminal Prosecutions for Industrial Accidents." *Harvard Law Review,* 101 (December 1987), pp. 535–54.

GOLD, M. E. "The New Right-to-Know Act." *Pennsylvania Bar Association Quarterly,* 56 (January 1985), pp. 53–59.

"The Good Faith Exception to the Exclusionary Rule in OSHA Proceedings." *University of Florida Law Review,* 35 (Fall 1983), pp. 738–63.

GOUGH, R. G., "Toxic Substances in the Workplace." *Florida Bar Journal,* 59 (January 1985), pp. 25–29.

"Hazardous Chemicals—Right to Know in Iowa." *Drake Law Review,* 36 (1986/1987), pp. 419–42.

"A Hazardous Mix: Discretion to Disclose and Incentives to Suppress Under OSHA's Hazard Communication Standard." *Yale Law Journal,* 97 (March 1988), pp. 581–601.

"Health in the Workplace: A Symposium." *Notre Dame Law Review,* 62 (1987), pp. 807–1062.

MANGUM, GARTH L. "Murder in the Workplace: Criminal Prosecution v. Regulatory Enforcement.'' *Labor Law Journal.* 39 (April 1988), pp. 220–31.

MANGUM, GARTH L. ''Warning! This Job May Be Hazardous to Your Life; Perhaps Employers Should go to Jail for Workplace Deaths.'' *Personnel Administrator,* 32 (November 1987), pp. 76–80.

''Murder, Inc.: The Criminal Liability of Corporations for Homicide.'' *Seton Hall Law Review,* 18 (1988), pp. 378–404.

OLEINICK, A., W. J. FODOR, and M. M. SUSSELMAN. ''Risk Management for Hazardous Chemicals: Adverse Health Consequences of Their Use and the Limitations of Traditional Control Standards.'' *Journal of Legal Medicine,* 9 (March 1988), pp. 1–103.

''Pursuit of the Corporate Criminal: Employer Criminal Liability for Work-Related Deaths as a Method of Improving Workplace Safety and Health.'' *Boston College Law Review,* 29 (March 1988), pp. 451–80.

''Reckless Endangerment of an Employee: A Proposal in the Wake of Film Recovery Systems [*People* v. *Film Recovery Systems* No. 83-11091, slip op. at 5 (Cook County, Ill. Cir. Ct. June 14, 1985)] to Make the Boss Responsible for His Crimes.'' *University of Michigan Journal of Law Reform,* 20 (Spring 1987), pp. 873–905.

SUSSER, P. A. ''The OSHA Standard and State 'Right-to-Know' Laws: The Preemption Battle Continues.'' *Employee Relations Law Journal,* 10 (Spring 1985), pp. 615–34.

UZYCH, L. ''Illinois' New Chemical Disclosure Law.'' *Illinois Bar Journal,* 73 (April 1985), pp. 444–46.

WELLS, C. ''The Decline and Rise of English Murder: Corporate Crime and Individual Responsibility.'' *Criminal Law Review* (December 1988), pp. 788–801.

''Workplace Exposure to Toxic Chemicals: Information Disclosure Versus Trade Secret Protection.'' *New York University Review of Law and Social Change,* 13 (1984/ 1985), pp. 149–72.

·V·

Corporate Actions
and Employee Rights

C. ITOH & CO. (AMERICA), INC., AND SUMITOMO CORPORATION OF AMERICA

Conflicts between the personnel policies of foreign multinational corporations (MNCs) in the United States and application of U.S. civil rights laws

One manifestation of the decline in America's once-vaunted international competitiveness and manufacturing strength has been the enormous growth of imports from foreign nations. Foreign products and brand names like Sony, Matsushita, Phillips, and Braun have become household words. While American consumers and even industrial companies increasingly seem to prefer foreign goods because of their perceived quality and price advantages over U.S.-made goods, U.S. manufacturers have been losing ground not only at home but also abroad. The result has been massive. In 1987, the United States international trade deficit totaled a whopping $171 billion.[1]

These large trade deficits have had to be paid for through borrowing from foreigners and also through selling U.S. assets to foreign investors. Thus, the United States has moved from a positive net investment position in the early 1980s to a negative international investment status in the latter part of the decade (see Figure 1). While the U.S. creditor position was a negative $402 billion in 1987, Japan's creditor status was a positive $260 billion (see Figure 2). Although the number of investments in the U.S. was slightly less in 1987 than in 1980 (see Figure 3), the net dollar value was greater. Of 1,051 foreign investments in the U.S. in 1987, Japan led the way with 351 (see Figure 4.).

In this they have been bolstered by the declining price of the U.S. dollar in terms of their own currencies, and a decline in the price of U.S. companies because of their poor profits and difficult financial conditions. Of the 351 Japanese investments in 1986, 68 were acquisitions, 58 new ventures, 31 joint ventures, 23 plant constructions, and 5 equity investments. The other 104 went to branches, agencies, warehouses, offices, and so forth.[2]

The increased presence of foreign multinationals in the U.S. as employers has raised a host of operational problems (treatment of minorities, job discipline) for U.S. workers and society at large.[3] In an ironical twist of circumstances, foreigners are accused of being like the "Ugly Americans" of an earlier era, when American companies were chastised for acting arrogantly abroad and being insensitive to local cultures and sensibilities. Foreign multinationals bring with them their own unique set of management and personnel policies developed and perfected in their respective homelands, just as the U.S. multinationals took their management systems and applied them to their overseas operations. In one sense, it it not unnatural to do so because the foreign MNC is both comfortable with its policies and believes them to be superior to local policies and, thereby, finds in them a competitive advantage. Of course, enlightened employers would want to adapt their management and personnel policies to conform to local laws and mores. However, this is not always possible because of the conflicting intents and social objectives that underlie specific laws and a foreign MNC's operational policies. These may make strict compliance with local (U.S.) laws almost impossible except at the cost of abandoning or radically altering the MNC's unique practices and thereby losing their inherent "superiority."

Nowhere is this dilemma more profoundly illustrated than in the case of the Japanese and other Asia-based companies, on the one hand, and the compliance with U.S. civil rights laws in their personnel policies, on the other hand. Because of their almost monoracial national make-up and their highly distinctive cultural traits, such societies have evolved management systems that are quite dissimilar to those practiced by companies based in industrialized Western Europe and the United States. These companies strongly believe that their superior manufacturing systems cannot be separated from their distinctive management and personnel policies, and to do so in any substantial de-

gree would jeopardize the inherent soundness of their management infrastructure.

At the same time, U.S. civil rights laws reflect a strong desire to correct a historical wrong. They also represent a fundamental American belief in the equality of opportunity and elimination of injustice. Moreover, their scope is currently being widened to cope with changing societal needs and to protect individuals from new sources of discrimination as they emerge. Thus, any perceived violation of these laws evokes not only a legal but also a strong emotional response.

The frontiers of the civil rights laws and their expanded application are constantly being tested in issues such as reverse discrimination, on the one hand, and the desire to have American multinationals operating overseas (in South Africa, for example) implement the intent of the law, on the other hand.[4] The latest, but certainly not the last, twist to the expanding scope of the civil rights statutes is the case of American employees suing Japanese multinationals for discrimination.

The two cases presented here illustrate a plethora of issues arising out of the working of foreign MNCs in the United States. These cases were brought against C. Itoh Corporation by their management-level employees who were U.S. citizens, and against Sumitomo Corporation of America by the female American employees working in clerical positions. Although these cases deal with Japanese companies, they are atypical only in terms of the scope of their coverage and not necessarily in terms of the types of problems encountered. As a matter of fact, the U.S. Equal Opportunities Commission has become quite active in this area and is currently in various stages of investigation or litigation involving a number of foreign companies based both in Western European and Pacific Basin countries.

On February 21, 1975, three white American executives filed charges against the U.S. affiliate of C. Itoh (*Spiess et al.* v. C.

Itoh & Company [America], Inc.), alleging job discrimination because of their race and national origin.[5] The plaintiffs, Michael E. Spiess, Jack K. Hardy, and Benjamin Rountree, were all American citizens and white Caucasians of non-Japanese national origin. Spiess had worked for Itoh since January 10, 1972, Hardy since September 22, 1969, and Rountree from June 12, 1970, until September 30, 1973. The plaintiffs performed middle management duties. At the time their complaint was filed, all worked in Itoh's Houston offices. The suit was settled out of court in September, 1985. As part of the settlement, and at the insistence of C. Itoh, it was agreed that the terms of the settlement would not be disclosed in public by the plaintiffs.

In the Sumitomo case, 12 present and former female employees working as secretaries filed charges of national origin and sex discrimination.[6] On November 21, 1977, they sued as individuals and as representatives of a class, charging Sumitomo with unlawful sex and national origin discrimination in employment under the Equal Employment Opportunity Act of 1964, 42 U.S.C. 2000 et seq. (Title VII), 42 U.S.C. 1981, and the Thirteenth Amendment to the Constitution. Compensatory and punitive damages were sought. The 12 plaintiffs were all employed in Sumitomo's New York office in clerical or secretarial positions. The Sumitomo case was settled out of court in a consent decree in February 1987.[7]

These cases are unusual and without any legal precedent. Therefore, the court decisions at various stages of litigation, as well as the nature and scope of settlements ultimately reached, would have a significant impact on the personnel practices of multinational corporations in the United States and abroad. Multinational corporations must contend with two factors in their overseas personnel policies and practices. One, they must conform to the local laws and customs that define the industrial relations of the foreign (host) country where their operations

are located. Two, they must pay competitive wages and benefits to employees from the country of headquarters (home country) to persuade them to work in an overseas location. MNCs have been able to accomplish both objectives through a dual personnel policy by which all host country employees are treated in accordance with the local employment laws. Employees from the MNC's home office are treated according to the laws and competitive conditions prevailing in the home country.

ISSUES FOR ANALYSIS

The issues involved are by no means simple, either as to fact or as to law.

1. Should a foreign multinational have a right to bring its own people (foreign nationals) into the United States for specific management jobs, or must it hire local people in the U.S. if similar qualified people are available?

2. The comparative similarity of candidate qualifications and the job functions may be more apparent than real. A foreign multinational may have a different management philosophy and operational style that are the product of the particular sociocultural milieu of the home country and people. This difference in management philosophy and operating style may make it difficult, if not impossible, for any direct comparisons of job specifications or individual qualifications as to suitability for certain jobs. What criteria can be used for comparing job performance and individual qualifications under those circumstances?

3. When a foreign multinational uses its own people for certain jobs with its U.S. affiliate because it considers those jobs "highly sensitive" and important not only in terms of its U.S. operations but also in terms of its overall global operations, how must it justify those decisions to avoid charges of job discrimination?

4. A foreign multinational may have a psychological predisposition to hire its own people for certain top management jobs in its U.S. and other overseas operations. Should this be

FIGURE 1. U.S. International Investment Position, 1980-87

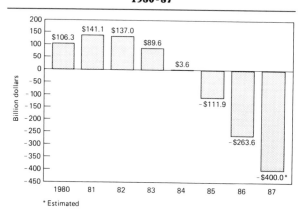

* Estimated

FIGURE 3. Total Number of Foreign Direct Investments, 1977-1986

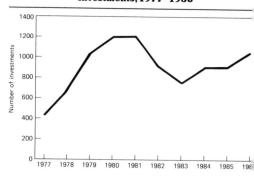

FIGURE 2. Year-end 1987 International Investment Position (estimated)

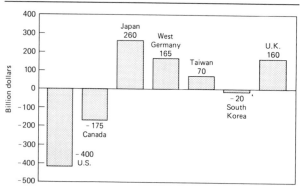

FIGURE 4. Number of Investments by Source Country, 1986 (total 1051 = 100.0%)

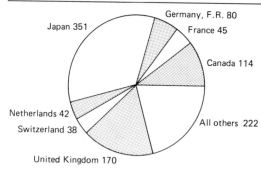

considered a prerogative of the owners, or should it be considered a job restriction based on national origin?

5. The civil rights laws were essentially a societal response to a dramatic change in the national climate as regards domestic discrimination by U.S. firms against blacks. In many instances, expatriate personnel of foreign multinationals are members of a racial, color, or national origin minority group by statutory definition. Considering these factors, should foreign multinationals doing business in the United States be subject to the civil rights laws in their employment practices?

6. Foreign multinationals are entitled to operate in the United States under treaties of friendship, commerce, and navigation that carefully define the rights each nation will render to the nationals and products of the other. Distinctions are made in many of the treaty provisions between U.S. subsidiaries of foreign firms incorporated under U.S. laws and branch offices of foreign multinationals. Essential to the successful operation of a multinational is the ability to use nationals from the home country of the parent firm for ''sensitive'' positions, a right recognized by treaty. Do these treaties permitting such commercial activities exempt or qualify the applicability of the civil rights laws to foreign multinationals?

7. Not all discrimination is prohibited under the civil rights laws; discrimination resulting from a bona fide occupational qualification (BFOQ) is permitted. Do expatriate personnel job positions constitute a bona fide occupational qualification? Are there other exemptions by which expatriate employment practices can be legally justified?

8. If U.S. affiliates of foreign multinationals are subject to U.S. civil rights laws, what changes in expatriate employment policies and practices are required to achieve compliance with the laws?

BACKGROUND OF THE U.S. CIVIL RIGHTS LAWS

The Civil Rights Act of 1866 and, particularly, the Civil Rights Act of 1964, Title VII, were designed primarily to protect minority groups in the United States from job discrimination.[8] As should be the case, these laws were passed specifically to satisfy societal needs and circumstances unique to the United States.[9]

At the time the 1964 Act was passed, there was little question about what groups needed the most protection.[10] The legal scope and enforcement effort was gradually expanded to other groups that faced job discrimination—Hispanic Americans, women, and the aged. It also became apparent that discrimination may result not only from intentional discriminatory acts, but also from business practices that have unintentional discriminatory consequences.[11] In addition, eradication of discrimination arising out of historical antecedents and past practices may not be instant because of a paucity of qualified candidates in the minority groups. Thus, remedial attention was focused on affirmative action plans and good-faith efforts on the part of employers.[12]

THE CASE AGAINST ITOH: PLAINTIFFS' ALLEGATIONS

On February 21, 1975, three white male executives of C. Itoh (America), Inc. sued as individuals and as representatives of a class, charging Itoh with unlawful deprivation of civil rights of the plaintiffs and others similarly situated.[13] The civil action was brought under 42 U.S.C. Section 1981 (1974), formerly the Civil Rights Act of 1866 (hereafter Section 1981), and Title VII of the Civil Rights Act of 1964, as amended, 42 U.S.C. Section 2000e (1974) et seq. (hereafter Title VII). Compensatory damages of $8 million and punitive damages of $5 million were sought. The plaintiffs in the Itoh case alleged that except for participation in the management of defendant (Itoh), from which they had been unlawfully excluded, they performed the same types and quality of work as did certain of Itoh's nonsecretarial employees who were of Japanese national origin. In many instances, primarily involving negotiations and servicing of major contracts with U.S. corporations and various agencies of the U.S. government, plaintiffs contended that their understanding of American business and social practices enabled them to outperform their Japanese counterparts. Yet, despite their accomplishments, the plaintiffs charged that defendant Itoh discriminated, intentionally and otherwise, against them and in favor of employees of Japanese national origin with respect to compensation, terms, conditions, and privileges of employment.[14]

They alleged that this discrimination, in direct violation of Title VII, included, but was not limited to, the following practices:

1. paying monthly salaries to the Japanese at least 20% greater than the monthly salaries paid to the non-Japanese;

2. paying midyear summer bonuses in excess of $4,000 to Japanese employees but not making such payments to the non- Japanese;

3. paying year-end bonuses to the Japanese substantially greater than those paid to the non-Japanese;

4. providing direct reimbursement of substantially all medical and dental expenses, in excess of that provided by insurance, to Japanese but not to non-Japanese employees;

5. paying personal automobile insurance premiums for Japanese but not for non-Japanese employees;

6. providing loans to Japanese employees to enable them to purchase automobiles, homes, and speculative securities for their personal accounts, but not making any such funds available to non-Japanese employees;

7. providing automatic pay increases of up to 50% of monthly compensation based on marital status and size of family to Japanese but not to non-Japanese employees;

8. providing to each Japanese employee but not to non-Japanese employees a subsidy for the rental of personal living quarters in amounts equal to one-half of the excess of such rental payments over 20% of monthly net salary;

9. unlawfully segregating and classifying its employees according to whether they are of Japanese or non-Japanese national origin, as demonstrated by the initials *J* (standing for "Japanese") and *A* (standing for "American") appearing after each employee's name on the monthly payroll records;

10. limiting the employment opportunities of its non-Japanese employees by refusing to promote them to managerial positions; and

11. regularly holding evening staff meetings to discuss and plan management policies which only the Japanese employees were permitted to attend.

The plaintiffs further charged that these discriminatory employment practices were in existence during the entire tenure of their employment and continued thereafter. Plaintiffs also insisted that these discriminatory employment practices remained a closely guarded secret among Itoh's Japanese employees until one employee unintentionally indicated the existence of these practices to plaintiff Hardy. At no time before the plaintiffs accepted the Itoh job offers did any representative of Itoh inform them of these practices. To the contrary, the plaintiffs, as intelligent and capable American businesspeople, were induced to work for Itoh by company representations that it treated its employees with fairness and impartiality and that positions of management and responsibility could be attained by dedication and hard work, regardless of one's national origin. The plaintiffs were thus induced to spend what could otherwise have been some of the most personally and financially rewarding years of their lives working for Itoh. Furthermore, Itoh allegedly refused to train its non-Japanese employees for higher management-level positions. Itoh evaluated its employees on the basis of a double standard, one for Japanese and another for non-Japanese, which effectively precluded non-Japanese employees from attaining management positions. The plaintiffs contended that had they known of these discriminatory employment practices, they would never have accepted jobs with Itoh.

Rountree left Itoh's employment shortly after the civil action was filed. Spiess and Hardy were notified on December 30, 1975, that Itoh was terminating their employment as of January 9, 1976. Itoh's reason was that Spiess and Hardy had removed from company files certain documents designated as confidential information not to be removed without permission from company officials. Spiess and Hardy alleged that Itoh had engaged in "retaliatory firing" in violation of their civil rights. They sought a temporary restraining order contending that the documents in question were furnished only to plaintiff's counsel to be used in furtherance of their Title VII suit.

The district court refused to grant the temporary restraining order. An employee, the court held, may not engage in unlawful or unethical conduct under the guise of promoting the public interest favoring nondiscriminatory employment practices. Nor would the court countenance the "theft" of confidential data based on an attorney-client relationship rationale, since the plaintiffs' counsel could have sought the documents in question through discovery. The court concluded: "Judicially protecting an employee's assistance and participation equitably is one thing; protecting the taking of documents unauthorizedly is another."[15]

THE CASE AGAINST SUMITOMO PLAINTIFFS' ALLEGATIONS

The plaintiffs in the Sumitomo case alleged that Sumitomo was guilty of national origin and sex discrimination by denying women promotions to executive, managerial, and sales positions in favor of Japanese males.[16] According to the complaint:

Plaintiffs bring this as a class action to 23(a) and (b) (2), of the Federal Rules of Civil Procedure, on their own behalf and on behalf of all women who have worked for the defendant, are working for the defendant, have left employment of the defendant because of its discriminatory policies, or may seek employment with the defendant. The members of this class, or classes, are discriminated against in ways which deprive them or have deprived them of equal employment opportunities by reason of their sex, and/or nationality.

The specific cause of action was that Sumitomo Corporation of America (SCOA) restricted the plaintiffs to clerical jobs and refused to train or promote them to executive, managerial, and/or sales positions on the basis of both sex and racial discrimination. At the time the suit was filed, the plaintiffs alleged that Sumitomo had no women employees above the clerical level, and no training programs in the U.S. to qualify women (or American males) for higher-level jobs. The plaintiffs also alleged that even though they may have had as much education, and were doing the same work, they were denied promotion to higher-level jobs held by Japanese males. In the words of Lisa Avigliano:

> You just knew you weren't going to get anywhere. I was doing the same job as most of the Japanese men, but I knew it was useless to think I could have the same opportunities, even though I had as much education. All the women were in clerical jobs. I think they really honestly thought women were inferior.[17]

THE COMPANIES: C. ITOH AND SUMITOMO

C. Itoh & Company (America), Inc. is a wholly owned subsidiary of C. Itoh & Company, Ltd. of Japan, which in 1988 had total trading transactions of $123.97 billion, gross trading profits of $2.2 billion, and a net profit of \$202 million. It is the leading integrated trading company (*sogo sosha*) ''with a fully integrated worldwide network of 187 offices in 85 nations, including 41 in Japan, 585 affiliated companies, and over 10,000 employees located throughout the world.''[18] It trades in many areas, including communications, textiles, machinery and construction, metals and ore, food and agriculture, forest products, energy and chemicals, and general merchandise. C. Itoh and Company (America), Inc. is a flagship subsidiary of the parent and is a general trading company. Although separate financial statements are not issued, it does business of several billion dollars a year, of which approximately 65% constitutes exports from the U.S. to Japan and other countries, and 35% involves imports from Japan and other countries. Itoh (America) and the parent company deal in some 50,000 commodities. Itoh (Japan) maintains locally incorporated companies in 12 major countries in the world and also branches and representative offices in more than 100 principal cities in Japan and overseas.

According to a company brochure, Itoh (Japan) has ''a positive attitude on capital and trade liberalization in Japan.'' The company states its management philosophy thus:[19]

> The general trading companies fulfill all round and diversified functions for the promotion of trade, efficiency of distribution and performance of various development projects. In line with the rapid changes of circumstances at home and abroad and in accordance with the new demands of society, C. Itoh will become increasingly dynamic in its functions. Recently, the social and economic environment has become subject to rapid changes on an international scale, and all the peoples of the world have come to expect their share of the world's riches. Therefore, C. Itoh has become very much aware of its mission and the role which it must perform with regard to changes of social and economic environment, and is also very much aware of the need for social responsibility in

business activities. C. Itoh earnestly desires to contribute to the betterment of social welfare with due regard to international activities, on the basis of its desire for international cooperation. C. Itoh strives to foster the harmonious development of the world and betterment of the quality of life of its inhabitants.

Sumitomo Corporation of America is a subsidiary of Sumitomo Corporation (Japan), a member of the Sumitomo Group, which is similar in structure and operation to C. Itoh. In 1987, the parent company's gross trading volume stood at \$89.4 billion. Gross profits were \$1.4 billion and net profits \$201,527 million.

Both companies are integrated general trading companies. Sumitomo put its overall business philosophy this way:[20]

> A business principle of Sumitomo Corporation of America is that the interests of people and society should be placed before that of individual enterprises. Increasingly, American industry strives to accommodate public interest and we are uniquely equipped to cooperate, because we are long experienced at combining public and business interests for the benefit of both.
>
> *Sogo sosha* possess vast communications networks that span the world, collecting and transmitting data on day to day commodity prices, markets, areas of surplus and storage, and everything that bears on trade. But a *sogo sosha's* undertakings may spread beyond trade and distribution of goods to financing, engineering and construction, to transportation and natural resources development. . . .
>
> *Sogo sosha* differ from other companies in that they are supply/demand oriented and work to solve such problems. When a demand for goods and services is identified, *sogo sosha* immediately look for a way to satisfy it.

Japanese trading companies are already a big factor among the Japanese businesses operating in the United States. During 1981, American subsidiaries of Japan's *sogo sosha* accounted for close to 10% of total trade.

According to brochures and interviews with representatives of both companies, they claim to contribute to United States trade and investment in three ways:

1. as a conduit through which American capital goods, coal and minerals, wood pulp, grain, raw cotton, chemicals, construction machinery, scrap metal, computers, aircraft, and foodstuffs flow to Japan and other nations;

2. as a supplier to the American market of industrial and consumer goods—textiles, steel, electronic equipment, footwear, radio and television sets, phonographs, plywood, foodstuffs, bicycles, automobiles—produced in Japan and other countries; and

3. as an active partner or as the creator, sponsor, and organizer of joint ventures and licensing arrangements in the United States, Japan, and elsewhere for American companies.

Organizational Structure: Parent-Subsidiary Relationships

Corporate organizational charts are provided as Exhibits 1, 2, and 3. We use C. Itoh to clarify the general picture. The point of organizational authority proved to be very important, as is the geographic place of incorporation.

For C. Itoh, the hierarchy of authority begins with the board of directors (*yakuin*) and continues through the president (*sochihainin*); executive vice-president (*sochihainin daiko*); managers of divisions (*bucho*), who are considered vice-presidents; in some cases, assistant managers of divisions (*buchodaiko*); managers of departments (*kacho*); in some cases, assistant managers of departments (*kachodairi*); supervisors (*kakaricho*); in some cases, assistant supervisors (*kakaricho daiko*); and finally, the section members, the low-level employees, plus secretaries, clerks, and porters. This is in addition to various staff departments commonly found in any large business organization.

The relationship between Itoh (America) and Itoh (Japan) is that of a subordinate-

superior. Decisions regarding management staff (particularly top management and Japanese staff) rests almost exclusively with Itoh (Japan). In choosing an executive vice-president to the president of Itoh (America), the board of directors has authority, theoretically, to approve a candidate. In reality, the candidate is selected by and sent from Itoh (Japan).[21] Thus, even though a business unit may be incorporated in the United States—as both SCOA and Itoh (America) are—real organizational authority rests with Japan.

EMPLOYMENT AND OTHER PERSONNEL POLICIES

Although indigenization of employees has increased significantly in the last decade, expatriates continue to play an important role in overseas operations, especially with the continuing increase in international trade and the liberalization of investment policies by most nations. Both C. Itoh and Sumitomo claim to have a flexible personnel policy, which is determined in light of perceived competitive advantage, given the nature of the business itself. It is these factors, not discrimination, which determine policy.

Itoh had a stated policy of nondiscrimination set forth in the American staff's employee's manual.[22]

> It is the policy of C. Itoh & Company (America), Inc., and its subsidiaries that all applicants for employment are considered only on the basis of merit, without discrimination because of race, creed, national origin, age or sex. Our employment practices ensure equal treatment to all employees without distinction in pay or opportunity because of an employee's color, religion, national origin, age or sex.

The Job and Tasks

In an interview, Sumitomo representatives explained how their historical personnel pol-

EXHIBIT 1. Organizational Chart of C. Itoh & Company (America), Inc.

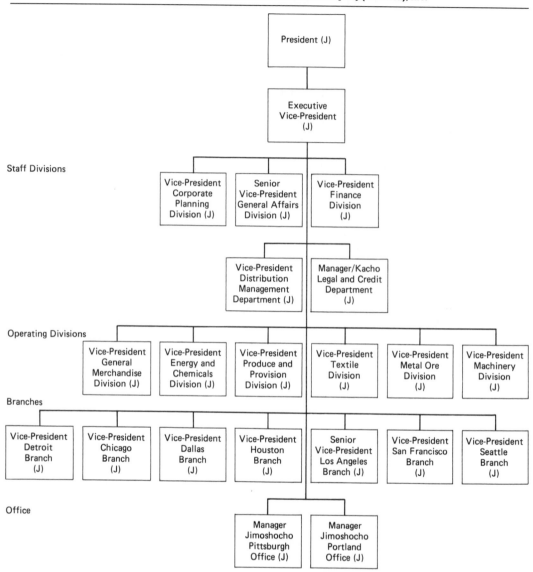

icies were in part a function of the nature of the business of being a trading company.[23] Beginning from the 1960s, the nature of their trading was primarily marketing Japanese goods in the U.S. The products were easy to sell because of high quality and low price. It was also easy to find American outlets to market them. The key strategic relation, therefore, was with the supplier, who was Japanese. As far as SCOA was concerned, the key persons in their operations were the "rotating staff" who were Japanese. It is, in fact, *their expertise* the suppliers were buying.

The primary job of rotating staff amount-

EXHIBIT 2. Organizational Chart of a Typical Staff Division

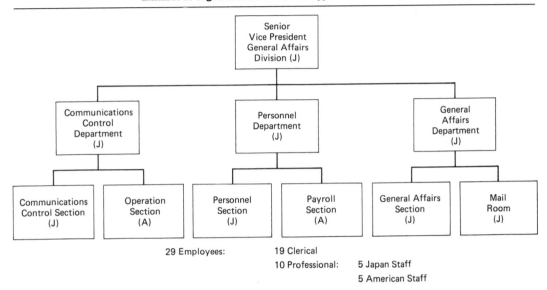

29 Employees: 19 Clerical
                       10 Professional: 5 Japan Staff
                                           5 American Staff

EXHIBIT 3. Organizational Chart of a Typical Operating Division

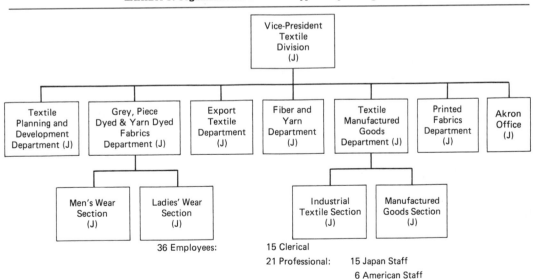

36 Employees: 15 Clerical
                       21 Professional: 15 Japan Staff
                                            6 American Staff

ed to responsibility for a customer's account or project to satisfy the supplier by channeling goods to markets. *Job* understood in this sense could entail any number of tasks—whatever was necessary to handle the project. Secondary positions were filed by support staff, the key word being *support*. In the SCOA offices, they were called secretaries; in fact, they were supposed to do anything required to support the work of the rotating staff. This included administrative tasks such as customs clearance and documentation, communication with customers, handling minor complaints, as well as clerical tasks.

Difficulties arose at SCOA when the support staff personnel realized that they were doing many of the same tasks as rotating staff and yet did not have the same career or job opportunities. According to SCOA representatives, it was not unusual for rotating staff to negotiate a deal and come back and type up the documentation attendant to it—it would all be the same job. The secretaries' impression that they were doing the same job was further underlined by the physical organization of a typical Japanese office, where everyone sits in one open room. In the American office, a secretary understands that he or she does not do and does not have the ability to do what the boss does. Furthermore, in the U.S., a secretary generally has a good grasp of the boss's business. Such was not the case at SCOA, where most of the real business was handled internally in Japanese. Thus, as far as tasks were concerned, there was a clear overlap between what the rotating and support staff did. But for the Japanese, the job responsibilities were clearly distinct.

However, Itoh also made a fundamental distinction between their Japan staff and American staff. Japan staff were employees sent by the parent company to work in the United States. American staff were all other employees and included Orientals of Chinese and Korean origin. American staff also included Japanese who were born and raised in the United States. Although of Japanese national origin, as that term is used in the

civil rights laws, they were not considered Japan staff by Itoh. According to the testimony of Sadao Nishitomi, secretary and EEO coordinator of Itoh (America), taken during the course of depositions by the plaintiffs' attorney in September 1975, this staff distinction appeared on payroll records.[24] When asked how far up in the ranks of C. Itoh (America) a member of the American staff can climb, Sadao Nishitomi, the EEO coordinator for Itoh (America), responded: "As far as I understand it, any employee can climb up in rank, all the way up, excepting for the position of president."[25]

The testimony of Sadao Nishitomi was to the point. He indicated that Japan staff were favored over American staff in management positions because Japan staff were believed to possess *shosha*. Literally translated as "intensive industry knowledge" or "moving think tank," *shosha* describes an individual with extensive knowledge about his or her industry. Such a person possesses the ability to collect relevant information, analyze this information, and apply the results to a business transaction on a higher level. Nishitomo testified that while the American staff could, "with good effort on their part," acquire this capability, there were very few who had that capability. When asked how an American would acquire *shosha*, Nishitomi responded that the American would have to apply for a position with Itoh (Japan), after overcoming very stiff employment competition, and work up the employment ladder with Itoh (Japan).[26]

In filing the lawsuit, C. Itoh's American managerial employees contended that training courses for Americans to develop *shosha* were not available, and Americans were not transferred to Japan with the parent company for experience. Although Japanese-language training through the Berlitz schools was subsidized for all employees by Itoh (America), no formal notification of the availability of the program was circulated to the American staff.

Itoh (America)'s stated nondiscriminatory policy notwithstanding, there was no established procedure or criteria by which management staff were selected to head departments or fill other supervisory positions. The result, as demonstrated through Nishitomi's testimony, was a general systematic exclusion of Americans from higher managerial positions. Nishitomi himself had never chosen an American manager. Only one American in the Itoh (America) organization served at the level of vice-president or above, and this title was largely illusory since the employee functioned only as *shitencho daiko,* or assistant manager of a branch office. After some years of service, the employee was still performing the same job and exercised the same authority as he did when first employed by Itoh (America). Significantly, his position as vice-president did not appear on a formal list of the executive officers of Itoh (America).

The disadvantages under which American staff operated in rising to managerial positions is demonstrated by the appointment of Ogata, formerly with Itoh (Japan), as *kacho* or department manager of the personnel department.[27] Prior to his appointment in February 1975, Ogata was with Itoh (Japan). Because the *kakaricho* of the personnel department related to both Japan and American staff, Itoh (America) felt that the position should be filled by a Japan staff member. Testimony by Nishitomi established that while Ogata lacked knowledge about American personnel matters, this deficiency could be overcome by appointing a knowledgeable American staff member to assist him. Conversely, there was a reluctance to appoint an American staff member as *kacho* and give him a knowledgeable Japan staff member to compensate for a lack of expertise in Japanese personnel matters. Thus, if a Japanese candidate with suitable qualifications could not be found within the Itoh (America) organization, a request was made to the personnel department of the parent company for some Japanese candidates who might be transferred to the U.S. Recruitment from outside the organization was not even considered.

It was not at all unusual for a Japanese to hold a number of unrelated functional positions within the Itoh organization until a certain position could be filled by the parent company. Nishitomi's many roles—secretary of Itoh (America), manager of the general affairs division, manager of the communication control department, and EEO coordinator—illustrates this tendency. Nor did it appear to be essential that the Japan staff member have special training in the activity he was managing. Thus, American staff members may have had better credentials than the Japan staff members. However, since the Japan staff members were considered to be on 24-hour duty (while the Americans worked between designated hours), Itoh felt that the nature of the Japan staff's work was different.

At Itoh, an essential difference between Japan staff and American managerial staff resulted from special skills "not able to be acquired in the United States." Nishitomi testified that Japan staff were " . . . mostly engaged in the transaction or the business transaction within Japan which would require in-depth knowledge of customs and habits of business transactions in Japan, which would not be too easy for American staff to acquire. . . . " The converse, however, is not necessarily true. American staff were not assumed to have a "correspondingly greater knowledge of American business practices and companies than members of the Japan staff" when doing business in the United States. As Nishitomi testified, " . . . those who are back in Japan might have a long-standing business relationship with foreign countries and they might have knowledge of foreign countries from that way, as well. . . . "[28]

Career Path

Both Sumitomo and Itoh had a more complicated personnel policy than the aforementioned model. In understanding the difference between the treatment of Japan staff and American staff, it is important to recognize the distinction that exists in the Japanese management system between "status levels" and "functional authority."[29]

Functional authority is a familiar concept for American managers and describes the typical chain of command found in organization charts. It is based on a job description in terms of specific tasks each person is to perform. Each position on the chart has certain assigned job responsibilities in terms of functions. Distinctions are drawn between line and staff functions. Hierarchical relationships between members of the organization, the degree of authority within the organizational structure, and compensation are all determined by the functional position of the individual within the organization.

Status is a Japanese concept and reflects an individual's standing in the organization based on such factors as length of service (seniority) and level of achievement or accomplishment. A correlation between status and functional position is not necessary. Status is best described as similar to an attitudinal response that American firms may informally display toward an "old and trusted" employee who is given supervisory responsibilities, special assignments, and additional compensation because of long and faithful service to the company that may not be reflected in the actual functional job position occupied by the employee. The concept of status is a formalized, organizational response to the traditional Japanese system of lifetime employment. Once an individual is employed, he or she remains with the firm until retirement age is reached, unless employment is terminated for breach of company rules and regulations.

Itoh (America), like its parent, has eight status levels, ranging from *sankyu* to *sanyo* (see Appendix). *Sankyu* is the lowest level and is assigned to an employee who has just graduated from college and joined the Itoh (Japan) staff. His or her position is that of a recruit or, in the words of Nishitomi, a private in a military organization.[30] *Sanyo* is the top level awarded to employees who have been with Itoh (Japan) for a number of years and contributed to the firm's welfare through loyal and dedicated service. This position can best be described as that of a commissioned officer. Though it is possible that a person of higher status may report to a person of lower status because of difference in functional authority, Itoh makes an effort to avoid this kind of conflict. Thus, individual positions exist in Itoh (America) with no functional titles, and individuals occupying those jobs perform managerial functions. A Japan staff member will rarely be in a subordinate position reporting to an American staff member, a policy that minimizes the inherent potential conflict between status and function.

Compensation

Itoh's management system resulted in a dual personnel compensation and promotion system, one for the Japan staff and one for the American staff, each with its own employee operating manual. This dualism did not apply in the Sumitomo case, for, as the plaintiffs alleged, they were confined to a clerical level and precluded from management. But, taking the dual management tracks at C. Itoh, Japanese staff were paid primarily on the basis of status and Americans on the basis of functional authority. The result was a notable difference in pay and benefits.

Americans started at a salary level substantially lower than that of a Japanese at the same functional level. Americans were paid a gross salary; Japan staff were guaranteed a net salary. Itoh therefore followed a practice of "grossing up" for its Japan staff. All taxes—federal, state, and local—were estimated and, that amount was added to the Japanese staff's salary so that the employee would receive the guaranteed net. In addition, midyear bonuses were paid to Japanese staff but not the American staff. The amount of the midyear bonus was determined by Itoh (Japan) but charged against the accounts of Itoh (America).

Medical insurance was available for both American staff and Japanese staff. However, the Japanese staff was immediately eligible for benefits, while the American staff first had to satisfy a three-month eligibility requirement before benefits could be received.

Until March 31, 1974, Itoh sponsored a program of rental subsidies for the Japanese staff only. Although that program was discontinued, the Japanese staff still had available to them a lease termination subsidy not open to the American staff. Automobile purchase and vehicle insurance were subsidized by Itoh (America) only for its Japanese staff. While loans were available to all Itoh employees, only the Japanese staff was officially notified of the availability of assistance.

The Japanese staff also received a family allowance—30% of the base salary for the spouse, 10% for each child of school age and above, and 5% for each child under school age, not to exceed 50% of the base salary. The allowance was paid, if necessary, directly to the family member who remained in Japan. Thus, Itoh (Japan) would pay an allowance in yen to children of Japan staff attending college in Japan. Itoh (Japan) would then charge Itoh (America) for the amount of this allowance in dollars to be included in the salary of the employee. The allowance paid by the parent company appeared on the withholding tax statement furnished to the employee by Itoh (America) for income tax purposes. This family allowance was not available to American staff, since their salaries were paid according to what is practiced generally in the U.S. business environment, based on the assumption that the American staff employee had taken into consideration the amount needed as a family allowance.

ITOH'S AND SUMITOMO'S DEFENSE

The civil action against Itoh began in the U.S. District Court at Houston (where the plaintiffs won) and was appealed to the Fifth Circuit Court of Appeals (where they lost 2 to 1). The Supreme Court did not hear the Itoh case, for in the meantime the Court agreed to hear the Sumitomo case, which had been brought two years after the Itoh case but which moved more quickly through the court system.

Both Itoh and Sumitomo initially moved for dismissal and lost. Itoh mounted a two-pronged defense. The company first questioned the right of the plaintiffs to bring suit under Title VII of the Civils Rights Act. Secondly, it claimed that Itoh was protected by the Treaty of Friendship concluded by the United States and Japan in 1953.

Itoh's interpretation of civil rights laws led it to challenge the plaintiff's standing to sue.[31] Itoh filed a motion to dismiss on March 6, 1975, in which it contended that the plaintiffs, as white citizens, were not protected by Section 1981 of Title VII. Section 1981 provides: "All persons within the jurisdiction of the United States shall have the same rights . . . to the full and equal benefit of all laws . . . as is enjoyed by white citizens. . . . "

Itoh argued that since the standard set forth in Section 1981 is rights "enjoyed by white citizens," only nonwhites have standing to sue under Section 1981 and Title VII. Itoh claimed that the plaintiffs, by the clear and unequivocal terms of Section 1981, must demonstrate as whites that they had been denied the same rights given by Itoh to its other white employees. Since Itoh treated all its white employees equally, which means its American staff, the plaintiffs failed to satisfy the statutory burden imposed under Section 1981. The motion was denied by the district court on January 29, 1976, since the statute eradicates "all social discrimination in the enumerated rights rather than merely [elevating] nonwhite citizens above white citizens to a privileged legal status because of race." The cutting edge of Section 1981, the judge held, was "protection against discrimination on the basis of race, not protection against discrimination by numerical majorities.''[32]

Five months later, the Supreme Court would rule in the McDonald case that both Section 1981 and Title VII prohibit racial discrimination in private employment against white persons as well as nonwhite:[33]

> . . . we cannot accept the view that the terms of Section 1981 exclude its application to racial discrimination against white persons. On the contrary, the statute explicitly applies to ''all persons.'' . . . While a mechanical reading of the phrase ''as is enjoyed by white citizens'' would seem to lend support to respondents' reading of the statute, we have previously described this phrase simply as emphasizing ''the racial character of the rights being protected.''

The second legal defense raised by Itoh (America), in a motion to dismiss filed on May 10, 1978, was that Itoh's employment practices were ''immunized'' under the terms of the U.S.-Japan Treaty of Friendship, Commerce, and Navigation. Sumitomo also employed this defense.[34]

Itoh argued that the effect of the U.S.-Japan Treaty was to create an absolute right on the part of American and Japanese firms to employ in each other's countries managerial and specialized personnel of their choice to the exclusion of nationals of their host country. Since the treaty predates Title VII and the reenactment of Section 1981, and since the legislative history of both acts is devoid of any reference to treaty commitments, the treaty thus immunizes Itoh from the impact of Section 1981 and Title VII to the extent that Itoh discriminates in favor of its nationals. Accordingly, Itoh contended that the plaintiffs had not stated a cause of action on which relief could be granted.

Sumitomo's Defense

Sumitomo followed a similar tack.[35] Dismissal was sought by Sumitomo pursuant to F.R.Civ. P. 12(b)(6) on the ground that the 1953 Treaty of Friendship, Commerce, and Navigation between the United States and Japan '' . . . exempts Japanese trading companies and their wholly-owned subsidiaries incorporated in the United States from the application of Title VII.''[36]

The chronology of events in the Sumitomo legal proceedings was as follows: In December 1976, SCOA was charged by the Equal Employment Opportunity Commission (EEOC); in September 1977 it brought the treaty agrument; and in December of that year it was faced with a class action lawsuit. In May 1978, the company filed a motion to dismiss, which was denied in June of the following year. In May 1980, the second circuit agreed to hear the case, and in January 1981 it gave its judgment. In June 1981, Sumitomo appealed to the Supreme Court. The Court accepted to hear the case in November 1981, and the hearing took place in April 1982, with a decision handed down in June 1982. In February 1982, the plaintiffs filed a motion for class certification, and by August 1982, Sumitomo filed for dismissal. Class certification was granted in November 1984. In January 1986, settlement talks started. An agreement was reached in January 1987, the Court approved it in March, and it became effective in June 1987.

The treaty defense argument in the Sumitomo case was decided by the Supreme Court on June 15, 1982. The attorney for the Itoh plaintiffs pointed out in an interview that the Supreme Court opinion borrowed significantly from Judge Reavely, who was the dissenting judge in the Houston Fifth Circuit Court of Appeals. The essence of the argument is that the nationality of a corporation depends on where it is incorporated. For the Court's purposes, Sumitomo was an American corporation. Chief Justice Burger stated, in part:[37]

> The purpose of the treaties was not to give foreign corporations greater rights than domestic companies, but instead to assure

them the right to conduct business on an equal basis without suffering discrimination based on their alienage.

And, because the company is a subsidiary incorporated in the state of New York:

> We are persuaded, as both signatories agree, that under the literal language of Article XXII(3) of the Treaty, Sumitomo is a company of the United States: we discern no reason to depart from the plain meaning of the Treaty language. Accordingly, we hold that Sumitomo is not a company of Japan and is thus not covered by Article VIII(1) of the Treaty.

The Supreme Court thus reached an extremely limited decision and left many questions unanswered. Moreover, it explicitly did not rule on a line a defense which, by implication, may have been the most fruitful for both Itoh and Sumitomo to employ: the bona fide occupational qualification (BFOQ). In a footnote to the decision, Chief Justice Burger explicitly addressed this issue when he stated:

> We express no view as to whether Japanese citizenship may be a bona fide occupational qualification for certain positions at Sumitomo or as to whether a business necessity defense may be available. . . . Whether Sumitomo can support its assertion of a bona fide occupational qualification or a business necessity defense is not before us.

Itoh saw that its prospects for victory under the treaty defense were limited indeed. Sometime after the Supreme Court decision, it moved to settle. By September 1985, it had concluded a confidential settlement with the plaintiffs.

Sumitomo's problem was a bit more complex. The plaintiffs' suit against it was certified as a class action suit. After the Supreme Court decision, Sumitomo had a change of strategy and was bent on settling, as manifested by its change in legal counsel.

The company declined to pursue the case in court on the question of bona fide occupational qualifications and eventually entered into a consent decree effective March 30, 1987. In declining to pursue the case further, company representatives cited transaction costs, the adverse effects on company image and on the morale of personnel, and that the nature of the business had changed sufficiently to call for a new personnel policy anyway. (In fact, company representatives maintained that, had litigation not been pending, they would have initiated new policies in many of the areas of complaint much sooner.)

Sumitomo described the conditions of the consent decree in a press release to announce the settlement:[38]

> The settlement agreement contains various monetary provisions, good faith staffing goals and objectives, a job titling and compensation program, career development actions, a process for the resolution of any dispute by a court-appointed special master and customary monitoring and reporting provisions. Sumitomo Corporation of America will make all career development programs available to all personnel at its cost. It has agreed to dedicate $1 million for participation in various employee programs by female employees. The agreement runs for three years. . . . In the settlement, the company did not admit to any violations of law nor did the court make any such findings. Throughout the case SCOA consistently and emphatically denied allegations of discrimination on the basis of sex, national origin or race. Agreed-on goals, which are not quotas, in the agreement provide that the company will make a good faith effort to ensure that female employees hold 23 to 25 percent of the management and sales jobs at the company, including some senior management and senior sales positions, by the end of the three- year period.

Under the terms of the decree, Sumitomo retains the right to determine all employees' qualifications for promotion.

This point seems to affirm that, indeed, there is something of substance to bona fide occupational qualifications. The consent decree emphasizes training programs to improve the qualifications of female employees.

APPENDIX

Glossary of Japanese Terms with English Equivalents

JAPANESE TERMS AS USED BY ITOH[a]	ENGLISH EQUIVALENTS AND/OR EXPLANATIONS
Organizational Titles	
yakuin	Member of the board of directors
sōshihainin	President
sōshihainin daikō	Executive vice-president
buchō	Division manager (vice-president)
shitenchō (equivalent to *buchō*)	Branch office manager (equivalent to vice-president)
buchō daikō	Assistant division or department manager (equivalent to assistant vice-president)
shitenchō daikō (equivalent to *buchō daikō*)	Assistant branch office manager (equivalent to assistant vice-president)
kachō	Department manager/section chief
kachō dairi	Assistant department manager/section chief
jimushochō	Manager of a subbranch office
kakarichō	Assistant section manager or supervisor
kakarichō daikō	Assistant supervisor
SM	Section members (low-level employees within a section, excluding secretaries, clerks, and porters)
daikō (the term *dairi* was used prior to April 1, 1975)	Assistant
Status Levels—Old and New Systems	
Old System (before April 1, 1975):	
sanyo	Head
ittōshain	Level 1
nittōshain	Level 2
santōshain	Level 3
yontōshain	Level 4
gotōshain	Level 5
New System (effective April 1, 1975):	
sanyo	Head
buchō-yaku	Chief (equivalent in military hierarchy to a commissioned officer)
buchō-ho	Assistant chief (commissioned officer status)
kachō-yaku	Manager (equivalent in military hierarchy to a noncommissioned officer)
kachō-ho	Assistant manager (noncommissioned officer status)
ikkyu	First grade status (equivalent in military hierarchy to enlisted personnel—i.e., corporal)
nikyu	Second grade status (private first class)
sankyu	Third grade status (recruit right out of college)

Miscellaneous Terms

Dowa Kaijō Kasai Hoken	Marine Fire and Casualty Insurance Company in Japan
gyōmuhonbu	Administrative and coordinating division of C. Itoh Japan
hikitsugi-sho	Document verifying transfer of authority upon resignation
honbusho	A unit consisting of several divisions
jimusho	Office
ka	Departments (sections under the old status system)
kaigaisojatsu-bu	Overseas department
kaigaitenshukansha	Emergency expense approved by the manager of an overseas branch office
kanrishoku-kyū	Management positions
kanrishoku	All status levels above kachō- ho that allow employees to receive certain allowances
karibaraikanjō	Suspense account—an account used for purchases of items that do not bear a clear purpose
kyuyogakari	Personnel in charge of payrolls
naiki	Company regulation—policy giving guidance as to whether a loan will be extended
saigaihukyūhi	Repair expense for damages related to the employee's property
sangokukan	Third country transaction—transaction with countries other than Japan and the United States
shiten	Branch office
shosha	In Japan, the term usually refers to a "general trading company." Itoh management uses the term to designate knowledge-intensive industry—ability to look at an entire industry, absence of a narrow perspective, "moving think tank."
shōyo	Bonuses
sōgokaihatsubu	Project development department
sōmubu	General affairs division—department that pays salaries
torishimariyaku	A level of employment above sanyo—equivalent to members of the board of directors, or yakuin
ukewatashi	Delivery of general machinery
zaimubu	Finance department
zaikinkyū	Overseas base salary—base salary plus family allowances

[a]Other Japanese companies may use slightly different titles.

NOTES

1. United States Department of Commerce, International Trade Administration, *United States Trade: Performance in 1987*. Washington, D.C.: U.S. Government Printing Office, 1988, pp. 11–13.

2. United States Department of Commerce, International Trade Administration, *Foreign Direct Investment in the United States: 1986 Transactions*. Washington, D.C.: U.S. Government Printing Office, 1987, p. 25.

3. Jacob. M. Schlesinger, "Fleeing Factories." *Wall Street Journal* (April 12, 1988), p. 1.

4. Section 1981 explicitly applies to "all persons" including white persons. The phrase "as enjoyed by white citizens" simply emphasizes the racial character of the rights being protected. *McDonald* v. *Santa Fe Trail Transportation Company*, 427 U.S. 273.96 S. Ct. 2574 (1976); see also *Regents of University of California* v. *Bakke*, U.S. 98 S. Ct. 2574 (1978).

5. *Michael E. Speiss, Jack K. Hardy, and Benjamin F. Rountree* v. *C. Itoh and Co. (America)*. Civil Action No. 75-H-267, United States District Court for the Southern District of Texas Houston Division.

6. *Lisa M. Avigliano, et al.* v. *Sumitomo Shoji*

America, Inc., 77 Civ. 5461, United States District Court, Southern District of New York.

7. 77 Civ. 5641, 82 Civ. 4390—consent decrees in full settlement of civil actions.

8. 42 U.S.C. Section 1981 (1974) and 42 U.S.C. Section 2000 (1974).

9. Debate by Senator Hubert H. Humphrey, reported in *Statuary History*, p. 1236. Therefore, the initial enforcement thrust on the part of the Equal Employment Opportunity Commission (EEOC) and the courts was directed to the protection of black minorities.

10. The first case to be considered by the Supreme Court involved a refusal of a Georgia motel to rent rooms to blacks. A bare five months after enactment of the 1964 Civil Rights Act, the Supreme Court upheld the constitutionality of the act, specifically Title II dealing with discrimination in public accommodations, *Heart of Atlanta Motel* v. *United States*, 379 U.S. 241M 85 S. Ct. (1964).

11. The current emphasis on sex discrimination is illustrated by many recent court decisions, including *Webster* v. *Secretary of Health Education & Welfare*, 43 F. Supp 127 C.N.Y. 1976), reversed on other grounds, 430 U.S. 313 97 S Ct. 1192, striking down differences in Social Security payments paid to men and women; see also the Age Discrimination in Employment Act of 1967, 29 U.S.C. Section 623.

12. Title VII proscribes not only overt discrimination but also practices that are fair in form but discriminatory in operation without regard for intent or motivation; *Griggs* v. *Duke Power Co.*, 401 U.S. 424, 91 S. Ct. 849 (1971); *Albermarle Paper Co.* v. *Moody*, 422 U.S. 405, 95 S. Ct. 2362 (1975).

13. Courts have broad remedial powers not only to issue injunctions but also to order such affirmative action as may be appropriate to remedy unlawful employment practices. *Alexander* v. *Gardner-Denver Co.* 415 U.S. 36.94 S Ct. 1011 (1974) and *Franks* v. *Bowman Transportation Co., Inc.* 424 U.S. 747.96 S. Ct. 1251 (1976).

14. Michael E. Speiss, et al., cited in note 5.

15. U.S. District Court for the Southern District of Texas Houston Division, Court's memorandum and order, filed January 9, 1976, Court's memorandum and order, filed September 2, 1977.

16. *Avigliano, et al.* v. *Sumitomo Shoji America, Inc.*, USDC SNY, No. 77 Civ. 5641, 1977.

17. Tamar Lewin, "A Complex Sex Bias Case." *New York Times* (April 4, 1982), pp. D1, D6.

18. C. Itoh and Co., Ltd., *Annual Report*, 1988, pp. 1, 20ff.

19. Sumitomo Corporation, *Annual Report*, 1987, pp. 1, 30–31.

20. Sumitomo Corporation, "Sumitomo Corporation of America, annual brochure, p. 21.

21. Deposition of Sadao Nishitomo, secretary and EEO coordinator at Itoh America, taken at the offices of C. Itoh and Co., New York, N.Y. by the plaintiffs' attorneys during the period September 10–26, 1975, pp. 571–78; 594–95.

22. Cited in S. Prakash Sethi, Nobuaki Namiki, and Carl L. Swanson, *The False Promises of the Japanese Miracle*. Boston, Mass.: Pitman Publishing Co., Inc., 1984, p. 68.

23. Sumitomo Corporation, interview with Prof. Sethi, September 1987.

24. Nishitomo, *Deposition*, pp. 633–58.

25. Ibid.

26. Ibid., pp. 433–36, 453–55, 697–702.

27. Ibid., pp. 643–53.

28. Ibid., pp. 590–91.

29. Ibid., pp. 184–87.

30. Ibid., pp. 172–84.

31. Ibid., pp. 143–45, 249–50, 257–58, 272–77, 286–92, 304–18, 356–67.

32. U.S. District Court for the Southern District of Texas, "Memorandum and Opinion," January 29, 1976, cited in *Lexis Nexis*, pp. 13–14, 22.

33. Ibid., pp. 22–31.

34. Ibid., pp. 27–30.

35. U.S. District Court for the Southern District of Texas Houston Division, "Opinion, March 1, 1979," cited in *Lexis Nexis*, pp. 4–12; "Order, April 10, 1979," cited in *Lexis Nexis*, pp. 1–3.

36. Sumitomo Corporation, interview, September 1987.

37. Supreme Court of the United States, 80-2070 and 81- 24, "Opinion," by Chief Justice Burger, June 15; 1982, p. 13.

38. Hill and Knowlton, Inc., "News Release for Sumitomo Corporation of America," February 24, 1987, April 6, 1987; U.S. District Court Southern District of New York, *Consent Decree in Full Settlement of Civil Actions*, 77 Civ. 5641 (CHT); 82 Civ. 4930 (CHT)

C. ITOH & CO. (AMERICA), INC.

BIERMAN, L. "International Economics and American Employment Relations." *Boston College Law Review*, 28 (December 1986), pp. 27–39.

BROWN, STANLEY J. "The Japanese Approach to Labor Relations: Can It Work in America?" *Industrial Relations* (April 1986), pp. 20–29.

CARR, W. Z., JR., and D. M. KOLKEY. "Labor Relations for Multinational Corporations Doing Business in Europe." *Loyola of Los Angeles International and Comparative Law Journal*, 7 (1984), pp. 1–26.

CARR, W. Z., JR., and D. M. KOLKEY. "Labor Relations Implications for Private Investments Abroad." *Private Investors Abroad* (1982), pp. 171–211.

"Civil Rights Laws and United States Treaties: Stagnating in Judical Limbo." *Houston Journal of International Law*, 5 (Spring 1983), pp. 323–38.

"Corporate Governance in Japan: The Position of Shareholders in Publicly Held Corporations." *University of Hawaii Law Review*, 5 (Spring 1983), pp. 135–206.

FOX, G. D. "Discovery from Japanese Companies: Oral Depositions Should Be Allowed Once Jurisdiction is Established." *Trial*, 22 (August 1986), pp. 18–21.

GROSHEN, ERICA L. *The Structure of the Female/Male Wage Differential: Is It Who You Are, What You Do, or Where You Work?* Research Department, Federal Reserve Bank of Cleveland, Ohio: 1987.

HILLER, J. S. "Civil Rights Enforcement and Japanese Subsidiaries." *American Business Law Journal*, 21 (Winter 1984), pp. 463–74.

"Investment in United States Property by Controlled Foreign Corporations: A Proposal for Reform." *Rutgers Law Journal*, 19 (Winter 1988), pp. 367–87.

"Japanese Companies on United States Soil: Treaty Privileges vs. Title VII Restraints." *Hastings International & Comparative Law Review*, 9 (Winter 1986), pp. 377–406.

"Jurisdiction over Alien Corporations Based on the Activities of Their Subsidiaries in the Forum: Whither the Doctrine of Corporate Separateness?" *Fordham International Law Journal*, 9 (1985/1986), pp. 540–95.

KEOTAHIAN, AVAK. "National Origin Discrimination in Employment: Do Plaintiffs Ever Win?" *Employee Relations Law Journal*, 11, no. 2 (1986), pp. 467–91.

MATSUMURA, Y. "Attitudes of Canadian Subsidiaries of Japanese Firms towards the Law and the Legal System in Canada." *University of British Columbia Law Review*, 21 (1987), pp. 209–22.

MILLER, K. C. "The Practical Aspects of Litigating against Foreign Corporations." *Journal of Air Law and Commerce*, 54 (Fall 1988), pp. 123–59.

PARCEL, TOBY L. *Ascription and Labor Markets: Race and Sex Differences in Earnings.* New York: Academic Press, 1983.

PICKAR-GRAY, ELIZABETH. "The National Origin BFOQ under Title VII: Limiting the Scope of the Exception." *Employee Relations Law Journal*, 11, no. 2 (1986), pp. 311–21.

SCULNICK, MICHAEL W. "The Supreme Court's 1986–1987 Equal Employment Opportunity Decisions: A Review." *Employment Relations Today*, 14 (Autumn 1987), pp. 213–23.

SETHI, S. PRAKASH. "Are Foreign Multinationals Violating U.S. Civil Rights Laws?" *Employee Relations Law Journal*, 4, no. 4 (1979), pp. 484–95.

"Sumitomo Shoji America, Inc. v. Avagliano, 102 S. Ct. 2374." *Boston College International and Comparative Law Review*, 7 (Winter 1984), pp. 67–89; *North Carolina Journal of International Law and Commercial Regulation*, 10 (Spring 1985), pp. 515–31; *New York Law School Journal of International & Comparative Law*, 5 (1983), pp. 167–82; *Thurgood Marshall Law Review*, 8 (fall 1982), pp. 111–28.

TAISHIRO SHIRAI. "Recent Trends in Collective Bargaining in Japan." *International Labor Review*, 123, no. 3 (May/June 1984), pp. 235–46.

"Title VII and Treaty Rights Battles: The Verdict is Still Out." *ASLIS International Law Journal*, 10 (Winter 1986), pp. 77–107.

TSUMURI, YOSHI. *The Japanese Are Coming.* Cambridge, Mass.: Ballinger Publishing Co., 1976.

TUNG, ROSALIE, ed. *Strategic Management in the United States and Japan.* Cambridge, Mass.: Ballinger Publishing Co., 1986.

United States Equal Employment Opportunity Commission. *Job Patterns for Minorities and Women in Private Industry.* Washington, D.C.: 1985.

"U.S. Incorporated Subsidiaries of Japanese Companies May Not Invoke Provisions of FCN Treaty, Sumitomo Shoji America, Inc. v. Avagliano, 102 S. Ct. 2374." *Suffolk Trans-national Law Journal,* 7 (Spring 1983), pp. 279–94.

WESTBROOK, J. L. "Theories of Parent Company Liability and the Prospects for an International Settlement." *Texas International Law Journal,* 20 (spring 1985), pp. 321–31.

WISE, SUE. *Georgie Porgie: Sexual Harassment in Everyday Life.* New York: Pandora, 1987.

YOSSHINO, MICHAEL. *Japan's Managerial System: Tradition and Innovation.* Cambridge, Mass.: MIT Press, 1968.

COMPARABLE WORTH

*A new approach to eliminating sex-based wage inequities
in employment*

The doctrine of comparable worth holds "that if individuals of different sexes have jobs that differ in duties yet are comparable in worth, the jobs should be paid the same regardless of external market value."[1]

Although very recent in its origin, this doctrine has been gaining rapid ground in public awareness. It has especially strong emotional appeal to the women's movement, segments of organized labor, and population groups who view it as an important tool with which to fight job discrimination and wage inequities. Comparable worth is said to be the issue of the 1980s. In an introduction to one of the best surveys of the issue, Helen Remick, director of the Office for Affirmative Action at the University of Washington, says: "Comparable worth addresses the sex difference in compensation that cannot otherwise be explained; when we advocate comparable worth, we mean that wages should be based on the worth of the work, not upon the sex of the person

doing it."[2] As an issue, comparable worth rides in the wake of a profound sociocultural change which occupies the forefront of public debate in the "modernized" Western world: Are women truly the equals of men? This is an idea which is not well established in the West and hardly rates mention in traditional societies. Comparable worth, nonetheless, is a policy which is rooted in the new thinking of the eighties. In its present state it remains exploratory and unfinished.

The notion of comparable worth, however, is surrounded by intense controversy encompassing the validity of the concept itself, difficulties in its measurement and application, and its potential consequences for growth in the U.S. economy and employment as well as the global competitiveness of American business. Although the methodological and process-related issues are quite serious, they can eventually be resolved. But there remains the most fundamental question posed by the comparable worth doctrine. That is, comparable worth strikes at the very core of the market economy by asserting that wages should be determined administratively, largely without regard to factors of supply and demand and market pricing. In the process, comparable worth may create an entire array of new inequities and market dysfunctioning while attempting to eradicate one set of inequities.

The debate on the issue, however, has only just begun, and the intellectual arguments are likely to rage for quite some time. The issue is gaining greater immediacy and is being looked at closely as more and more women enter the work force. To date, 17 states have passed legislation that tries to deal with the issue.[3] Thirteen states use the term *comparable worth* directly in their legislation. Representative Olympia Snowe of the Joint Economic Committee stated that ''The lack of pay equity for the women of this country is the most urgent problem facing women in the labor force.''[4] While these arguments would provide shape and substance to the future debate, eventual solutions must emerge in the political and legal arena. For eventually it is the political will of the people expressed through a democratic system that can alter the distributive effects of the market economy.

COMPARABLE WORTH: THE FIRST VICTORY

The proponents of comparable worth achieved their first significant victory in a case filed by the American Federation of State, County, and Municipal Employees (AFSCME) against the state of Washington. On December 14, 1983, an employer, the state of Washington, was for the first time found guilty of discrimination under Title VII for personnel policy disparities in functionally unrelated jobs. The case grew out of a 1974 survey of state personnel which revealed massive pay discrimination against women. The court's judgment culminated

10 years of debate, and it assumed national significance.[5]

The antecedents of this case, however, were building up through the legal system, where the concept of job discrimination was being litigated and refined in terms of bona fide occupational qualifications (BFOQ), disparate treatment, and disparate impact. An important precedent was set in *County of Washington* v. *Gunther,* decided in 1981, wherein the United States Supreme Court resolved the threshold legal issue of whether sex-based wage discrimination claims can be brought under Title VII without satisfying the equal work standard of the Equal Pay Act. In a significant but narrowly written opinion, the Supreme Court ruled that compensation discrimination claims brought under Title VII are not restricted to claims for equal pay for ''substantially equal'' work.[6]

The Gunther case set a precedent for the *AFSCME* v. *The State of Washington* case.[7] In this case, the county of Washington's market study showed that female jail matrons, based on relative skills, effort, responsibility, and working conditions, should have received 95% of what male jail guards received in pay. The county, however, only paid the matrons 70% of the amount paid to guards. Four female matrons filed a suit claiming they were paid less than their evaluated worth. The United States Supreme Court decided that ''a claim of intentional wage discrimination can be brought under Title VII even when jobs are not considered substantially equal under the Equal Pay Act.''[8]

The *Gunther* decision represented a crucial first step toward development of the concept of comparable worth as a means of achieving pay equity through litigation. *Gunther* established that women may challenge systematic sex-based wage discrimination under Title VII without the necessity of showing that the employer had hired male workers at higher wages to perform substantially equal work.[9]

The Supreme Court indicated that Title VII should be interpreted more broadly and that claims under it are not restricted to equal pay for substantially equal work. Instead, they cover the entire spectrum of sex-based employment discrimination practices.

Although this case did set precedents for future claims, the court at this point stressed the narrowness of its ruling. These jobs were only slightly different, not unrelated. The court did not lay down any guidelines or conditions for future claims. However, the ruling did give precedence for future claimants that decisions would be different when brought under the Equal Pay Act versus Title VII.

ISSUES FOR ANALYSIS

1. How substantive are the intellectual, legal, and operational arguments made by the proponents and opponents in the *AFSCME* v. *The State of Washington* case? To what extent and along what dimensions are the merits of opposing arguments relevant in other situations?

2. What does *worth* mean in the context of the employers' options and those of employees? Should an employer be forced to pay more for a job if it employs predominantly female workers? If the logic of the argument of comparable worth is to be held across-the-board, why should it not be argued in favor of other job classifications that are predominantly occupied by blacks, Hispanics, or other identifiable disadvantaged groups?

3. What are some of the measurement problems that arise in trying to compare jobs that are functionally distinct so as to determine their relative worth?

4. What administrative mechanisms can be used in comparing the relative worth of different jobs? What are the limitations and biases built into these systems?

5. What proof is needed to show discrimination in the case of functionally unrelated jobs? Does the fact that employers' self-studies on this issue have been used against them in suits discourage employers from doing such studies?

6. How might one evaluate the role of unions in fighting for comparable worth for female employees? Is comparable worth a concern for pay equity, or is it another device to protect union members from market and competitive pressures?

7. Is the issue of social equality of women being improperly mixed up with the pay equity issue, or are the two the same?

8. To what extent are market wage rates biased by cultural factors and, therefore, do not respond to the scarcity of valuable skills? Is an administratively determined wage rate for comparable worth the best approach? If not, how might the wages for different jobs be made more responsive to the market?

9. What are some of the possible costs to the economy, and the implications for the labor market, if the doctrine of comparable worth is accepted and/or legislated?

AFSCME v. STATE OF WASHINGTON

The state of Washington has two systems of classified service. One is the civil service, and the other is higher education. Each of these systems has a personnel board which is responsible for any changes in the classification of jobs within the system. All jobs are classified, and those having the same classification receive the same pay. Pay rates must also be comparative to the rates of other private and public institutions. To determine this comparability, that state does salary surveys of specific benchmark positions every two years. Once rates are formulated by the personnel boards, they are adopted in open hearings; the governor uses them in the state budget; and the state legislature appropriates the required funds.

AFSCME International, or the American Federation of State, County, and Municipal Employees, is the largest union of public employees. Of its 1 million members, 400,000 are women. Half of these women perform clerical jobs, with the remainder found in other traditional female occupations.[10] In 1982, one third of their local presidents and 45% of their local union officers were women.[11]

In 1974, at AFSCME's urging, the Governor of Washington State at the time, Daniel J. Evans, asked that the two personnel boards do an internal study of the disparities between female-dominated jobs and male-dominated jobs. Both boards did a small study, and following this, the governor had the two boards meet together with an outside consultant, Norman D. Willis, and conduct a much larger study.

The Willis study evaluated jobs based on four factors: skills/knowledge; mental demands; accountability; and working conditions. It studied those jobs which were 70% or more female versus those jobs which were 70% or more male-dominated. The study's major conclusion was that those jobs which were equal according to the factors, but were female-dominated, paid on the average 20% less than male-dominated jobs.

In 1976, Governor Evans put just over $7 million into the budget to start to correct these disparities. Soon after, he left office, and the newly elected governor withdrew the money. Four more studies were done from 1974 to 1982 with basically the same results. AFSCME asked both the new governor and his successor to replace the money in the budget. The Willis Plan was never instituted, partially due to financial considerations involved. So, in 1981, nine AFSCME members filed charges of discrimination with the Equal Employment Opportunity Commission on behalf of all workers employed in female-dominated jobs. In 1982, when the EEOC did not respond to the claim, AFSCME filed a suit.

Just prior to the trial in 1983, the state legislature voted to modify the classification process to include not only market ratings but also increases to obtain comparable worth. The state maintained that the disparities were not illegal, just unfair. Both of the personnel boards were to set up 10-year comparable worth schedules to be started between 1983 and 1985 and completed by June 1993. The legislature defined *comparable* as being jobs similar in responsibilities, judgments, knowledge, skills, and working conditions.

Even with this step toward the goal of pay equity, criticism remained. The Engrossed House Bill 1079 gave one-and-a-half million dollars to this end. There were, however, no specifics on how to accomplish this goal, just time limits on its completion. The money appropriated worked out to be only $100 per person with respect to the 15,000 to 20,000 people employed in those jobs. Critics maintained that it would take 80 to 90 years to accomplish pay equity at that rate. And so the trial ensued.

AFSCME went to trial on behalf of all individuals who were employed in jobs comprised of 70% or more females as of November 20, 1980. AFSCME based its suit on four claims:

1. The studies done had shown disparities of 20% differences in income. In 1983, this disparity had even increased. Disparities were also found in closely related jobs such as barber and beautician. In addition, these studies showed that even entry-level jobs which required the same qualifications were paid differently depending on the sex of the employee. Positions filled by men, which required no high school education, were paid approximately 10% more than female positions requiring no high school. Male jobs which required a high school degree paid about 22% more, and jobs requiring one year of college paid men 19% more.[12]

2. The state failed to act promptly to correct the disparity, and even when it did (1983), the action was inadequate.

3. The state had a history of sex-segregating jobs. Employment ads placed in newspapers were put in columns labeled "men" and "women" from the 1950s to 1973. The state also had "protective" laws prohibiting women from certain jobs.

4. Statements were made by public officials and

administrators on the problem and efforts to correct it. In addition, there were personnel board reports and the governor's Affirmative Action Committee's statements concerning the situation.

The state defenses included:

1. The system used was legal as well as nondiscriminatory. Salaries were based on a fair, legitimate system, and provided the most for the taxpayers' dollars. Changing the system could alter the state's ability to recruit and keep workers. Changing would also seriously disrupt the labor force.

2. The studies that were undertaken were only informational studies used by the state to look into the comparable worth idea. Before the results of these studies could be implemented, the validity, feasibility, and implications had to be considered.

At the trial, Judge Tanner allowed only 2 of the 14 witnesses on behalf of the state to testify. He did not accept any of the state arguments about possible flaws in the study. The judge found that the state had acted in bad faith and should have known the legal implications of the studies when it began to conduct them. In addition, he felt the evidence proved "pervasive and intentional discrimination."[13]

When claiming discrimination, there are two avenues of proof: disparate treatment, and disparate (adverse) impact. Disparate treatment holds that the employer intentionally discriminated against its employees. Disparate impact states that just because an employer does nothing, and the practice is discriminatory, even without intent, the employer is liable. AFSCME sought relief under both disparate treatment and disparate impact. The state argued that in all previous cases of comparable worth, primarily *Gunther* v. *County of Washington*, proof of intent was required. Therefore, AFSCME could not claim disparate impact. The court "held that the plaintiffs in fact had established a prima facie case of discrimination

under either a disparate impact or disparate treatment theory using direct or indirect evidence."[14]

Even the award made by the judge proved quite controversial. Through previous cases, the Supreme Court had set precedents for the District Court in determining relief. The guidelines concerned: the extent to which an award would be economically damaging to the defendants; any adverse effects the award could have on the economy or any innocent third parties; and lastly, whether the defendants had reasonable time with which to correct their wrongdoings. The judge found these guides to be irrelevant to this case and ordered the following:

1. all practices of discrimination would be stopped;

2. all plaintiffs would be paid the amount they were due under a plan adopted as of May 1983;

3. further evaluation studies would be conducted listing completely all employees who were entitled to backpay;

4. the court would appoint a master who would have broad access to state buildings and files and would report back in 90 days on the extent of progress in implementing the plan; and

5. the state would pay for the master's fees.

Estimates are that this case will cost the state anywhere from $500 million to $1 billion. Two-thirds of this amount is backpay the state might have avoided had it shown greater and quicker action concerning the controversy. Had the state taken such action, it could have used as little as 2% of its budget to bring pay equity.[15]

THE CONTROVERSY CONTINUES: ARGUMENTS FOR AND AGAINST COMPARABLE WORTH

The proponents of the comparable worth doctrine assert that women have historically earned less and continue to do so compared to men in general, and also in particular where two jobs require essentially similar levels of competence and skills and may be of equal value to the employer. They also point out that occupational categories such as teachers and nurses, where women predominate, tend to have lower wages. Moreover, when a particular job category or occupation starts having more women workers, the average level of wages has a distinct tendency to fall when compared to previous levels and in relation to other job categories that have been historically used in wage rate comparisons.

In 1939, women earned 63¢ for every dollar that a man earned. In 1950, the figure dropped to 62¢ and has not changed since.[16] In addition, female-dominated occupations typically earn significantly lower wages than male-dominated occupations (see Table 1).

The issue is complicated by society categorizing certain types of jobs and professions by sex. For example, 81% of clerical workers, 96% of nurses, and 82% of elementary teachers are women. These are also the occupations that are typically found at the lower end of the pay structure. On the average, a secretary earns $4,000 less per year than a truck driver. Not only are women paid less, but there is evidence that women

are also generally employed by lower-paying firms.

The proponents of comparable worth also reject the two arguments made most often by their critics: the market pricing of a job's relative worth, and the difficulty in determining alternative pricing mechanisms that would overcome the alleged market pricing deficiencies and provide a more efficient and socially equitable criterion for determining the wage base for various jobs and occupational categories.

Market pricing, in its simplest form, assumes that a job is worth as much as an employer is willing to pay for and an employee is willing to work for. Thus, an employee performing exactly the same work may accept lower wages when there are too many people competing for work, and may demand and receive higher wages when jobs are plentiful and there are not enough people available to take them. If the workers demand too high a price for their services, the employers will hire fewer workers to do only the most valuable or profitable work; find a substitution for workers, i.e., become more capital intensive; or go out of business. In all these cases, the effect would be to reduce the demand for labor to a point where at a given wage rate the demand and supply for workers balances out. Conversely, if employers offer wages that are too low compared to the alternatives available to workers, the workers will be inclined to leave that occupation; fewer new workers will enter that occupation; and employers in other businesses will tempt these workers to come work for them at higher wages. In all these cases, the effect would be to reduce the supply of workers so that employers are forced to raise wages to a level where they can get the number of workers they need. Thus, employers use the market to determine the going rate for a particular job on the basis of actual supply and demand of workers for that job. This entails a survey of various occupations and job classifications within them. Basically, wages are based on what

TABLE 1. The Wage Gap: Figures for Full-time Workers in Selected Occupations

	WOMEN AS PERCENT OF ALL WORKERS		EARNINGS RATIO, FEMALE TO MALE	
	1979	1986	1979	1986
Accountants and auditors	34	45	0.60	0.72
Computer programmers	28	40	0.80	0.81
Computer systems analysts	20	30	0.79	0.83
Lawyers	10	15	0.55	0.63
Managers and administrators	22	29	0.51	0.61
Sales of business services	28	34	0.58	0.79
Teachers, elementary school	61	82	0.82	0.95

SOURCE: Robert Pear, "Women Reduce Lag in Earnings But Disparities with Men Remain," *New York Times* (September 4, 1987), p. A13.

everyone else is paying. Those trying to validate market ratings as a measure of job worth propose that the law of supply and demand will ensure that a job is paid what it is worth.

Opponents argue that this may not be the case for women, and they use the example of the recent shortage of nurses. Based on the increased demand and decreased supply, their wages should have risen considerably, yet this did not occur to any significant degree. "Many compensation professionals feel that the market truly does not reflect the internal worth of jobs"[17] and that in effect the market both embodies and prolongs discrimination.

The market theory also assumes that the labor market is freely competitive. This is a critical assumption which may be flawed.[18] Consider the following:

1. Because of the necessary skills and training, people are not free to change jobs at will.

2. Because of family or other considerations, restrictions exist geographically.

3. Information is not openly accessible; therefore much of the information an individual does possess is inadequate.

4. Institutional structures, such as seniority rather than merit, inhibit pure competition.

5. Employers often fill vacancies internally rather than on the open market.

6. Supply and demand of the labor force is influenced by other institutions such as unions and government.

The second method of job evaluation is to determine a job's internal worth. The Committee on Women's Employment and Related Social Issues concluded that job evaluation systems hold much promise as an equitable, consistent method of evaluating a job's intrinsic value. "Women are concentrated in low paying jobs, not solely out of choice—though choice may play some role—and not because these jobs would be low paying regardless of who did them but

rather as the result of earlier traditions of discrimination that have become institutionalized—as well as possible current intentional discrimination."[19] Using this method an employer ranks jobs on the basis of several factors which are taken as representative of a job's worth. Those jobs which have equal total points should be paid the same wage.

In reviewing the study which underpinned the *AFSCME* v. *State of Washington* case, Helen Remick wrote:

> Examples bring the issue to life. A Food Service Worker I, at 93 points, earned an average salary of $472 per month, while a Delivery Truck Driver I, at 94 points, earned $792; A V Clerical Supervisor III, at 305 points, earned an average of $794. A Nurses Practitioner II, at 385 points, had average earnings of $832, the same as those of a Boiler Operator with only 144 points. A Homemaker I, with 198 points and an average salary of $462, had the lowest earnings of all evaluated jobs.[20]

Obviously, the methodology used in assigning points is a very hotly disputed issue. Although the job evaluation idea may hold promise, it needs development. First, current systems in use do not reflect the advances in social science measurement techniques which could greatly enhance validity. Secondly, many job evaluation systems incorporate market rates which, as mentioned previously, may be discriminating in themselves. Thirdly, the system must be used firm-wide, and often different systems are used for different classifications or levels within an organization.

Judy Fulgham has proposed some guidelines for conducting a job evaluation.[21] She gives considerable attention to both defining the evaluations tools as well as to the organizational interaction of the parties involved. Her work is helpful in pointing out some of the pitfalls to be expected.

ARGUMENTS
FOR COMPARABLE WORTH

The notion of comparable worth has been strongly criticized by a number of scholars and public and private institutions on grounds that it is inherently flawed as logic, would introduce more politics and ideology into the wage determination system and thus make it more and not less equitable, and would be an administrative nightmare.

The chairman of the U.S. Civil Rights Commission calls comparable worth "the looniest idea since Looney Tunes."[22] The Commission, in an early policy statement, by a 5 to 2 vote, had rejected the comparable worth concept as a remedy for sex bias in the workplace. It went so far as to urge that Congress and federal enforcement agencies oppose the notion of equal pay for men and women employed in different jobs of comparable value. "Implementation of the unsound and misplaced concept of comparable worth would be a serious error." The latest policy statement, an outgrowth of hearings the panel held in June 1985, supported the Reagan Administration's opposition to the comparable worth concept. In its statement, the Commission contended that salary differences between men and women often were caused by factors other than discrimination, such as unequal educational backgrounds and skills. It also suggested that the evaluation studies frequently used to implement the comparable worth concept "are inherently subjective" and do not prove wage bias. Civil rights laws do not prevent employers "from relying on market factors" to set pay, the statement adds. Speaking for the Commission, Morris Abram, vice-president, stated that the comparable worth concept would amount "to permanent government wage control over a substantial, if not the majority, of the working population and I don't think this country is ready for it."[23]

Furthermore, in a case dealing with alleged sex discrimination, the Equal Employment Opportunity Commission (EEOC) held that the payment of lower wages to employees in the female-dominated administrative branch than to those in the male-dominated maintenance branch of an employer's operations did not amount to unlawful sex discrimination, especially where there was no evidence that employees were assigned on the basis of sex or that there were barriers to movement between the job categories. Further, there is no statutory basis for a claim of increased wages based on a comparison of the intrinsic worth of jobs in one category with that of other jobs in the same organization.[24]

Similar views were also expressed by the Appeals Court judges in their decision rejecting AFSCME's claims in reversing the lower court's decision against the state of Washington. The Appeals Court stated that "Neither law nor logic deems the free market a suspect enterprise" in overturning a decision that required the state of Washington to pay 15,500 mostly female workers as much as $1 billion in damages.[25]

The critics of comparable worth argue that despite its deficiencies, market-based pricing of human labor still offers the most efficient and equitable system and that any other system would lead to inefficiencies and would be inherently more inequitable. The rationale for a market-based wage is as follows:

To begin with, the determination of the worth of anything is individual and relative. It is individual in that values differ among individuals, resulting in different assessments of worth of any object of exchange. Were this not so, no exchange of goods or services would occur; the purchaser in any exchange must judge the object of exchange as worth more than does the supplier of the object. Judgments of worth also are relative; they reflect comparison between the anticipated outcomes of one exchange and the most attractive alternative to that exchange. The market concept as elaborated in economic theory provides a potential mechanism for identifying some common measure of value of exchanges. Individual buyers and sellers seek out beneficial exchanges, and the various rates of exchange observed in the market influence the valuations of opportunity cost of both buyers and sellers. Alternative rates of exchange available in the market represent to both buyers and sellers an element of what is foregone when entering into any specific exchange. Another major element of opportunity cost is the valuation of nonmarket uses such as work in the home or leisure. Both alternative wage rates in the labor market and personal valuation of time spent homemaking or skiing influence the opportunity cost to the worker of accepting a specific wage and employment offer.[26]

In the competitive market, the actions of both buyers and sellers seeking their personal advantage tend to converge on a single rate of exchange, a market rate at which all who wish to buy and sell are accommodated. In a similar manner, a market wage is generated through the actions of buyers and sellers in a competitive labor market. Each employer and employee considers alternatives and the opportunity cost associated with each and enters into exchanges of work and wages which are considered worthwhile. Alternatives available to the employer include hiring other persons with greater or lesser potential productivity, losing production and sales, subcontracting to other employers, and making technological substitutions for labor. Alternatives available to the employee include other job opportunities, investment in education and training, nonmarket work in the home, and consumption or leisure. Only exchanges judged worthwhile by both parties are consummated, and the rates of exchange converge on a common market wage rate through competitive action. The market wage rate is, therefore, the best available measure of job worth, reflecting as it does the collective valuations of worth by employers and employees.

In theory, a market wage is associated with each job or occupation, and the wage differential between any two occupations reflects the collective judgments of relative worth of these occupations by employers and employees. One occupation is paid more than another as necessary to attract the desired number of applicants and to the extent that it is viewed as producing greater economic value for the employer. It is this structure of wage differentials obtained in a competitive labor market that reflects the relative worth of different occupations. Furthermore, the structure of wage differentials can be expected to change as labor demands and supplies change as a result of employers and employees altering their valuations of different jobs.[27]

The worst part of the comparable worth concept is that it tends to perpetuate job rigidities and thus condemns women to the same "undesirable" jobs that they seek to get out of. To the extent that no overt or covert discrimination is involved, wages in occupations with excess supply over demand would tend to be more depressed than the prevailing wages in other occupations. And should women, or any other identifiable group, be concentrated in that particular occupation, it would, as a group, receive lower wages. Suppose, for the sake of argument, we decide that primary school teachers who are predominantly women, and who are also underpaid, should receive higher wages. In the absence of any restriction to job mobility based on sex, the more competent among these women would move to other jobs, leaving those who, for one reason or another, are unmovable. In case these reasons are personal, this is an individual choice and nothing needs to be done. However, in other cases employees are staying because they cannot find better, higher-paying jobs. Thus, employers would be forced to upgrade jobs and attract better people, or they would receive poor performance.

Should we raise the wages of these people that are above the market rate, it would have the effect of keeping people in these jobs when they would have been more productive elsewhere. It would also pay the less efficient people more money since they have no incentive to move. Finally, it would attract more people to these jobs when in fact the demand for their services would be declining, for the employers would be constantly seeking alternative ways to accomplish these tasks and thereby avoid paying above-market wages.

Although couched in male versus female and primarily white-collar terms, the issue of comparable worth pervades examination of every kind of wage differential. Basically, the issue of comparable worth relates to the determination of relative worth of any two jobs or occupations. Most pilots are men. Most typists are women. In the name of fairness, as proponents of comparable worth see it, employers should raise the salaries of typists. The private sector implications are obvious. If it is discriminatory for the federal government to pay a female typist less than a male pilot, isn't it true for American Airlines as well? And wouldn't it be up to the federal government to ensure that such discriminatory practices are rectified? It is also argued that any implementation of a comparable worth plan would not so much pit women against men as blue-collar workers against white-collar workers. Most comparable worth studies favor white-collar occupations over blue-collar occupations, assessing points for degrees and credentials while ignoring such factors as working conditions and market demand. To comparable worth advocates, it does not seem fair that a truck driver with no high school degree could earn more than a systems analyst with a college education.[28]

George F. Will, the noted conservative syndicated columnist, criticizes comparable worth in terms of an ideological play by the liberal left in America. He argues that "comparable worth might have the retrograde effect of reinforcing a 'pink collar' ghetto of jobs considered women's work. Advocates of comparable worth say comparable jobs are of comparable worth to employers. Ad-

vocates are not content to let employers say what that worth is."[29]

Will outlines four criteria by which advocates of comparable worth would ascertain the worth of a job. One is the amount of knowledge and skills required, meaning the "total amount of information or dexterity" involved. This requires an assessment of the comparable worths of mental and manual capabilities—of information relative to dexterity. The second criterion is mental demands. However, Will argues that the distinction between mental demands and knowledge is at best arbitrary and at worst subjective, i.e., nonscientific. Rather than paying more for jobs making high mental demands, Will suggests (albeit facetiously) that "a job that is dull because it is simple and repetitive should be considered a job that makes especially difficult mental demands. A dull job can be difficult because attention and zest are difficult to maintain." A third criterion is accountability, meaning the amount of supervision the job involves. A fourth criterion is working conditions. However, supervision could be a pleasure and not necessarily a chore. Similarly, a job performed outdoors would, presumably, get special "worth points" because working outdoors is less pleasant than working inside—unless, of course, the worker prefers working outdoors. But, then, who asked the worker? It is the manufacturers of criteria—the social scientists formulating formulas—who will be asked.[30]

Finally, Will alludes to the ideological leanings of the proponents of comparable worth and observes:

Comparable-worth looks like part of the not-very-hidden agenda of the left. It serves the goal of giving control of almost everything—in this case, everyone's wages or salary—to a small priestly class of "experts." Computing the comparable worth of every activity would inevitably be the work—the profitable work—of a particular class. Comparable worth would be a jobs program for an articulate, theorizing class of intellectuals.

And not surprisingly, that formula gives special value—extra "worth points"—to the kind of work done by the kind of person who devises such formulas, work involving "knowledge" skills. Surprise! The formula enhances the economic value of formula makers. And, of course, it lowers the relative "worth," moral and monetary, of the labor performed by the neediest women.

When society's least pleasant work is considered, someone might ask a really radical question: should not nurses be paid more than doctors? Doctors have the psychic income of intellectual stimulation and social prestige. Nurses have bedpans and subordination. Surely nurses should have more money. Michael Walzer, a political philosopher, goes a step farther: perhaps citizens should be conscripted to collect the garbage.

Onerous Jobs: There are other jobs that must be done but are onerous. Garbage collection is one. Caring for the very aged is another. Such jobs often are filled by people of whom Walzer says, felicitously, this: "When they were growing up, they dreamed of doing something else." Anything else. Walzer argues that "negative" but necessary jobs should not be allotted by economic forces to "negative" categories of people such as the poor or recent immigrants. Walzer is not saying that collecting the garbage is work without dignity. He says the physical nature of such unpleasant work cannot be changed, but its moral nature can be. It can be accorded due dignity by distributing it as a duty of citizenship, rather than leaving it for those at the bottom of society's status system.[31]

LEGISLATION: EQUAL PAY ACT AND TITLE VII

There are two major pieces of legislation which govern pay equity. The first of these is the Equal Pay Act of 1963 (29 U.S.C. 206[d]), which is an amendment to the Fair Labor Standards Act of 1938. This act guarantees that employees of different sexes doing the same job are required to receive equal pay.[32]

There are four factors which determine job similarity: first, skill which includes experience, training, education, and ability; second, effort, which can be both physical and mental; third, responsibility, or how much accountability is required to do the job; and fourth, the working conditions of the employee. If these four conditions are equal, and there is disparity in pay, then discrimination may be evident.

However, there are four defenses which can excuse an employer from liability under the Equal Pay Act: disparity due to seniority; disparity due to merit; disparity due to differences in productivity in which earnings are distributed based on quantity or quality of output (an example of this would be a salary based on commission according to sales volume); and disparity due to any factor other than sex.

To use these defenses, the systems must be formalized and used in a sex-blind manner. Title VII of the Civil Rights Act of 1964 (42 U.S.C. 2000E) is the second major piece of legislation dealing with pay equity. Title VII makes it unlawful to discriminate in hiring, job classifications, promotion, compensation, fringe benefits, discharge, and any other terms of employment.

The Bennett Amendment (Section 703[h]) of Title VII incorporates the provisions of the Equal Pay Act into Title VII. This Amendment has caused considerable controversy. Two interpretations of its meaning have been expressed. The first interpretation stresses that in order for wage discrimination to be tried under Title VII, it must satisfy the conditions of equal work as in the Equal Pay Act. The second interpretation holds that only the four exceptions or defenses are incorporated into Title VII. This distinction is a major one for the issue of comparable worth. The way in which the courts interpret the Bennett Amendment has significant impact on the decisions of future comparable worth cases.

NOTES

1. Elizabeth Cooper and Gerald V. Barrett, "Equal Pay and Gender Implications of Court Cases for Personnel Practices." *Academy of Management Review*, 9 (January 1984), pp. 84–92; and *Wall Street Journal*, "Pay Equity, Born In Public Sector, Emerges as an Issue in Private Firms" (July 8, 1985), p. 15.

2. Helen Remick, ed., *Comparable Worth and Wage Discrimination*. Philadelphia, Pa.: Temple University Press, 1984, p. x.

3. Judy B. Fulgham, "The Employer's Liabilities under Comparable Worth." *Personnel Journal*, 62 (May, 1983), pp. 396–419.

4. U.S. Congress, Joint Economic Committee, *Hearing On Women in the Workforce: Pay Equity*, 98th Congress, 2nd Session, 1984, p. 2.

5. Gary R. Siniscalso and Cynthia L. Remmers, "Comparable Worth in the Aftermath of AFSCME vs. State of Washington." *Employee Relations Law Journal*, 10 (summer 1984), pp. 6–29.

6. Mary Heen, "A Review of Federal Court Decisions under Title VII of the Civil Rights Act of 1964." In H. Remick, *Comparable Worth*, p. 198.

7. Barbara R. Bergman and Mary W. Gray, "Economic Models As a Means of Calculating Legal Compensation Claims." in H. Remick, *Comparable Worth*, pp. 155–72; Heen, "Review," pp. 197–202, 212–13.

8. Gary R. Siniscalso and Cynthia L. Remmers, "Comparable Worth." *Employee Relations Law Journal*, 9 (winter 1983–1984), pp. 496–99.

9. Heen, in H. Remick, *Comparable Worth*, p. 1984.

10. Ibid., p. 4.

11. Committee on Post Office and Civil Service, U.S. House of Representatives, *Hearing on Federal Pay Equity Act of 1984*, 98th Congress, 2nd Session, 1984, p. 63.

12. Ibid., p. 204.

13. Ibid., p. 134.

14. Siniscalso and Remmers, "Comparable Worth," p. 497.

15. Ibid., p. 13.

16. Committee on Post Office and Civil Service, *Hearing*, p. 204.

17. Committee on Post Office and Civil Service, U.S. House of Representatives, *Joint Hearing on Pay Equity: Equal Pay for Work of Comparable Value*, 97th Congress, 2nd Session, 1983, pp. 1–2; and Robert Pear, "Women Reduce Lag in Earnings But Disparities with Men Remain." *New York Times* (September 4, 1987), pp. A1, A13.

18. Fulgham, "Employer's Liabilities," p. 404.

19. Joint Economic Committee, *Hearing*, pp. 12–14; Thomas A. Mahoney, "Market Wages and Comparable Worth." *ILR Report*, Cornell University (spring 1982), pp. 15–19.

20. Joint Economic Committee Report, Supra note 4, p. 5.

21. Remick, *Comparable Worth*, p. 103.

22. Judy B. Fulgham, "The New Balancing Act: A Comparable Worth Study." *Personnel Journal*, 63 (January 1984). pp. 32–38.

23. "Business and the Law—States Leading on Pay Equity," *New York Times* (June 22, 1987), p. D2.

24. Joann S. Lubin, "Use of Comparable-Worth Idea to Fight Job Sex Bias Opposed by Rights Panel." *Wall Street Journal* (April 12, 1985), p. 60.

25. EEOC, Decision 85-8, June 17, 1985, as reissued July 12, 1985. Commerce Clearing House (1985), pp. 7044–48.

26. David L. Kirp, "Comparable Worth Debate Lives On—Courts Not the Place to Set Job Values and Pay," and Michael Evan Gold, "Federal Court Decision Blind to New Realities." *Sunday Press*, Binghampton, NY (September 15, 1988), pp. 1, 4E.

27. Thomas A. Mahoney, "Market Wages and Comparable Worth." *ILR Report* (spring 1982), pp. 15–19.

28. Ibid., p. 56.

29. Dick Armey, "Comparable-Worth: A Bad Idea That Won't Die." *Wall Street Journal* (September 26, 1988), p. 26.

30. U.S. Supreme Court, 29 U.S.C. 206 [d] June 1988.

31. Ibid.

32. Ibid.

COMPARABLE WORTH

"AFSCME v. State of Washington [770 F.2d 1401]: The Future of Equal Pay for Comparable Worth." *New England Law Review*, 21 (1985/ 1986), pp. 673–96.

"AFSCME v. Washington [770 F.2d 1401]: Comparable Worth Suffers a Set Back." *Detroit College of Law Review* (Fall 1986), pp. 915–33.

"AFSCME v. Washington [770 F.2d 1401]: The Death of Comparable Worth?" *University of Miami Law Review*, 40 (May 1986), pp. 1039–74.

BECKER, GARY S. "Human Capital, Effort and the Sexual Division of Labor." *Journal of Labor Economics*, 3, no. 1 (January 1985), pp. 533–58.

BERGMANN, BARBARA R. *The Economic Emergence of Women*. New York: Basic Books, 1988.

BERGMANN, BARBARA R., and MARK ROBERTS. "Income for the Single Parent: Work, Child Support and Welfare," in Clair Brown and Joseph Pechman, eds., *Gender in the Workplace*. Washington, D.C.: Brookings Institution, 1987.

BROWN, CLAIR, and JOSEPH PECHMAN, eds. *Gender in the Workplace*. Washington, D.C.: Brookings Institution, 1987.

EBERTS, RANDALL W., and JOE A. STONE. "Male-Female Differences in Promotion: EEO in Public Education." *Journal of Human Resources* (Fall 1985), pp. 504–21.

ENGLAND, PAULA. "The Failure of Human Capital Theory to Explain Occupational Sex Segregation." *Journal of Human Resources* (Spring 1982), pp. 358–70.

"Equal Protection I: Sex Discrimination in Employment." 1986 *Annual Survey of American Law* (May 1987), pp. 419–40.

FISCHEL, D. R., and E. P. LAZEAR. "Comparable Worth and Discrimination in Labor Markets." *University of Chicago Law Review*, 53 (Summer 1986), pp. 891–918.

"The Future of Comparable Worth: Looking in New Directions." *Syracuse Law Review*, 37 (1987), pp. 1189–218.

GOLD, MICHAEL EVANS. *A Debate on Comparable Worth*. Ithaca, N.Y.: Industrial and Labor Relations Press, 1983.

GUTEK, BARBARA A. *Sex and the Workplace*. San Francisco, Calif.: Jossey-Bass, 1985.

HARRIMAN, ANN. *Women, Men, Management*. New York: Praeger, 1985.

McCRUDDEN, C. "Comparable Worth: A Common Dilemma." *Yale Journal of International Law*, 11 (Spring 1986), pp. 396–436.

"Meritor Savings Bank v. Vinson [106 S. Ct. 2399]: Sexual Harassment at Work." *Harvard Women's Law Journal*, 10 (Spring 1987), pp. 203–24.

SHAW, B. "Comparable Worth and its Prospects: AFSCME v. State of Washington [770 F.2d 1401]." *Labor Law Journal*, 38 (Fall 1987), pp. 100–18.

SMITH, ROBERT S. "Comparable Worth: Limited Coverage and the Exacerbation of Inequality." *Industrial and Labor Relations Review*, 41 (January 1988), pp. 227–39.

"Symposium: Comparable Worth." *University of Michigan Journal of Law Reform*, 20 (Fall 1986), pp. 1–215.

TAEUBER, CYNTHIA M., and VICTOR VALDISERA. *Women in the American Economy*. Washington, D.C.: United States Department of Commerce, 1986.

WILLIAMS, ROBERT E. *A Closer Look at Comparable Worth: A Study of the Basic Questions to be Addressed in Approaching Pay Equity*. Washington, D.C.: National Foundation for the Study of Equal Employment Policy, 1984.

UNITED AIRLINES, INC.

*A case of age discrimination or a concern for the safety
of the flying public* *

The United States has been in the fore-front of nations protecting the rights of its citizens against discrimination in places of work, pleasure, and habitation, i.e., in all walks of life. Enshrined in various civil rights laws, American citizens are protected from discrimination based on sex, race, national origin, age, or other disabilities that are not directly related to the specific performance of tasks at hand, do not adversely affect job performance, or do not threaten public safety.

The primary intent of these laws has been to protect individuals from arbitrary and capricious behavior on the part of other individuals or institutions, i.e., employers, builders and landlords, and owners of restaurants and other places of entertainment.

*We gratefully acknowledge the helpful comments on an earlier draft provided by Dr. Bruce Avolio of the School of Management of the State University of New York at Binghamton.

Discrimination, however, can and does take place even where it is not motivated by racial or other prejudicial motives. This situation arises when an individual is denied certain rights because he or she falls into a general class that may have a high statistical propensity to fail expected standards of performance. Thus, women as a group may be required to pay higher life insurance premiums than men because women *as a group* live longer and thus require annuity payments for a longer time than men *as a group* of comparable age. Similarly, young unmarried men under age 26 are charged higher car insurance premiums than women of similar age and marital status because men in this group as a class are involved in more accidents than women.

All group-based discrimination affects individual rights. It is immaterial whether the impact is derived as a consequence of prejudice or society's inability to isolate individuals from within a particular group where such a group may be generally more prone to engage in activities that are perceived as harmful to the legitimate interests of others. In the United States, public opinion, political and legislative action, and legal proceedings have consistently eroded such barriers to individual rights based on some group or class characteristic. Thus, as a matter of public policy, group-based discrimination has been effectively outlawed even where it can be shown that to do so would adversely affect those who are not part of such a group.

Age-based discrimination raises similar and even more controversial issues. Age has long been used as a determining factor for suitability in employment where a job is perceived to require certain physical attributes for satisfactory performance, employee safety, or public safety. The rationale is that a person's responses and reflexes deteriorate with age, and that since individual rates of deterioration are difficult to determine, it is imperative that an employee retire involuntarily from the job.

There are, however, other reasons based on history and tradition that support involuntary retirement at a predefined age: for example, a society's desire to allow its senior citizens to enjoy their golden years in relaxation through accumulated pension and other retirement benefits; to create career advancement opportunities for younger generations; and to minimize discriminatory actions against individual workers by imposing generally uniform conditions of retirement on all workers. These conditions have been enforced by custom as well as law and employment contracts.

The issue, therefore, is not that of age-based job discrimination per se but that of balancing the competing interests of employers, employees, and society at large in a manner that is fair and equitable to the individuals and institutions involved and to society. The issue has become even more important in the United States because this country's population, as that of most other industrially advanced countries, is becoming gradually older. This is due to a declining birth rate, improvement in medical and health care technologies, and increases in life expectancy. The latter two factors have made it possible for most people to live longer and remain healthier well into their seventies and even later years. The United States currently is in the midst of a major demographic change. By the year 2010, 25% of the population is projected to be age 55 or older. People in this category numbered 47.4 million in the 1980 census. They are estimated to reach 58.8 million in the year 2000, and 74.1 in 2010.[1] At the same time, while the number of young workers entering the work force stood at 3 million in the early 1970s, it has now fallen to 1.3 million per year.[2]

The case of United Airlines and certain of its pilots and flight engineers amply demonstrates the nature of these conflicting claims. It also shows the process by which these claims may be balanced to arrive at more equitable and socially desirable solutions. Equally important, it suggests that such a balancing of interests need not be permanent and irreversible. In fact, changes in the technology of specific jobs, improvements in medical and health care, and advances in diagnostical and statistical evaluation techniques may allow society to discard older group-based measures in favor of conditions that apply to specific individuals.

THE CASES OF AGE DISCRIMINATION AGAINST UNITED AIRLINES

On January 31, 1979, a number of flight engineers filed an age discrimination action against United Airlines and the Airline Pilots Association challenging United's policy of retiring all flight engineers at age 60. Another action was filed by certain of United's pilots because of the airline's refusal to allow the pilots to transfer to flight engineer's positions when they reached age 60. The action was joined by the Equal Employment Opportunity Commission. The combined cases became known as *Gerry V. Monroe and Lee E. Higman, et al., and Equal Employment Opportunity Commission* v. *United Airlines Inc., and Airline Pilots Association International.*[3] The plaintiffs asserted that United's policy of involuntary retirement at 60 was in contravention of the Age Discrimination in Employment Act of 1967 (ADEA) in that the mere fact of age could not be shown as a bona fide occupational qualification (BFOQ) that could be considered reasonably necessary for satisfactory job performance. United, in its defense, agued that a flight engineer's age (second officer) indeed met the criterion of reasonably necessary for the safe operation of the aircraft. It further argued that it was impractical to screen out, through vigorous periodical medical examinations, individual officers who could become incapacitated or otherwise become unable to perform their duties during the period between regularly scheduled medical examinations. In the case of the pilots, United argued that it was the company policy and the binding union agreement that disallowed pilots from down-bidding for jobs, regardless of age, except in very specific, clearly defined, and contractually agreed circumstances between the company and the Airline Pilots Association.

ISSUES FOR ANALYSIS

1. How are the rights of employees affected in hiring people based on age? Under what conditions should these criteria be considered reasonable, and where might they be considered contrary to public interest?

2. Under what circumstances should employers be allowed to discriminate among employees on the basis of age for purposes of promotion and retention?

3. Where issues of public safety and social pol-icy are raised, how might the balancing of rights be achieved as between the employees, employers, and society at large?

4. In addition to airline pilots, what other job categories raise substantive issues of public safety based on an employee's age, health, and medical fitness?

5. Age-based hiring, promotion, and retention issues have serious economic implications for certain employers as well as general social concerns. Under conditions of economic downturn or severe market competition, an employer may be under tremendous pressure to reduce costs or face business failure. Other things being equal, older employees with longer tenure on the job command higher wages that may not be necessarily associated, on a one-to-one basis, with increased productivity. Thus, it would be economically prudent for the employer to effect savings in labor costs by laying off older employees. It would also allow the company to retain younger workers, who may be in a more vulnerable economic position and thus less able to survive extended periods of unemployment. Under what circumstances may it be legally or morally justified to retain younger employees at the expense of older workers?

6. How are the issues raised in items 1 through 5 related to the United Airlines case and the relative arguments made by the airline, the pilots and the flight engineers, the Airline Pilots Association, and the Equal Employment Opportunity Commission? Are the lower court's verdict and the decision of the Appeals Court reasonable and fair based on your analysis of the facts of the case and your understanding of the concepts of equity and fairness as applied to different parties in the case?

7. Where age-based hiring and promotion criteria become necessary, how might employers and society at large help those who become the unintended victims of these standards? What measures, if any, can be taken to help those who, because of age, might be unable to perform satisfactorily in their current jobs, but are otherwise healthy, anxious to work, and need employment to survive and maintain their standard of living?

OLD AGE AND EMPLOYMENT PRACTICES: SOCIAL AND LEGAL FRAMEWORK

It has long been assumed in Western countries that people would retire at age 65. This arbitrary age was apparently selected in 1889 by Otto Von Bismarck, Chancellor of the German Republic.[4] Bismarck was establishing the first formal national old-age pension program. He himself was 74 at the time. There do not appear to be documented scientific or health reasons which prompted him to choose that age. Be that as it may, it was not long before other Western countries followed suit.

The United States opted for the retirement age of 65 with the passage of the Social Security Act of 1935. The choice of that plateau by Congress also appears to have been arbitrary.[5] There were a number of different motivations surrounding the law. One was to make room for younger workers.[6] Another was the desire to create an independently financed retirement system based on employee contributions which would also be free of the political process.[7] In Japan, the mandatory retirement age has been 55 years for a long time and has only recently been raised to 58 years. Japanese life expectancy, on the other hand, has been rising steadily and now exceeds 72 years for males and 74 years for females. In contrast to most Western countries, Japanese social security payments do not start until the age 60, and retirement benefits are generally meager compared to Western standards. Thus, Japan alone among all the industrially advanced countries has more people over the age of 60 who work full-time out of necessity rather than choice. In large parts of the Third World, 55 is still the age at which mandatory retirement takes place.

Elderly Americans have become a very potent political force, represented by powerful lobbying groups. Largely due to their efforts, several important pieces of legislation were passed. First came the Age Discrimination in Employment Act (ADEA) of 1967. This Act outlawed discrimination based on age with respect to workers who were between 40 and 65. It applied to all establishments employing 25 persons or more and also included the policies of employment agencies and labor unions.[8] It became unlawful for an employer to take any personnel action—including hiring, promotions, demotions, or firing—because of an individual's age. Personnel actions which proved to be adverse to older workers had to be justified in terms of a bona fide occupational qualification (BFOQ). The BFOQ clause specifies that actions be based on reasonable factors other than age.

The Federal Aviation Administration (FAA) has implemented the "age 60 rule" under the Federal Aviation Act of 1958. This rule prohibits airlines from employing pilots who are over age 60. Prior to the United case, the FAA was sued some eight times between 1959 and 1978, but in each case the courts upheld the age 60 rule. The rule became the subject of congressional hearings in July of 1979 and was further put in jeopardy by 1975 and 1978 amendments to the Age Discrimination in Employment Act of 1967, which raised the mandatory retirement age to 70.[9]

The BFOQ has been the subject of considerable, and often contentious, debate. Employers have increasingly sought to use it to defend certain employment practices, including age-based differential treatment of employees. At the same time, employees have consistently and increasingly challenged BFOQ exceptions in employment practices by forcing employers to defend their practices on specific grounds of performance standards. In the case of airlines, BFOQ was unsuccessfully used to limit flight attendant jobs to female employees and to ground female employees in the event of marriage or pregnancy. The intensity of legal conflicts and court cases led Congress to amend the ADEA in 1975 by deleting the vague term *reasonable*. In 1978, further amendments extended protection from age discrimination to age 70 and expanded coverage both to private industry employees as well as to those in state and local governments.[10]

In January 1987, H.R. 4154 was approved. It further extended protection to workers over the age of 70 and eliminated mandatory retirement at age 70. In approving this measure, Congress included a seven-year exemption with respect to public safety and welfare employees, such as police and prison guards, as well as college professors. During this period, the EEOC and the Department of Labor are charged with the responsibility of conducting studies to see if reliable tests of physical and mental fitness of older employees may be devised. The elderly have thus won the right to work as long as they are willing and able.[11] Employees also have the right to a jury trial should they choose one, and, if victorious, they are entitled to double damages in cases of willful violations of the ADEA.

The Legal Framework

The law provides two avenues through which a person can establish the fact of discrimination, i.e., disparate treatment and disparate impact. Under the disparate treatment doctrine, a person must show that the discrimination was intentional, i.e., the employer purposefully applied terms or conditions of employment that led to less favorable employment consequences for older workers. Evidence of discrimination can be either direct or indirect. Direct evidence in ADEA cases includes organizational policies or procedures where the employer can be shown to be treating older workers differently, such as mandatory retirement policies or the refusal to hire individuals over a certain age. Indirect evidence suggests a showing of intent by inference.

Statistical evidence is also used to dem-

onstrate discriminatory intent on the part of an employer under ADEA's disparate treatment doctrine. For example, statistical disparities establishing that those treated less favorably are significantly older than those treated favorably are often used to help establish an employer's discriminating motivation. However, there are two reasons why statistical proof is not conclusive in ADEA cases. First, natural occurrences may better explain the statistical discrepancies where age is the implied discriminating variable. Second, age discrimination is often based on assumptions about the effects of age on ability and efficiency. Thus, the possibility of a justifiable relationship between age and reduced performance renders age-related statistical disparities inconclusive. Courts hearing age discrimination cases typically require large statistical discrepancies. Therefore, statistical evidence is more helpful in establishing a claim of age discrimination when it is combined with other evidence.[12]

Under the disparate impact doctrine, it is only necessary to show that the employment practices in question have a differential effect on older workers regardless of employer motivation. For example, if the plaintiffs in an ADEA suit were able to show a statistically significant difference between the number of old and young employees laid off during a reduction in force, this would be sufficient for a prima facie showing under the requirements of the disparate impact doctrine. Also, "Employment critiera that are age neutral on their face but which nevertheless have a disparate impact on members of the protected group must be justified as a business necessity."[13] There are of course defenses against these claims. Not every personnel decision which had negative consequences for older workers is a violation of the ADEA. It is not unlawful for employers to base personnel decisions on age "where age is a bona fide occupational qualification (BFOQ) reasonably necessary to the normal operation of the particular business" (29 U.S.C. s623 [f] [1]). Employers are also protected against personnel decisions that result in age differentials where the decisions are based on reasonable factors of age (FOA)—for example, seniority systems or discharge or discipline of an employee for a ''good'' cause.

Employers raising the BFOQ defense admit that their personnel decisions were made on the basis of age but seek to justify them by showing that those decisions were reasonably necessary to normal business operations. When treated as a BFOQ, age is commonly used as a generalization about the ability level of all older workers. For example, a BFOQ defense might be based on a showing that all workers below a certain age would be more effective than those above that age limit. This is called a *factual showing*. Another possible defense is to show that it was impossible or impractical to make such decisions based on individual evaluations. For instance, an airline that could not make a factual showing might be able to justify a BFOQ by showing that there was no accurate or efficient way to determine which of its pilots ought to retire except by reference to age. The test case was provided by *Usery v. Tamiami Trail Tours, Inc.*, 531 F.2d 224 (5th Cir. 1976). According to Rosenblum:

> Under the so-called *Tamiami* test, the age-based classification (1) must be reasonably necessary to the essence of the employer's business, and (2) the employer must have reasonable cause, i.e., *a factual basis* for believing either (a) that *all* or *substantially all* persons within the excluded class would be *unable to perform safely and efficiently* the duties of the job or (b) that it is *impossible or impractical* to deal with persons over the age limit on an individualized basis (emphasis in original).[14]

Safety-related businesses using the BFOQ defense present a special problem for the courts. Any increase in the risk to others resulting from the abandonment of age-related employment criteria has come to be viewed as an important legal consideration.[15]

An employer who raises the FOA (factor of age) defense asserts that its actions were reasonable and based on some factor other than age. The defendant's only legal burden is to articulate clearly the specific nature of the FOA.

Employers can use two broad categories of defenses to refute charges of age discrimination: noneconomic and economic considerations. Included among those not directly related to economic considerations are violations of company policy, uncooperativeness, poor performance, lack of confidence in an employee's ability, and lack of training. Defenses directly related to economic considerations include reductions in force and other cost-cutting gestures as well as other personnel decisions directly made on the basis of employment costs. Thus, it would be appropriate under the ADEA for an employer to terminate all employees whose compensation was more than a prescribed amount, even though the practice would result in the discharge of a greater number of older workers.[16]

Since ADEA cases are often resolved based on research evidence that examines the relationship between age and organizational variables, it is important to appreciate the role of research in investigative efforts in ADEA-related cases. Furthermore, since age-related research findings are not uniform and methodologies suspect, caution should be exercised when using the results of age-related research to justify relationships between age and important organizational variables.[17]

THE FLIGHT ENGINEERS' AND PILOTS' CASE: ARGUMENTS IN SUPPORT OF CHARGES OF AGE DISCRIMINATION

On January 31, 1979, the three named *Monroe* plaintiffs, who served as flight engineers, brought suit claiming that their forced retirement at age 60 violated the Age Discrimination in Employment Act of 1967 (ADEA), as amended (29 U.S.C. sec. 621 et seq.). The *Higman* plaintiffs, who were captains seeking to transfer to flight engineer positions at age 60, filed their complaint on April 18, 1979. During the course of the proceedings, many additional pilots and flight engineers joined the complaint, bringing the number of individual plaintiffs to 112.[18]

The individual plaintiffs brought suit claiming that their forced retirement at age 60 violated the ADEA. Two groups of plaintiffs were suing. The *Monroe* plaintiffs were suing as flight engineers at the time of their involuntary retirement and sought to continue in that position beyond their sixtieth birthdays. The *Higman* plaintiffs served as captains, copilots, flight instructors, or flight management pilots until age 60, the age at which Federal Aviation Administration (FAA) regulations require that they cease to serve as pilots on commercial flights. They sought to transfer to the position of flight engineer, for which the FAA imposes no age requirement. The Equal Employment Opportunity Commission (EEOC) intervened in this action, seeking an injunction to prohibit United from continuing these age-based policies. The EEOC alleged that United had violated the ADEA by denying plaintiffs and other employees the opportunity to work as flight engineers solely because of their age (60).[19]

All the plaintiffs were seeking either to continue in or transfer to the flight engineer position at age 60. All were fully qualified in terms of medical qualifications and airman proficiency up to their sixtieth birthdays, when they were forced to retire by United. United, however, refused to permit them to continue their employment, citing a company policy prohibiting any flight engineer to work past the sixtieth birthday. (*Plaintiffs' Brief*, pp. 4–7)

In 1975, United Airlines performed a detailed study of the effect of incapacitation of the flight engineer on flight safety and concluded that such incapacitation did not interfere with the safe operation of the flight. Consistent with the findings of this study, United had, on numerous occasions, permitted individuals recently recovered from serious medical conditions to return to flight duties but limited them to the position of flight engineer.

United has an elaborate and very sophisticated system of testing the current proficiency of its flight crew, including its flight engineers. All of United flight deck crew members pass through a training center once a year for proficiency training and checking conducted by United flight instructors and check pilots. During these sessions, the flight engineer's performance is evaluated using a computerized flight simulator. Thus, even United's vice-president for flight standards and training admitted that United's system of proficiency checking provided an objective measure of the proficiency of the flight crew member which is effective regardless of the age of the individual tested. (*Plaintiffs' Brief*, pp. 10–14)

In addition, United's flight engineers are not permitted to continue in duty status unless they pass two physical examinations per year (one by the FAA and the other by United). Therefore, United's doctors have a longitudinal medical history detailing any significant changes or patterns in the health of each individual. United's doctors have admitted that these tests are effective in screening crew members of all ages, including those aged 59. They also admitted that as far as they were aware, all of their medical procedures could be used to test flight engineers over age 60.

All experts agree, even those from United, that there is enormous variability in aging between individuals. There is no specific point at which aging begins or accelerates. Therefore, from a medical point of view, age 60 has no special significance in the aging process. A deterioration in function is caused by specific, identifiable diseases and not by the aging process itself.

Thus, conditions that could impair a flight engineer's ability to perform his or her job duties are capable of detection through medical and performance testing. (*Plaintiffs' Brief*, pp. 14–18) For many years, United had used tests to assess, on an individual basis, the ability of pilots and flight engineers to perform their jobs safely and efficiently. The FAA and United have permitted numerous pilots to return to flight duty following serious ailments provided they can first pass appropriate medical and psychological tests. Since these tests can be used to evaluate individuals regardless of age, an upper age limit of 60 for employment for United flight engineers is not reasonably necessary for safety. (*Plaintiffs' Brief*, pp. 21–23)

In 1960, the FAA adopted the age 60 rule. The FAA repeatedly ruled, however, that this regulation was not applicable to flight engineers and that no other FAA regulation required that a flight engineer be below age 60. Therefore, United's only reason for enforcing the age 60 rule for flight engineers was that such employment was contrary to the terms of their pension plan. However, in 1978, Congress amended the ADEA to eliminate the pension plan exception and prohibit involuntary retirement based on age. For United to continue this practice, it would have to prove that age was a BFOQ reasonably necessary to the normal operation of its business. United did not present any evidence that they conducted studies or prepared any reports in 1978 to evaluate whether their policy with respect to flight engineers was necessary for safety. Thus, it must be concluded that United was in violation of the ADEA. (*Plaintiffs' Brief*, pp. 26–28)

The *Higman* plaintiffs were captains who wanted to down-bid to flight engineers. The collective bargaining agreement did contain certain restrictions on down-bidding by the captains. In general, crew members were limited to bidding up to higher-ranking positions or to higher-status equipment. However, down-bidding was permitted where a pilot wished to bid onto a higher-status plane as a second officer. In fact, a very substantial number of pilots had been permitted to down-bid over the last 10 years. United never gave any serious consideration to the request of age 60 pilots to down-bid to second officer positions when they became unable, solely because of the FAA rule, to continue in their positions as captains. Although United permitted down-bidding in all situations ranging from reductions in force to performance failure, they would not permit a captain to down-bid. United could not even show that there was even one other instance, aside from pilots affected by the age 60 rule, where a pilot who became unable to continue in his present position was denied the opportunity to down-bid to a position he could hold. (*Plaintiffs' Brief*, pp. 33–33A)

There is no dispute in this case that United refused to allow flight engineers to work past their sixtieth birthdays. Such an age-based employment policy is a prima facie violation of the ADEA. Thus, it was United's burden to prove that its policy of barring all persons over the age of 60 from the flight engineer's position is a BFOQ reasonably necessary for the safe transportation of passengers, and that fitness could not be determined on an individual basis. As to the reasonable necessity of United's policy, there is no evidence showing that the flight engineer's position was critical to safety. The flight engineer has no responsibilities for flying the plane or manipulating the flight control. In fact, United did not consider it necessary to use a flight engineer at all on two of its jets. This is why the FAA has never imposed any age limitation for the position of flight engineer.

As to the inability to determine fitness of a person on an individual basis, even United admitted that their systems were fully capable of identifying unfit crew members at all ages through age 59. They also knew of no procedures that became ineffective beyond age 60. United's capacity to test fitness on an individualized basis is underscored by its well-established policy of permitting crew members to return to flight duties following serious illness provided that they pass appropriate medical tests. There is no explanation why United could not perform similar tests or determine whether otherwise healthy 60-year-olds were experiencing any loss of function. (*Plaintiffs' Brief*, pp. 35–40)

Moreover, United's ability to detect deterioration in function was not limited to its periodic medical exams and performance evaluations. The flight engineer does not work in isolation. The job requires continuous interaction with other individuals. Several times on every flight, the captain, copilot, and flight engineer check their instrument panels by calling out challenges and responses to each other. Any deterioration in cognitive function would be apparent to the flight engineer's coworkers. Thus, there was ample evidence for a jury to conclude that United's requirement that flight engineers retire at 60 was not reasonably related to or necessary for the safe transportation of passengers, and that individualized testing of fitness was possible. (*Plaintiffs' Brief*, pp. 40–41)

United's refusal to permit pilots affected by the FAA age 60 rule to down-bid, while permitting down-bidding by pilots displaced from their positions for non-age-related reasons, constitutes disparate treatment. The ADEA makes it unlawful for an employer to treat employees differently on account of their age. The evidence previously stated demonstrated that the plaintiffs were indeed treated differently because of their age, and that age was a determining factor in the rejection of their transfer requests. United could not demonstrate that there was even one circumstance, other than disqualification by the FAA age 60 rule, where the airline had refused to permit down-bidding by a pilot displaced from his or her current job. There is no nondiscriminatory, age-neutral reason for this difference in treatment. Therefore, one must conclude that pilots over age 60 were discriminated against on account of their age. (*Plaintiffs' Brief*, pp. 65–68)

The FAA age 60 rule does not require retirement at age 60; it merely requires that pilots cease to occupy captain or copilot positions at that age. The FAA rule presents no bar to pilots transferring to flight engineer positions at age 60. Although the ADEA does not require that older workers be afforded special working conditions in order to allow them to remain employed, it does require that older workers be granted the same opportunity as younger employees to transfer to other jobs when they are forced to vacate their current positions. Therefore, since age 60 pilots were denied the right accorded to younger employees to transfer to lower-status positions when displaced from their pilot jobs, United violated the ADEA by engaging in disparate treatment on account of age. (*Plaintiffs' Brief*, pp. 70–73)

UNITED'S DEFENSE

Since the plaintiffs' action involved the collectively bargained agreements between United and the Airline Pilots Association (ALPA), United counterclaimed against the ALPA. United claimed that it had the lawful right to require all crew members to retire at age 60. For over 30 years, United, for publicly asserted reasons of safety, had a policy of requiring flight engineers to retire at 60. It asserted a bona fide occupational qualification (BFOQ) defense permitted under the ADEA to all the plaintiffs. As to the *Higman* plaintiffs, it also asserted defenses based on age-neutral terms of the ALPA-United collective bargaining agreement.[20] In the 1950s, United adopted a retirement policy requiring each cockpit member to retire at age 60.

In 1960, the FAA adopted its own rule prohibiting captains and copilots from serving after age 60 because of the inability of medical science to predict declining function on an individual basis. In addition, in 1981, the National Institute of Aging concluded as part of a congressionally mandated inquiry that the FAA rule should not be changed since the decline in pilot functions could not be accurately predicted or measured. Furthermore, United could not predict or detect conditions that result in medical groundings after the annual extensive examination. In the five-year period from 1976 to 1981, United medically grounded 209 flight officers. Only 53 were detected in the annual examination. Stated another way, 146 of the 209 were not discovered. The medical condition developed after the detailed examination given by United Airlines. (*Defense Brief,* pp. 5–9)

The inability of medical science to predict an individual's reaction to, for example, stress, is illustrated in United's attempt to follow FAA exemption policies. The FAA identifies certain illnesses or medical conditions which require grounding. With changed scientific procedures, including sophisticated stress tests, the FAA adopted an exemption practice in which a grounded pilot who had presumably recovered could subject himself or herself to expert professional physical examination to seek reinstatement from the medical grounding. United allowed 20 such pilots who were granted exemptions after the most extensive physical examination available to return to the cockpit. However, many of the test group, far from having recovered, had recurrent serious difficulties resulting in subsequent grounding. In short, United's experience was that the supposed ability to predict, on an individual basis, was invalid. (*Defense Brief,* p. 11.)

Barring Flight Engineers from Working Beyond Age 60 Met the BFOQ Criteria

A BFOQ was established if United's age policy was reasonably related to safety and if, further, the evidence demonstrated that a blanket rule must be used because of the inability to rely on individualized analysis. United contended that the facts of the case and its actions proved that it was so in the present case. As to the duties of the flight engineer, United contended that they were crucial to the safety of the plane. It was important in this respect to look at flight handbooks of various planes. The ''Irregular Procedures'' and ''Emergency Procedures'' portions of these handbooks are significant in this case. The B-747 handbook specifies about 15 emergencies that require the flight engineer to respond appropriately and 50 emergencies where he or she has very specific duties. In the DC-10 handbook, there are about 22 emergency procedures. Every witness on the subject had stated that if the flight engineer was unable to perform his or her duties properly, it could have an adverse impact on safety. This assertion was in direct conflict with the plaintiffs' claim that the flight engineer did not contribute to safety. (*Defense Brief,* p. 21)

United, therefore, contended that its 1950 policy that required all crew members to retire at age 60 was lawful. It was reasonably related to the essential operation of its business. Furthermore, it was impossible or impractical to decide who should retire through individual analysis.

United asserted that its policy met the BFOQ criteria that required a two-step order of proof. First, the rule must be reasonably related to the defendant's business. The essence of United's business is safe transportation. Second, it must be determined that the defendant cannot handle the retirement issue by individual or case-by-case review. Every witness who had been asked to comment on the importance of the flight engineer conceded that the flight engineer performed duties that were necessary to safety. A sampling of National Transportation Safety Board (NTSB) reports on the causes of major accidents also disclosed that the failure to perform flight engineer duties had been responsible for some major accidents.

In addition, the courts in a number of cases have held that flight attendants with limited safety duties, under the BFOQ defense exception in Title VII, may be required if they become pregnant, to take involuntary leaves of absence. If the law treats flight attendants in this manner, surely a B-747 flight engineer who has very specific duties in about 50 emergency situations which, if not performed properly, could lead to disaster, has an adequate legal relationship to safety. Passenger safety is the essence of United's business. Congress has mandated that United must operate its business with the highest possible degree of care. Thus, safe is not sufficient; rather, the safest possible air transportation is the ultimate goal. (*Defense Brief*, pp. 25–30)

Contractual Obligations under the Collective Bargaining Agreement

The application of the age 60 policy was based in part on the fact that all cockpit crew members were pilots under the collective bargaining agreement. The contract provision against down-bidding impacted equally on all crew members regardless of age. The bona fide seniority system established by United's collective bargaining contract was, as a matter of law, a valid defense calling for judgment against the *Higman* plaintiffs. The *Higman* plaintiffs alleged that they retained sufficient seniority to be employed as flight engineers. United denied this, pleading that contract provisions barred plaintiffs' transfer to the flight engineer positions. (*Defense Brief*, pp. 33–37)

Prior to 1978, United's age policy was expressly sanctioned by the ADEA as part of its pension plan. Congress withdrew this exemption. The key issue, therefore, was United's decision in 1978 to continue and reaffirm a medical policy that was established in 1950 before there was an ADEA. The evidence provided by United's medical department was not contradicted at the trial. Among other things, it showed that as of the

end of 1978, over 50% of medical groundings were unanticipated. It would be inconceivable that United, with the finest medical department in the industry, would not detect and remove from flight those hundreds of cases at the time of the examination if techniques for such detection were available. In short, United contended that it could not predict and, therefore, control through individual testing, such unanticipated occurrences. Furthermore, the FAA rule, while limited to two crew members, was based on the inability to predict psychological and physical failure. Thus, there should be a judgment for the defense since there was no evidence to consider contradicting United's strong medical case. (*Defense Brief*, pp. 51–53)

Stated again, in 1978 Congress amended the ADEA to bar the use of retirement plans or seniority systems to require involuntary retirement because of age. However, Congress did not amend the ADEA as it applied to promotion and transfer opportunities affected by terms of a bona fide seniority system. In the absence of United's age 60 policy, the eligibility and bidding rule applicable to all United pilots would not have allowed captains, at age 39 or 69, to transfer to flight engineer positions without extraordinary circumstances not applicable to plaintiffs. In 1978, Congress did not intend to require that employees disqualified from continuing in a position subject to a BFOQ be given statutory right to transfer to positions not subject to a BFOQ. Lack of seniority rights, not age, caused plaintiffs to be denied transfers to flight engineer positions. Whether or not the age 60 policy precluded service by flight engineers after 60, the *Higman* plaintiffs would have been denied transfers to flight engineer positions in observance of the terms of a bona fide seniority system, which is not a subterfuge to evade the purposes of the ADEA. (*Defense Brief*, pp. 67–68)

Furthermore, a court has held (in *United Airlines, Inc.* v. *McMann*, 434 U.S. at 203) that a retirement plan provision established prior to the enactment of the ADEA, and maintained without material changes thereafter, could not be considered a subterfuge to evade the purposes of the ADEA. The seniority system as it existed in the 1965–1966 pilot agreement limited bidding rights in the same manner as subsequent agreements, except for post-1967 modifications, which allowed greater use of length of service. Therefore, plaintiffs were in no worse position under any agreement negotiated after 1967 than they were under the 1965–1966 agreement. The challenged provisions of the seniority system had not been materially modified since the enactment of the ADEA. Therefore, the failure to amend the seniority system could not be deemed to constitute a subterfuge. (*Defense Brief*, pp. 53 and 67) United, therefore, asserted that it had not violated the ADEA by engaging in disparate treatment and that the company's policy was reasonable and not in violation of the ADEA.

LEGAL PROCEEDINGS: OUTCOME OF THE LAWSUIT

On September 29, 1982, the jury in a district court returned a verdict for the plaintiffs. It also found that United's violation of the ADEA was willful. Based on the finding of willfulness, the district court doubled the damages awarded by the jury. In four following decisions in 1983, the district court issued rulings to force compliance with the jury decision by the defendants. On January 6, 1984, United and other defendants appealed to the Seventh Circuit of the United States Court of Appeals (736 F.2d394 [1984]). In its appeal, United claimed that the district court had erroneously instructed the jury in several crucial respects, thereby denying United its right to proper defense. In particular, United argued that the trial court should not have denied the airline a method of establishing its defense of BFOQ to which it was entitled. United also claimed that the trial court erroneously instructed the jury on the role of pretext in evaluating the airline's claims; and that the airline was not liable to judgment, notwithstanding the verdict with respect to the claim of one career second officer who claimed that the officer's retirement was required by the terms of the airline's bona fide retirement plan.

In proceedings that dragged on until August 10, 1984, the Appeals Court reversed the lower court verdict. The Appeals Court agreed with United's contention that the lower court had erred against United in denying its lawful defense. On February 25, 1985, the United States Supreme Court refused to hear a further appeal (No. 84-916; No. 84-958, 470 U.S.).

In the end, the age 60 rule remains in effect, albeit ambiguously. At the same time, general practice allows pilots to downgrade to the flight engineer job (to which the age 60 rule does not apply). In 1985, United Airlines agreed to pay some $11 million in damages to over 100 pilots in the job downgrading issue. Pan Am Airways fought a similar issue in the courts from 1981 to 1988 with essentially the same results.[21]

NOTES

1. Robert Clark, *Reversing the Trend Towards Early Retirement.* Washington, D.C.: American Enterprise Institute, 1981.

2. Alan Halcrow, "Age Old Problem of Discrimination." *Personnel Journal* (April 1985), p. 11.

3. 736 *Federal Reporter*, 2nd Series, p. 394.

4. V. Louviere, "The Fight over Mandatory Retirement: How Old Is Old?" *Nation's Business* (March 1978), pp. 48–54.

5. J. Roger O'Meara, "Retirement." *Across the Board* (January 1977), pp. 4–8.

6. R. N. Butler, "The Relation of Extended

Life to Extended Employment Since the Passage of Social Security in 1935.'' *Health and Society*, 61 (1983), pp. 420–29.

7. Barnet N. Berin, ''From the Penny Express to the Pension Express.'' *Across the Board* (June 1978), pp. 42–47, 50–53.

8. Stanley Yolles, *The Aging Employee*. New York: Human Sciences Press, Inc., 1984; U.S. Government Printing Office, *Laws of 90th Congress, 1st Session*, ''Age Discrimination in Employment Act of 1967,'' (Public Law 90-202; 81 Stat. 602), pp. 658–65.

9. United States House of Representatives, Subcommittee on Aviation of the Commimttee on Public Works and Transportation, *To Eliminate Age Limitations Presently Imposed on Certain Pilots of Aircraft*, Hearings, 96th Congress, 1st Session (July 18–19, 1979). Washington D.C.: U.S. Government Printing Office pp. 5–10.

10. Robert MacDonald, *Mandatory Retirement and the Law*. Washington, D.C.: American Enterprise Institute, 1978.

11. Stephen Cabot, ''Living With the New Amendments to the Age Discrimination in Employment Act.'' *Personnel Administrator*, 31, no. 12 (January 1987), p. 53.

12. Robert H. Faley, Lawrence S. Kleiman, and Mark L. Lengnick-Hall, ''Age Discrimination and Personnel Psychology: A Review and Synthesis of the Legal Literature with Implications for Future Research.'' *Personnel Psychology*, 37 (1984), pp. 329–31.

13. Equal Employment Opportunity Commission, ''Final Interpretations: Age Discrimination in Employment Act.'' *Federal Register*, 46, no. 188, pp. 47724–28.

14. Marc Rosenblum, ''The Role and Influence of Technology on Enforcement of the Age Discrimination in Employment Act of 1967.'' *Aging and Work* (fall 1983), p. 305.

15. Faley, et al., ''Age Discrimination,'' pp. 332–35.

16. Ibid., pp. 335–37.

17. Ibid., pp. 343–45.

18. *Gerry W. Monroe and Lee F. Higman, et al., Plaintiffs-Appellees and Equal Employment Opportunity Commission, Intervening Plaintiff-Appellee v. United Airlines, Inc., and Airline Pilots Association, Defendants-Appellants*, United States Court of Appeals, Seventh Circuit, August 10, 1984, 736 *Federal Reporter*, 2nd Series, p. 394.

19. ''Brief for Appellees Gerry W. Monroe and Lee F. Higman, et al., and the Equal Opportunity Employment Commission,'' submitted to the United States Court of Appeals, Seventh Circuit (October 28, 1983). (Hereafter cited as *Plaintiffs' Brief*.)

20. ''Brief and Appendix for Appellants United Air Lines, Inc., Airline Pilots Associated International,'' submitted to the United States Court of Appeals, Seventh Circuit (April 1984). (Hereafter cited as *Defense Brief*.)

21. Katherine Bishop, ''Pan Am to Pay Retired Pilots in Age Bias Suit.'' *New York Times* (February 4, 1988), p. A18.

UNITED AIRLINES, INC.

American Bar Association's Commission on Legal Problems of the Elderly and The National Council on Aging, Inc. *Age Discrimination in Employment Act: A Symposium Handbook for Lawyers and Personnel Practitioners*. Washington, D.C.: ABA, 1983.

BUCK, T., and B. FITZPATRICK. ''Age Discrimination in Employment: Legal Protection in the United States and in the United Kingdom.'' *Anglo-American Law Review*, 15 (July/Sept. 1986), pp. 192–217.

CHAMPION, W. T., JR. ''The Age/Experience Dilemma and the ADEA.'' *Thurgood Marshall Law Review*, 9 (Fall 1983/Spring 1984), pp. 51–64.

CHRISTENSEN, A. S. ''Are Early Retirement Offers Coercive?'' *New York University Conference on Labor*, 41 (1988), pp. 13.1–22.

EGLIT, H. ''The Age Discrimination in Employment Act's Forgotten Affirmative Defense: The Reasonable Factors Other Than Age Exception.'' *Boston University Law Review*, 66 (March 1986), pp. 155–226.

EGLIT, HOWARD C. *Age Discrimination*. New York: Shepard's and McGraw Hill, 1987, three volumes.

FRIEDMAN, LAWRENCE MEIR. *Your Time Will Come: The Law of Age Discrimination and Mandatory Retirement.* New York: Russell Sage Foundation, 1984.

HATANO, DARYL G. "Employee Rights and Corporate Restrictions: A Balancing of Competing Interests." *California Management Review* (Winter 1981), pp. 5–13.

KALET, JOSEPH E. *Age Discrimination in Employment Law.* Washington, D.C.: Bureau of National Affairs, 1986.

KASS, R. G. "Early Retirement Incentives and the Age Discrimination in Employment Act." *Hofstra Labor Law Journal,* 4 (Fall 1986), pp. 63–109.

KAUFMAN, R. L., and S. SPILERMAN. "The Age Structures of Occupations and Jobs." *American Journal of Sociology.* 87, no. 4 (1982), pp. 827–51.

KENDIG, WILLIAM L. *Age Discrimination in Employment.* New York: American Management Association, 1978.

LAWRENCE, BARBARA S. "New Wrinkles in the Theory of Age: Demography, Norms and Performance Ratings." *Academy of Management Journal,* 31, no. 2 (1988), pp. 309–27.

McMORROW, JUDITH A. "Retirement and Worker Choice: Incentives to Retire and the Age Discrimination in Employment Act." *Boston College Law Review,* 29 (March 1988), pp. 347–90.

"Metz v. Transit Mix. 828 F.2d 1202." *Illinois Bar Journal,* 76 (June 1988), p. 570.

MILONE, F. M. "Age Discrimination: Proving Pretext under the ADEA." *Employee Relations Law Journal,* 13 (Summer 1987), pp. 104–21.

MINKLER, MEREDITH, and CARROLL L. ESTES, eds. *Readings in the Political Economy of Aging.* Farmingdale, N.Y.: Baywood Publishing Company, 1984.

MOORE, TERENCE J. "Individual Rights of Employees within the Corporation." *Corporation Law Review,* 16, no. 1 (Winter 1983), pp. 39–48.

"Protecting at Will Employees against Wrongful Discharge: The Duty to Terminate Only in Good Faith." *Harvard Law Review,* 93 (1980), pp. 1816–44.

"*Seredinski v. Clifton Precision Products Co.,* 776 F.2d 56." *Duquesne Law Review,* 25 (Fall 1986), pp. 171–85.

SCULNICK, MICHAEL W. "Early Retirement Plans and ADEA." *Employment Relations Today,* 14 (Autumn 1987), pp. 203–10.

SCULNICK, MICHAEL W. "The Supreme Court's 1986–1987 Equal Employment Opportunity Decisions: A Review." *Employment Relations Today,* 14 (Autumn 1987), pp. 213–23.

"Title VII and the Age Discrimination in Employment Act: Should Partners be Protected as Employees?" *University of Kansas Law Review,* 36 (Spring 1988), pp. 581–609.

"To Arbitrate or not to Arbitrate? The Protection of Rights under the Age Discrimination in Employment Act: Steck v. Smith Barney, Harris Upham & Co. [661 F. Supp. 543]." *Missouri Journal of Dispute Resolution.* (1988) pp. 199–218.

"TWA v. Thurston [105 S. Ct. 613]: The Balance of Age Disqualification against Age Discrimination." *Wisconsin Bar Bulletin,* 60 (January 1987), p. 37.

United States House of Representatives, Subcommittee on Aviation of the Committee on Public Works and Transportation, Hearings. *To Eliminate Age Limitations Presently Imposed on Certain Pilots of Aircraft.* 96th Congress, 1st Session (July 18–19, 1979). Washington D.C.: U.S. Government Printing Office.

United States Senate, Special Committee on Aging, Hearings. *Working Americans: Equality at Any Age.* 99th Congress, 2nd Session, 1986. Washington D.C.: U.S. Government Printing Office.

"Waiver of Rights under the Age Discrimination in Employment Act of 1987." *Columbia Law Review,* 86 (June 1986), pp. 1067–92.

"Willfulness, Good Faith, and the Quagmire of Liquidated Damages under the Age Discrimination in Employment Act." *Journal of Corporation Law,* 13 (Winter 1988), pp. 573–619.

SEARS, ROEBUCK AND CO. VERSUS EQUAL EMPLOYMENT OPPORTUNITY COMMISSION

Employment discrimination and affirmative action

On January 31, 1986, the U.S. District Court for the Northern District of Illinois Eastern Division dismissed the case against Sears, Roebuck and Co. by ruling that the EEOC failed to prove that the company had discriminated against women in hiring, promotion, or pay in its employment practices.

The Sears case deals with one of the major attempts by the government to create a broad-scale pattern of enforcement of the law. This enforcement would not base itself so much on proving individual discrimination, but on proving general broad patterns of implicit discrimination based on the existence of certain employment categories. The ideal, prior to this case, was that most government attempts at equal employment were on a case-by-case basis. Critics believed that during the early 1970s this approach was not very efficient and productive because individual cases were time-consuming and did not create broad patterns of compli-

ance. The strategy of the EEOC at the time was for the government to initiate a new approach, i.e., to go after major corporations and create settlements that involved large numbers of employees. The *EEOC* v. *AT&T* case, which was settled without litigation, was the last of this kind. This would thereby set national patterns for hiring and employment practices.

BACKGROUND TO THE SEARS CASE

The major struggle which began in 1973 intensified on January 24, 1979, when Sears, Roebuck and Co., the nation's largest retailer, filed an unprecedented class action suit against 10 federal agencies (see Table 1) charging that various federal laws and actions (see Table 2) had contributed to the creation of an "unbalanced civilian work

TABLE 1. Federal Agencies Charged in Sears Suit

Attorney General of the United States
Secretary of Labor
Chairman of Equal Opportunity Employment Commission (EEOC)
Secretary of Commerce
Secretary of Health, Education, and Welfare (HEW)
Secretary of Housing and Urban Development (HUD)
Director of the Office of Federal Contract and Compliances Programs (OFCCP)
Office of Federal Statistical Policy and Standards
Bureau of Census
Federal Agency Council on the 1980 Census

TABLE 2. List of Constitutional Provisions, Statutes, and Executive Orders Cited in Sears Suit

Article I, S1 of the Constitution of the United States
Article I, S2, cl. 3 of the Constitution of the United States
Article II, S1, of the Constitution of the United States
Fifth Amendment of the Constitution of the United States
Section 10 of the Administrative Procedure Act, 5 U.S.C. SS701-706
Equal Pay Act of 1963, 29 U.S.C. S206 (d)
Age Discrimination in Employment Act of 1967, 20 U.S.C. SS623, 633a
Rehabilitation Act of 1973, 29 U.S.C SS791 (b)–(c), 793(a)
Comprehensive Employment and Training Act of 1973, 29 U.S.C. SS848 (f), 983, 991 (a)
Vietnam Era Veterans' Readjustment and Assistance Act of 1974, 38 U.S.C. SS2012(a), 2014, 2021
Title VI, Civil Rights Act of 1966, 42 U.S.C. SS2000d et seq.
Title VII, Civil Rights Act of 1964, 42 U.S.C. SS2000d et seq.
Title VIII, Civil Rights Act of 1968, 42 U .S.C. SS3601 et seq.
Title IX, Education Amendments of 1972, 20 U.S.C. SS1681 et seq.
Housing and Community Development Act of 1974, 42 U.S.C. SS5309(a)
Age Discrimination Act of 1975, 42 U.S.C. SS 6101, 6102
Budget and Accounting Act, 31 U.S.C. S18b
Executive Order No. 11,246, 30 Fed. Reg. 12,319 (1965), reprinted U.S.C. S2000e note, at 1232 (1976) (prohibits discrimination by federal contractors on the basis of race, color, religion, sex, or national origin)
Reorganization Plan No. 1 of 1978, 43 Fed. Reg. 19,807 (1978)

Departments of State, Justice, and Commerce, the Judiciary, and Related Agencies Appropriation Act, 1979, Pub. 95-431, Title V, 92 Stat. 1021 (1978)

force which restricts employment opportunities of American citizens.''[1]

Although the notion of equality for its citizens is embedded in the U.S. Constitution and is one of the cornerstones of U.S. society, the efforts to convert this principle into reality has entailed a very tortuous and often tumultuous history, as witnessed in the American Civil War and subsequent efforts to abolish slavery and its consequences. The first concrete step to convert to a new kind of reality or to conform the law to the new reality of the situation was witnessed in the passage of the Equal Employment Opportunity Act of 1964, commonly known as Title VII. Over a number of years, its scope has been considerably expanded and the strategies for its implication have changed, in general reflecting both the programs of different administrations and also the political climate prevailing at the time.

The most active period of equal employment opportunity was during the Johnson era. During this era, a major number of initiatives were created and some landmark settlements were made. More recently, it has been stated that the Reagan Administration diminished these initiatives and took the position that affirmative action programs are contrary to the law rather than compatible with it.

The Reagan Administration believed that the activity level in Title VII enforcement showed that the major issues had been resolved and discrimination had been outlawed. The practices of fair and equal treatment had been institutionalized and, therefore, it was not necessary to launch broad pattern cases.

A number of cases were filed based on the notion that there were employment categories where the number of employees from different races or sexual categories were disproportionate to the number of employees in the ''relevant'' group. This led to the assumption of discrimination. Most of the cases did not come to trial; like GM and AT & T, all were settled out of court. Therefore, Sears was the first major case where the concept of broad pattern of discrimination was put to a judicial test.

Lengthy investigations of the charges against Sears followed until 1977, when EEOC commissioners, in a 2 to 1 vote, found reasonable cause to believe that the firm had discriminated against women, blacks, and other minorities. The investigation had been based largely on 1973 employment data provided by Sears. The charges were part of an EEOC enforcement and strategy aimed at large employers, seeking to duplicate a job bias settlement with AT&T.

Sears and the government had been in disagreement over EEOC policies for some time prior to the initiation of the case. The company had previously settled two cases with the Labor Department over its alleged violations of the Equal Pay Act, and with the Office of Federal Contract Compliance Programs over its national affirmative action plan. In all these cases, it was found that Sears had not met the requirements of the law. Sears sued to block the release of the 1977 EEOC's finding as well as the disclosure of the company's affirmative action plan and employment data on individual facilities. The EEOC, in responding to the Sears suit, issued a statement stating that the litigation was part of a series of court cases initiated by Sears in an effort to defend its current practices for hiring and firing. The company responded that its affirmative action plan and program was better than anything that EEOC could point to for other companies. Sears also proclaimed that the lawsuit was not a delaying tactic, as some had claimed, and that regardless of the outcome of its suit, the company would continue to provide equal opportunity for all Americans.

During the proceedings of the EEOC case against Sears, it was revealed that the EEOC's acting general counsel at one stage recommended that the Commission prepare the suit primarily as a bargaining strategy with Sears with no intention of filing it in court. It was believed that an out-of-court settlement would be considerably to EEOC's advantage and would significantly enhance EEOC's enforcement efforts. As it turned out, the EEOC was not to follow this advice, with consequences which adversely affected all parties concerned and failed to advance any public interest.

The Sears, Roebuck case was intended to create a settlement that would set broad patterns to be applied to other cases. This was a different approach than handling cases based on individual complaints. It was hoped that this approach would save the government both money and time in implementing its public policy goals. The initial successes in terms of out-of-court settlements at GM and AT&T suggested that this approach had ample merit. However, as can be seen in the case of Sears, this strategy also ran the risk of becoming mired in very expensive and time-consuming litigation if a company decided to challenge EEOC in court. Note that in the case of Sears, it took almost 13 years and countless millions of dollars for the litigation to be concluded.

One of the important assumptions underlying this strategy was that any significant difference between the composition of a company's work force and of the relevant qualified population pool from which such a work force is drawn is evidence of a pattern of discrimination that must be corrected.

The public policy and political motivation behind such a strategic move was to achieve broad gains in employment and upward mobility for various minority groups. The government was also counting on broad public support for such a move and the relative reluctance of major corporations to confront the government where there were serious risks of adverse publicity, regardless of the eventual ending of the case.

This strategy had some serious drawbacks because it was based on certain assumptions about the nature of underlying factual data and its casual relationship with the eventual outcome in employment practice. That the reasoning proved to be somewhat faulty is reflected in the eventual dismissal of the government's case against Sears, Roebuck. However, of even greater importance, this case reflects the complex nature of defining and correcting discriminatory employment practices on the one hand, and creating greater job opportunities for minorities and other disadvantaged groups on the other. The two objectives may not be one and the same thing. Finally, the case should lead us to explore other more proactive ways of ensuring equal employment opportunities for all U.S. citizens.

ISSUES FOR ANALYSIS

The Sears defense against the EEOC charges has been a bone of contention between American business and federal regulatory agencies for a number of years. Notwithstanding the merits of the Sears defense, the case raises important issues of corporate strategy and public policy that merit serious consideration.

1. It is true that public priorities must change with changing social needs. However, there is a clear need for setting priorities when the interests of various groups, protected under different laws, come into conflict and cannot be satisfied simultaneously:
   a. Where should the responsibility lie for setting such priorities, and how can they be established?
   b. What are the options available to business firms when caught between conflicting pressures for compliance of various laws and agency regulations representing different constituencies?

2. In case business firms are forced to set priorities on their own, what standards of performance can be accepted as a measure of good-faith effort?

3. What is the proper use of statistical data in establishing the existence and magnitude of job discrimination? The statistics challenged by Sears are the backbone of many government cases against employers. What other factors should federal agencies and courts take into consideration in weighing the credibility of statistical data?

4. What are some of the elements of Sears strategy and tactics during the period the lawsuit was in progress? To what extent can these strategies and tactics be followed in similar

and different areas of business-government relations or business-social policy issues? What more could Sears have done to achieve even greater success and more expeditious resolution of the case?

FACTS AND CIRCUMSTANCES OF THE CASE

Headquartered in Chicago, Illinois, Sears maintains more than 2,500 facilities in all 50 states, the District of Columbia, and Puerto Rico. It employs approximately 400,000 people and is the nation's second largest employer of women. The suit, entitled *Sears* v. *The Attorney General,* was filed in U.S. District Court in Washington, D.C., on behalf of Sears and all other general merchandise retailers with more than 15 employees. In its suit, Sears pointed out that the laws protecting veterans, the handicapped, and the aged limit the number of jobs and promotions available for women and minorities. Yet, government agencies have in the past decade pressed employers for compliance with employment opportunities laws favoring women and minorities. Sears charged that there existed a conflict among many federal employment laws and that Federal agencies were trying to hold private employers liable for the work force the government itself created. Sears and similarly situated employers, therefore, found it impossible to satisfy the government even if they were committed to equal employment opportunities for all Americans.

In its complaint, Sears strongly defended its hiring and promotion record despite the burdens created by the company's compliance with veterans' laws. According to then chairman and chief executive officer, Edward Telling:

Of our more than 400,000 employees at the end of 1977, 19.9 percent were minorities compared with 8.7 percent in 1965. Minorities represented 10.5 percent of our officials and managers—up from 1.4 percent in 1956. And 36 percent of the officials and managers were women, compared with 20 percent in 1965.

According to the latest information available from the EEOC, the percentage of women at Sears in the officials and managers category is more than double the average of all other employers reporting to the EEOC. This includes 38,000 companies, employing 34 million workers. And with respect to minorities, we lead other reporting companies by more than a third in the officials and manager category.

We believe this demonstrates our commitment to the spirit and letter of the law. We also believe it is time to end government practices which are working at cross purposes, hampering real progress and discouraging voluntary efforts.[2]

Despite this outstanding record, the company found itself embroiled in conflict with the EEOC for years and could not come to an agreement with the agency. Sears stated that it had filed the lawsuit to "cut through the impossible conflicting regulations, to force a clarification of irreconcilables, to help to refocus national goals and achievable means towards these goals." The action taken by the firm was not an impulsive decision, according to company officials, but "came as a culmination of exasperating circumstances experienced" by Sears.[3]

The Sears Complaint

In 1977, following a lengthy investigation initiated in 1973, the EEOC agreed on settlements with American Telephone & Telegraph Company; five other employers (Ford, General Motors, General Electric, the International Brotherhood of Electric Workers, and Sears) were charged with nationwide employment discrimination by the EEOC chairman. Sears sued to block the release of the 1977 EEOC's findings, as well as the disclosure of the company's affirmative

action plan and employment data on individual facilities. They asserted that neither these findings nor the underlying proprietary information could be made public by the EEOC. Sears also asserted that the EEOC had made pledges of confidentiality, which the EEOC denied. Critics wondered what Sears had to hide, since on a comparative basis, the company had "the best" equal employment record in the country. Further, decrying the EEOC charges against the firm, Sears observed that it said "something dreadful" about the future of voluntary efforts if a company with the best, or one of the best, records could be dragged into court and assessed with massive backpay.[4]

According to one federal official, "Sears doesn't want to [release the report] because it contains so much damaging information."[5] EEOC investigators had allegedly found that women and minorities were underrepresented in Sears management and in better-paying sales jobs and largely confined to clerical and part-time sales jobs. Critics also contended that Sears's progress in hiring and promoting minorities and women had been too slow. According to one federal official, "When you've got a work force so predominantly white male, you'll never catch up with a representative work force until sometime in the 21st century at the rate Sears is going."[6] Overall 1,850 discrimination charges had been filed against the company with the EEOC since 1965. This amount represents approximately 200 charges a year, which is a small figure when compared to the large number of employee decisions made by Sears. According to Ray J. Graham, director of Equal Opportunity at Sears, some of the EEOC charges were dismissed by the Commission. In addition, about 50 employment discrimination lawsuits were then pending against the company.

Sears contended that the EEOC charges were unfair because the agency had not taken into account the progress Sears had made or the effects of federal policies on its work force. After informing the company of its findings in 1977, the EEOC was required by law to try to negotiate a settlement out of court. The agency demanded that Sears agree to a large dollar payment, which would be allocated on a proportional basis to all minority and female employees, irrespective of whether or not they had been discriminated against. When no agreement could be reached between thè parties, the EEOC broke off the negotiations on January 16, 1977. Eight days later, Sears filed its suit.

The thrust of the lawsuit was the firm's claim that employers had been denied "the right to comply" with various federal anti-discrimination statutes and policies because of conflicts between these guidelines as well as the confusion existing in their interpretation and enforcement. Sears requested an injunction requiring the coordination of all equal opportunity laws and demanded the issuance of uniform guidelines in order "to resolve the existing conflicts between affirmative action requirements based on race and sex and those based on veterans' status, age and physical or mental handicap."[7]

Conflicting Requirements in Federal Law

The complaint lists a long series of actions by federal agencies that imposed conflicting employment policies on private employers.

Until 1964, the federal government actively supported, by statutes and regulations, the family unit with a single breadwinner. Moreover, the federal government, by setting military and civilian policy and by enacting laws pursuant to those policies, had undertaken to create and to shape the national labor force from which private employers must hire.

After World War II, the United States adopted an affirmative action policy which called for a national effort to integrate returning veterans into civilian life by providing them benefits such as job preferences and subsidized educational opportunity

under the GI Bill of Rights. Congress also enacted statutes that required private employers to reemploy returning World War II veterans. Similar statutes were enacted during the Korean and Vietnam wars.

Sears complied with government policies by hiring veterans. Trained under the GI Bill, these veterans were able to fill managerial and skilled technical positions. About 97% of these veterans were male, and approximately 92% were white. After the Korean conflict and the Vietnam era, Sears again "complied with and exceeded the requirements" of legislation which provided for reemployment of veterans. Although these veterans were almost exclusively males, a greater proportion than before was now black. Of the Vietnam veterans, for example, less than 4% were women, but 20% were black. Of both Korean and Vietnam veterans, a much smaller percentage took advantage of educational benefits offered by the government than after World War II. The impact this group of veterans had on supervisory and management positions at Sears was consequently less dramatic than that of the World War II veterans. As of the filing of the lawsuit, of 31 senior executives, 27 were veterans. Of these, 23 were veterans of World War II.

In 1964, the federal government altered its stand on employment policy by including women and minority members in the group that should be given special consideration. In that year, Title VII of the Civil Rights Act[8] had been enacted, and in the following year President Johnson issued Executive Order No. 11,246[9] prohibiting discrimination in employment on the basis of race, color, religion, sex, or national origin by federal contractors and requiring them to implement affirmative action plans. Sears, as a federal contractor, voluntarily instituted a formal affirmative action program in 1968. As part of this program, the company inaugurated its Mandatory Achievement Goals (MAG) Plan in 1974. This plan requires, among other things, that each Sears unit "hire one underrepresented group member for every white male hired until the presence of the underpresented group in a particular job groupings equals or exceeds its presence in the local trade hiring area.''[10]

The Age Discrimination in Employment Act (ADEA) of 1967 protects people between the ages of 40 and 65 by prohibiting employers from exercising employment judgments on the basis of the age of the applicant or employee. The 1978 amendment to this act extends the coverage to individuals up to age 70 and raises the mandatory retirement age from 65 to 70. In compliance with the ADEA, Sears in 1978 suspended its mandatory retirement policies under which all hourly personnel had to retire at 65 years of age and most salaried personnel at 63 years of age. Before the suspension took effect, Sears had estimated that over a six-year period there would be a loss of 20,000 hourly job opportunities and 3,800 salaried job change opportunities, because in the past each retirement had triggered four hourly and six salaried promotional opportunities. At that time, Sears had estimated that about one-third of its employees would choose to remain beyond their normal retirement age, a figure that was only about half the number of those who actually chose to stay.

Sears claimed that the ADEA amendment considerably slowed its progress in hiring and promoting women and members of minority groups. The company was also disturbed by yet another inconsistency in the EEOC's charge about the dominance of women in the part-time worker pool. Sears contended that the government had consistently encouraged part-time employment. The Equal Pay Act of 1963 allows employers to pay part-time employees on a different basis from full-time employees. In 1978, Congress enacted legislation to encourage flexible work schedules and part-time careers in federal employment situations. In 1977, women comprised approximately 75% of part-time federal government workers. Thus, if the government encourages part-time employment and condones that women fill about three-fourths of these jobs at federal agencies, why should the EEOC object to a similar situation in the retail industry, where women comprise about 77% of the Sears part-time force, a rate that is approximately equal to the national average of women in nonagricultural and salaried part-time jobs?

With regard to the government's failure to provide a diverse work force, Sears charged that the government's "failure, refusal or inability" to enforce antidiscrimination provisions concerning housing, education, training, and employment had exacerbated the inability of qualified members of minority groups and women to gain employment in management and skilled jobs and the inability of minorities to receive the education and training necessary to secure employment. It has also "deprived employers of an available pool of qualified minority and female applicants" and subjected employers "to liability for employment discrimination in spite of their good faith efforts to comply with the federal government's antidiscrimination mandates." (Complaint, Sec. VII Para.56)

Statistics

A core argument underlying Sears's complaint is the government's reliance on statistical sources of information, which Sears claimed are often inadequate and inaccurate. (Complaint, Sec. VII) For example, there is no central source of valid and appropriate statistical data collected and disseminated, or recommended, by the federal government. Statistical data are maintained by diverse federal agencies in diverse ways and in diverse locations. EEOC instructed federal equal employment compliance officers and private employers to use state and local employment and unemployment estimates to measure an employer's compliance with the laws. The National Commission on Employment and Unemployment Statistics and the General Accounting Office (GAO) found that state and local employment and unemployment estimates lack the accuracy of national estimates. EEOC depends on the EEO-1 system of data development, reporting, and collection for use in its educational, litigative, and research work. However, the EEO-1 database was not representative of the private industry civilian force; it was developed without the required participation of public users to ensure maximum usefulness; the published equal employment opportunity reports do not include an appraisal of the accuracy of the statistics; and the EEO-1 reports are not compiled and disseminated promptly.

No statistical data collected and maintained, or recommended, by the federal government could be used by the agencies to make an accurate determination of the relevant labor market for retail sellers of general merchandise. Neither the EEOC nor other federal agencies that use statistics selected by the federal government were able to determine the relevant labor market for retail sellers of general merchandise because appropriate statistics either were not compiled or, if compiled, were inconsistent, inappropriate, inaccurate, obsolete, or otherwise unavailable.

Federal agencies and the courts relied primarily on the sure compliance with equal employment laws. Some of the reasons that made the Bureau of Census's labor statistics inadequate for the determination of an employer's relevant labor market were:

1. Statistics on the time and distance traveled to work, most frequently used mode of transportation, recent turnover and mobility rates, the characteristics of multiple job holders, actual hours and weeks worked, actual earnings base rate, and joint income were necessary to determine an employer's relevant civilian labor sources, but are not collected by the bureau.

2. Bureau of Census tabulations of civilian labor force statistics did not allow for the exclusion of groups within categories, such as government workers, multiple job holders, non-salaried workers, agricultural workers, and the self-employed. These groups could not be included in the determination of the relevant labor market actually available to a retail seller of general merchandise.

3. Tabulations of civilian labor force statistics produced by the Bureau of the Census, including special tabulations, did not contain breakdowns of the civilian labor force by race and Hispanic ethnicity, sex, occupation, industry, etc.

Relief Sought by Sears

Because of the government's conflicting employment rules and regulations, their haphazard administration, and the use of inaccurate statistical data to measure an employer's compliance with these guidelines, the Sears suit sought court orders that would:

1. prohibit the use against employers of any statistical disparities from the civilian labor force traceable to compliance with veterans acts and the Age Discrimination in Employment Act;

2. prohibit enforcement of the 1978 amendment of the Age Discrimination in Employment Act;

3. declare that the EEOC's contention that employment of women in part-time jobs violates Title VII is an incorrect and invalid interpretation of applicable laws;

4. prohibit the use of a statistical approach to show compliance until the government has taken steps to reshape the national work force and has produced adequate statistics;

5. declare that Sears's voluntary Mandatory Achievement of Goals Plan complies with the law;

6. require the defendants to issue uniform guidelines to instruct employers how to resolve existing conflicts between affirmative action requirements based on race and sex

and those based on veteran's status, age, and physical or mental handicap; and

7. bar federal agencies from seeking backpay or other damages from Sears until they have made compliance possible.

THE FEDERAL GOVERNMENT'S RESPONSE

On March 26, 1979, the Justice Department filed a petition for the dismissal of the Sears complaint on grounds of "lack of jurisdiction over subject matter," and Sears's "failure to state a claim upon which relief can be granted."[11] The thrust of the Justice Department's argument was that in the absence of a government's formal charge, Sears had no case against which it sought the protection of the court. Simply put, "the complaint is a political essay, not a lawsuit, and it is nonjusticiable." (*Government's Response*, p. 1)

The federal government argued that the issues raised by Sears, i.e., of the allegedly conflicting requirements of various federal antidiscrimination statutes and regulations, were traditionally the province of the legislature and the executive. Moreover, the relief which Sears sought called on the court to assume continuing regulatory jurisdiction over the national antidiscrimination program. The Constitution (Article III) does not give the court a roving commission to inquire generally into the activities of the two other branches, or to provide government by injunction.

In pursuing its charge of lack of a justiciable claim on the part of Sears, the government charged that Sears was unable to point to a single instance in which the government had taken enforcement action against it for violations of antidiscrimination statutes, or in which Sears had been denied an opportunity to defend itself on grounds of its compliance with other statutes. Sears could not identify a single instance in which the government had used "statistical disparities" in

an enforcement action to prove that Sears had not complied with civil rights acts.

DISMISSAL AND APPEAL

On May 15, 1979, the court issued an order concluding that Sears had failed to present a justiciable case or controversy and that the case must be dismissed. In its order, the court essentially relied on the arguments made by the Justice Department and stated that Sears must recognize that personnel policies reflecting earlier and more limited national attitudes must be modified to widen employment opportunities for all: "To be sure, realization of national policy of genuine equal opportunity for all citizens is a formidable task, but not beyond the notable skill and competence of Sears."[12]

Sears appealed the dismissal of its suit on July 13, 1979. The firm saw its prospects of a court resolution brighten by the Supreme Court's decision in the *Weber* case.[13] This case resolved the legality of voluntary affirmative action programs after Kaiser Aluminum's plan had been challenged in court. Edward R. Telling, then chairman and chief executive officer at Sears, said: "The Weber decision supports our own affirmative action program and should allay the concern of a number of black leaders who feared that our suit would delay affirmative action."[14]

EEOC FILES A COMPLAINT AGAINST SEARS

On October 17, 1979, the EEOC finally filed a series of complaints against Sears charging the company with intentionally engaging in unlawful employment practices in violation of Title VI of the U.S. Civil Rights Act of 1964.[15]

The legal broadside against Sears consisted of a nationwide sex discrimination suit brought in a Chicago federal court and four race discrimination suits brought in federal courts in New York, Atlanta, Memphis, and Montgomery, Alabama. The race bias complaints charged Sears with discriminating against blacks in its hiring practices at seven specific facilities. The New York suit also alleged discrimination against Hispanic Americans. The lawsuits came more than six years after the date when the EEOC had filed a charge with the commission alleging violation of Title VII by Sears.[16]

The major suit against Sears's home office in Chicago, Illinois, dealt with the issue of sex discrimination and charged that:

1. Since at least July 2, 1965, and continuously to date, Sears had intentionally engaged in unlawful employment practices in the Northern District of Illinois and in each and every state of the Continental United States in violation of Section 703 of Title VII 42 U.S.C. SS2000e-2, including, but not limited to, the following:

   Maintenance of recruitment and selection practices, assignment and transfer practices, training and promotion practices, paying women lower wages than are paid to male employees in the same etablishment for equal work, and in general, organizing and conducting its employment practices in a manner that denied female employees employment opportunities, earnings, and on-the-job treatment enjoyed by male applicants and employees.

2. EEOC charged that since at least June 11, 1964, and continuously up until the present time, Sears, an employer having employees subject to the provisions of Section 6 of the FLSA, 29 U.S.C. S206, had willfully violated Sections 6(d) (1) and 15(a) (2) of the FLAA, 29 U.S.C. SS206(d) (1) and 215(a) (2), by discriminating between such employees on the basis of sex in the above mentioned manner.

EEOC requested that the court:

1. Grant a permanent injunction enjoining Sears from engaging in any employment practice which discriminates because of sex in violation of Title VII and FLSA.

2. Order Sears to institute and carry out policies, practices and affirmative action programs which provide equal employment opportunities for females and which eradicate the effects of its past and present unlawful employment practices.

3. Order Sears to make whole those persons adversely affected by the unlawful employment practices described herein, by providing appropriate back pay, with interest, in the amount to be proved at trial and other affirmative relief necessary to eradicate the effects of its unlawful employment practices.

4. Grant such further relief as the Court deems necessary and appropriate.

5. Award the Commission its costs in this action.

USES AND ABUSES OF NEWS MEDIA BY SEARS AND EEOC AND THE REACTION OF THE BUSINESS COMMUNITY

The nature of the issues raised by Sears and the magnitude of their potential impact was so significant that the case attracted considerable national attention. The legal merits of the case notwithstanding, public opinion was likely to play an important role, for the resolution of some of the underlying issues would take place in the political and legislative arena, where the opinion of the public carried considerable weight. It was, therefore, not surprising that both Sears and the EEOC made conscientious use of the news media to cultivate favorable opinion for their respective positions and viewpoints.

To make its case, Sears hired a well-known civil rights attorney, Charles Morgan, Jr., with a record of fighting desegregation cases for over a decade with "a mixture of law, politics and public relations . . . a mixture designed to change the way the government thinks and acts at least as much as it is designed to win a victory in court."[17] The majority view voiced in the news media proclaimed that the filing of the lawsuit by Sears was mainly a preemptive legal and public relations strike to gain the offensive. It was a tactic designed to win sympathy for the firm before the EEOC would file discrimination charges, or "to steal thunder from an anti-Sears suit" by the EEOC.[18] Sears certainly did not drop off the lawsuit quietly at the federal courthouse. Instead, it promoted the action as "loudly as a sale on dishwashers"[19] and billed the suit as a fundamental challenge to big government at news conferences and private press briefings in New York and Washington. Sears publicists distributed over 13,000 press kits to news organizations across the country. The company's president, A. Dean Swift, flew to Washington for briefings, where he announced that his company had filed the suit not only because of its own problems with various federal regulators, but for all corporations and for the country as a whole.

In filing a preemptive suit against the government and doing it with maximum media blitz, Sears was "ignoring a cardinal rule of retailing: "Don't make enemies for that can hurt sales.""[20] According to the *Wall Street Journal,* Sears had already alienated women's groups and their sympathizers—hundreds and thousands of potential customers—but in the eyes of Sears's management there was no evidence of this being true. It was also not surprising that regulators in Washington did not take kindly to the suit. Federal officials viewed it as an effort to get in a roundhouse punch before the EEOC filed its own suit charging Sears with hiring discrimination. There was also skepticism in government circles and even among a few knowledgeable attorneys about the fundamental merits of Sears's claim. A federal official familiar with Sears's hiring practices was quoted in the *Wall Street Journal* as saying: "That suit is as spurious as a $7 bill, and any lawyer who would tell you otherwise is a horse's ass."[21]

When Sears filed its suit, the text of the EEOC 1977 decision was still under court seal. The EEOC by law could not disclose its findings against Sears nor discuss the case publicly until legal action had been taken by the commission against the company. The *Washington Post,* however, reported that shortly after Sears launched its legal attack, EEOC officials hinted that the case against Sears would be one of the most far-reaching job discrimination suits ever. Moreover, the EEOC's case began leaking to the press. Secret documents accused the company of violating job bias law in 69 different ways.[22] Finally, in February 1979, most of the charges against Sears appeared in an article in the *Washington Post.*[23]

Another news leakage by the EEOC occurred in August 1979. The content of an internal memo written by the EEOC acting general counsel, Issie L. Jenkins, found its way to the press. The memo, published by the *Employment Relations Report,* revealed that teams of EEOC lawyers, who in early 1979 had reinvestigated and analyzed the charges against Sears, had found "flaws" and "errors" in the 1977 findings of "reasonable cause." Thus, the case against Sears would be weaker and narrower than had first been assumed. According to this memo, Jenkins recommended that the EEOC prepare the suit with no intention of filing it, and then use it as a bargaining chip to negotiate a settlement with Sears. The memo also noted that an EEOC out-of-court settlement with Sears would provide a more reasonable remedy, based on the EEOC's more complete understanding of the merits of the case, than a court would likely award. This settlement with Sears "would do more to enhance EEOC enforcement efforts than would immediately filing the suit," the Jenkins memo said.[24]

Before the EEOC filed its case against Sears, the commission issued a statement which said that further analysis of the Sears case had revealed additional information which superseded the earlier analysis and prompted the commission to proceed with the filing of the suit. An EEOC source said, however, that there was really no new information and that EEOC chairwoman Eleanor Holmes Norton was merely trying "to keep the dam from breaking and from preempting her commissioners" before the suit was filed.[25] Norton was known to favor quick settlements of cases and to prefer bringing several small suits against a firm's individual facilities rather than a nationwide suit. She seemed to believe that nationwide cases are more dramatic than effective. This may account for the EEOC's action of filing five suits against Sears facilities in various localities. After the EEOC had brought its legal action against Sears, the firm announced that it welcomed the suit. Sears would now have an opportunity for a fair hearing before the courts, something it had not been able to get in six years of dealing with the EEOC staff.

SEARS FILES A MOTION TO DISMISS THE EEOC SUIT

Sears's key argument in its motion to dismiss the EEOC lawsuit[26] was based on the Commission's alleged misconduct in handling the Sears investigation before the agency filed its suit. Sears stated:

> The EEOC engaged in a carefully orchestrated pattern of leaks, disclosures, and other unfair and prejudicial acts designed to undermine Sears' business reputation, to coerce and harass Sears into settlement by attempting to "fuel private lawsuits" and to force Sears to forego its right to have its innocence determined by a court of law. It did this by attempting to create "a carefully cultivated public image" of guilt . . . by publicizing the filing of the charge against Sears in violation of Title VII; by intentionally or negligently allowing the Commission Decision to fall into the hands of the National Organization for Women (NOW) and another women's rights group which had charges pending against Sears (despite the existence of a federal Court order forbidding release) and by allowing portions of the decision to be

published. (*Memorandum to Dismiss*, C.A. 79-C-4373, 3)

The EEOC actions, according to Sears, were not based on a valid charge: They denied Sears due process of law, and did not permit conciliation. The EEOC, therefore, had deprived the court of subject matter jurisdiction or, alternatively, had failed to state a claim on which relief could be granted. Consequently, the suit should be dismissed.

Sears's most important allegation of misconduct by the EEOC, however, arose from the dual positions of David A. Copus as deputy chief and later acting director of the Commission's national programs division, while at the same time being an active member of the board of directors of the NOW Legal Defense and Education Fund (NOW-LDEF). Sears stated: "His name appears on a document entitled 'A Litigation strategy for NOW' with the names of others who were in charge of NOW's anti-Sears campaign."[27] (*Memorandum to Dismiss*, C.A. 79-C-4373, 12)

In its motion to dismiss the case, Sears thus charged that EEOC members' close affiliation with NOW and the leaks to this and other similar organizations led to harassment of Sears, "subjected it to economically and politically motivated punishment," fueled private lawsuits against Sears, and hindered conciliation of individual claims against the firm.

In addition to accusing EEOC of misconduct, Sears claimed that the Equal Pay Act allegations made by the commission should be dismissed, since the issue of equal pay had already been decided in an earlier suit by the government against Sears.[28] The court had denied the government's request for an equal pay injunction on a nationwide basis. Sears concluded that the EEOC had no case against it, and charged EEOC with "having sought to brand Sears and having led outside interests groups to expect a large monetary settlement or a lawsuit." Apparently, the EEOC could not resist the political pressure thus created, even when its acting general counsel's review of the record revealed basic flaws in the case. (*Memorandum to Dismiss*, C.A. 79-C-4373, 21)

Sears Victory in the Court

In Chicago, the location of the major case, Judge Grady denied the motion to dismiss while expressing himself as sharply critical of the EEOC. The trial judge in New York also granted Sears's motion to dismiss, and his judgment in favor of Sears was sustained in the Federal Court of Appeals for the Second Circuit. Judge Freeman in Atlanta also denied the motion in May of 1980, but in the same month Judge Varner in Montgomery, Alabama, granted the motion based on the failure to verify the charges and the EEOC's refusal to engage in a bona fide conciliation issue. The following February in Tennessee, a magistrate also recommended dismissal, finding that there had been no good-faith investigation. All of the cases were eventually dismissed, except for the Chicago case, and all counts of prejudice were cleared. This left the EEOC's case to be resolved in the Chicago courtroom. This was finally resolved on January 31, 1986, following a 10-month protracted trial, when the Federal Court dismissed the EEOC's case against Sears.[29]

It would appear that the government's case was in trouble from the very beginning of the trial. Federal judge John A. Norberg began whittling away at the discovery motions that were filed and pushed the parties to a final statement of the issues. The EEOC tried to postpone the trial by responding late to deadlines and claiming that Sears was being unreasonable in not answering questions.

As this process continued, the EEOC began to dismiss claim after claim, including several so-called suitable individual charges. At the time of the original complaint, the suit involved 42 distinct claims of nationwide sex discrimination by Sears. By the time of the trial, EEOC had abandoned all of its Equal Pay Act claims under Title VII. The two allegations EEOC sought to prove at the trial were that Sears engaged in a nationwide practice of sex discrimination:

1. by saying that female applicants for all selling positions, commission or straight salary, should be deemed to have applied for a commission-selling position and be deemed to be fully qualified for commission-selling whether or not they indicated interest in commission selling.

2. by paying female checklist management employees in certain job categories lower compensation than similarly situated male checklist management employees.

SUMMARY OF THE COURT'S DECISION

Legal Standards Applied to the Case

Two separate legal analyses are applied to this case and Title VII cases in general. These are: disparate treatment and disparate impact, each of which has distinct elements of proof. The EEOC claimed that the choice of a theory was unimportant. Under 703(a) (1) of Title VII, 42 U.S.C. 52000e2(a) (1), the disparate treatment theory, employers are prohibited from treating an employee less favorably than the employee's peers because of an employee's sex, color, religion, or national origin.[30] Here the plaintiff must prove that unlawful discrimination has been the regular policy of the employer, that "discrimination was the company's standard operating procedure and the regular rather than the usual practice." The focus is on the pattern of discriminatory decision making, not on individual employment decisions.

Under the disparate impact theory, the plaintiff must show that a facially neutral standard for hiring excludes a disproportionate number of members of a protected class. The EEOC admitted to not being able to identify any specific employment practice of Sears which was discriminatory to women, but instead contended that there was something subjective in the process at Sears.

The court concluded that disparate impact theory could be applied only when a policy had been identified by the plaintiff. Since the EEOC had admitted to not having identified any specific neutral policy of Sears which disproportionately excused women from the job at issue in this case, the court chose to apply only the disparate treatment theory to this case.

Court's Ruling on the Use of Statistical Data by EEOC

An overwhelming majority of the proof given by the EEOC was statistical in nature, and statistical evidence is an acceptable form of evidence for discrimination. The statistics were analyzed in terms of the level of statistical significance of the results. The primary statistical analyses used by the EEOC were multiple regression analyses; the court critically examined the variables in the model and their ability to measure the variables accurately, the weights of the variables, and the importance of variables not included.

In evaluating the EEOC's evidentiary data, the court carefully analyzed the quality of the data, the type of statistical analyses used, the basic assumptions underlying the use of data and analyses, and the credibility of expert witnesses offered by both EEOC and Sears. The court found the Commission's position deficient and unsustainable on all these grounds.

Evidence and Possible Biases in the EEOC Data on Hiring

One of the most serious flaws in the EEOC's statistical analyses was in the selection of the applicant pool for commission sales jobs at Sears. EEOC's analysis arbitrarily included in its sales applicant pool anyone who checked the sales box and assumed that they were seeking a sales position. The EEOC presented no evidence to support this, and Sears presented evidence to prove it was false.

A second major flaw was the failure to include in its analysis the many important factors that significantly affect hiring. The EEOC chose only six factors: (a) job applied for; (b) age; (c) education; (d) job type experience; (e) product line experience; and (f) commission product expenses. These factors in no way represent the necessary or most important factors. However, other factors were ignored which could be considered quite important in choosing an employee for a particular position, e.g., applicant's interest in sales and in the product to be sold, or characteristics which could be determined only from an interview.

Evidence and Inadequacies in EEOC Data and Variables on Promotion

The EEOC relied exclusively on statistical analyses to prove that Sears discriminated against women in promotions from non-commission to commission sales jobs. The EEOC only performed two analyses: one on the expected proportion of female promotions for each year using each score separately, and one based on the division. Z-scores were calculated for each analysis. This analysis led to highly imprecise and misleading conclusions and evidence that was so flawed that it could not meet the burden of proof.

There were also many coding problems, such as the EEOC failing to code for the amount of prior experience, or for interruptions in work history, or the failure to code other relevant experience on the job application.

Faulty Basic Assumptions

EEOC also made certain specific assumptions about the data-base which, on analysis, turned out to be unsustainable. These assumptions were as follows: (1) All male and female sales applicants were equally likely to accept a job offer for all commission sales positions at Sears; and (2) all male and female sales applicants were equally qualified for commission sales positions at Sears.

The EEOC offered no credible evidence to support these assumptions, whereas Sears proved, with many different kinds of evidence, that men and women tended to have different interests and aspirations regarding work, and the differences partially explained the lower percentage of women in commission sales jobs.

With regard to equal qualifications for men and women, the EEOC's own report, "Commission Sales Report," demonstrated this to be false. This, in addition to other deficiencies, e.g., creating artificial territorial and nationwide applicant pools, left the statistical analyses with no real value. Sears did not perform any of its own analyses, but instead offered other evidence to disprove the EEOC's analyses and to prove that a number of women hired and promoted into commission sales at Sears reflected its affirmative action efforts, not discrimination. Sears presented data on hiring and promotion figures that demonstrated the success of the company's efforts in promoting women.

Judge John A. Norberg stated: "Viewing all of the evidence together, and considering the credibility of the witnesses and the reasonableness of their testimony, the court finds that EEOC has failed to carry its burden of persuasion on the claim of hiring discrimination. Its statistical evidence is wholly inadequate to support its allegations."[31]

The most flagrant flaw in the EEOC's case was its failure to have "one employee or applicant witness" who claimed to be discriminated against. EEOC also did not account for the interests of applicants in commission sales and products sold on commission at Sears. In addition, the EEOC had also failed to counter Sears's highly convincing evidence of its affirmative action programs and failed to have one witness that could claim discrimination. The judge contended that the EEOC failed to prove its case of discrimination in hiring against women and found that Sears had proven that it did not have such a pattern as practice.

In regards to promotion, the court stated:

> The EEOC has failed to prove its claims of a nationwide pattern or practice of intentional discriminations against women in promotions into commission sales at Sears. To the contrary, the court finds that Sears has proven that it did not have any such pattern as practice. Moreover, Sears has proven legitimate, nondiscriminatory reasons for the alleged disparities and the EEOC has not proven them pretextual.[32]

Both Sears, Roebuck and EEOC Appeal the Lower Court Decision

The EEOC appealed the lower court judgment on the disparate treatment claims and its denial of partial summary judgment regarding a provision that had existed in the Sears personnel manual until 1974 allowing a male employee a day off with pay when his wife gave birth.[33] Sears cross-appealed the district court's refusal to dismiss the case on the alleged ground of conflict of interest.

On January 14, 1988, the Appeals Court for the Seventh Circuit decided in favor of Sears, Roebuck by affirming the findings and decision of the lower court. In their judgment, the Court stated that "the performance of EEOC [with regards to all aspects of the case] was disappointing and did a disservice not only to Sears, but also to the public and even to NOW and its causes." The Appeals Court also upheld the lower court's decision with regard to the issues raised in Sears's cross-appeal.[34]

APPENDIX

SUMMARY OF AFFIRMATIVE ACTION PROGRESS AT SEARS, 1965 TO 1977

Title VII of the Civil Rights Act of 1964 became effective July 2, 1965. This appendix reviews the highlights of actions taken by Sears from that date through 1977 in its efforts to comply with this new law. These efforts were undertaken, despite a lack of clear government direction for implementing the Act, because Sears believed that Title VII, as reflected in congressional intent, was sound social and business policy. (Implementing the law became difficult at best because of overlapping and sometimes conflicting guidelines from various enforcement bodies.)

During the mid-1960s, the subject of equal employment was reviewed at numerous Sears board of directors meetings and at many management-level conferences. Even before passage of the Act, Sears took such steps as surveys of minority employment, issuance of guidelines to administrative units on increasing minority employment, and desegregation of lunch and restroom facilities. These early moves, made in anticipation of the impending legislation, helped to position the company for the difficult task that all employers were required to undertake beginning in 1965. In addition, these actions were the basis for what was to become a new dimension of executive responsibility at Sears, as reflected in the significant increases in black employment from 1962 to 1965.

1962		1963		1964		1965	
8,020	3.8%	10,404	4.3%	14,384	5.3%	16,766	5.9%

By late 1967, it became apparent to Sears's officers that the issues raised by rapidly changing and ever-expanding equal opportunity guidelines and judicial pronouncements were becoming so complex that they required the development of staff with special expertise to deal with them. Consequently, in early 1968 a new department of equal opportunity was established in Sears's national personnel department. A director of equal opportunity, reporting to the vice-president of personnel, was appointed. Other important developments followed rapidly:

1. In the spring of 1968, Sears made the voluntary decision to declare itself a government contractor subject to the equal opportunity requirements of Executive Order No. 11,246. For the next 10 years, Sears was the sole retailer of general merchandise in the country to take that action. Despite doing less than 1% of its total sales volume in government business, Sears worked closely with its reviewing agency, the General Services Administration, which conducted approximately 2,000 reviews of Sears's facilities across the country during that time without any serious problems.

2. In the fall of 1968, the company issued to its more than 2,500 individual facilities a "Guide for the Development of an Affirmative Action Program." Follow-up visits were made by territorial executives (Sears operates through five administrative offices called "territories") to provide guidance and assistance in developing affirmative action programs in each unit.

3. To ensure uniformity of procedures and progress, Sears, in the spring of 1970, issued a comprehensive affirmative action manual to every unit, setting up a detailed record keeping procedure and requiring regular reporting of progress to territorial and headquarters officers. The program ensured that women of all races as well as minority men were included.

4. Goals and timetables as required of government contractors were developed for each facility, reflecting the government's estimates of local minority population. The company expressed its goal-setting intent in these words to its managers: Employment, training, and upward mobility of minorities and women at all levels of the Sears work force is a legal requirement as well as a moral obligation assumed by your company. The ultimate goal of Affirmative Action is a balanced work force which accurately reflects the various elements of the society in which each Sears unit is located.

5. Sears was expending significant resources, both in dealing with its internal problems and in sharing its experience with many other employers. Evidence of Sears's commitment to this effort is found in the record of an equal opportunity meeting Sears conducted in June 1971. The two-and-a-half day meeting was called by the president of the company for the purpose of updating the top officials of its major suppliers (about 50 companies represented) on their legal obligations, Sears's program, and Sear's concern that its supplies not be interrupted by compliance failures. This pragmatic approach typifies the company's overall attitude toward the achievement of a balanced work force: This is a matter of business necessity, not simply an effort to improve society; it requires the same attention and effort as other major corporate business goals such as improved sales and profits.

William H. Brown III, chairman of the EEOC, two other commissioners, the general counsel, and 15 to 20 staff members participated actively with Sears in the planning phases and for one full day of the conference. The EEOC's annual report for 1986 while not identifying the employer contained the following acknowledgment of this event:

> An example of the private forum was a model hearing and seminar on Equal Employment Opportunity conducted with one of the nation's largest retailers and top corporate officials of 50 of its major suppliers. Witnesses from the corporation subjected themselves to questions from the Commissioners to show the suppliers the kinds of issues they needed to deal with in testing, recruitment, and upward mobility of women and minority group persons.[35]

From the outset, Sears believed that no amount of commitment, no amount of personnel, and no amount of dollars spent were meaningful without measurable statistical progress toward its goal of a reasonably balanced work force. The following is statistical proof, as reported to the EEOC, of the success of the company's efforts from 1965 to 1973.

	1965		1973	
Black, total	16,766	5.9%	44,293	11.1%
All minorities, total	24,470	8.7%	61,561	15.4%
All minorities, officials and managers	458	1.4%	2,976	6.3%
Women, officials and managers	6,681	20.0%	13,149	27.6%

Because of continuing top management concern, board chairman A. M. Wood convened a meeting in May 1973 of Sears's top 250 officers and senior managers to review progress and problems in the company's affirmative action efforts. This was the first such meeting in 23 years, and it was devoted entirely to the subject of equal employment opportunity. This important event occurred four full months prior to the issuance of the commissioner's charge against Sears by EEOC chairman Brown (similar charges were issued concurrently against GM, Ford, and GE).

Flowing directly from this May 1973 meeting was a new element of Sears's affirmative action program, the Mandatory Achievement of Goals (MAG) Plan, which became effective in early 1974. The following is an excerpt from a 1978 report, *Training and Jobs Programs in Action*, by the Committee for Economic Development, which conducted an independent study of a number of corporate affirmative action programs, including Sears:

> Sears Roebuck is the nation's largest retail employer. Its Affirmative Action (AA) program is unique in the country: it is a *voluntary* compliance program that matches any court-imposed AA plan in its sweeping long-range goals; its mandatory requirements wherever groups are under-represented in its work force; its comprehensive implementation system; and its rapid proportional gains for women and minorities in most job categories in the last few years.

Intended only as a means of bringing lower level management's attention to the seriousness of corporate intent, the use of the term *mandatory* cannot be taken literally. While the basic purpose of MAG is to fill 50% of all job openings where underrepresentation exists with minorities and women, a bypass or relief from this requirement was provided (after careful documentation of good-faith efforts). Such requests must be approved by the territorial office and are granted where clear evidence shows the unavailability of a qualified applicant or incumbent needed to move the facility toward its long-range goals. Requests may also be granted in those instances where, because of obviously superior qualifications such as experience, demonstrated ability, or length of service, an individual representing the majority in a particular job category may be chosen. The effect of MAG has been to accelerate Sears's progress toward its long-range goals, as demonstrated by its progress since the plan's implementation in 1974 (see the following chart). The flexibility of the plan has enabled Sears to keep the intent of its affirmative action program uppermost in its managers' minds while avoiding the charge of a possible illegal fixed quota system.

Beginning with its annual report to shareholders for 1973, Sears (to the best of its knowledge) became the first corporation in the United States to publish its consolidated "EEO-1 report." This disclosure has continued as a way of communicating to employees, shareholders, and the general public the company's equal opportunity progress. For example, Sears's annual report for 1977 devoted a full page to "Progress in Equal Opportunity." The latest (January

	1974		1977	
Blacks, total	46,039	12.0%	59,942	13.9%
All minorities, total	64,092	16.7%	85,658	19.9%
All minorities, officials and managers	3,186	6.9%	5,506	10.5%
Women, officials and managers	13,529	29.4%	18,909	36.0%

1978) EEO-1 information was presented and compared to figures for 1965 (for example, black employment was 5.9% in 1965, 13.9% in 1977; black officials and managers were 0.4% in 1965, 7.2% in 1977; women officials and managers were 20% in 1965, 32% in 1977). The report stated: "While Sears' total employment rose 143,400 or 52% in the last 13 years, its minority employment increased 61,000 or 250%. Today minorities represent 19.9% of all company employees."[36]

Sears believes that underrepresentation of minorities and women is plainly a national problem, permeating all segments of society—government, education, the professions, religion, as well as business. Sears is approaching the problem in a businesslike manner, setting targets to get minorities and women into management positions in as short a period as practicable, maintaining a reporting system that measures progress and identifies strengths and weaknesses—just as the company does in any other important phase of its business. It has informed all its managers that future evaluations, compensations, and promotions will be based on how well these equal opportunity responsibilities and other company objectives are met.

It is precisely because of this businesslike approach that the Sears program is succeeding. An equal commitment by the government is needed for any employer to ac-

complish the full objectives of an affirmative action program.

NOTES

1. Sears, Roebuck and Co., News Release, January 24, 1979.

2. Ibid.

3. Ibid.

4. Lawrence J. Tell, "EEOC's Secret Struggle with Sears." *Business and Society Review* (summer 1979), pp. 29–34.

5. Ibid.

6. Lawrence Ingrassia, "Sears' Suit Challenging Enforcement of Anti-Bias Laws Raises some Key Issues." *Wall Street Journal* (March 7, 1979), p. 38.

7. *Sears, Roebuck and Co., etc.* v. *Attorney General of the United States, et al.*, Civil Action No. 79-244, U.S. District Court, District of Columbia, January 1979.

8. Title VII of the Civil Rights Act of 1964, as amended by the Equal Employment Opportunity Act of 1972, forbids discrimination in employment (including firing, upgrading, salaries, fringe benefits, and other conditions of employment) on the basis of race, color, religion, national origin, or sex. Title VII also established the information-gathering and conciliation agency. The EEOC, however, could not enforce any discrimination provisions until 1972, when Congress gave it the power to bring suits to federal district court when it found a pattern of discrimination within a company or other working establishment.

9. Executive Order 11,246, as amended by 11,375, requires government contractors to take "affirmative action" to ensure equality for women and minorities. The Office of Federal Contract Compliance (OFCC) of the Department of Labor was established to enforce this law. Enforcement was almost impossible, however, until the OFCC introduced Order 4. This required every employer with a government contract worth $50,000 or more to file written affirmative action plans with the agency, listing minority categories to be broken down by "utilization rate." Revised Order 4 includes women in these minor-

ity categories. It requires companies to set specific goals and timetables for hiring and promoting women on all levels of their work forces. If the company fails to comply, the government can revoke contracts with federal agencies.

10. Sears News Release, January 24, 1979.

11. *Sears, Roebuck and Co., etc.* v. *Attorney General of the United States*, Civil Action No. 79-244, motion to dismiss, filed March 26, 1979.

12. *Sears, Roebuck and Co., etc.* v. *Attorney General of the United States*, Civil Action No. 79-244, filed May 15, 1979.

13. *Steelworkers of America AFL-CIO* v. *Bryan F. Weber et al.* U.S. 621 L. Ed. 2d. 99 S. Ct. 2721 (1979). The United Steelworkers of America, the AFL-CIO, and Kaiser Aluminum and Chemical Corporation entered into a master collective bargaining agreement that contained an affirmative action plan designed to eliminate conspicuous racial imbalances in Kaiser's almost exclusive white craft work force. At Kaiser's Gramercy, Louisiana, plant, for example, the craft work force was 39%, black. Black craft hiring goals and on-the-job training programs were established for each plant. At the Gramercy plant, Kaiser selected trainees on the basis of seniority, with the provision that at least 50% of the new trainees would be black until the percentage of black skilled craft workers in the Gramercy plant approximated 39%, the percentage of blacks in the unskilled labor force. During the first year of operation, the most junior black trainee selected had less seniority than several white production workers whose bids for admission to the program were rejected. Weber instituted a class action alleging that the affirmative action program discriminated against him and other similarly situated white employees in violation of Sections 703(a) and 703(d) of Title VII of the Civil Rights Act of 1964.

The Supreme Court held in a 5 to 2 decision, two justices abstaining, that private, voluntary, race-conscious affirmative action plans do not necessarily violate Sections 703(a) and 703(d).

Kaiser's affirmative action plan, designed to eliminate traditional patterns of conspicuous racial segregation in the crafts, was permissible under Title VII since it did not require the discharge of white workers and their replacement with new black employees, did not create an absolute bar to the advancement of white employees, and was only a temporary measure designed to eliminate a manifest racial imbalance. The two dissenting justices contended that Kaiser's racially discriminatory quota was flatly prohibited by Title VII and was sanctioned neither by the act's legislative history nor its "spirit."

14. "News from Sears," July 13, 1979.

15. *Equal Employment Opportunity Commission* v. *Sears, Roebuck and Co.*, Northern District of Illinois, Civil Action No. 79-C-4373; Middle District of Alabama, C.A. No. 79-507-N; Southern District of Georgia C.A. No. C79-1957; Southern District of New York, C.A. No. 79-CIV-5708; and Western District of Tennessee, C.A. No. 79-2695-B, filed October 17, 1979.

16. The original charge filed on August 30, 1979.

17. "Sears' Sweeping Challenge," editorial in *Washington Post* (January 29, 1979), p. A22.

18. "A Sears Suit: Calls for Clarification," *Time* (February 5, 1979), pp. 127, 128. Other articles used in preparing this section include the following: Lawrence J. Tell, "EEOC's Secret Struggle with Sears," *Business and Society Review* (summer 1979), pp. 29–34; "Sears and the EEOC Dig in for a Long War," *Business Week* (February 12, 1979), p. 41; "Sears Roebuck Charges U.S. Action Hurt Firm's Efforts to Hire Women, Minorities," *Wall Street Journal* (January 25, 1979), p. 2; Lawrence Ingrassia, "Sears Suit Challenging U.S. Enforcement of Anti-Bias Laws Raises Some Key Issues." *Wall Street Journal* (March 7, 1979), p. 42; Allan Sloan and John J. Donovan, "The Sears Case of Equal Job Opportunity." *New York Law Journal* (February 5, 1979), pp. 86–87; Edward Cowan, "Sears Loses Its Suit Over Job-Bias Rules." *New York Times* (May 16, 1979), pp. A1, D18.

19. *Wall Street Journal* (March 7, 1979), p. 42.

20. Ibid.

21. Ibid.

22. Jerry Knight, "EEOC Hits Sears with Job-Bias Suits." *Washington Post* (October 23, 1979), pp. E1, E6.

23. "EEOC Report on Sears Job-Bias Practices," *Washington Post* (February 25, 1979), p. A1.

24. "The EEOC May Settle Its Case against Sears," *Business Week* (August 20, 1979), p. 24. For further information on this issue, see "EEOC's Lawyers Cushion Plan to Sue Sears over Job Bias," *Wall Street Journal* (August 3, 1979), p. 21; Keith Richburg, "EEOC Staff Recommends Dropping Suit against Sears." *Washington Post* (August 2, 1979), p. A3; "Job-Bias Agency Decides to Proceed in Sears Suit," *Washington Post* (August 14, 1979), p. A7; "Sears Is Charged in Series in EEOC Suits with Discrimination," *Wall Street Journal* (October 23, 1979), p. 12.

25. *Washington Post* (August 2, 1979), p. A3.

26. *Equal Employment Opportunity Commission* v. *Sears, Roebuck and Co.*, Civil Action No. 79-C-4373, N.D. Illinois, November 1979. Memorandum of Points and Authorities in Support of Defendant's Motion to Dismiss. (This source will hereafter be referred to as *Memorandum to Dismiss*, C.A. 79-C-4373, followed by the appropriate page number.)

27. Another name appearing on the document was that of Whitney Adams, an active member of NOW and a special assistant to the chairman of EEOC.

28. *Usery* v. *Sears, Roebuck and Co.*, 421, F. Supp. 411, supplementing *Brennan* v. *Sears, Roebuck and Co.*, 410 F. Supp. 84 (N.D. Iowa, 1976).

29. The U.S. District Court for the Northern District of Illinois Eastern Division, *EEOC* v. *Sears, Roebuck and Co.*, No. 79-C-4373, Judge John A. Nordberg, Jan. 31, 1986.

30. Ibid.

31. Ibid.

32. Ibid.

33. The motion for partial summary judgment contained four other claims. The EEOC withdrew two of those claims before the court ruled on the motion and decided not to pursue on appeal the court's denial of regarding the two other claims, which involved pregnancy policies.

34. *EEOC* v. *Sears Roebuck and Co.*, 86-1519 and 86-1621, U.S. Court of Appeals, 7th Circuit.

35. EEOC, *Annual Report*, 1986.

36. Sears, Roebuck and Co., *Annual Report*, 1985.

SEARS, ROEBUCK AND CO.

ABRAM, MORRIS B. "Affirmative Action: Fair Shakers and Social Engineers." *Harvard Law Review,* 99 (April 1986), pp. 1312–26.

"Affirmative Action: A Symposium." *Iowa Law Review,* 72 (January 1987), pp. 255–85.

"Applying Disparate Impact Theory to Subjective Employer Selection Procedures." *Loyola of Los Angeles Law Review,* 20 (January 1987), pp. 375–419.

DURVAGE, V. "The OFCCP under the Reagan Administration: Affirmative Action in Retreat." *Labor Law Journal,* 36 (June 1985), pp. 360–68.

DWYER, P. "Affirmative Action: After the Debate, Opportunity [Supreme Court Decision; Santa Clara County v. D. Joyce Case]." *Business Week* (April 13, 1987), p. 37.

DWYER, P. "Clearing the Confusion over Affirmative Action." *Business Week* (July 14, 1986), pp. 26–27.

"Equal Protection II: Affirmative Action Programs in Employment." 1986 *Annual Survey of American Law* (May 1987), pp. 441–68.

FISHER, A. B. "Businessmen Like to Hire by the Numbers." *Fortune* (September 6, 1985), pp. 26–28.

FRIEDMAN, J. W. "Redefining the Equality, Discrimination and Affirmative Action Under Title VII: The Access Principle." *Texas Law Review,* 65 (November 1986), pp. 41–99.

GAMSON, WILLIAM A., and Andre Modigliani. "The Changing Culture of Affirmative Action." *Research in Political Sociology,* 1 (1987), pp. 37–77.

JEFFERSON-PATERSON, EVA. "The Future of Affirmative Action." *California Lawyer* (February 1986), pp. 28–33.

JOST, K. "Precedent, Race and the Court." *California Lawyer,* 9 (January 1989), pp. 47–51.

LEACH, D. E. "Affirmative Action Guidelines: An Appropriate Response." *Labor Law Journal,* 27 (September 1978), pp. 555–61.

LEVINGER, GEORGE, ed. "Black Employment Opportunities: Macro and Micro Perspectives." *Journal of Social Issues,* 43 (spring 1987), pp. 1–132.

"Limiting the Role of Statistical Evidence in Affir-mative Action Cases." *Boston College Law Review,* 27 (December 1985), pp. 168–73.

MORRIS, A. A. "New Light on Racial Affirmative Action." *U.C. Davis Law Review,* 20 (winter 1987), pp. 219–71.

MOSKOWITZ, D. B., and S. W. SETZER. "High Court Backs Racial Quotas." *Engineering News Record,* 218 (March 5, 1987), p. 42.

O'MEARA, J. C. "Whither Affirmative Action?" *Personnel Administration,* 32 (January 1987), pp. 54–55.

PARCEL, TOBY L. *Ascription and Labor Markets: Race and Sex Differences in Earnings.* New York: Academic Press, 1983.

ROBINSON, JAMES C. "Trends in Racial Inequality and Exposure to Work-related Hazards, 1968–1986." *Milbank Quarterly,* 65 (September 2, 1987), pp. 404–20.

ROSENFELD, MICHEL. "Affirmative Action, Justice and Regulation: A Philosophical and Constitutional Appraisal." *Ohio State Law Journal,* 46 (fall 1985), pp. 845–924.

SCULNICK, MICHAEL W. "The Supreme Court's 1986–1987 Equal Employment Opportunity Decisions: A Review." *Employment Relations Today,* 14 (autumn 1987), pp. 213–23.

SELIGMAN, D. "It Was Foreseeable (No Change in Republican Policy of Affirmative Action Quotas)." *Fortune* (July 22, 1985), p. 119.

STEWART, D. O. "The System on Trial: Racism, Discretion and the Will of the Court." *American Bar Association Journal,* 73 (July 1987), p. 38.

SULLIVAN, KATHLEEN M. "Sins of Discrimination: Last Term's Affirmative Action Cases." *Harvard Law Review,* 100 (November 1986), pp. 78–98.

United States Equal Employment Opportunity Commission. *Job Patterns for Minorities and Women in Private Industry.* Washington, D.C.: 1985.

"U.S. Finds for AT&T in Equal Employment Cases." *CPA Journal* (April 1979), pp. 72–73.

VERNON-GERSTENFELD, S., and E. BURKE. "Affirmative Action in Nine Large Companies: A Field Study." *Personnel,* 62 (April 1985), pp. 54–60.

·VI·

Consumer Protection

THE RISE AND FALL OF GM'S X-CAR

*Politicization of the regulatory process:
the role of activist groups and the news media*

On March 8, 1988, a three-judge panel in a federal appeals court ruled that the U.S. government had failed to meet its burden of demonstrating a class-wide defect and other violations of the National Highway Traffic and Motor Vehicle Safety Act, arising out of the alleged defective brakes in the 1980 model X-cars of General Motors Corporation.[1] The United States was appealing the decision of a lower court (April 14, 1987) in an earlier trial in favor of GM.[2] In that case, the National Highway Traffic Safety Administration of the Department of Transportation (NHTSA) had charged, among other things, that GM had manufactured an entire generation of cars, its 1980 X-cars,* that were predisposed to a phenomenon known as ''premature rear wheel lock-up.'' The gov-

ernment further argued that GM either determined or should have determined ''that the rear braking system, for reasons relating to several distinct components of that system, caused premature rear wheel lock-up with consequent loss of vehicle control.'' NHTSA also alleged that during postproduction, GM learned that deterioration of front braking components in service was exacerbating the problem. However, in each such instance, the company failed in its legal duty to notify the Secretary of Transportation and the cars' owners of, and to remedy, the defect. As to the two recalls that GM did conduct in 1981 and 1983, with respect to some 1980 X-cars, the government deemed them to be inadequate. Finally, the U.S. government charged that GM failed to submit accurate and complete information in response to NHTSA's queries in the course of its administrative investigation of the 1980 X-cars. Furthermore, GM violated a NHTSA regulation

*The term X-car has no significance other than as an internal designation assigned by GM to that particular car body.

by omitting NHTSA's hot line telephone number in the recall letters the company sent to X-car owners in the 1981 recall campaign. (*District Court's Decision*, pp. 1–2) These latter two charges were made the subject of a separate trial on GM's request. The U.S. asked for a judgment requiring GM to recall and effectively repair all of its 1.1 million 1980 X-cars. In an unprecedented move, the government also sought $4 million in civil monetary penalties from the company. However, once the court had decided against NHTSA on all other charges, the government agreed to withdraw its complaint on the remaining counts against GM "with prejudice," i.e., the government forfeited its right ever to sue GM again in future on these charges.[3]

This has been a long case and one of the sorrier sagas in the annals of U.S. regulations. It demonstrates the excesses to which a regulatory process can be pushed by political and activist group pressures, to the extent that concerns for consumer safety are subordinated for high-profile victories in the press. It also shows how the news media is often abused by various parties, including government agencies, to create favorable public opinion without regard for accuracy or fair treatment of other parties' positions.

The investigation started before the first X-cars hit the showrooms and continued for more than three years. The trial commenced on March 13, 1984, and continued, with intermittent recesses, until May 16, 1985, with the Court's decision rendered in April 1987. Instead of the six weeks originally allotted, the trial eventually consumed 113 court days. Testimony was received from 33 trial witnesses, including 20 experts. The trial record consisted of 16,000 pages of transcripts and about 3,700 exhibits. This does not include the time allowed for appeals, which would take another year to resolve. The costs to both GM and the government must be counted in tens of millions of dollars, and it is doubtful whether any more lives were saved as a consequence. Both GM and the

government could have spent this money more productively.

GM had won a victory. However, it came too late. By then, the X-car had become a casualty of constant controversy, numerous recalls, and bad publicity. GM discontinued building the X-car in 1985. The X-car was GM's hope of producing an answer to the Japanese competition for a small, fuel-efficient car, designed and built from scratch, with state-of-the-art manufacturing and equipment. When the last car came off the assembly line at GM's Willow Run assembly plant, the company had built a total of 3,314,349 cars. The discontinuance of X-car production caused a layoff of about 5,000 workers. Although sales decline may have been partially due to the normal life cycle of a model and other market factors, the adverse publicity and government lawsuit no doubt played an important part in the demise of the X-car.

ISSUES FOR ANALYSIS

The GM case raises a variety of issues concerning the nature of regulatory processes that are not only relevant to NHTSA but may have more general applicability to the work of other regulatory agencies. They also illuminate the role of political leaders and activist groups in influencing the direction of regulatory processes and, even more importantly, in short-circuiting the regulatory procedures that are designed to ensure an orderly investigation and disposition of consumer complaints. Finally, the case shows the vulnerability of companies, even ones as large as General Motors, to adverse news media publicity regardless of the merits of their position. Some of the questions for analysis are as follows:

1. To what extent is NHTSA's mandate adequate in protecting car owners' and drivers' safety against manufacturing defects? To

what extent and in what direction does NHTSA help or hinder the market-related and other legal (e.g., tort) remedies available to car owners?

2. How adequate and effective are NHTSA's procedures in initiating and conducting investigations? Why did it take NHTSA so long to complete its investigation of GM's X-cars?

3. How would one evaluate the use of voluntary, self-initiated consumer complaints as the basis for launching regulatory investigations? How can these processes be made effective in reflecting more realistically the true magnitude of the problem rather than merely the consumer perception?

4. What are some of the other means, e.g., more timely and accurate information on manufacturing defects, that might make markets more effective in protecting consumer interest by affecting the sales of particular cars or other products?

5. How would one evaluate the role of congressional intervention in the regulatory process? Clearly, any political leader has a right, and an obligation, to air his or her concerns and to seek expeditious resolution of problems that concern his or her constituents and are also in the arena of broad public policy. These concerns, however, can also be manipulated for short-term political gains and thus subvert the regulatory processes that were designed to insulate them from such unwarranted political interventions. How can these two competing tendencies be balanced?

6. How would one evaluate the role of activist groups intervening in the regulatory process? In U.S. society, do these groups have the right and the obligation to represent public interest as they see it? In their zeal to advance a cause, they can overlook the need for substantive evidence and the risk of potential injury to other parties. Is there a need to make these groups more accountable for their actions? If so, what are some of the measures that might be taken in this regard?

7. What was the role of the news media, and journalists in particular, in creating public awareness and fanning public concern in the X-car controversy? Was this role merely informative, or did it go beyond that in the direction of influencing public opinion? It is clear

that adverse news publicity can have severe consequence on the fortunes of a company. Witness the more recent cases of Audi and Suzuki, which were severely injured by news reports of alleged defects, later found to be unsubstantiated.[4] In the X-car case, to what extent did various news media attempt to verify the accuracy of their information before publishing it, and when found incorrect, to report their errors?

8. How would one evaluate the adequacy of GM's testing procedures for car defects, and its responsiveness in warning consumers of potential hazards and in correcting them promptly and satisfactorily? What measures might one suggest in improving these procedures and in making GM more responsive to customer complaints?

9. What measures might be taken to make the regulatory process less confrontational and time-consuming so that consumer interests are protected more efficiently and expeditiously?

GENERAL MOTORS

General Motors Corporation (GM) is the largest manufacturer of automobiles in the world. For the year 1988, GM ranked at the top of the *Fortune* 500 list of largest U.S. industrial corporations. Total sales amounted to $121 billion, with profits of $4.8 billion.[5]

GM's passenger car production in the U.S. includes the Chevrolet, Pontiac, Oldsmobile, Buick, and Cadillac lines. The company also produces products and services in the defense and other nonautomotive sectors, which are marketed through distributors and dealers overseas. For the year 1980, GM's total sales of all products was $57 billion, lower than the 1979 sales of $66 billion, whereas income had dropped to a loss of $762 million from a 1979 profit of $2.9 billion. The market shares have dropped from about 46% of U.S. new car sales in 1980 to about 36% in 1988.[6]

THE BIRTH OF THE X-CAR

The X-car was a long time in the making. The project started in 1973 as GM faced drastically different market conditions for fuel-efficient cars following the first oil crisis. The first action taken by GM was to appoint Robert J. Eaton as the chief of engineering of the X-car project center and responsible for coordinating the resource allocations. In August 1975, Chevrolet Motor Division got the authorization for the engineering design work.[7] In January 1979, James McDonald, executive vice-president of North American Automotive Operations of General Motors, was quoted by *Ward's Auto World* magazine: "There was an absolute dedication that this X-car would have the highest quality of any car we ever brought to market."[8]

The X-car was to be GM's technologically innovative response to the emerging energy crunch. It had an all-new X-body front-wheel drive configuration. Although GM did not have much prior experience with the front-wheel drive technology, especially as coupled with the newer transverse layout, it was, nevertheless, willing to make a frontal attack on the challenge facing it. Thus, X-car got a sophisticated, state-of-the-art computer-designed technology to develop its components. About 200 suppliers and hundreds of plant people were trained so that the assembled car would be perfect. The new trans-axle was to prove itself in a nearly 1 million kilometer (about 600,000 miles) test on roads and tracks. The X-car also led the onset of GM's alphabetic naming of cars.[9]

After four years of research and development and an estimated $3 billion expenditure to build its first small front-wheel drive cars, the X-cars reached the GM dealer showrooms on April 19, 1979. The X-car was well-received; one auto magazine even awarded it the "1980 Car of the Year" honor.[10] Barely two months earlier, in February 1979, the Shah of Iran was ousted, thus precipitating the second energy crisis of the 1970s. Every car customer wanted a fuel-efficient small car, and GM had the hottest, newest, high-mileage car at just the right time. X-car became the crucial new configuration for the Chevrolet, Pontiac, Oldsmobile, and Buick divisions. In 1980, GM announced its estimated corporate fuel average as approximately 23 miles per gallon, which was more than 1981 federal requirements.[11] The car represented a prominent part of GM's product policy. Its different configurations were marketed as Chevrolet Citation, Pontiac Phoenix, Oldsmobile Omega, and Buick Skylark and were promoted as roomier, fuel-efficient alternatives to hot-selling Japanese small cars.

NATIONAL TRAFFIC AND MOTOR VEHICLE SAFETY ACT OF 1966

The National Traffic and Motor Vehicle Safety Act was enacted by Congress in 1966 for the purpose of reducing traffic accidents and deaths and injuries to persons resulting from such accidents.[12] The Act requires automobile manufacturers to notify both NHTSA and vehicle owners when they discover safety-related defects, and then to remedy those defects without charge to the owners. The term *defect* is defined under Section 1391 in a circular manner, as including any defect in performance, construction, components, or materials. A prima facie proof of a defect in a class of vehicles requires only a showing that a "significant number of them have failed in consequence of the defect," a significant number being merely a "non-*de minimis*" quantity; it need not be "a substantial percentage of the total."[13] The manufacturer may assert in its defense, among other things, that the failures resulted from unforeseeable owner abuse or neglect of vehicle maintenance.

Under Section 1411, the government must also show that the manufacturer not only knows of the supposed defect in its vehicles, but that it made a good-faith determination that the defect relates to motor vehicle safety as well. A defect is "related to motor vehicle safety" if it presents an "unreasonable risk of accidents." As in the matter of determining the existence of a vehicle "defect," a "commonsense analysis to be employed is ascertaining what constitutes an unreasonable risk, but, as a general proposition, any defect that involves a loss of control presumptively presents an unreasonable risk of accidents as a matter of law. (*District Court's Decision*, pp. 4–6)

Section 1414 of the Act defines the procedures to remedy the defect by any of the alternative routes of repairing the vehicle, replacing it, or refunding the purchase price less depreciation. The Act gives the secretary of transportation authority to order the manufacturer to take remedial action if the secretary (i.e., NHTSA) determines that certain vehicles contain a defect relating to safety. This order is judicially enforceable. Vehicle manufacturers are required to maintain information, and to produce it on request, in conjunction with an investigation. If an investigation develops evidence of a violation, the secretary may refer the matter to the attorney general, who may bring an enforcement action in a United States district court to recover civil penalties as well as to obtain appropriate injunctive relief.

NHTSA's Defect Investigation Procedures

NHTSA has well-defined procedures to follow during different phases of a safety investigation.[14] They are designed to ensure a systematic and objective analysis of complaints; determination of present and potential defects and the scope of likely public injury; and implementation of remedial measures. At the same time, they are also intended to provide car manufacturers with a reasonable opportunity to respond to complaints and offer contrary evidence refuting the allega-

tions in the complaints, and to propose their own corrective measures. The entire process is designed to protect the consumer, balance competing interests, and ensure due process. Equally important, the regulatory process is designed to insulate it from undue political interference.

NHTSA's defect investigation is carried out by the Office of Defect Investigation (ODI) through its three divisions: defects information systems, engineering analysis, and defects evaluation.

Defects Information Systems Division. This division gathers and organizes all information NHTSA receives relating to possible safety defects in motor vehicles, vehicle equipment, or tires. The information is received in many forms and is the primary source from which NHTSA first learns of possible safety defects. The division operates a toll-free 24-hour auto safety hot line (800-424-9393) which allows consumers to report motor vehicle safety problems or request information on recalls. NHTSA sends a qustionnaire to each consumer who calls the hot line about his or her potential safety defect so that vital information NHTSA needs in its investigations can be recorded.

The division staff initially reviews and sorts all consumer complaint letters and questionnaire forms for trends and then enters those complaints not related to a formal investigation but determined to be safety-related into the division's computerized database. Copies of the complaint letters and questionnaire forms are then sent to the respective manufacturers for their records. NHTSA's computerized database contains other information—such as manufacturers' service bulletins that describe specific repair procedures to be followed by dealers, motor vehicle warranty data, and past defect recall reports—which can also be used to support safety defect investigations.

Engineering Analysis Division. This division reviews numerous consumer complaints and other documents to analyze and identify potentially dangerous safety defects. This is accomplished by two types of evaluations—inquiries and engineering analyses. Such an enquiry or analysis may lead the staff to proceed with an engineering analysis, close the inquiry without additional work, or continue the inquiry to obtain more information on the potential problem.

During this phase, a manufacturer may agree to conduct a recall and thereby resolve the issue and close the investigation. However, if a manufacturer decides not to take any action, a NHTSA panel may decide to open a formal investigation, perform additional engineering analysis work before making a final decision, or close the engineering analysis.

Defects Evaluation Division. This division conducts formal investigations after NHTSA's review panel decides to proceed beyond the engineering analysis phase. ODI also notifies the manufacturer. NHTSA issues a press release to inform the public that it is conducting a formal investigation and to solicit relevant information. This is intended to develop documentary evidence which will bridge the gap between an alleged motor vehicle defect and the official determination that a safety-related defect does or does not exist.

Both the chief counsel of NHTSA and its deputy administrator must approve any course of recommended action. Should NHTSA and the manufacturer find no resolution to the problem, and the manufacturer refuses to conduct a recall, NHTSA can order the manufacturer to do so, and when this is not forthcoming, NHTSA will proceed with a court action against the manufacturer.

NHTSA and Automotive Recalls

There are three types of product recalls pertaining to automobiles. Type I recall includes problems associated with mislabeled or missing placards as well as tire-related troubles. These are classified as minor recalls.

Type II, also called intermediate recalls, include defects such as loosened or missing bolts to major assemblies on the automobiles, and the different windshield wiper-related troubles. Type III, or the major recalls, are for severe magnitude major defects affecting the safety of the vehicle, such as vehicular fire or the loss of steering and braking operations. Other troubles included in Type III are repeated engine stalling and problems which severely affect vehicle driveability.[15]

It would, however, be incorrect to assume that the number of recalls are an indication of poor product quality. A company may voluntarily recall some of its cars simply because it is conscious of its responsibility to the consumer and, therefore, acts in anticipation of potential problems. Voluntary recalls have traditionally constituted about 90% of total automotive recalls. On the other hand, a company may indeed have defective cars on the road and be forced to recall them for corrective action. A number of recalls may also be related to genuine disagreements between the manufacturer and NHTSA about the existence of a potential defect and the appropriate corrective action desired.

The effect of recalls and the number of cars affected varies from manufacturer to manufacturer. For GM, the largest automobile manufacturer, a major recall involves 40,000 to 50,000 cars; for Ford, the corresponding magnitude would be about 20,000 cars; and for Chrysler it would be about 10,000 cars. Between 1967 and 1981, 116 recalls met the aforementioned criteria of major recalls.[16] Table 1 provides data on recalls for major automobile manufacturers.

Automotive Recall Announcement Process

Information regarding automotive recalls is generally given out to people via two public announcements. In the case of voluntary recalls, the process gets into motion when a

TABLE 1. Domestic Vehicle Recalls

	1978	1979	1980	1981	1982	1983	1984	1985	1986	1987
American Motors	749,362 / 8	28,641 / 7	11,369 / 2	85,261 / 9	23,741 / 3	40 / 1	71,938 / 7	211,197 / 6	58,056 / 6	219,513 / 4
American General Corporation	21,123 / 2	6,913 / 2	1,143 / 2	399 / 1	3,227 / 1	2,545 / 1	497 / 1	334 / 1	—	24,627 / 3
Chrysler	1,574,244 / 17	227,572 / 14	2,396,533 / 9	290,046 / 5	77,243 / 8	167,403 / 7	445,760 / 10	328,800 / 4	51,506 / 6	59,573 / 7
Ford	3,608,620 / 37	1,405,146 / 34	1,002,852 / 25	399,099 / 18	274,576 / 20	1,621,979 / 21	2,303,924 / 23	1,165,668 / 18	443,967 / 20	3,909,089 / 16
General Motors	1,739,136 / 20	4,813,313 / 36	320,256 / 15	6,476,445 / 15	938,461 / 15	1,214,915 / 20	3,326,057 / 25	3,105,248 / 27	828,303 / 25	2,757,591 / 32
Total	1,141,342 / 72	6,997,667 / 218	,3,939,035 / 129	7,379,189 / 129	1,401,192 / 107	3,071,321 / 109	6,283,303 / 127	4,995,186 / 137	1,730,657 / 139	729,717 / 150

NOTE: x = total number of cars recalled (upper number)
y = number of times recalls were made (lower number)

SOURCE: A statement prepared from summary tables in NHTSA's "Annual Reports on Safety-Related Recall Campaigns for Motor Vehicles and Motor Vehicle Equipment, Including tires," 1978–1987. Washington, D.C.: U.S. Government Printing Office.

manufacturer discovers a design defect or flaw in the material or workmanship used. The company notifies NHTSA with a recall notification memo describing the identity and number of automobiles involved, the specific reasons behind the recall, the ramifications with respect to safety, and the proposed corrective procedure to alleviate the problem. On receipt of this memo, NHTSA posts it publicly for general reference. Thus, certain special interest groups keep track of such developments for their possible impact on stock prices, etc., and may share the information with their own clientele before others know about it.

Another public announcement regarding the automotive recalls occurs when the manufacturer has been able to organize its dealer network for the proposed remedial actions for the affected consumers. Dealers are notified through technical notices and are supplied with the necessary parts. This may take up to a few weeks. Thus, the manufacturer issues a corporate press release explaining the relevant information to consumers. Media, such as *the Wall Street Journal*, publish these materials on the next business day.

DEVELOPMENT AND TESTING OF THE X-CAR

As noted, GM introduced the 1980 X-car for public sale in April 1979, under the trade names of Chevrolet Citation, Pontiac Phoenix, Oldsmobile Omega, and Buick Skylark. About 1.1 million X-cars were sold during the 1980 model year ending in September 1980. Like all new cars, the X-car went through an extensive period of engineering studies and field testing. Since certain aspects of these testing procedures and their adequacy in relation to the X-car became the subject of controversy of NHTSA complaint, it is important to review the history of X-car engineering studies and field testing.

Formal planning for the 1980 X-car began in 1975. This car was to be GM's first high-volume front-wheel drive automobile with a transversely mounted engine to be sold as a "coordinated car line." Because an X-car model was to be offered by each of GM's four car divisions, its design and development was coordinated through a project center, established in early 1976, to which engineers from both car and component divisions were assigned. The project center was administratively part of GM's corporate engineering staff, but all engineering decisions were ultimately the responsibility of the chief engineers of the several car divisions: Chevrolet, Pontiac, Oldsmobile, and Buick. (*District Court's Decision*, p. 6)

Particular divisions were assigned lead responsibility for the evolution of specific vehicle systems. In the case of brakes, GM brake engineers first selected the generic type of brake components and sized them based on projected vehicle mass. This is standard operating procedure for any GM car program. The procedure started with engineering designs and proceeded to the development of prototype components, laboratory testing, and field testing on similar-sized peer cars (called "component" cars). As development progressed, the evolving system was installed on various preproduction versions of the proposed X-car itself (called successively, "prototype," "pilot," and "lead unit build" cars). Test results were reviewed, and designs were modified to improve performance as the tests indicated. GM at all times contemplated that the 1980 X-car would be equipped with front disc brakes and rear drum brakes, a combination common then and now on both GM and non-GM automobiles. (*District Court's Decision*, pp. 6–7).

Commenting on their field testing procedures, a GM executive stated:

> In the pre-production and pre-announcement period on any car, in the design period, extensive testing is done with cars that are not production cars but are, in various ways, representative, at least for engineering purposes, of what we expect to be manufacturing. Cars were being run on a durability schedule that was itself in the process of being developed.[17]

GM thus developed new ways to test these models. It was decided that rather than develop tests as needs arose, GM would develop tests that would monitor car performance under actual driving conditions. According to a GM executive:

> We selected a group of potential customers at random, and for a nominal compensation, asked them to drive these cars under different driving conditions. Each car was equipped with a black box monitoring device placed in the trunk to monitor the braking of the customer, the system monitored, among other things, the speed at which the brakes were applied, the rate of deceleration, how long the deceleration occurred, etc. Our objective was to develop a test from the driving pattern of the customer, incorporating the most severe driving conditions.[18]

For the X-cars, the comprehensive durability test was identified as R1523, to comprise 100,000 miles and 11 months, from Detroit, over the Rocky Mountains to Arizona, and back via a different route. The route included Alaska, for cold temperature conditioning. GM engineers also developed a modified R1523, with reduced mileage of 57,000, thereby eliminating some areas not requiring extensive use of brakes. This route had 11 different cycles—rural, city, etc.—involving different extents of braking. Having chosen the front disc/rear drum brake design for the X-car, GM brake engineers elected to use semimetallic linings for the disc brakes, believing them to offer superior resistance to fade at the higher brake temperatures they expected to occur at the heavier front end of the vehicle. Organic linings were to be employed on the rear drum brakes on the supposition that they would be less susceptible to environmental degradation. The 1980 X-car was also to be equipped with two fixed-slope proportioning valves in its hydraulic system (one valve per rear wheel) to limit the line pressure going to the rear brakes in moderate to heavy braking. The valves compensate for dynamic force transfer by proportioning rear line hydraulic pressure to incremental front line pressure above a certain "break," or "knee," point which, in the X-car, was set at 350 psi (pounds per square inch). (For example, a 41% fixed-slope proportioner valve allows, in theory, 41% of the amount of the incremental line pressure applied to the front brakes above the break point to reach the rear brakes as well.) In harder brake applications, therefore, more line pressure would be directed to the front brakes relative to the rear to compensate for the dynamic transfer of normal force to the front. (*District Court's Decision*, pp. 8–9)

GM engineers were generally satisfied with the X-car brake system they had settled on. Pilot and lead-unit built cars passed FMVSS-105 certification tests using either the 3198/3199 or the 4035/4050 rear lining combinations, and the system achieved what GM engineers considered to be acceptable ratings on the Pike's Peak schedule for effectiveness, wear temperature behavior, and overall performance. (*District Court's Decision*, p. 12)

During test driving of X-cars, some of the drivers reported rear-wheel lock-up in their "Test Incident Report." Engineers then looked at the cars and found that the linings of the rear wheels were cracked, baked, or burned, and the steel shoes had been glued from excessive heat generation. This created a divisive crisis within GM. Test engineers said that something was wrong with the cars, while the design engineers felt that the test was too severe.

The incidence of wheel lock-up was brought to the attention of a management group gathered in Mesa, Arizona, in December 1978, a month before the actual production of the X-car was to commence. This was an annual meeting to review the driving tests of cars likely to be produced in the coming year. In this meeting, Pete Estes, GM's president, set up a task force to evaluate the X-car situation in detail. The loosely defined task force included 15 to 20 members from various departments involved with different aspects of the braking system. On January 23, 1979, the task force unanimously recommended against a delay in the production of the 1980 X-cars as designed, and to proceed with production on schedule. The task force, however, expressed concern that there could be complaints from drivers who drove very excessively and/or braked extremely hard. Consequently, the task force recommended various design changes to take care of these potential problems.

The prop valve setting was recommended to be changed from 41% to 27% in order to change the brake balance and reduce the amount of braking done by the rear wheel in moderate to heavy braking. The task force also recommended a change in the brake lining in automatic transmission cars from 4035/4050 to 4050/4050. The two numbers correspond to the number of linings in a primary and a secondary shoe. The secondary shoe does the principal amount of work, and the 4050 lining had slightly lower friction than the 4035 lining. The brake drum was recommended to be changed from a smooth drum to a finned drum to facilitate quicker dissipation of the heat generated during braking. The recommended changes were introduced in production during the course of the 1980 model year and at different times depending on the extent of change involved or the availability of new components.

ORIGINS OF THE CONTROVERSY

According to a General Motors spokesman, the controversy started in May 1979 when a 1980 model X-car with green brakes was turned over to an automotive magazine reporter for evaluation before the cars were put on the road. A just-manufactured car requires braking for a few times to get the brakes burnished and to develop a good mating between the drum (for rear brakes) or the rotor (for front brakes). The 1980 model X-cars rolled off the assembly line in mid-January 1979, and the magazine reporters started writing critical articles about the brakes between May and July 1979. GM believed that these articles had some influence on the number of public complaints about rear-wheel lock-up.[19]

Rear-Wheel Lock-Up

The alleged defect was the premature rear-wheel lock-up. Here *lock-up* refers to skidding, when a wheel or wheels slide across the road surface instead of rotating. Wheels typically lock up when the brakes are applied so hard that the braking force at the tire exceeds the frictional adhesion between the tire and the road. Skidding leads to the driver's loss of control, because while the tire is locked up steering is ineffective, and it takes longer for skidding tires to slow down.

Rear-wheel lock-up refers to the situation when the rear wheels lock up before either of the front wheels do. This is also referred as "fishtailing," "spin-out," or "yawing," and may cause a rotation around the car's vertical axis. *Premature lock-up* refers to the car skidding before the driver would ordinarily expect it to in view of the level of braking force applied. This is the crucial issue in the case, as the District Court explained that skidding results from the interaction of the driver, the brake system, and the tire-road surface, and in itself it is not a failure of vehicle performance nor indicative of a brake defect. An ideal braking system should lock up all four wheels simultaneously, which, the District Court observed, "can never be achieved by any brake design throughout the entire range of operating and evading conditions to which a car is subjected." (*District Court's Decision*, p. 29)

NHTSA's own regulation implicitly encourages rear lock-up bias design over the front-wheel lock-up bias design. The United States government stresses that cars stop quickly, that is, a stopping distance over stability as the paramount objective of effective braking.

In November 1979, NHTSA initiated an engineering analysis of the 1980 X-car when compliance testing conducted by NHTSA

raised suspicion that these cars might be predisposed to unanticipated lock-ups of the rear wheels while being braked. By the time the engineering analysis was completed in June 1981, NHTSA had received 212 consumer complaints, 58 of them culminating in accidents. A search of NHTSA's computers revealed 54 additional complaints compared to none for any other front-wheel drive cars, including GM's own 1981 X-cars. (*District Court's Decision*, p. 32)

On July 6, 1981, the ODI director wrote to GM stating that NHTSA believed "the rear brake system of the 1980 X-body vehicles (utilizing the 41% valves and aggressive brake linings) contains an engineering defect which has safety-related implications. . . ." and urged GM to commit itself to "corrective action . . . within five (5) working days." GM immediately agreed to a recall of 47,371 manual transmission X-cars fitted with a 41% proportioning valve to be replaced with a 27% proportioning valve, while not conceding the existence of any defect. (*District Court's Decision*, p. 32)

NHTSA continued its investigation and issued an initial determination in January 1983. NHTSA stated that all 1980 X-cars, manual as well as automatic transmission, with the more aggressive rear-brake linings, were defective. NHTSA also released a film clip of an X-car spinning out of control to the TV networks, which was featured prominently on nightly news broadcasts and was watched by an estimated 53 million viewers. GM, faced with the adverse publicity, promptly agreed to recall all 1980 X-car manual transmission models and some of its automatics.

Between March 1979 and February 1983, GM undertook a total of 10 recalls involving 717,042 cars. Of the 10, the first 8 recalls involving 429,872 cars were voluntary, while the last 2 dated August 5, 1981, and February 18, 1983, were initiated at the direction of NHTSA and involved 287,170 cars (see Table 2).

On March 4, 1983, NHTSA issued GM a

formal administrative subpoena called "Special Order and Documentation Production Request" for production of internal documents relating to premature rear-wheel lock-up. GM responded in three installments between March 25 and 31, 1983. According to NHTSA, the material revealed for the first time that "not only had GM's own test drivers reported 'rear wheel lock-up' incidents on pre-production X-body prototypes more than two years before, but also that GM management had felt compelled to create an unprecedented 'task force' to deal with the very problem NHTSA was investigating." (*District Court's Decision*, pp. 34–35)

Although NHTSA was following its own internal procedures, it decided to abort the administrative proceedings and instead asked the Department of Justice to take legal action against GM. By the time the legal action was filed against GM, NHTSA claimed that it had more than 2,000 consumer complaints of premature wheel lock-up. These complaints included multiple instances of accidents, injuries, and fatalities. Furthermore, where these "incidents were attributable to a vehicle defect, the defect was indisputably safety-related." (*District Court's Decision*, p. 35)

U.S. LAWSUIT AGAINST GENERAL MOTORS

On August 3, 1983, the Justice Department, on behalf of NHTSA, filed a suit against GM and sought that GM would recall and repair its 1.1 million 1980 model X-cars. The U.S. complaint charged that "GM had filed false and misleading responses to its inquiries in at least 18 instances." The suit claimed that GM itself had doubts about the braking system in 1978, but made no changes to avoid the problem. It alleged that GM had received 1,740 complaints about wheel-locking incidents, numerous accidents, 71 injuries, and 15 deaths. The suit further charged that GM had given the government false or misleading information about the X-cars and had failed to tell federal officials and car owners about the defects. The government felt that GM conducted two recalls which it knew would not correct the problem. (*District Court's Decision*, p. 33)

TABLE 2. Recall Campaigns For GM's 1980 X-cars

MANUFACTURER'S NOTIFICATION TO NHTSA	INITIATOR OF RECALL	MAKES AND MODELS	VEHICLES RECALLED	LIKELY PROBLEM
1. March 19, 1979	Voluntary by GM	B, C, O	35	Nonconformity to FMVSS 207 "Anchorage of Seats."
2. April 3, 1979	'	B, C, O. P	4,382	Interference between clutch control cable and brake pipe.
3. April 3, 1979	'	B, C, O, P	4,626	Incorrect position of fuel hoses, interfering with front axle.
4. April 3, 1979	'	C, P	10,751	Longitudinal body bars not properly welded.
5. April 12, 1979	'	B, C, O, P	23,725	Over diameter of front suspension coil spring.
6. September 19, 1979	'	B, C, O, P	224,892	Voids in automatic transmission cooler hoses.
7. September 19, 1979	'	B, C, O, P	161,225	Fatigue cracks on steering gear mounting plate.
8. October 19, 1979	'	B	236	Incorrect turn signal flasher unit installed.
9. August 5, 1981	NHTSA influenced	B, C, O, P	47,371	Rear-brake lock-ups in moderate to hard braking of manual transmission cars.
10. February 18, 1983	NHTSA influenced	B, C, O, P	239,799	All manual transmission and automatic transmission cars produced before mid-March 1979 for lock-up in braking.

B = Buick Skylark; C = Chevrolet Citation; O = Oldsmobile Omega; P = Pontiac Phoenix; FMVSS = Federal Motor Vehicle Safety Standard

SOURCE: GAO Report by the Comptroller General of the United States, GAO/RCED-83-195, August 5, 1983. "Department of Transportation's Investigation of Rear Brake Lockup Problems in 1980 X-body cars should have been more timely." Where these "incidents were attributable to a vehicle defect, the defect was indisputably safety-related." (*District Court's Decision*, p. 35)

According to J. Paul McGrath, assistant attorney general, "this was the first time that the U.S. Government was asking for civil penalties against an auto maker for providing false data to the safety agency during a defect investigation."[20]

William L. Webber, Jr., GM's assistant general counsel in Detroit, responded to the government's 1983 Washington suit with the following statement:

> We are surprised by the unexpected filing of the Justice Department suit. It is especially unwarranted in view of the fact that GM has cooperated extensively with NHTSA to develop the facts which will show clearly that no further recall or corrective action is appropriate. . . . We categorically deny the Government's assertion of misrepresentation. Accordingly, we will vigorously defend the lawsuit.[21]

Elmer W. Johnson, GM vice-president in charge of the public affairs group, said:

> The lawsuit was filed despite our clear understanding with counsel for NHTSA which had been conducting an administrative investigation, that we would be given the opportunity to present our case through cross-examintion of witnesses before that agency.
>
> That opportunity was never provided (to GM). The issue has been taken to the courts by the government. We are confident of the merits of our case, and we will vigorously contest this action in the courts. It would now be inappropriate to debate these issues in another forum.[22]

NEWS MEDIA AND POLITICAL PRESSURES ON NHTSA

On January 5, 1983, Congressman Timothy E. Wirth, chairman of the Subcommittee on Telecommunications, Consumer Protection, and Finance, Committee on Energy and Commerce, asked the U.S. government's general accounting office (GAO) to investigate the National Highway Traffic Safety Administration in connection with possible brake defects in the 1980 General Motors X-body cars. Wirth stated, "I am deeply concerned that NHTSA's delay in determining whether there is a defect or ordering a recall of these vehicles may have grave and serious repercussions for the driving public."[23] Congressman Wirth's concern had been raised because of a news story that appeared in *The New York Times* on the same day with regard to X-car's alleged defects.[24] Congressman Wirth stated that he had recently received reports that NHTSA was unnecessarily delaying resolution of the various issues pertaining to possible brake defects in the X-car and, most importantly, might be covering up the existence of very serious defects.

Wirth asked NHTSA to provide answers to the following questions:

1. If NHTSA had known about the possibility of a defect since 1979, why had the agency taken so long to order a recall of the X-car or, alternatively, to close the defect investigation?

2. What further information was needed in order to reach a conclusion regarding the presence of a safety defect, or lack thereof?

3. Why did NHTSA allow General Motors to recall only a small number of X-cars—those with manual transmissions produced before July 1979—and not recall other 1980 X-cars with both manual and automatic transmissions?

4. In those cars that were recalled, was the remedy chosen adequate or did NHTSA have information which indicated that more should be done to ensure public safety?

In early 1983, NHTSA was also receiving complaints from the Center for Auto Safety, an activist consumer group privately financed and headed by its director, Clarence Ditlow.[25] Ditlow called the NHTSA action "a preemptive strike" and asked "why it had taken NHTSA two years and 15 deaths to act against GM." Ditlow claimed that NHTSA had tried to cover up the full extent of the brake defect "at the expense of the consumer lives."[26] NHTSA administrator Raymond A. Peek, Jr. denied the charge and said that "safety was not a partisan question and it was law enforcement."[27]

The GAO Report

The GAO submitted its report on August 5, 1983.[28] Its main findings included the following:

1. NHTSA did not follow its established procedures for conducting safety defect investigations.
2. Although NHTSA had information that indicated that General Motors' remedy for the braking defect might not be adequate, NHTSA did not formally advise GM of its concern when GM proposed a remedy, aggressively pursue testing affected cars, or initiate an audit of the recall's effectiveness as soon as possible.
3. By delaying or not taking these and related required actions, NHTSA delayed the recall of cars with potential safety defects. Decisions regarding most of these actions were made by a single Safety Administration official, with no apparent review by top agency officials.

The Safety Administration's review of the rear-brake lock-up on X-body cars was conducted in two phases—engineering analysis and formal investigation. GAO found that although NHTSA's goal was to complete the engineering analysis within 6 months, this phase took 19 months, from November 26, 1979, to July 1, 1981.

Essentially, the only action NHTSA took during the first 13 months of the engineering analysis was to send a letter to GM requesting basic information for investigating the brake problem. This letter was sent six months after the engineering analysis began. NHTSA guidelines state that such letters should be sent to the manufacturer within two weeks of starting an engineering analysis.

The formal investigation phase was from July 1981 to January 1983. From July 1981 through October 1982, numerous actions called for under NHTSA guidelines were not taken or were delayed. These included the following:

1. A press release, which is normal practice, was not issued when the formal investigation was opened.
2. The information request letter to the manufacturer was not sent until December 17, 1982, almost 18 months after the formal investigation was opened on July 2, 1981. This letter is usually sent soon after a formal investigation begins.
3. A contract to obtain information from consumers directly affected by the defect problem was not awarded until March 22, 1983, nearly 21 months after the formal investigation was opened. This contract is usually awarded to a private contractor early in the investigation.
4. An audit of GM's August 1981 recall of 47,371 cars to determine, among other things, the adequacy of the remedy to correct the rear-break lock-up problem was delayed about five months from when it was originally proposed.
5. Although NHTSA tested 1980 GM X-body cars in July and November 1981 to identify the conditions under which rear-brake lock-up occurred and the causes of such lock-ups, it did not indicate in the public record until January 1983 that these tests were conducted. Normal practice is to disclose that such tests were conducted soon after their completion.

Congressman Wirth said that the GAO report and his preliminary review showed that "NHTSA breached its obligation to the public as required by law." Wirth observed that it was part of a "pattern of non-enforcement and repeal of safety rules which has characterized NHTSA since 1981," and that "it was a sorry state of affairs and an inexcusable track record for an agency whose primary obligation under the law is to remove dangerous vehicles from our roads."[29] Wirth hoped that the secretary of transportation and a new administrator would return NHTSA to its "congressionally-mandated purpose of protecting the public."[30]

At the same time, Congressman Wirth was receiving information from a staff source in NHTSA. Later, in January 1984, Wirth was reported to have gone over the head of the then NHTSA chief, Diane Steed, to ask Transportation Secretary Elizabeth H. Dole to look into the X-car brake issue personally.[31]

As a result, Robert Helmith, chief of the defects evaluation division at NHTSA, felt that there was considerable congressional pressure on NHTSA. To alleviate the pressure, NHTSA administrator Raymond A. Peek sent a new request in December 1982 to GM for more information and thus escalated the investigation activities.

NHTSA's January 1983 initial determination (ID) was made under the coordination of Peek. The normal procedure in the agency is that recommendation progresses up from the individuals doing the analysis at the working level to the associate administrator of the NHTSA agency, who is then responsible for making the initial determination.

In the case of the X-car, GM felt that there were many clear departures from the set procedure. For instance, as early as June 1982, NHTSA defects engineers had recommended that the X-car case be closed on the grounds that consumer complaints had dropped 75% after GM had voluntarily changed the proportioning valves on 47,000 manual transmission cars. Furthermore, typically the NHTSA chief administrator stays out of a controversy until the final decision-making stage. The chief administrator hears the manufacturer to determine the correctness of the initial determination made by the associate administrator. But, with respect to the X-car, in December 1982 NHTSA chief Raymond A. Peek, Jr. ordered an initial

defect determination as soon as possible just before he faced stiff questioning on the X-car at a congressional hearing.

When GM sought information to investigate the internal process pursued in NHTSA, the government claimed the Deliberative Process Privilege, which is the legal right of a governmental agency to keep its internal processes from being discovered in lawsuits.

In the case of the X-car, at the time of making the initial determination, the public relations office of NHTSA (on January 13, 1983) released a film clip to the television networks showing an X-car spinning out of control. In the film, the X-car was proceeding on a wet surface, and as the driver applied the brakes, the car went through a 270- to 360-degree spin. According to NHTSA, this was clear evidence supporting the government's determination that the X-car had a rear-brake lock-up defect. The film was shown on the nightly newscasts of all three major networks, and it resulted in an immediate avalanche of added complaints to GM and NHTSA.

However, with the film clip, NHTSA did not mention that the driver was told not to steer, and the ground surface was wetted to facilitate skidding. The brakes were mechanically applied and adjusted to induce rear-brake lock-up. The brake linings were also taken from a car that had been cited in a consumer complaint. Despite these intentional adverse conditions, in only 19 out of a total of 189 trials (that is, about 10%) the test drivers were able to get the X-car to skid—a fact that was withheld from the television stations and the viewers.

As a result of the broadcast, GM received an immense amount of complaints and criticism from customers, and management started getting calls from dealers about their continued sales. GM realized that defending itself against the government would take time, and dealers would be forced to bear enormous losses in the market sales.

Since the government had filed the lawsuit against GM, the company decided not to appear and testify at the hearing held by Congressman Timothy E. Wirth's Subcommittee on Telecommunications, Consumer Protection, and Finance, Committee on Energy and Commerce.

NHTSA'S LEGAL ARGUMENTS AGAINST GM

The government built its case against GM primarily on the evidence of X-car consumers and their personal experiences. This evidence took several forms, including: (1) in-court testimony of 12 live-witness consumers who had lost control of their 1980 X-cars while attempting to slow or stop; (2) depositions of absent consumers in which similar incidents were described; (3) unsolicited written complaints sent to the government or directly to GM; (4) statistical analysis of the complaint data establishing a relationship between reported accidents and early wheel lock-ups; and (5) comparisons between complaint rates for X-cars and other cars.

According to the government, the 1980 X-car had been the subject of the largest number of reports of "yaw instability" of any car in NHTSA's history. When the trial began, the number of complaints had exceeded 3,500 and went over 4,000 by the end of February 1985, more than two months before the end of the trial. In contrast, the number of similar complaints about other cars were negligible.

The centerpiece of the government's circumstantial proof-of-defect-by-failure-alone evidence was the testimony of 12 "typical" consumers who appeared at the trial. These consumers were considered representative of the variety of the car owners and driving conditions confronted by the totality of complaints. (*Federal Court Decision*, pp. 37–40)

The government also asserted to have corroborated this evidence with the docu-

mentation that it secured from GM under subpoena. According to the ODI's analysis of the thousands of documents supplied by GM, from the very beginning of the field testing, test drivers had begun to submit reports of rear-brake or rear-wheel lock-ups and that these reports had been circulated throughout the corporation to the considerable consternation of senior management. These reports had led GM to take the unprecedented step of establishing a task force and making a series of design and manufacturing changes in the X-car both during the testing period as well as in various production phases of the car.

As evidence of GM's knowledge of and difficulty with the X-car brakes, NHTSA introduced an internal GM memorandum by a senior vice-president of engineering, which stated, among other things:

> Don't you know that you never lock the rear wheel brakes first?!
>
> How are such product decisions made?
>
> What event caused the division responsible for design to change their minds on this matter?
>
> How could we miss something so obvious?!
>
> How can GM put out such a system?
>
> Engineering staff is not doing its job!

As late as May 7, the same vice-president wrote, "Every time I ask, I am told the X-car brakes are fixed. These tests do not indicate they are. What do we have that does?" (*District Court's Decision*, p. 43)

According to the government's complaint, GM began receiving complaints soon after the X-cars went on sale in April 1979. In 1980, GM began to catalog the complaints according to the various brake component configurations then in service. Its records revealed that X-cars with 27% proportioning valves, 4050/4050 rear linings, and finned drums were generating fewer complaints from the field than any of the other configurations. Yet the company made no effort to do anything about those cars otherwise equipped until its first recall the following year.

This phase of the trial was followed by an extensive submission of engineering data by NHTSA and GM. The District Court considered the vehicle test data "to be most objective, least ambiguous or equivocal, and hence the most convincing evidence adduced" and considered the evidence to be the primary basis for its decision. (*District Court's Decision*, pp. 44–45)

Based on its review, the court concluded that the results of engineering analysis and field tests that were conducted both by NHTSA and General Motors conclusively disproved the existence of any common engineering idiosyncrasy in the braking performance of 1980 X-cars, no matter how configured. (*District Court's Decision*, p. 46) In particular:

1. The percentage of competitive cars found to be rear biased in the "as received" condition, lightly loaded, was not only substantial; it exceeded that of the X-cars.

2. The braking efficiencies of rear-biased competitive cars in customer service were found to be generally lower than the efficiencies of rear biased X-cars, including so-called complaint cars.

3. The brake balance of all X-cars measured in terms of their braking efficiencies fell well within the brake balance envelope established by the extremes of the competitors from the same and later model years.

4. When the design intent brake balance of current configuration X-cars was tested with the brakes rebuilt and burnished, it was revealed to be front biased, even in the lightly loaded condition.

In short, it appeared that it was the unique character of each application of each vehicle's brakes, and a combination of other factors, never to be replicated, that would ultimately determine whether, and to what

extent, a braked vehicle would "yaw." There was simply no engineering evidence of any peculiar property of X-cars in general that would render them in any way exceptional insofar as having a predisposition to "yaw." (*District Court's Decision*, p. 36)

Since NHTSA could not demonstrate that 1980 test X-cars displayed greater degrees of rear bias than competitive cars, or exhibited any particular propensity to rear-brake lock-up, it postulated the existence of worst-case vehicles somewhere in the undiscovered X-car universe by combining the extremes of adverse brake torque measurements made on different X-car tests. "Such projections, however, are not only purely hypothetical, and do not even remotely approach by the measurements actually made on more than 100 X-cars, they were all but disavowed by NHTSA engineers who acknowledged that worst-case projections are essentially speculation rather than a valid engineering analysis." (*District Court's Decision*, pp. 50–51)

GM'S DEFENSE

GM denied that its cars experienced any of the functional failures alleged by the government. It also asserted that neither skidding nor rear-brake lock-up per se constituted a functional failure, since all cars could be expected to lock wheels under some circumstances, and that the X-car had not been shown to have any peculiar propensity to lock up, rear or front, more frequently than cars generally. (*District Court's Decision*, pp. 56–57)

In addition to the engineering analysis and field test data, GM also presented the court with a risk analysis comparing the relative rates of accident involvement of 1980 X-cars with three groups of competitive cars, drawing on accident data from two of NHTSA's own sources and 10 state compilations. Only in the case of safety-related defects did the manufacturer have a duty to notify and repair vehicles under the Act. GM's risk analysis disclosed that, in each database surveyed, 1980 X-cars consistently exhibited a relevant accident rate no worse than, and in most instances better than, the rate for not only peer car groups but also all 1980 models.

It is interesting to note that the government did not present its own risk analysis and instead argued that this data was not significant to the case. It asserted that incidents of rear-brake lock-up were relatively rare and would likely be masked by the vastly greater number of accidents for which "driver error" was responsible. The court, however, concluded that the risk analysis data were consistent with the engineering test data in tending to prove the absence, not the presence, of a safety-related defect in the X-car. (*District Court's Decision*, pp. 52–54)

GM also challenged NHTSA's assertion of large numbers of consumer complaints and accidents related to X-cars. The company asserted that the majority of these complaints had poured in after the release of the film clip showing an X-car spinning out of control.

GM argued that in releasing the film in conjunction with the 1983 preliminary finding of defects, NHTSA had withheld a number of salient features of the demonstrated car: (1) the test driver of the car was instructed not to steer; (2) the brakes were mechanically applied to induce the desired rear-brake lock-up; (3) the road surface was specially coated for slickness of watered down ice; and (4) under the aforementioned conditions, the X-car skidded out of the prescribed lane only 18 out of 179 instances.

The government's position, according to the District Court, could be summarized as follows:

1. a failure of the vehicle simply to perform as expected was a "defect";

2. consumer experiences alone were sufficient to prove performance failure; and

3. the government was not required to come forward with an "engineering explanation" for that failure of performance.

Moreover, according to the government, the comparative performance of peer cars was irrelevant. That a manufacturer had built to the state of the art was not a defense if there were a significant number of failures to perform as expected. The *only* defense, according to the government, was "gross vehicle abuse" by the owner.

DISTRICT COURT'S DECISION

Based on all the evidence, the court concluded that the government had "failed to meet its burden" that X-cars ever presented an "unreasonable risk of accidents due to a 'defect' in the car." The court found that the government had stressed "the anecdotal accounts of consumer's personal experiences," whereas the court looked at the NHTSA's voluminous accident and fatality data showing the front-wheel drive compact X-car to be one of the safest cars on the road.

The court concluded that the government did not establish that the X-car braking system represented an unreasonable risk of accidents and injuries of "significance" in either the severity or frequency. The court rejected the government's allegation of GM's prior knowledge of X-car defects and complicity in withholding this information by stating that the internal documents simply demonstrated that despite continuous efforts, the engineers had failed to find an ideal braking system that would be foolproof under every and all driving conditions. In terms of the recalls, the court also rejected the government's charges that GM had failed to notify X-car owners, as required by regulations, of NHTSA's toll-free auto safety hot line. Instead, the court decided that GM's notification was not required. (*District Court's Decision*, pp. 66–71)

NHTSA LOSES AGAIN ON APPEAL

Dissatisfied with the lower court's decision, the U.S. government filed an appeal before the United States Court of Appeals for the District of Columbia. In its appeal, the government challenged the lower court's verdict on the following grounds:

1. The District Court should not have considered the evidence of consumer complaints in establishing the case of defect as insufficient.
2. The District Court was wrong in relying on the engineering data developed during the litigation in response to claims of defect arising before the litigation.
3. The District Court erred in holding that GM's 1981 and 1983 recalls were adequate.

Evidence of Consumer Complaints

The case of defect was made primarily on consumer complaints with causation established through the unusual nature of complaints and their large number. The Appeals Court sided with the District Court and stated that although consumers may have experienced rear-wheel lock-ups, it could not be established by the evidence alone that they were either premature or were the result of a defect in the car. The Appeals Court cited the District Court's observation that the government must demonstrate that *"failures* had occurred, not merely that consumers had complained." (*Appeals Court Decision,* p. 25)

The Appeals Court also rejected the government's argument about the large number of complaints by indicating that a statistical analysis of complaints showed that these complaints were not large when compared with similar cars, and that a rise in complaints was linked to tremendous adverse publicity generated by NHTSA's film on the X-car test crash. The effects of the adverse publicity were all too obvious. Out of the sampling of complaints that NHTSA ana-

lyzed as consistent with rear-wheel lock-up, 91% alluded to the complainants' awareness of adverse publicity about the X-car. Furthermore, GM and NHTSA received more reports of X-car skidding in the two weeks following the television newscast than in the previous three-and-a-half years combined.

The point, according to the Appeals Court, was not that consumers who complained about the X-car did not in fact experience the events complained of, but that they were led to complain in such *relatively* large numbers because of the adverse publicity surrounding the X-car's brake system. It is important to note that the government's evidence failed to show that the actual incidence of the phenomenon complained of was greater for the X-car than for comparable vehicle classes. (*Appeals Court Decision,* p. 31)

Use of Engineering Analysis Data

The Appeals Court rejected the government's argument against the inapplicability of engineering analysis data developed during the course of litigation. Since the government's case was based on circumstantial evidence of consumer complaints, which were held to be insufficient, it was indeed appropriate for the trial court to consider GM's testing data in rebuttal to the charge that vehicle malfunction was responsible for the incidents described by the consumer complaints. In that respect, GM's evidence tended to show, first, that causes other than vehicle malfunction could (indeed, usually) cause the skidding phenomenon about which consumers complained; and second, through examining the X-car's braking performance in comparison with competitive cars, that the X-car was no more likely than other vehicles to be involved in such incidents. Indeed, it would have been odd for the District Court to have dismissed all this data as irrelevant in assessing the probabilities that the vehicle, rather than other factors, was responsible for the mishaps. (*Appeals Court's Decision*, pp. 32–33)

Inadequacy of Recalls

The Appeals Court also accepted the trial court's decision in concluding that GM's actions as to both 1981 and 1983 recalls were voluntary. According to the Appeals Court, under the regulatory framework established by the National Traffic and Motor Vehicle Safety Act of 1966, GM never incurred an obligation to conduct either recall.

NOTES

1. *United States of America* v. *General Motors Corporation*, U.S. Federal Court, District of Columbia, Civil Action No. 83-2220 (References to this citation in the text appear as the *District Court's Decision* followed by the appropriate page numbers.)

2. *United States of America* v. *General Motors Corporation*, Federal Court, District of Columbia, Civil Action, 656, F. Supp. 1555 (D.D.C. 1987), Dated March 8, 1988. (References to this citation in the text appear as *Appeals Court Decision* followed by the appropriate page numbers.)

3. *United States of America* v. *General Motors Corporation*, Civil Action No. 83-2220, Stipulation and Final Order of Dismissal, U.S. District Court for the Dismissal, U.S. District Court for the District of Columbia, June 14, 1989.

4. See: *Business Week*, "If It Has Wheels and Carries People, Shouldn't It Be Safe?" (June 20, 1988), p. 48; and *Business Week* "Revving Without a Cause: When the Car Has a Mind of Its Own" (April 4, 1988), pp. 66–67. Also see for Audi: News Release by U.S. Department of Transportation, dated March 7, 1989, "NHTSA Announces Results of 'Sudden Acceleration Study'"; and John Tomerlin, "Solved: The Riddle of Unintended Acceleration," *Road & Track*, February 1988. For Suzuki case, see a letter from George L. Parker, Associate Administrator for Enforcement of NHTSA to Samuel H. Cole of Center for Auto Safety, dated September 1, 1988, denying a petition to open a defect investigation and order a recall of the Suzuki Samurai and its variants.

5. "The Fortune 500, Largest U.S. Industrial Corporations," *Fortune* (April 24, 1989), pp. 354–55.

6. Paul Ingrasia and Jacob M. Schlesinger, "GM's Market Share Declines Last Year, Even as Net Set a Mark," *Wall Street Journal* (February 15, 1989), pp. 1, 7.

7. See: *Newsweek*, "Slamming the Brakes on GM's X-car" (January 17, 1983), p. 25 ff.

8. *Ward's Auto World*, January 1979, quoted in an editorial in *Ward's Auto World*, September 1983, p. 6.

9. *Fortune*, "X-Cars Exit. GM Plans to Close the Line" (February 21, 1983), p. 12.

10. John E. Peterson, "Recall Order Denied in GM X-Cars Case; US Claimed Brake Defects." *Business Week*, (April 15, 1987), p. 56 ff.

11. General Motors Corporation, Annual Report, 1980, p. 7.

12. 15 U.S.C. 1381; see generally 1966 U.S. Code Cong. & Admin. News at 2709.

13. *United States* v. *General Motors Corporation*, 518 F 2d. 420, 438 & N. 84 (D.C. Cir. 1975). Cited in District Court's Decision, p. 5.

14. Comptroller General of the United States (GAO), GAO/RCEP-83-195, *Department of Transportation's Investigation of Rear Brake Lockup Problems in 1980 X-Body Cars Should Have Been More Timely.* (Washington, D.C.: GAO, August 5, 1983).

15. George E. Hoffer, Stephen W. Pruitt, and Robert J. Reilly, "Automotive Recalls and Informational Efficiency." *Financial Review*, 22, no. 4 (November 1987), pp. 433–42.

16. George E. Hoffer, Stephen W. Pruitt, and Robert J. Reilly, "116 Recalls Between 1967–1981: The Impact of Product Recalls on the Wealth of Sellers; a Reexamination." *Journal of Political Economy*, 96, no. 3 (1988), p. 664.

17. Interview with the author. Unless other-

wise specifically stated, all direct quotes and paraphrased statements from different people are
based on personal interviews or written communications to the author.

18. Ibid.

19. See also, *Appeals Court's Decision*, p. 6ff.

20. Helen Kahn, "NHTSA Sues GM to
Force 1.1 Million X-car Recall." *Automotive News*
(August 8, 1983), p. 1.

21. Ibid.

22. Ibid.

23. Letter from Congressman Timothy E.
Wirth, chairman, House of Representatives, Subcommittee on Telecommunications, Consumer
Protection, and Finance of the Committee of Energy and Commerce, to Charles A. Borosher,

comptroller general, General Accounting Office,
dated January 5, 1982, p. 3.

24. Ibid.

25. *Newsweek*, "Slamming the Brakes on
GM's X-Cars" (January 17, 1983), p. 18.

26. Kahn, "NHTSA Sues," p. 1.

27. *Newsweek*, "Slamming the Brakes," p. 18.

28. Kahn, "NHTSA Sues," p. 8.

29. Comptroller General, *Investigation*, pp.
18ff.

30. *Automotive News*, "Wirth Wants DOT to
Prove GM Brakes" (January 2, 1984), p. 3.

31. Ibid.

THE RISE AND FALL OF GM'S X-CAR

BURNHAM, S. J. "Remedies Available to the Purchaser of a Defective Used Car." *Montana
Law Review*, 47 (Summer 1986), pp. 273–334.

COBEN, L. E. "Safety on the Road: Evaluating
Crashworthiness." *Trial*, 24 (February 1988),
pp. 18–32.

"Comparative Fault and Products Liability: A
Dangerous Combination." *Missouri Law Review*, 52 (Spring 1987), pp. 445–65.

CONLEY, NED L., and ERIC P. MIRABEL. "The Expanding Personal Liability of Corporate Officers and Directors for Patent Infringement,"
IDEA, 28, no 4 (1988), pp. 225–47.

GOLDBERG, J. "New Mexico's 'Lemon Law': Consumer Protection or Consumer Frustra-
tion?" *New Mexico Law Review*, 16 (Spring
1986), pp. 251–82.

HOWELLS, G. G. "Finding Fault with New Cars."
Solicitors Journal, 131 (May 22, 1987), pp. 682–
84.

"Illinois Lemon Car Buyer's Options in a Breach
of Warranty Action" *J. Mar. Law Review*, 20,
(Spring 1987), pp. 483–508.

KRIZ, MARGARET E. "Liability Lobbying: Borrowing a Page from Consumer Activists, Business Groups Seeking a National Standard
Governing Product Liability Cases are Having Success With Grass-Roots Organizing."

National Journal, 20 (January 23, 1988), pp.
191–93.

"'Lemon Laws' in Ohio Turn Sour for the
Dealer." *Cap. U. Law Review*, 13 (Winter
1984), pp. 611–43.

MCGUIRE, E. Patrick. *The Impact of Product Liability.* New York: The Conference Board, Research Report no. 908, 1988.

NAPOLEON, V. J. "An Annotated Bibliography of
'Lemon' Laws and Other Related Publications." *Journal of Law and Commerce*, 4 (1984),
pp. 517–31.

NAPTHINE, B. "A New Deal for Used Car Buyers." *Law Institute Journal*, 61 (May 1987), pp.
435–36.

NEELY, RICHARD. *The Product Liability Mess: How
Business Can Be Rescued from the Politics of
State Courts.* New York: Free Press, 1988.

"New Jersey's 'Lemon Law,' A Statute Ripe for
Revision: Recent Developments and a Pro-
posal for Reform." *Rutgers Law Journal*, 19
(Fall 1987), pp. 97–129.

"New York's Used-car Lemon Law: An Evaluation." *Buffalo Law Review*, 35 (Fall 1986), pp.
971–1020.

NICKS, S. J. "Lemon Law II." *Wisconsin Bar Bulletin*, 60 (July 1987), pp. 8–11.

NICKS, S. J. "Remedies for Motor Vehicle Purchasers.'' *Wisconsin Bar Bulletin*, 58 (March 1985), pp. 25–26.

PLATT, L. S. ''Lemon Auto Litigation in Illinois.'' *Illinois Bar Journal*, 73 (May 1985), pp. 504–9.

REITZ, C. R. ''What You Should Know about State 'Lemon Laws.' '' *Practicing Lawyer*, 34 (April 1988), pp. 83–89.

''Returning the 'Balance' to Design Defect Litigation in Pennsylvania: A Critique of Azzarello v. Black Brothers Company [391 A.2d 1020 (Pa.)].'' *Dickenson Law Review*, 89 (Fall 1984), pp. 149–74.

RIGG, M. S. ''Lemon Laws.'' *Clearinghouse Review*, 18 (February 1985), pp. 1147–64.

SCHWARTZ, ALAN. ''Proposals for Products Liability Reform: A Theoretical Synthesis.'' *Yale Law Journal*, 97 (February 1988), pp. 350–415.

''A Sour Note: A Look at the Minnesota Lemon Law.'' *Minnesota Law Review*, 68 (April 1984), pp. 846–80.

''Strict Products Liability and the Risk-utility Test for Design Defect: An Economic Analysis.'' *Columbia Law Review*, 84 (December 1984), pp. 2045–67.

THORNTON, G. R. ''A Case History of the 'X' Car.'' *Trial*, 21 (July 1985), pp. 22–34.

United States Senate, Committee on Commerce, Science, and Transportation, Subcommittee on the Consumer. *Product Liability Reform.* Hearing, September 18, 1987 (100th Congress, 1st Session). (S. hearing 100-342)

''Vaughn v. General Motors Corporation [466 N.E 2d 195 (Ill.)]: Limiting Defective Product Tort Loss Recovery.'' *J. Mar. Law Review*, 18 (Winter 1985), pp. 525–39.

WIDDOWS, R. ''Consumer Arbitration as a Dispute Resolution Mechanism in Customer-seller Disputes over Automobile Purchases.'' *Arbitration Journal*, 42 (March 1987), pp. 17–24.

CIGARETTE SMOKING AND PUBLIC HEALTH: PART I

The role of the tobacco industry in the United States

More than 42,000 people die in the United States every year from chronic obstructive lung disease caused by smoking. Heavy smokers are estimated to be 30 times more at risk than nonsmokers.[1] In the early 1980s, cancer-related deaths averaged 350,000 per year (Table 1). Cigarette-related cancer deaths were in the range of 65%, with 85% of lung cancer linked to tobacco (Table 2). Deaths from lung cancer rose from a reported 4,000 in 1935 to some 121,000 in 1984. The Surgeon General's 1982 report identified smoking as the principal cause of lung cancer; the more one smoked the greater was the likelihood of cancer. Furthermore, tobacco was found to work synergistically with alcohol and workplace hazards (such as asbestos) in increasing the likelihood of cancer.[2] According to the U.S. Surgeon General, Dr. C. Everett Koop, "Smoking is responsible for well over 300,000 deaths annually in the United States," more than 30 times all narcotics-related fatalities combined.[3]

Regarding cardiovascular disease, the 1983 Surgeon General's Report estimated that the death rates from coronary heart disease for smokers were 70% higher than for nonsmokers, and that 30% of all coronary heart disease deaths (about 170,000 per year) could be attributed to smoking.[4]

These results also held true for women and were even heightened if women smokers were using birth control pills. Furthermore, studies of maternal and fetal health link smoking to weight reduction, long-term growth prospects, intellectual development, future respiratory diseases, and greater risk of miscarriage and infant death syndrome.[5]

Allegations that tobacco use causes disease are almost as old as use of the plant itself. From 1953 to 1984, some 45,000 studies of the health impact of tobacco were conducted.[6] The results of such studies show a high correlation between tobacco use and a number of heart, lung, fetal, and other diseases. The crux of the debate is whether such correlations establish cause. The health issues involved are cancer, cardiovascular disease, lung disease, maternal and fetal health, and fire danger and burn injuries. The debates rage not only over ordinary full-flavor cigarettes but also over ''safer'' cigarettes with less tar and nicotine and even over passive or environmental smoke.

It is hard to imagine anyone in the United States who is not familiar with the notion that smoking is injurious to one's health. That this awareness has had some effect on public consciousness is undeniable. Increasing numbers of public and private institutions have imposed restrictions on smoking on the premises, encouraging smokers to quit. Nonsmokers have also become more vociferous in their protests

TABLE 1. Estimated Annual Cigarette-Related Deaths in the U.S.

CAUSE	NUMBER
Cancer	130,000
Heart disease	170,000
Chronic lung disease	50,000
Total	350,000

SOURCE: Surgeon General's Reports, 1982, 1983, and 1984

TABLE 2. Estimated Cigarette-Related Cancer Deaths, 1982

TYPE OF CANCER	1982 DEATHS	TOBACCO-RELATED (%)	TOBACCO-RELATED (#)
Lung	111,000	85	94,350
Larynx and oral cavity	13,000	50–70	7,800
Esophagus	8,300	50+	4,150
Bladder and kidney	50,000	30–40	17,500
Pancreas	22,000	30	6,600
Totals	204,300		130,400

SOURCE: U.S. Dept. of Health and Human Services. *The Health Consequences of Smoking: Cancer.* Washington, D.C.: U.S. Government Printing Office, 1982. (Right-hand column calculated using average figures in middle column.)

against smokers among them in order to create a healthy and smoke-free environment.

Notwithstanding, the tobacco industry continues to argue that scientific evidence linking smoking to cancer and other health hazards is inconclusive. The tobacco industry has constantly fought a fierce battle against any restrictions on smoking. In this, they have been helped by the immense profits that cigarette sales generate in the United States. The industry maintains that as long as the product is legal, it has every right to manufacture and sell it. The issue is also presented in terms of freedom of choice: Since adults are aware of the alleged health hazards of smoking, they do so at their own free will and, thereby, absolve the industry of even an indirect responsibility. The latest controversies center around environmental (or passive) smoke and the addictive nature of smoking. The tobacco industry vigorously disputes these allegations. However, passive smoke (inhaling the smoke of others) has also been found by the Surgeon General and other investigators to constitute a health hazard.

The following excerpts from the Tobacco Institute's report, ''Tobacco Smoke and the Nonsmoker: Scientific Integrity at the Crossroads,'' illustrate the point.[7]

Three major scientific conferences have concluded within the last five years that there is no persuasive evidence that cigarette smoke in the air, or environmental tobacco smoke (ETS), poses any significant risk to the health of nonsmokers . . . .

When the weekly newspaper of the American Medical Association reported on scientific testimony presented to a committee of the National Academy of Sciences, and referred to the evidence on the health effects of ETS as ''inconclusive,'' the report was denounced as ''outrageously wrong'' by officials of the heart, lung and cancer associations. As one of the anti-smoking organizations' officials outlined the issue in political —rather than scientific—terms: ''It would be truly unfortunate if the AMA's efforts [in opposition to ETS] were undermined by this report. . . . The continued focus on unfounded claims that tobacco smoke compromises the health of nonsmokers will only intensify the current climate of emotionalism and impede the progress of scientific inquiry.''...

ETS is but one of many potential elements of indoor air. As a matter of scientific fact, exposure to ETS has not been shown to cause lung cancer in nonsmokers. The two most recently published reports on the subject make it clear that the findings are conflicting and inconclusive.

While some regulations on the promotion and smoking of cigarettes have been publicly imposed, they have not unduly hurt the industry. A declining trend among current smokers is balanced by young adults who continuously join the ranks of smokers. Furthermore, the addictive nature of smoking makes smokers insensitive to price increasing, thus allowing tobacco companies to reach ever greater profit margins from unit sales. A far more ominous charge against cigarette smoking was leveled in the 1988 Report of the U.S Surgeon General, which labeled tobacco as an addictive entry-level drug.[8]

The addiction charge has significantly increased the stakes in the controversy. For one thing, if addiction is involved, the freedom of smokers to choose to smoke or not would be severely impaired. For another, it calls for a reassessment of the tobacco industry as a legitimate business and opens the door to an entirely different type of product liability suit.

Notwithstanding the mountainous accumulation of data and research findings, no end is in sight to the controversy. The tobacco industry continues to dispute the research findings, maintaining that (1) research methodology has been flawed and even biased; and (2) statistical correlation does not prove causality.[9]

The battle has clearly moved beyond the scientific community, and many new fronts have been opened, most notably legal liability lawsuits, local ordinances restricting smoking, hostility of nonsmokers resulting in smoking being viewed as an antisocial activity, higher insurance rates for smokers, and activities of public interest groups seeking further regulation of marketing and promotion of cigarettes. Adversaries include private voluntary groups, state and local governments, as well as the formidable departments of the Federal Trade Commission (FTC), the Federal Communications Commission (FCC), and the Surgeon General's Office. These critics are appalled by the industry's steadfast denial of any causal link between cigarette smoking and cancer and other diseases. Says Dr. Alan Blum, editor of the New York Journal of Medicine and founder of ''Doctors Ought to Care'' (an antismoking organization): ''We have more evidence to prove that cigarettes cause cancer and heart disease than we have concerning the cause of virtually any other disease entity.''[10]

Nevertheless, the industry shows no sign of giving up the fight. Strongly represented in Congress, the tobacco producers are aggressive lobbyists against restrictive legislation based on what they term irreponsible and insufficient medical research. In 1958, the cigarette industry formed the Tobacco Institute, which became its primary lobbying arm and provided a single agency to deal with health-related matters. The Tobacco Institute has taken the lead in efforts to limit the power of the Federal Trade Commission to regulate cigarette advertising and to assure that cigarette warning regulations enacted by Congress are acceptable to the industry. It has also consistently asserted that government action has been based on political rather than scientific motives.[11]

While all this negative publicity has sent shock waves through the industry, cigarettes are still a big money maker.[12] Emboldened by fat coffers and unwilling to give up enormous profits generated by cigarette sales, the industry is taking on all challengers. From all indications, the battle is likely to be fierce, and it is not all clear as to what outcomes will emerge.

ISSUES FOR ANALYSIS

1. What are the standards of evidence, both scientific and medical, that must be met in cases involving large-scale serious dangers to public health before a strong case can be made for imposing restrictions on the sale, promotion, and even consumption of a product such as cigarettes? To what extent have these standards been met in the case of cigarette smoking?

2. How should the tobacco industry, in general, and individual companies, in particular, conduct themselves? What posture should businesses outside the industry (e.g., health insurance companies, the media, retailers) adopt?

3. Should there be any self-imposed constraints on promoting certain kinds of cigarettes or promoting them to certain groups, such as teenagers?

4. What role should the government play, and what is the rationale for such a role? Should the government be a mediator? Policy maker and Regulator? Disseminator of information?

5. What are the rights and responsibilities of smokers and nonsmokers in and out of public places or workplaces? Can employers insist that employees not smoke at all—even in private—in the interest of keeping their insurance premiums down?

6. What information about smoking should be available? In what form? Presented by whom? To what audience? To what end? Should certain demographic groups (e.g., teens) receive special attention?

7. What are the rights and duties of producers and antismoking groups to argue their positions? Is it all right to allow antismoking ads while banning advertisements for cigarettes, a legal product?

The Surgeon General's Report of 1964 brought to a head the long dispute between health authorities and the tobacco industry. The antecedents linking smoking to cancer go back to 1900, when statisticians noted an increase in lung cancer associated with smoking. Their data are usually taken as the starting point for studies on the possible relationship of smoking to lung cancer, to diseases of the heart and blood vessels, and to noncancerous diseases of the lower respiratory tract. In contemporary terms, the benchmark study arguing in favor of public regulation of the industry is the Surgeon General's Report of 1964. As a result the public was informed that cigarette smoking is causally related to lung cancer in men and that the magnitude of the effect of cigarette smoking far outweighs all other factors. The report also found that the risk of developing lung cancer increased with the duration of smoking and the number of cigarettes smoked per day, and diminished with discontinuing smoking. According to the report, the risk of developing cancer of the lung for the combined groups of pipe smokers, cigar smokers, and pipe and cigar smokers is greater than for nonsmokers, but much less than for cigarette smokers. In addition, the report stated that cigarette smoking was the greatest cause of chronic bronchitis in the United States and greatly increased the risk of death from that disease and from emphysema. For most Americans, cigarette smoking was a much greater cause of chronic bronchopulmonary disease than atmospheric pollution or occupational exposure. The report also concluded that cigarette smoking was related to cardiovascular diseases.

Subsequent reports have reconfirmed the original findings and added precision to the arguments regarding cancer, cardiovascular, and lung diseases. In addition, more attention has been paid in recent years to issues of maternal and fetal health and the question of tobacco as an addictive drug.[13] The U.S. Department of Health and Human Services publishes hundreds of documents a year. The Surgeon General's reports have a clear policy focus, serving to summarize research and disseminate it to a larger public. They do not so much inform the medical community as provide a basis for public policy initiatives. Such reports appear regularly. During the 1980s, they have taken a thematic approach: women (1980), the changing cigarette (1981), cancer (1982), cardiovascular disease (1983), lung disease (1984), passive smoke (1986), and addiction (1988).

FEDERAL GOVERNMENT ACTION

Following the Surgeon General's 1964 Report, there was tremendous pressure on Congress for action. Issues of primary concern included (1) warning labels, (2) advertising, (3) the "equal time" provision, and (4) selective bans on smoking.

Health Warnings

The first official government reaction came from the FTC, when it announced on January 18, 1964, that it was scheduling hearings for March 16.[14] Following these hearings, the FTC announced proposed trade regulation rules to require a warning on cigarette packages and advertisements, the actual wording to be left to the manufacturers. FTC chairman Paul Rand Dixon notified the House of the Commission's decision and said that the labeling requirement would become effective January 1, 1965. There was so much opposition from the tobacco industry, however, that chairman Dixon postponed the labeling requirement to July 1, 1965, so that the Eighty-ninth Congress, which convened on January 4, 1965, would have time to examine the proposal. The FTC also dropped its regulation on two other ad directives regarding claims of good health and statements that one brand may be less harmful than another.

As the debate ensued, three sets of arguments came to dominate discourse: economics, the free market, and health and human habits.[15]

The FTC's position was initially set forth in the congressional hearings of 1964. Chairman Paul Dixon contended that the Commission had authority to regulate cigarette advertising under Section 5 of the Federal Trade Commission Act, which authorizes the commission "to proceed against any actual or potential deception in sale, or offering for sale, of any product in commerce. . . . Such deception may result either from a direct statement concerning a product or a failure to disclose any material fact relating to such a product." Dixon stated that "the Commission had completed its consideration of the record in this proceeding and has determined that the public interest required the promulgation of a trade regulation rule for the prevention of unfair or deceptive advertising or labeling of cigarettes in relation to the health hazards of smoking." The chairman, however, was more anxious that Congress take the initiative in such a politically sensitive and explosive area.

At the hearings, the industry's position was presented by Bowman Gray, chairman of the board of directors of R. J. Reynolds Tobacco Company, Winston-Salem, North Carolina. The industry opposed the FTC regulations regarding labeling and advertising for three reasons: (1) The FTC did not have the authority to issue such a trade regulation and the Commission, therefore, acted unlawfully; (2) the matter was of such importance that it should be resolved by Congress and not by an agency: "the Commission's rule would not have preemptive effect, and the industry would be exposed to the possibility of diverse State and municipal laws"; and (3) "We oppose it because we believe the Commission's warning requirement is unwise, unwarranted and is not a fair factual statement of the present state of scientific knowledge."

Should Congress consider that a warning label was absolutely necessary, Gray emphasized the following points:

1. Any such legislation should make it absolutely clear that the congressional statute pre-

empted the field. If there was to be a caution notice, it should be uniform and nationwide in scope.

2. The required caution notice should be fair and factual. It should be phrased in a way that reflected the lack of scientific clinical and laboratory evidence of the relationship between smoking and health.

3. If a warning was to be required on the package, it certainly should not be required in cigarette advertising.

Congress ultimately passed S.559, which required that all cigarette packages bear the label "Caution: Cigarette Smoking May Be Hazardous to Your Health." The bill provided for a uniform and overriding federal labeling requirement that was not expected to affect sales seriously. All action on control of advertising was suspended until July 1969. In its final form, the bill called for a fine of $10,000 for violations and required periodic reports from the FTC and HEW. The bill was strongly opposed by many who saw it as too soft on the industry. The law that was finally passed had little effect on the tobacco industry's sales. A 1965 FTC study reported that 82% of respondents felt the warning label had no effect. For the fiscal year ending June 1965, consumption was at a record level of more than 5.33 billion cigarettes.

The U.S. Public Health Service also noted that, although a million Americans were giving up smoking each year, they were replaced by 1.5 million new smokers, mostly youngsters. In addition, it urged a stronger warning on cigarette packages: "Caution: Cigarette Smoking is Dangerous to Your Health and May Cause Death from Cancer and Other Diseases."

The FTC also recommended to Congress that the Public Health Cigarette Smoking Act be amended to require that the following statement appear clearly and prominently on all cigarette packages: "Warning; Cigarette Smoking Is Dangerous to Health, and May Cause Death from Cancer, Coronary Heart Disease, Chronic Bronchitis, Pulmo-

nary Emphysema and Other Diseases." The Commission also recommended that Congress consider a system of rotational label warnings similar to the present Swedish system. Beginning in 1977, Sweden introduced a labeling system requiring 16 different warning statements on cigarette packages, to be used interchangeably. In 1979, following an assessment that the system had increased knowledge, 16 new statements were substituted, and the rotational warning requirement was extended to cigarette advertising as well.[16]

Regulation of Advertising

Further hearings were held before both the House and Senate Commerce Committees during the first session of the Eighty-ninth Congress, March 22 to April 1, 1965. The testimony in these hearings emphasized regulation of advertising. The tobacco industry argued, on the basis of the proper role of government and the proper relationship between government and business, that it should not be the government's role to attempt to change the behavior of individual citizens.[17] When an industry demonstrated a willingness to regulate itself, as the cigarette industry had done through its voluntary code, government regulation represented undue interference with business and free enterprise. The government, furthermore, had no right to prohibit the advertising of a product that could be legally manufactured and sold. If action was considered necessary, a warning on the label and not in advertising would be the proper form. The label was the traditional and most effective place for hazard warnings.

Testimony was also given on the nature and purposes of advertising in the cigarette industry. Advertising, it was argued, was a basic means of competition, and prohibiting it would restrict competition in the industry. The intent of cigarette advertising was not to encourage people to smoke, since half the people in the country were already smoking, but to encourage smokers to change brands—that is, to increase a company's market share. The industry was mature and had a mature marketplace. The aim, therefore, was selective and not primary demand.

The FTC, although always in favor of regulating cigarette advertising, had consistently argued that the political and economic implications of such a regulation made Congress the proper initiating body.[18] Congress was also reluctant. In a pressure play in 1965, the FTC announced that it would require a stiffer warning on cigarette packages unless Congress took action. Such a tactic precipitated the 1965 Act (which would expire on June 30, 1969). The FTC again used the same tactic it had employed in the labeling debate. In June 1968, in a 3 to 2 decision, it voted to ban all cigarette advertising from radio and television and strongly suggested to the Senate committee that Congress legislate on the matter. Later in the summer, the surgeon general's Task Force for Smoking and Health charged that the tobacco industry was encouraging death and disease with its advertising practices and that it was unwilling to face up to the health hazards of smoking.

On February 5, 1969, the FCC, in a 6 to 1 decision, moved to ban cigarette advertising from radio and television. Chairman Hyde indicated that the Commission would be satisfied only with a complete ban and not with the voluntary restrictions. In defense of its legal power, the Commission said: "In the case of such a threat to public health, the authority to act is really a duty to act"; it would appear "wholly at odds with the public interest for broadcasters to present advertising promoting the consumption of a product imposing this unique danger."[19]

The cigarette industry considered the decision arbitrary, and the National Association of Broadcasters charged that the FCC was outside its normal jurisdiction. Despite the heated reaction to the FCC proposal, however, there could be no actual ban without extensive hearings, and there remained the possibility of contrary legislation. Thus, the FTC and FCC made it clear that Congress would have to act.

The Equal Time Provision

On June 2, 1967, the FCC ordered radio and television stations to allow time for antismoking advertisements. The seven commissioners said that their decision was based on the fairness doctrine, which states that the public should have access to conflicting viewpoints on controversial issues of public importance.[20] This fairness doctrine, a basic principle of the broadcasting field, was made a part of the Communications Act of 1959, although it was not applied to product advertising until 1967.

Thus, stations running cigarette ads had to turn over a significant amount of free time to antismoking commercials—one antismoking for every three smoking commercials. Antismoking groups such as the American Cancer Society filled the air with effective antismoking ads. After the ruling, the American Cancer Society distributed 8,900 antismoking commercials in 16 months. The counterads were, in effect, the reverse of the cigarette ads. Instead of looking happy and vigorous, smokers were presented as miserable and unhealthy. A number of celebrities were used to advocate quitting smoking, and others refused to perform on programs sponsored by cigarette companies.

The person largely responsible for the FCC's application of the fairness doctrine to cigarette advertising was John F. Banzhaf III, a 28-year-old New York attorney known as "the Ralph Nader of the cigarette industry."[21] In January 1967, Banzhaf had filed a formal complaint with the FCC against WCBS-TV. The complaint maintained that the fairness doctrine required the station to give equal time to "responsible groups" to present the case against cigarette smoking. Although the FCC rejected the equal time contention, its June 3 ruling responded to Banzhaf's complaint. Banzhaf then formed two organizations. The first, ASH (Action on Smoking and Health), sponsored by noted physicians, raised more than $100,000 to conduct litigation on the fairness doctrine and to enforce its application by monitoring TV stations and filing complaints against those failing to comply. The other organization, LASH (Legislative Action on Smoking and Health), raised funds and enlisted support for the congressional battles.

Despite the voluntary advertising code, the tobacco industry continued to represent smoking as an enjoyable and even healthful activity. Also, much of the advertising was done during prime broadcasting hours and consequently was reaching young people. The industry also fought the fairness doctrine, which mandated equal time for opposing views in television advertising. However, since industry regulation was proving ineffectual, Congress finally acted in March 1970, and cigarette advertising on radio and television was banned as of January 21, 1971.[22] The debate continues over whether all forms of advertising should be banned on the grounds that it is both harmful and deceptive.[23,24]

Taxes and Selective Bans on Smoking

In January 1983, federal cigarette taxes were raised for the first time in 30 years. The tax was doubled from 8 cents to 16 cents in an effort to discourage consumption. Some studies suggested negative price elasticities of −0.42 for adults to −1.42 for teenagers. Some advocates of increased taxes favored using the revenue to defray public health costs due to smoking. The industry objected to the tax and also disputed the public health cost structure rationale. The original legislation promised to rescind the tax in 1985. These taxes, however, still remain in force.[25]

Other government agencies have also gotten into the act. The Civil Aeronautics Board moved in January 1979 to restrict smoking aboard airplanes. The rules require that airlines create as many nonsmoking seats as passengers demand, that each passenger class have at least two rows, that seating for cigar and pipe smoking be completely banned, and that nonsmoking passengers between smoking sections not be "unreasonably burdened" by smoke. By 1988, most airlines had banned smoking in all flights lasting under two hours, while Northwest Orient has banned smoking on all its domestic U.S. flights.[26]

REGULATION BY STATE AND LOCAL GOVERNMENTS

A majority of state legislatures have dealt with the regulation of smoking over the past decade. Many local governments have also become active in this area. Legislation has centered around certain topics: (1) limitations on smoking in public places, (2) commerce, (3) smoking and schools, (4) advertising of tobacco products, (5) selling to minors, and (6) insurance. By far the two most important topics have been limitations on smoking in public areas and distribution of cigarette tax revenue.

Those who wish to ban smoking in the workplace cite two reasons: (1) the health hazard of environmental smoke, and (2) the increased productivity of workers in a nonsmoking environment. The tobacco industry vigorously disputes the facts behind those proposals and, in addition, has spoken out for "smokers' rights."[27]

The question of labor productivity was raised by the Surgeon General in a 1985 address in which he asserted that smoking employees cost American industry $39 billion a year.[28] Some observers question whether adequate studies have been carried out to justify such an assertion. Micro-level studies, which serve as the basis for broader generalizations, are cited by both sides. At the very least, however, a new battlefield has been demarcated in the seemingly endless smoking controversy. Antismoking activists have succeeded in mobilizing public opinion. In a 1988 poll conducted by the National Center for Health Statistics, 55% of those polled favored a complete ban on smoking in all public places, while 43% were opposed and 2% had no opinion. Among nonsmokers, 69% favored the ban and 30% opposed it. Among smokers, 25% favored the ban while 72% opposed it. The handwriting on the wall is ominous for the tobacco industry and smokers. Even if they think antismokers are misinformed about the scientific facts, it may not matter. For the U.S. population, when grouped by cigarette smoking status, breaks down as follows: 45% have never smoked, 24% are former smokers, and 31% are current smokers.[29]

THE CONTINUING DEBATE OVER THE PUBLIC INTEREST

In addition to the activities of the federal government, nonsmokers' rights organizations have become increasingly active in the early 1980s. They proved to be successful in achieving restrictions on public smoking in many states and localities. The most controversial areas have been smoking in the workplace as related to the passive or "second smoke" controversy, and product liability suits.

Smoking in the Workplace

A number of smaller companies are becoming involved in the antismoking campaign by offering incentives to their employees to quit smoking. Neon Electric Corporation of Houston banned smoking among its employees and offered a 50-cent-per-hour pay raise to any worker who got rid of the habit. The Alexandria, Virginia, fire department no longer hires smokers as firefighters because 16 of 22 men who retired with disabilities from 1973 to 1978 were smokers. Cybertek Computer Products, Inc., pays $500 to each employee who will quit. In all, about 30% of U.S businesses have some sort of policy restricting smoking, and about 3% pay their employees not to smoke. Large companies are more reluctant to ban smoking or to offer bonuses to quitters. One company, AT&T's Bell Laboratories at its Whippany, New Jersey, plant, is experimenting with prohibiting smoking in 70% of its plant. Dow Chemical, Continental Illinois, Kimberly-Clark, and others sponsor educational programs and poster campaigns urging smokers to quit. Larger companies also depend to a certain extent on peer pressure to encourage smokers to quit. At least in one instance, however, smokers have filed suit to reinstitute smoking.

Civil Suits: Product Liability

A new threat to the tobacco industry has appeared in the form of a wave of product liability lawsuits by victims of lung cancer and other diseases allegedly caused by cigarette smoking.[30]

The most celebrated case is that brought by the family of Rose Cipollone, because for the first time ever a tobacco company lost a case. The liability issue has been brewing for some time. In 1963, legal considerations emerged when the question of cigarette manufacturers' liability was raised in the case of *Green* v. *The American Tobacco Company*. A district court in Miami held that, although smoking was a cause of cancer, the company was not liable since it could not have foreseen the consequences. As a result, however, the industry began to give serious consideration to a warning on cigarette packages in order to limit companies' liability. In December 1963, the American Cancer Society issued the results of a survey of more than 1 million Americans. Its conclusion was that ''the evidence continues to pile up, and the burden of proof that there is not a causal relationship could soon shift over to the cigarette companies.''

Since 1954, 321 liability suits have been filed against tobacco companies; 207 have been dismissed or withdrawn and, until the Cipollone case, none had been lost. Prosecutors, however, are pinning their hopes on juries in a society more conscious than ever of the hazards of smoking.

INDUSTRY RESPONSE AND STRATEGY

The industry has objected to the singling out of cigarettes for regulation while the liquor industry escapes such censorship. In denying the aforementioned health allegations, the tobacco industry mounted a vigorous strategy of defense against both the onslaught of legislation and the undermining of consumer confidence. The principal measures they adopted aimed at (1) preventing erosion of the industry itself, and (2) building a vigorous political lobby.

Preventing erosion of the industry involved making the product safer; vigorously promoting the product; diversifying lines of business; and expanding overseas. (This last point is treated in a separate accompanying case.) Building a powerful political lobby called for a voluntary adoption of a marketing and advertising code to handle critics' demands; continuing to challenge the scientific validity of the antismoking research and sponsoring independent research; enlisting the active support of economic stakeholders in the industry; and making use of corporate philanthropy.

Product Alterations

Over 25 years ago, the industry began intensive research on the nature of the product itself with respect to the three most toxic byproducts of smoking: tar, nicotine, and carbon monoxide. In February 1964, Dr. Raymond McKeon, American Medical Association president, announced that six tobacco companies had given the AMA $10 million for research, without any restrictions whatsoever. In addition, all the tobacco companies began or intensified their own filter research as well as other product innovations.

There was considerable debate over establishing appropriate criteria and procedures for testing. Yet this line of research led to the transformation of the industry. The industry introduced various types of filters, light cigarettes, and the 100-millimeter cigarette—up to half an inch longer than the regular cigarette.

From 1963 to 1985, the nonfilter share of the market fell from 42% to 6%, while filters rose from 58% to 94%. Charcoal filters reached a high of 6% market share from 1968 to 1972 but fell to 1% by 1985. The most innovative change came with the smokeless cigarette, which was announced in 1987 and test marketed in 1988. This product promised to be safer for the smoker and also not to harm those in the smoking environment.[31]

Marketing

In 1970, total advertising was $314.7 million, with $217.4 going to television and radio. In 1971—after the ban on TV and radio advertising—the total dropped to $251.26 million. By 1975, total advertising was $491; 10 years later it had increased five times to $2,476 million. Advertising budgets of the industry are presented in Table 3.

Marketing did not succeed in increasing the number of cigarettes sold per capita (see Table 4). Per capita consumption dropped from 208 packs in 1966 to 164 packs in 1986 and is projected to decrease by about another 50 packs in the next decade; it peaked with 207 packs in 1973. Overall volume

**TABLE 3. Domestic Cigarette Advertising and Promotional Expenditures
For Years 1985 and 1986
(thousands of dollars)**

TYPE OF ADVERTISING	1985	% OF TOTAL	1986	% OF TOTAL
Newspapers	203,527	8.2	119,629	5.0
Magazines	395,129	16.0	340,160	14.3
Outdoor	300,233	12.1	301,822	12.7
Transit	33,136	1.3	34,725	1.5
Point of sale	142,921	5.8	135,541	5.7
Promotional allowances	548,877	22.2	630,036	26.4
Sampling distribution	140,565	5.7	98,866	4.1
Distribution bearing name[a]	211,429	8.5	210,128	8.8
Distribution not bearing name[a]	—	—	—	—
Public entertainment[b]	57,581	2.3	71,439	3.0
All others[c]	443,043	17.9	440,011	18.5
TOTAL[d]	2,476,441	100.0	2,382,357	100.0

[a]In 1979 through 1983, one company did not provide separate data for categories "Distribution bearing name" and "Distribution not bearing name." The entire amount is included in "Distribution bearing name." Also, beginning in 1985 advertising expenses allotted to "Distribution bearing name" and "Distribution not bearing name" are combined into the "Distribution bearing name" category. For this reason, no figures are shown opposite the "Distribution not bearing name" category for 1985 and 1986.

[b]This category previously was referred to as "Special events." Sporting, musical, etc., are included in "Public entertainment." Some of these previously had been included in the "All others" category.

[c]Expenditures for direct mail, endorsements, testimonials, and, now, audio-visual are included in the "All others" category to avoid disclosure of individual company data.

[d]Because of rounding, sums of percentages may not equal 100.

stood at 522.5 billion cigarettes in 1966, peaked in 1981 at 640 billion, and declined to 582 billion in 1986, with another loss of 130 billion estimated by 1995.

At the same time, the industry has been able to effect significant price increases, especially at manufacturing and wholesale levels. The result is that the cigarette industry has proven to be very profitable. Total retail sales in 1986 stood at $33.7 billion, up 47% over 1981. The industry leader, Philip Morris's U.S. tobacco division, reported operating gross profits of $2.4 billion on sales of $7.1 billion. R. J. Reynolds earned a gross $1.4 billion on sales of $4.7 billion. These two companies account for nearly 70% of the market.[32]

Industry Diversification and Overseas Expansion

A growing trend in the cigarette industry is a move toward diversification.[33] American Brands produces alcohol, snack foods, fruit products, and office supplies. It owns 27.5% of the outstanding shares of Franklin Life Insurance Company. RJR Nabisco, in addition to tobacco and food, owns a shipping and oil production firm, and acquired Del Monte Corporation. A comparatively smaller company, Liggett Group Inc., markets wines and liquors, pet foods, cereals, and leisure-time products. Liggett's cigarette market share is the smallest, and there are rumors that Liggett may withdraw from the U.S. cigarette market. Philip Morris has diversified into industrial products, land development, soft drinks (7-Up®), and Miller beer. It also owns General Foods, one of the leading companies in the packaged food industry in the United States. More recently, it bought Kraft Co., another major packaged food company with several leading national brands. This acquisition has made Philip Morris the largest packaged food company in the United States.

Advertising Code

On April 27, 1964, the major tobacco companies announced the formulation of a voluntary advertising code to become effective in January 1965.[34] It outlawed any advertising that would appeal to those under 21, thus barring cigarette commercials before and after television programs designed for minors. It forbade any advertising that portrayed smoking as being essential to social prominence, distinction, success, or sexual attraction. The broadcasting industry also established codes to regulate cigarette advertising. The National Association of Broadcasters' television code board stated that cigarette advertising should not contain false claims and that neither programming nor advertising was to depict smoking as promoting health or as being necessary or desirable to young people. The industry agreed to subject itself to self-regulation, to be enforced by an independent administrator capable of leveling fines of $100,000 for infractions.

Critics questioned the sincerity of the industry and asserted that the aforementioned initiative was nothing more than an elegant public relations enterprise. In a sense, these critics have prevailed as regulation of the industry has increased rather than subsided. Proponents of the code suggest that it at least kept things from getting worse.

Challenging the Scientific Evidence

The tobacco industry has never retreated from its stance of challenging the validity of the scientific evidence. This defense has always appeared to lack credibility, and the scientific community and public have generally ceased to pay any attention to the industry's claims. Nevertheless, the industry has continued to support their argument as a defensive posture for fear that a reversal of this position may expose the tobacco firms to further product liability lawsuits. The industry has pinned its research hopes on the "safer" cigarette (without, however, admitting that ordinary full-flavor cigarettes are unsafe). The industry has also bared its fists over environmental smoke and the question of how smoking relates to worker productivity. Perhaps the most critical research issue facing the industry, however, is the contro-

versy over addiction, for it may undermine the legal basis of the industry. That charge may prove to be the most potent weapon in the antismoking arsenal.

Enlisting Econmic Stakeholders

The tobacco industry has been hard at work trying to rally all those who make their living in the industry to become active on its behalf. Tobacco is a major part of the U.S. economy. In addition to its advertising budget of $2.5 billion, the tobacco industry employed 46.1 thousand workers in 1986 and met a payroll of $1,308 million. It paid $6,341 million to suppliers, including small farmers, local transporters, warehousemen, and so forth. It invested $658 million, added value of $12,724 million, and shipped products worth $19,073 million.[35]

The tobacco industry's health is vital to many states and local communities, not only because of investments and jobs but also because the industry accounts for millions of dollars in tax revenues. Aside from the 16 cent federal tax per pack, considerable revenue in sales, property, and income taxes is generated.

Philip Morris Corporation also has stressed the "trillion dollar" economic clout of the nation's 55 million smokers.[36] In so doing, it has tried to create an upscale image of smokers as well as to warn establishments such as restaurants not to discriminate against smokers.

The Use of Philanthropy

The tobacco industry has come to realize that a good deal of its prospects for success depend on how it is perceived—its image rather than scientific data. To this end, it has coupled philanthropy with its marketing efforts.[37] In addition to subsidizing the arts, the industry has also been attentive to the needs of minorities. All of this at least helps buy the silence of influential groups in society, if not win their active support.

NOTES

1. Joe B. Tye, "A Note on Public Policy Issues in the Cigarette Industry." Stanford Graduate School of Business (xerox), 1985, p. 15.

2. Ibid., pp. 10–14; Lawrence A. Loeb, Virginia L. Ernster, Kenneth E. Warner, John Abbotts, and John Laszlo, "Smoking and Lung Cancer: An Overview." *Cancer Research,* 44 (December 1984), pp. 5940–58.

3. Peter Schmiesser, "Pushing Cigarettes Overseas." *New York Times Magazine* (July 10, 1988), p. 16.

4. Tye, "Note," p. 14.

5. Ibid., p. 17; Warren E. Leary, "Even a Few Puffs Raise Women's Heart Risk." *New York Times* (November 17, 1987), p. B13.

6. Tye, "Note," p. 11.

7. Tobacco Institute, *Tobacco Smoke and the Non-Smoker:* Scientific Integrity at the Crossroads. Washington, D.C.: Tobacco Institute, 1987; B. Bruce Briggs, "The Health Police Are Blowing Smoke." *Fortune* (April 25, 1988), pp. 349–51; Stephen Labaton, "Denting the Cigarette Industry's Legal Armor." *New York Times* (June 19, 1988), p. E28.

8. Martin Tolchin, "Surgeon General Asserts Smoking Is an Addiction." *New York Times* (May 17, 1988), pp. A1, C4.

9. Tobacco Institute, *Cigarette Smoking and Chronic Obstructive Lung Disease: The Major Gaps in the Knowledge; and Tobacco Institute, Smoking and Health, 1964–1979: The Continuing Controversy.* Washington, D.C.: Tobacco Institute, 1979.

10. Tye, "Note," p. 15.

11. Tobacco Institute, *The Tobacco Observer.* This monthly publication provides an update of issues of interest to the industry.

12. U.S. Department of Commerce, *U.S. Industrial Outlook 1988,* "Tobacco Products," pp. 1–6. Washington, D.C.: Tobacco Institute, 1987.

13. Ed Bean, "Surgeon General's Stature Is Likely to Add Force to Report on Smoking as Addiction." *Wall Street Journal* (May 13, 1988), p. 21.

14. *Congressional Quarterly 1967 Almanac* (1967).

15. U.S. Congress, House Committee on In-terstate and Foreign Commerce, *Hearings, Cigarette Labeling and Advertising,* 88th Congress, 2nd Session, 1964.

16. Fedral Trade Commission, *Report to Congress Pursuant to the Federal Cigarette Labeling and Advertising Act, 1986.* Washington, D.C.: May 1988, pp. 1–6.

17. U.S. Congress, House Committee on Interstate and Foreign Commerce, *Hearings, Cigarette Labeling and Advertising,* 91st Congress, 1st Session, 1969.

18. San Francisco Chronicle, "Move to Ban Cigarette TV Ads" (February 6, 1969), p. 1.

19. *U.S. News and World Report,* "A Move to Limit Cigarette Ads" (February 17, 1969), p. 12; *New York Times,* "Showdown in Cigarette Advertising" (May 4, 1969), p. 36ff; Federal Trade Commission, *Report to Congress for the Year 1981.* (1984), p. 12; Joe B. Tye, *STAT! (Stop Teenage Addiction to Tobacco).* (Xerox draft). Palo Alto, Calif., 1985.

20. Federal Communication Commission, "Television Station WCBS-TV," *Federal Communication Commission Reports,* 2nd series, vol. 8 (May 19–August 4, 1967), pp. 381–87.

21. *Banzhaf* v. *FCC,* U.S. Court of Appeals, D.C. Circuit, Case 21285, November 21, 1968.

22. *Wall Street Journal,* "House, Senate Conferees Agree to Abolish Broadcast Cigarette Ads" (August 10, 1970), p. 9.

23. Irvin Molotsky, "Ban on Cigarette Ads to be Urged in Congress." *New York Times* (January 19, 1987), pp. A1, A13; Slade Metcalf, "Will Cigarette Advertising Be Banned?" *Folio* (May 1987), pp. 135–36.

24. Joe B. Tye, "Cigarette Marketing: Ethical Conservatism of Corporate Violence." *New York State Journal of Medicine* (July 1985), pp. 324–27.

25. Tye, "Note," pp. 20–22.

26. Laurie McGinley, "Airline Anti-Smoking Drive Gains But Still Faces Strong Opposition." *Wall Street Journal* (August 7, 1987), p. 23.

27. Lawrence Ashe, Jr., and Dennis H. Vaughan, "Smoking in the Workplace: A Management Perspective." *Employee Relations Law Journal,* 11, no., 3, pp. 383–406; Thomas E. Smith,

Jr., "Public Smoking Laws: Who Needs Them? Who Wants Them?" *Legislative Policy*, 3, no. 2 (1982), pp. 51–62; Ann LaForge, "Snuffing Out Smoking in the Office." *New York Times* (February 22, 1987), pp. K1, K2; Ronald Sullivan, "New York Adopts Wide Restrictions on Public Smoking." *New York Times* (January 7, 1987), pp. 1, 30.

28. Alan Herbert, "Cigarette Industry Faces Problems." *Journal of Commerce* (April 17, 1985), p. 5.

29. Alix M. Freedman, "Smokers' Rights Campaign Suffers from Lack of Dedicated Recruits." *New York Times* (April 11, 1988), p. 29.

30. Teri Agins and Alix M. Freedman, "Tobacco Firms Misled Public, U.S. Judge Says." *Wall Street Journal* (April 28, 1988), pp. 2, 26; Laurie P. Cohen and Alix M. Freedman, "Cracks Seen in Tobacco's Liability Dam." *Wall Street Journal* (June 15, 1988), p. 27; Alfonso A. Narvaez, "Scientists Fault Tobacco Company." *New York Times* (February 14, 1988), p. 43; Jesus Rangel, "Tobacco Company Testifies It Published Cancer Research." *New York Times* (May 8, 1988), p. 27; Matthew L. Wald, "Using Liability Law to Put Tobacco on Trial." *New York Times* (February 14, 1988), p. F11.

31. FTC, 1988 *Report*, p. 15; Alison Leigh Cowan, "Smoke Cut in Reynolds Cigarette." *New York Times* (September 15, 1987), pp. D1, D5.

32. Daniel P. Wiener, "Puffing Up a Second Wind." *U.S. News and World Report* (September 27, 1987), pp. 79–81.

33. Robert Miles, *Coffin Nails and Corporate Strategies*. Englewood Cliffs, N.J.: Prentice Hall, 1985.

34. Ibid., pp. 58, 72, 89, 92, 101, 238.

35. U.S. Department of Commerce, Bureau of the Census, *Annual Survey of Manufacturers— Value of Product Shipments*, Table 2. (1986).

36. Alix M. Freedman, "Philip Morris Ads Tout Demographics of Smokers to Alter 'Low Class' Image." *Wall Street Journal* (June 29, 1988), p. 28.

37. Alix M. Freedman, "Tobacco Firms, Pariahs to Many People, Still Are Angels to the Arts." *Wall Street Journal* (June 8, 1988), pp. 1, 22; Nick Ravo, "Tobacco Companies Gifts to the Arts: A Proper Way to Subsidize Culture?" *New York Times* (March 8, 1987), p. 32.

CIGARETTE SMOKING AND PUBLIC HEALTH: PART I

ABERNETHY, AVERY M, and JESSE E. TEEL. "Advertising Regulation's Effect upon Demand for Cigarettes." *Journal of Advertising*, 15 (1986), pp. 51–55.

"Adding Smoke to the Cloud of Tobacco Litigation—a New Plaintiff: The Involuntary Smoker." *Valparaiso Univeristy Law Review*, 23 (Fall 1988), pp. 111–44.

BACKINGER, CATHY L. "Smokeless Tobacco Use in the United States: Health Implication and Policy Options." *Journal of Public Health Policy*, 9 (Winter 1988), pp. 485–502.

BARRY, D. T., JR., and E. C. DEVIVO. "The Evolution of Warnings: The Liberal Trend Toward Absolute Product Liability." *Forum*, 20 (Fall 1984), pp. 38–58.

Bibliography on Smoking and Health. Washington, D.C.: U.S. Department of Health and Human Services, 1987.

BRADGATE, J. R., and N. SAVAGE. "The Consumer Protection Act 1987." *New Law Journal*, 137 (October 2, 1987), pp. 929–32; October 9, 1987, pp. 953–54; October 30, 1987, pp. 1025–26; November 6, 1987, pp. 1049–50.

FRIEDMAN, KENNETH MICHAEL. *Public Policy and the Smoking-Health Controversy: A Comparative Study*. Lexington, Mass.: Lexington Books, 1975.

LEVIN, B. A. "The Liability of Tobacco Companies—Should Their Ashes Be Kicked?" *Arizona Law Review*, 29 (1987), pp. 195–245.

"The Liability of Cigarette Manufacturers for Lung Cancer: An Analysis of the Federal Cigarette Labeling and Advertising Act and

Preemption of Strict Liability in Tort against Cigarette Manufacturers.'' *Kentucky Law Journal*, 76 (Winter 1987/88), pp. 569–96.

MCLEOD, KATHLEEN M. ''The Great American Smokeout: Holding Cigarette Manufacturers Liable for Failing to Provide Adequate Warnings of the Hazards of Smoking.'' *Boston College Law Review*, 27 (September 1986), pp. 1033–74.

MILES, ROBERT H. *Coffin Nails and Corporate Strategies*. Englewood Cliffs, N.J.: Prentice Hall, 1985.

National Research Council (U.S.) Committee on Passive Smoking. *Environmental Tobacco Smoke: Measuring Exposures and Assessing Health Effects*. Washington, D.C.: National Academy Press, 1986.

O'SHEA, J. D. ''Alcohol and Tobacco Manufacturers and Sellers: Liability in a Post-Alvis [*Alvis v. Ribar*, 421 N.E.2d 886 (Ill.)] Era.'' *Illinois Bar Journal*, 73 (May 1985), pp. 510–15.

OSTER, GERRY. *Economic Costs of Smoking and Benefits of Quitting*. Lexington, Mass.: Lexington Books, 1984.

''An Overview of Current Tobacco Litigation and Legislation.'' *University of Bridgeport Law Review*, 8 (1987), pp. 133–82.

POMERLEAU, OVIDE F. *Nicotine Replacement: a Critical Evaluation*. New York: Liss, 1988.

''Product Liability for Smokeless Tobacco: Should Tobacco Companies Be Liable for a Failure to Warn?'' *Suffolk University Law Review*, 21 (Fall 1987), pp. 769–809.

TAYLOR, PETER. *Smoke Ring: Tobacco, Money and Multinational Politics*. New York: New American Library, 1985.

THOMPSON, ROGER. ''Tobacco under Siege.'' *Editorial Research Reports* (October 5, 1984), pp. 739–56.

TILLEY, NANNIE M. *The R. J. Reynolds Tobacco Company*. University of North Carolina Press, 1985.

''Tobacco Law Symposium.'' *Tennessee Law Review*, 54 (Summer 1987), pp. 551–725.

TOLLISON, ROBERT D. *Clearing the Air: Perspectives on Environmental Tobacco Smoke*. Lexington, Mass.: Lexington Books, 1988.

TOLLISON, ROBERT D. *Smoking and the State: Social Costs, Rent Seeking, and Public Policy*. Lexington, Mass.: Lexington Books, 1988.

''Symposium on Product Liability.'' *Journal of Legislation*, 14 (1987), pp. 127–274.

United States House of Representatives, Committee of Energy and Commerce, Subcommittee on Health and the Environment. *Designation of Smoking Areas in Federal Buildings* (June 12, 27, 1986), Serial 99-135.

WHITE, LARRY C. *Merchants of Death: The American Tobacco Industry*. New York: Morrow, 1988.

·VII·

Multinational Corporations and Developing Countries

CIGARETTE SMOKING AND PUBLIC HEALTH: PART II

The role of the tobacco industry in the Third World

Depending on who you talk to, smoking is either an insidious habit causing untold harm to one's health and well-being, or it is a harmless habit enabling frazzled people to relax. In either case, it takes on ominous proportions in the poverty-stricken countries of the Third World. These countries, which do not have adequate means to feed their teeming populations and which are often unable to provide even the most basic health care for their people, should be doing everything to discourage smoking, whether for health or economic reasons. Unfortunately, this is not so. While the consumption of cigarettes in most of the industrially advanced countries of the world, with the exception of Japan, is either stagnant or declining, the consumption of cigarettes is increasing in most of the Third World.[1]

Whether it is cynicism, gross indifference, or the need for current revenues to meet other more pressing needs, the fact remains that in most Third World countries governments are active participants in the production and sale of tobacco products. In a number of countries, tobacco is a state-owned monopoly, while in most others it is a significant source of tax revenues. Therefore, the governments of these countries do not discourage cigarette smoking regardless of its long-term costs in human lives, health, and misery.

To this tragedy we must add the growing role of Western tobacco companies, among which U.S.-based companies are some of the biggest, in modernizing the production, manufacturing, distribution, and consumption of cigarettes. Often helped by their governments, these companies have dramatically expanded Third World markets through sophisticated mass-marketing and promotion techniques. They have, thereby, condemned the people of these countries to a double jeopardy. Not only are they increasingly persuaded to become smokers, but they must also use their precious foreign

ISSUES FOR ANALYSIS

Some would argue that it is unreasonable to blame foreign multinationals for smoking-related concerns in the Third World when all these companies have done is to compete for a share of those markets on a fair and equitable basis. And in most cases they have provided the consumer with a better product at a relatively lower cost. If smoking is alleged to cause any health-related problems, which tobacco companies consistently deny, it should be up to the governments of these countries to impose restrictions. Furthermore, it is suggested that it would be the height of cultural arrogance to assume that the governments of these countries do not know what is best for their own people, and that the Western countries are always there to tell the Third World countries what is good for them.

Such cynicism has a large measure of truth to it. The problem, however, is not that simple and, in any case, it is loaded with serious economic, political, and moral issues.

1. What is the responsibility of the governments of various countries to protect the health and welfare of their people? Does the world community have a right to raise such a question and hold various governments accountable with respect to the rights of their people? Are governments ignoring a hazardous situation in the interest of foreign exchange, jobs, and tax revenues? Or, in places where poverty is endemic, is smoking a rich man's issue?

2. Should the governments of industrially advanced developing countries, e.g., South Korea and Taiwan, be expected to uphold standards of public health that are higher than those of poorer and less developed countries? If so, why and by what criteria?

3. To what extent, and under what circumstances, should the governments of industrially advanced countries be expected to regu-

late the behavior of multinationals in overseas marketing practices? There are precedents where the U.S government, and even United Nations agencies, have forbidden companies and countries from undertaking activities which are condoned by the host countries but considered unacceptable by the home countries. The U.S. government has in the past restricted the sale abroad of textiles and synthetic materials that were banned for use in the United States. Similarly, the use of the pesticide DDT has been banned under the auspices of the World Health Organization (WHO) because of its serious side-effects on the environment; despite that many underdeveloped countries confronted with the serious problem of controlling mosquito-related diseases would prefer to use it.[2]

4. On what basis, if any, should the U.S. government require the U.S-based tobacco companies to carry health warnings on their cigarettes sold abroad when no such warnings are required by the laws of the host countries, and when the domestic producers, often local government-owned entities, and other foreign producers are unlikely to follow these standards?

5. What is the proper role of the World Health Organization in this issue? Should it be more concerned with more basic health care needs in countries where people have a low life expectancy due to diseases long controlled in the West?

6. Can we justify an inherently immoral behavior on the part of U.S. tobacco companies on economic and competitive grounds, or should we hold ourselves to standards that we consider right and proper at home regardless of their economic and social consequences? An example of this type of action is the case of South Africa, where U.S. laws have severely restricted investments by American companies because of South Africa's policies of apartheid. (South Africa's major investment partners, i.e., the United Kingdom and West Germany, have refused to go along with us.)

7. U.S. tobacco companies have argued, and with some justification, that their expansion in overseas markets has come at the expense of domestic monopolies and that they are simply better and more efficient marketers.

However, equally cogent arguments can be made that, through sophisticated and high-pressure mass marketing and advertising techniques, these companies have helped in the glamorization of smoking, especially among the young and have thereby further aggravated an already serious problem. Who is right? What would be most morally defensible?

8. Is it ethical for First World investors (such as large insurance companies and pension funds) to invest their funds in cigarette companies doing business abroad, especially in poorer Third World countries?

9. The primary, and perhaps the only, significant opposition to the American tobacco companies' marketing practices in Third World countries has been mounted by social activists and public interest groups based in the United States and Western Europe. These groups do not appear to have any constituency in Third World countries or have any mandate, direct or indirect, from Third World governments or their peoples. Why should these groups be so interested in this issue while there are equally, if not more, important social issues (e.g., the plight of the homeless, crime, drug addiction) that cry for help and attention within their own countries? The cynics would argue that these concerns reflect the prevailing fads and the need for new and exotic issues.

THE INTERNATIONAL TOBACCO ECONOMY AND THE THIRD WORLD

The bulk of world tobacco production is consumed domestically, with only about one-quarter entering world trade.[3] Global production of tobacco reached 6 million tons in 1985, and is expected to attain 6.9 million tons in 1990 and 7.9 million tons in 1995. Thus, between 1985 and 1995, global production is expected to increase by 31.7% (see Table 1).

Nearly 70% of production comes from developing countries, with nearly 35% from Asian centrally planned economies (principally China).[4] On average, developing countries exported 16% of their production (715,000 tons), while developed countries exported 31% (635,000 tons). In 1985, 12 countries accounted for 4.7 million tons or 78% of production (see Table 2). With 25% of world production, China only exports 10% of its crop, while the United States with 10% of world production exports 37% of its crop.

World imports of tobacco stood at some 1,414,000 tons in 1985, showing little change throughout the 1980s (see Table 3, A and B). Of this, North America took 14% (202,000 tons), Europe imported 46% (662,000 tons), and developing countries accounted for 16% (238,000 tons). The values of developing countries' imports was approximately $805 million versus exports of $1,789 million. Most regions were net exporters. The major net importers were the Eastern European Socialist countries; China was also a net importer.

Table 4 estimates the percentage of smokers in various countries as well as the amount of consumption regionally from 1966 to 1985. During that period, consumption rose throughout the world, ranging from an increase of 54% in developing countries to 12% in Europe. Only in North America did it decline (12%).

World consumption is divided between the developed Western countries (30%), the U.S.S.R. and Eastern Europe (10%), and the developing countries 60%, of which the Asian centrally planned economies constitute one-half (or 30% of world consumption). Developing countries' statistics do not usually include the smokers, who do not enter the marketplace, but provide for themselves.[5] In Pakistan, the average per capita consumption of cigarettes has increased 8% each year since 1975. In China, the world's largest producer and consumer of tobacco, there has been an astronomical increase in cigarette consumption. Despite a total ban on advertising, there are an estimated 300 million smokers in that country, and some reports have put the annual rate of increase at close to 10%.[6] Cigarette sales have increased rapidly in Bangladesh, more than

TABLE 1. Tobacco: Production, Utilization, and Trade

	PRODUCTION[a]				IMPORTS[b]		
	1981–1983 average	1984	1985	1986	1981–1983 average	1984	1985
	(thousand tons)						
World total	6,271	6,456	6,939	6,587	1,466	1,423	1,395
Developing countries	4,085	4,249	4,825	4,559	253	235	238
Latin America	718	736	718	655	20	14	19
Africa	241	304	295	292	30	46	43
Near East	267	242	230	253	69	79	66
Far East	1,075	1,058	1,059	1,104	73	68	64
Asian CPE	1,785	1,908	2,523	2,255	—	—	—
Developed countries	2,156	2,207	2,114	2,028	1,213	1,188	1,157
North America	927	875	774	666	233	215	203
Western Europe	445	479	488	396	673	665	673
EEC(12)	372	400	405	394	603	600	599
E. Europe and USSR	627	664	682	786	196	202	184
Other developed countries	187	189	171	180	112	106	97
World total by type[c]	6,271	6,456	6,939	6,587			
Flue-cured Burley							
and other light leaf	4,139	4,261	4,580	4,216			
Oriental	878	904	971	988			
Dark leaf	1,254	1,291	1,388	1,383			

	EXPORTS[b]				VALUE OF EXPORTS		
	(thousand tons)				*(million US dollars)*		
World total	1,419	1,393	1,342	1,350	4,404	4,144	4,030
Developing countries	806	767	743	715	2,004	11,770	1,744
Developed countries	613	627	599	635	2,400	2,374	2,286

	CLOSING STOCKS				AUCTION PRICES		
	(thousand tons)				*(national currency/kg)*		
World[d]	6,980	7,314	7,800		United States (cents)		
					Flue-cured	385	400	379
United States[d]	1,681	1,726	1,685		Burley	397	414	352
United States[e]	962	982	944		Zimbabwe (cents		
					Flue-cured	180	207	281
					Turkey (lira)		
					Oriental[f]	516	1,178	1,677

[a]Farm sales weight basis
[b]Dry weight basis
[c]Based on production figures published by the U.S. Department of Agriculture
[d]At 31 December
[e]At 30 June for domestic flue-cured only.
[f]Export unit value
SOURCE: United Nations Food and Agriculture Organization (FAO). *Commodity Review and Outlook, 1986–1987*, (Rome, Italy), p. 98.

doubling over the last 10 to 15 years.[7] Almost 70% of adult males and 20% of females smoke some form of tobacco product.[8] Consumption in Kenya has been rising at 8% annually. And in Indonesia, per capita cigarette consumption quadrupled between 1973 and 1981.[9]

MARKET STRUCTURE

The world's tobacco business is dominated by six international companies: British American Tobacco (U.K.), Philip Morris (U.S.), R. J. Reynolds (U.S.), American

TABLE 2. Leading Tobacco Producers and Exporters, 1985

COUNTRY	OUTPUT (TONS)	EXPORTS
China	1,770,000	178,000
United States	670,450	250,000
India	450,000	80,700
Brazil	388,000	198,000
USSR	376,000 (1984)	12,000
Turkey	196,000	102,700
Bulgaria	155,511	60,400
Italy	155,000	85,000
Greece	138,960	86,800
Indonesia	128,000	20,200
Zimbabwe	121,050	1,400
Japan	121,020	98,300

SOURCE: *Tabak Journal International* (April 1986), pp. 158–65; April 1985, pp. 152–54.

Brands (U.S./U.K.), Imperial Tobacco (U.K.), and Rupert/Rothmans (West Germany/U.K./U.S.).[10] The biggest U.S. companies are Philip Morris, with 40% of the U.S. market and about 7% of the world's market, and Reynolds, with 32% of the U.S. market and less than 1% of the world's market. Philip Morris has since acquired Liggett's international operations and also holds a 25% stake in Rothmans International. American Brands is nearly 80% European in its tobacco operations (see Tables 5 and 6).

These six producers account for almost 40% of the world's cigarettes. If communist countries and those with state-owned monopolies are excluded, their share rises to 80%.[11] Philip Shephard has provided an insightful historical perspective to the structural change that took place in the industry in the twentieth century. According to Shephard, during the first half of the twentieth century:

> Growth in domestic consumption and output was so spectacular that none of the firms showed any real interest in developing foreign operations or exports. The *quid pro quo* U.S. cigarette firms obtained for not entering foreign markets was protection in exploiting the large, rapidly-growing U.S. market. The long period of expansive domestic growth had made overseas markets pale in comparison. . . . [Gradually,] The growth rate of the

domestic market began to shrink as the market became relatively saturated at high levels of consumption, [so small firms] began to explore the possibilities of foreign operations and increased exports as a way to hedge against uncertainty.[12]

In 1964, the cigarette package labeling controversy broke out in the United States; the leading cigarette companies moved almost immediately to expand overseas where the climate was more favorable. According to one observer, as sales continued to stagnate, the scramble intensified:

> Historical spheres of influence were abandoned under the immense pressure to diversify out of the U.S. cigarette market. Large-scale demand creation efforts constituted the basic advantage of U.S. cigarette firms. Cigarette companies did not necessarily seek large markets; they went everywhere, large and small.[13]

In general, the strategy that was favored was to acquire existing companies rather than starting from scratch. In so doing, the companies made themselves an attractive sector of the economy by helping local farmers produce tobacco, injecting advertising money into the economy, helping the balance of payments, and providing government revenues. Tobacco firms have made judicious use of government policies as well as their industry strengths and opponents' weakness in crafting their strategies.[14]

THE ROLE OF THE U.S. GOVERNMENT IN CREATING A COMPETITIVE ADVANTAGE

U.S. government policy has been a major element in the competitive strategy of tobacco companies. These companies have honed in on both domestic policies of taxes and price supports and foreign policies of "Food for Peace" and economic aid.

Table 3. A. Tobacco Exports — Major Regions
Years 1981, 1983, and 1985

	QUANTITY (000 METRIC TONS)			VALUE (MILLONS $US)		
	1981	*1983*	*1985*	*1981*	*1983*	*1985*
World	1490.8	1341.0	1389.4	4400.4	4191.9	4054.7
Developed market economy countries	493.9	495.1	512.9	2001.3	2044.1	2020.1
America (Canada and United States)	299.8	263.9	276.6	1575.5	1556.9	1598.7
Europe	187.4	220.3	227.3	407.0	465.3	407.9
South Africa	5.9	7.3	7.5	14.8	11.4	9.6
Oceania	.6	.8	0.0	3.4	4.6	0.1
Developing countries and territories	883.7	730.1	775.5	2118.2	1856.3	1789.3
Africa	188.9	141.6	172.0	463.1	375.6	360.2
America (excluding major petroleum exporters	271.0	276.0	304.0	596.5	660.9	674.2
Asia	401.3	284.1	283.9	987.0	711.9	695.7
Europe	22.5	28.4	15.6	71.3	107.7	59.2
(Malta and Yugoslavia)						
Oceania (Papua New Guinea	0.1	0.0		0.3	0.2	
Socialist countries of Western Europe	89.8	84.7	80.1	444.0	241.8	209.6
Socialist countries of Asia	23.3	31.1	21.0	36.9	49.6	35.7

SOURCE: United Nations Conference on Trade and Development (UNCTAD) *Commodity Yearbook, 1987,* (Geneva, Switzerland, pp. 190–91.

Domestic Policies

The tobacco industry has pursued two government policies that it viewed as contrary to its interests insofar as they impeded its overall ability to compete in the global marketplace, for they affected capital accumulation. The first was taxation. An important side-effect of cigarette taxation has been the increasing dependence on cigarette tax revenues. (See the preceding case, "Cigarette Smoking and Public Health: Part I"; Table 3.) From 1978 to 1982, all levels of government took in over $6 billion per year in taxes on tobacco products. After the tax rate was raised from 8 cents to 16 cents in 1983, revenues rose to $8.9 billion in 1983 and to $9.6 billion in 1987.[15] Not only did the industry want lower domestic taxes, it also wanted pressure on foreign governments to lower taxes. For example, between 1981 and 1985, Japan lowered the import tariff on foreign cigarettes from 90% to 20%, but it slapped on a retail tax equivalent to 41% of the price of cigarettes.

The second concern has been price supports. Tobacco price supports historically have been established at levels high enough to assure farmers greater profits than they could realize from any other crop. The USDA tobacco program rose from a net cost of $80 million in 1985 to $279 million in 1987. (See the preceding case, "Cigarette Smoking and Public Health: Part I"; Table 4.)[16] Such policies maintained domestic prices at higher levels than world prices, with the curious result that they subjected American farmers to intense foreign competition. The tobacco industry has not openly opposed price supports, but it has shifted its suppliers to Third World countries when producing overseas. Philip Morris, however, maintains that American farmers are its primary suppliers (*Annual Report*, 1987). Many developing nations receive substantial assistance from the cigarette companies in establishing their own tobacco agricultural programs. If need be, the seven largest companies, which control 40% of the world market, can increasingly internationalize their sources of supply of raw materials. This may be an ominous sign for the U.S farmers.

B. Tobacco Imports — Major Regions
Years 1981, 1983, and 1985

	Quantity (000 metric tons)			Value (Millions $US)		
	1981	1983	1985	1981	1983	1985
World	1448.2	1379.8	1413.9	4392.8	4668.1	4767.3
Developed market economy countries	961.2	946.8	962.1	3016.2	3361.7	3350.9
America	175.6	163.0	202.3	433.0	484.3	539.5
Europe	671.8	672.9	662.3	2054.2	2318.5	2296.4
South Africa	9.9	12.6	8.4	30.1	33.5	17.1
Oceania	15.4	13.8	23.3	70.2	66.0	101.8
Developing countries and territories	244.2	233.3	237.9	730.2	714.5	805.6
Africa	84.4	104.0	98.1	229.0	314.8	306.1
America	25.0	19.2	17.3	78.3	56.0	44.5
Asia	125.4	99.9	106.1	393.5	318.9	421.9
Europe	7.5	9.6	15.9	20.0	22.1	29.9
Oceania	1.9	0.6	0.6	9.4	2.8	3.2
Least developed countries	15.1	17.3	22.0	40.2	47.1	46.9
Socialist countries of Eastern Europe	196.2	189.2	184.8	504.4	561.4	518.9
Socialist countries of Asia	42.6	10.5	29.0	128.0	30.5	92.0

U.S. GOVERNMENT FOREIGN AID POLICIES

The initial overseas expansion of U.S. tobacco companies was partially a result of the "Food for Peace" campaign and other United States governmental interventions to help feed the world after World War II. In 1933, the Agricultural Adjustment Act classified tobacco as a basic agricultural commodity. This defined tobacco as a necessity to the farm economy and the general U.S. economy and paved the way for support payments and for export under the Lend Lease Act during World War II. Through the Commodity Credit Corporation and the price support system, the U.S. Department of Agriculture spent more than $337 million on the U.S. tobacco industry in 1979 alone, compared to less than $50 million spent on antismoking efforts.[17] When the U.S. government began the "Food for Peace" campaign, its most publicized aim was to feed hungry people. Its other goals, sometimes pursued more vigorously, were to get rid of surplus commodities, to advance U.S. government policy, and to create markets for agricultural products. Since 1955, more than $700 million worth of tobacco was sent to South Vietnam, the Philippines, Cambodia, Egypt, and other Third World countries. As North Carolina Senator Jesse Helms argued, these sales were important because historically they developed new markets for tobacco. In 1980, tobacco was removed from the "Food for Peace" program. A program of loan guarantees to commercial lenders who financed tobacco exports was substituted in its place.[18]

A second way the U.S. government has helped the tobacco industry is through contributions to international development agencies to facilitate further market growth. The U.S. government uses taxpayers' money to finance support of Third World growers both through World Bank funds and support of the United Nations Development Program.[19]

TABLE 4. Worldwide Smokers[a]

COUNTRY	MALE %	FEMALE %	COUNTRY	MALE %	FEMALE %
China	90	3	Switzerland	50	37
Morocco	90	—	Turkey	50	50
Nepal	87	72	Ghana	50	—
Papua New Guinea	85	80	Ireland	49	36
Philippines	78	—	Guyana	48	4
Indonesia	75	10	Austria	46	13
Bangladesh	70	20	Hungary	45	23
Thailand	70	4	Mexico	45	18
France	70	50	Chile	45	26
Denmark	68	49	Venezuela	46	26
Republic of Korea	68	7	Israel	44	30
Spain	66	10	Soviet Union	44	10
India	66	26	Czechoslovakia	43	11
Poland	63	29	Cuba	40	—
Zambia	63	56	Norway	40	34
Japan	63	12	Egypt	40	1
Uruguay	60	32	East Germany	40	29
Argentina	58	18	U.K.	38	33
Tunisia	58	6	Canada	37	29
Yugoslavia	57	10	Australia	37	5
Netherlands	57	42	Hong Kong	37	5
Malaysia	56	2	Guatemala	36	10
Italy	56	32	United States	35	28*
Brazil	54	37	New Zealand	35	29
Nigeria	53	3	Peru	34	7
Kuwait	52	12	Uganda	33	—
Colombia	52	18	Sweden	30	30
Rumania	52	9	Ivory Coast	24	1

[a]Prevalence of smoking among adults—late 1970s, early 1980s
—data not available
*current data (1987)
SOURCE: World Health Organization.

THE U.S. TOBACCO INDUSTRY'S STRATEGY FOR OVERSEAS EXPANSION

In overseas expansion, the U.S. tobacco companies pursue two principal strategies: investment and trade.

Investment

Beginning in the 1950s and accelerating after the Surgeon General's Report of 1964, the United States tobacco companies have moved abroad. Actual export of tobacco products has never been the main feature of their strategy. Instead, they opted for marketing arrangements with foreign firms, licensing agreements, and the establishment of their own manufacturing and production facilities.[20] When they moved to establish their own production facilities, the tobacco companies committed themselves to the modernization of a country's entire tobacco industry in order to ensure adequate supply of quality tobacco. In a survey of the role of tobacco companies in developing countries, the Economist Intelligence Unit identified six functions:[21] (1) pioneering and developing new areas for tobacco production and subsequent economic growth; (2) providing extension services and materials (usually at cost) to farmers; (3) buying the leaf produced; (4) supporting (overall) family-owned farms; (5) providing financial support and investment on a variety of levels; and (6) conducting research and training. The study is generally benign in interpreting the effects of the

TABLE 5. How the Producers Rank

1988 SHARE	1987 SHARE	1986 SHARE	1986–1988 PERCENTAGE POINT CHANGE	BILLIONS OF CIGARETTES			1986–1988 ANNUALIZED COMPOUND GROWTH RATE[a]
				1988 SALES	1987 SALES	1986 SALES	
Philip Morris 39.33%	37.83%	36.77%	2.56	218.7	215.5	214.2	0.8%
Reynolds 31.73%	32.53%	32.33%	−0.60	176.4	185.3	188.3	− 2.0%
Brown & Williamson 10.95%	10.97%	11.67%	−0.72	60.9	62.5	68.0	− 5.1%
Lorillard 8.26%	8.23%	8.15%	0.11	45.9	46.9	47.5	− 1.6%
American Brands 6.85%	6.88%	7.18%	−0.33	38.1	39.2	41.8	− 5.3%
Liggett 2.88%	3.56%	3.90%	−1.02	16.0	20.3	22.7	−18.0%
Total 100.00%	100.00%	100.00%		556.0	569.7	582.5	− 2.2%

[a]Base year 1985; 1987 figures revised.
SOURCE: *Business Week,* January 23, 1989, p. 59.

companies' activities on the local economy. Critics are not so optimistic.

Trade Policy

A more recent, and quite significant, source of leverage has been the U.S. trade policy to pressure Japan and some of the newly industrializing countries, ˙e.g., South Korea and Taiwan, to remove their discriminatory import and marketing policies against the U.S tobacco companies and to allow for greater import of U.S. tobacco products. The relevant legislation is Section 301 of the revised 1974 Trade Act.[22] The procedure is straightforward and simple. If a company feels that it has been subjected to unfair or discriminatory trade, it files a complaint with the U.S. trade representative. Specialists from the departments of commerce, trade, and agriculture are called in to map out a bargaining strategy. The trump card is to threaten tariffs or boycotts of the goods of the nation in question.

The tobacco industry was driven toward export markets because of stagnant demand and even declining sales in the United States. At home, it has used a combination

of defensive and offensive strategies (see the preceding case, "Cigarette Smoking and Public Health: Part I"). These have included advertising and lobbying campaigns to slow down the regulatory onslaught, on the one hand, and product innovation and diversification, on the other hand. Furthermore, to compensate for setbacks in their domestic markets, the U.S tobacco companies began an aggressive drive to expand their overseas sales by (1) entering new markets, and (2) fighting against entry barriers in countries with large markets where their sales were arbitrarily restricted by local regulations and discriminatory trade practices.

To open up the markets in Japan and other Pacific Rim countries, in 1986 the U.S. Cigarette Export Association enlisted the support of the Reagan administration. The trade group hired as lobbyists Richard Allen, former national security director, Michael Deaver, former presidential deputy chief of staff, and Michele Laxalt, the daughter of former Nebraska Senator Paul Laxalt, a close personal friend of the President. As a result, Section 301 was vigorously applied in the cases of Japan, Taiwan, and South Korea.[23]

The combined effect of these actions has

TABLE 6. Profile of Large, Multinational Tobacco Companies

COMPANY	TURNOVER (BILLIONS $)	EMPLOYEES (NUMBER)	CIGARETTE PRODUCTION (BILLIONS)
BAT	$14.6	280,000	550
Philip Morris	8.3	72,000	400
R. J. Reynolds	8.9	83,000	280
Rothmans Int.	4.5	19,000 (Europe)	190
American Brands	6.8	52,000	110

REGIONAL SALES ANALYSIS (% TURNOVER)

	NORTH AMERICA	EUROPE	ASIA	SOUTH AMERICA	AFRICA
BAT	24%	46%	7%	19%	4%
Philip Morris	75%	21%	—	—	—
R. J. Reynolds	79%	13%	—	—	—
Rothmans Int.	25%	56%	15%	—	4%
American Brands	36%	62%	—	—	—

	MAIN BRANDS	%TURNOVER FROM TOBACCO
BAT	Benson and Hedges State Express 555	57%
Philip Morris	Marlboro	64%
R. J. Reynolds	Winston, Camel	56%
Rothmans Int.	Rothmans, Dunhill	90%
American Brands	Benson and Hedges (in U.K.), Pall Mall	63%
Carlton		

MAIN DIVERSIFIED PRODUCTS
(IN ORDER OF TURNOVER IMPORTANCE)

BAT	Retailing, paper/ packaging/ printing, cosmetics, home improvements
Philip Morris	Brewing, soft drinks, industrials
R. J. Reynolds	Food and beverages, transport, energy
Rothmans Int.	Brewing, luxury goods, energy
American Brands	Food, hardware, office equipment

SOURCE: David Tucker, *Tobacco: An International Perspective.* London: Euromonitor Publications, Ltd., 1982, p. 70.

resulted in phenomenal success for the U.S tobacco industry in overseas markets both in terms of absolute growth and in terms of penetrating specific markets where hitherto the tobacco companies had restricted access (see Table 7). In the first six months of 1987, Japan quadrupled consumption of U.S. cigarette exports (by volume) compared with the same period of 1986, approaching nearly half the volume of the European Community, which is the largest export market for U.S.-made cigarettes. Japan has recently liberal-ized pricing and distribution restraints on cigarette imports and, as a result of negotiations with the United States, has suspended its tariffs on cigarettes. These developments have allowed imports to become more price competitive and to increase their share of the Japanese market.

Japan has a very large and enticing tobacco market, but U.S. and other foreign cigarette makers were effectively locked out of it by the Japanese government and its tobacco monopoly. Japan's 120 million people

TABLE 7. U.S. Cigarette Exports
(in Millions of Cigarettes)

IMPORTING COUNTRY	1981	1985	1986	JAN.–JUNE 1986	1987
Japan	5,177	6,455	9,638	3,705	14,710
Taiwan	88	238	209	96	2,140
South Korea	160	111	281	71	45
European Community	23,828	15,454	20,162	8,738	10,142
Others	53,329	36,689	33,655	16,835	17,095
Total	82,582	58,947	63,945	29,445	44,132

SOURCE: U.S. Department of Commerce, *U.S. Industrial Outlook 1988*, ''Tobacco Products,'' pp. 43–1, 43–3, 43–5.

smoke over 300 billion cigarettes annually. Over 63% of Japanese males and 12% of Japanese females are smokers. Before the Japanese market was pried open by American negotiators under the pressures of Section 301, the U.S. tobacco companies' market share had hovered around 2% despite spending over $200 million in product promotion. After the application of Section 301, U.S. cigarette sales in Japan had a phenomenal increase, rising from 3% in 1986 to 10% in 1987, with sales predicted to rise between 15% and 20% by 1992.[24]

Other areas of growth have been the newly industrialized countries (NIC) of East Asia, e.g., South Korea, Taiwan, and Singapore, in East Asia where U.S. government negotiators have pushed open markets under Section 301 of the revised 1974 Trade Act. At the same time, exports to the Common Market and other countries where there is greater protection of local markets as well as thriving domestic industries have declined.

In 1987, Taiwanese smokers, according to the U.S. Department of Agriculture, bought 5.1 billion American-made cigarettes worth $119 million, compared with a mere $4.4 million in 1986. Currently, imports account for 18% of cigarette sales in Taiwan, with American cigarettes accounting for over 83% of total imports or a 15% market share.

South Korea is another case in point. In May 1988, the U.S. was able to persuade South Korea to liberalize its cigarette mar-

kets and allow U.S. companies to compete with the domestic government monopoly. The agreement lowered taxes on imported cigarettes, allowed the U.S. companies to market their products independent of the government monopoly, and allowed them to advertise and engage in other promotions. As a consequence, it is estimated that the U.S. share of the South Korean market, which was $1.3 million in 1987 (representing little over 0.5% of the market), was likely to increase to ''several hundred million dollars of new sales'' in the foreseeable future.[25] Indeed, Asian sales accounted for most of the growth in American cigarettes in 1987. According to the Brown & Williamson Tobacco Corporation, exports of all American-made cigarettes to Asia rose 76% in 1987, resulting in $1 billion in new sales.[26] At present, however, Europe is still the major market for U.S. companies, but it does not possess the potential for growth that the developing countries do. One can, therefore, expect to see a major thrust of U.S. tobacco companies into developing countries.

As pointed out in Table 6, the major portion of American Brand's sales are in Europe. In 1987, its domestic sales were $1,403 million, while international (notably U.K.) were $4,740 million. Surprisingly, however, domestic sales generated operating income of $430 million, nearly double the $244 million earned by international tobacco sales. (It is uncertain what precise role exchange rates played).[27]

Philip Morris and R. J. Reynolds are the

two major U.S. companies with a predominantly American base and considerable sales overseas. Philip Morris claims 7% of the world market and sales of 4.500 billion units. Reynolds claimed sales of 98 billion units in 1987, wich would give it but 0.15% of the world market. This nonetheless represented a 10% increase over the previous year, and its Camel® brand reached 3.6% of the European market. Sales of Salem® cigarettes grew by about 18% during the same period in Europe; but in Asia, which accounts for half of the brand's unit volume, sales zoomed 40%. Reynold's local brands (such as Mustang® in Brazil) posted a 10% unit volume increase. More revealing, however, were management's comments on R. J. Reynolds Tobacco International's future. The future markets tagged were Taiwan, South Korea, China, Turkey, and Thailand and other major "government-controlled markets."[28]

Of Philip Morris's $27 billion operating revenues, $6.3 billion (23%) derived from Europe; only 6% derived from sources other than the United States. Exports from the United States also totaled only 6%, leaving roughly 66% from U.S. product sales (which achieved a 74% increase in revenues in 1987, due primarily to price increases). Philip Morris International, however, increased its revenues by 25.4% due primarily to increases in unit volume and to currency translation. Philip Morris also owns slightly less than 25% of Rothmans International but is involved in proceedings over its ownership with the European Community. The most interesting aspect of strategy is the targeting of developing country markets as the areas of high-growth potential. To gain access, the industry is clearly counting on the U.S. government to bring pressure to bear in order to open markets.[29]

SMOKING AND THE THIRD WORLD

There is no question that the smoking habit is increasing among the people of most developing countries. It is also expanding in highly industrialized countries such as Japan, and many newly industrialized countries, e.g., South Korea, Taiwan, Hong Kong, and Singapore. The adverse health effects are, of course, ominous.

It is important to consider why people smoke. In general, smokers find the habit pleasant, at least initially. The pleasure is more than physical. The social aspects of smoking in developing countries include such dynamics as (1) being "American" and "with-it," for foreigners, (2) peer pressure, and (3) for some, symbolic of savoir-faire, adulthood, and modernity.[30] These psychosocial dynamics of smoking are not lost on the major tobacco companies. The tobacco industry claims that it advertises to increase market share and influence brand choice, not to incite smoking. This is questionable, for advertising is also prevalent in quasi-monopoly markets.[31]

It is legitimate to examine the activities of U.S. tobacco companies in promoting cigarette smoking in foreign countries, especially when they use marketing and promotion strategies that have been banned in the United States as endemic to public health and contrary to public policy. However, the issue of public health cannot be viewed in isolation and without regard to the policies and activities of the governments of those nations. Clearly, the governments of the countries where cigarettes are sold through nationally controlled monopolies must be seen in the same light as private multinational companies, or even domestically controlled private companies. The motives of governments in developing countries are mixed. The characteristics of cigarettes' addictiveness and insensitivity to price elasticities make them prime sources of tax and tariff revenues, with which these governments can meet other important economic and national security needs.

According to a World Health Organization report, a large part of the world's production of cigarettes is accounted for by state-owned monopolies in centrally planned economies or socialist countries (37%), and by state-owned monopolies in nonsocialist countries, such as France, Italy, Austria, and Kenya (17%). The six major international tobacco companies account for about 60% of the global production *outside* the centrally planned economies, and almost 80% of the output in the private sector, i.e., *exclusive* of centrally planned economies and state-owned monopolies in other parts of the world.[32]

The principal contrast in analysis is between those who take an economic view (emphasizing income, jobs, foreign exchange, tax revenue) and those who take a health view. The health problem has not surfaced in a major way among Third World leaders; no one really knows what the people think if, indeed, they are concerned about the issue. One reason is that the health problems related to smoking often do not arise in a stark way due to prevalent malnutrition and low life expectancies in Third World countries. People do not live long enough to develop smoking-related health problems. In addition, the health establishments in those countries are not looking for such data in the first place.

ECONOMIC CONSIDERATIONS: BENEFITS AND COSTS

According to Michael Reich, their are four types of revenues associated with tobacco, and all of them have important political aspects.[33] These revenues are: tax revenues, income to farmers, income to processors, and foreign exchange. There do not seem to be precise aggregate data available for developing countries in all of these areas. We approach them in terms of country examples and some aggregate data generated by the United Nations' Food and Agriculture Organization.

In many countries, tobacco companies are welcomed because the industry produces jobs, export earnings, and a taxable product. Tobacco is one of the most heavily taxed commodities in the world. In the United States, for example, the Tobacco Institute claims that in 1983 tobacco accounted for $15.7 billion in federal, state, local, and export taxes. During the same year, the industry generated directly and indirectly 2.3 million jobs. Such patterns are repeated and often intensified throughout the world. In China, 8% of the government's revenues come from tobacco sales. In financially strapped Brazil, the tobacco industry contributes 1.6% of the country's revenue. ''The most important taxpayer in Brazil is the cigarette industry, which contributes 37 to 40 percent of the total amount collected by the Industrialized Products Taxation,'' reported Dr. Fernando C. Barros of Brazil in the *New York State Journal of Medicine*. Brazilian tobacco consumers pay the highest rate of sales tax in the world, twice that which U.S. consumers pay. In 1983, as much as 75% of the price of a pack of cigarettes in Brazil went to government coffers. Brazil earned $300 million in tobacco exports in 1983 and almost $1 billion in tax revenue, and the tobacco industry provided some 3 million jobs.[34]

The industry's support is crucial to tobacco farmers, who could be making less costly, though not as profitable, use of their land cultivating food crops. Ten years ago, the Food and Agriculture Organization reported that 10.9 million acres of arable land worldwide had already been converted from food to tobacco production. Approximately 69% of this land was located in the Third World. For example, though surrounded by farmland, Santa Cruz, Brazil, must now import the majority of its supply of fresh vegetables and fruits from areas which are more than 100 miles away.[35]

In Egypt, the tobacco monopoly, Eastern Company, produces 180 million cigarettes a day, 30 million over demand. Of the surplus, 7 million is exported (primarily to the Arabic world), and the remainder is used for the production of eight foreign brands by special arrangement with Philip Morris (Marlboro and Merit), R. J. Reynolds (Camel® and Winston®), BAT and B and W (Kent® and Du-Maurier®), and two brands for Rothmans.[36]

China, the world's largest tobacco producer, also follows a primarily economic strategy.[37] Its present monopoly, China National Tobacco Corporation, was formed in January 1982. About 300 million Chinese smoke regularly (roughly 55% of adults—some say 90% of the men and only 3% of the women). Demand is growing by about 10% a year (from a young demographic base). Some 1.05 trillion cigarettes packaged in 2,500 brands are produced in about 140 plants; some 200 small, uneconomical plants have been closed. China does not allow foreign cigarettes to be marketed to the ordinary population. Of domestic brands, only 13% are filtered, and tar delivery is between 20 and 35 milligrams. By 1985, China was a net exporter of tobacco. It hopes to expand in this direction. For this, it is dealing with industry leaders. China's most advanced machines produce about 1,000 cigarettes per minute, as compared to 6,500 and even 8,000 cigarettes per minute in world-class factories. China has contracted with Philip Morris and R. J. Reynolds to build state-of-the-art facilities in its special economic zones of Shenzen and Xiamen. The government set aside more than $200 million in foreign exchange for the acquisition of plants and materials. China's counties collected more than $450 million in local tobacco levies (40% of the price received by the farmer) in addition to taxes from cigarettes.

Evidence suggests that outside of areas of state control of tobacco (such as in China, Egypt, and Brazil), trends of international market concentration will continue. Transnational corporations dominate virtually all the major markets outside the state monopoly and socialist nations. Such seller concentration is the result of barriers which prevent potential competitors from entering an industry over relatively long periods of time. In the opinion of Philip Shepherd,[38]

Bain (1956) identified three basic sets of barriers to entry: (1) absolute cost advantages of existing firms; (2) economies of scale (or other advantages of large-scale production); and, (3) consumer preferences for the products of existing producers. The latter is far and away the most important in the cigarette industry. Process (as opposed to product) technology is not a reason for barriers to entry in the cigarette industry, nor are the supply of raw materials. Process technology does not constitute a barrier to entry because it is not subject to large economies of scale. Small-scale operations are feasible and as efficient as much larger ones. While [a supply of] oligopsonistic pressure on growers maintains fairly low prices, so it could be afforded by new entrants in most markets.

The primary barriers to entry may be found, instead, in the factors making for enduring consumer preferences for the products of existing firms: (1) through the location of plants or sales outlets; (2) through the provision of exceptionally good service; (3) by means of physical differences in the product supplied; and, (4) through the creation of a favorable subjective image in the minds of consumers for the product. These demand creation efforts prevent new entry and permit above competitive profits.

There are critics of the economic view: Scarce capital resources should be devoted to food production; pricing policy diminishes prospects for meeting basic needs.[39]

Tobacco production also has serious environmental costs. Throughout the Third World, tobacco production leads to accelerated rates of deforestation and erosion as farmers cut trees for the fuel needed to cure tobacco. It can take an acre of woodland to cure a single acre of tobacco in developing countries. Two to three hectares of forest are required to cure 1 ton of tobacco.

Third World leaders do not seem to be persuaded.[40] Typically, less than 1% of arable land is devoted to tobacco, and then only for about six months. While food imports do command foreign exchange, cheap food is available (to pro-U.S. countries) via Public

Law 480 subsidy imports. Comparatively, in the view of developing country governments, tobacco contributes more to capital development.

PUBLIC HEALTH: REGULATION OF PROMOTIONAL ACTIVITIES

Where do local public health agencies stand in reference to economic development? They seem to be in a secondary position. Table 8 provides some indication of antismoking policies in various countries. However, there is not much data available. The lack of data may indicate neglect of smoking as a health issue. Five of the eight countries listed in Table 8 as totally banning cigarette advertising are socialist and do not feature advertising for much of anything anyway. Furthermore, six of the eight show evidence of increased smoking rates. Ten of 16 countries with package warning labels show increased rates of cigarette use. It is difficult to sort out demographic factors from implementation and enforcement factors. The truth seems to be that aside from North America and Western Europe, smoking is not an issue that is given high priority.[41] Susan Motely has gathered some interesting examples.[42]

Brazil, where cigarette consumption grows at a rate of 6% each year, provides an excellent example of the laissez-faire environment in which the tobacco industry operates in some countries. There are no restrictions on tobacco promotion. Billboards litter the countryside. More importantly, the advertising is aggressive and aimed at the young, providing no health warnings but promising success, happiness, and social status. Throughout the Third World, labels on cigarette packages warning of health hazards are the exception rather than the rule. And the cigarettes sold may "contain twice as much tar as cigarettes sold in western countries," notes the International Organization of Consumers' Unions.[43] In countries where

restrictions on advertising have been initiated, tobacco companies have found ways around them. When the Sudan banned all advertising, Philip Morris altered its billboards: Cigarette packs were replaced with cigarette lighters displaying the Marlboro logo.

But despite the sobering prospects, there are encouraging signs. Throughout the world, antismoking groups are springing up, pressuring their respective governments for warning labels and advertising curbs. In the Middle East, health ministers from several Gulf states joined together to call for mandatory health warnings on all cigarette packages as well as a listing of tar and nicotine contents. The Zambian government has banned cigarette-related advertising.

The investments are large and the stakes high. More than 2 million people worldwide now die each year because of tobacco-related ailments. Indeed, if the Third World's consumption of tobacco continues to increase, malnutrition and infectious diseases may soon become secondary to smoking-related diseases.

The tobacco industry "is expanding unchecked" throughout the Third World and the results are cause for alarm. A World Health Organization document asserts that there is a "probability that the smoking epidemic will have affected the developing world within a decade and that a major avoidable public health problem will have been inflicted on countries least able to withstand it."[44]

UNRESOLVED POLICY ISSUE

Several major problems in countering the sale of cigarettes in Third World countries are related to living conditions. Specifically:

1. Life expectancies are not long, so a problem that will affect a person in their later years will not have a great effect on the choices a person makes regarding smoking, since he or she

TABLE 8. Cigarette Use and Antismoking Policies in Selected Countries, 1974-1984

COUNTRY	ANNUAL CHANGE IN USE OF CIGARETTES %	PACKAGE WARNING LABEL	ADVERTISING BAN		BANS IN PUBLIC PLACES	
			Total	Partial	Strong	Weak
Argentina	+0.1					
Australia	+0.9	X		X		
Brazil	+1.6	X				
Bulgaria	−0.2	X	X		X[a]	
China	+6.2		X			X
Egypt	+8.7	X		X		X
Finland	+0.8	X	X		X	
France	+0.6	X		X	X	
Hungary	+0.4	X	X		X	
Italy	+1.6		X		X	
Japan	+0.6	X				X
Kenya	+3.9					X
Mexico	+1.0	X		X		
Netherlands	−3.3	X		X		
Norway	−1.6	X	X			
Poland	+0.3		X		X[a]	
Soviet Union	+0.8	X	X		X	
Spain	+1.6			X		
Sweden	−0.3	X	X			
United Kingdom	−3.1	X	X			
United States	0	X	X			X

[a]Includes restrictions on smoking in the workplace.
SOURCE: William U. Chandler, "Tobacco—Strong Words Are Not Enough," in *World Health Forum*, 7, no. 3 (1986), pp. 217–24.

will not live long enough to have the problem.

2. The children end up becoming malnourished. The money used for cigarette consumption will come out of the household budget. With barely enough money to get by as it is, the loss of money to cigarette purchases results in fewer funds available for food.

3. A major source of energy is wood. But wood is removed to make space available to grow tobacco, leaving an energy deficit.

4. Using land for tobacco growing means the land cannot be used for farming, which dims the prospects of self-sufficiency.

Some lay the distortion of society's priorities at the door of tobacco multinationals.

The six largest U.S. cigarette manufacturers spend about $2.6 billion a year on advertising. But, charge antismoking advocates, the money goes much farther than just encour-aging smoking and countering the small plain box containing the Surgeon General's warning. They say it also ensures that the carrier of the advertising does not write about smoking and health before it thinks about the ad money that could conceivably be lost.[45]

Compound this with the fact that "The big six tobacco companies, all conglomerates, wield much more power when they throw in the advertising budgets of their non-tobacco lines." Tobacco companies also alter their advertising images in Third World countries. Realizing the high illiteracy rates, the picture is the primary means of selling; copy is relatively unimportant. Thus, efforts are concentrated on portraying the proper visual image. Also, in different countries tobacco companies will adjust the tar levels of their cigarettes; although they will not admit in which countries.[46]

When entering a foreign market, cigarette companies find a way around local advertising regulations. As noted, in the Sudan, when Marlboro could not advertise their cigarettes, they began advertising Marlboro lighters.

An additional social problem of selling to Third World countries is related to currency. "[Third World countries] are not able to pay in hard currency. This calls for new financing methods and a whole lot of innovation. It's a question of whether the industry will be able to adapt."[47]

Add to this that First World governments are largely indifferent to the health issues of the Third World, concentrating instead on the balance of payments. In the United Kingdom, Rothman's International was given the 1983 Queens' Award for Export Achievements.[48]

As the World Health Organization claimed in a 1978 report,

In the absence of strong and resolute government action, we face the serious probability that the smoking epidemic will have affected the developing world within a decade and that a major avoidable public health problem will have been inflicted on countries least able to withstand it for the twin reasons of commercial enterprise and government inactivity.[49]

And Albert Huebner observed:

If Third World nations follow the example of industrialized countries, antismoking efforts won't begin until lung cancer is epidemic. The scenario has brought untold misery to people in the developed world. For the Third World, it will entail, in addition, an overwhelming economic burden.[50]

NOTES

1. R. Masironi and K. Rothwell, "Smoking in Developing Countries." Geneva: World Health Organization, 1985 (Photocopy: WHO/ SMO/85.1); Uma Ram Nath, *Smoking: Third World Alert*. Delhi, India: Oxford University Press, 1986.

2. Thomas R. Dunlap, *DDT: Scientists, Citizens and Public Policy*. Princeton, N.J.: Princeton University Press, 1981; Brian Toyne, *The Global Textile Industry*. London: George Allen and Unwin, 1984; United States Congress, *The Foreign Corrupt Practices Act of 1977*. Washington, D.C.: U.S. Government Printing Office, 1977.

3. T. M. Burley and L. N. Chilvers, "Trends in Leaf Tobacco Production and Trade: Retrospect and Prospect," in W. F. Forbes, R. C. Frecker, D. Nostbakken, eds., *Proceedings of the Fifth World Conference on Smoking and Health, Winnipeg, Canada*. Ottawa: Canadian Council on Smoking and Health, 1983, pp. 281–85.

4. M. Kohr Kok Peng, "The Urgent Need to Control the Smoking Epidemic in the Third World," in Forbes, Frecker, Nostbakken, eds., *Proceedings*, pp. 561–66.

5. Masironi and Rothwell, "Smoking," pp. 5–10.

6. Thomas W. Netter. "W.H.O. Increasing Anti-Smoking Fund." *New York Times* (January 25, 1987), p. L15.

7. *Multinational Monitor* (July/August 1987), p. 10.

8. *New York State Journal of Medicine* (July 1985), p. 442.

9. Steve Mufson, "Cigarette Companies Develop Third World As a Growth Market." *Wall Street Journal* (July 5, 1985), p. 1.

10. David Tucker, *Tobacco: An International Perspective*. London: Euromonitor Publications, Ltd., 1982, p. 68ff; Robert Miles, *Coffin Nails and Corporate Strategies*. Englewood Cliffs, N.J.: Prentice-Hall, 1982; Philip Morris, Inc., *Annual Report*, 1987.

11. *The Economist* (March 26, 1988), p. 70; Gregory Connolly, "Smoking or Health: The International Marketing of Tobacco," *Tobacco and Health: International Issues in Tobacco Trade and Policy*, Proceedings of a Symposium sponsored by

the Institute for the Study of Smoking Behavior and Policy, John F. Kennedy School of Government and The Takemi Program in International Health, Havard School of Public Health, (December 8, 1987), pp. 3–4, citing P. Taylor, *The Smoke Ring*, New York, Mentor Press, 1988.

12. Philip L. Shepherd, ''Transnational Corporations and the International Cigarette Industry,'' in Richard S. Newfarmer, ed., *Profits, Progress and Poverty—Case Studies of International Industries in Latin America*. Notre Dame, IN: University of Notre Dame Press, (1985), pp. 63–112, quoted material appears on pages 78 and 80.

13. Ibid., p. 81.

14. Miles, *Coffin Nails*, chap. 1; U.S. Department of Commerce, *U.S. Industrial Outlook 1988*, ''Tobacco Products,'' (1987), pp. 43–1, 43–3, 43–5.

15. United States Department of Agriculture, Economic Research Service, *Tobacco Situation and Outlook Report*, June 1988, p. 35.

16. Ibid., p. 29.

17. Albert Huebner, ''Tobacco's Lucrative Third World Invasion.'' *Business and Society Review* (fall 1980), p. 51ff.

18. Joe B. Tye, *A Note On Public Policy Issues in the Cigarette Industry*. Stanford, Graduate School of Business, Palo Alto, CA (April 15, 1985), (xerox), p. 21–22.

19. Michael Crosby, ''Selling Cigarettes to the Third World.'' *Christianity and Crisis* (May 13, 1983), p. 213.

20. Miles, *Coffin Nails*, p. 125ff.

21. The Economist Intelligence Unit, *Tobacco Study, II* (April 13, 1984), pp. 6–8, 10, 12–14.

22. Peter Schmiesser, ''Pushing Cigarettes Overseas.'' *New York Times Magazine* (July 10, 1988), p. 18.

23. *The Economist*, ''Cigarettes—Trade Liberalisation's Dark Shadow'' (March 28, 1988), pp. 70–71; Connolly, ''Smoking or Health,'' p. 9ff; and United States District Court for the District of Columbia, *United States* v. *Michael K. Deaver*, CR-87-0096. November, 3, 1987. Washington, D.C., pp. 766–814.

24. Susan Chira, ''U.S. Cigarette Makers Gain in Asia.'' *New York Times* (May 10, 1988), p. D1.

25. Ibid., p. D5.

26. Ibid., p. D1.

27. American Brands, *Annual Report,* 1987.

28. RJR Nabisco, *Annual Report,* 1987.

29. Philip Morris, Inc., *Annual Report,* 1987.

30. Huebner, ''Third World Invasion,'' p. 52.

31. S. Chapman and R. Vermeer, ''Tobacco Marketing Monopolies That Advertise.'' *Lancet* (March 30, 1985), p. 758.

32. Connolly, ''Smoking or Health,'' pp. 3–4.

33. Michael Reich, ''Tobacco Production and Export Policies in the Third World.'' (Unpublished article) Cambridge, MA, 1988.

34. Susan A. Motely, ''Burning the South: U.S. Tobacco Companies in the Third World.'' *Multinational Monitor* (July/ August 1987), p. 12.

35. Ibid., p. 9ff.

36. M. R. Naguib, ''Increased Cigarette Production and Exports in Egypt.'' *Tabak Journal International* (April 1986), p. 96.

37. M. Ahmad, ''Leaf Situation In China.'' *Pak Tobacco* (January 1984), pp. 23–25; *Tobacco International*, ''CNTC, World's Largest Cigarette Maker, Seeks Advice'' (September 20, 1985), pp. 7–10; M. Ahmad, ''Special Report: The New China.'' *Tobacco Reporter* (March 1985), pp. 46–48, 50, 52; *Tabak Journal International*, ''China Puts Tobacco Regulations Into Effect'' (April 1984), pp. 134, 136–37; A. Shelton, ''The Quest for Better Quality.' *Tobacco Reporter* (March 1986), pp. 26–29.

38. Shepherd, ''Transnational Corporation,'' pp. 65, 72ff.

39. D. Femi-Pearse, ''Aspects of Smoking in Developing Countries in Africa.'' *New York State Journal of Medicine* (December 1983), pp. 1312–13.

40. Ruth Roemer, *Recent Developments in Legislation to Combat the World Smoking Epidemic.* Geneva: WHO, 1986.

41. Susan Motely, ''Burning the South,'' p. 9ff.

42. Ibid.

43. Morton Mintz, ''The Smoke Screen: Tobacco and the Press—An Unhealthy Alliance.'' *Multinational Monitor* (July/ August, 1987), pp. 15, 18.

44. Mufson, ''Cigarette Companies,'' pp. 1, 16.

45. Colleen Lowe Morna, ''Zimbabwe's Tobacco Addiction.'' *Multinational Monitor* (July/ August 1987), pp. 12–14.

46. Ibid.

47. *Lancet*, "Third World Smoking—The New Slave Trade" (January 7, 1984), pp. 23–24.

48. Ibid.

49. Huebner, "Third World Invasions," p. 51; See also R. Masironi, "The Role of WHO in Smoking Control," in Forbes, Frecker, Nostbakken, eds., *Proceedings*, pp. 99–102.

CIGARETTE SMOKING AND PUBLIC HEALTH: PART 2

BOESEN, JANNIK, and A. T. MOHELE. *The 'Success Story' of Pleasant Tobacco Production in Tanzania*. New York: Holmes & Meier, 1983.

CHANDLER, W. U. *Banishing Tobacco*. Washington, D.C.: Worldwatch Institute, 1986.

CHEN, HAN-SENG A. *Industrial Capital & Chinese Peasants: A Study of the Livelihood of Chinese Tobacco Cultivators*. Edited by Ramon H. Myers. New York: Garland Publications, 1980.

DE JESUS, Ed C., ed. *The Tobacco Monopoly in the Philippines: Bureaucratic Enterprise & Social Change*. New York: Cellar, 1981.

ECKHOLM, ERIK. *Cutting Tobacco's Toll*. Washington, D.C.: Worldwatch Institute, 1978.

HARRISON, PAUL. *Inside the Third World*. Harmondsworth, England: Penguin, 1979.

HEISE, LORI. "Unhealthy Alliance: With U.S. Government Help, Tobacco Firms Push Their Goods Overseas." *World Watch*, 1 (September/October 1988), pp. 19–28.

MULLER, MIKE. *Tobacco and the Third World: Tomorrow's Epidemic?* London: War on Want, 1978.

NATH, UMA RAM. *Smoking: Third World Alert*. New Delhi, India: Oxford University Press, 1986.

RAMSTROM, LARS M., ed. *The Smoking Epidemic*. Stockholm: Fourth World Conference on Smoking and Health, 1980.

TAYLOR, PETER. *The Smoke Ring: Tobacco, Money & Multinational Politics*. Rev. ed. New York: New American Library, 1985.

TILLEY, NANNIE M. *The R. J. Reynolds Tobacco Company*. Charlotte. NC: University of North Carolina Press, 1985.

TUCKER, DAVID. *Tobacco: An International Perspective*. London State Mutual Bk., 1985.

UNCTAD. *Marketing and Distribution of Tobacco*. Geneva: United Nations, 1978.

WHELAN, ELIZABETH. *A Smoking Gun: How the American Tobacco Industry Gets away with Murder*. New York: G. F. Stickley Co., 1984.

WHITE, LARRY C. *Merchants of Death: The American Tobacco Industry*. New York: Morrow, 1988.

WHO (World Health Organization). *Controlling the Smoking Epidemic*. Technical Report Series 636, Geneva, 1979.

WHO. *Legislative Action to Combat Smoking around the World*. Geneva, 1976.

WHO. *Smoking and its Effects on Health*. Technical Report Series 568, Geneva, 1975.

WHO. *Smoking Control Strategies in Developing Countries*. Report of the WHO Committee, Technical Report Series 695, Geneva, 1982.

WICKSTROM, B. *Cigarette Marketing in the Third World*. Gothenburg University, 1979.

UNION CARBIDE CORPORATION

Industrial plant accident in Bhopal, India:
responsibility of the multinational corporation

In the middle of the night on December 3, 1984, J. Mukund, the factory manager of the Union Carbide (India) Ltd. (UCIL) pesticide plant in Bhopal, was woken up by a telephone call from the night shift supervisor informing him that an accident had occurred at the plant causing a large amount of methyl isocyanate (MIC) gas to leak out from the underground storage tanks. The lethal gas was causing havoc in the plant neighborhoods, injuring and killing untold numbers of people as they tried to escape the area. Within a short time, Mukund had driven to the plant and initiated damage control and emergency procedures. He telephoned the company headquarters in Bombay, which in turn notified divisional offices in Hong Kong, and the parent company headquarters in Danbury, Connecticut. Within a few hours, news of the disaster had reached all key personnel in the company. The worst corporate crisis in history had just hit Union Carbide Corporation.

The morning of December 4, 1984, found death strewn over the stunned Bhopal city. Bodies and animal carcasses lay on sidewalks, streets, and railway platforms, and in slum huts, bus stands, and waiting halls. Thousands of injured victims streamed into the city's hospitals. Doctors and other medical personnel struggled to cope with the chaotic rush, knowing neither the cause of the disaster nor how to treat the victims. Groping for anything that might help, they

This case was prepared by Dr. Paul Shrivastava, Associate Professor of Business, New York University and Executive Director Industrial Crisis Institute, Inc., New York. It was developed from Dr. Shrivastava's book entitled *Bhopal: Anatomy of a Crisis* (Cambridge, Mass.: Ballinger, 1987). Prepared for publication in Sethi and Steidlmeier, *Up Against the Corporate Wall*, 5th ed. (Englewood Cliffs, N.J.: Prentice Hall, 1991).

treated immediate symptoms by washing their patients' eyes with water and then soothing their burning with eyedrops; giving the victims aspirins, inhalers, muscle relaxants, and stomach remedies to provide temporary relief. Before the week was over, nearly 3,000 people had died. More than 300,000 others had been affected by exposure to the deadly poison. About 2,000 animals had died, and 7,000 more were severely injured. The worst industrial accident in history was over. But the industrial crisis that made the city of Bhopal international news had just begun.

The impact of the disaster on Union Carbide Corporation was devastating. At the time of the accident, in 1984, Union Carbide had sales revenues of $9.5 billion, net income of $323 million, and total assets of $10.5 billion. Three years later, the sales revenues had fallen to $6 billion, assets had shrunk to about $6.5 billion, and shareholders' equity fell from $4.9 billion to under $1 billion. This drastic reduction in size occurred without a single penny being paid in compensation to victims of the disaster.

During these turbulent three years, the company's financial survival was threatened more than once. First, in 1985, a few months after the disaster, Carbide stock price plunged from about $48 a share to about $33 a share. At the depressed price, speculators and arbitrageurs acquired large amounts of the company stock. On August 14, 1985, the GAF Corporation announced that it had acquired a significant stake in Carbide and would try to take it over. Samuel Heyman, chairman of GAF, said he would sell off Carbide units that contributed about 40% of its revenues. With the money from those sales (estimated by GAF to be $4.5 billion), he would settle the Bhopal victims' claims. This immediately put the company in play in the take over game. This was followed by frantic bidding and counterbidding wars between GAF and Union Carbide management.

Six months later, GAF gave up its takeover attempt, but only after Carbide management had been maneuvered into a radical financial restructuring. The restructuring involved selling off 25% of the most profitable assets of the company, closing several marginally profitable plants, and laying off about 4,000 people.

After more than four years of legal proceedings and acrimonious and contentious charges and countercharges, a settlement was reached in early February 1989 between the government of India and Union Carbide. The agreement called for Union Carbide to pay $470 million. The agreement resolves all outstanding issues and claims by any and all parties against Union Carbide. The Supreme Court of India, in settling the claim, did not address the issue of who was to blame for the accident. Also as part of the settlement, the Indian Supreme Court ordered dismissal of all criminal charges and other civil suits in India against Union Carbide.[1]

In the years since the accident, a great deal has happened and yet a great deal remains unchanged. Union Carbide went through the shock of a long, drawn-out hostile takeover battle which left the company severely battered, highly leveraged, and financially constrained. The accident also attracted worldwide attention to the broad scope of hazards associated with industrial accidents in general, and those in the Third World in particular. Although this accident was the most severe in history, it was by no means unique.

Large-scale industrial accidents have created crises for corporations and the public regularly throughout this century. Since the beginning of this century, there have been 28 major industrial accidents in fixed facilities in the free world. These accidents do not include transportation accidents, such as airliner crashes or train derailments. These accidents have occurred in both industrialized countries as well as developing countries. In the U.S., the explosion of a ship with a cargo of ammonium nitrate caused the deaths of over 530 people in Texas City in 1947. In 1948, the explosion of confined dimethyl ether in Ludwigshafen, Germany, killed nearly 250 people. In 1970, an accident at an underground railway construction site in Osaka, Japan, killed 92 people. In 1984, accidents in Mexico City and Cubatao, Brazil, killed about 500 people each.

Major industrial accidents can occur anywhere—in industrialized as well as developing countries, in small as well as large organizations, in the public as well as the private sectors. Accidents such as, Bhopal, Chernobyl, and the NASA Challenger explosion have fundamentally changed the public's awareness of the technological hazards facing society. They have highlighted the very limited scope of our knowledge about these hazards and the extreme inadequacy of our ability and resources to cope with such major accidents.

Another sad realization to emerge out of the Bhopal case is that four years after the accident and despite an apparent settlement, the case is still mired in courts and there is no solution in sight for the victims. None of the victims have received a single penny in compensation for damages. While Union Carbide Corporation and the Government of India fight in the courts, the plight of the victims largely goes unnoticed. The survivors of those who died remain desperately poor and destitute with no alternative means of supporting themselves. Those who were partially or totally disabled suffer from a lack of adequate medical care and rehabilitation, loss of employment, and financial hardships. One thing is certain, many more will die before seeing justice done, and those who live long enough to see the courts resolve the case may not have much time left to make use of the compensation they eventually receive in any settlement.

ISSUES FOR ANALYSIS

The Bhopal case raises a number of important issues concerning public disclosure of potential hazards, appropriate technology transfers to developing countries, corporate responsibility and liability for overseas' plant safety, and the role of host country governments in direct foreign investments. In addition, it highlights the importance of developing expeditious and equitable systems for resolving postaccident conflicts and payment of compensation to victims.

1. What are the responsibilities of multinational corporations for their overseas operations, especially in developing countries, to ensure that these plants are operated safely with regard to workers, communities, and the environment? Can companies adopt a single uniform safety standard for all their plants around the world?

2. To what extent did Union Carbide Corporation (U.S.) and its Indian subsidiary exercise due care in this regard? What more could each of them have done to ensure plant safety?

3. How should environmental and safety concerns be incorporated in strategies for technology transfer to developing countries?

4. How can multinational corporations (MNCs) control the safety performance of their overseas operations?

5. To what extent can majority of other forms of ownership be used to ascertain the liability of various parties in case of major industrial accidents?

6. How do issues 3, 4, and 5 apply to the Bhopal case?

7. What should be the responsibility of government in ensuring plant safety? To what extent should government agencies be held responsible for losses to human lives and property? What should be done if such responsibility is poorly or inadequately discharged?

8. How do the issues raised in item 7 apply to the government of India, the state government of Madhya Pradesh, and the local city government agencies in Bhopal?

9. What criteria should be used in determining compensation to victims? What kinds of compensation systems should be designed to ensure speedy and fair compensation? How much compensation can Union Carbide pay without going bankrupt?

10. Which country's courts should be responsible for handling cases involving multicountry accidents and liability disputes, and why? What role can the International Court of Justice play in this regard?

11. To what extent and under what circumstances are courts an appropriate forum for resolving international liability cases? What alternative forms of dispute resolution mechanisms can be recommended?

12. What corporate and business policies should firms adopt in order to minimize the occurrence of major accidents? How can they trade off between the expense of being safe versus cutting costs to be competitive?

13. What ethical issues does the Bhopal case raise? What ethical standards should be applied in making corporate policies regarding the case?

14. In light of Bhopal-type disasters, how should corporate responsibility toward environmental protection and worker and community safety change? What additional actions should corporations undertake voluntarily that were not warranted before Bhopal?

UNION CARBIDE CORPORATION (UCC)

The organizational context of this accident may be understood by examining the position of the Bhopal plant in the overall business of Union Carbide Corporation. In 1984, Union Carbide Corporation (UCC) was the seventh largest chemical company in the United States with total assets of $10.51 billion and sales approaching $10 billion. It owned or operated businesses in 40 countries and employed over 33,000 people worldwide. Its main product lines included dry cell batteries, chemicals, industrial gases, specialty alloys, and agricultural products.

The early 1970s were a turbulent period for the chemical industry and Union Carbide. The highly cyclical chemical industry became even more volatile because of oil price fluctuations during the early 1970s. The oil embargo created an artificial shortage of petrochemicals and related products and sent their prices skyrocketing. In 1973 and 1974, UCC's sales grew at unprecedented rates of 21% and 35% respectively. This created an upbeat mood at the company, and an aggressive program of growth and expansion was started. Capital expenditure increased annually until 1975. In 1975, the company got the first of a series of jolts. While its sales increased 6% over 1974, world recession triggered by the 1973 oil embargo reduced demand, resulting in a decline in sales and total employment. Inflation caused reductions in net earnings and led to cost-cutting measures and strategic reorientation. The company outlined three strategies: first, to strengthen its position in businesses with a good future and in areas where it had a strong market position; second, to withdraw from businesses which did not meet Carbide's criteria for financial performance; and third, to shift the business mix to include a greater proportion of performance products (e.g., Sevin® and Temik® pesticides). It also decided to diversify into related and unrelated businesses, and identified the areas of health, food products, environment, and energy as its future focus. The company estimated that about 60% of its business in 1975 was in growth categories, and it planned to allocate about 80% of its capital expenditure from 1975 to 1979 on these growth businesses. Specifically, pesticides and other agricultural products were considered as having high growth potential, whereas old and mature chemical businesses were considered to be less desirable.

In 1976, Congress passed the Toxic Substances Control Act, placing more stringent requirements on the corporation's chemical businesses. Union Carbide set up a new corporate-level Health, Safety, and Environmental Affairs Department to ensure compliance with the new Act and centralize internal administration.

The year 1977 saw a change in the top management of Union Carbide. W. S. Sneath took over as chairman of the company, and Warren Anderson became the new president. Together, they restructured Carbide's business portfolio and started divesting some of its businesses. These decisions resulted in divestiture of over a billion dollars worth of assets over the next four years, including Carbide's petrochemical business in Europe and the entire medical business, in which the company had developed a number of new products.

In 1979, Union Carbide once again benefited from the steep oil price hike by OPEC. Sales jumped 17% and earnings jumped 41%, and the total number of employees reached an all-time high of 115,763. In the 1980s, Union Carbide continued to refocus its portfolio of businesses away from chemicals, and concentrated on industrial gases and batteries. It had divested almost three dozen business units and product ventures in the late 1970s, to dilute its chemical operations in the U.S. This was done in acknowledgment of increasing competition in the chemicals industry and lackluster financial performance of the company during the past decade.

In 1982, Warren Anderson took over as chairman while Alec Flamm became president. The early 1980s were a period of declining performance. Sales dropped, earnings declined, capital expenditures and working capital was reduced, maintenance expenditures were cut back, assets were stripped, and employment level was curtailed. These trends are apparent in the financial figures presented in Tables 1, 2, and 3.

UNION CARBIDE (INDIA) LTD.

Union Carbide (India) Limited (UCIL) was incorporated in Calcutta under the name of Eveready Company (India) Ltd. on June 20, 1934. Its name was changed to National Carbon Company (Ltd.) and then to Union Carbide (India) Ltd. in December 1959. The company's most important product is dry cells (batteries). In 1984, more than 50% of the company's revenues came from this product. But over the years, as its product lines in batteries, chemicals, and plastics matured, the company sought out new markets to maintain its growth.

The industries UCIL entered were typically technology-and-capital-intensive. They catered to mass markets and required large-scale production and technically skilled labor. Most often, UCIL would enter industries still in their early stages of development and gain a dominant market position by using the superior technology of its parent company. One such industry was pesticides. In the 1960s, large-scale use of agricultural pesticides was promoted by the Indian government as part of its "green revolution" campaign to modernize agriculture. Pesticides quickly became popular among farmers, and their use tripled between 1956 and 1970.

The Agricultural Products Division was established in 1969. It developed Carbaryl (Sevin) using methyl isocyanate (MIC) as the active agent for a range of pesticides. The Bhopal plant also began operating in 1969. It was located on the north side of Bhopal, about two miles from the railway station and bus stand—the hub of local commercial and transportation activities. Since the plant was initially used only for formulation (the mixing of different stable substances to create pesticides), it did not pose a grave danger to surrounding areas. In 1974, however, it was granted an industrial license to manufacture pesticides and began production of both Sevin and MIC in 1977. While these developments occurred inside the company, the pesticide industry underwent major changes. Many small manufacturers entered the industry as formulators. They were less capital intensive and served small market niches.

The Bhopal plant was the key manufacturing facility of the Agricultural Products Division of the company. At the time of the accident in December 1984, Union Carbide (India) Limited was the twenty-first largest company in India. Of UCIL shares, 50.9%

TABLE 1. Selected Financial Data for Union Carbide Corporation

DOLLARS AMOUNTS IN MILLIONS (EXCEPT PER SHARE FIGURES)	1984[a]	1983[a]	1982[a]	1981	1980
From the Income Statement					
Net sales	$ 9,508	$ 9,001	$ 9,061	$ 10,168	$9,994
Cost of sales	6,702	6,581	6,687	7,431	7,186
Research and development expense	265	245	240	207	166
Selling, administrative, and other expenses	1,221	1,243	1,249	1,221	1,152
Depreciation	507	477	426	386	326
Interest on long-term and short-term debt	300	252	236	171	153
Other income (expense)—net	77	120	162	164	41
Nonrecurring charge—closing of facilities	—	241	—	—	—
Income before provision for income taxes	590	82	385	916	1,052
Provision for income taxes	227	(10)	58	258	360
Income before extraordinary charge and cumulative effect of change in accounting principle	341	79	310	649	673
Extraordinary charge	(18)	—	—	—	—
Cumulative effect of change in accounting principle for ITC	—	—	—	—	217
Net income	323	79	310	649	890
Income per share before extraordinary charge and cumulative effect of change in accounting principle	4.84	1.13	4.47	9.56	10.08
Extraordinary charge per share	(0.25)	—	—	—	—
Cumulative effect per share of change in accounting principle for ITC	—	—	—	—	3.28
Net income per share[c]	4.59	1.13	4.47	9.56	13.36
From the balance sheet (at year-end)					
Working capital	1,548	$ 1,483	$ 1,747	$ 2,147	$2,124
Total assets	10,518	10,295	10,616	10,423	9,659
Long-term debt	2,362	2,387	2,428	2,101	1,859
Total capitalization	7,962	7,999	8,305	8,018	7,282
UCC stockholders' equity	4,924	4,929	5,159	5,263	4,776
UCC stockholders' equity per share	69.89	69.95	73.54	76.74	70.90
Other data					
Funds from operations—sources	$ 964	$ 708	$ 715	$ 1,172	$1,211
Dividends	240	240	235	224	206
Dividends per share	3.40	3.40	3.40	3.30	3.10
Shares outstanding (thousands at year-end)	70,450	70,465	70,153	68,582	67,367
Market price per share—high	65¼	73⅞	61	62⅛	52½
Market price per share—low	32¾	51	40⅛	45¼	35¼
Capital expenditures	670	761	1,179	1,186	1,129
Number of employees (at year-end)	98,366	99,506	103,229	110,255	116,105
Selected financial ratios					
Total debt/ total capitalization (at year-end)	33.7%	34.0%	33.9%	30.3%	29.9%
Net income/ average UCC stockholders' equity	6.6%	1.6%	6.0%	12.9%	15.3%[b]
Net income + minority share of income/ average total capitalization	4.5%	1.4%	4.3%	9.1%	10.6%[b]
DIvidends/ net income	74.3%	303.8%	75.8%	34.5%	30.6%[b]
Dividends/ funds from operations—sources	24.9%	33.9%	32.9%	19.1%	17.0%

[a]Amounts for 1982 and subsequent years reflect the adoption of Statement of Financial Accounting Standards No. 52.
[b]Net income in these ratios excludes the nonrecurring credit for the cumulative effect of the change in accounting principle for the investment tax credit (ITC).
[c]Net income per share is based on weighted average number of shares outstanding during the year. *Funds from operations—sources* includes income before extraordinary charge and noncash charges (credits) to income before extraordinary charge. *Total debt* consists of short-term debt, long-term debt, and current installments of long-term debt. *Total capitalization* consists of *total debt* plus *minority stockholders' equity in consolidated subsidiaries* and *UCC stockholders' equity.*

were owned by Union Carbide Corporation, New York. Remaining shares were held by individuals and institutions in India.

The company manufactured a wide range of products including agricultural products, chemicals and plastics, marine products, battery products, and special metals and gases. It had five operating divisions.

TABLE 2. Consolidated Statement of Income and Retained Earnings for UCC

MILLIONS OF DOLLARS (EXCEPT PER SHARE FIGURES), YEAR ENDED DECEMBER 31	1984	1983	1982
Net sales	$9,508	$9,001	$9,061
Deductions (additions)			
Cost of sales	6,702	6,581	6,687
Research and development	265	245	240
Selling, administrative, and other expenses	1,221	1,243	1,249
Depreciation	507	477	426
Interest on long-term and short-term debt	300	252	236
Other income—net	(77)	(120)	(162)
Nonrecurring charge—closing of facilities	—	241	—
Income before provision for income taxes	590	82	385
Provision for income taxes	227	(10)	58
Income of consolidated companies	363	92	327
Less: Minority stockholders' share of income	39	32	36
Plus: UCC share of income of companies carried at equity	17	19	19
Income before extraordinary charge	341	79	310
Extraordinary charge	(18)	—	—
Net income	323	79	310
Retained earnings at January 1	4,509	4,670	4,595
	4,832	4,749	4,905
Dividends declared	240	240	235
Retained earnings at December 31	$4,592	$4,509	$4,670
Per share			
Income before extraordinary charge[a]	$4.84	$ 1.13	$ 4.47
Extraordinary charge[a]	$(0.25)	$ —	$ —
Net income[a]	$4.59	$ 1.13	$ 4.47
Dividends declared	$3.40	$ 3.40	$ 3.40

[a]Based on 70.478.524 shares (70.347.418 shares in 1983 and 69.305.609 shares in 1982), the weighted average number of shares outstanding during the

In addition, it owned majority interest in a joint venture—the Nepal Battery Company Limited.

UCIL was a well-respected company in India. It was considered a good business customer and a responsible and desirable employer. The company worked closely with local, state, and central government agencies to promote the government's family planning and other social programs. It thus developed strong contacts in the government. This excellent relationship with the government facilitated company-government interactions at many levels of operations. The company was easily able to get government permissions for dealing with a variety of operating issues. For example, the parent company was allowed to retain 51% of the stock in the Indian company, even after the revised Foreign Exchange Regulations Act (FERA) required foreign companies to hold less than 40% of a domestic (Indian) company's stock.[2] On another occasion, the company was able to get Bhopal government's objection to its site overruled by the state government.[3]

UCIL had 32.58 million outstanding shares. Of these, 16.58 million shares (50.89%) were held by Carbide Corporation, U.S.A., the holding company. The company had issued and subscribed share capital of Rs.325.83 million and accumulated reserves and surplus of Rs.293.89. In 1983, company revenues were Rs.2100 million, ($1 US = Rs.12.8 in 1984), excluding products used internally and valued at Rs.540 million. It re-

TABLE 3. Consolidated Balance Sheet for UCC

MILLIONS OF DOLLARS AT DECEMBER 31	1984	1983
Assets		
Cash	$ 28	$ 46
Time deposits and short-term marketable securities	68	72
	96	118
Notes and accounts receivable	1,512	1,460
Inventories		
Raw materials and supplies	468	473
Work in process	409	421
Finished goods	669	616
	1,546	1,510
Prepaid expenses	152	157
Total current assets	3,306	3,245
Property, plant, and equipment	11,131	10,708
Less: Accumulated depreciation	4,748	4,426
Net fixed assets	6,383	6,282
Companies carried at equity	288	300
Other investments and advances	139	121
Total investments and advances	427	421
Other assets	402	347
Total assets	$10,518	$10,295
Liabilities and stockholders' equity		
Accounts payable	$ 470	$ 492
Short-term debt	217	240
Payments due within one year on long-term debt	104	91
Accrued income and other taxes	124	114
Other accrued liabilities	843	825
Total current liabilities	1,758	1,762
Long-term debt	2,362	2,387
Deferred credits	1,119	865
Minority stockholders' equity in consolidated subsidiaries	355	352
UCC stockholders' equity		
Common stock		
Authorized—180,000,000 shares		
Issued—70,600,810 shares (70,567,283 shares in 1983)	756	755
Equity adjustment from foreign currency translation	(419)	(333)
Retained earnings	4,592	4,509
	4,929	4,931
Less: Treasury stock, at cost—150,579 shares (101,784 shares in 1983)	5	2
Total UCC stockholders' equity	4,924	4,929
Total liabilities and stockholders' equity	$10,518	$10,295

ported profit before taxes of Rs.148 million, and profit after taxes and Investment Allowance Reserves of Rs.87 million. It declared a dividend of Rs.1.50 per share. Net worth per share was Rs.19.02, and earnings per share were Rs.2.86. The company employed over 10,000 people, of whom nearly 1,000 earned incomes of over Rs.3,000 per month, making the company one of the best-paying employers in India.[4]

UCIL MANAGEMENT AND ORGANIZATION

UCIL was managed by an 11-member board of directors, with Keshub Mahindra, a well-known industrialist, as chairman. The vice-chairman was J. B. Law, who also served as the chairman of Union Carbide Eastern, Inc., Hong Kong. V. P. Gokhale served as the managing director (chief executive) of the company. He took this position on December 26, 1983 and was responsible for overall management of the company. A mechanical engineer by training, he had been with the company since 1959. Each of the five operating divisions were headed by a vice-president reporting to the managing director. Each division was a profit center, organized internally on a functional basis.

Management of the Agricultural Products Division was characterized by frequent changes in top management. During the past 15 years, it had eight different division heads. Many of them came from nonchemical businesses of the company. Discontinuity in top management created frequent changes in internal systems and procedures, and uncertainty for managers. Many of the more talented managers, particularly those trained in the United States for operating the MIC plant in 1980, had left the company by 1984.[5]

OPERATIONS

The company had 13 manufacturing facilities located in major Indian cities such as Bombay, Calcutta, Madras, Hyderabad, Bhopal, and Srinagar. Production technologies used in these facilities were modern and supplied by the parent corporation. For example, the Bhopal facility contained plants to manufacture methyl isocyanate (MIC), and to formulate MIC-based pesticides. The company operated 20 sales offices and sold through a network of 3,000 dealers, who in turn sold to 249,000 retailers all over India. It had dominant market share in its main product (batteries) and was a significant competitor in other product lines, including pesticides, carbons, special metals, chemicals, and plastics. Differences in product lines, marketing philosophies, and operations made each division distinct and independent. For example, the Battery Division operated through a network of distributors and dealers and advertised intensively. The Agricultural Products Division sent distributors to geographical areas

where customers (private farmers) were concentrated. Promotion involved programs for farmers aimed at educating them about the usefulness of pesticides.

INDUSTRIAL ENVIRONMENT IN BHOPAL AND INDIA

Bhopal is the capital of the state of Madhya Pradesh and the most centrally located city in India. It has a good agricultural and forest base and two large lakes that ensure a steady supply of water to the city. The government controls the most important segments of the local economy. It is the largest employer, the largest producer, and the largest consumer. More than 90% of India's productive industrial resources are controlled directly or indirectly by agencies of the city, state, and central (federal) governments. Virtually all service organizations are nationalized, including banks, insurance companies, postal and telephone systems, radio and television stations, energy production and distribution, railways, airlines, intercity bus service, medical services, and education.

Urbanization and industrialization in Bhopal were not integrated with rural development of hinterlands. Agricultural production in rural areas was stagnant, while the state's population grew at a rate of more than 2% per year. These conditions forced the rural unemployed to seek work in urban areas—turning Bhopal into a rapidly growing urban area. Bhopal's population grew from 102,000 in 1961, to 385,000 in 1971, and to 670,000 in 1981—a growth rate almost three times the average for the state and for the nation as a whole.

Migrants from rural areas were hardly equipped to deal with the difficulties of urban life. In 1971, almost two-thirds of the migrants were unemployed. Of these, half had not completed high school and 20% were totally illiterate. Bhopal's rapidly rising population, coupled with high land and construction costs, caused a severe housing shortage in the city. Government efforts to build housing resulted, for the most part, in the construction of expensive dwellings. Unable to afford housing, many migrants became squatters, illegally occupying land and creating slums and shantytowns. Most of these slums cropped up around industrial plants and other employment centers. Slum dwellers served as a pool of cheap labor for industry, construction, offices, and households seeking domestic help. By 1984, Bhopal had 156 slum colonies, home for nearly 20% of the city's population. Two of them—Jaya Prakash Nagar and Kenchi Chola—were located across the street from Union Carbide's plant, even though the area was not zoned for residential use.

In 1974, UCIL was granted an industrial license by the central government to manufacture, rather than simply formulate, pesticides. By 1977, UCIL had begun producing more sophisticated and dangerous pesticides in which carbaryl was the active agent. Component chemicals such as methyl isocyanate (MIC) were imported from the parent company in relatively small quantities. Within a short period of time, however, the pesticides market became very competitive. Fifty different formulations and more than 200 manufacturers came into existence to serve small, regional market niches. Increased competition forced manufacturers to cut costs, improve productivity, take advantage of economies of scale, and resort to "backward integration" (that is, not only formulate the final products but manufacture the raw materials and intermediate products as well).

While competitive pressures were mounting, widespread use of pesticides declined. Agricultural production peaked in 1979, declined severely in 1980, and then recovered mildly over the next three years. Weather conditions and harvests during 1982 and 1983 were poor, causing farmers to cut costs temporarily by abandoning the use of pesticides. As a result of reduced demand, the pesticides industry became even more competitive in the early 1980s. The expansion and underutilization of production capacity, coupled with a decline in agricultural production, further fueled competition.

During this period of industry decline, UCIL decided to backward integrate into the domestic manufacture of MIC. Until this time, MIC was imported in small drums and did not need to be stored in great quantities. In 1979, the company expanded its Bhopal factory to include facilities that manufactured five pesticide components, including MIC. Using this strategy, UCIL hoped to exploit economies of scale and save transportation costs. Manufacture of MIC required the establishment of a new, hazardous plant and storage facility for MIC. More specifically, this arrangement required MIC to be stored in three large underground tanks with a capacity of about 60 tons each. This made the plant much more hazardous than it had been before.

Municipal authorities in Bhopal objected to the continued use of the UCIL plant at its original location. The city's development plan had earlier designated the plant site for commercial or light industrial use, but not for hazardous industries. With the addition of the MIC facility, this plant had clearly become a hazardous industry. However, at the behest of UCIL the central and state government authorities overruled the city's objections and granted approval of the backward integration plan.

THE ACCIDENT AND ITS POSSIBLE CAUSE

At the core of any industrial crisis is a triggering event. In Bhopal, the triggering event was the leakage of a toxic gas, MIC, from storage tanks. Human, organizational, and technological failures in the plant paved the way for the crisis that ensued. The events leading to the accident are murky, which is not unusual when major accidents like the one in Bhopal occur. Moreover, the attributable causes of such accidents become highly contentious because of their impact in establishing culpability and payment of damages to the victims.

MIC is a highly toxic substance used for making Carbaryl, the active agent in the pesticide Sevin. It is also very unstable and needs to be kept at low temperatures. UCIL manufactured MIC in batches and stored it in three large underground tanks until it was needed for processing. Two of the tanks were used for MIC that had met specifications, while the third stored MIC that had not met specifications and needed reprocessing.

THE PLANT

A schematic layout of the storage tanks and various pipes and valves involved in the ac-cident is shown in Figures 1 and 2. MIC was brought into storage tanks from the MIC refining still through a stainless steel pipe that branched off into each tank (see Figure 2). It was transferred out of storage by pressurizing a tank with high-purity nitrogen. Once out of storage, MIC passed through a safety valve to a relief-valve vent header, or pipe, common to all three tanks. This route led to the production reactor unit. Another common line took rejected MIC back to storage for reprocessing and contaminated MIC to the vent-gas scrubber for neutralizing. Excess nitrogen could be forced out of each tank through a process pipe that was regulated by a blow-down valve. Though they served different purposes, the relief-valve pipe and the process pipe were connected by another

FIGURE 1. Schematic Layout of Common Headers of MIC Storage Tanks

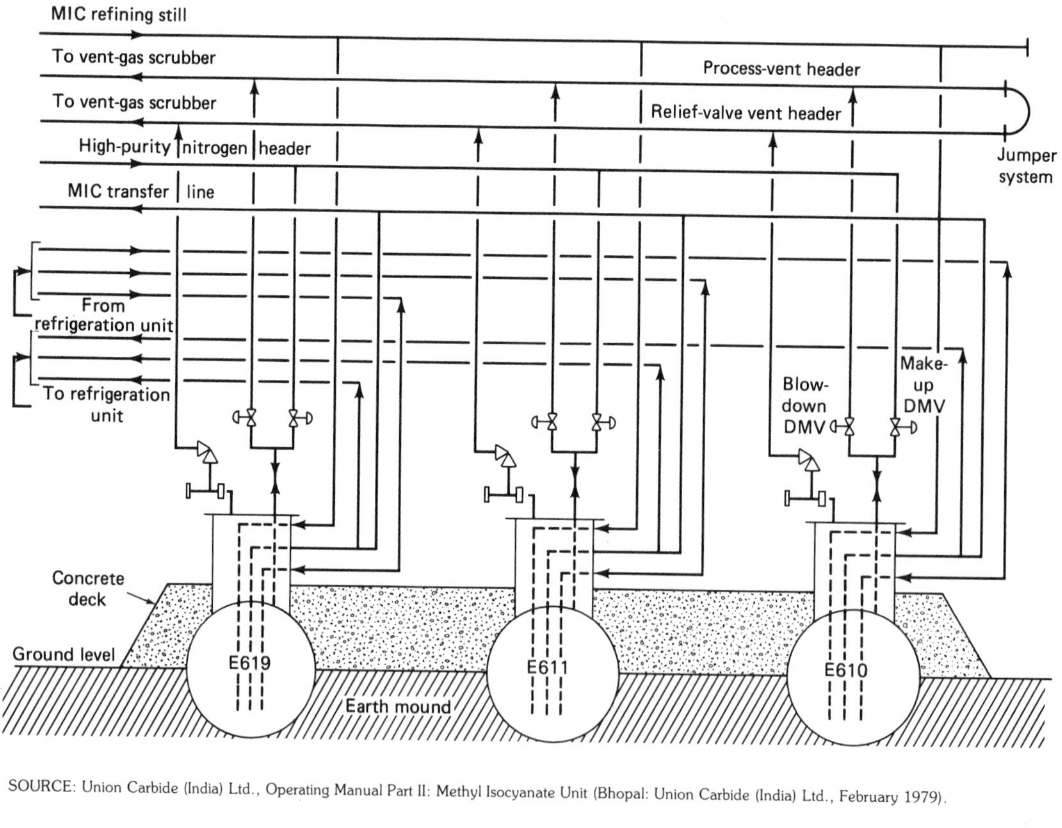

SOURCE: Union Carbide (India) Ltd., Operating Manual Part II: Methyl Isocyanate Unit (Bhopal: Union Carbide (India) Ltd., February 1979).

FIGURE 2. MIC Storage Tank

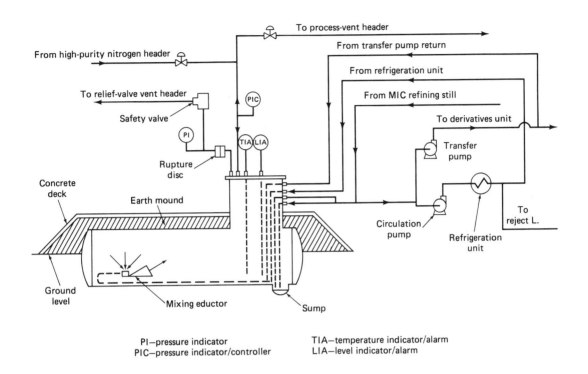

PI—pressure indicator
PIC—pressure indicator/controller

TIA—temperature indicator/alarm
LIA—level indicator/alarm

SOURCE: Bhopal Methyl Isocyanate Incident Investigation Team Report (Danbury, Conn.: Union Carbide Corporation, March 1985).

pipe, called the jumper system. This jumper system had been installed about a year before the accident to simplify maintenance.

Normal storage pressure, maintained with the aid of high-purity nitrogen, was 1 kilogram per square centimeter (kg/ sq cm). Each storage tank was equipped with separate gauges to indicate temperature and pressure, one local and the other inside a remote control-room. Each tank also had a high-temperature alarm, a level indicator, and high- and low-level alarms.

The safety valve through which MIC passed on its way to the Sevin plant operated in conjunction with a mediating graphite rupture disk, which functioned like a pressure cooker—holding the gas in until it reached a certain pressure, then letting it out. The rupture disk could not be monitored from a remote location. Checking it required frequent manual inspection of a pressure indicator located between the disk and the safety valve.

The plant had several safety features. The vent-gas scrubber was a safety device designed to neutralize toxic exhausts from the MIC plant and storage system. Gases leaving the tank were routed to this scrubber, where they were scrubbed with a caustic soda solution and released into the atmosphere at a height of 100 feet or routed to a flare. The gases could also be routed directly to the flare without going through the scrubber. The flare tower was used for burning normally vented gases from the MIC section and other units in the plant. Burning would detoxify the gases before venting them into the atmosphere. However, the flare was not designed to handle large quantities of MIC vapors. A few weeks before the accident, the scrubber was turned off to a standby position.

Two additional features of the plant were relevant for safety. The first was a refrigeration system, used to keep MIC at low temperatures, particulary in the summer when the ambient air could reach temperatures as high as 120°F. However, the refrigeration system was shut down in June of 1984, and its coolant was drained for use in another part of the plant, thus making it impossible to switch on the refrigeration system during an emergency. The second important feature was a set of water-spray pipes that could be used to control escaping gases, overheated equipment, or fires.

A CHRONOLOGY OF EVENTS

The last batch of MIC manufactured before the accident was produced between October 7 and October 22, 1984. At the end of the manufacturing cycle, one storage tank, called tank E610, contained about 42 tons of MIC, while the second tank, E611, contained about 20 tons. After the MIC production unit was shut down, parts of the plant were dismantled for maintenance. The flare tower was shut down so that a piece of corroded pipe could be replaced. On October 21, nitrogen pressure in tank E610 dropped from 1.25 kg/sq cm, which was about normal, to only 0.25 kg/sq cm. Because the first storage tank lacked sufficient pressure, any MIC needed in the manufacturing process was drawn from the other tank—E611. But on November 30, tank E611 also failed to pressurize because of a defective valve. Plant op-

erators attempted to pressurize tank E610 but failed, so they temporarily abandoned it and, instead, repaired the pressure system in tank E611.

In the normal course of operation, water and MIC react with each other in small quantities in the plant's pipes, creating a plastic substance called trimer. Periodically, the pipes were washed with water to flush out all the trimer that had built up on pipe walls. Because the mixture of water and MIC was so volatile, the pipes were normally blocked off with a physical barrier, known as a slip blind, to prevent the water from going into the storage tank.

On the evening of December 2, the second-shift production superintendent ordered the MIC plant supervisor to flush out several pipes that led from the phosgene system through the MIC storage tanks to the scrubber. Although MIC unit operators were in charge of the flushing operation, insertion of the slip blind was the responsibility of the maintenance supervisor, a position that had been eliminated several days earlier, and no worker had yet been given responsibility for inserting the slip blind. The flushing operation began at 9:30 P.M. Because several bleeder lines, or overflow devices, downstream from the flushing were clogged, water began to accumulate in the pipes. Many of the valves in the plant were leaking, including one that was used to isolate the lines being flushed, so water rose past that valve and into the relief-valve pipe. When the operator noticed that no water was coming out of the bleeder lines, he shut off the flow, but the MIC plant supervisor ordered him to resume the process. The relief-valve pipe was about 20 feet off the ground, causing the water to flow downhill toward tank E610. First it flowed through the jumper system to the process pipe. From that pipe, which is normally open, the water flowed to the blow-down valve, which should have been closed. However, the blow-down valve is part of the system used to pressurize the tank with nitrogen—the same tank whose pressurization system had not been working for weeks. It is possible that this valve had been inadvertently left open or was not sealed properly.

With the blow-down valve open, about 1,100 pounds of water flowed through another isolation valve, normally left open, and entered tank E610, where it began to react with the MIC being stored there. At 10:45 P.M., a change of shift took place. At 11 P.M., Suman Dey, the new control-room operator, noticed that the pressure in tank E610 was 10 pounds per square inch (psi), well within the operating range of 2–25 psi. One-half hour later, however, a field operator noticed a leak of MIC near the scrubber. Workers inspected the MIC structure and found MIC and dirty water coming out of a branch of the relief-valve pipe, on the downstream side of the safety valve. They also found that another safety valve, called the process-safety valve, had been removed, and the open end of the relief-valve pipe had not been sealed for flushing. They informed the control room about this. By 12:15 A.M., Dey saw that the pressure in tank E610 had risen to between 25 and 30 psi and was still rising. Within 15 minutes, it showed a reading beyond 55, which was the top of the scale.

Dey ran to the tank. He heard a hissing sound from the safety valve downstream, indicating that it had popped. Local temperature and pressure gauges showed values beyond their maximums of 25°C (77°F) and 55 psi. Dey heard loud rumbling and screeching noises from the tank and felt heat radiating from it. He went back to the control room and tried to switch on the scrubber, which had been in a standby mode since the last MIC manufacturing run. But Dey's instruments indicated that the caustic soda, the neutralizing agent used in the scrubbers, was not circulating within the scrubber. In the meantime, field operators saw a cloud of gas gushing out of the stack.

Supervisors notified the plant superintendent, who arrived immediately, suspended operation of the MIC plant, and turned on the toxic-gas alarm to warn the community around the plant. A few minutes later the alarm was turned off, leaving only the in-plant siren to warn workers inside the plant. Operators turned on the firewater sprayers to douse the stack, the tank mound, and the relief-valve pipe to the scrubber. Because of low water pressure, the water spray did not reach the gases, which were being emitted at a height of 30 meters. The supervisors tried to turn on the refrigeration system to cool the tanks, but since the coolant from the system was drained, the refrigerator could not work. The safety valve remained open for two hours. A mixture of gases, foam, and liquid escaped at a temperature in excess of 200°C (close to 400°F) and a pressure of 180 psi.

Because the plant was so close to the slums, many thousands of people were affected by exposure to this lethal mixture. Nearly 3,000 people died, although the exact number would never be fully determined. A few months after the accident, the Indian government officially put the death toll at 1,754. But various sources suggest a wide range of higher figures, and the best conclusion one can draw is that the death toll was probably close to 3,000. Thousands more were harmed in some way, many of whom experience illnesses that linger to this day. More than 2,000 animals were killed, and environmental damage was considerable. Bhopal was not equipped to handle an accident of this magnitude. Hospitals and dispensaries could not accommodate the flow of injured victims; likewise, government officials and registered mortuaries could not keep up with the certification and burial of the dead.

There were many reasons for discrepancies in death toll figures. There was no systematic method to certify and accurately count the dead as they were discovered or brought to government hospitals and cremation or burial grounds. For the first three days after the accident, all available medical personnel were engaged in caring for the injured. Few people were left to care for the dead, register them, perform inquests and autopsies, issue death certificates, or arrange for systematic disposal of bodies.

Dead bodies piled up, one on top of another, in the only city morgue and in temporary tents set up outside of it. Many bodies were released to relatives for disposal without death certificates. Bodies were buried or cremated at unregistered facilities. Graves and funeral pyres registered as single burial units were made to accommodate many corpses because of worker and material shortages. Many people ran from Bhopal and died on roads outside the city and were buried or cremated by the roadside.

THE LONG-TERM HEALTH EFFECTS

The long-term health consequences of exposure to MIC and other toxic gases remain largey unknown and are the subject of considerable controversy in scientific and medical circles. They are likely to be far more serious than originally anticipated.

The most serious permanent damage among the injured was in the respiratory tract. Many victims died of oedema (fluid in the lungs). MIC also damaged mucus membranes, perforated lung tissue, inflamed lungs, and caused secondary lung infections. Many survivors could not be employed because they suffered from bronchitis, pneumonia, asthma, and fibrosis and were physically unable to work. Long-term epidemiological studies have been hampered by unwilligness of various government agencies in charge of medical studies to share their data with outsiders. It was expected that this data would be produced in courts as medico-legal evidence. However, even four years after the accident, no comprehensive study of health effects of the disaster was available.

ECONOMIC AND SOCIAL DISRUPTION

The accident did tremendous damage to the local economic and social structures. In addition to the shutdown of the UCIL plant, two mass evacuations—the first at the time of the accident, the second during a fear-ridden "scare" two weeks later—led to the closure of factories, shops, commercial establishments, business and government offices, and schools and colleges. These closures, and labor scarcity resulting from death and injury, disrupted essential services and civil supplies. Establishments that remained open had few employees and few clients.

Estimates of business losses ranged from $8 million to $65 million. The closure of the Union Carbide plant alone eliminated 650 permanent jobs and approximately the same number of temporary jobs—jobs that were particularly important to the local economy because Union Carbide paid high wages. The plant shutdown also dismantled a $25 million investment in the city, which had provided secondary employment to about 1,500 persons. State and local governments lost untold thousands of dollars in taxes. The city, the nation, and the entire developing world suffered a loss of business potential because the accident damaged Union Carbide's business image.

To make matters worse, relief efforts following the accident distorted prices and the availability of goods. At one point, almost 50% of the city's population was receiving free grain from the government. This caused grain prices to decline and labor prices to increase abnormally.

ENVIRONMENTAL CONSEQUENCES

Damage to plant and animal life, while equally devastating, was not studied systematically because most available resources were deployed for mitigating human losses. Animal deaths probably exceeded 2,000 and included cows, buffaloes, goats, dogs, cats, and birds, although official government records put the figure at only 1,047. About 7,000 animals were given therapeutic care. Postmortems on farm animals suggested the possible presence of an undetected toxin, lending credence to the view that cyanide poisoning was involved. MIC exposure destroyed standing vegetation in surrounding areas. Of 48 plant species examined after the accident, 35 were affected to some degree, and 13 appeared free from damage.

LEGAL PROCEEDINGS

On hearing about the accident, Union Carbide called an emergency meeting of its top executives to develop a crisis management plan. It rushed some medical supplies and teams to Bhopal. Chairman Warren Anderson himself rushed to Bhopal to oversee relief and help to victims. Upon arrival, he was immediately arrested by the local police and confined at the Union Carbide Guest House. After a few hours and the intervention of the central government, he was released and flown to New Delhi. He returned to the United States without making any headway on the relief mission. On the contrary, his visit and arrest served to create the ferociously adversarial mood that governed the subsequent relations between the company and the government of India.

Government agencies mounted a massive relief and rehabilitation effort to deal with the disaster. However, given their limited resources and the vast magnitude of the accident, they were barely able to give first aid treatment to victims. The government made interim relief payments of $80 to $800 to help victims tide over their immediate financial needs. Once the immediate crisis subsided, however, relief efforts lost their intensity. Since then, government agencies

have been criticized in the local press for their indifference and insensitivity to the plight of the victims.

CONSEQUENCES FOR UNION CARBIDE

The accident threatened Union Carbide's very survival. In its aftermath, the company was subject to worldwide humiliation. The day after the accident, the Bhopal plant was shut down and local managers were arrested on criminal charges. When Union Carbide's chairman, Warren Anderson, and UCIL's top management rushed to Bhopal, they too were arrested. The company's reputation came under intense attack by the news media worldwide.

The Bhopal accident triggered a series of sanctions and protests against Union Carbide all over the world. Public interest and activist groups initiated a variety of grassroots campaigns against the company. In Breziers, France, where Union Carbide used MIC made in the United States to make pesticides, the local community objected to reopening the plant after it was shut down following the Bhopal accident. In Rio de Janeiro, Brazil, the state government decreed that MIC could not be produced, stored, or transported within the state. In Scotland, despite a local unemployment rate of 26%, the city of Livingston rejected Union Carbide's proposal to set up a plant to manufacture toxic gases.

During this period of scrutiny and backlash, several accidents occurred at Union Carbide in U.S. plants and deepened the company's crisis. On March 28, 1985, the chemical mesityl oxide leaked from the Institute, West Virginia, plant, sickening eight people in a nearby shopping mall. Then, on August 11, 1985, another chemical, aldicarb oxyme, leaked from a storage tank at the same plant, injuring 135 people, 31 of whom were admitted to local hospitals. Two days later, another leak occurred at a sister plant in Charleston, West Virginia. Although no one was injured, the leak was highly publicized and spawned further investigations into company operations. Investigations also revealed that 28 major MIC gas leaks had occurred at the Institute, West Virginia, plant during the five years preceding the Bhopal accident. One of them occurred just a month before the Bhopal leak, releasing 14,000 pounds of an MIC/chloroform mixture into the atmosphere.

LEGAL CONSEQUENCES

Soon after the accident, lawyers from the United States arrived in Bhopal, formed partnerships with Indian lawyers, and started arranging to represent victims in multimillion-dollar personal injury lawsuits against Union Carbide. The chronological development of the legal ramifications of the accident is shown in Table 4. Union Carbide was not the only party taken to court. Many victims also sued the government of India, charging it with negligence in allowing the disaster to occur. Some lawsuits pointed out the delays, incompetence, and corruption involved in relief efforts. Others argued that government was partly responsible because it had allowed Union Carbide to locate and operate the hazardous facility, and because it had legalized the slums around the plant early in 1984. Critics faulted the government for failing to act on the recommendation of its own Labor Department, which had urged a safety investigation at the plant, and for failing to prepare for the possibility of an emergency at the plant.

In March of 1985, the Indian government passed a law conferring on itself sweeping powers to represent victims in the lawsuit and to manage all aspects of registering and processing legal claims. The following month it filed a lawsuit in the United States, charging Union Carbide with liability in the deaths of 1,700 persons, the personal

injury of 200,000 more persons, and property damages.

Union Carbide Corporation developed a multilayered defense strategy. First, it argued that the suits should be dismissed from U.S. courts because the accident happened in India, victims were mostly Indians, and most material evidence and witnesses were in India. It also suggested that Indian law and compensation standards should be applied in determining victim compensation in this case. The government of India countered this argument, saying that U.S. courts were an appropriate forum for the case because the parent company was a U.S. corporation. This claim was supported by private victim lawyers, who were interested in keeping the case in the U.S., where they could legally represent victims. The battle over the correct forum for trial of cases extended over several months. During this time, Carbide began negotiating an out-of-court settlement of the case with the government of India and the private lawyers. The government of India had bestowed on itself all rights to represent the victims. It did not accept the role of private lawyers in the case. These lawyers had also lost legitimacy in the eyes of the victims and the world media because of the insensitive way they had descended upon Bhopal to sign up clients after the accident. They had obtained clients by running newspaper advertisements with affidavit forms attached, which the victims could fill out and mail back to the lawyers' respective offices. Some of them never even met their clients or discussed with them the nature or extent of the damages. Their main interest was in the extremely lucrative attorney fees that were likely to result from the case if it were decided in an American court.

Judge Keenan, the presiding judge in this case, attempted to balance the power of the opposing parties in order to keep them negotiating, but was not very successful. For example, in April of 1985, the court ordered Union Carbide to pay immediately $5 million for interim relief, deductible from the

TABLE 4. Developments in Lawsuits Against Union Carbide

December 1984 and January 1985	Over 45 suits filed against Carbide in various state and federal courts; 482 personal injury suits filed against UCIL in Bhopal; a $1 billion representative suit filed in Bhopal against UCIL and UCC; a suit in India's Supreme Court against UCIL and the government of India and Madhya Pradesh. Federal suits against UCC consolidated for pretrial proceedings in the Federal Court of the Southern District of New York under Judge J. F. K. Keenan.
March–April 1985	The Bhopal Gas Leak Disaster (Processing of Claims) Ordinance, 1985 passed by Indian Parliament conferring on the government of India powers to secure claims arising out of the disaster. Government of India files **parens patriae** action against UCC.
May 1985	UCC offers $5 million for relief, to be deducted from payment of final settlement. It attaches stringent accounting requirements and demands detailed information on victims' health.
July 1985	UCC moves to dismiss cases against it on **forum non conveniens** grounds.
Through 1985	Out-of-court negotiations
March 1986	Union Carbide and private victim lawyers reach a tentative settlement of $350 million for compensation. Government of India is not party to this settlement and rejects it as absurdly low.
May 1986	Judge Keenan rules on the forum issue sending the case to be tried in Indian courts.
August 1986	Government of India refiles case in Bhopal District Court.
April 1987	Judge Deo of the Bhopal Court revives the attempt to bring about a settlement.
December 1987	Bhopal Court orders UCC to pay to victims $270 million in interim payment. UCC appeals.
April 1988	Madhya Pradesh High Court upholds the Bhopal Court ruling, but reduces amount to $190 million.
February 14, 1989	Supreme Court of India orders a settlement of the case whereby Union Carbide agrees to pay $470 million as full and final settlement of all claims arising out of the accident and subsequent litigation. The court also dismisses all criminal and civil charges then pending in India against the company and its executives.

final settlement amount. But the government of India refused to accept the money, saying the corporation had imposed ''onerous conditions'' on its use. The court was unable to give away the money for seven months because the litigants could not agree on a plan for using it. This delay was embarrassing for all parties because, all the while, media reports detailed the woefully inadequate relief being provided to the victims.

Initial negotiations led to Union Carbide's offer in August of 1985 of about $200 million to be paid out over 30 years for a total and final settlement of the case. The government rejected the offer without explanation. Two detailed estimates of damage made public in 1985 suggested that the compensation to the victims should range from $1 billion to $2 billion.

In late March of 1986, *The New York Times* reported that a tentative settlement of $350 million had been reached between Union Carbide and the private lawyers. The lawyers had a strong economic motive for settling the case early, because if the case was moved to India, they would loose all their fees, which amounted to millions of dollars. But the Indian government's attorneys had not been involved in the negotiations, and they once again rejected the offer as absurdly low. Indeed, even if the agreement were sanctioned by the court, it would be virtually impossible to implement without the cooperation of the government, which was the only party with access to the information and administrative procedures needed to distribute the compensation money fairly.

In May of 1986, Judge Keenan ruled on the forum issue, deciding to send the case to India for trial. In so doing, he imposed three conditions on Union Carbide. First, the corporation had to submit itself to the jurisdiction of Indian courts. Second, Carbide had to agree to satisfy any judgments rendered by Indian courts through due process. And third, the company had to agree to submit to discovery under the U.S. law, which allowed more exploration of company-held information than Indian laws did. This last condition was appealed by Union Carbide, which requested the court to make discovery under U.S. law a reciprocal condition and impose it on the government of India, too.

Union Carbide's second line of defense was to argue that it was not legally liable for the accident. It said that the parent company was not responsible for the accident, because the plant in which it occurred was designed, constructed, owned, and operated by the Indian company Union Carbide (India) Ltd. It argued that the parent company had no control over its Indian subsidiary in matters of day-to-day operations. It suggested that the "corporate veil" between parent and subsidiary prevent it (the parent) from controlling the causes of the accident. Thus, it blamed the accident on the Indian company, which had total assets of only about $80 million. The government of India argued against this position on the basis of Union Carbide's 51% ownership of its subsidiary, and on the legal doctrine of strict liability. This doctrine says that as long as the source of damage or injury originates within a facility owned by a company, the company is strictly liable for the damages, regardless of whose fault led to the accident. The acceptability and applicability of this doctrine was contested by Union Carbide.

Finally, the company argued that the accident was caused by sabotage. It said that a disgruntled employe had deliberately poured a large quantity of water into the MIC tank to cause the runaway reaction. However, it did not provide the identity of the saboteur. It argued that since the parent company was not in control of the day-to-day operations of the Indian subsidiary, it should not be held liable for the accident. This issue was being debated in courts in India even four years after the accident.

DRIVE TOWARD A SETTLEMENT: THE UNSETTLED FATE OF VICTIMS

As the case moved slowly through the court system in the U.S., and then in India, the pressure on both parties to reach an out-of-court settlement increased. The government of India wanted a settlement to prevent political backlash from the dissatisfied victims. UCC wanted a settlement to shake off the legal liability and protect its assets. The differences in their motives and objectives, and the backlash from the lawsuits, kept them from reaching a settlement even four years after the accident.

The board of directors of Union Carbide decided to sell assets of the company and distribute to shareholders the net pretax sale proceeds above the net book value of the businesses. In 1985, the company divested about $2 billion worth of assets. In early 1986, it sold its battery division to Ralston Purina for $1.42 billion and announced intentions of selling its home and automative products division for $800 million. It later sold its corporate headquarters building for $345 million and its agricultural chemicals business for $575 million.

These divestitures alarmed the Indian government. It asked the Bhopal court to bar the company from stripping asets, paying dividends, or buying back debt until a review ensured that these activities would not disadvantage the victims. The company was able to have the injunction lifted by agreeing to maintain at least $3 billion in assets, which could be used to settle the Bhopal claims.

In the Bhopal District Court, the Indian government had demanded $3 billion as compensation for damages. In April 1987, the District Judge, M. W. Deo, suggested that the company make an interim relief payment of $4.6 million and urged the litigants to reach an agreement on the final amount of the settlement. In August 1987, the company agreed to distribute the $4.6 million interim aid and a few months later offered about $500 million as a final settlement amount. This money was to be paid over a 30-year period. The net present value of this amount was not different from the earlier offer made by the company. The offer was rejected by the government.

Frustrated by the unyielding positions of both sides and the increasing complexity of the litigation, Judge Deo ordered Union Carbide to pay $270 million as interim aid to victims in December 1987. This money was to be placed with the Commissioner of Claims named by the Indian Government. He suggested that this amount be distributed to victims as follows: $15,500 per death, $8,000 per severe injury, and lesser amounts for remaining victims.

Union Carbide appealed this interim payment on the grounds that it amounted to "a judgment and decree without trial." The issue was moved up to the High Court in Jabalpur. The High Court Judge S. K. Seth in April 1988 upheld the order of the lower court but reduced the interim relief amount from $270 to $190 million. He also said that it was not necessary to hold a trial to determine damages to thousands of victims. He suggested that $7,800 should be paid to families of those killed or injured seriously, $3,900 be paid to those injured less seriously, and $1,050 to those with minor injuries.

One problem with implementing this order was the incomplete medico-legal documentation for determining which victims were injured seriously, less seriously, and in a minor way. A more serious problem, as previously stated, was that Union Carbide refused to pay.

Unfortunately for the victims, even the Indian Supreme Court may not be the final arbiter of this case. Even after the Supreme Court rules on it, the judgment must be implemented in the U.S. There is the possibility of the case being appealed in the U.S. Even four years after the accident, the compensation issue was no closer to being resolved in the legal system. In the meantime, the victims who are poor and unable to work because of their medical conditions continue to die of their ailments and malnourishment.

In light of the agonizing plight of the victims, the issue of who is responsible becomes a crass legalistic exercise. Union Carbide argues that the accident was caused by sabotage by a disgruntled employee. But it refuses to reveal the identity of the saboteur. It also claims that despite its 51% ownership of the Indian subsidiary, it did not control the Indian operation. Hence, it should not be held legally liable for damages. The Indian government argues that since the accident occurred at the company's premises, the company is liable for all damages accruing out of it. There are few legal doctrines and legal precedents available to decide a case as complex as this one. Legal experts estimate that the case could continue in courts for many more years. Settling the case out of court is the legal, moral, and ethical challenge facing the company and the Indian government.

NOTES

1. Sanjay Hazarika, "Bhopal Payments Set at $470.0 Million for Union Carbide." *New York Times* (February 15, 1989), p. 1. See also "Union Carbide Agrees to Settle All Bhopal Litigation for

$470.0 Million in Pact With India's Supreme Court," *Wall Street Journal* (February 15, 1989), p. A-3.

   2. *India Today*, "City of Death," December 31, 1984, p. 2.

   3. Ward Morehouse and Arun Sub-ramanyam, *The Bhopal Tragedy*. New York: Council on International and Public Affairs, 1986, pp. 18, 32.

   4. Union Carbide Corporation and Union Carbide (India) Limited, annual reports, 1983, 1984.

   5. Personal interviews with the author.

UNION CARBIDE CORPORATION

ABRAHAM, MARTIN. "The Lessons of Bhopal: A Community Action Resource Manual on Hazardous Technologies." International Organization of Consumer Unions (IOCO), September 1985.

ALDER, STEVEN J. "Carbide Plays Hardball." *The American Lawyer* (November 1985).

BANG, RANI, and MIRA SADGOPAL. *Effects of the Bhopal Disaster on Women's Health*. Study Report. SEWA, Bhopal, February 1985.

BIVENS, TERRY. "Union Carbide Expected to Pay Out $500 Million." *The Journal of Commerce* (December 13, 1984).

BOFFEY, PHILLIP. "Bhopal's Doctors Given High Praise." *New York Times*, December 18, 1984.

————. "Few Lasting Health Effects Found Among Indian Gas-Leak Survivors." *New York Times*, December 20, 1984.

DE GRAZIA, ALFRED. *A Cloud Over Bhopal*. The Kalos Foundation, Bombay, 1985.

DIAMOND, STUART. "The Bhopal Disaster" 4 articles series, *New York Times*, January 28, 29, 30, and February 3, 1985.

EVEREST, LARRY. "Behind The Poison Cloud—Union Carbide's Bhopal Massacre." Chicago: Banner Press, 1986.

GOMP (Government of Madhya Pradesh) "Treatment Arrangements Made for the Affected Cases of the Poisonous Gas That Leaked Out From the Union Carbide Factory on December 2-3, 1984." Internal Memo Prepared by the Directorade of Health Services, Bhopal, December 1984.

KURZMAN, DAN. "A Killing Wind: Inside Union Carbide and the Bhopal Catastrophe." New York: McGraw-Hill Book Co., 1987.

McFADDEN, ROBERT D. "India Disaster: Chronicle of a Nightmare," *New York Times*, December 10, 1984, pp. A1–A6.

Report on Scientific Studies on the Factors Related to Bhopal Toxic Gas Leakage, Report Results from Studies, December 1985.

ROGERS, W. P. *Report to the President by the Presidential Commission on the Space Shuttle Challenger*. Washington, D.C., 1986.

SHRIVASTAVA, PAUL. *Bhopal: Anatomy of a Crisis*. Cambridge, MA: Ballinger Publishing Company, 1987.

SUFFERING, SIDNEY C. *Bhopal: Its Setting, Responsibility and Challenge*. New Delhi: Ajanta, 1985.

Union Carbide Corporation. *Operational Safety Survey, CO/MIC/SEVIN Units, Union Carbide India Ltd., Bhopal Plant*. South Charleston, WV, 1982.

Union Carbide (I) Ltd. *Action Plan-Operational Safety Survey, May 1982*. Bhopal, India, October 5, 1982, and June 7, 1983.

Union Carbide Corporation and Union Carbide (I) Limited Annual Reports, 1980 to 1985.

VARADARAGAN, S., et al. *Report on Scientific Studies on Factors Related to Bhopal Toxic Gas Leakage*. New Dehli Council—Scientific and Industrial Research, December 1985.

WEIR, DAVID. "The Bhopal Syndrome: Pesticides, Government, and Health." San Francisco: Sierra Club Books, 1987.

WEISMAN, STEVEN. "Medical Problems Continue in Bhopal." *New York Times*, March 31, 1985.

————. "Doctors in India Disagree on Drug." New York Times, April 10, 1985.

U.S. COMPANIES IN SOUTH AFRICA

Witness for change or instrument of oppression?
The Sullivan Principles as a voluntary system
of introducing socially responsible behavior

On October 21, 1986, the front page of *The New York Times* carried this headline: "G.M. Plans to Sell South Africa Unit to a Local Group." Roger B. Smith, chairman of the board, issued this statement:

There were several factors behind this decision, but our main objective was to create a financially sound organization which will have a greater chance for long-term viability and will continue to be a positive force in the ending of apartheid.

G.M.S.A. [General Motors South Africa] has been losing money for several years in a very difficult South African business climate and, with the current structure, we could not see our operations turning around in the near future.[1]

This case study was prepared by Dr. Karen Paul, Associate Professor of Management, Rochester Institute of Technology.

Although a number of American companies had been withdrawing from South Africa or gradually reducing their investment there, this withdrawal was the largest yet. The reverberations of this announcement would soon fulfil the worst fears of the South African government. U.S. companies, under continuing pressure from activists at home protesting apartheid, were beginning to pull out in droves. (Apartheid is the practice of requiring individuals to be registered as white, black, colored, or Asian. Racial classification determines where one may live, go to school, get medical attention, and enjoy recreational facilities and is embodied in the laws and institutions of South Africa.) Smith went on to allude to other reasons for withdrawal and expressed his disappointment at the relative lack of progress in dismantling apartheid and solving South Africa's continuing political problems:

We have been disappointed in the pace of change in ending apartheid. Decisions about our investment in South Africa have depended on an assessment of the economic, social and political environment in that area.

We had hoped conditions would permit a continued presence there. We have worked hard to maintain a solid business, provide equal economic opportunity and a better quality of life, and also to help move South Africa away from apartheid and toward a society open to all South Africans. In short, we feel our presence there has been a force for constructive change.[2]

Smith blamed the imposition of sanctions on "the slowness of ending apartheid" and referred to "the ongoing recession in that country," concluding that "the interests of our employees and dealers in South Africa and our own stockholders are better served by local ownership and control."[3]

Smith made no mention of any of the moral arguments that GM and other companies had asserted previously in defense of their determination to stay in South Africa. The basis of the Sullivan Principles, of which GM was a charter signer, was rooted in the conviction that it was morally justifiable to continue operating in South Africa because companies were doing good by staying there. Nor did the press release make any reference to the continuous pressure that social critics in the U.S. had exerted for the past 15 years to force GM to cease South African operations. Nevertheless, social activists welcomed the announcement that the U.S. company with the second-largest investment in South Africa (Mobil Oil had the largest) had decided to withdraw. "This is a tremendously significant decision," said Timothy Smith, director of the Interfaith Center on Corporate Responsibility. "Business will understand the symbolism of the action, and we expect to see the trickle of companies leaving to turn into a flood."[4]

During 1984 and 1985, respectively, 4 and 40 U.S. companies had withdrawn from South Africa. The trickle did indeed turn into a flood, with 50 companies leaving in 1986 and 53 in 1987.[5] However, many of the companies retained licensing, franchise, or distribution agreements in South Africa. Although GM, Ford, Xerox, IBM, and Coca Cola had formally withdrawn from South Africa, their products remained available in the South African market. Eastman Kodak was the only U.S. corporation to announce that it was halting sales of its products in South Africa. However, even in this case, middlemen continued to distribute most of the company's film and camera products. The impact of the withdrawals on the South African economy was not immediately apparent, but would surely be long-term and indirect rather than immediate and dramatic. Locally owned companies continued to do business much as they had under U.S. ownership, although in time they might come to be at a disadvantage due to reduced access to technology, international markets, or international lending. Social activists in the U.S. and to some extent in other countries had been campaigning for multinational corporations to withdraw from South Africa in order to pressure the country to change its practice of apartheid. Yet even after so many corporate withdrawals, the South African government showed little inclination to make the one essential change desired by social activists—to give South African blacks the right of political participation. Indeed, political repression in South Africa grew increasingly severe during the period from 1984 to 1988 when economic sanctions were being applied by the U.S. and multinationals were withdrawing.

ISSUES FOR ANALYSIS

This case raises questions about the moral, legal, and pragmatic considerations a multinational company must face when operating in host countries whose society differs greatly from the home country. In the case of South Africa, that country's unique system of institutionalized racial discrimination is abhorrent to most Americans. Social activists in churches, trade unions, and universities have maintained that U.S. companies should either withdraw in order to demonstrate their support for the oppressed majority of the population, or should challenge the South African government to change its practice of apartheid, or at the very least should serve as a witness for change, demonstrating in their own subsidiaries the extent of their commitment to black empowerment. These demands put multinationals in a new and unique position. Generally, they face the demand that they stay out of host country politics and abstain from attempting to influence government officials, but with their operations in South Africa, they are pressured from the U.S. to mobilize in order to become an effective lobby for change. This unparalleled situation raises the following issues.

1. How should a multinational corporation represent the moral, cultural, or political ideals of its home country in a host country? Under what circumstances should it attempt to refrain from imposing home-country standards on a host country? How should a U.S.-based multinational cope with the moral, cultural, and political values of its home country that are universally desirable but are not respected in a large number of Third World countries?

2. The decision to make new investments calls for different criteria than the decision to withdraw from existing commitments or to close an ongoing operation. In the former case, the choice may be among competing investment alternatives and may be easier to make. In the latter case, it is a question of balancing competing interests among different stakeholders and honoring existing commitments. How should a company develop standards to resolve these situations?

3. An associated issue, and the one that is equally important especially in the case of existing commitments, concerns the potential loss that a company might incur as a result of such a withdrawal. What if a withdrawal inflicts a significant harm to the company's stockholders? Suppose such a withdrawal has not been forced on the company because of a legal directive from a government, e.g., the imposition of sanctions forbidding continued investment. Should managers be held responsible for losses to their shareholders accruing from such a withdrawal? What is the responsibility of social activists under these circumstances when they inflict losses on a company's stockholders but do not stand to make any economic sacrifice of their own as a result of their own ethical, political, or social values?

4. How much responsibility does a multinational have to obey the laws of a host country even if they seem unjust and oppressive? Under what circumstances should a corporation violate such laws or support employees who violate such laws?

5. When should U.S. corporations exceed local expectations as to working conditions and wages paid to employees? How much responsibility does a business have to pay its work force at a just rate, even when the prevailing local norm is less?

6. What should U.S. companies do to respond to social activists who criticize their presence in South Africa? Can the companies develop any strategies to cope with the pressures of divestment, purchasing restrictions, and the sanctions movement?

7. What contributions have the Sullivan Principles made to the operating practices of U.S. companies and to the people in South Africa? How can the monitoring system be managed in future years? What changes are necessary, and what changes might be useful?

U.S. INVESTMENTS IN SOUTH AFRICA: A BRIEF HISTORY

U.S. multinationals have invested in South Africa for many decades, but their investment increased dramatically in the 1950s and 1960s and peaked in 1981. However, periodically U.S. business was forced to confront troubling moral questions about the treatment of black workers in South Africa. Economic concerns reinforced moral considerations. While U.S. multinationals benefited in some ways from having available a large work force of low-paid black workers, there were disadvantages as well. Large-scale markets for manufactured goods could not develop until blacks were paid at a level sufficient to permit them more purchasing power. As businesses became more dependent on skilled rather than unskilled labor, the inadequacy of the education system for blacks, the low level of housing available to them, and the long commutes they had to the workplace became serious hindrances to productivity.[6]

South Africa's economy is highly dependent on international linkages. Foreign direct investment has been of major importance to the South African economy. In 1984, Great Britain was represented by 364 companies in South Africa, with total investments probably approaching 40% of South Africa's direct foreign investment. The United States and West Germany each held about 20% of South Africa's foreign direct investment, with the U.S. share declining and the West German share increasing.[7] For 1986, exports (mainly gold, other minerals, and base metals) amounted to 30% of the Gross Domestic Product (GDP) of South Africa, down about 15% from the previous year. Imports (mainly machinery, vehicles and aircraft, chemicals, and base metals) for 1986 were 25% of the GDP, down about 12% from 1985. Both figures declined due to the weakness of the South African economy, the devaluation of their currency, and the gradual imposition of sanctions by some trading partners including the U.S., several Scandinavian countries, and members of the European Economic Community.[8] Great Britain was South Africa's largest trading partner in the 1950s, 1960s, and 1970s, but then was overtaken by the U.S., which was in turn surpassed by Japan in 1987. Despite its historical reliance on international linkages, South Africa has the potential to be a fairly

self-sufficient economy because of its highly developed economic infrastructure, its position as a net exporter of agricultural goods, and its capacity to supply all raw materials except oil. Even with regard to its oil needs, it has large stockpiles as well as a massive gas-to-oil project underway to meet its own energy needs, albeit at high cost.

THE ORIGINS OF THE SULLIVAN PRINCIPLES

Beginning in the 1960s and intensifying in the 1970s, U.S. companies in South Africa were under pressure to defend their involvement in that country. Church groups were particularly biting in their criticism, asserting that by their very presence there, U.S. companies were supporting the government of South Africa and helping to prop up apartheid.

General Motors was under special pressure to get out of South Africa as a result of Project GM, an effort by a group of young lawyers and campus activists to "democratize the corporation" in 1970. One demand was that they withdraw from South Africa. A shareholders' resolution to this effect attracted little support, but the company did nominate a black clergyman from Philadelphia to sit on the board of directors. For five years this clergyman, the Reverend Leon Sullivan, pressed General Motors to withdraw from South Africa. Then he developed a unique system of corporate social monitoring to guide U.S. companies in South Africa.

The Sullivan Principles, issued in March 1977, called on U.S. companies to follow these guidelines:

1. nonsegregation of the races in all eating, comfort, and work facilities;

2. equal and fair employment practices for all employees;

3. equal pay for all employees doing equal or comparable work for the same period of time;

4. initiation of and development of training pro-

grams that will prepare, in substantial numbers, blacks and other nonwhites for supervisory, administrative, clerical, and technical jobs;

5. increasing the number of blacks and other nonwhites in management and supervisory positions; and

6. improving the quality of employees' lives outside the work environment in such areas as housing, transportation, schooling, recreation, and health facilities.

The original signatories of the Principles included GM, Union Carbide, Ford, Otis Elevator, 3M, IBM, International Harvester, American Cyanamid, City Bank, Burroughs, Mobil, and Caltex. Signatories were obliged to provide reports in which they detailed the extent of their efforts to comply with each of these principles. Their reports were compiled and evaluated by Arthur D. Little, Inc., a consulting firm, and a report was issued annually in which a rating was assigned to each company.

Three ratings were possible—Making Good Progress, Making Progress, and Needs to Become More Active. Each company was assigned to one of these categories on the basis of data submitted in response to a questionnaire which was then analyzed by Arthur D. Little. The "goalposts" changed each year, and companies were evaluated in comparison to the entire set of signatories. While individual companies knew of the areas in which they achieved high and low markings in the evaluation process, for the outside public the only information released was each company's final rating.

This set of principles was quite controversial when it was introduced in South Africa. First, it obligated the companies to undertake certain activities that went beyond normal employee practices and in many cases breached existing legal restrictions or social conventions in South Africa. For example, the second principle called for the representation of employees in trade unions, legal for whites but not legal for blacks at the time

the principles were introduced. Second, it required businesses to undertake activities *outside* the plant that involved not only their workers but the larger black community as well. Third, it subjected a company's social performance to outside auditors, public reporting, and disclosure.

The Sullivan Principles evolved over the years, with the Reverend Sullivan providing several amplifications that emphasized actions he thought U.S. companies should be taking. His first amplification, issued in 1978, called on companies to desegregate the workplace and all its facilities immediately. The second amplification, issued in 1979, stated that companies should support changes in influx control laws to provide for the right of black migrant workers to a normal family life. (Influx control was the system of restrictions maintained which required blacks to remain outside urban areas unless they could present proof of employment by means of a pass issued by employers.) The third amplification, issued in 1982, required that companies have several items verified by their own accounting firms. However, the fourth amplification, dating from 1985, constituted a significant expansion in the activities expected from signatories. This amplification required that companies press the South African government to end the laws and regulations which constituted apartheid. This last amplification was institutionalized as a seventh principle, "Working to eliminate laws and customs that impede social and political justice" in the Tenth Report, issued in December 1986.

This last amplification put signatories in the position of outright defiance of the South African government. Normally, multinationals operating abroad are expected to stay out of politics, to refrain from attempting to exert undue influence on the government, and to respect local laws and customs. But U.S. companies in South Africa were being asked to lobby actively to create changes in South African laws, to support those who challenged the government, and to take a public stand on social issues—in short, to become an instrument for social change.

By the middle of the 1980s, the majority of U.S. companies had joined the Sullivan program as signatories, with the number subscribing to the principles increasing to 184 in 1986.[9] However, the number of U.S. companies in the Sullivan program decreased to 90 by the end of 1987, mainly because 52 of the signatory companies withdrew from South Africa.[10]

DISILLUSION
WITH THE SULLIVAN SYSTEM

Critics charged that despite the efforts of the U.S. companies to improve working conditions for blacks, nevertheless the basic reality was that blacks had the lowest-paying jobs, few chances for advancement, and far from equal opportunity in the workplace. Furthermore, the conditions of life for blacks under apartheid remained oppressive. Questions were raised about the goals of the Sullivan Principles—did they merely serve to promote incremental change which would make the conditions of work life more tolerable for blacks in South Africa, but would they never lead to fundamental change in the distribution of power or the recognition of basic human rights?[11] Were South African blacks themselves represented in the process, or did the companies formulate goals and objectives mainly on the basis of what made sense in boardrooms in the United States, and with little attention to the actual needs defined by the victims of apartheid?[12]

Methodological problems were also raised about the reports. Data which formed the basis for the reports were represented as being "independently verified," but in reality only a very few items were verified, leaving unverified such critical items as the number of job vacancies in various categories, the total number of people in trainee positions, and the total number of blacks in various occupational categories, all critical factors in

assessing whether or not blacks were being prepared for and moved into jobs requiring higher skills. Even if no intentional distortion were present, this system left much room for individual interpretation and hence inconsistency.

Companies were evaluated on the basis of a check-off system covering a myriad of areas. Hence, efforts tended to become fragmented. The yearly evaluation lead many companies to make short-term donations rather than more enduring investments in social responsibility projects.[13]

The emphasis was on inputs to the process—the amount of expenditure in each of this wide variety of categories—rather than on outcome. Companies tended to throw money at projects rather than to engage in careful planning, implementation, and evaluation, since their rating points came from the donations they made rather than through the effectiveness of their projects. The timing of the monitoring process exacerbated this problem. Companies had to spend their target amounts very quickly in order to be able to report that they had met objectives.

Although the companies were obliged as a part of the monitoring process to inform employees of their rating categories, and to review the implementation of the Principles with employee groups several times a year, many black employees felt that they were not consulted adequately. Too, they sometimes resented that the system was managed by white American management consultants from Arthur D. Little, Inc. Were no blacks qualified to do the monitoring? Why were black South Africans not represented in the process? Their exclusion made the monitoring system seem a paternalistic gesture on the part of U.S. business.

CHANGES IN SOUTH AFRICA

At the end of the 1970s, the South African government made some changes that modified economic and social relations between the races. Whereas Job Reservation had restricted skilled and managerial jobs to whites, now blacks were to be allowed to serve as apprentices, to gain skills, and to occupy positions where they would work beside whites and even supervise whites, which had previously been forbidden. Acknowledgment was made that perhaps some blacks might be entitled to be permanent residents of urban areas, rather than just temporary sojourners permitted only as long as they held jobs in these areas. The hated pass books which blacks were required to carry and to produce on demand were replaced by identity books now issued to all races. Existing immorality laws were scrapped, permitting interracial marriage and sexual contact. However, a mixed-race couple would still have no place to live, since residential areas remained limited to one race only. A new Constitution adopted in 1983 provided for a limited form of political representation for Asians and Coloureds, although still no representation for blacks.

The United Democratic Front (UDF) was formed to oppose the constitutional changes that had continued to leave blacks unrepresented. Too, labor unions were been made legal for blacks. These two organizational mechanisms, together with growing grassroots militancy, created an explosive potential for mobilization among township blacks in South Africa. By 1985, U.S. companies in South Africa were facing strident challenges from activists in both the United States and South Africa. A new sense of urgency was created by the state of emergency declared by the South African government in response to increasing mobilization in the townships. Rising levels of violence in townships were met by brutal repression by police and military. Thousands of persons were detained without formal charges being filed, and police were not even required to acknowledge who they had in custody. In the black townships, there was increasing hostility toward those who were thought to be collaborating with the government. ''Neck-

lacing'' became a means of punishment, the necklace being a tire filled with gasoline placed around the neck of the person judged guilty of some offense, and set alight. Schools ceased to function, and a rent boycott spread rapidly. Within a year, the South African government was to declare a state of emergency, impose press censorship, and detain 20,000 individuals, including thousands of children.

THE U.S. CONGRESS TAKES ACTION

Under the Carter administration, from 1976 to 1980, there had been considerable pressure from the U.S. government for isolating the South African economy. However, after Reagan took office in 1981, the U.S. government became rather supportive of the continued participation of U.S. business in South Africa. The idea that U.S. business could be a liberalizing force in South Africa, and that orderly political change would result from continued economic development, was generally accepted in the executive branch. The constructive engagement policy emphasized the need for continued U.S. participation in South Africa to lead that country toward job creation and black socioeconomic advancement. The Reagan administration renewed military contracts and restored nuclear cooperation with South Africa, and relaxed existing regulations restricting trade with security forces in South Africa.[14]

When constructive engagement failed to produce any positive changes in the actions of the South African government, strong sentiment developed in Congress for sanctions. Proposals ranged from the relatively mild demand that trade in *krugerrands* (South African gold coins) be halted, to the more substantive demand that new investment in South Africa be prohibited or even that all trade be prohibited. Partly in order to forestall congressional action, President Reagan imposed very mild sanctions by executive order at the end of 1985, banning U.S. imports of *krugerrands*, restricting bank loans to South Africa, and limiting computer sales to that country.

In September 1986, the Comprehensive Anti-Apartheid Bill was passed by the House of Representatives and the U.S. Senate, vetoed by President Reagan, and passed by a two-thirds vote over his veto. It banned new investment, prohibited the import of such South African goods as uranium, coal, textiles, steel, and agricultural products, stopped the sale of weapons and computers used by agencies that enforce apartheid, and terminated the landing rights of South African Airways in the United States. The bill went so far as to threaten a cut-off of U.S. aid to countries who continued to supply South Africa with weapons, with Israel as the intended target. This bill did not go as far as it could have—for example, if all trade had been cut off, and particularly if imports of gold had been blocked, since gold provides the largest part of South Africa's export earnings.

SOCIAL PRESSURE CONTINUES TO BUILD

The movement continued on the part of some religious groups, unions, and social activists to press for increased sanctions against South Africa. Yet it was far from clear that sanctions were achieving their intended impact on the South African government. Advocates of sanctions asserted that in time capital investment, both direct and portfolio investment, from outside South Africa would be reduced; therefore, within South Africa there would have to be an increased use of internal savings for investment, or less investment; which would lead to reduced productive capacity; and a decline in the ability to import goods; and a

massive currency devaluation; diminished per capita GDP; a continuation of the brain drain that already existed; and a lag of technology.[15]

There was a question as to the extent of compliance with international sanctions on the part of all nations. No doubt sanctions busting would be promoted by both South African government and business interests. And gold, South Africa's main export, was extremely susceptible to this type of trade.

Sanctions could have the following confounding effects: Supplies of vital minerals to the Western world could be harmed, since South Africa ranks first among exporters not only of gold, but also chrome ore, ferrochrome, and vanadium, and the second-largest for platinum, manganese, ferromanganese, and titanium.[16] Also, the "front-line states," the nations surrounding South Africa, are dependent on that country's transportation lines for importing goods as well as shipping local products to overseas markets. In addition, a decline in the economic situation in South Africa would mean fewer jobs for blacks.

Finally, there was the question of what kind of political change could be expected even if sanctions did have their intended economic effect. Thus far, the South African government has shown little inclination to liberalize apartheid even in the face of international pressure. Indeed, some statements by government leaders seemed to indicate that the pressures just generated a hardening of attitudes and a worsening of repression by government officials.

SOUTH AFRICAN RESPONSES TO THE CALL FOR DISINVESTMENT

From South Africa came conflicting responses to the call for disinvestment. The United Democratic Front (UDF), representing more than 600 church, trade union, student, and community organizations, issued this statement in 1983: ''The UDF welcomes the disinvestment campaign and its gains, especially in so far as it has succeeded in rendering Reagan's Constructive Engagement policy hollow and unrepresentative of the majority of American citizens.''[17]

The exiled leadership of the banned resistance movements generally favored disinvestment. The African National Congress (ANC) adopted two resolutions in favor of disinvestment in 1985. AZAPO, the Azanian Peoples' Organization, representing the Black Consciousness tradition of Steve Biko, opposed all foreign investment and all foreign involvement in South Africa. However, within South Africa, there was more caution. Among trade union leaders, there was concern that jobs might be lost as a result of disinvestment. And yet the call for disinvestment had a powerful rallying effect in townships. The result was somewhat cautious support for selective disinvestment, but a general hesitancy to come out unequivocally for total withdrawal of multinationals.

In November 1985, the Congress of South African Trade Unions (COSATU) was formed and soon emerged as the most powerful representative of organized black labor interests in South Africa. Its membership quickly reached 600,000. At its inaugural conference in 1985, COSATU announced its support for disinvestment.[18]

Black leaders came out both for and against disinvestment. Archbishop Desmond Tutu, Nobel-prize winning Anglican Archbishop, was a supporter of economic sanctions. On the other hand, Chief M. Buthelezi, head of the Zulu ''nation,'' opposed corporate withdrawals. Helen Suzman, who for many years was the single representative of the opposition party in the South African Parliament, also opposed disinvestment, observing:

The Pretoria regime will not fall because of sanctions. It will make the changes it intended to make, which will fall far short of

what it believes is demanded of it by the undefined expression, 'dismantling apartheid and sharing power.' Thereafter, if continued pressure is put on it, the Pretoria regime will retreat into the *laager*, bringing with it an even more oppressive system than has been experienced up to now in South Africa.[19]

Various surveys were done purporting to represent black opinion on disinvestment. One commentator observed:

Anti-sanctions academics tend to ask black people whether they are prepared to support sanctions which will cost them their jobs (they aren't). Sanctioneers ask them whether they will back sanctions which will end apartheid (they do). Both questions are loaded. . . .[20]

POLITICAL DEVELOPMENTS AND BUSINESS PRESSURE

Political unrest continued at high levels throughout South Africa during 1985 and into 1986. Probably 1 million black students were participating in the school boycott. Rent strikes were attracting wide support, especially since the South African government had decided that local township councils should become self-supporting, and rents and payments for various services had to be increased. The industrial sector was hard hit by labor unrest. There had been 469 strikes during 1984, and the beginning of 1985 brought new strikes at about twice that rate. Loosely organized community groups, workers' groups, and student groups in the black townships were confronting security forces on a continuous basis.

For many years, outdoor gatherings had been banned in South Africa, and now this ban was extended to any meeting, indoors or outdoors, where criticism of the government was aired. The Minister of Law and Order described the ban as applying to

. . . all gatherings held where any government or any principle or any policy principle or any actions of the government, or any statement, or the application or implementation of any act is approved, defended, attacked, criticized or discussed, or which is in protest against or support or in memoriam of anything.[21]

In August 1985, major international banks, led by Chase Manhattan and other U.S. institutions, refused to roll over short-term loans to the private sector in South Africa. Almost two-thirds of South Africa's foreign debt, now amounting to more than $20 billion, was affected. The exchange rate of the rand dropped to an all-time low. The government was left with little choice but to suspend payments. With this set of circumstances, virtually no new foreign capital came into South Africa. Capital investments and modernizing of existing manufacturing plants, mining facilities, and other operations were generally halted. The economy poised on the brink of a severe contraction.

In August 1985, South Africa's State President P. W. Botha reaffirmed the government's commitment to maintaining apartheid: ''I am not prepared to lead white South Africans and other minority groups on a road to abdication and suicide. . . . Destroy white South Africa and our influence and this country will drift into factions, strife, chaos, and poverty.''[22] The message was clear that an end to apartheid was neither anticipated nor desired by those who ruled the country.

Later that fall, 91 South African business leaders issued a statement saying,

There is a better way. As responsible businessmen committed to South Africa and the welfare of all its people, we are deeply concerned about the current situation. We believe that the reform process should be accelerated by:

—Abolishing statutory race discrimination wherever it exists;

—Negotiating with acknowledged black leaders about power sharing;

—Granting full South African citizenship to all our peoples;

—Restoring and entrenching the rule of law.

We reject violence as a means of achieving change and we support the politics of negotiation. We believe that there is a better way for South Africa and we support equal opportunity, respect for the individual, freedom of enterprise and freedom of movement.

We believe in the development of the South African economy and the benefit of all of its people and we are, therefore, committed to pursue a role of corporate social responsibility and to play our part in transforming the structures and systems of the country toward fair participation for all.[23]

Signers of the statement were mainly CEOs of South African companies, although some South African subsidiaries of U.S. and European companies were represented. In the U.S., 44 CEOs of multinationals endorsed the statement, running full-page advertisements in *The Wall Street Journal* as well as in South African newspapers to publicize their stand.

In the U.S. and in most countries with a market economy, this lineup of business leaders would have been regarded as having a formidable influence on government policy. But not so in South Africa. Indeed, the national government seemed almost to become even more determined to handle the demand for reform in its own way and at its own pace.

In the face of this intransigence, a small group of South African business leaders determined to reach out to the banned African National Congress (ANC) to try to establish their own communications with the black political movement commanding the most widespread allegiance among South African blacks. In September 1985, a delegation of businesspeople and journalists flew to Lusaka, Zambia, to meet with ANC leaders, reportedly infuriating State President Botha. The position of the South African government was that the ANC stood for the violent overthrow of the existing government and its replacement by a regime which perhaps would embody the worst totalitarian features of Soviet communism, and quite likely would exhibit the same ineptitude for ruling that had been shown in many other African countries which had experienced years or even decades of misrule, exploitation, tribal conflict, and economic disaster following independence.

PRESSURES ON U.S. COMPANIES

U.S. companies were facing considerable pressure from various constituencies in their home country to play a more active role in working for social and political change in South Africa. The Reverend Sullivan announced in early 1985 that if apartheid were not abolished by May of 1987, he would call on U.S. companies to withdraw from South Africa.

One issue confronting U.S. corporations was how they could effectively challenge the government of a host country. In most situations, the posture of U.S. companies was to respect and to conform with the laws of the nation where subsidiary operations were located. However, in this case they had historically skirted the edge of legality, not obeying all apartheid laws at least in the workplace, and they were being called on to do more, to go farther in defying the law. Secondly, U.S. companies wondered how they could do more given the system of economic, social, and political oppression that existed in South Africa. The Sullivan Principles required that they train and promote more black managers and supervisors, but the educational system of South Africa systematically failed to prepare blacks for these positions.

Another issue was whether or not it was worthwhile to put the time, the managerial attention, and the investment into the compliance effort. The Reverend Sullivan was threatening to withdraw his own moral authority from the monitoring system he had created, and that would leave U.S. companies even more exposed to charges of exploitation and propping up an illegitimate government. A number of cities and states had adopted resolutions putting restrictions on purchasing from companies with operations in South Africa. Cities and states buy a wide range of products—copiers, fleets of vehicles, computers, software, swimming pool chemicals, generators, food products—so these purchasing restrictions were of considerable importance.

The divestment movement was picking up steam. Colleges and universities, labor unions, church groups, and a number of pension funds were joining the act. Resolutions to rid portfolios of companies with holdings in South Africa would not in themselves depress stock prices—after all, if ready buyers came along at the going price, divestment would have no impact on stock prices. However, it was one more consideration for managers of U.S. companies.

SULLIVAN CALLS FOR WITHDRAWAL; THE MONITORING PROCESS CHANGES

In June 1987, the Reverend Sullivan created further pressure on companies to withdraw. He followed through on the threat he had made two years earlier when he had said that if apartheid had not been dismantled by May of 1987, he would call for U.S. corporations to leave South Africa. Ironically, although Sullivan dissociated himself from the monitoring process, the Sullivan Principles were now institutionalized in the Comprehensive Anti-Apartheid Bill. This legislation required U.S. companies remaining in

South Africa to be monitored either through the Sullivan Principles or by the U.S. Department of State, which developed a similar set of guidelines. A number of the purchasing restrictions adopted by states and municipalities and the portfolio divestment resolutions specified that companies would be given preferential treatment if they scored acceptably on the Sullivan Principles.

The Signatory Association, now reduced in numbers, had to devise a new way of managing their social responsibility programs and of reporting their ratings to the public. For the next year, the companies agreed to work with what had been called the Sullivan Principles but now were known as the Signatory Principles. Arthur D. Little,

Inc. agreed to continue to perform the monitoring function. However, the task forces that the Sullivan Companies had formed in South Africa to work on various aspects of the principles ceased to function. The number of companies working in the Signatory Association was greatly reduced, and many companies were reexamining the extent of their support for the projects previously supported. Some companies even looked at the possibility of opting for State Department monitoring, since this would reduce costs, and the demands being made under this system were considerably less than the demands that had been made in recent years under the Sullivan system.

NOTES

1. "G.M. Statement on Sale," *The New York Times* (Oct. 21, 1986), p. D1.

2. Ibid.

3. Ibid.

4. "G.M. Plans to Sell South Africa Unit to a Local Group," *The New York Times* (October 21, 1986), p. 1.

5. Data from Investor Responsibility Research Center, Washington, D.C.

6. Merle Lipton, *Capitalism and Apartheid*. Claremont, Cape Province, South Africa: David Philip, 1986.

7. Merle Lipton, *Sanctions and South Africa*. London: The Economist Intelligence Unit, 1988, p. 40.

8. *S.A. Barometer*, vol. 1 and 2. March 27, 1987, p. 19.

9. According to the U.S. Department of State, there were 29 U.S. companies in South Africa remaining outside the Sullivan program at the end of 1986.

10. Of the remaining companies, eight withdrew from the program, two were dropped for nonpayment of dues, and in a merger Burroughs and Sperry became a single company, Unisys.

11. Elizabeth Schmidt, *One Step in the Wrong Direction: An Analysis of the Sullivan Principles as a Strategy for Opposing Apartheid*. New York: Episcopal Churchpeople for a Free South Africa, 1985.

12. David Beaty and Oren Harari, "Divestment and Disinvestment from South Africa: A Reappraisal." *California Management Review*, 29 (summer 1987), pp. 31–50.

13. Karen Paul, "The Inadequacy of Sullivan Reporting." *Business and Society Review*, no. 57 (spring 1986), pp. 61–65.

14. Elizabeth Schmidt, "Marching to Pretoria: Reagan's South Africa Policy on the Move." *TransAfrica Forum*, 2, no. 2 (1983), pp. 1–12.

15. J. P. Hayes, *Economic Effects of Sanctions of Southern Africa*. London: Trade Policy Research Centre, 1987.

16. Merle Lipton, *Sanctions and South Africa*. London: The Economist Intelligence Unit, 1988, p. 42.

17. Jack Brian Bloom, *Black South Africa and the Disinvestment Dilemma*. Johannesburg: Jonathan Ball Publishers, 1986, p. 86.

18. "A New Political Force," *Financial Mail* (December 6, 1985), p. 1.

19. Helen Suzman, "The Folly of Economic